The Handbook of ALTERNATIVE INVESTMENT STRATEGIES

Published by Institutional Investor, Inc.
488 Madison Avenue
New York, NY 10022

Editorial production: Design Plus, Koehli/LeBrun
Cover design: Design Plus, Koehli/LeBrun

Printed and bound in the United States of America by Braun-Brumfield, Inc.

ISBN 0-9619-446-8-4

Articles 3, 4, 6, 12 and 16 have been reprinted with permissions from the original publishers whose names are listed in the endnotes of each chapter.

THE HANDBOOK OF ALTERNATIVE INVESTMENT STRATEGIES

Edited by:
THOMAS SCHNEEWEIS
University of Massachusetts

and

JOSEPH F. PESCATORE

IBOOKS

INSTITUTIONAL INVESTOR, INC.
NEW YORK

To *Alison Sundgren* and *Joanne Carroll Pescatore*

For letting us be their best investments

TABLE OF CONTENTS

FOREWORD I

Over the past decade, the transformation of financial markets has lead not only to wide changes in the financial industry but to increased opportunities for individual investment. Investment professionals who used to trade primarily for proprietary trading desks or mutual funds now offer their investment strategies directly to investors. Even for those investments which are not traded outside of financial institutions, investment houses, insurance companies and other financial firms are using new forms of investment structures to sell their exposure (and resulting returns) to investors through new forms of product design. Within the past ten years alone, the managed futures (investment professionals trading primarily in the foreign exchange, futures and option markets), hedge funds (investment professionals trading in both the cash and derivative markets) and traditional private and public equity/debt investment industry have all witnessed dramatic increases in institutional, endowment, and individual investor interest. Today, more and more investors are looking to alternative investments as a means to increase return opportunities while reducing risk. The increased globalization of the investment world has also reduced the benefits of diversification among stocks and bonds as global capital markets become increasingly integrated.

The question remains which investment vehicles provide the ability to obtain unique return opportunities while decreasing portfolio risk exposure in uncertain market environments. This book proves that investors must add additional "non-correlated" asset classes to their traditional long stock and bond portfolios. This book shows that alternative investments provide unique risk and return properties not found easily in traditional stock and bond investment. Moreover, the book removes a number of myths commonly held about the use of these investment vehicles. It shows that:

1) There is sound theoretical and empirical evidence for the ability of the strategies underlying the various alternative investments.
2) There exists a well founded means of tracking and measuring proper asset allocation to these instruments.
3) Most importantly, investors can benefit from alternative investments through increased returns as well as reduced risk in a number of market environments.

In contrast to many other books on alternative investments, this book takes a straightforward approach to understanding the benefits of alternative investments. Most of the articles in this book are academic/practitioner in nature and have gone through a rigorous referee process. As a result the reader can take comfort in the fact that the information has at least passed the first test of creditability. Second, the book concentrates on empirical evidence of the performance of a wide range of these vehicles.

The Handbook of Alternative Investments illustrates the maturing of the industry. As the authors mention, other excellent books exist which summarize the structure and background of the alternative investment industry. This is the first book, to my knowledge, which stresses the empirical academic and practitioner evidence of interest to the investor. In that it truly provides an investor's guide to the alternative investment area. While there is still much to be learnt and explored in future years, I thank the authors for their efforts in bringing this collection of readings and their own insights into the area. Investors as well as the industry benefit from their efforts.

SOHAIL JAFFER
Chairman, Alternative Investment Management Association (AIMA)

FOREWORD II

One of the principal goals of the Managed Funds Association is education of the investing public through dissemination of information on the managed funds industry (hedge funds, managed futures and funds of funds). For managed funds or alternative investments to become successful, however, additional voices are required to further investor education. This book offers the basic information required to understand a wide range of alternative investment products, the reasons why alternative assets should be part of every investor's portfolio, and how investors can include them into their portfolios and evaluate their performance.

This book brings together a host of academic research demonstrating that managed futures, hedge funds, and other alternative investment strategies provide direct exposure to return patterns obtained from international financial and non-financial asset sectors not available from traditional stock and bond portfolios. This book will help investors to appreciate that the investment benefits of managed futures are well founded in financial theory and empirical evidence. While it is impossible in any one book to convey all the details of the benefits of managed futures, hedge funds and a wide range of other alternative investment strategies, it should be clear to any reader of this book that academic evidence has shown that alternative investments potentially provide a means to 1) reduce portfolio volatility, 2) enhance portfolio returns in economic environments in which traditional stock and bond investments offer limited opportunities or produce losses, and 3) participate in a wide variety of new financial strategies and markets not available in traditional stock and bond portfolios.

The Handbook of Alternative Investments offers potential investors (including endowments, family offices, and corporate and public pension funds), as well as academic researchers, investment managers and investment consultants, an important review and debunking of the many myths and concerns surrounding alternative asset investments. The articles and discussions in this book show that portfolios of managed futures, hedge funds and other alternative investments are in many ways less risky than traditional investments, offer significant return opportunities compared to traditional equity and bond markets, *especially* when those traditional markets experience their worst returns, and offer significant diversification benefits when added to existing stock, bond, or stock and bond portfolios. In short, they are a highly beneficial addition to any investor's portfolio. I recommend that all investors regardless of their present views take the time to read this book. They will benefit from a better understanding of this growing area.

GEORGE E. CRAPPLE
Chairman, Managed Funds Association

PREFACE

Despite their over twenty year history, managed futures, hedge funds, and traditional alternative investments such as private equity and private debt have only recently begun to gain acceptance as investment vehicles. This is not surprising. Behavioral studies have shown the reluctance of individuals to accept new products or ideas. Despite the acceptance of equity securities today as investment vehicles, stocks were not always regarded as suitable investment vehicles. Only after the bull market of the 1980s were stocks regarded as a suitable investment for many investors. Similarly, despite years of financial theory and empirical evidence that indicated the importance of international investment in reducing risk and increasing potential investor return, international investment has only recently become regarded as a central part of an overall investment portfolio.

Behavioral research and market structure explains this seeming lag in investor acceptance of new investment products. While investors have witnessed greater losses in cash, bond and stock markets than in alternative investments, such as managed futures or hedge funds, those losses were also felt by most other market participants. However, during the past decade, the investment management industry has undergone numerous changes. New forms of investment products have come into existence to meet the needs of changing financial regulation, information technology, and investor demands. Today, while most investors continue to concentrate on traditional stock and bond investment, an increasing number of alternative investment products are becoming available which offer the investor new means of increasing return while reducing risk through diversification.

In this book, we offer a brief review of academic and practitioner research covering the theoretical basis of, and empirical evidence for, the benefits of a wide range of alternative investments. Simply put, results show that a wide range of alternative investment strategies such as managed futures, hedge funds, commodity investments and the like offer unique risk and return opportunities not easily found in other traditional investment vehicles such as stocks and bonds. The articles printed or reprinted in this handbook provide ample evidence of the need for investors to better understand the unique contributions of an ever increasing range of investment opportunities and how they may best fit their investment objectives.

We especially thank the members of the Managed Funds Association (MFA), the Alternative Investment Management Association (AIMA), fellow faculty and students at the Center for International Security and Derivatives Markets (CISDM) at the University of Massachusetts, especially Richard Spurgin and George Martin, as well as friends and associates at the various exchanges, investor roundtables and seminars of the New York Mercantile Exchange during which a wide range of these ideas were discussed. We thank the writers of these articles for their efforts and their permission in printing their work. We realize that as time passes some of these earlier efforts may seem limited. However, like a good wine, many of them simply get better with age. Lastly, we thank Pady Jalali of CISDM and the staff of II, Randi Stoopler and Gauri Goyal, for bearing with us and for their support in this effort.

THOMAS SCHNEEWEIS

JOSEPH F. PESCATORE

Editors

INTRODUCTION

In recent years, investors have witnessed a rapid increase in investment alternatives. In addition to traditional stock and bond investments, investors are now asked to consider a wide range of alternatives including foreign stock and bond funds, managed futures funds, and hedge funds, to name only a few. More importantly, as financial markets become internationalized, the breadth of new investing opportunities will further increase.

The 1960s have been called the era of the stock markets, the 1970s were the decade of the bond market, the 1980s gave rise to growth in international investments, while the 1990s saw the rise of new products such as hedge funds, managed futures and other funds based on more exotic securities. All new investment alternatives now provide the institutional investor with greater choices regarding risk and return tradeoffs and opportunities not easily obtainable through traditional stock and bond investment vehicles.

While this new array of 'alternative' investments has been shown to offer investors a wide range of risk and return benefits, many investors are still uncertain about their benefits or unfamiliar with a growing body of academic and practitioner research which supports their inclusion in a diversified portfolio. Some of this research is published in refereed journals or by non-profit academic research centers and thus lends itself less to a pure 'industry perspective'. Therefore, the purpose of this book is to offer the reader a summary of recent research in the field that is, in particular, most relevant to the institutional investor and to provide the text of articles which offer a full presentation of the issues in question. In this book, we show that of these investment products, commodity investments, managed futures funds (or commodity trading advisors), hedge funds, traditional alternatives such as real estate, private equity and private debt, as well as new financial products perform well as stand alone investments or as additions to existing stock and bond portfolios. We hope that this book will enable investors to understand these markets and use alternative investments with confidence.

I ALTERNATIVE ASSET RETURNS: THEORETICAL BASES AND EMPIRICAL EVIDENCE

INTRODUCTION

The past decade has witnessed a continued increase in investors' use of stock and bond investments as stand-alone investments or as part of a diversified portfolio. At the same time, however, the continued integration of international capital markets has resulted in a decrease in the potential diversification advantages of international investment. If investors wish to increase their exposure to assets which provide unique return opportunities in unique market environments while decreasing their portfolio risk exposure in uncertain market environments, they must add additional assets classes which are "non-correlated" to their traditional long stock and bond portfolios.[1] Investments that provide unique risk and return properties not found easily in traditional stock and bond investment are often classified as alternative investments. Despite rapid growth in traditional alternative investments such as private equity, leveraged-buyouts and venture capital and nontraditional alternative such as managed futures and hedge funds, the level of dollar investment in alternative investment products remains small compared to investment in traditional stock and bond funds.[2]

One is not able in this collection of readings to cover the complete range of alternative asset strategies.[3] For our purposes, alternative assets may be categories into a series of possible alternative asset classes as given in Exhibit 1. Simplified definitions for the various asset classes are given in Appendix I. In this section on "Alternative Asset Returns: Theoretical Basis and Empirical Evidence," a wide range of practitioner and academic evidence indicates that alternative investments may be regarded as separate asset classes in that they offer unique risk and return opportunities not easily available through investment in traditional asset classes.

One reason given for the relative difference in investment dollars between traditional and alternative investments is that investors may not be aware of the investment benefits of a wide range of alternative investments or that a number myths exist about several alternative investment strategies[4]. For instance, despite the fact that many investors regard managed futures as extremely risky investments, academic research [Schneeweis, 1998] has shown that the risk (annualized standard deviation of return) of the average commodity trading advisor (e.g., managed futures trader) is similar to that of the average standard deviation of a firm listed in the Dow Jones 30 industrials. Even at the portfolio level, academic research has shown the standard deviation of a portfolio of commodity trading advisors is similar to that of the S&P 500. More importantly, for a wide range of alternative investments, the return movements of alternative investments have been shown to offer a low correlation with traditional stock and bond investments as well as a low correlation with other alternative investments. This low level of correlation indicates that many alternative investments may be regarded as offering unique risk and return tradeoffs not easily available through investment in traditional stock and bond investment or though investment in other more traditional alternative investments.

As important, this low correlation between alternative investments and between alternative investments and traditional stock and bond investments enables investors to reduce the long term uncertainty in their final investment value. Among many investors, there is a common fallacy known as "time diversification"; that is, investors may

EXHIBIT 1 ALTERNATIVE INVESTMENT UNIVERSE

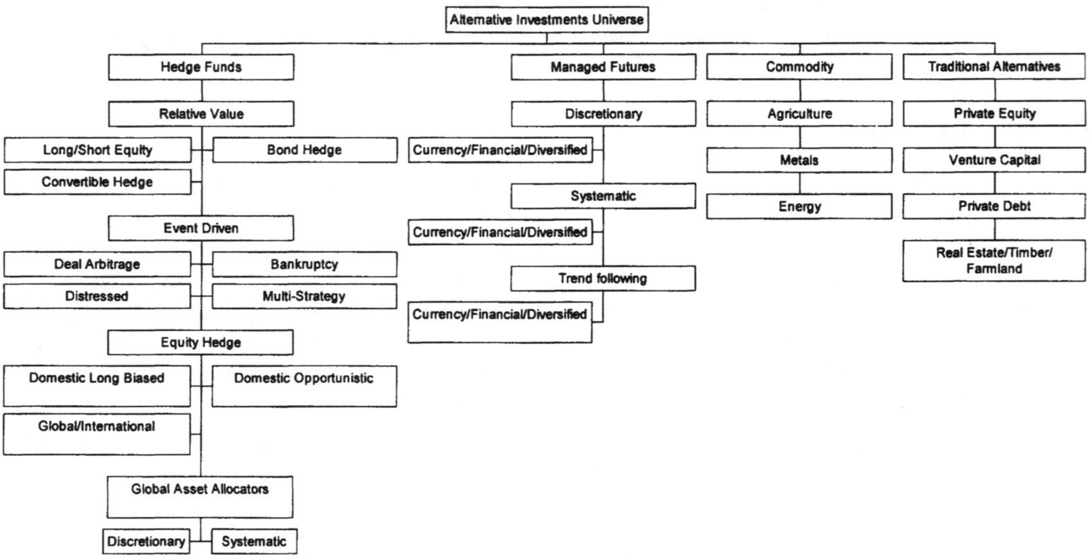

incorrectly believe that the risk of holding an equity position declines in the long run [Gastineau and Kritzman, 1996]. Academics have long shown that even if it is true that the per year average rate of return has a smaller standard deviation for a longer time horizon, the yearly standard deviation of the dollar return becomes more uncertain the longer the investment horizon.[5] As a result, what investors really should want are ways to keep their annual expected return with lower annual standard deviation.

The articles in this section provide empirical evidence on the potential benefits of alternative investments in diversified investors' portfolios and the theoretical and empirical bases for enlarging investors' choice to include alternative investments.

ARTICLE REVIEW

What is an investment's expected rate of return and is there an economic basis for a wide range of traditional and alternative investments? One may argue that there is positive expected return to stocks or bonds and that return is based on a claim on corporate earnings and the expected risk premia or compensation for risk. Within the past several years, stock returns have been historically high. However, since 1900, the Dow Jones industrial average has experienced long periods of relative low growth. For instance, at the end of 1964 the Dow Jones 30 Industrials were at 875. Over fifteen years later, at the end of 1981, the Dow Jones 30 Industrials were again at 875. Thus, despite evidence that investors' base investment primarily on recent performance academic research are cautious on using a limited historical period as a true indication of future return.[6]

In the first article in this section, Peter Bernstein reflects on "Are Stocks The Best Place to Be in the Long Run? A Contrary Opinion". As discussed above, recent equity returns are not necessarily predictors of future returns. Bernstein raises various concerns; first, theoretical arguments exist that raise concerns over the simple use of past stock or stock/bond data to argue for investment in a single asset classes. Second, given reasonable assumptions about future earnings growth, it is possible to expect stock returns to continue to obtain their recently high historically returns? Lastly, market psychology, which provides evidence of over reaction (e.g., market momentum), gives one concern as to stocks as the only place to be. [7]

So what of alternative investments? Are they any different than stocks and bonds? Private equity, private debt, and venture capital may be said to derive their returns from the same general source (economic growth) as stocks and bonds albeit with a risk premia for illiquidity and information costs. Similarly, a wide range of hedge funds which also hold primarily long positions in stock or bond positions may likewise have a claim on economic growth. Long only cash commodity investment may likewise link expected returns with economic growth, in that unexpected increases in demand may lead to increases in price until increased supplies or production can be raised. In addition, futures based long only commodity investment may capture returns (convenience yields) as a result of various hedging activities of cash market commodity managers.[8]

In contrast, several alternative investment strategies may not have claim on 'natural' returns due to long term economic growth and instead may hold essentially market neutral positions or trade in what may be regarded as "zero sum" game markets[9]. First, many 'fully market neutral' hedge fund strategies may not be exposed to systematic market/sector based risk and therefore market/sector returns. Second, while futures and options markets may provide economic benefits to the underlying users of their markets, managed futures primarily trade in futures and options markets in which the market provides a net zero sum investment position; that is, where investor losses equal investor gains on any given day.

However, the existence of a 'single market' neutral investment position or zero sum game futures and option markets does not restrict certain hedge fund strategies and futures and options based investment strategies from offering positive expected rates of return. First market neutral hedge funds, while reducing the risk of a single or multi market exposures, may still remain exposed to a series of systematic risk based factors. For investors who solely trade futures and option markets, cost of carry and put/call parity models insure that futures and options can be used to create similar if not identical investment positions to the underlying cash instruments. Moreover, given the lower transaction costs of trading in futures and options markets, these trading strategies may be superior to the underlying cash markets for comparable long positions. Secondly, institutional characteristics and differential carry costs among investors, may permit managed fund traders from taking advantage of short-term pricing differences between theoretically identical stock, bond, futures, options and cash market positions. Thus, managed funds traders, in contrast to a large number of traditional stock fund managers, who are restricted by convention or regulation from taking short or arbitrage positions, have opportunities for arbitrage profits under a number of varying market conditions.

Arbitrage profits and risk/return positions which replicate the underlying cash markets, however, are not the only potential positive risk/return strategies of managed funds. In cash and futures/options markets, speculative positions are often required as a means of meeting the risk management or hedging demands of cash market participants. This hedging demand may create investment situations were hedgers are required to offer speculators a 'risk' premia for holding open long or short positions even in a world of arbitrage traders. This positive return to holding investment positions which are opposite that of the desired hedgers, may result positive rates of return in various cash markets as well as the underlying futures and options markets. This return to traders for offering liquidity to hedgers desiring to limit losses may exist not only in futures markets but may exist in a wide range of derivative and cash market products. For instance, option traders may be able to create positions which offer a 'risk premium' for holding various options contracts when cash market participants increase purchases of options to protect themselves in markets with trending prices or volatility. This return (e.g., convenience yield) can be earned simply by buying and holding a derivative portfolio and is, arguably, the basis for the positive long term return in various futures markets based publicly available commodity index products (e.g., JPMorgan or Goldman Sachs commodity indices).

The return to managed funds can also stem from the ability of managers to exploit 'imperfections' in the markets for futures and options as well as the markets for the underlying cash instruments. Research on traditional investment vehicles (e.g., stocks, bonds, and currency) indicates that investors may underreact to information and consequently trends are present in various financial prices. In addition, except in the case of purely "unexpected" information releases market prices may incorporate market or security information before that very information is made public to the general market. Lastly, research has shown that the approach of government policy intervention in interest rate and currency markets may result in trending currency and interest rate markets. Similarly, various firm risk management approaches may result in security trading which may, by themselves, create short-term market trends. Trading techniques based on capturing these price trends may be profitable. Evidence that investors under react to information and consequently trends are present in security prices is discussed in greater detail in the research review later in this article.

In the second article, "Technical Trading: When it Works and When it Doesn't," William Silber tests out-of-sample simulations of the profitability of popular moving average trading rules on different groups of futures contracts. His results show that, for the time period of his analysis, technical trading rules generate abnormal returns for foreign currencies and interest rate contracts. His results are consistent with a wide range of academic research [see Exhibit 2] which supports the existence of profitable trading rules in markets characterized by government intervention. In short, to the extent the individuals (e.g., hedgers) or governments have a different loss function than other market participants and are willing to hold positions that provide opportunities for speculators, abnormal returns in various market conditions may be obtained by following simple technical trading rules.

Since various alternative investment strategies provide access to economic factors similar to that existing in traditional stock and bond markets (albeit with differential returns due to exposure to additional risk factors such as illiquidity etc.), replicate many of investment available in the spot market more cheaply (e.g., replication of cash indices), and provide exposure to some things that cannot be easily achieved in spot markets (e.g., ability to short), ex ante return models must be based not only on factors which explain traditional asset class returns but also the factors unique to trading opportunities of manage funds' traders. In the last article article, "The Benefits of Managed Funds," Thomas Schneeweis provides a review of recent empirical data on the risk and return relationships between various managed funds investments (hedge funds and commodity trading advisors) and traditional long only stock and bond investments. While the alternative sources or drivers of the stock, bond, and managed funds returns are not detailed in this article (See article in section III of this book, entitled "Multi-Factor Analysis of Hedge Funds, Managed Futures, and Mutual Fund Risk and Return Characteristics"), results illustrate that over a long time frame and in different market conditions, hedge funds and managed futures may provide unique return opportunities not available in traditional stock and bond investment.[10]

EXHIBIT 2 SUMMARY OF SELECTED RESEARCH REGARDING TECHNICAL TRADING RULES AND FINANCIAL MARKETS ANOMALITIES

Bibliography	Title	Topic	Major Results
Acar, E. and S. Satchell eds., (Butterworth/Heinemann, 1998)	"Advanced Trading Rules"	Series of articles dealing with forecasting techniques to predict direction of price movements.	Tests of various technical trading rules in foreign currency/stock markets Results show evidence of abnormal returns
Lequex, P. ed. (Wiley, 1999)	"Financial Markets Tick by Tick."	Series of articles which focus on high frequency data analysis as basis for profitable trading strategies and price processes..	Presentation of a wide variety of statistical techniques and tests which capture intraday pricing processes a wide range of financial futures and currency markets.
Neely, Christopher, FRB of Chicago Review, (1997)	"Technical Analysis in the Foreign Exchange Market: A Layman's Guide"	Reviews various technical trading methods, evaluates ten simple technical trading rules for the currency markets.	Concludes the weight of evidence now suggests that excess returns have been available to technical foreign exchange traders over long time periods.
Thaler, Richard (Free Press, 1992)	"The Winners Curse: Paradoxes and Anomalies of Economic Life"	Analysis of research which demonstrates that markets do not always operate in the real of total market efficiency.	Summarizes academic evidence which reflect existences of mean reverting stock prices (chp.12) as well as existences of return anomalies and evidence on individual behavior which is consistent with differential expectations and trading behavior.

Malz, Allan, FRB NYStaff Reports (1997)	"Option-Implied Probablity Distributions and Currency Excess Returns,"	Analysis of extracting probability distribution of Futures Exchange rates from Option price	Results indicate that investors can earn excess returns from holding currencies for which option prices indicate positive skewness
Bates, D.S. JF (1991)	"The Crash of '87: was its expected? Evidence from Option Markets"."	Investigation of out-of the money and in - of the money option prices as predictor of stock return probabilities	Use of option prices and to forecast probability of stock market returns.
Fabozzi, F. et al., JPM (1995)	"Predicting Intraday Price Reversals,"	Study of stocks intraday pricing patterns	Presents evidence that large intraday price movements are often followed by price reversals within the same day. In additions cites many academic articles indicating existence of weekly trends in stock prices as well as daily patterns in stock prices.
Conrad, J. and G. Kaul,, RFS (1998)	"An Anatomy of Trading Strategies"	Explores the sources of profits to a wide spectrum of equity return-based trading	A momentum strategy is usually profitable at the medium (3 - 12 month) horizon while a contrarian strategy works at long horizon. Results however, are based on monthly data and is not related to shorter return interval price forecasting patterns.
Fung, W. and D. Hsieh FMDR (1998)	"Pricing Rend Following Trading Strategies: Theory and Empirical Evidence"	Develops an option trading stratgy designed to capture 'trend followoing'.	Trendfollowing strategies reflect lookback straddle (maximum range of the market over a fixed time interval) and replilcate key features of CTA payouts.

Journal abbreviations: FMDR — Foundation for Managed Derivatives Research; RFS — Review of Financial Studies; *JF* — Journal of Finance; *JPM* — Journal of Portfolio Management.

Simply put, managed funds may offer risk/return patterns that differ from underlying traditional cash markets. Specifically, the differing investment styles and investment areas enable investors to create asset allocated portfolios which offer expected positive returns in various market cycles and market conditions not easily available through traditional stock or bond market investment.

RESEARCH IN MANAGED FUNDS

In addition to the articles presented in this handbook, investors should be aware of a wide range of additional sources of information on recent research in the area of empirical evidence of the ability of various fundamental information based or technical trendfollowing based hedge fund and managed futures strategies to offer access to positive expected returns. A wide range of books exists which cover both practical management issues as well as academic/practitioner research in the area of returns to fundamental research as well as technical trading rules. Investors are referred to a list of readings and books listed in the bibliography and reference section of this chapter.

The Efficient Market Hypothesis and Alternative Investments

Traditionally, academics have questioned the ability of both traditional stock and bond markets as well as alternative investments to obtain superior risk adjusted returns. This market efficiency literature (Fama, 1970) has been divided into tests of weak form efficiency (use of historical price series), semi-strong efficiency (use of public information), and strong form efficiency (use of private information). Given that markets are considered to be at least semi-strong form efficient, (inside information is required to beat the market), it may be surprising to some the extent of effort spent on designing trading strategies based solely on the analysis of historical price patterns or public information.

However, academics have questioned the extent of "market efficiency". For instance, even if market agents are rational and utility (wealth) maximizing, it is possible that prices will not *fully* reflect a given set of information. The reason is that acting on information is not costless; accordingly, market agents will rationally only choose to buy or sell a security if the *net* benefit of the trade exceeds the costs (broadly defined to include transaction costs, information gathering costs, taxes, and other relevant costs) of executing the trade [Grossman and Stiglitz, 1980]. Thus firms with lower transaction costs, information costs and the like may obtain relative superior profits if, at the margin, their trade does not remove the profitable opportunity. Secondly, considerable research exists on the extent to which all market agents are considered to have equal access to information or react 'rationally' in similar manners to market information [DeBondt and Thaler, 1985, and Hershleifer and Subrahmanyam, 1997].

Source of Returns to Technical Trading

Weak-form price efficiency implies that security prices reflect all information in past security prices and returns (including past prices and returns of other securities). Efficiency of this form would preclude, for example, profitable trading strategies based upon serial- or cross-correlations in past security returns (so-called technical analysis).[11] While the existence of market trends (upward or downward) has been debated in academic literature, evidence exists that due to institutional factors (e.g., end of month window dressing, portfolio rebalancing, specialist risk positions, government actions), markets may trend upward or downward for varying time periods in various markets.[12]

For instance, research on traditional security markets also has shown that market prices react to unexpected changes in micro (e.g., earnings) or macro (e.g., interest rates, GNP) information. In a very short window of time surrounding the release of price-relevant information, it is conceivable that there will be some delay before prices reflect the new information. To the extent that there is no immediate consensus regarding the value implications of the information, there can be a period of time during which, for individual securities, prices fail to completely reflect the information. Unlike many traditional money managers, managed futures traders and hedge fund managers face no restrictions on taking short positions or ability to sell short unless the asset market first moves up (uptick rule). Therefore, managed funds' traders may take both long and short positions depending on market environments.[13]

Traditional cash markets and derivative markets have shown short term as well as longer term market movements due to both governmental action to support a particular market position despite economic fundamentals as well as evidence of "herd" buy/sell actions among investors (e.g., August credit quality fund movement). While results on profitable technical trading strategies in cash security markets have been questioned [Fama, 1991], in part due to high transaction costs in cash markets, the low transaction costs combined with the ability to go short may permit the use of technical trading rules by managed futures traders to obtain positive returns. In fact, intraday, daily and longer-term market cycles embedded in cash market prices and transfered to the corresponding futures and option markets has been used to explain some portion of the return to a technically based commodity futures trading system. Two recently published collections of readings [Acar and Satchell, 1998 and Lequeux, 1999] offer extensive analysis of various technical trading rules which show evidence of outperforming passive strategies even after transaction costs and information costs are considered.[14] Moreover, research on the source of managed futures traders' returns is consistent with their obtaining their returns in months in which market prices move up or down (due to trends or absolute moves) but during which the overall market volatility is low [Fung and Hsieh, 1998; Schneeweis and Spurgin, 1998].

The ability to take short positions in futures and option markets also permit managed funds traders to create positions which offer potential returns due to changes, not in market trends, but in market volatility. At present, few publicly traded financial instruments exist that permit individuals to trade market volatility directly. As a result, investors must create investment positions which allow them to take advantage of forecasts in changing market volatility (e.g., straddle positions or option based contracts).[15] Research has also indicated the ability of managers to use various implied option pricing volatility forecast models to trade on changes in implied market volatility.[16]

Thus the return to managed funds can stem in part from the ability of managers to exploit systematic inefficiencies in the behavior of security prices over time. In short, a wide range of research [Exhibit 2] exists which indicates both the theoretical possibility and the empirical reality of trending prices and the ability of managed funds traders to capture those price movements.

Sources of Returns to Fundamental Traders

Semi-strong form price efficiency implies weak form efficiency, plus it implies that prices reflect all publicly available information. Under this characterization, trading strategies based, for example, on published financial statement information would not yield risk-adjusted returns. Strong form efficiency implies that prices reflect all private information. Under this characterization, there would not be abnormal returns to strategies based on public information, or information such as management's internal forecasts of earnings and unannounced corporate strategic plans. The vast majority of capital markets research is premised on the semi-strong form of the efficient markets hypothesis, which predicts that observed stock prices should be consistent with those that would be obtain if all market participants possessed the same publicly available information. Many studies have tested this hypothesis by investigating whether market prices reflect publicly available accounting information such as earnings per share quickly (primarily event window research) and completely (primarily long-term association studies). Such research has uncovered several "anomalies" — instances of apparent market mis-pricing.

EXHIBIT 3 SUMMARY OF SELECTED RESEARCH REGARDING FUNDAMENTAL ACCOUNTING INFORMATION AND PRICE ANOMALIES

Bibliography	Title	Topic	Major Results
Bernard, V., and J. Thomas. *JAR* 27 (1989)	"Post-Earnings-Announcement Drift: Delayed Price Response or Risk Premium."	Examination of anomalous returns based on sign of past earnings surprises.	Replication of prior evidence of supernormal returns
Bernard, V., and J. Thomas. *JAE* 32 (1994)	"Evidence that Stock Prices Do Not Fully Reflect the Implications of Current Earnings for Future Earnings."	Further investigation of drift in post-earnings-announcement returns.	Supernormal returns appear to be consistent with the market using the naive expectations.
Ou, J., and S. Penman. *JAE* 11 (1989)	"Financial Statement Analysis and the Prediction of Stock Returns."	Analysis of the predictability of earnings and returns using financial statement ratios.	A trading strategy using earnings predictions derived from *Pr* appears to generate supernormal returns.
Holthausen, R., and D. Larcker. *JAE* 15 (1992)	"The Prediction of Stock Returns Using Financial Statement Information."	Prediction of stock returns using statistically-selected financial statement ratios.	Evidence of supernormal returns to trading strategy based on summary statistic derived from financial statement ratios.
Abarbanell, J., and B. Bushee *AR* 73 (1998)	"Abnormal Returns to a Fundamental Analysis Strategy."	Investigation of trading strategies based on Lev and Thiagarajan fundamental signals.	Trading strategies based on fundamental signals constructed using financial statements earn supernormal returns of 13.2% per year.
Sloan, R. *AR* 71 (1996)	"Do Stock Prices Fully Reflect Information in Accruals and Cash Flows About Future Earnings?"	Study of market's incorporation of known differences in the persistence of cash flow and accrual components of earnings.	Trading strategy based on this delayed impounding of true persistence yields supernormal returns in excess of 10% in the year of implementation.

Journal abbreviations: *JAR* — Journal of Accounting Research; *JAE* — Journal of Accounting and Economics; *AR* — The Accounting Review; *FAJ* — Financial Analysts Journal; *JF* — Journal of Finance; *JFE* — Journal of Financial Economics.

The academic research on the ability of information traders to obtain positive excess risk adjusted rates of returns would fill volumes (See Exhibit 3). In fact, the very existence of a wide range of information based trading rules and managers is indicative of the ability of certain traders and strategies to obtain information less costly than others or to use that information in a way that permits investors to share in the returns to that information gathering. The overall conclusions that can be drawn from those studies are that (subject to caveats regarding the measurement of abnormal returns) there appears to be reliable evidence of delayed responses to publicly available accounting data — in contrast to extant academic theories about the efficiency of the stock market — and these delayed responses appear to provide opportunities for trading strategies that can earn returns that exceed compensation for known risk factors. As important if both positive and negative abnormal returns exist, spread trades at the micro and macro level may provide positive risk adjusted returns even after removing market trends and market impacts, thus leading to the profitability of various market neutral strategies. Lastly, the returns to private information or costly public information may form the basis for some of the risk/return offered to investors of various traditional alternative investments such as private equity and private debt.

CONCLUSION

Investors may ask, however, what is one's expected natural return to holding managed fund products which try to capture the convenience yields, mispricings or arbitrage returns, trend-following programs, on changing volatility patterns? Moreover, does one get a consistent monthly or yearly rate of return from such investments? If one means as consistent and natural the situation in stock markets where if all goes as expected, the price of the stock should rise by its discounted rate of return, the answer most likely is no. If by consistent and natural one means that over time, conditions may be expected to exist in the future (as they have in the past) where individuals will offer a convenience yield or suitable risk premia to cash market or futures and option speculators, where individuals and institutions may face trending markets due to the unique trading patterns of institutions with unique risk/return concerns, or where mispricing may exist in cash and futures and options markets that permit reasonable risk/return tradeoff to exist for alternative long and short positions, the answer is yes. In short, for different reasons individuals will often sell correctly priced assets. Individuals who offer to provide liquidity to such investors by buying or selling in such markets may obtain a return for offering such liquidity services.

What investors must come to appreciate is that a low return, a negative return, or failure to achieve a unreasonably high return in many alternative investment strategies is not evidence of a poor investment decision, just as a low stock return is not evidence of a poor ex ante investment decision. If one believes that the future earnings or economic cycle is not conducive to forecasted return/risk tradeoff available in equity investment, reduction in asset allocation to that area is appropriate. Likewise, if one believes that markets will not trend, that mispricings will not exist, that returns to volatility positioning do not exist, then major investment into the managed funds area based on fundamental expected pricing patterns is not appropriate. However, if one believes, as past academic research has shown, that alternative investments provide potential unique return/risk opportunities, then investment into these asset classes may be regarded as natural.

ENDNOTES

[1] For our purposes an asset class is defined as an investment vehicle which offers unique returns in unique market environments which are not easily obtained by investment in other investment vehicles. For a more thorough discussion of asset class see [Gastineau and Kritzman, 1996].

[2] For instance, according to the Goldman Sachs/F. Russell report [1997] the large institutions increased investment in traditional alternatives by over 57% between 1995 and 1997, while similar increases were also found in managed futures and hedge fund investment [MAR Reports].

[3] For a series of recent books on various areas of alternative investments see S. Jaffer ed., Alternative Investment Strategies [Euromoney Books, 1998]; J. Nicholas, Investing Hedge Funds [Bloomberg Press, 1999], Peters and Warwick, Handbook of Managed Futures [Irwin, 1997].

[4] See Schneeweis, Dealing with Myths of Managed Futures *The Journal of Alternative Investments* [Summer, 1998] and Dealing with Myths of Hedge Funds, *The Journal of Alternative Investments* [Winter 1998]

[5] For a discussion of time diversification see Z. Bodie, A. Kane, and A. Marcus, Investments. [Irwin, 1996].

[6] *Pension Benefits*, Vol. 8 No 1 (January 1999). In a 1995 survey conducted by the IAI mutual fund group, over 55% of the 1600 respondents replied that they expected to obtain at least 15% per year. While this is in line with recent returns over the past decade, it is not consistent with returns over the last 70 years.

[7] For additional academic research on the use of economic theory to forecast futures stock returns see John C. Cochrane, "Where is the Market Going? Uncertain facts and Novel Theories," Federal Reserve Bank of Chicago. Economic Perspectives (November/December, 1997) and Peter Bernstein, "What Rate of Return Can You Reasonably Expect . . . or What Can the Long Run Tell Us about the Short Run," *Financial Analysts Journal* (March/April, 1997), 20-27. Bernstein notes that bond investment also does not remove the risk of investment. In fact, because of a lack of mean reversion in the bond market, bonds may have a greater uncertainty about the long run rate of return beyond that assumed in the current duration of the security.

[8] See section 4.

[9] Refers to the fact that derivatives markets reallocate uncertain cash flows among market participants without enhancing aggregate cash flows in any way [Gastineau and Kritzman, 1996].

[10] While an oversimplification, long-only stock and bond strategies may be said to gain when market volatility falls (sell volatility) while several alternative managed futures strategies or hedge fund strategies offer the potential for positive returns when market volatility increases (buy volatility).

[11] Much of the recent predictability debate has centered on explaining autocorrelations and mean reversion in asset returns. At least three competing arguments concerning evidence of this form of predictability exist: 1) it is in reality only the result of measurement error and market imperfections; 2) there is time variation in the risk premium [Fama 1991]; and, 3) markets are characterized by irrationality [DeBondt and Thaler, 1985, and Hershleifer and Subrahmanyam, 1997]. However, predictability in asset prices has manifest itself in many markets [See Exhibit 2] such as mean reversion in long-horizon asset returns and positive autocorrelation in short horizon returns [Poterba and Summers, 1988].

[12] Readers should note that in many countries restrictions on short sales in traditional markets are even more restrictive than in the United States. To the degree that these restrictions exist, futures and option(s) traders may find investment opportunities in foreign markets not generally found in the United States.

[13] For equity markets, market microstructure effects are held largely accountable for the autocorrelations found in short horizon returns. Using additional explanatory variables, mean reversion in asset returns has also been linked to the business cycle [Gangopadhyay, 1996 and Gangopahhyay and Reinganum,1996]. Other studies link serial correlation in short-horizon returns to autoregressive conditional heteroscedasticity models [LeBaron, 1992]. Explanations consistent with rational time variation in expected returns actually describe deviations that are indistinguishable from the movements caused by irrational bubbles (temporary price swings away from fundamental values) , that is, Poterba and Summers [1988] show how both time variation in risk premiums and irrational markets can imply the same mean-reverting return patterns.

[14] For a recent example of academic research on the profitability of pure price based momentum or contrarian trading strategies see Conrad and Kaul [1998]. Conrad and Kaul show that less than 50% of the 120 strategies analyzed yield statistically significant profits and the profitability of the various

strategies were time dependent. It is also important to point out that the analysis was not conducted using very short time period (e.g., high frequency) data.

[15] For new methods of volatility trading see Jarrow Ed., Volatility: New Estimation Techniques for Pricing Derivatives [Risk Books, 1998].

[16] Volatility [Risk, 1999].

SELECTED REFERENCES

Section I Articles

Bernstein, P. "Are Stocks the Best Place to Be in the Long Run:A Contrary Opinion," *The Journal of Investing* (Summer, 1996), pp. 6-11.

Silber, William. "Technical Trading: When it Works and When it Doesn't," *The Journal of Derivatives* (Spring, 1994), pp. 39-44.

Schneeweis, Thomas and Richard Spurgin, "Benefits of Managed Fund Strategies: Managed Futures and Hedge Funds" CISDM/SOM, 1998.

Returns to Fundamental Information

Alexander, J., and J. Ang. "Do Equity Markets Respond to Earnings Paths?" *Financial Analysts' Journal* July/August (1998), pp. 81-94.

Bernard, V., and J. Thomas. "Post-Earnings-Announcement Drift: Delayed Price Response or Risk Premium." *Journal of Accounting Research* 27 (1989), pp. 1-36.

Bernard, V., and J. Thomas. "Evidence that Stock Prices Do Not Fully Reflect the Implications f Current Earnings for Future Earnings." *Journal of Accounting and Economics* 13 (1990), pp. 305-340.

Debondt, W., and R. Thaler. "Does the Stock Market Over-React?" *The Journal of Finance* 40 (1985), pp. 793-805.

Dechow, P., and R. Sloan. "Returns to Contrarian Investment Strategies: Tests of Naive Expectations Hypotheses." *Journal of Financial Economics* 43 (1997), pp. 3-27.

Freeman, R., and S. Tse. "A Nonlinear Model of Security Price Responses to Unexpected Earnings." *The Journal of Accounting Research* 30 (1992), pp. 185-209.

Holthausen, R., and D. Larcker. "The Prediction of Stock Returns Using Financial Statement Information." *Journal of Accounting and Economics* 15 (1992), pp. 373-411.

Jegadeesh, N., and S. Titman. "Returns to Buying Winners and Selling Losers: Implications for Market Efficiency." *The Journal of Finance* 48 (1993): pp. 65-91.

Kothari, S., and R. Sloan. "Information in Prices about Future Earnings." *Journal of Accounting and Economics* 15 (1992), pp. 143-171.

Lakonishok, J., A. Shleifer, and R. Vishny. "Contrarian Investment, Extrapolation, and Risk." *The Journal of Finance* 49 (1994), pp. 1541-1578.

Lo, Andrew ed. *Market Efficiency: Stock Market Behaviour in Theory and Practice.* Lyme, N.H.: Edward Elgar Publishing, 1997.

Ou, J., and S. Penman. "Financial Statement Analysis and the Prediction of Stock Returns." *Journal of Accounting and Economics* 11 (1989), pp. 295-329.

Pfeiffer, Ray J. Jr., "The Implications of Accounting Research for Accounting Based Investment Strategies," *The Journal of Alternative Investments* (Winter, 1998), pp. 68-77.

Returns to Technical Trading

Acar, E. and S. Satchell. Advanced TradingRules. Butterworth Heinemann, Oxford, 1998.

Bessimber, H. and K. Chan. "Market Efficiency and the Returns to Technical Analysis." *Financial Management* Vol. 7 No. 2: (1998) pp. 5-17.

Bessimber, H. and K. Chan. "The Profitability of Technical Trading Rules in Asian Stock Markets." *Pacific-Basin Finance Journal* (July 1995), pp. 257-284.

Boudoukh, J., M. P. Richardson, and R. F. Whitelaw. "A Tale of Three Schools: Insights on Autocorrelations of Short Horizon Returns." *Review of Financial Studies* Vol. 7 No. 3 (1994), pp. 539-573.

Brock, W., J. Lakonishok, and B. LeBaron.. "Simple Technical Trading Rules and the Stochastic Properties of Stock Returns." *The Journal of Finance* (December 1992), pp. 1731-1764.

Debondt, W. F. M. and R. M. Thaler. "Does the Stock Market Overreact? *The Journal of Finance*, 3: (1985), pp. 793-805."

___________. "Further Evidence on Investor Overreaction and Stock Market Seasonality." *The Journal of Finance*, 3 (1987), pp. 557-581.

Conrad, Jennifer and Gautam Kaul. "An Anatomy of Trading Strategies," *The Review of Financial Studies*, Vol. 11, No. 3 (Fall, 1998), pp. 489-520

Copeland, Maggie and Tom Copeland, "Leads, Lags, and Trading in Global Markets," *Financial Analysts Journal* (July/August, 1998), pp. 70-80.

Fama, E.F. "Efficient Capital Markets: A Review of Theory and Empirical Work.". *The Journal of Finance* 25 (1970), pp. 383-417.

Fama, Eugene, "Efficient Capital Markets: II", *The Journal of Finance*,(December, 1991), pp. 1575-1618.

Fung, William and David Hsieh, "Price Trend Following Trading Strategies: Theory and Empirical Evidence," Paradigm Financial Products and Duke University, 1998.

Gangopadhyay, P.. "Macroeconomic Variables and Seasonal Mean Reversion in Stock Returns," *The Journal of Financial Research*, Vol. 19, No. 3 (1996), pp. 395-416.

Gangopadhyay, P., and M. R. Reinganum. "Interpreting Mean Reversion in Stock Returns," *Quarterly Review of Economics and Finance*, Vol. 36, No. 3 (1996), pp. 377-394.

Gastineau, Gary and Mark Kritzman,. *Dictonary of Financial Risk Management.* Frank Fabozzi Associates, 1996.

Grossman, Sanford J.. "Dynamic Asset Allocation and the Informational Efficiency Markets." *The Journal of Finance*, No.3 (1995), pp. 773-787.

Hershliefer d. and Subrahmanyam. "A Theory of Overconfidence, Self-Attribution, and Security Market Under- and Over-reactions." Working Paper, University of Michigan. 1997.

Jegadeeesh, N. "Seasonality in Stock Price Mean Reversion: Evidence from the U.S. and the U.K," *The Journal of Finance*, 46 (1991), pp. 1427-1444.

Jegadeesh, N. and S. D. Titman.. "Returns to Buying Winners and Selling Losers: Implications for Stock Market Efficiency." *The Journal of Finance*, No. 1 (1993), pp 65-91

Knez, P. and M. Ready. "Estimating Profits from Trading Strategies." *Review of Financial Studies* (Winter, 1996), pp. 1121-1164.

Lakonishok, J., A. Shleifer, and R. W. Vishney.. "Contrarian Investment, Extrapolation, and Risk." *The Journal of Finance*, No. 5 (1994), pp 1541-1578.

Lamourex, C. G., and G. Zhou. "Temporary Components of Stock Returns: What Do the Data Tell Us?" *The Review of Financial Studies*, No. 4 (1996), pp. 1033-1059.

Lequeux, Pierre. Financial Markets: Tick by Tick, Wiley, 1999.

LeBaron, B. "Some Relations between Volatility and Serial Correlations in Stock Market Returns," *Journal of Business*, Vol. 59, No. 2 (1992), pp. 199-219.

McQueen, G.. "Long-Horizon Mean Reverting Stock Prices Revisited," *Journal of Financial and Quantitative Analysis* Vol. 27 (1992) pp. 1-18.

Neely, Christopher, "Technical Analylsis in the Foreign Exchange Market: A Layman's Guide," Federal Reserve Bank of St. Louis *Review*, (September/October, 1997), pp. 23-38.

Poterba, J. A., and L. M. Summers. " Mean Reversion in Stock Prices: Evidence and Implications." *Journal of Financial Economics*, Vol. 5 (1988), pp. 323-348.

Schneeweis, T. and R. Spurgin, "MultiFactor Analyses of Hedge Fund, Managed Futures and Mutual Fund Return and Risk Characteristics." *The Journal of Alternative Investments* (Fall, 1998), pp. 1-25.

Appendix I

Commodity, Managed Futures, and Hedge Fund Performance Indices

Goldman Sachs Commodity Index, AIG, Chase Manhattan Commodity Indices: Measure the performance of actively traded, dollar-denominated commodity futures contracts

Managed Account Reports (MAR), TASS, Barclays: Track the performance of individual CTAs as well as CTA Funds and Pools that invest in individual CTAs. Classify CTAs into a number of different groups, and publish each group's performance index. These groups include currency, energy, financial, diversified, discretionary, and trend-following.

Evaluation Associates Capital Management (EACM); HFR, Hennessee, Van Hedge: Compile performance records for individual hedge funds and classify hedge funds into categories based on style and markets traded.

Sample Hedge Fund Classifications

Relative Value: Balanced, or hedged, long and short positions with subindices such as *Long/Short equity* (long undervalued equities/short overvalued equities usually on an equal dollar bases), *Convertible hedging* (long convertible bonds or preferred stock, short underlying common), B*ond Hedging* (yield curve arbitrage or long/short debt positions), and *Rotational* (multiple relative value strategies, including all of the above).

Event Driven: Corporate transactions and special situations subindices. Includes *Deal Arbitrage* (long/short equity securities of companies involved in corporate transactions), B*ankruptcy/Distressed* (long undervalued securities of companies in financial distress), and *Multi-strategy* (multiple event-driven strategies).

Equity Hedge: Long and short securities with varying degrees of exposure and leverage, such as *Domestic Long Equity* (long undervalued US equities, short selling is used sparingly), *Domestic Opportunistic Equity* (long and short U.S. equities with ability to be net short overall), and *Global International* (long undervalued global equities, short selling used opportunistically).

Global Asset Allocators (including CTAs): Opportunistically long and short financial and/or non-financial assets, typically by using derivatives. Sub-indices include *Systematic* (long or short markets using on trend-following or other technical trading strategies) and *Discretionary* (long or short markets based on qualitative/fundamental analysis, often with technical input)

Short selling: Short sale of U.S. equities with expectation of price declines.

1 ARE STOCKS THE BEST PLACE TO BE IN THE LONG RUN? A CONTRARY OPINION

PETER L. BERNSTEIN
Peter L. Bernstein, Inc.

Editor: *The Journal of Portfolio Management*

INTRODUCTION

This presentation is more of an exploration than a set of didactic statements. The case against which I am going to be contrary is a powerful case, not easily subject to attack when examined from the perspective of many decades of history. Nevertheless, this contrary opinion can stand up in the face of the facts. It finds additional and compelling support from both theory and the current psychological environment.

The focus of my attack is the familiar phrase: In the long run, stocks are the best place to be. Once upon a time, in my lifetime if not in yours, that was the contrary opinion, which is itself proof that this popular prediction is not a verity permanently set in cement.

Yet today it has become a mantra. All believers in contrary opinion should be skeptical of mantras.

I am going to define the long run as twenty-five years. This is not a number out of a hat. I assume that the average age of this audience is somewhere around forty, because the peak of the baby boom was forty years ago. Therefore, I also assume that this average person has about twenty-five years to retirement.

The topic of discussion, then, is how you plan to manage your retirement funds, whether in some kind of 401(k) vehicle, an IRA, or just plain money you are putting aside now to take care of your old age. If you are over forty, and your time horizon is shorter than twenty-five years, my case will be all the stronger, because you will have less of a long run working in your favor.

LOOK AT THE FACTS FIRST

The facts on long-run investing in common stocks are mighty impressive. I shall cite only a few of these facts, but you can find a cornucopia of them in Jeremy Siegel's *Stocks for the Long Run*, which I highly recommend. Siegel makes the most complete case for common stocks that anyone has ever made, along with more facts than you have ever seen before. I do not lightly take issue with him.

Siegel's data begin with 1800. Here is in a nutshell what he has to say.

- There has not been even one out of 169 twenty-five-year periods over this time span nearly two centuries in which you would have lost money on common stocks, even in periods that ended in 1930.
- The average annual total return in those twenty-five-year periods has been 7.7%, with a standard deviation of only 2.6% (the annual standard deviation was 18%); the compound growth rate was nearly the same, doubling every 9.5 years and growing over sixfold in twenty-five years.
- As the long-, long-run rate of inflation in this country has been only about 1.0% –

the inflation rate averaged just 0.3% a year from 1800 to 1940 – the real annual return over the twenty-five-year periods since 1800 works out to a fat average of 6.4%.

- Stocks beat long-term bonds by an average of 3.1% a year. Bonds won on only twenty-six occasions – or in 15% of the periods – all of which were twenty-five-year periods ending before 1900. An amusing fact: The smallest equity risk premium over a twenty-five-year period since the end of World War II was the 1.6% earned in the twenty-five years ending 1993, just the other day. In that period, stocks compiled 10.5% a year. But the bonds set their all-time record for twenty-five-year intervals by scoring 8.9% a year.

In the face of all that evidence, only a fool would tell you that investing in stocks over the long run is a bad idea. The absolute returns should satisfy the most greedy among us, while the consistent superiority over lower-risk assets should satisfy the most fearful among us.

SO WHY GO ON?

Three reasons. First, there is a powerful theoretical argument that diminishes the future relevance of all these facts. Second, looking forward from the level of stock prices at this moment [Fall 1995], the implicit assumptions in the case for equities are less solid than history by itself would suggest. Third, the current psychological environment has to make a contrarian uneasy: The case for stocks is just too pat.

THEORY

The theoretical issues are profound, even if they are simple and obvious. I take them with utmost seriousness.

The popular game today is to look at Siegel's data, or, more frequently, to look at the far more favorable Ibbotson data from the end of 1925 onward, and construct probabilities of various rates of return. The Association for Investment Management and Research recently published an elegant presentation along these lines by William Reichenstein and Dovalee Dorsett. The Fall 1995 issue of *The Journal of Portfolio Management* has a similar analysis by Jack Wilson and Charles Jones.

These studies have a problem. We can depend upon future probabilities extracted from past frequencies only when the past frequencies are derived from independent observations like rolls of the dice or spins of the roulette wheel.

Although stock returns display a remarkable resemblance to independent observations — they are by and large lognormally distributed — that "by and large" is a critically important qualification. The outliers are few in number, but they lie way out, with most of them falling in negative rather than positive territory. Hence, if stock prices are not truly independent, all this evidence is only suggestive, not something on which you can bet the ranch.

This point is so important that it deserves further elaboration. The ancient Greek word for "probability" was *eikos*, which means essentially "to be expected with some degree of certainty." Socrates defined *eikos* as "likeness to truth." The modern German word for "probable" is *wahrscheinlich*, which also means "appearance of truth."

A subtle point of great importance is involved in these definitions. *Likeness to truth is not the same thing as truth.* The Greeks felt so strongly about that distinction that they refused to recognize any truth that could not be proven by logic and axioms. Empirical research proved nothing.

Nobody can prove that the distribution of future returns in the stock market must be the same as the distribution of historical returns. Paul Samuelson makes the point in a few words: "We have only one sample of the past."

Unless you can look Socrates right in the eye and assert that these 169 twenty-five-year periods from history were truly throws of the dice, or unless you know some other reason based in theory for stock patterns to repeat themselves flawlessly, your facts are only one sample, not 169 truly independent observations. In real life, as Wordsworth pointed out, the child is father to the man; the present is never independent of the past.

In short, no matter how imposing the story from the past may be — no matter how consistently the case holds up across wildly differing economic environments — we still cannot with complete confidence project that experience into the future. Facts are not theory.

IMPLICIT ASSUMPTIONS ABOUT THE NEXT 25 YEARS

You can buy a twenty-five-year U.S. Treasury zero today for a return on the order of 6.5%. That return is as close to riskless as you can get. Can you expect the stock market to do better for you from here, and with what degree of confidence?

The nature of your expectations will depend a lot on precisely how long you want to define long-run experience to be. I mentioned earlier that the Siegel data show that total returns for twenty-five-year periods average 7.7% a year, with a standard deviation of 2.6%. The riskless bond return of 6.5% is about a half standard deviation below the 7.7% average. This super-long-run experience suggests that you would have something less than one chance in ten of falling short of 6.5% over the next twenty-five years — small, but large enough to be worrisome.

On the other hand, if you argue that all that ancient history is irrelevant and only the sixty-nine years of Ibbotson data are what matter, the game appears to be a cinch. The rolling twenty-five-year total returns since the end of 1925 (first period being the twenty-five years ending 1951) average 10.8% a year with a standard deviation of merely 2.2%, a ratio of return-to-volatility of five, substantially higher than the Siegel ratio of three. On that basis, failing to beat the bond would require close to a two-sig event, or about one chance in twenty.

Beating out the zero-coupon bond looks like a no-brainer, but consider this. My friends, Rob Arnott of First Quadrant and Jack Bogle of Vanguard, are both fond of pointing out the peculiarity in the long-run Ibbotson numbers. A portion of those rich twenty-five-year average returns come from the upward revaluation of a conservatively valued market in 1926 to a less conservatively valued market in 1995. In 1926, the dividend yield on the S&P 500 was 5.5%. Today, it is about 2.5%.

The average yield over these sixty-nine years is 4.4% with a standard deviation of 130 basis points. Thus, the 1926 yield of 5.5% is clearly on the high side of history. If we were to value today's dividend of about $14 at 5.5% instead of at 2.5%, the S&P would be at 254 instead of 570!

Bonds have suffered the opposite fate. Bond yields in 1925-1926 were at 4.0%; now they are in the region of 6.5%. On a thirty-year bond, that means a price loss of some 37 points.

If valuations had held at the 1926 level, stock returns would have averaged about 110 basis points per year less than reported, while bond returns would have averaged 90 basis points a year more than reported. It is instructive to look back over the recent twenty-five years from 1969 to 1994.

In 1969, stocks yielded just under 3.0% and bonds were at a 6.4% basis — both roughly the same as today's valuation levels. Stocks beat bonds by only 230 basis points over that time period, far less than the average excess compound return of roughly 540 basis points from 1925 to 1994. Given the greater volatility of stocks compared to bonds, the relative attractiveness of the two assets at today's valuations is not nearly as clear-cut as the sixty-nine years of gross Ibbotson figures would lead us to believe.

I must make one important point that favors the argument against my case. A lot of people make an issue that the income on stocks is now so piddling that you just cannot hope to accumulate enough money over twenty-five years to meet your future needs. Note that this is not at all the same point I have been making, which relates to the change in valuation, not its absolute level.

This issue fails to hold up to careful examination, despite its superficial appeal. You can argue that today's dividend yield of 2.5% is too low and that yields in 2020 will be higher than that, but you cannot argue that 2.5% is too low a dividend yield to give you the retirement nest egg that you seek. Quite aside from the interesting observation that a zero-coupon bond offers zero income, while stocks produce at least piddling current income, something quite different is involved here.

Recent work I have done suggests that dividends really do not matter over the long run. What the shareholder gains from the cash distribution is fully offset by a reduction in the assets of the corporation that pays the dividend. That quarterly ex-dividend cut in stock prices reflects a genuine hit to the underlying value of stocks, a hit that accumulates over the years to a significant amount of money.

My calculations show that, taxes aside — which they are in IRA or 401(k) plans — aggregate investor wealth today, without having received any dividends since 1925 and with all earnings reinvested, would be almost identical to what it has become with dividend distributions. Stock prices would be much higher than they are because they would not have sustained any of those quarterly ex-dividend hits.

Now let me return briefly to the argument that total returns on stocks might fail to match the long-run Ibbotson compound average of 10% or even the longer-run Siegel average of nearly 8%. A lot of uncertainty lurks out there. The 2% standard deviation of twenty-five-year periods in the Ibbotson record sounds like too little to worry about, but a 2% deviation from the average becomes real money when it is spread over twenty-five years.

If we look out twenty-five years, and your wealth grows at the 10% average rate, you will end up with $13 for every dollar you started with. If you are lucky, and come in one standard deviation above that average, you would be worth $21 instead of $13. But if you hit the lower end of the band, you would have only $8 in the kitty when you retire. As Zvi Bodie has recently demonstrated with great care, the mathematics of option premiums proves that expected volatility of returns increases with the passage of time, rather than diminishing.

I must admit that even $8 would still leave you ahead of the bond, which would have grown your capital to only $4.83. But you would inevitably have some missed heartbeats along the way. And I must repeat my theoretical point: How relevant are the long-run averages anyway?

PSYCHOLOGY

Back in 1968, Jerry Goodman, a.k.a. "Adam Smith," observed that the money managers of that time believed that the best way to preserve capital was to double it. Goodman was being funny, but his wisecrack resonates in today's world.

I am not referring to the frantic boom now under way in technology stocks, but to a much broader attitude about common stocks today: the conviction that equities, not bonds, are the risk-free investment for the long-run investor. If risk, as Robert Jeffrey has so wisely defined it, means not having the cash when you need it to pay your bills, and if you can let the long run work its wondrous ways for you over twenty-five years, where is the risk in equity ownership?

This confident view of equity investing is held by millions of investors who never heard of Roger Ibbotson, Jeremy Siegel, or any other academic. It is also held by millions of investors in foreign markets, although some Japanese and Mexican investors may be having some second thoughts about what the long run can do for them.

The popular perception of equities as a riskless asset springs from a source closer to us than the academics and their fancy computer models: namely, the experience of 1987. Imagine, the stock market dropped over 20% in one single day in markets all around the world, and the world kept right on turning.

This experience surely proves that one, and only one, investment strategy makes sense — Buy on Weakness. In other words, the level of the stock market is irrelevant: No matter how high the market is today, prices will be delightfully higher some years from now. Market timing and tactical asset allocation strategies are for dummies.

Do I exaggerate? I do not think so.

In response, I shall quote from someone whom I believe everyone here would accept as a great authority on the stock market, Benjamin Graham. Graham speaks these words to us today from forty-three years in the past, but they have lost no relevance with the passage of time.

The quotation is from an article called "Toward a Science of Security Analysis," which Graham wrote for the *Financial Analysts Journal* (then *The Analysts Journal*) of August 1952.

In that article, Graham makes a powerful case for stocks as "an essentially undervalued security form," largely because investors at that time failed to understand that the risk in a diversified group of common stocks is far less than the risk in any single stock. That notion is second nature to most investors in today's world.

But then Graham goes on to say this:

> The reasoning I have just indulged in is, I believe, both scientifically valid and psychologically dangerous.... If — as happened in the 1920s — this very thesis is twisted into the slogan that common stocks are attractive investments, regardless of how high they sell, then we would find ourselves beginning as scientists and ending as heedless and ill-starred gamblers.

QUITE CONTRARY

I make this case with some trepidation. Many people are intuitive bulls who see the bearish view as the opinion to which they will hold a contrary view. I also am an intuitive bull. The resiliency of our economic system has proven to me, over and over, that the doomsayers deserve little credence. Hence, I would be hesitant to predict that 2020 will be the same as 1930.

But merely by stating the words in that fashion, I summarize my argument. Can we be certain?

ENDNOTE

This article was published in *The Journal of Investing*, Summer 1996. It is an address delivered to the 33rd Annual Contrary Opinion Forum, Vergennes, Vermont, September 29, 1995.

2 TECHNICAL TRADING: WHEN IT WORKS AND WHEN IT DOESN'T

WILLIAM L. SILBER
New York University

INTRODUCTION

When everyone knew that markets were efficient, proponents of technical trading rules were the objects of scorn. Now that the notion of market inefficiency has become somewhat more fashionable, technical trading is making a comeback.

The most convincing argument against the continued success of technical rules is that the process of exploiting the abnormal returns destroys the trading rule. But this does not seem to be the case in foreign exchange markets, where filter rules (Sweeney [1986]) and moving averages Levich and Thomas [1991]) seem to work over long periods of time.

Some have conjectured that foreign exchange is different from other markets because under the system of managed floating exchange rates, central banks spend money trying to smooth price fluctuations. Fears of central bank activity coupled with occasional massive expenditures by central banks, such as occurred in the second half of 1992, might introduce sluggish price adjustments that could be exploited by traders. In a sense, the price-smoothing behavior of central banks subsidizes private participants in the foreign exchange market.

There are other markets that operate under conditions similar to foreign exchange. In particular, central banks spend considerable effort maintaining and manipulating short-term interest rates. If technical trading works in foreign exchange markets because of government intervention, then it might also work in trading short-term interest rates such as Federal funds, Treasury bills, and Eurodollar time deposits. Moreover, if that were the only reason for the success of technical trading, technical trading should not work in markets without significant government intervention, such as gold, equities, and perhaps long-term Treasury bonds.

This study tests these conjectures by simulating the profitability of the popular moving average trading rule as applied to futures contracts on foreign currencies, short-term interest rates, and other actively traded commodities. The advantage of futures contracts is twofold: 1) historical prices are available that reflect actual transactions prices; and 2) financing costs are embedded in futures prices.

Unlike other studies, our simulations roll forward each futures contract as it approaches the settlement date, just as a futures trader would. Thus, our results reflect the transaction costs and "spread trading" that someone exploiting these profit opportunities would encounter.

Technical trading encompasses a wide variety of techniques designed to identify and exploit recurrent patterns in historical prices. Our tests focus on moving averages primarily because the buy and sell signals generated are unambiguous. Other technical trading rules, such as "head and shoulders" patterns and Elliot Waves, cannot be tested properly because they require trader interpretation: that is, they do not produce unambiguous buy and sell signals.

We find considerable evidence that abnormal returns from following moving average trading rules exist and are not unique to the foreign exchange market. More specifically, the profitability of moving average trading rules is highly correlated with the presence of price-smoothing participants in the market.

MOVING AVERAGE TRADING RULE

The popular moving average trading rule generates buy and sell signals based on the relationship between a short-term and long-term moving average of prices (see Kaufman [1987, Chapters 4 and 5]). The rule requires a long position when the shorter average moves above the long average, and dictates a short position when the shorter average falls below the long average.

For example, on Day 1, if the average of the last seven days' closing prices for gold is \$352.50, while the average of the last sixty days' closing prices is \$350.50, the rule requires a long position in gold. On Day 2, if the seven-day average is \$349 while the sixty-day average is \$350, the long position must be sold out and a short position established.

Thus, the moving average rule is essentially a trend-following system because in a rising price environment the shorter average tends to have larger values than the longer average, requiring a long position; when prices are falling, the shorter average tends to have lower values than the longer average, requiring a short position.

Although the moving average trading system is mechanical, there is presumably some skill in choosing the best moving average. For example, does a seven-day-sixty-day combination do better than a six-day-one-hundred-day combination?

Some practitioners test for the best moving average by simulating the profitability of hundreds of alternative combinations during a particular historical period, choosing the one that has done best. Moreover, they cite the historical profitability of the "winner" as evidence that the system works.

The problem with this approach is, of course, selection bias: if enough combinations of moving averages are tried, at least one is likely to work simply by chance. Out-of-sample simulations are required to determine whether the trading rule works in general and to identify which combination works best in particular.

For each futures contract in our sample, we follow a two-step procedure for selecting optimal moving averages and for simulating their profitability. Daily futures closing prices are used as the raw data. We start by searching for the most profitable moving average for Year 1 of our sample. We then use that optimal combination to simulate returns for Year 2.

The next step is to reoptimize by searching for the most profitable moving average for Years 1 and 2 combined. We then use that new optimal combination to simulate returns for Year 3. This sequential optimization and simulation is continued through the end of the sample period.

More specifically, let MA (i, j) represent the moving average strategy of short average i and long average j. We arbitrarily restrict our search for the optimal moving average to combinations represented by i = 1, 2, 3, ..., 15 and j = 16, 18, 20, ..., 200.

Suppose that following the buy/sell signals for MA (5, 50) produces the largest average daily return from among all 1,395 possible combinations for the first year of our sample. We then use MA(5, 50) to generate buy/sell signals for Year 2, and we record the daily returns from that strategy. Note that the simulations for Year 2 are out-of-sample simulations that are not contaminated by selection bias.

We then repeat the optimization procedure by searching over MA(i, j), i = 1, 2, 3, ..., 15, j = 16, 18, 20, ..., 200, with data for Years 1 and 2 combined, and then simulate the returns from employing the winner's signals for Year 3.

If there are n years of data (including 200 observations prior to what we have labeled Year 1), we have n - 1 years of out-of-sample daily returns simulations from following a moving average trading strategy.

SIMULATIONS AND PERFORMANCE MEASURES

Our optimization/simulation technique is based on data from futures markets. The great advantage of futures prices is that for actively traded contracts, closing prices represent actual transaction prices. In addition, financing costs are embedded in futures prices, so that separate interest rate data are not needed to incorporate carrying costs into the returns calculation.

On the other hand, because futures contracts expire, so-called rollover transactions are needed simply to maintain existing positions. Moreover, performance measures must take account of the fact that purchases and sales of futures contracts do not require exchanges of cash. We must deal with these complications in the simulations.

Implementing buy/sell decisions in futures markets according to the moving average rule requires that we choose from among outstanding contracts with different maturities. We simulate the buy/sell decisions in the nearest contract because it is usually the most liquid contract. As the settlement date approaches, however, liquidity shifts to the next-nearest contract.

Thus, simply to maintain an existing position the simulation must close out the position in the near contract and open a position in the next-nearest contract. Buy/sell transactions therefore occur not only following on moving average signals but also to roll over existing positions. The number of these transactions depends on the cycle of the particular commodity, with quarterly rollovers the most common.

To evaluate the performance of the moving average trading rule requires that we calculate the risk and return associated with following the buy/sell signals. To generate parameters consistent with cash market portfolios, we measure returns on futures prices as the natural logarithm of the closing price on Day t(p_t) divided by the closing price on Day t - 1 (p_{t-1}). This statistic is multiplied by 1 if the trading rule specifies a long position and multiplied by -1 if the rule requires a short position.

We then calculate the mean of the daily log returns associated with the moving average rule and annualize, assuming 250 trading days per year. The annualized standard deviation of the daily log returns is calculated as $\sigma \sqrt{t}$, where σ is the standard deviation of the trading rule's daily log returns, and t equals 250.

To determine whether the moving average trading rule generates abnormal returns requires a risk-adjusted measure of returns to compare with alternative investments, such as a buy-and-hold strategy for the S&P 500. As a first step we use the so-called Sharpe ratio, $(r_p - r_f)/\sigma_p$, with r_p signifying the returns on the portfolio p, which in our case are the returns generated by following the moving average trading rule for a particular futures contract; σ_p is the standard deviation of r_p; and r_f is the risk-free rate.

Because holding futures contracts requires no cash outlay, the returns are all in excess of the risk-free rate, so that total returns to the moving average trading position are $r_p + r_f$. Therefore, the relevant Sharpe ratio is simply r_p / σ_p, or the return divided by its standard deviation.

TRADING RULE SIMULATIONS FOR SELECTED FUTURES CONTRACTS

Moving average buy/sell signals were generated for twelve actively traded futures contracts. We include the major foreign currencies traded on the Chicago Mercantile Exchange (CME), i.e., the German mark, Swiss franc, Japanese yen, British pound, and Canadian dollar. We also include two actively traded short-term interest rate contracts: Eurodollar time deposits from the CME, and three-month sterling from the London International Financial Futures Exchange (LIFFE). Although the Treasury bill and Federal funds rate contracts would better reflect the potential price-smoothing behavior of central banks, neither is sufficiently liquid to warrant inclusion in our analysis.

Finally, to represent actively traded contracts without significant government price-smoothing behavior, we chose gold and silver from the Comex, U.S. Treasury bonds from the Chicago Board of Trade, crude oil from the New York Mercantile Exchange, and the S&P 500 from the CME. We should recognize, however, that both the Treasury bond market (because of central bank activity at the short end of the yield curve) and crude oil (because of OPEC) might contain elements of price-smoothing that could be exploited by trading rules.

We begin our optimization/simulation in 1979, except for those contracts that started trading after that date (Eurodollar time deposits, three-month sterling, S&P 500, and crude oil). The simulations end in 1991. Note that we could not include a number of short-term interest rate contracts currency trading on LIFFE (Euromark, Euroswiss, and Eurolira) because less than three years of data were available.

EXHIBIT 1 SIMULATIONS OF THE MOVING AVERAGE TRADING RULE

	(1)	(2)	(3)	(4)	(5)	(6)	(7)	(8)	(9)
	Number of Years	Average Annual Returns	Standard Deviation of Returns	Column 2 ÷ Column 3	Average Number of Trades per Year	Average Annual Returns After Transaction Costs	T-Statistic on Column 6 Returns	Average Annual Returns: Buy and Roll Over	Column 6 ÷ Column 3
German Mark	12	0.0980	0.1176	0.8333	17.08	0.0937	2.76	-0.0197	0.797
3-Month Eurodollar	8	0.0034	0.0038	0.8947	16.75	0.00298	2.53	0.0036	0.785
Swiss Franc	12	0.10103	0.1311	0.7727	12.25	0.0982	2.67	-0.0268	0.749
Japanese Yen	12	0.0742	0.1112	0.6673	17.08	0.0699	2.17	0.020	0.629
British Pound	12	0.0580	0.1198	0.4841	16.58	0.0539	1.55	0.0047	0.4495
Canadian $	12	0.0253	0.0429	0.5897	25.50	0.0189	1.52	0.0148	0.441
Crude Oil	7	0.199	0.4151	0.479	31.71	0.1673	1.07	0.117	0.403
3-Month Sterling	8	0.0024	0.0054	0.4444	28.63	0.00168	0.88	-0.0046	0.312
U.S. T-Bonds	12	0.0450	0.1406	0.3201	24.42	0.0377	0.93	0.0371	0.267
Silver	11	-0.003	0.3159	-.009	30.18	-0.0271	-0.28	-0.2224	-0.086
Gold	12	-0.0270	0.2337	-0.1155	18.92	-0.0364	-0.54	-0.121	-0.15
S&P 500	8	-0.1120	0.2195	-0.5103	15.88	-0.1152	-1.48	0.0672	-0.524

Exhibit 1 presents the relevant summary statistics. Column 1 records the number of years available for out-of-sample simulations. Most contracts have twelve years of simulations, with 1979 providing the first optimization year, and 1980 through 1991 available for simulation. For the S&P 500, three-month sterling, and three-month Eurodollar contracts, simulations were performed over eight years, and for crude oil simulations were done over seven years. (Although data for silver were available in 1979, we eliminate 1980 from the simulation because we did not want the Hunt family price manipulations during 1980 to contaminate the results.)

Column 2 shows the average annual return produced by following the moving average buy and sell signals, column 3 records the standard deviation of returns, and column 4 shows the relevant Sharpe ratio, i.e., the mean return from column 2 divided by the standard deviation of return from column 3.

Note that the returns in column 2 are positive for all contracts, except silver, gold, and the S&P 500. This result provides initial support for the proposition that technical trading profits occur only in markets where price-smoothing behavior is present.

Although the returns data are based on closing prices in each of the markets, the results in column 2 do not take account of the bid-ask spread encountered when trading. One problem is that the relevant bid-ask spread varies with the number of contracts that must be bought and sold.

For simplicity, we assume the bid-ask spread is equal to one tick (the smallest price increment) for each of the contracts in the Exhibit, except for crude oil and gold, where the bid-ask spread is assumed equal to two ticks. These numbers certainly reflect the cost of trading up to ten contracts in these markets; in many cases, hundreds of contracts can be traded with no change in these bid-ask spreads.

To adjust returns for transaction costs we first expressed the bid-ask spread as a percent of price, then multiplied by the average number of trades per year (including rollovers) in column 5 of the Exhibit, and subtracted that sum from the annual returns recorded in column 2. The resulting average returns after transaction costs are recorded in column 6.

The message from column 6 is identical with that of column 2: returns are positive in markets where price-smoothing behavior is present, but not elsewhere (gold, silver, and the S&P 500).

To determine whether price-smoothing is associated with statistically significant positive returns after transaction costs, we form a t-statistic on the mean returns by dividing column 6 by $\sigma\sqrt{t}$, where σ is the standard deviation from column 3, and t is the number of years from column 1. The t-values are recorded in column 7. Four of the seven returns on currencies and short-term interest rate futures are significantly positive at the 5% level.

Of greater interest is a test of the joint hypothesis that all seven means are significantly different from zero. Making the simplifying assumption that the moving average returns follow jointly normal distributions permits us to perform a Hotelling T^2 test (see Morrison [1976, p. 131]). Our calculation gives a T^2 statistic of 13.62, which has a p-value of less than 0.0001 under the distribution of $F_{7,1756}$. Thus we can strongly reject the hypothesis that the positive mean returns observed for the currencies and short interest rates are really equal to zero.

To what extent can the positive returns from the moving average rule be accomplished by a naive strategy of simply buying and holding (and rolling over) each futures contract? Comparing column 6 with column 8, which records the annual average return (after transaction costs) from a "buy and roll over" strategy, shows that for those contracts with positive returns, the moving average rule dominates in each case except for three-month Eurodollars. Thus the moving average rule seems to add value over and above a naive buy and roll over strategy.

To determine whether the moving average rule generates excess returns relative to the risk incurred, we turn our attention to column 9, which reports the new Sharpe ratio (column 6 divided by column 3). Recall that the Sharpe ratio equals the return over and above the risk-free rate divided by the standard deviation of returns. Thus, the ratio measures the excess return per unit of risk. The contracts are listed in the Exhibit from highest to lowest according to the Sharpe ratio recorded in column 9. Thus, the German mark has the highest Sharpe ratio, three-month Eurodollars the next highest, and so on, until the S&P 500, with the lowest Sharpe ratio.

The relative values of the Sharpe ratio support the hypothesis that returns per unit risk are related to the existence of price-smoothing behavior in the market. With the single adjustment of changing the relative position of three-month sterling and crude oil, the Sharpe ratio is highest for currencies and short interest rates, next highest for markets with some potential price-smoothing (crude oil and Treasury bonds), and lowest for markets without obvious price-smoothing behavior (gold, silver, and the S&P 500).

How do these returns per unit risk compare with investing in the stock market? Between 1980 and 1991, the Sharpe ratio for investing in the S&P 500 was approximately 0.43. Using that criterion, the returns on all the currencies and on three-month Eurodollars can be considered abnormal relative to the risk incurred.

An alternative measure of performance suggested by Jack Treynor scales the excess return by beta to calculate risk-adjusted return. The betas (relative to the S&P 500) of each of the moving average strategies in the Exhibit are all between ±0.04. Thus for practical purposes, all the contracts with positive returns seem to earn abnormal returns. In other words, the moving average trading rule produces abnormal returns in all markets, except for those without any price-smoothing behavior, i.e., gold, silver, and the S&P 500.

One important caveat is in order. Although technical trading generates abnormal returns in foreign currencies, short-term interest rates, and, to a lesser extent, Treasury bonds and crude oil, implementing the strategy is not so easy. This is not so much because the trading rules are complicated; they aren't. Rather, sticking to trading positions that may have little support from fundamentals simply because of trading rule "instructions" requires dedication and discipline that can be sorely tested by intermittent losses.

Trading rules in currencies and short-term interest rates fail frequently because they aren't followed. The abnormal returns are, after all, only expected returns; sufficient time must elapse before the probabilities assert themselves. As a practical matter, only those who have properly scaled their leveraged trading positions relative to available capital have the staying power necessary to succeed.

CONCLUSION

Academic arguments contradicting practitioner faith in technical trading systems have usually focused on two points. On a conceptual basis, the persistence of abnormal returns is inconsistent with the fact that rational market participants exploit the abnormal returns. On methodological grounds, most practitioner evidence suffers from selection bias.

This study of abnormal returns from following moving average rules in futures contracts on foreign currencies and short-term interest rates overcomes both of these objections. First, the existence of central bank price-smoothing behavior in markets for foreign currencies and short-term interest rates suggests that abnormal profits from following trading rules need not disappear over time. Second, our out-of-sample simulations demonstrating abnormal returns are carefully designed to eliminate selection bias.

Thus, even practitioners who believe in efficient markets need not apologize for the success of technical trading rules in futures contracts on foreign currencies and short-term interest rates.

ENDNOTES

This article was published in *The Journal of Derivatives*, Spring 1994, pp 39-44.

The author wishes to thank Jeff Heisler and Abbe Goldstein for their excellent research assistance. Helpful comments were received from Menachem Brenner, Kenneth Garbade, Richard Levich, Jainping Mei, and Roy Smith.

REFERENCES

Levich, Richard M., and Lee R. Thomas. "The Significance of Technical Trading Rule Profits in the Foreign Exchange Market: A Bootstrap Approach." NBER Working Paper #3818, August 1991.

Morrison, Donald F. Multivariate Statistical Methods, 2nd. ed. New York: McGraw-Hill, 1976.

Sweeney, Richard J. "Beating the Foreign Exchange Market." *Journal of Finance*, March 1986.

3 BENEFITS OF MANAGED FUND STRATEGIES: MANAGED FUTURES AND HEDGE FUNDS

THOMAS SCHNEEWEIS
University of Massachusetts

RICHARD SPURGIN
Clark University

INTRODUCTION

The alternative investment universe consists of a number of investment strategies that offer risk and return opportunities not commonly found in traditional long-only stock and bond investment. A natural way to differentiate between different alternative investment strategies is to examine the liquidity of the investment vehicle. The most illiquid are investment trusts such as venture capital funds, leverage buyout funds and natural resource partnerships that do not, as a general rule, allow selective redemptions. Hedge funds are moderately liquid alternative investments. *Hedge funds*, likewise, manage client assets on a discretionary basis and generally represent 'leveraged' investment strategies which use both global cash and global futures and options markets. They generally have three-month to one-year lock-up periods. The most liquid are managed futures accounts. M*anaged futures* refers to an industry comprised of professional money managers known as *commodity trading advisors* (CTAs) who use global futures and options markets as an investment medium. CTAs typically allow investors to withdraw capital with less than three months notice.

This article focuses on the benefits of adding hedge funds and managed futures to an investment portfolio. Managed futures provide direct exposure to international financial and nonfinancial asset sectors while offering (through their ability to easily take both long and short investment positions) a means to gain exposure to risk and return patterns not easily accessible with investment in traditional stock and bond portfolios. Hedge funds trade in both cash and derivative markets, and can provide returns based not only on market direction but also unique return opportunities available in individual markets and securities. However, for alternative investments such as hedge funds and managed futures to grow as an investment alternative, individuals need to increase their knowledge and comfort level regarding their use in investment portfolios. Exactly what are the benefits of managed funds as part of an investor's overall asset portfolio? While it is impossible in a short synopsis to convey all the details of the benefits of these assets, managed futures and hedge funds offer the opportunity to:

(1) reduce portfolio volatility risk,

(2) enhance portfolio returns in economic environments in which traditional stock and bond investments offer limited opportunities, and

(3) participate in a wide variety of new financial products and markets not available in traditional investor products.

GENERAL DESCRIPTION OF MANAGED FUTURES AND HEDGE FUNDS

Both managed futures and hedge funds have been described as skill-based investment strategies. Skill-based strategies obtain returns from the unique skill or strategy of the trader. Managed futures and hedge funds have also been described as *absolute return* strategies, as these returns do not depend on the long-term return in underlying traditional stock and bond markets. Because managed futures and hedge funds are actively managed, trader skill is certainly important, as are the basic trading strategies behind most fund investments. However, more recently, some hedge fund and managed futures returns have been shown to be driven also by market factors such as trends, so one can think of their returns as a combination of manager skill and of an underlying return to the strategy itself. With the increased use of managed futures and hedge fund vehicles in investment management, industry practitioners and academics have created indices that can be used as benchmarks for managed futures and hedge fund investors. These indices are constructed to show managed futures and hedge fund performance by investment style. Investors should note that there are several different benchmarks, each with its own approach to performance presentation, manager selection, and investment

EXHIBIT 1A PERCENTAGE OF ASSETS IN ALTERNATIVE MAR CTA STRATEGY (12/1998)

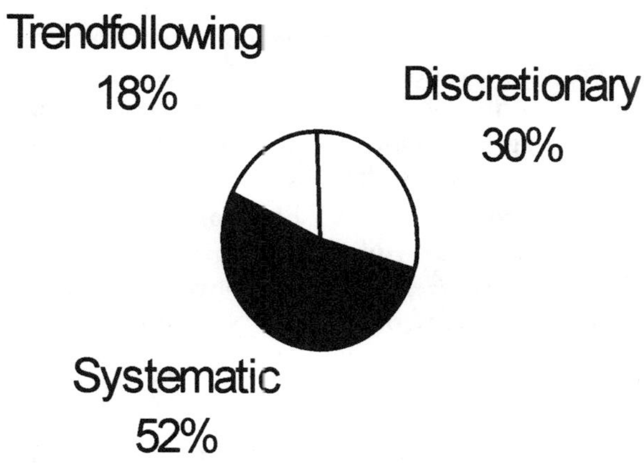

EXHIBIT 1B PERCENTAGE OF ASSETS (SECTOR ALLOCATION) IN ALTERNATIVE MAR CTA STRATEGY (12/1998)

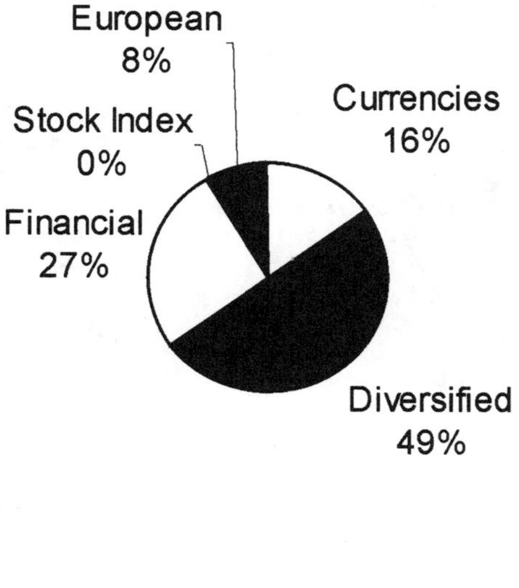

style classification. In this article, we use primarily the managed futures indices compiled by Managed Accounts Reports (MAR) and hedge fund indices compiled by Evaluation Associates Capital Markets (EACM). A short description of the managed futures and hedge fund indices follows:

MANAGED FUTURES INDICES (Managed Accounts Reports)

Commodity Trading Advisors (CTAs) are often classified into equal-weighted and dollar-weighted indices as well as sub-groups based on markets traded (for example, diversified, currency, and financial), or based on investment style (discretionary, systematic and trend-following). As of 1998, MAR reports that over $40 billion is managed under the managed futures fund, pools, and commodity trading advisor classification. For commodity trading advisors, Exhibits1a and 1b illustrate the percentage invested according to financial markets or investment style.

HEDGE FUND INDICES (Evaluation Associates Capital Markets)

Hedge funds are first classified according to investment style (for example, relative value). Within each style category, funds are classified according to the underlying markets traded. For example, within the relative value style classification, there are a number of sub-groups, including long/short equity, convertible hedging, and bond hedging. EACM classifies hedge funds into the following categories.

(1) **Relative Value**: Balanced, or hedged, long and short positions with subindices such as *Long/Short Equity* (long undervalued equities/short overvalued equities usually on an equal dollar bases); *Convertible Hedging* (long convertible bonds or preferred, short underlying common); *Bond Hedging* (yield curve arbitrage or long/short debt

EXHIBIT 1C PERCENTAGE OF ASSETS IN ALTERNATIVE HFR HEDGE FUND CLASSIFICATIONS (12/1998)

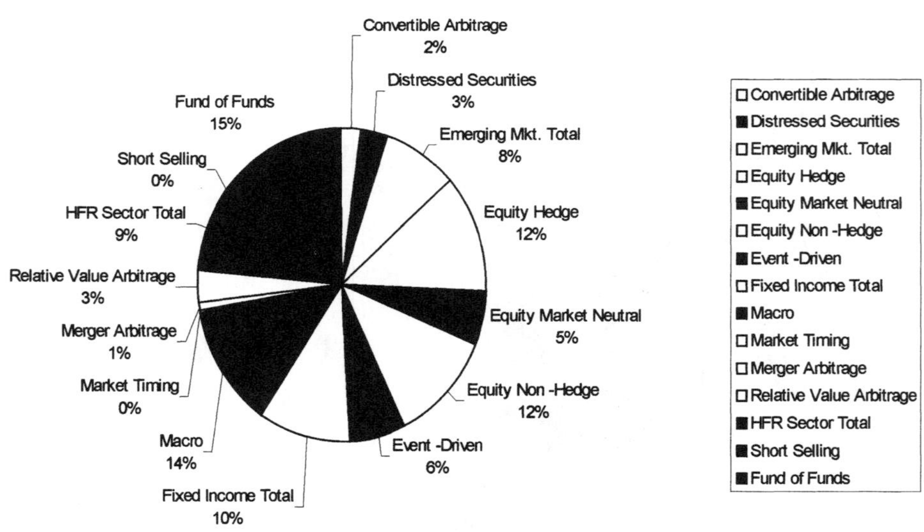

positions); *Rotational* (multiple relative value strategies, including all of the above).

(2) **Event Driven**: (Corporate transactions and special situations) sub-indices including *Deal Arbitrage* (long/short equity securities of companies involved in corporate transactions; B*ankruptcy/Distressed* (long undervalued securities of companies usually in financial distress or operating under Chapter 11). Multi-strategy includes deal funds dealing in both deal arbitrage and bankruptcy.

(3) **Equity Hedge Funds**: Long and short securities with varying degrees of exposure and leverage such as *Domestic Long Equity* (long undervalued US equities; short selling is used sparingly); *Domestic Opportunistic Equity* (long and short U.S. equity with ability to be net short overall) and *Global International* (primarily long undervalued equities with the ability to use short selling opportunistically)

(4) **Managed Futures/Global Asset Allocators**: Opportunistically long and short multiple financial and/or non financial assets. Sub-indices include *Systematic* (long or short markets based on trend-following or other quantitative analysis) and *Discretionary* (long or short markets based on qualitative/fundamental analysis often with technical input)

(5) **Short Selling**: Short sale of U.S. equities with expectation of price declines.

Other firms which provide active manager indices, such as Managed Accounts Reports and Hedge Fund Reports provide similar groupings as well as additional subset groupings. For instance, for HFR Hedge Fund indices, Exhibit 1c illustrates the percentage invested according to financial markets or investment style.

THE GROWTH AND BENEFIT OF ALTERNATIVE INVESTMENTS

Futures and options have been used for centuries both as a risk management tool and return enhancement vehicle. Investment firms have always followed proprietary trading strategies involving both cash market and derivative positions. More recently, institutional investors such as corporate and public pension funds, endowments and trusts, and bank trust departments have been including hedge funds and managed futures as one segment of a well-diversified portfolio.

The dollars under management in the Managed Futures industry have grown from less than $5 billion under management in 1990 to approximately $40 billion in 1998 while for the hedge fund industry have grown from under $25 billion in 1990 to over $250 billion in 1998. Growth in investor demand for managed futures and hedge fund products indicates investor appreciation of the potential benefits of trading in derivatives markets. There are also a number of advantages that derivatives markets have over cash markets, including lower transaction costs, lower market impact costs, and access to leverage. In addition, certain trading strategies that rely primarily on exchange-traded derivatives offer the additional benefits of market integrity, safety, and government oversight.

MANAGED FUTURES AND HEDGE FUNDS: RISK AND RETURN PERFORMANCE

Results in Exhibit 2 show the performance of a number of assets and combinations of assets over the past nine years (1990-1998).[1] These assets include the EACM 100 index, which is an alternative investments index consisting of hedge funds and commodity trading advisors, the MAR CTA index, and several measures of U.S. and global stock and bond performance. The EACM 100 index has a higher Sharpe ratio than any of the other assets. Managed futures reported a Sharpe ratio that is about equal to that

EXHIBIT 2 PERFORMANCE MEASURES FOR MANAGED FUTURES AND OTHER ASSET INDICES AND PORTFOLIOS

Nine Year Performance of Indices: January, 1990 - December, 1998	EACM 100	MAR$CTA	GSCI	S&P 500	Salomon Treasury Bond	MSCI
Average Annual Return	13.95%	12.6%	0.4%	16.5%	8.3%	10.0%
Standard Deviation	4.09%	10.8%	16.7%	13.5%	4.2%	14.2%
Sharpe Ratio	2.19	0.71	-0.27	0.85	0.77	0.35
Minimum Monthly Return	-4.6%	-6.2%	-13.0%	-15.6%	-2.3%	-14.3%
Maximum Monthly Return	4.7%	13.5%	20.7%	10.8%	4.0%	10.0%
Correlation With EACM 100			0.11	0.41	0.18	0.33
EACM 100 Excess Annual Breakeven			9.1%	7.5%	8.4%	8.5%
Correlation With MAR$CTA			0.10	-0.06	0.27	-0.10
MAR$CTA Excess Annual Breakeven			7.9%	8.1%	5.4%	8.0%

Nine Year Performance of Asset Portfolios: January, 1990 - December, 1998	Port I US Stock, Bond, Commodity and EACM 100	Port II US Stock, Bond, and Commodity	Port III US Stock and Bond	Port IV Wrld. Stock, Bond, Commodity and EACM 100	Port V Wrld. Stock, Bond, and Commodity
Average Annual Return	11.7%	10.4%	12.6%	9.5%	8.2%
Standard Deviation	6.4%	6.7%	7.7%	7.0%	7.3%
Sharpe Ratio	1.04	0.81	0.98	0.64	0.44
Minimum Monthly Return	-5.9%	-6.1%	-6.1%	-5.4%	-5.6%
Maximum Monthly Return	5.6%	5.6%	7.2%	5.4%	5.3%
Correlation With EACM 100		0.42	0.40		0.30
EACM 100 Excess Annual Breakeven		7.6%	7.4%		8.4%
Correlation With MAR$CTA		0.08	0.03		0.03
MAR$CTA Excess Annual Breakeven		6.9%	7.3%		7.5%

EXHIBIT 3 RISK AND RETURN OF STOCK, BOND AND HEDGE FUNDS: 1990-1998

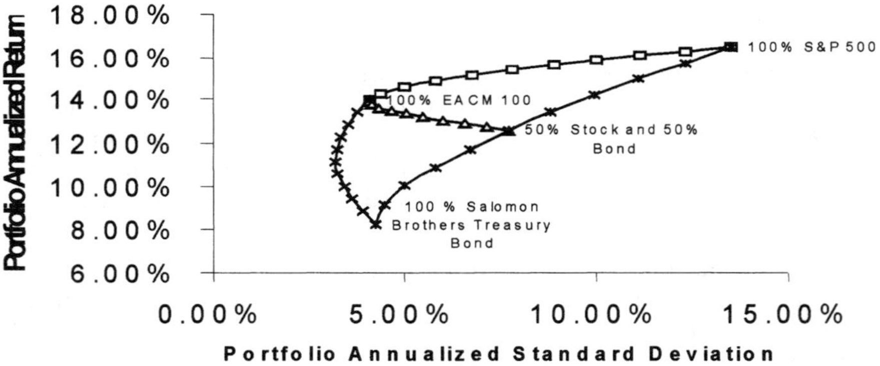

of U.S. stocks and bonds over the time period. However, relative to the EACM 100, the lower low correlation with stocks and bonds means that managed futures may offer superior diversification benefits.[2]

The benefit of including hedge funds and managed futures in diversified portfolios is illustrated in Exhibit 3. When the hedge fund/managed futures index (EACM 100) is added to the U.S. stocks, Treasury Bonds, or a portfolio of U.S. stocks and bonds, the risk/return profile improves.

RISK/RETURN OPPORTUNITIES IN PERIODS OF MARKET UNCERTAINTY

The correlation between alternative investments and most traditional investments are close to zero (Exhibit 2). However, when the correlation between asset returns is segmented according to whether the traditional asset rose or fell, certain hedge funds and managed futures are often negatively correlated in months when traditional asset returns are negative while being positively correlated when traditional asset returns are positive.

For instance, as shown in Exhibit 4, for the period 1990 through 1998, managed futures are negatively correlated (-. 25) with the S&P 500 when the S&P 500 posted its 30 worst months and yet are positively correlated (.33) when the S&P 500 reported its best 30 months. Thus, as shown in Exhibit 5, various managed funds strategies have different correlations in varying S&P 500 return periods. For instance, many hedge

EXHIBIT 4 CORRELATIONS WITH THE S&P 500 (1/1990 TO 12/1998)

		All Months	Mid Ranked SP 500 Months	Worst 30 SP 500 Months	Best 30 SP 500 Months
EACM	Long/Short Equity	-0.19	-0.21	0.02	0.06
EACM	Convertible Hedge	0.08	0.02	0.41	-0.17
EACM	Bond Hedge	0.02	0.13	0.61	-0.18
EACM	Rotational	0.07	0.13	0.57	0.05
EACM	Arbitrage	0.54	0.05	0.68	-0.04
EACM	Bankruptcy	0.37	-0.04	0.53	0.03
EACM	Multi-Strategy	0.53	0.19	0.76	-0.14
EACM	Domestic Long	0.80	0.31	0.78	0.33
EACM	Domestic Opportunity	0.26	0.30	0.29	0.05
EACM	Global/International	0.62	0.18	0.72	0.40
EACM	Discretionary	0.25	-0.13	0.52	-0.05
EACM	Systematic	-0.07	-0.04	-0.26	0.32
EACM	Short	-0.76	-0.39	-0.68	-0.38
MSCI	World	0.78	0.30	0.74	0.62
Sal. Bros.	Treasury Bond	0.36	-0.02	-0.01	0.17
MAR	CTA$	-0.04	-0.07	-0.25	0.33

EXHIBIT 5 CORRELATIONS IN BEST AND WORST 30 MONTHS IN S&P 500 (1/1990 TO 12/1998)

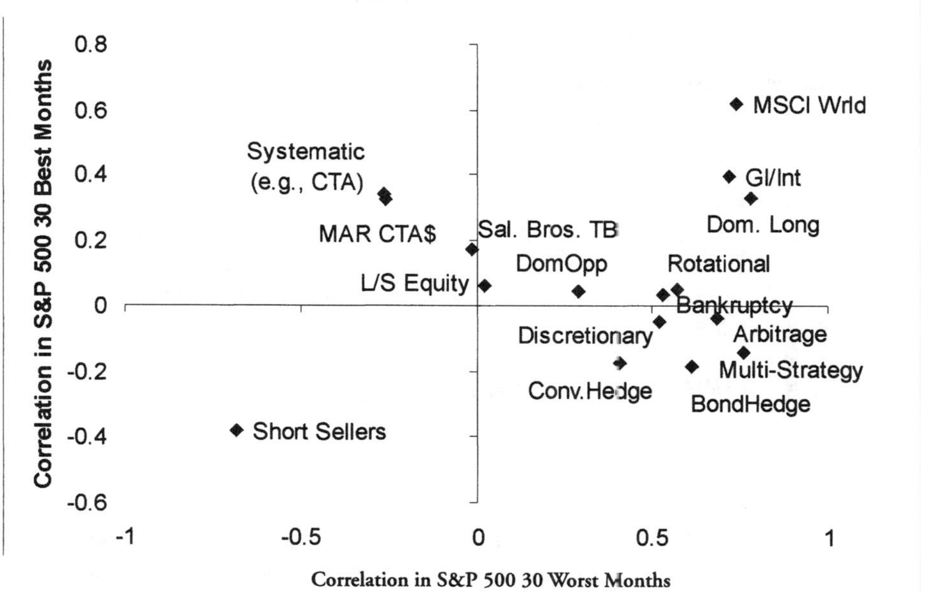

funds often have low correlations with the S&P 500 when it is rising and high correlations when it is falling. Thus the benefits of several hedge fund strategies with equity or bond exposure may arise less from their diversification advantages than their higher expected return/risk tradeoffs.

In contrast, Exhibit 6 indicates that when S&P 500 returns are ranked from low to high and divided into nine subperiods for the period 1990 through 1998, managed futures offered positive returns in months in which the S&P 500 provided its greatest negative returns as well as positive returns in months in which the S&P 500 reported its highest positive returns.

EXHIBIT 6 RANKING BY S&P 500 (1990-1998)

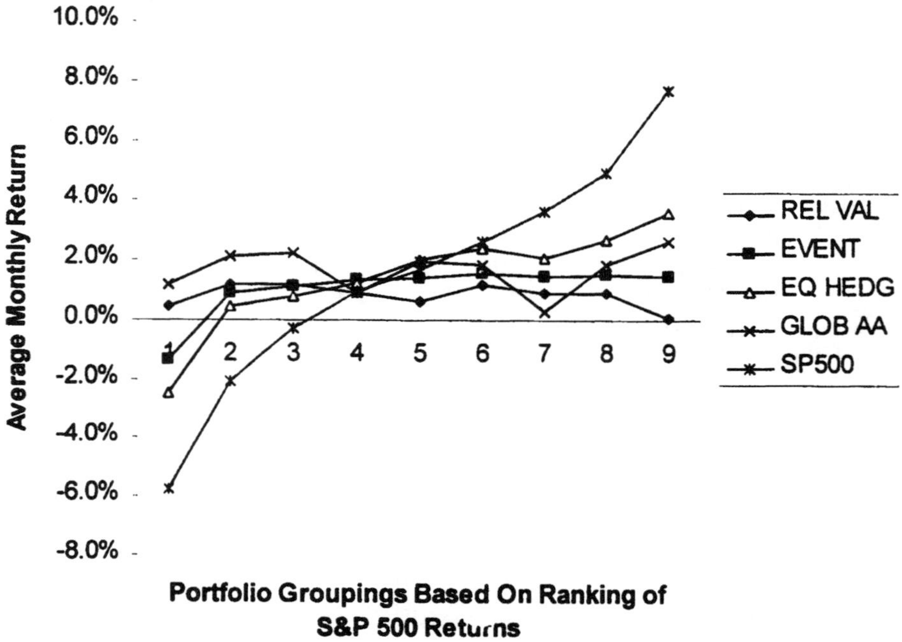

EXHIBIT 7 RISK AND RETURN OF STOCK, BOND AND HEDGE FUNDS: 1995-1998

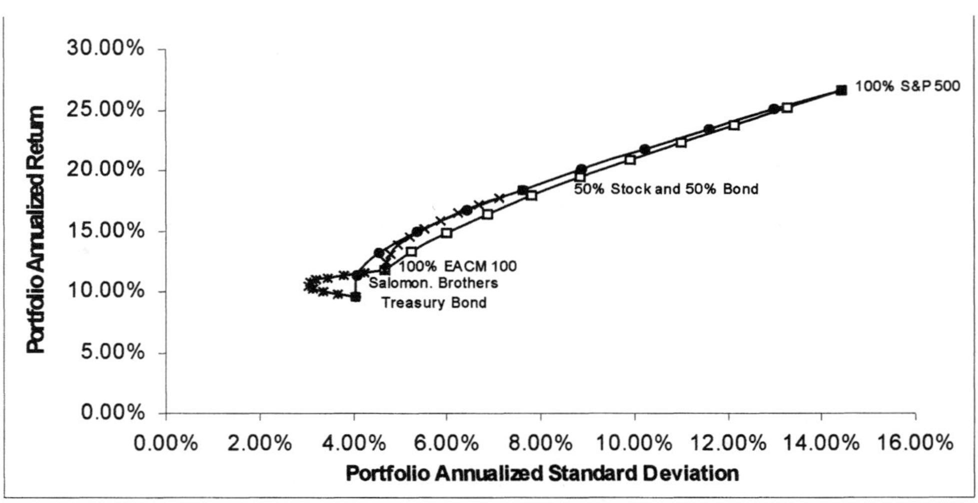

RECENT PERFORMANCE

The benefits of adding hedge funds to a diversified portfolio may, however, be affected by the historical high returns achieved by hedge funds during the first half of the 1990s. In Exhibit 7, the return and risk frontier of adding the EACM 100 to the S&P 500 and Salomon Brothers Treasury Bond index portfolio is given for the recent four-year period, 1995-1998. As shown in Exhibit 8, in the period 1995-1998, the return of the EACM 100 was lower and the risk was higher than for the full period 1990-1998.[3]

EXHIBIT 8 PERFORMANCE MEASURES FOR MANAGED FUTURES AND OTHER ASSET INDICES AND PORTFOLIOS

Four Year Performance of Indices: January, 1995 - December, 1998	EACM 100	MAR$CTA	GSCI	S&P 500	Salomon Treasury Bond	MSCI
Average Annual Return	11.8%	11.4%	-2.9%	26.6%	9.6%	17.4%
Standard Deviation	4.4%	9.4%	17.3%	14.4%	4.1%	13.3%
Sharpe Ratio	1.48	0.66	-0.47	1.48	1.07	0.92
Minimum Monthly Return	-4.6%	-4.9%	-13.0%	-15.6%	-2.0%	-14.3%
Maximum Monthly Return	3.5%	7.9%	9.7%	7.9%	4.0%	8.7%
Correlation With EACM 100			0.23	0.63	-0.02	0.61
EACM 100 Excess Annual Breakeven			7.0%	2.4%	6.6%	4.1%
Correlation With MAR$CTA			0.18	0.11	0.47	0.10
MAR$CTA Excess Annual Breakeven			7.0%	4.7%	1.4%	5.4%

Four Year Performance of Asset Portfolios: January, 1995 - December, 1998	Port I US Stock, Bond, Commodity and EACM 100	Port II US Stock, Bond, and Commodity	Port III US Stock and Bond	Port IV Wrld. Stock, Bond, Commodity and EACM 100	Port V Wrld. Stock, Bond, and Commodity
Average Annual Return	15.8%	14.4%	18.4%	11.8%	10.4%
Standard Deviation	6.8%	7.3%	7.6%	6.6%	7.2%
Sharpe Ratio	1.55	1.26	1.73	0.99	0.72
Minimum Monthly Return	-5.9%	-6.1%	-6.1%	-5.4%	-5.6%
Maximum Monthly Return	5.0%	5.6%	5.3%	4.6%	4.8%
Correlation With EACM 100		0.59	0.58		0.47
EACM 100 Excess Annual Breakeven		3.3%	2.1%		5.0%
Correlation With MAR$CTA		0.28	0.24		0.23
MAR$CTA Excess Annual Breakeven		2.9%	2.4%		4.6%

In both periods, managed funds increased the return/risk of the investment frontier.

As important, as shown in Exhibit 9, the S&P 500 experienced a negative return of -14.5% while the Morgan Stanley World Equity Index also fell -13% during the recent period of international turmoil in August, 1998. International diversification among equity securities failed to provide diversification. Hedge funds with equity exposure or hedge funds with extensive credit risk exposure also experienced poor performance in August, 1998. However, various market neutral and commodity futures programs had relatively low negative returns or, in the case of managed futures, even a positive return performance

COMPARISON OF TRADITIONAL AND ALTERNATIVE INVESTMENT VEHICLES

While alternative and traditional investment may differ in terms of their strategies and investment goals, there is very little difference in the methods of structuring and packaging the returns. For instance, in the managed futures/hedge fund area, as in the traditional asset area, investors can obtain 1) passive indices reflecting the expected return of a particular investment strategy or active investment position and 2) open and closed-end funds that track a particular investment strategy offered by managers. These open and closed end funds may be single or multiple manager in form, private pool/ limited partnerships and segregated accounts (private investment trusts).

EXHIBIT 9 MONTHLY RETURNS IN RECENT PERIOD OF MARKET CRISIS (AUGUST 1998)

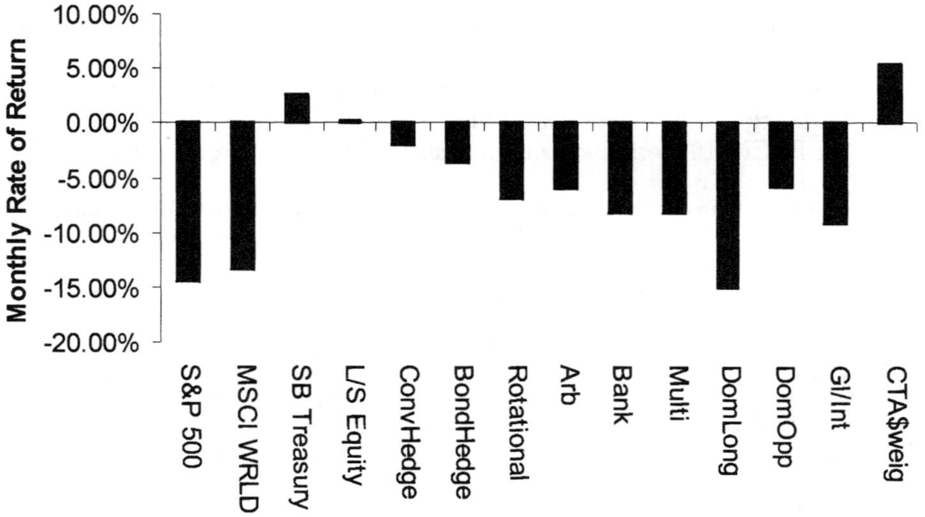

Many new alternative investment products have also been developed to assuage investor concerns. For example, guaranteed investment structures remain a principal source of investment offerings. These products eliminate or minimize the risk of loss of principal if held to maturity. Guaranteed products have a lower return than direct investment in the underlying fund.

The recent near-collapse of Long Term Capital Management has raised the concern of many investors on the trading and oversight risks of investing in alternative investments. Many alternative investments are not materially different from traditional stock and bond investments in terms of market structure, product structure, or security design. Stock and bond investments share many common features with alternative assets. These features include institutional issues such as government regulation and professional oversight. While some hedge funds trade primarily on relatively unregulated over-the-counter markets, most hedge funds and commodity trading advisors trade on regulated exchanges such as the New York Mercantile Exchange or the Chicago Board of Trade in which financial products are traded in real-time liquid markets.

Investors must appreciate that the essential difference between alternative and traditional investments is not how they are governed, marketed or even measured in terms of market performance, but that alternative investments offer unique risk and return properties not easily available though traditional investment securities or investment products. These return opportunities stem from the expanded universe of securities available to trade and the strategies that can be employed. Funds can access both financial and nonfinancial (commodity) markets and can easily take long, short, spread and option positions in any of these markets. Expanding the set of investment opportunities results in providing diversification benefits to a portfolio that cannot be replicated through traditional stock, bond and real estate investment strategies.

ENDNOTES

This article was published by CISDM/SOM, University of Massachusetts, and is reprinted with permission.

[1] The annual and monthly returns presented in the exhibits are derived from natural logs. Investors who wish to calculate holding period returns from the above returns should use the antilogarithm of x (reported return).

[2] In this study, Portfolio I is a portfolio comprised of the EACM 100 (10%), GSCI (10%), S&P500 (40%), and Salomon Brothers Treasury Bond (40%) Indices. Portfolio II is a portfolio comprised of GSCI 20%), S&P500 (40%), and Salomon Brothers Treasury Bond Index (40%). Portfolio III is an equal weighted stock and bond portfolio. Portfolios' IV though VI are similar to Portfolios I through III with the substitution of the MSCI World equity and Salomon Brothers World Bond Index for the S&P 500 and Salomon Treasury Bond Index. Lastly, Excess Annual Breakeven is a measure of the difference between the actual return achieve and the return required for the cited investment (EACM 100 or MAR$CTA) to be included (at some weight) with the cited asset (e.g., S&P 500) or portfolio (e.g., Portfolio III) such that the Sharpe ratio of the comparison asset or portfolio increases.

[3] Similar improvements in the return/risk frontier result from using the MAR$CTA index. See Benefits of Managed Futures, AIMA, 1999.

REFERENCES

Chance, D. *Managed Futures and Their Role in Investment Portfolios* (Institute of Chartered Financial Analysts, 1994).

McCarthy, D., Thomas Schneeweis, and R. Spurgin, "Investment in CTAs: An Alternative Managed Futures Investment," *The Journal of Derivatives*, Vol.3, No.4 (Summer, 1996), pp. 36-47.

McCarthy, D. and R. Spurgin. "A Review of Hedge Fund Performance Benchmarks," *The Journal of Alternative Investments* (Summer, 1998), pp. 18-28.

Peters, C.C. ed. *Managed Futures: Performance Evaluation and Analysis of Commodity Funds, Pools and Accounts* (Probus Publishing, 1992).

Schneeweis, T. *The Benefits of Managed Futures.* AIMA, 1998.

Schneeweis, T. "Dealing with Myths of Managed Futures," *The Journal of Alternative Investments* (Summer, 1998), pp. 9-17.

Schneeweis, T. "Dealing with Myths of Hedge Funds," *The Journal of Alternative Investments* (Winter, 1998), pp.11-15.

Schneeweis, T. and R. Spurgin. Alternative Investments in the Institutional Portfolio, AIMA, 1998.

Schneeweis, T., R. Spurgin and M. Potter. "Managed Futures and Hedge Fund Investment for Downside Equity Risk Management", *Derivatives Quarterly*, (Fall, 1996), pp. 62-72.

Schneeweis, T. and R. Spurgin. "Comparisons of Commodity and Managed Futures Benchmark Indices." *The Journal of Derivatives*, (Summer, 1997), pp. 33-50.

II MANAGED FUTURES

INTRODUCTION

During the past decade the investment management industry has undergone numerous changes. New forms of investment products have come into existence to meet the needs of changing financial regulation, information technology, and investor demands. While most investors continue to concentrate on traditional stock and bond investment, managed futures (investment funds which use foreign exchange and international futures and options markets as their primary investment vehicles) are attracting the interest of institutional investors as a means of increasing return while reducing risk through diversification.

Both practitioner and academic research has addressed the importance of futures and options in global asset management as well as the potential return from holding passive and active positions in global foreign exchange and futures and options markets. While theoretical bases for profitable return to risk managed futures' strategies exist, ultimately the question of whether managed futures can obtain these benefits for their investors is an empirical one.

Previous analyses of the benefits of managed futures in asset management have principally focused on the benefits of commodity trading advisors (CTAs) and private and public commodity funds [Elton et al., 1987, 1990, 1992; Irwin et al., 1993]. Some of these studies have concluded that while direct investment with CTAs appears profitable, individual accounts with publicly traded commodity funds may provide poor investments as stand alone vehicles and may only provide marginal value as additions to traditional asset classes [Edwards and Park, 1996; Edwards, 1998]. However, some of these earlier studies' results may not reflect either the number of new futures/option contracts available or the current structure of these funds (e.g., single manager versus multiple manager forms).[1]

Moreover, academic research results based on fund performance during the early 1980 to the early 1990s may not fully represent the risk/return tradeoffs available today in a widening variety of global financial and commodity markets. Lastly, results that concentrate on public managed futures funds and pools performance may be based on a select set of commodity trading advisors and not on the larger commodity trading advisor universe, many of whom prefer not to offer their investment services through public funds or private pools.[2]

In fact, futures and options have been used for centuries both as a risk management tool and return enhancement vehicle. Managed futures have been used as an investment alternative since the late 1960s.[3] More recently, institutional investors such as corporate and public pension funds, endowments and trusts, and bank trust departments have been including managed futures as one segment of a well-diversified portfolio. As shown in Exhibit 1, the dollars under management in the managed futures industry has grown from less than $1 billion under management in 1980 to approximately $40 billion in 1998.[4]

However, despite empirical evidence [Schneeweis, 1996] that supports the investment benefits of managed futures as stand alone investments and, more impor-

EXHIBIT 1 MANAGED FUTURES ASSETS UNDER MANAGEMENT, 1980 TO 1998

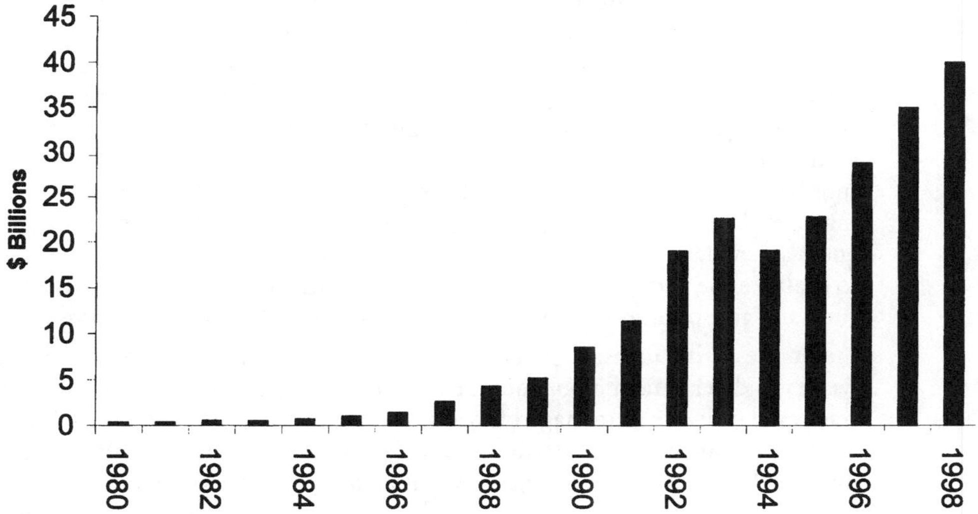

Source: Managed Accounts Reports

tantly, as part of investors' diversified portfolios, investment research has continued to concentrate on the performance characteristics of traditional asset products. In order for managed futures to become an increasing portion of investors' portfolios, individuals need to increase their comfort level regarding their use. As discussed in the previous section, investment in various commodity trading advisor investment strategies is linked both to financial theory and empirical evidence. Unfortunately, several myths still exist among investors which prevent them from better understanding the investment properties of managed futures investment. For instance, while few investors would question if stocks were riskier than bonds (although in certain market environments such as high interest rate volatility some bonds are expected to be riskier than some stocks), the question remains if investment in commodity trading advisors (CTAs) is by nature riskier than investment in stocks.

While CTAs have often been regarded as high risk investments, over the period 1990-1998, both individual CTAs and individual firms Dow Jones 30 industrials had, on average, annualized standard deviation of approximately 25%. Also, for the period 1990-1998, a portfolio of CTAs tracked by Managed Accounts Reports had an annualized standard deviation (13.6%), similar to that of the Dow Jones 30 Industrials (13.8%).[5] The articles reprinted in this section address some of the myths of investment in managed futures. Articles are presented which offer information on the existence of suitable investment benchmarks, the creation of managed futures portfolios through both passive and active manager choice, and the risk and return performance of managed futures.

ARTICLE REVIEW

Investment benchmarks have formed the basis for both performance analysis and asset allocation in the traditional stock and bond investment area.[6] For stocks and bonds, benchmark indexes exist that reflect the performance of both passive (e.g., S&P 500) and active (Lipper mutual fund manager indexes) investment styles. Likewise, investment benchmarks exist for managed futures that are similar in form to those available in traditional stock and bond markets. For instance, a number of indexes have been proposed as benchmarks for both passive commodity investment and active management of derivatives. In the first article, "Comparison of Managed Futures Benchmarks," Thomas Schneeweis and Richard Spurgin review the relative risk/return performance of the principal managed futures benchmarks and their correlation with other commonly used commodity futures and hedge fund-based benchmark indexes. While these managed futures indexes are generally similar within each benchmark category, differences are evident. To select an appropriate benchmark, either for passive investment or to evaluate the performance of active managers, one must understand the unique structural and computational differences in commonly used managed futures benchmarks.[7]

For the active investor, a trader based investment benchmark is important if one wishes to determine if a portfolio of commodity trading advisors can be created which tracks the universe of managed futures managers, just as portfolios of stocks and bonds have been shown to track traditional passive stock and bond benchmarks. In the second article, "Naive and Optimal Diversification For Managed Futures", George Martin and Thomas Henker provide empirical evidence that a naïvely (e.g., randomly) chosen CTA portfolio replicates comparable CTA benchmark indexes. For instance, Henker and Martin show that a portfolio of randomly selected CTAs has a correlation in excess of .90 with that of a commonly cited benchmark (MAR dollar-weighted CTA index). Moreover, their research on multi-manager CTA portfolios indicates that the benefits of increased portfolio size for CTAs is similar to that for stocks.

Modern portfolio theory points out that the true measure of risk for investors who hold portfolios of assets is the expected standard deviation of a portfolio of investments. Martin and Henker also show that for CTAs, as for equity securities, a randomly selected equal-weighted portfolio of 8-10 CTAs has a standard deviation similar to that of the population from which it is drawn. Thus, as for multi-firm equity portfolios, multi-manager CTA portfolios may have risk levels similar to that of a larger population of CTAs. Thus, the historical returns of the corresponding MAR CTA index may be a suitable proxy for a diversified CTA index and can be used to determine optimal asset allocation.[8] Lastly, Martin and Henker also measure the number of randomly selected CTAs needed to achieve the optimal mean/variance portfolio consisting of equities and CTAs. They report results similar to that of Billingsley and Chance [1996], which indicate that fewer than ten CTAs are needed to achieve most of the benefits of including CTAs to an existing stock and bond portfolio.

While active and passive benchmarks exist which provide information on the investment performance of managed futures strategies, questions still exist regarding the actual performance of managed futures. In the third article, "The Benefits of Managed Futures," Thomas Schneeweis [1996] shows that managed futures may offer improved return/risk tradeoffs to that existing in traditional stock and bond or stock, bond and commodity portfolios. Schneeweis shows that the potential benefit of adding managed futures to an existing portfolio may be measured by an asset's excess breakeven return; that is, the difference between its actual return and the return required to improve an asset's or portfolio's Sharpe ratio. Schneeweis also provides evidence of the benefits of managed private pools and public funds. The results show that, depending on the time period analyzed, even higher-cost fund structures such as public funds have the ability to improve an investor's return/risk tradeoff.

In the fourth article, "Managed Futures and Hedge Fund Investment for Downside Equity Risk Management", Thomas Schneeweis, Richard Spurgin, and Mark Potter

EXHIBIT 2 SUMMARY OF SELECTED RESEARCH REGARDING MANAGED FUTURES

Bibliography	Title	Topic	Major Results
Peters, C. and B. Warwick eds. (Irwin, 1997)	"The Handbook of Managed Futures"	Series of articles dealing with the performance, evaluation and analysis of managed futures.	Articles provides evidence of profitability in technical trading rules and review historical evidence of the case for managed futures
Epstein, C. ed. (Wiley, 1992)	"Managed Futures in the Institutional Portfolio."	Series of articles dealing with the performance, evaluation and analysis of managed futures.	Articles review historical evidence of the case for managed futures
Peters, C. eds. (IIR, 1992)	"Managed Futures"	Series of articles dealing with the performance, evaluation and analysis of managed futures.	Articles provides evidence of profitability in technical trading rules review historical evidence of the case for managed futures
Schwager, J. (Wiley, 1996)	"Managed Trading Myths and Truths"	Review of research on Managed futures.	Practitioner based presentation of major issues of managed futures trading
Chance, D. (AIMR, 1994)	"Managed Futures and Their Role in Investment Portfolios"	Review of research on Managed futures.	Academic/Practitioner based presentation of major issues of managed futures performance
Fung, W. and D. Hsieh, FMDR (1998)	"Price Trend Following Trading Strategies: Theory and Empirical Evidence,"	Reviews the performance of managed futures traders as lookback options	Lookback strategy can replicate key features of CTA performance
Schneeweis, T., (AIMA, 1996)	"The Benefits of Managed Futures,"	Summary Review of the Performance of Managed Futures, Private Pools, and Public Funds	Presents evidence that CTAs and other managed fund products have the potential to increase the return to risk tradeoff for U.S. and international investors.

McCarthy et al .(JAI, 1998)	"Informational Content in Historical CTA Performance."	Explore the use of historical CTA returns to forecast future performance	Result show that in addition to a historical benchmark forecast, historical CTA returns may be used to offer information as to future performance in unique market conditions.
Fung, W. and D. Hsieh (JPM, 1997)	"Survivor Bias and Investment Style in the Returns of CTAs	Test of impact of survivor bias on CTA performance.	Results are consistent with Schneeweis and Spurgin (1996) of an annual bias of approximately 4% between full sample and survivor sample
Lintner, J. (FAA/Toronto-1983)	"The Potential Role of Managed Commodity - Financial Futures Accounts (and/or Funds) in Portfolios of Stocks and Bonds	First recognized study the impact of managed futures investment on stock and bond portfolios	First recognized academic evidence of the diversification benefits of managed futures
Elton et al., (JB, , 1987, 1989, FAJ 1992)	Multiple articles: (e.g., Professionally Managed, Publicly Traded Commodity Funds,","	Series of articles on the performance of managed futures products relative to stock and bond investment and the performance persistence of managed futures returns	Presents evidence that CTAs and other managed fund products have the potential to increase the return to risk tradeoff for U.S. and international investors, however, the performance in period of analysis (1980's) showed little benefits for public funds.
Schneeweis et al., JAI (1998)	"Dealing With Myths of Managed Futures"	Series of articles on the performance of managed futures products relative to stock and bond investment and the performance persistence of managed futures returns	Reviews series of articles by author on questions of CTA performance, CTA survivior bias, return persistence, return drivers, and risk management properties.

Journal abbreviations: *JAI* — Journal of Alternative Investments; *JB* — Journal of Business; AIMA — Alternative Investment Management Association; *FAJ* — Financial Analysts Journal; *JF* — Journal of Finance; JPM— Journal of Portfolio Management; AIMR — Association of Investment Management Research; FMDR-Foundation for Managed Derivatives Research

EXHIBIT 3A PERFORMANCE MEASURES FOR MANAGED FUTURES AND OTHER ASSET INDICES AND PORTFOLIOS

Fourteen Year Performance of Indices:
January, 1985 - December, 1998

	MAR$CTA	MAR$FP	GSCI	S&P 500	Salomon Treasury Bond	MSCI	Salomon World Bond
Average Annual Return	14.8%	10.0%	6.7%	17.2%	9.3%	15.3%	10.8%
Standard Deviation	13.6%	13.9%	15.7%	15.4%	4.9%	14.8%	6.9%
Sharpe Ratio	0.67	0.31	0.06	0.75	0.73	0.65	0.74
Minimum Monthly Return	-6.4%	-11.0%	-13.0%	-24.3%	-2.7%	-18.6%	-4.1%
Maximum Monthly Return	17.8%	14.0%	20.7%	12.7%	4.7%	11.1%	6.5%
Correlation With MAR$CTA			0.02	0.11	0.24	0.07	0.16
MAR$CTA Excess Annual Breakeven			9.0%	7.9%	6.7%	8.4%	7.4%
Correlation With MAR$FP			-0.01	0.16	0.25	0.14	0.20
MAR$FP Excess Annual Breakeven			4.3%	2.6%	1.7%	3.0%	2.2%

Fourteen Year Performance of Asset Portfolios:
January, 1985 - December, 1998

	Port I US Stock, Bond, Commodity and CTA	Port II US Stock, Bond, and Commodity	Port III US Stock and Bond	Port IV Wrld. Stock, Bond, Commodity and CTA	Port V Wrld. Stock, Bond, and Commodity	Port VI Wrld. Stock and Bond
Average Annual Return	13.2%	12.4%	13.5%	13.0%	12.3%	13.3%
Standard Deviation	7.3%	7.3%	8.6%	7.7%	7.8%	9.1%
Sharpe Ratio	1.04	0.92	0.92	0.96	0.84	0.84
Minimum Monthly Return	-6.9%	-7.1%	-9.2%	-4.4%	-5.6%	-5.4%
Maximum Monthly Return	7.4%	6.7%	7.2%	7.5%	6.8%	7.6%
Correlation With MAR$CTA		0.17	0.17		0.12	0.12
MAR$CTA Excess Annual Breakeven		6.9%	6.9%		7.7%	7.7%
Correlation With MAR$FP		0.20	0.22		0.17	0.19
MAR$FP Excess Annual Breakeven		1.7%	1.5%		2.2%	2.1%

EXHIBIT 3B PERFORMANCE MEASURES FOR MANAGED FUTURES AND OTHER ASSET INDICES AND PORTFOLIOS

Nine Year Performance of Indices: January, 1990 - December, 1998	MAR$CTA	MAR$FP	GSCI	S&P 500	Salomon Treasury Bond	MSCI	Salomon World Bond
Average Annual Return	12.60%	8.4%	0.4%	16.5%	8.3%	10.0%	9.1%
Standard Deviation	10.77%	9.7%	16.7%	13.5%	4.2%	14.2%	6.0%
Sharpe Ratio	0.71	0.35	-0.27	0.85	0.77	0.35	0.68
Minimum Monthly Return	-6.2%	-6.6%	-13.0%	-15.6%	-2.3%	-14.3%	-3.7%
Maximum Monthly Return	13.5%	13.7%	20.7%	10.8%	4.0%	10.0%	5.8%
Correlation With MAR$CTA			0.10	-0.06	0.27	-0.10	0.18
MAR$CTA Excess Annual Breakeven			7.9%	8.1%	5.4%	8.0%	6.3%
Correlation With MAR$FP			0.06	-0.03	0.30	-0.04	0.22
MAR$FP Excess Annual Breakeven			3.6%	3.7%	1.2%	3.6%	2.0%

Nine Year Performance of Asset Portfolios: January, 1990 - December, 1998	Port I US Stock, Bond, Commodity and CTA	Port II US Stock, Bond, and Commodity	Port III US Stock and Bond	Port IV Wrld. Stock, Bond, Commodity and CTA	Port V Wrld. Stock, Bond, and Commodity	Port VI Wrld. Stock and Bond
Average Annual Return	11.6%	10.4%	12.6%	9.4%	8.2%	9.8%
Standard Deviation	6.4%	6.7%	7.7%	6.9%	7.3%	8.6%
Sharpe Ratio	1.04	0.81	0.98	0.63	0.44	0.56
Minimum Monthly Return	-4.9%	-6.1%	-6.1%	-4.4%	-5.6%	-5.4%
Maximum Monthly Return	6.5%	5.6%	7.2%	5.6%	5.3%	6.7%
Correlation With MAR$CTA		0.08	0.03		0.03	-0.02
MAR$CTA Excess Annual Breakeven		6.9%	7.3%		7.5%	7.7%
Correlation With MAR$FP		0.09	0.06		0.07	0.05
MAR$FP Excess Annual Breakeven		2.8%	2.9%		3.1%	3.2%

EXHIBIT 3C PERFORMANCE MEASURES FOR MANAGED FUTURES AND OTHER ASSET INDICES AND PORTFOLIOS

Four Year Performance of Indices:
January, 1995 - December, 1998

	MAR$CTA	MAR$FP	GSCI	S&P 500	Salomon US Treasury Bond	MSCI	Salomon US World Bond
Average Annual Return	11.4%	8.7%	-2.9%	26.6%	9.6%	17.4%	8.9%
Standard Deviation	9.4%	8.1%	17.3%	14.4%	4.1%	13.3%	6.1%
Sharpe Ratio	0.66	0.43	-0.47	1.48	1.07	0.92	0.60
Minimum Monthly Return	9.6%	-4.2%	-13.0%	-15.6%	-2.0%	-14.3%	-3.5%
Maximum Monthly Return	9.3%	6.2%	9.7%	7.9%	4.0%	8.7%	5.8%
Correlation With MAR$CTA			0.18	0.11	0.47	0.10	0.21
MAR$CTA Excess Annual Breakeven			7.0%	4.7%	1.4%	5.4%	5.0%
Correlation With MAR$FP			0.18	0.07	0.49	0.05	0.17
MAR$FP Excess Annual Breakeven			4.2%	2.7%	-0.7%	3.1%	2.7%

Four Year Performance of Asset Portfolios:
January, 1995 - December, 1998

	Port I US Stock, Bond, Commodity and MAR$CTA	Port II US Stock, Bond, and Commodity	Port III US Stock and Bond	Port IV Wrld. Stock, Bond, Commodity and MAR$CTA	Port V Wrld. Stock, Bond, and Commodity	Port VI Wrld. Stock and Bond
Average Annual Return	15.8%	14.4%	18.4%	11.8%	10.4%	13.4%
Standard Deviation	6.8%	7.3%	7.6%	6.6%	7.2%	7.4%
Sharpe Ratio	1.55	1.26	1.73	0.99	0.72	1.10
Minimum Monthly Return	-4.9%	-6.1%	-6.1%	-4.4%	-5.6%	-5.4%
Maximum Monthly Return	5.1%	5.6%	5.3%	5.1%	4.8%	5.8%
Correlation With MAR$CTA		0.28	0.24		0.23	0.18
MAR$CTA Excess Annual Breakeven		2.9%	2.4%		4.6%	4.4%
Correlation With MAR$FP		0.25	0.20		0.18	0.12
MAR$FP Excess Annual Breakeven		1.0%	0.7%		2.4%	2.4%

offer evidence on the portfolio benefits of commodity trading advisors in periods of poor equity market performance. In short, since managed futures strategies (in contrast to many long only stock and bond investments) permit both long and short positions in financial markets, commodity trading advisors may provide "good" diversification; that is, positively correlated with stock and bond markets when those traditional assets are performing well and negative correlation with stock and bond markets when those traditional assets are performing poorly. In contrast, many stock and bond strategies offer what may be called "bad diversification"; that is, low correlation in flat or rising equity and bond markets, with positive correlation in falling stock and bond markets.

The benefits of managed futures are often discussed in terms of their unique distributional return form; that is, commodity trading advisors are often described as having skewed return distributions that offer greater upside than downside probability of return than assumed by a perfectly normal distribution. In the final article, "Skewness in Asset Returns: Does it Matter," George Martin and Richard Spurgin address the benefits of skewness in commodity trading advisors' returns in stand alone comparisons and in a portfolio context. Martin and Spurgin show that while skewness may exist in the returns of individual CTAs and can be of use when comparing individual managers, CTA skewness may not necessarily be useful in a diversified CTA portfolio.[9]

RESEARCH IN MANAGED FUTURES

In addition to the articles presented in this handbook, investors should be aware of a wide range of additional sources of information on recent research in the area of managed futures. A number of books cover both practical management issues as well as academic/practitioner research in the area of managed futures. Investors are referred to a list of readings and books listed in Exhibit 2 and reference section of this chapter. These references refer to additional issues on the performance of managed futures including performance persistence, survivor bias, and additional evidence of risk and return performance.

Updated Risk and Return Performance

Recent risk and return analysis of managed futures performance generally supports the results discussed in the articles in this section. Results in Exhibits 3a, 3b and 3c show that using recent data, investment in a portfolio of commodity trading advisors (e.g., MAR$CTA) provides not only similar risk and return benefits to existing passive and actively managed stock and bond investments (e.g., S&P 500, Salomon Brothers U.S. Treasury bond indices, Salomon Brothers World Government bond indices and MSCI world stock indices), but also offers the investor an increased return to risk ratio when considered as an addition to widely diversified asset portfolios.[10] The benefits of managed futures in a diversified portfolios is illustrated in Exhibits 4, 5, and 6 in that when the MAR$CTA is added to a S&P 500, Salomon Brothers Treasury Bond index, as well as a S&P 500 and Salomon Brothers Treasury bond portfolio, increased opportunities exist for risk reduction and return enhancement.

Results in Exhibit 7a and 7b also show the importance of managed futures in months in which traditional stock benchmarks have had their worst performance. Results show that managed futures have consistently performed well in just those months that equity issues have had their worst performance. Various reasons may exist for this relationship including the impact of increasing interest rates and changes in market volatility which may be captured by various CTA trendfollowing or volatility capture programs. Investors, however, may be concerned that the risk and return performance of managed futures may be impacted either by performance persistence or survivor bias.

EXHIBIT 4 RISK AND RETURN OF STOCK, BOND AND MANAGED FUTURES: 1985-1998

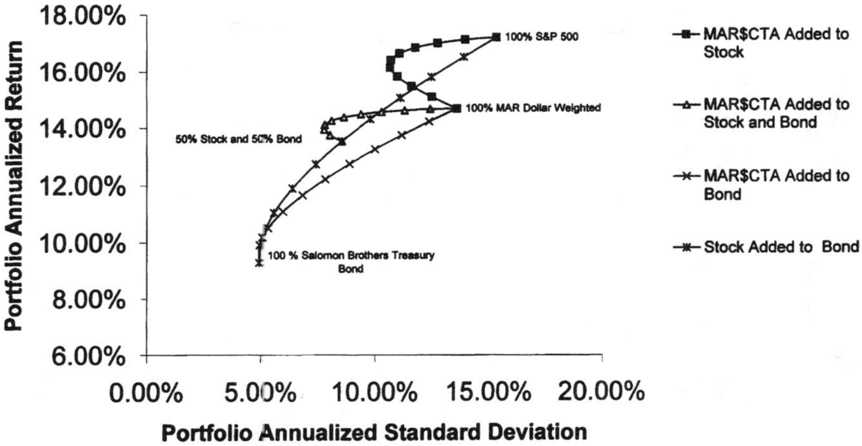

EXHIBIT 5 RISK AND RETURN OF STOCK, BOND AND MANAGED FUTURES: 1990-1998

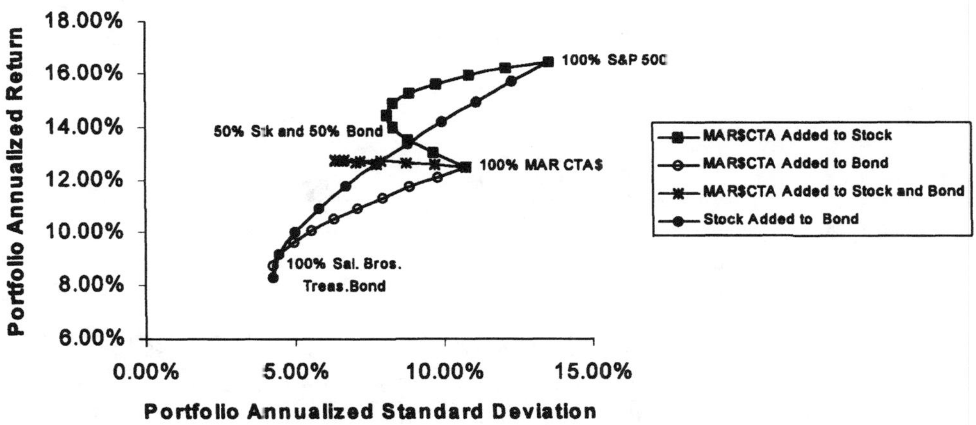

EXHIBIT 6 RISK AND RETURN OF STOCK, BOND AND MANAGED FUTURES: 1995-1998

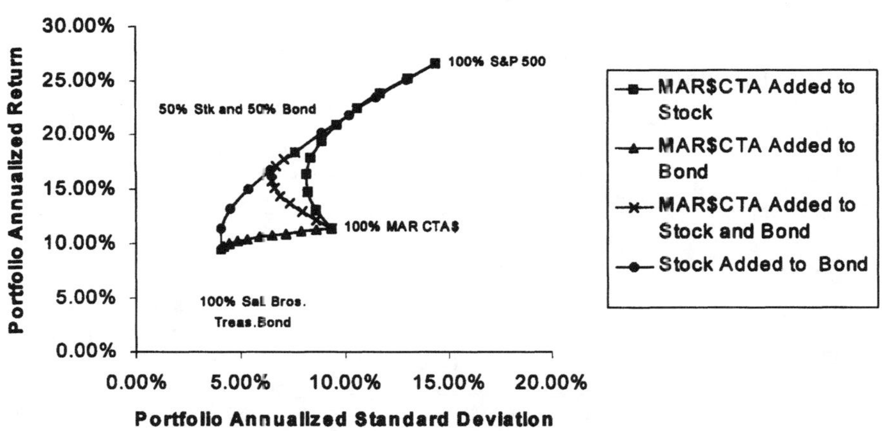

EXHIBIT 7A PERFORMANCE OF MAR$CTA INDEX RELATIVE TO S&P 500 (1985-1998)

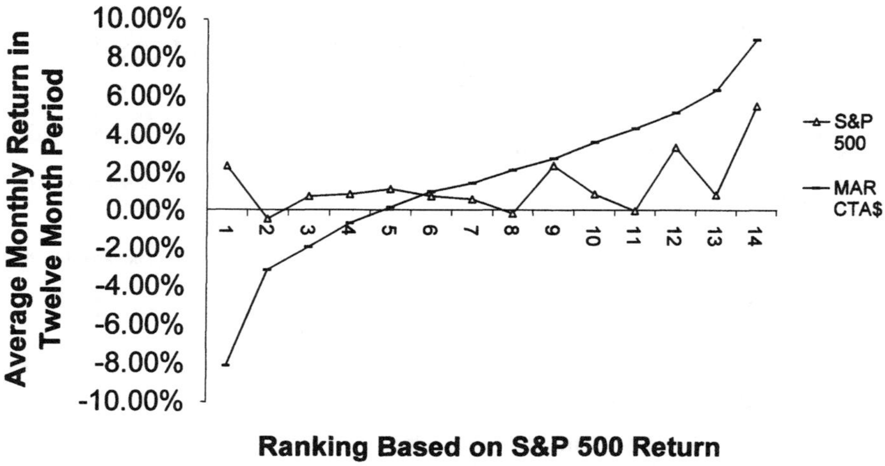

EXHIBIT 7B PERFORMANCE OF CTA IN 10 WORST S&P 500 MONTHS (1/90 TO 12/98)

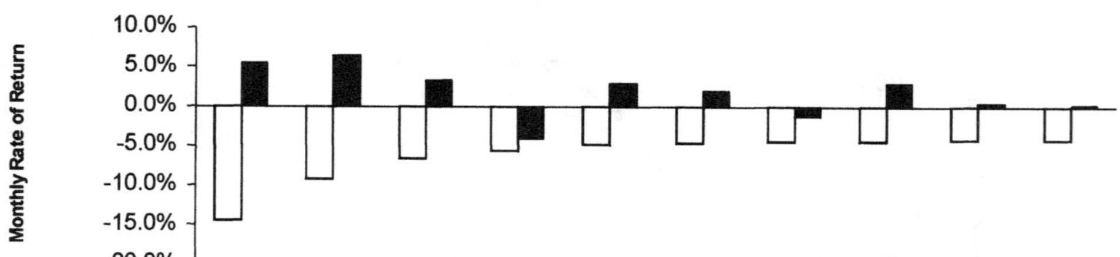

	Aug-98	Aug-90	Jan-90	Aug-97	Sep-90	Jun-91	Jul-96	Mar-94	Nov-91	Mar-97
□ S&P 500	-14.5%	-9.1%	-6.6%	-5.6%	-4.8%	-4.6%	-4.4%	-4.3%	-4.2%	-4.1%
■ MARCTA	5.4%	6.5%	3.2%	-4.1%	2.9%	2.0%	-1.3%	2.9%	0.2%	-0.1%

Ranked by S&P 500 Monthly Return

EXHIBIT 8 CUMULATIVE SURVIVOR AND NONSURVIVOR PERFORMANCE IN 12 MONTHS PRIOR TO DISSOLUTION

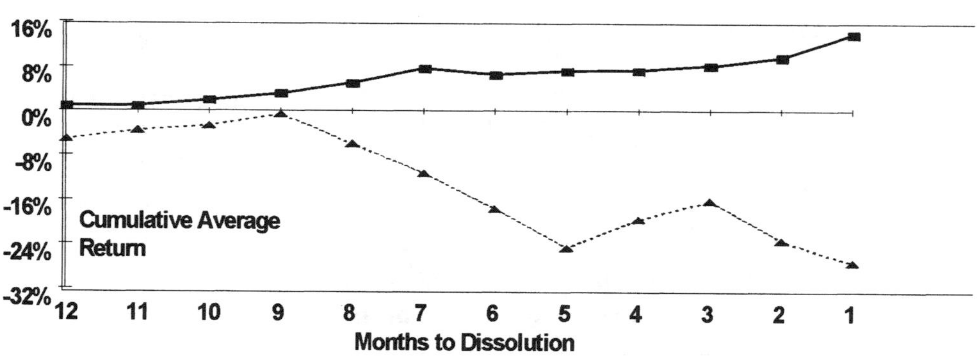

Performance Persistence

Performance persistence in CTA managers has been actively debated in the academic community [Brown and Goetzmann, 1995]. While there is little evidence that a strategy of investing in winners and avoiding losers will be successful over time, there is some evidence of performance persistence. McCarthy et al. [1996] provide evidence that the relative riskiness of a CTA — the CTA's beta with respect to an index of CTAs — is a good predictor of future relative returns.[11] Thus past CTA performance is valuable in forecasting CTA and multi-advisor CTA portfolios' return and risk parameters, especially at the portfolio level. In terms of public policy, public disclosure of individual CTAs as well as relative benchmark information may be of benefit to potential investors who desire to forecast expected risk-adjusted public commodity fund performance.

Survivor Bias

Despite the research presented in the articles, other issues remain of concern to managed fund investors, including issues of survivor bias and risk measurement. The impact of survivorship bias on empirical studies of equity mutual fund performance has received considerable attention [Brown et. al, 1995; Malkiel, 1995]. For equity funds, survivorship bias implies that analysis of only existing equity investment managers or funds may result in an upward bias estimate (1.5%) of the actual performance of a randomly chosen investment over the historical period of analysis. Likewise, for managed futures, empirical studies have attempted to assess the impact of survivorship bias on studies of commodity fund performance. In Fung and Hsieh [1997] and McCarthy et al., [1996], the differential performance of survivor and nonsurvivor CTA subsamples is analyzed. Pairwise comparison results indicate that significant return differences exist (3.5%) between the surviving CTAs and the full sample. However, when held in a portfolio with other risky asset classes, this return bias may be offset by a lower correlation of a full sample of CTAs relative to a survivor sample.

In addition, as shown in the Exhibit 8, using traditional abnormal return methodology, McCarthy et al. show that the return differential between survivor and nonsurvivor samples (on an absolute and risk-adjusted basis) is shown to be due primarily to return performance in the months just prior to CTA dissolution and not necessarily due to differential returns over extended past investment. The ability of investment professionals to forecast which managers may not survive could result in dramatic differences in relative return performance.[12]

CONCLUSION

It is important to note that neither this nor any synopsis can capture nor review all possible questions relating to the future or past performance of various investment products such as managed futures and hedge funds. It is hoped that the results of the above and future studies will put to rest many of these concerns. Traditional asset managers use futures and options markets in numerous ways (e.g., rebalance portfolios, manage currency risk, trade bonds with option features such as convertibility or callability). Most traditional money managers, however, are restricted by regulation or convention from using more actively traded futures and option contracts.

Moreover, as new financial products come into existence, such as futures contracts traded on S&P 500 value or growth stocks, managed futures may provide the most logical means of quickly taking advantage of the potential returns from such new products. The logical extension of using investment managers with specialized knowledge of traditional markets to obtain maximum return/risk tradeoffs is to add specialized managers who can obtain the unique returns in market conditions and types of securities not generally available to traditional asset managers; that is, managed futures.

ENDNOTES

[1] The previous results were given net of expenses, such that the impact of manager fees are directly considered in the empirical results. At the same time, concern has been raised regarding the level of fees in the managed futures industry. Several reasons exist for the relative fee differential between managed futures and other investment media. First, as indicated in previous sections, to the degree that investment managers control downside risk, the fee paid to managers may in part be seen as a payment for a protective put. However, compensation costs do affect relative performance. Investors must compare the after fee return structure to evaluate the comparison returns. Likewise, other relative cost considerations should be considered in more detailed analyses including tax, liquidity and personal timing of investment needs. Today, fund management in the derivative products area includes not only investment through public commodity funds but investment directly with commodity trading advisors for which the management fees charged by certain public commodity funds do not reflect the negotiated fees applicable to large investors or portfolio managers.

[2] The ability of commodity funds, in contrast to direct investment in commodity trading advisors, has also been questioned in more recent studies by Schneeweis [1996] and Edwards and Liew [1998]. Schneeweis, however, also concludes that the results are strategy and time period dependent. Given that commodity funds are often multi-manager in form, the benefits of commodity fund investment relative to multiple commodity trading advisor investment is primarily a function of the fee structure.

[3] Books which include information on the structural and performance history of managed futures include Fox-Andrews and Meaden [1995], Peters and Warwick [1996], and Chance [1996].

[4] These numbers do not include the large amount of funds traded through hedge funds (e.g., global asset allocators) or proprietary trading desks of large investment houses, insurance companies or banks which trade using similar strategies as independent CTAs.

[5] The annual returns are derived from natural logs. Investors who wish to calculate holding period returns from the above returns should use the antilogarithm of the reported return.

[6] Benchmark indexes are commonly used in studies of investment performance to provide a performance index which reflects the particular style of an investment manager. Benchmark indexes are also use in determination of asset allocations across asset classes.

[7] For a summary of a wide variety of managed futures benchmark indexes see "Managed Futures Benchmarks." AIMA, 1998.

[8] See also Park and Staum [1998].

[9] The use of drawdown (time period of a managers worst loss) as a commonly used measure of manager performance is likewise of value primarily when comparing individual managers with similar strategies over similar time periods and is of less use at determining the value of a CTA manager in a diversified portfolio. The use of drawdown as a risk measure has other problems including bias induced by survivor bias. Managers who have the highest variance may have high drawdowns relative to low risk managers. However, those 'high risk" managers who exist today have survived large historical drawdowns while many with similar drawdowns are not longer part of the public record.

[10] In this study, Portfolio I is a portfolio comprised of the MAR$CTA (10%), GSCI (10%), S&P500 (40%), and Salomon Brothers Treasury Bond (40%) Indices, Portfolio II is a portfolio comprised of GSCI (20%), S&P500 (40%), and Salomon Brothers Treasury Bond Index (40%), and Portfolio III is an equal weighted stock and bond portfolio. Portfolios' IV though VI are similar to Portfolios I through III with the substitution of the MSCI World equity and Salomon Brothers World Bond Index for the S&P 500 and Salomon Treasury Bond Index. Lastly, Excess Annual Breakeven is a measure of the difference between the actual return achieve and the return required for the cited investment (MAR$CTA) to be included (at some weight) with the cited asset (e.g., S&P 500) or portfolio (e.g., Portfolio III) such that the Sharpe ratio of the comparison asset or portfolio increases.

[11] Similar results are reported by Brorsen [1998].

[12] For research in the area of manager default see Diz [1999].

SECTION II ARTICLES

Schneeweis, Thomas. and Richard Spurgin, "Comparison of Managed Futures Benchmarks," CISDM/ SOM, 1998

Henker, Thomas. and G. Martin, "Naive and Optimal Diversification For Managed Futures", *The Journal of Alternative Investments* (Fall, 1998), pp 25-49.

Schneeweis, Thomas, "The Benefits of Managed Futures," (AIMA, 1998).

Schneeweis, Thomas, R. Spurgin, and M. Potter, "Managed Futures and Hedge Fund Investment for Downside Equity Risk Management", *Derivatives Quarterly*, (Fall 1996), pp 62-72.

Martin, George and Richard Spurgin, "Skewness in Asset Returns: Does it Matter," *The Journal of Alternative Investments* (Fall, 1998), pp 66-75.

SELECTED REFERENCES

Billingsley, R. S. and D. Chance, "Benefits and Limitations of Diversification Among Commodity Trading Advisors," *The Journal of Portfolio Management* (Fall, 1996), pp. 65-80.

Brown, S. and W. Goetzmann, and S. Ross, "Survival", *Journal of Finance* (July, 1995), pp. 853-875.

Brown, S. and W. Goetzmann. "Performance Persistence," *Journal of Finance*, Vol. 50, No. 2 (1995), pp. 679-698.

Brorsen, B. Wade. "Performance Persistence for Managed Futures," Foundation of Managed Derivatives Research, 1998.

Chance, D. Managed Futures and Their Role in Investment Portfolios. AIMR, 1996.

Diz, Fernando. "How do CTA's Return Distribution Characteristics Affect their Likelihood of Survival?" *The Journal of Alternative Investments* (Forthcoming, 1999).

Edwards, Franklin R. and Jimmy Liew, "Managed Futures As an Asset Class." Foundation for Managed Derivatives Research 1998.

Edwards, Franklin and C. Ma. "Commodity Pool Performance: Is the Information Contained in Pool Prospectuses Useful?" *Journal of Futures Markets*, Vol.8., No. 5 (1988), pp. 475-517.

Edwards, Franklin and J. Park, " Do Managed Futures Make Good Investments," *Journal of Futures Markets*, Vol. 16, No. 5, (1996), pp. 475-517.

Elton, E.J., M.J. Gruber, and J.C. Rentzler. "Professionally Managed, Publicly Traded Commodity Funds," *Journal of Business* (April 1987), pp. 177-199.

Elton, E.J., M.J. Gruber, and J.C. Rentzler. "New Public Offerings, Information, and Investor Rationality: The Case of Publicly Offered Commodity Funds," *Journal of Business*, Vol. 6, No. 1, (1989), pp. 1-15.

Elton, E.J., M.J. Gruber, and J. Rentzler, "The Performance of Publicly Offered Commodity Funds," *Financial Analyst Journal* (July-August, 1990), pp. 23-30.

Elton, E.J., M.J. Gruber, and J. Rentzler, "The Performance of Publicly Offered Commodity Funds " in C. Peters ed. *Managed Futures* (Probus Publishing, 1992), pp. 387-401.

Epstein, C. ed., Managed Futures in the Institutional Portfolio. Wiley, 1992.

Fox-Andrews, F. and N. Meaden. Derivative Markets and Investment Management. Prentice Halll, 1995.

Fung, William and David Hsieh, "Survivor Bias and Invstment Style in the Returns of CTAs," *The Journal of Portfolio Management.* (Fall, 1997), pp. 30-41.

Fung, William and David Hsieh, "Price Trend Following Trading Strategies: Theory and Empirical Evidence, " The Foundation for Managed Derivatives Research (September, 1988).

Irwin, Scott, C. R. Zulauf, and Barry W. Ward, "The Predictability of Managed Futures Returns," *The Journal of Derivatives* (Winter, 1994), pp. 20-27.

Irwin, Scott, C. R. Zulauf, and Barry W. Ward, "Investment Performance of Public Commodity Pools: 1979-1990." *Journal of Futures Markets*, 13 (1993), pp. 799-820.

Henker, T. and G. Martin, "Naive and Optimal Diversification For Managed Futures", *The Journal of Alternative Investments* (Fall, 1998), pp. 25-40.

Malkiel, B. "Returns from Investing in Equity Mutual Funds, 1971-1991," *Journal of Finance* (June, 1995), pp 549-572.

McCarthy, D., Thomas Schneeweis, and R. Spurgin, "Investment in CTAs: An Alternative Managed Futures Investment," *Journal of Derivatives*, Vol.3, No.4 (Summer, 1996), pp. 36-47.

McCarthy, D., and Schneeweis, T., R. Spurgin and "Informational Content in Historical CTA Performance." *The Journal of Futures Markets*, (May, 1997), pp. 317-340.

Park, James M. and Jeremy C. Staum, "Performance Persistence in the Alternative Investment Industry." Working Paper, Paradigm Capital Management, 1998.

Peters, C. ed., *Managed Futures.* Probus, 1992.

Peters, C. and B. Warwick ed. The Handbook of Managed Futures. Irwin, 1997.

Schneeweis, T. The Benefits of Managed Futures. AIMA, 1996.

Schneeweis, T. "Dealing with Myths of Managed Futures," *The Journal of Alternative Investments* (Summer, 1998), pp. 9-17.

Schneeweis, T. and R. Spurgin. "Comparisons of Commodity and Managed Futures Benchmark Indexes." *The Journal of Derivatives,* (Summer, 1997), pp. 33-50.

Schneeweis, T. and R. Spurgin, "Managed Futures, Hedge Fund and Mutual Fund Return Estimation: A Multi-Factor Approach", *The Journal of Alternative Investments* (Fall, 1998), pp. 1-24.

Schneeweis, T., R. Spurgin and D. McCarthy. "Survivor Bias in Commodity Trading Advisor Performance." *Journal of Futures Markets,* (October, 1996), pp. 757-772.

Schneeweis, T., R. Spurgin, and M. Potter. "Managed Futures and Hedge Fund Investment for Downside Equity Risk Management", *Derivatives Quarterly,* (Fall, 1996), pp. 62-72.

Schwager, J. Managed Trading: Myths and Truths. Wiley, 1996.

4 COMPARISON OF MANAGED FUTURES BENCHMARKS

THOMAS SCHNEEWEIS
University of Massachussetts

RICHARD SPURGIN
Clark University

INTRODUCTION

Security market benchmark indices are commonly used to provide a performance index which reflects the particular style of an investment manager. While benchmark indices are common in the areas of stock and bond investment, in recent years futures and options based commodity trading products have grown rapidly as alternative means of investing in cash market commodity and financial securities. While commodity and futures market based indices (e.g., Dow Jones Commodity index) have existed for years, other commodity based indices (Goldman Sachs, JP Morgan) and managed futures indices (e.g., MAR, Barclay, TASS, and EACM Global Asset Allocator indices,) based on the performance of commodity futures trading advisors (CTAs) have also recently been used in discussions of benchmark performance or asset class determination. Other performance indices have been created which attempt to provide an active futures market based return index which attempts to mimic the performance of active managed futures traders who hold both long and short positions. For instance, the Mount Lucas Management (MLM) index uses a trend-following technical trading rule to determine whether a particular futures contract should be held as a long or short position.

The purpose of this paper is to review the risk/return performance of the benchmarks based on commodity prices as well as the indices that track various managed futures based trading products. The next section reviews the composition and structure of popular commodity and managed futures based indices. The following section provides the data and methodology employed in this study. Results indicate that commodity and managed futures benchmark indices have sources of risk and return that are distinct from traditional assets such as stocks and bonds and offer investors an important area of diversification. However, commodity and managed futures indices differ in significant ways. There appears to be little connection between the returns of major commodity indices and the returns of CTA indices. Unlike stock and bond markets, where broad indices provide suitable benchmarks for the performance of an actively managed portfolio, results presented suggest that CTA-based indices provide a better benchmark for an actively managed futures portfolio than either passive or active (e.g., MLM) commodity based performance indices. Moreover, results indicate that the actual efficient frontier created from the inclusion of alternative CTA and commodity indices with an existing stand alone investment may differ depending on the CTA index used. Investors must therefore realize that to the degree that their own investment portfolio differs from the established benchmarks or for which the index is noninvestible, the relationships describe above may not be met. Conclusions and suggestions for future studies are discussed at the end of the paper.

COMMODITY AND MANAGED FUTURES INDICES IN ASSET MANAGEMENT

The increased use of commodity trading vehicles and managed futures products in investment management has led practitioners to create indices that offer performance benchmarks for purchasers of physical commodities as well as investors in managed futures products such as commodity funds, pools, and segregated commodity trading advisor accounts. As is true for stock and bond performance indices, commodity and managed futures-based indices have a variety of uses. They are a source of information on cash commodity and futures commodity market trends, are used as performance benchmarks for evaluation of commodity trading advisors and provide a historical track record useful in developing asset allocation strategies.

Classification of Benchmark Indices

Benchmark indices may be either noninvestable, and thus useful primarily as a measure of relative performance, or investible and of use both as a relative return index as well as a surrogate for actual investment performance. An index is termed inevitable if it is easily replicated through investment in the underlying securities. Until recently, most futures-based indices were not investable. However, most of the new commodity based futures price indices are designed to be investable and many commodity trading firms have begun to offer investment products based on the performance of managed futures indices.

The principal commodity and managed futures indices fall into three categories. The first category is long only commodity indices based on the returns of futures contracts and/or cash markets. Included in this group are the CRB, Goldman Sachs, Chase Manhattan Commodity Index, the Dow Jones-AIG Commodity Index, and JPMorgan. The second group contains indices based on the actual performance of commodity trading advisors. This group consists of MAR, Barclay, TASS, and Evaluation Associates (EACM Global Asset Allocators). A third index group provide returns comparable to passive long/short positions in listed futures contracts or, in the case of the MLM index, of long and short positions determined by a moving average trading rule.[1]

In addition to commodity indices based on the performance of actual cash/futures market contracts, a number of managed futures indices have been derived to track the performance of a select group of actively traded managed futures funds, pools, or commodity trading advisors (CTAs). At present, none of these indices is in investable form. There are two reasons for this. First, the firms that create these indices (e.g. MAR) do not release the exact composition of the indices. Second, since management and incentive fees for managed futures accounts are generally negotiable and CTAs may manage accounts differently for different clients, knowing the exact composition of the index is not sufficient to replicate the reported returns.

Commodity Indices

Commodity indices attempt to replicate the return available to holding long positions in agricultural, metal, energy, or livestock investment. Since the cost of carry model insures that the return on a fully margined position in a futures contract should mimic the return on an underlying spot deliverable, futures contract returns are often used as a surrogate for cash market performance. Futures contract based commodity indices have three separate sources of return: price, roll, and collateral return. Price return derives from changes in commodity futures prices. Roll return arises from rolling long futures positions forward through time and may capture a risk premium over time if futures prices are a downwardly biased forecast of future spot prices. Collateral return assumes the full value of the underlying the futures contracts are invested at a risk-free interest rate. This is equivalent to assuming an investor posts 100% margin with Treasury bills. Commodity indices, however, differ widely in purpose, composition, and weighting scheme.

Commodity indices use either arithmetic or geometric averaging to calculate the index return from the component returns. Most commodity indices use an arithmetic average of the commodity returns. Investors attempting to replicate the index must rebalance their portfolios monthly to maintain constant dollar weights. The CRB uses geometric averaging of the component returns (which are themselves calculated with arithmetic averaging).

Composition and Weightings

Each of the major indices contains a different group of underlying assets. For instance, the JPMCI is composed entirely of futures contracts based on industrial commodities (energy and metals). The Dow Jones-AIG, CRB and Goldman Sachs indices include industrials, grains, and soft commodities. The MLM index contains those groups as well as interest rate and currency futures. The composition of each index is periodically reviewed, typically annually, and contracts may be added or deleted based on previously announced criteria. For example, the composition of the MLM index depends on volume and open interest in the underlying contracts, and the GSCI depends on the importance of the underlying commodity to world production.

Commodity indices also differ in the relative emphasis placed on different commodities and the procedure used to determine the weightings in the index. The weights of the JPMCI are determined by an optimization procedure that maximizes an objective function that includes positive correlation with economic growth and unexpected inflation, negative correlation with stock and bond returns and a high Sharpe ratio. Equal weighting is used in the CRB. A world production weighting is used in the GSCI. Composition and weighting schemes are driven partly by liquidity considerations. An equal or production-weighted index that includes relatively illiquid contracts may be difficult to replicate. For example a $1 billion investment in the GSCI would represent an investment in live hog futures equal to 27% of the average open interest in live hog futures during 1993, making it difficult to roll a position forward without influencing the price.

Managed Futures Indices

Managed futures indices also differ widely in purpose, composition, and weighting scheme. The major differences are outlined in the Appendix to this chapter. Differences in composition arise because some indices require CTAs to have longer historical track records or larger asset size before inclusion. Indices also differ by type of managed futures accounts followed (e.g. CTAs, funds, pools, hedge funds). Managed Account Reports (MAR) tracks the performance of individual CTAs as well as CTA Funds and Pools while TASS and Barclays offer performance measurement for CTAs only. MAR produces both equal-weighted and dollar-weighted indices while TASS offers dollar weighted indices and Barclay and EACM provide equal-weighted indices. The proper benchmark for an investor thus depends in large part on whether the portfolio contains a large number of smaller CTAs, in which case an equally weighted index is appropriate, or invests primarily in the large, well-known CTAs, which calls for a dollar-weighted benchmark. Dollar-weighted indices are easier to replicate, however, as monthly rebalancing is not required. This is an important consideration, as rebalancing requires shifting assets among CTAs based on their end-of-month performance. Performance figures are often not publicly available for several days after month-end, and many CTAs require advance notice of redemptions. Thus replicating an arithmetic index will be very difficult.

Both Barclay and MAR provide subindices based on market sector (e.g., currency, energy, financial, stock, agricultural) and trading sector (e.g., discretionary and systematic). MAR also provides broad indices for commodity funds and pools and sector subindices (e.g., guaranteed, offshore, multi-advisor, single advisor, public, private). TASS, MAR, and Barclay are broad-based, and attempt to include all CTAs or Pools which meet listing requirements. The returns of an individual CTA or pool are calculated as a weighted average composite of the different accounts managed by each CTA, including public commodity funds, private pools, and individual managed accounts. Moreover, basing an index on composite returns and including a large number of CTAs with few assets under management may result in an index that is very difficult to replicate and may not closely track a typical institutional managed futures portfolio. EACM tracks the monthly performance of a preselected set of CTAs and hedge funds. The EACM equal weighted index is rebalanced only once each year. The initial investment is assumed to be invested with each trader for the full year. EACM recognizes that a lack of liquidity and fund investment rules prevent monthly rebalancing.

The EACM index is more susceptible to survivor bias than the general indices because much of the early return series for the index is hypothetical. Since inclusion in the index is a subjective decision made by EACM management, a historical reconstruction of the index is difficult. The EACM index is comparable to the Dow Jones Industrial average in that the CTAs and hedge funds included in the index tend to be the dominant players in the industry. Furthermore, EACM maintains frequent contact with the fund managers, and would likely remove a fund from the index well before the fund dissolved. A final difference between EACM and the other indices is the method of calculating returns. MAR, TASS, and Barclay rely on the CTAs to report monthly returns, either directly to the index managers or through disclosure documents, so data quality may be an issue. The returns in the EACM index are generated by its own tracking of investment managers who are following specifically designated programs. Thus potential problems resulting from self-reporting and from using composite returns are lessened.

DATA AND METHODOLOGY

Monthly returns were derived for a series of stock, bond, commodity, and managed futures indices for the time period from January, 1990 through December 1998. Data was obtained for each of the indices and relevant subindices described in Appendix I (JPMCI, GSCI, MAR, TASS, Barclay, EACM, MLM), as well as the Standard and Poors 500 Stock Index, the Salomon Brothers Treasury, Salomon Brothers Cov./Corp. Bond Index, Three-month Treasury bill yields are obtained from Datastream. CTA indices are obtained from respective index providers. Returns for all data series are expressed as annualized returns. Statistical tests include presentation of descriptive risk and return characteristics and return correlations between each of the primary and subindices. With a sample size of 108, correlations with absolute value greater than .19 are significant at the 5% level (*) and greater than .24 significant at the 1% level (**). In addition, several of the indices have been reconstructed at various times to better reflect a particular performance history. As a result the performance of an index reported in this paper may not strictly reflect the performance of that index in other research.

EXHIBIT 1 DESCRIPTIVE STATISTICS (1990-1998)

		Annualized Return	Annualized Standard Deviation	Monthly Minimum	Monthly Maximum	Sharpe Ratio
Tass	CTA $	10.2%	11.8%	-8.0%	7.6%	0.44
Tass	Currency	9.6%	15.0%	-7.8%	11.0%	0.31
MARCTA:	Dollar Wt.	12.5%	10.7%	-6.2%	7.9%	0.70
MARCTA:	Equal Wt.	10.1%	9.8%	-5.6%	7.0%	0.52
MARCTA:	Discretionary	12.9%	7.4%	-4.7%	6.6%	1.06
MARCTA:	Trendfollowing	11.9%	16.8%	-11.0%	11.2%	0.41
MARCTA:	Currency	11.4%	14.0%	-8.5%	10.0%	0.46
MARCTA:	Diversified	10.2%	12.5%	-7.8%	10.2%	0.41
MARCTA:	Financial	13.7%	13.6%	-8.9%	9.5%	0.64
MLM	Passive Trendfollowing CTA Index	8.9%	5.2%	-4.1%	5.2%	0.75
Barclay	CTA Index	7.6%	9.6%	-5.6%	6.2%	0.27
Barclay	Currency	10.0%	13.1%	-8.0%	7.2%	0.38
Barclay	Agricultural	7.0%	7.5%	-5.0%	7.4%	0.27
Barclay	Financial/Metals	8.9%	7.7%	-4.3%	6.1%	0.51
Barclay	Energy	-2.0%	19.4%	-34.6%	22.0%	-0.36
Barclay	Diversified	10.5%	12.7%	-6.8%	9.7%	0.43
Barclay	Systematic	10.6%	12.6%	-7.9%	7.2%	0.44
Barclay	Discretionary	3.9%	5.3%	-3.1%	4.3%	-0.20
MAR FP:	Dollar Wt.	8.4%	9.7%	-6.6%	6.2%	0.35
MAR FP:	Equal Wt.	6.7%	10.3%	-5.6%	8.1%	0.16
MAR FP:	Guaranteed	6.4%	8.5%	-7.2%	5.0%	0.16
MAR FP:	Multiadvisor	8.0%	13.4%	-9.0%	7.8%	0.23
MAR FP:	Offshore	8.9%	13.5%	-17.1%	6.0%	0.29
MAR FP:	Private Pool	14.3%	9.9%	-4.3%	7.9%	0.94
MAR FP:	Public	6.8%	12.1%	-8.0%	9.9%	0.15
MAR FP:	Single Advisor	10.6%	9.0%	-6.1%	5.6%	0.62
EACM	GLOB AA	18.9%	10.6%	-5.6%	8.4%	1.31
EACM	Discretionary	16.3%	10.3%	-17.5%	7.3%	1.10
EACM	Systematic	20.6%	17.2%	-10.4%	13.0%	0.91
EACM	100 Index	13.9%	4.1%	-4.6%	3.6%	2.19
S&P 500	Index	17.9%	13.5%	-15.6%	7.9%	0.95
SALOMON BROS.	Treasury	8.4%	4.2%	-2.3%	4.0%	0.81
SALOMON BROS	Govt/Corp	8.7%	4.2%	-2.5%	4.2%	0.87
Tbill	Three Mnth.	5.0%	0.4%	0.2%	0.5%	0.00
Mutual Funds	Aggressive Growth Index - Large	13.9%	16.5%	-21.1%	10.1%	0.54
Mutual Funds	Aggressive Growth Index Small	12.0%	13.6%	-15.4%	7.1%	0.52
Mutual Funds	Balanced Index	11.4%	8.6%	-9.8%	5.2%	0.75
Mutual Funds	Foreign Securities Index	8.0%	13.0%	-14.9%	8.2%	0.23
Mutual Funds	Growth and Income Index	14.3%	12.3%	-15.4%	7.2%	0.76
Mutual Funds	Government Securities Index	7.0%	3.6%	-2.1%	2.9%	0.57
Mutual Funds	Income Index	11.5%	7.8%	-8.7%	5.4%	0.83
Mutual Funds	Long Term Growth Index	14.9%	14.4%	-17.6%	7.9%	0.69
Mutual Funds	Total Return Index	12.0%	10.2%	-12.2%	5.6%	0.69
GSCI	Index	0.4%	16.7%	-13.0%	9.7%	-0.27
GSCI	Agricultural	1.7%	13.5%	-10.1%	10.7%	-0.24
GSCI	Energy	-2.5%	29.7%	-25.0%	17.4%	-0.25
GSCI	Industrial	1.9%	16.4%	-13.8%	10.6%	-0.19
GSCI	Livestock	2.4%	13.0%	-11.0%	10.3%	-0.20
GSCI	Non-energy	2.1%	9.0%	-6.5%	6.6%	-0.32
GSCI	Precious Metals	-2.5%	11.6%	-9.0%	8.4%	-0.65
JPMCI	Index	0.4%	16.6%	-14.5%	9.1%	-0.28
JPMCI	Base Metals	0.4%	15.9%	-13.5%	10.5%	-0.29
JPMCI	Energy	-1.1%	28.2%	-25.2%	14.1%	-0.22
JPMCI	Precious Metals	-1.6%	12.4%	-9.1%	9.5%	-0.53
GPR-LIFE	Nth. Amer. Real Estate Secs	3.7%	15.2%	-20.4%	9.2%	-0.09
GPR-LIFE	International Real Estate Secs	0.0%	17.6%	-16.4%	14.6%	-0.28

RESULTS

Analysis of Commodity and Managed Futures Indices as Stand-Alone Investments

In Exhibit 1 the annualized returns for the sample of futures products, stock, bond, and commodity indices over the 1/90-12/98 period are presented. Results in Exhibit 1 show that the annualized returns of the broad-based commodity indices all of the CTA indices (MAR CTA - Equal Weighted (MARCTAeq), 10.1%, MAR CTA - Dollar Weighted (MARCTA$), 12.5%, Barclay, 7.6%, TASS, 10.2%), and the trading index (MLM, 8.9%), were greater than the average return of the commodity (GSCI, 0.4%). Returns on many of the CTA indices performed below the traditional financial benchmarks such as the S&P 500 (17.9%). However, as in previous tests (Elton et al., (1992) and Irwin et al., (1992)), the average return of the MAR dollar weighted Public Fund/Pool Index (6.8%) and MAR Equal Weighted Fund/Pool Index (6.7%) were below stock and bond returns.

Results in Exhibit 1 also show that the monthly standard deviation of each of the CTA-based indices {MARCTAeq, 9.8%, MARCTA$, 10.7%, Barclay, 9.6%, and TASS, 11.8%), were greater than most of the futures-based commodity indices (MLM, 5.2%). CTAs indices were also more volatile than the returns of US Bonds (4.2%) but less than stocks (S&P 500 13.5%). Exhibit 2 plots the performance of selected indices in return/standard deviation space.

Managed Futures and Stock and Bond Correlation

The decision to add an investment product to an existing portfolio depends on the relative means and standard deviations of the investment vehicle and the existing portfolio as well as the correlation between the investment vehicle and the portfolio. The correlation between each of the comparison groups is given in Exhibit 3 (parts A and B). The correlation between the S&P 500 and the CTA-based managed futures indices and subindices are between 0.3 (financial) and -0.1 (discretionary). While most correlations are negative, only a few are statistically significant.

EXHIBIT 2 ANNUALIZED RETURN AND RISK TRADEOFF (1990-1998)

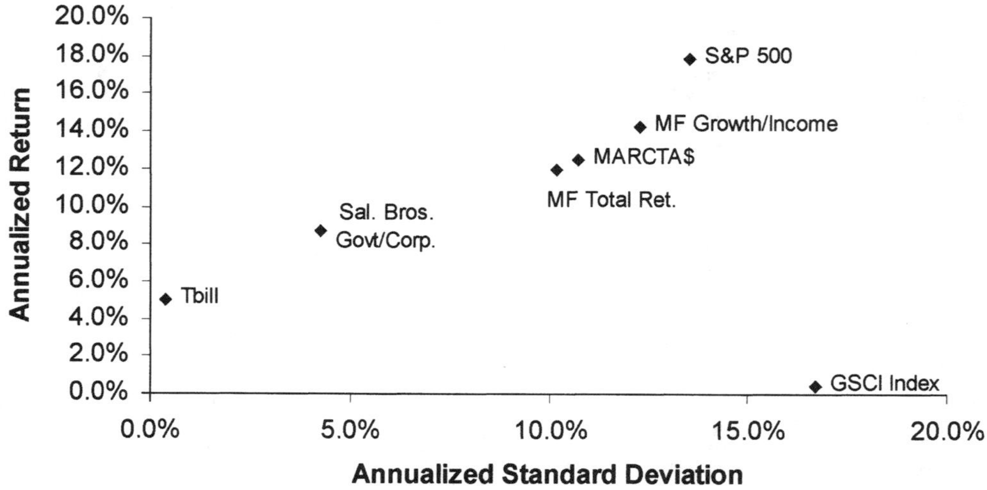

EXHIBIT 3

		Tass CTA $	Tass Currency	Barclay CTA Index	Barclay Currency	Barclay Agricultural	Barclay Financial/Metals	Barclay Energy	Barclay Diversified	Barclay Systematic	Barclay Discretionary
MARCTA:	Dollar Wt.	0.97	0.72	0.95	0.71	-0.01	0.88	0.17	0.92	0.95	0.56
MARCTA:	Equal Wt.	0.95	0.73	0.98	0.75	0.00	0.88	0.19	0.96	0.97	0.62
MARCTA:	Discretionary	0.54	0.42	0.56	0.40	-0.05	0.49	0.17	0.55	0.53	0.48
MARCTA:	Trendfollowing	0.97	0.74	0.95	0.74	-0.01	0.89	0.16	0.92	0.96	0.52
MARCTA:	Currency	0.70	0.87	0.68	0.91	-0.08	0.65	0.10	0.63	0.74	0.34
MARCTA:	Diversified	0.93	0.62	0.93	0.60	0.04	0.82	0.11	0.95	0.92	0.55
MARCTA:	Financial	0.93	0.67	0.85	0.67	-0.01	0.88	0.15	0.80	0.87	0.43
MLM	Passive Trendfollowing Index	0.25	0.08	0.25	0.01	0.20	0.14	-0.14	0.30	0.24	0.19
MAR FP:	Dollar Wt.	0.98	0.73	0.93	0.71	-0.01	0.84	0.14	0.90	0.94	0.51
MAR FP:	Equal Wt.	0.97	0.67	0.97	0.67	0.03	0.88	0.13	0.96	0.96	0.59
MAR FP:	Guaranteed	0.91	0.65	0.84	0.66	-0.04	0.80	0.06	0.80	0.87	0.41
MAR FP:	Multiadvisor	0.96	0.70	0.94	0.70	-0.01	0.86	0.17	0.92	0.94	0.53
MAR FP:	Offshore	0.67	0.71	0.60	0.69	-0.02	0.49	0.06	0.61	0.65	0.32
MAR FP:	Private Pool	0.77	0.49	0.75	0.50	0.04	0.71	0.19	0.75	0.71	0.54
MAR FP:	Public	0.96	0.70	0.93	0.68	-0.03	0.89	0.13	0.90	0.93	0.47
MAR FP:	Single Advisor	0.95	0.76	0.88	0.71	0.01	0.80	0.11	0.85	0.91	0.47
EACM	GLOB AA	0.85	0.67	0.83	0.68	-0.01	0.79	0.27	0.80	0.84	0.60
EACM	Discretionary	0.16	0.18	0.18	0.21	-0.09	0.17	0.31	0.14	0.16	0.35
EACM	Systematic	0.94	0.72	0.91	0.72	0.04	0.87	0.16	0.90	0.93	0.54
Tass	CTA $	1.00	0.75	0.95	0.72	0.00	0.87	0.10	0.93	0.96	0.51
Tass	Currency	0.75	1.00	0.71	0.92	-0.08	0.63	0.08	0.67	0.79	0.32
Barclay	CTA Index	0.95	0.71	1.00	0.72	0.03	0.88	0.18	0.98	0.97	0.66
Barclay	Currency	0.72	0.92	0.72	1.00	-0.10	0.67	0.17	0.67	0.79	0.43
Barclay	Agricultural	0.00	-0.08	0.03	-0.10	1.00	-0.07	-0.12	0.02	0.00	0.11
Barclay	Financial/Metals	0.87	0.63	0.88	0.67	-0.07	1.00	0.20	0.84	0.88	0.57
Barclay	Energy	0.10	0.08	0.18	0.17	-0.12	0.20	1.00	0.17	0.17	0.54
Barclay	Diversified	0.93	0.67	0.98	0.67	0.02	0.84	0.17	1.00	0.96	0.67
Barclay	Systematic	0.96	0.79	0.97	0.79	0.00	0.88	0.17	0.96	1.00	0.58
Barclay	Discretionary	0.51	0.32	0.66	0.43	0.11	0.57	0.54	0.67	0.58	1.00

		MARCTA: Dollar Wt.	MARCTA: Equal Wt.	MARCTA: Discretionary	MARCTA: Trendfollowing	MARCTA: Currency	MARCTA: Diversified	MARCTA: Financial	EACM GLOB AA	EACM Discretionary	EACM Systematic
MARCTA:	Dollar Wt.	1.00	0.94	0.63	0.97	0.72	0.92	0.92	0.88	0.23	0.95
MARCTA:	Equal Wt.	0.94	1.00	0.54	0.96	0.70	0.93	0.88	0.82	0.15	0.91
MARCTA:	Discretionary	0.63	0.54	1.00	0.51	0.45	0.56	0.47	0.62	0.44	0.51
MARCTA:	Trendfollowing	0.97	0.96	0.51	1.00	0.73	0.92	0.93	0.83	0.11	0.95
MARCTA:	Currency	0.72	0.70	0.45	0.73	1.00	0.57	0.65	0.67	0.21	0.70
MARCTA:	Diversified	0.92	0.93	0.56	0.92	0.57	1.00	0.83	0.79	0.11	0.90
MARCTA:	Financial	0.92	0.88	0.47	0.93	0.65	0.83	1.00	0.80	0.14	0.90
MLM	Passive Trendfollowing Index	0.19	0.21	0.17	0.20	0.02	0.32	0.08	0.13	-0.12	0.23
MAR FP:	Dollar Wt.	0.96	0.93	0.58	0.95	0.70	0.92	0.92	0.86	0.21	0.93
MAR FP:	Equal Wt.	0.95	0.97	0.55	0.95	0.64	0.94	0.89	0.82	0.15	0.92
MAR FP:	Guaranteed	0.91	0.85	0.54	0.91	0.68	0.83	0.89	0.82	0.25	0.86
MAR FP:	Multiadvisor	0.96	0.94	0.57	0.96	0.69	0.93	0.89	0.86	0.20	0.94
MAR FP:	Offshore	0.66	0.66	0.50	0.63	0.63	0.63	0.64	0.64	0.25	0.64
MAR FP:	Private Pool	0.76	0.74	0.56	0.71	0.48	0.76	0.69	0.73	0.23	0.76
MAR FP:	Public	0.96	0.93	0.50	0.97	0.68	0.92	0.92	0.82	0.14	0.93
MAR FP:	Single Advisor	0.92	0.89	0.53	0.91	0.70	0.87	0.90	0.83	0.21	0.90
EACM	GLOB AA	0.88	0.82	0.62	0.83	0.67	0.79	0.80	1.00	0.59	0.89
EACM	Discretionary	0.23	0.15	0.44	0.11	0.21	0.11	0.14	0.59	1.00	0.15
EACM	Systematic	0.95	0.91	0.51	0.95	0.70	0.90	0.90	0.89	0.15	1.00
Tass	CTA $	0.97	0.95	0.54	0.97	0.70	0.93	0.93	0.85	0.16	0.94
Tass	Currency	0.72	0.73	0.42	0.74	0.87	0.62	0.67	0.67	0.18	0.72
Barclay	CTA Index	0.95	0.98	0.56	0.95	0.68	0.93	0.85	0.83	0.18	0.91
Barclay	Currency	0.71	0.75	0.40	0.74	0.91	0.60	0.67	0.68	0.21	0.72
Barclay	Agricultural	-0.01	0.00	-0.05	-0.01	-0.08	0.04	-0.01	-0.01	-0.09	0.04
Barclay	Financial/Metals	0.88	0.88	0.49	0.89	0.65	0.82	0.88	0.79	0.17	0.87
Barclay	Energy	0.17	0.19	0.17	0.16	0.10	0.11	0.15	0.27	0.31	0.16
Barclay	Diversified	0.92	0.96	0.55	0.92	0.63	0.95	0.80	0.80	0.14	0.90
Barclay	Systematic	0.95	0.97	0.53	0.96	0.74	0.92	0.87	0.84	0.16	0.93
Barclay	Discretionary	0.56	0.62	0.48	0.52	0.34	0.55	0.43	0.60	0.35	0.54

		MAR FP: Dollar Wt.	MAR FP: Equal Wt.	MAR FP: Guaranteed	MAR FP: Multiadvisor	MAR FP: Offshore	MAR FP: Private Pool	MAR FP: Public	MAR FP: Single Advisor
MARCTA:	Dollar Wt.	0.96	0.95	0.91	0.96	0.66	0.76	0.96	0.92
MARCTA:	Equal Wt.	0.93	0.97	0.85	0.94	0.66	0.74	0.93	0.89
MARCTA:	Discretionary	0.58	0.55	0.54	0.57	0.50	0.56	0.50	0.53
MARCTA:	Trendfollowing	0.95	0.95	0.91	0.96	0.63	0.71	0.97	0.91
MARCTA:	Currency	0.70	0.64	0.68	0.69	0.63	0.48	0.68	0.70
MARCTA:	Diversified	0.92	0.94	0.83	0.93	0.63	0.76	0.92	0.87
MARCTA:	Financial	0.92	0.89	0.89	0.89	0.64	0.69	0.92	0.90
MLM	Passive Trendfollowing Index	0.22	0.28	0.19	0.23	0.05	0.23	0.18	0.21
MAR FP:	Dollar Wt.	1.00	0.95	0.92	0.98	0.71	0.79	0.97	0.96
MAR FP:	Equal Wt.	0.95	1.00	0.87	0.96	0.63	0.78	0.95	0.91
MAR FP:	Guaranteed	0.92	0.87	1.00	0.90	0.63	0.61	0.91	0.88
MAR FP:	Multiadvisor	0.98	0.96	0.90	1.00	0.65	0.76	0.97	0.90
MAR FP:	Offshore	0.71	0.63	0.63	0.65	1.00	0.57	0.61	0.76
MAR FP:	Private Pool	0.79	0.78	0.61	0.76	0.57	1.00	0.74	0.76
MAR FP:	Public	0.97	0.95	0.91	0.97	0.61	0.74	1.00	0.91
MAR FP:	Single Advisor	0.96	0.91	0.88	0.90	0.76	0.76	0.91	1.00
EACM	GLOB AA	0.86	0.82	0.82	0.86	0.64	0.73	0.82	0.83
EACM	Discretionary	0.21	0.15	0.25	0.20	0.25	0.23	0.14	0.21
EACM	Systematic	0.93	0.92	0.86	0.94	0.64	0.76	0.93	0.90
Tass	CTA $	0.98	0.97	0.91	0.96	0.67	0.77	0.96	0.95
Tass	Currency	0.73	0.67	0.65	0.70	0.71	0.49	0.70	0.76
Barclay	CTA Index	0.93	0.97	0.84	0.94	0.60	0.75	0.93	0.88
Barclay	Currency	0.71	0.67	0.66	0.70	0.69	0.50	0.68	0.71
Barclay	Agricultural	-0.01	0.03	-0.04	-0.01	-0.02	0.04	-0.03	0.01
Barclay	Financial/Metals	0.84	0.88	0.80	0.86	0.49	0.71	0.89	0.80
Barclay	Energy	0.14	0.13	0.06	0.17	0.06	0.19	0.13	0.11
Barclay	Diversified	0.90	0.96	0.80	0.92	0.61	0.75	0.90	0.85
Barclay	Systematic	0.94	0.96	0.87	0.94	0.65	0.71	0.93	0.91
Barclay	Discretionary	0.51	0.59	0.41	0.53	0.32	0.54	0.47	0.47

		S&P 500 Index	Salomon Brothers Treasury	Salomon Brothers Govt/Corp	Tbill Three Mnth.	JPMCI Index	GSCI Index
MARCTA:	Dollar Wt.	-0.05	0.27	0.25	0.05	0.16	0.11
MARCTA:	Equal Wt.	-0.08	0.23	0.21	0.10	0.18	0.14
MARCTA:	Discretionary	-0.10	0.18	0.18	-0.06	0.24	0.20
MARCTA:	Trendfollowing	-0.06	0.28	0.26	0.07	0.14	0.10
MARCTA:	Currency	0.00	0.18	0.17	0.13	0.04	0.01
MARCTA:	Diversified	-0.11	0.25	0.23	0.05	0.14	0.07
MARCTA:	Financial	0.03	0.37	0.35	0.03	0.09	0.06
MLM	Passive Trendfollowing Index	-0.29	-0.01	-0.03	0.14	0.10	0.05
MAR FP:	Dollar Wt.	-0.01	0.30	0.28	0.06	0.11	0.06
MAR FP:	Equal Wt.	-0.04	0.30	0.28	0.10	0.14	0.10
MAR FP:	Guaranteed	0.15	0.40	0.39	0.03	0.06	0.05
MAR FP:	Multiadvisor	-0.03	0.28	0.27	0.09	0.16	0.12
MAR FP:	Offshore	0.02	0.19	0.18	0.03	-0.16	-0.21
MAR FP:	Private Pool	-0.16	0.22	0.19	0.17	0.12	0.06
MAR FP:	Public	0.00	0.34	0.32	0.06	0.11	0.08
MAR FP:	Single Advisor	-0.03	0.31	0.30	0.05	0.08	0.01
EACM	GLOB AA	0.06	0.23	0.24	0.15	0.18	0.15
EACM	Discretionary	0.25	0.04	0.09	0.12	0.14	0.17
EACM	Systematic	-0.07	0.26	0.24	0.12	0.14	0.08
Tass	CTA $	-0.06	0.27	0.25	0.09	0.06	0.11
Tass	Currency	-0.13	0.10	0.09	0.20	-0.02	0.03
Barclay	CTA Index	-0.09	0.18	0.17	0.10	0.14	0.19
Barclay	Currency	-0.07	0.10	0.09	0.24	0.04	0.06
Barclay	Agricultural	-0.02	-0.01	-0.02	0.03	0.05	0.01
Barclay	Financial/Metals	-0.01	0.34	0.33	0.16	0.17	0.20
Barclay	Energy	-0.04	0.03	0.03	0.18	0.47	0.46
Barclay	Diversified	-0.13	0.18	0.16	0.12	0.12	0.17
Barclay	Systematic	-0.07	0.22	0.21	0.14	0.12	0.16
Barclay	Discretionary	-0.17	-0.01	-0.02	0.18	0.40	0.40

		Mutual Funds Aggressive Large	Mutual Funds Aggressive Small	Mutual Funds Balanced	Mutual Funds Foreign Sec.	Mutual Funds Growth and Income	Mutual Funds Gov. Securities	Mutual Funds Income	Mutual Funds Long Term Growth	Mutual Funds Total Return
MARCTA:	Dollar Wt.	-0.15	-0.14	-0.02	-0.13	-0.07	0.22	-0.03	-0.10	-0.07
MARCTA:	Equal Wt.	-0.19	-0.19	-0.06	-0.12	-0.11	0.19	-0.07	-0.14	-0.12
MARCTA:	Discretionary	-0.16	-0.14	-0.06	-0.08	-0.10	0.11	-0.05	-0.14	-0.09
MARCTA:	Trendfollowing	-0.16	-0.15	-0.03	-0.13	-0.08	0.24	-0.04	-0.11	-0.08
MARCTA:	Currency	-0.09	-0.10	0.02	-0.02	-0.03	0.17	-0.01	-0.06	-0.04
MARCTA:	Diversified	-0.20	-0.19	-0.08	-0.12	-0.13	0.20	-0.09	-0.16	-0.13
MARCTA:	Financial	-0.09	-0.09	0.07	-0.06	0.00	0.32	0.05	-0.03	0.00
MLM	Passive Trendfollowing Index	-0.31	-0.32	-0.30	-0.23	-0.31	-0.01	-0.30	-0.31	-0.32
MAR FP:	Dollar Wt.	-0.11	-0.11	0.02	-0.07	-0.04	0.26	0.00	-0.07	-0.04
MAR FP:	Equal Wt.	-0.15	-0.15	-0.02	-0.11	0.07	0.25	-0.02	-0.10	-0.07
MAR FP:	Guaranteed	0.02	0.02	0.20	0.05	0.13	0.37	0.18	0.09	0.13
MAR FP:	Multiadvisor	-0.13	-0.12	0.01	-0.08	-0.05	0.24	-0.01	-0.08	-0.05
MAR FP:	Offshore	-0.03	-0.04	0.04	0.12	0.00	0.16	0.02	-0.02	0.01
MAR FP:	Private Pool	-0.23	-0.23	-0.13	-0.18	-0.17	0.19	-0.14	-0.20	-0.19
MAR FP:	Public	-0.11	-0.10	0.04	-0.06	-0.02	0.29	0.03	-0.05	-0.02
MAR FP:	Single Advisor	-0.11	-0.12	0.01	-0.06	-0.05	0.28	0.00	-0.07	-0.04
EACM	GLOB AA	-0.01	-0.01	0.11	0.01	0.06	0.21	0.11	0.02	0.06
EACM	Discretionary	0.25	0.25	0.30	0.26	0.29	0.06	0.32	0.26	0.29
EACM	Systematic	-0.15	-0.16	-0.04	-0.13	-0.09	0.22	-0.05	-0.12	-0.10
Tass	CTA $	-0.17	-0.17	-0.04	-0.12	-0.09	0.23	-0.05	-0.12	-0.09
Tass	Currency	-0.22	-0.25	-0.13	-0.11	-0.17	0.08	-0.14	-0.19	-0.18
Barclay	CTA Index	-0.19	-0.19	-0.08	-0.14	-0.12	0.14	-0.09	-0.15	-0.13
Barclay	Currency	-0.13	-0.17	-0.06	-0.04	-0.10	0.09	-0.09	-0.12	-0.11
Barclay	Agricultural	0.02	0.03	-0.01	0.01	-0.01	-0.02	-0.01	0.00	0.01
Barclay	Financial/Metals	-0.13	-0.13	0.02	-0.09	-0.04	0.30	0.02	-0.07	-0.04
Barclay	Energy	-0.02	-0.03	0.00	-0.15	-0.02	0.02	-0.03	-0.03	-0.02
Barclay	Diversified	-0.22	-0.22	-0.11	-0.15	-0.16	0.14	-0.12	-0.19	-0.16
Barclay	Systematic	-0.17	-0.17	-0.05	-0.13	-0.10	0.18	-0.06	-0.13	-0.10
Barclay	Discretionary	-0.16	-0.16	-0.14	-0.18	-0.17	-0.02	-0.15	-0.17	-0.17

The correlation coefficients between the Salomon Brothers U.S. Government bond index and the CTA-based managed futures range from 0.40** (MAR Guaranteed) to .18* (MAR Discretionary). The high correlation in the MAR guaranteed subindex is consistent with the fact that a guaranteed fund typically place the bulk of its assets in zero-coupon bonds to ensure investors the return of principal at some point in the future.

CTA Index Correlation

Among CTA based indices, the broad indices have very high correlations. The MARCTA$, MARCTAeq, Barclay, TASS and EACM indices have correlations above 0.90. There is considerable variation among some of the subindices, however, particularly those which have a small population of CTAs. For instance, the MAR and EACM discretionary subindices have a lower correlation (0.44) than the systematic/trend following subindices (0.95**).

When subindices are compared to broad indices, the MAR discretionary index (0.54) offers the lowest correlation with the MARCTA$ index, while CTA trend-followers (0.98) have the highest correlation with the MARCTA$ index. Barclay subindex results are similar. These results suggest there is little difference between broad indices constructed by MAR, TASS, Barclay, and EACM, and furthermore that these indices would provide suitable benchmarks for the performance of a diversified or trend-following CTA. However, these broad indices will provide poor benchmarks for CTAs who concentrate in a single market (e.g., energy traders). Lastly, the low correlation offered by single-market CTAs suggests they offer more diversification benefit to a typical CTA portfolio than a trend-following or diversified CTA.

The broad CTA indices (MAR, Barclay, TASS, and EACM) are relatively uncorrelated with commodity indices. The MARCTA$ index has no correlation with the JPMorgan (.16), or Goldman Sachs (.01) indices. Low correlation between CTA returns and commodity index returns (correlations are below .25 across all cash and futures- based commodity indices) reflects fundamental differences in the return-generating processes: First;

EXHIBIT 4A RISK AND RETURN OF STOCK, BOND AND MAR$CTA INDEX: 1990-1998

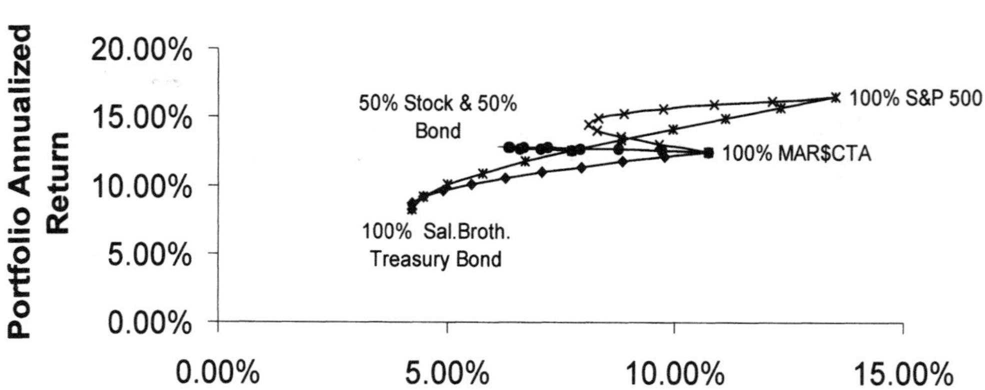

EXHIBIT 4B RISK AND RETURN OF STOCK, BOND AND BARCLAYB CTA INDEX: 1990-1998

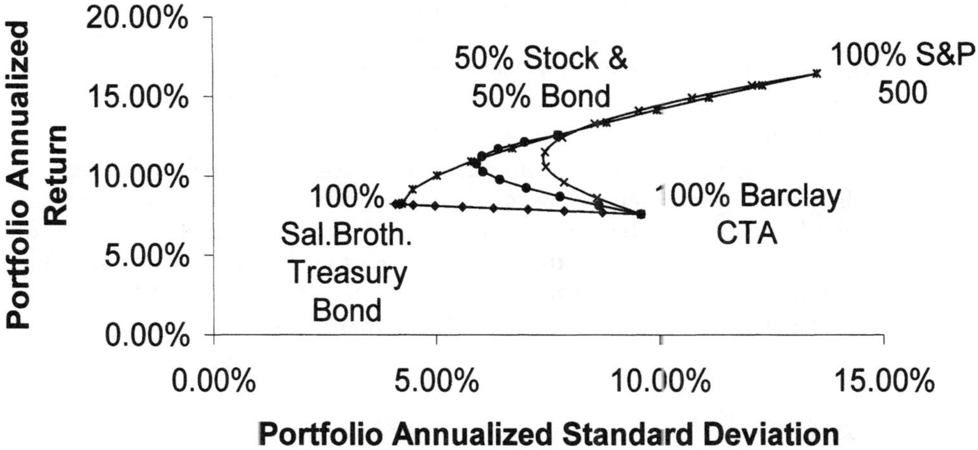

EXHIBIT 4C RISK AND RETURN OF STOCK, BOND AND TASS CTA INDEX: 1990-1998

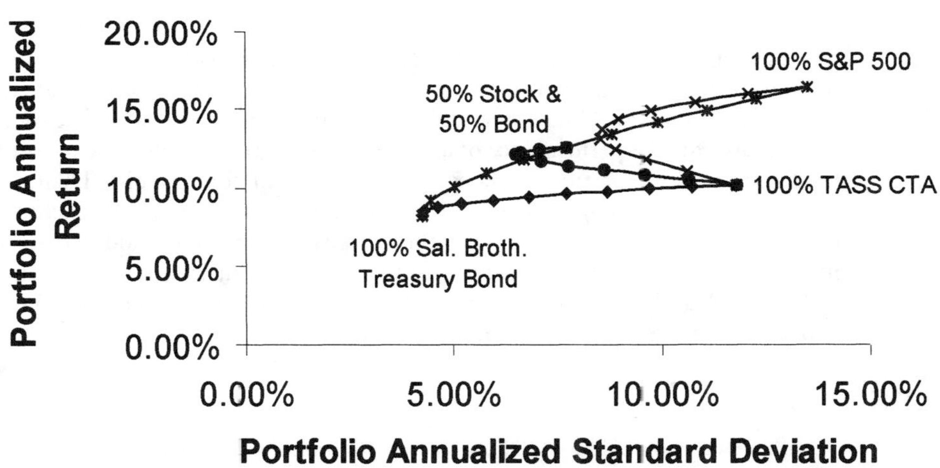

CTAs take long, short, and spread positions in both futures and options contracts, while indices are strictly long futures and do not include options. Second, commodity indices generally do not include fixed income, currency, or equity futures, while many CTAs actively trade in these contracts. An exception is the MLM Index, which takes short and long positions (but excludes spreads and options). This index correlates more highly with the MARCTA$ index (0.19) and other CTA indices, reflecting the predominance of trend-following traders in the MAR CTA index (Lukac [1985]).

Portfolio Impacts

The actual efficient frontier created from the inclusion of alternative CTA indices with an existing stand alone investment depend on the risk and return characteristics of the CTA index used. Results in Exhibits 4a-4c, reflect the asset allocation to CTA investment based on the alternative CTA index used. While differences exist, results show that the risk and return opportunity set expands for all the CTA indices used.

Investors must therefore realize that to the degree that their own investment portfolio differs from the established benchmarks or for which the index is noninvestible, the relationships described above may not be met. Investors must therefore determine the extent to which their own portfolios track the CTA index used in determining asset allocations. Research [Billingsley and Chance, 1996; Henker and Martin, 1998] have shown that approximately three to five CTAs are required for a portfolio to track existing CTA indices.

CONCLUSIONS

This study reviews the risk/return performance and relative tracking error of the various commodity indices and indices used to track managed futures performance. Results indicate that commodity and managed futures benchmark indices have sources of risk and return that are distinct from traditional assets such as stocks and bonds. Assuming this pattern continues, these indices offer investors an important area of diversification. Each index studied also has a unique construction that results in differential return correlation with alternative assets and thus each may be useful as a performance benchmark for unique portfolios, or, if the index is tradeable, as an addition to an existing portfolio.

However, commodity and managed futures indices differ in significant ways. There appears to be little connection between the returns of major commodity indices and the returns of CTA indices. Unlike stock and bond markets, where broad indices provide suitable benchmarks for the performance of an actively managed portfolio, the return to a buy and hold commodity investment strategy provides a poor forecast of CTA returns. Results presented therefore suggest that CTA-based indices provide a better benchmark for an actively managed futures portfolio than either passive or active commodity based performance indices. Moreover, results indicate that the actual efficient frontier created from the inclusion of CTA and commodity indices with an existing stand alone investment may differ depending on the CTA or commodity index used.

ENDNOTES

This article was published by CISDM/SOM, and is reprinted with permission.

[1] In this paper, results are presented solely on the Goldman Sachs and JPMorgan commodity indices, the TASS, MAR, Barclay, and EACM CTA based indices. Other commodity indices, the Chase Manhattan commodity index, the Dow-Jones-AIG commodity index also exist. Similarly, other CTA indices also exist including the ITR (International Traders Research) CTA index.

REFERENCES

AIMA. "Review of Methodology and Utilisation of Alternative Investment Benchmarks and Indices," (1997).

Billingsley, R. and D. Chance. "Benefits and Limitations of Diversifcation Among Commodity Trading Advisors." *The Journal of Portfolio Management,* (Fall 1996), pp. 65-80.

Chance, D. Managed Futures and Their Role in Investment Portfolios (Institute of Chartered Financial Analysts, 1994).

Edwards, F. and J. Park. "Do Managed Futures Make Good Investments," *The Journal of Futures Markets*, Vol. 16, No. 5 (August, 1996), 475-517.

Bailey, Jeffrey. "Evaluating Benchmark Quality," *Financial Analysts Journal* (May-June, 1992), 33-39.

Bodie, Zvi, and Victor Rosansky. "Risk and Return in Commodity Futures," Financial Analysts Journal 36 (May-June 1980), 3-14.

Edwards, F. and J. Park. "Do Managed Futures Make Good Investments," The Journal of Futures Markets, Vol. 16, No. 5 (August, 1996), 475-517.

Elton, E.J., M.J. Gruber, and J.C. Rentzler. "Professionally Managed, Publicly Traded Commodity Funds," Journal of Business (April 1987), 177-199.

Elton, E.J., M.J. Gruber, and J.C. Rentzler. "New Public Offerings, Information, and Investor Rationality: The Case of Publicly Offered Commodity Funds," Journal of Business, Vol. 6, No. 1, (1989) 1-15.

Elton, E.J., M.J. Gruber, and J. Rentzler, "The Performance of Publicly Offered Commodity Funds," in C. Peters ed. Managed Futures (Probus Publishing, 1992), 387-401.

Epstein, Charles ed., Managed Futures in the Institutional Portfolio, (Wiley, 1992).

Henker, T. and G. Martin, "Naïve and Optimal Diversification for Managed Futures," *The Journal of Alternative Investments*, (Fall, 1998), 25-39.

Irwin, S. "Further Evidence on the Usefulness of CTA Performance Information in Public Commodity Pool Prospectuses and a Proposal for Reform, "Advances in Futures and Options Research, Vol. 7 (1994).

Irwin, S., T. Krukemyer, and C. R. Zulaf, " Are Public Commodity Pools a Good Investment, " in C. Peters ed. Managed Futures (Probus Publishing, 1992),405-433.

McCarthy D, T. Schneeweis, and R. Spurgin. "Investment through CTAs: An Alternative to Public Commodity Funds", *Journal of Derivatives* (Summer, 1996), 36-47.

New York Stock Exchange. Commodity Futures as an Asset Class Report by Powers Research Associates, (January, 1990).

Peters, C.C. ed. Managed Futures: Performance Evaluation and Analysis of Commodity Funds, Pools and Accounts (Probus Publishing, 1992).

Reilly, F., G.W. Kao, and D. Wright, "Alternative Bond Market Indices", *Financial Analysts Journal* (May-June, 1992), 44-58.

Reilly and Rashid A. Akhtar, "The Benchmark Error Problem with Global Capital Markets," The *Journal of Portfolio Management* (Fall, 1995), 33-53.

Roll, R. " Performance Evaluation and Benchmark Error I.," *Journal of Portfolio Management* (Summer, 1980), 5-12.

Roll, R. "Performance Evaluation and Benchmark Error II." *Journal of Portfolio Management* (Winter, 1981), 17-22.

Rudd, A. and B. Rosenberg, "The Market Model in Investment Management," *Journal of Finance* (Vol. 35. No. 2 (1980), 597-607.

Schneeweis, T. "The Benefits of Managed Futures. European Managed Futures Association, August, 1996.

Schneeweis, T., U. Savanayana, and D. McCarthy, "Alternative Commodity Trading Vehicles: A Performance Analysis," *Journal of Futures Markets* (August, 1991), 475-490.

Schneeweis, T., U. Savanayana and D. McCarthy. "Multi-Manager Commodity Portfolios: A Risk/ Return Analysis," in C. Epstein ed. Managed Futures (Wiley, 1992), 81-102.

Schneeweis, T. and R. Spurgin. "Comparisons of Hedge Fund Indices," Working Paper CISDM, SOM, University of Massachusetts, (1996).

Schneeweis, T. and R. Spurgin. "Multi-Factor Models in CTA/Hedge Fund Return Estimation", Working Paper CISDM, SOM, University of Massachusetts, (1996).

Schneeweis, T., R. Spurgin, and D. McCarthy. "Survivor Bias in Commodity Trading Advisor Performance" *Journal of Futures Markets* (Forthcoming, 1996).

Schneeweis, T., R. Spurgin, and D. McCarthy. "Informational Content in Historical CTA Performance" *Journal of Futures Markets* (Forthcoming, 1997).

APPENDIX I

Description of Commodity and Managed Futures Indices

Goldman Sachs Commodity Index (GSCI) is an arithmetic measure of the performance of actively traded, dollar-denominated nearby commodity futures contracts. As of January 9, 1995, there were 22 commodities in the index. The weights assigned to individual commodities are based on a five-year moving average of world production. Weights are determined each July and are made effective the following January. All contracts are rolled on the fifth business day of the month prior to the expiration month of the contract. Subindices are calculated for agricultural, energy, industrial, livestock, and precious metals contracts. Two versions of the indices are available: a total return version, which assumes that capital sufficient to purchase the basket of commodities is invested at the risk-free rate, and a spot version, which only tracks movements in the futures prices. This study uses the total return measure. The GSCI was officially launched in 1992.

JPMorgan Commodity Index (JPMCI) is comprised of 11 highly liquid industrial commodity futures contracts. It excludes "softs," relying exclusively on energy, precious metals, and industrial metals. The two nearby contracts for each commodity are used, and rolls are conducted over a five-day period from the fifth to the ninth business day of the month. Component weights are rebalanced monthly according to a scoring system that seeks to maximize risk-return performance, track unexpected changes in inflation, provide a hedge against stock and bond investments, and correlate with economic growth measures. Subindices for energy, precious metals, and industrial metals are also available. The JPMCI is published in both spot and total return formats. This study uses the total return measure. The JPMCI was officially launched on September 21, 1994.

Mount Lucas (MLM) Index differs from other indices in two important ways. First, it allows both long and short positions in the underlying futures contracts. Second, it incorporates financial and currency futures (but not stock index futures) into the index, along with the commodities tracked by other indices. The index is an equally weighted average of the monthly returns from 25 separate futures contracts. Within each market (e.g., corn futures), the index will be long or short depending on whether the contract is above or below its trailing 12-month moving average. MLM is a total-return index. It was launched in May, 1989.

Managed Account Reports (MAR) tracks the performance of individual CTAs as well as CTA Funds and Pools that invest in individual CTAs. MAR produces several performance indices, the dominant being the CTA equal-weighted and dollar-weighted indices. MAR classifies CTAs into a number of different groups, and publishes each group's performance index. These groups are currency, energy, financial, diversified, discretionary, and trend-following. MAR also reports the following subindices for fund and pool performance: guaranteed, multi-advisor, single-advisor, private pools, and public pools. It was restructured in 1992.

Barclay Trading Group, publisher of the Barclay Managed Futures Report, also creates CTA performance indices. Indices are based on monthly returns of CTAs with established track records. Barclay publishes an equal weighted index of all CTAs as well as the following subindices: agricultural, currency, diversified, energy, financial/metal, discretionary, and systematic.

TASS offers historical managed futures performance similar to MAR or Barclays. It publishes a dollar weighted CTA index and one subindex of currency CTAs. Additional indices and subindices will be available in the future.

EACM offers historical managed futures/hedge fund performance on an array of indices and subdices designed to capture the return to unique managed futures/hedge fund strategies. These indices include relative value, event-driven, equity hedge funds, global asset allocators and short selling. Subindices include long/short equity, convertible hedge, bond hedge, rotational, deal arbitrage, bankruptcy, and multi-event. For managed futures, the principal subindices include discretionary and systematic. It has been publicly available since January, 1996.

5 NAIVE AND OPTIMAL DIVERSIFICATION FOR MANAGED FUTURES

THOMAS HENKER
University of New South Wales, Sydney

GEORGE MARTIN
University of Massachusetts

INTRODUCTION

The past decade has witnessed a dramatic increase in the use of alternative investment vehicles such as hedge funds and managed futures products as additions to traditional stock and bond portfolios. Academic and practitioner literature [Chance, 1994, Schneeweis, 1996] shows that the returns of hedge funds and managed futures have a low correlation with traditional investment vehicles such as stocks and bonds. This low correlation is due to the wide variety of markets traded by such alternative investment vehicles as well as their different trading methods (e.g., the ability to go long and short or use high leverage), and it provides a major reason for the use of these investments.

Specifically, the differing investment styles and investment areas enable Commodity Trading Advisors (CTAs) to create portfolios which offer risk and return tradeoffs not available through traditional stock, bond, or even hedge fund investments. Unfortunately, the differences in investment styles and markets traded between CTAs and traditional investment vehicles often hide the extent to which managed futures offer similar risk characteristics as traditional stock and bond investments and the degree to which investment management concepts which work for stock and bond portfolios are also true for CTA-based asset portfolios. In this paper, results are presented first on the number of randomly or "naively" selected and equally weighted CTAs that must be included in a portfolio for that portfolio to accurately track a variety of benchmark CTA and asset indexes [e.g., S&P 500, GSCI] Second, since historical managed futures performance is often used to determine *ex-post* optimal CTA selections and weightings in investor portfolios, the robustness of the level of inclusion of managed futures in mean-variance optimal multi-asset class portfolios is tested. Results show the potential benefits of managed futures investments in both naive and optimal portfolio determination.[1]

It is shown that the impact of random diversification on naively constructed (randomly chosen and equal weighted) CTA portfolios and the impact of CTA investment in mixed stock or bond portfolios are, as expected, similar to that shown to exist for traditional stock and bond investments. That is, depending on the homogeneity of the sample, between five and fifteen CTAs are generally required for the CTA portfolio to achieve a lower variance bound and to track representative managed futures or cash market performance indexes. Secondly, as with stock and bond portfolios, optimal diversification based on historical risk and return parameters results in "efficient" portfolios with CTA weightings is dramatically different from those implied in comparison CTA benchmark indexes. Thus, as with a stock and bond portfolio, a CTA portfolio constructed to optimize its historical return and risk tradeoff may differ dramatically from its benchmark.

The results indicate the close similarity between the problems of managed futures investment and the problems of traditional stock and bond investment allocations. To the degree that investors used "popular" asset allocation programs based on traditional passive or active manager indexes to determine investment allocation, investors must ensure that their stock, bond, or managed futures portfolios reflect the performance of the underlying indexes or portfolios used to construct the expected performance. Thus, for managed futures, as for stock and bond investments, a greater effort must be made to determine the underlying distributional factors of the portfolio and its performance under economic conditions expected to exist over the planned investment horizon.

MANAGED FUTURES, STOCK FUNDS, AND BOND FUNDS: NAÏVE AND OPTIMAL ASSET ALLOCATION

The past five years has witnessed a dramatic increase of research conducted on the potential benefits of managed futures products.[2] For the individual or institutional investor, asset allocation into any investment area is often based on two criteria. First, the theoretical arguments (e.g. the existence of unique expected positive risk/return tradeoffs) and, second, on past evidence that the actual creation of a fund or portfolio is consistent with empirical results based on previous fund or benchmark analysis. In this respect, the requirements for investor participation in managed futures products is similar to that for traditional investments; that is, investors require support for the belief that the risk and return benefits exist and that investable vehicles exist that offer this performance in a consistent fashion. For stock and bond funds, considerable research exists on the ability of a naively constructed stock and bond portfolio to mimic that of the passive market index or market sector (Elton et al. [1983]; Hill and Schneeweis [1981]) such that investors have the reasonable assurance that stock and bond portfolios can be constructed that will have the characteristics of the underlying passive market benchmark or the active portfolio sector performance.

Similarly, for managed futures, research shows a correspondence between historical and future risk and return as well as the importance of manager based benchmarks, in explaining managed futures return (Irwin et al. [1994] and Schneeweis et al. [1997]). As for stocks and bonds, Billingsley and Chance [1996] and Oberuc [1993] also have shown that naive diversification among as little as ten CTA managers results in a mixed (stocks, bond, and CTA) portfolio that approaches the lower portfolio variance bound. The benefits of adding CTAs to the traditional passive stock and bond portfolio is based on the low correlation between the CTAs and the traditional investment vehicles. The number of CTAs required to achieve the lower variance bound for the mixed traditional and non-traditional portfolio is determined by the correlation between the sample CTAs. The more similar the styles and markets traded are, the lower the impact of an increased number of CTAs on reducing the portfolio variance. Equally important is that the higher the correlation between CTAs in a sample, the lower the number of CTAs required to mimic the performance of the CTA universe used to construct the active performance benchmark that is representative for that CTA sample. As of importance is that previous research on naively determined stock and bond portfolios (Statman [1987]; Hill and Schneeweis [1981]) implies that a greater number of CTAs may be required if one wishes to reduce the tracking error of the naively determined portfolio to the representative benchmark or the alternative investment.

Although information on naive diversification is useful background to understanding the asset allocation decision, optimal asset allocation requires that one specify the criteria and constraints which govern an optimization procedure. Mean-variance optimization in the spirit of Markowitz is the traditional approach used in stock and bond allocation. However, for any asset allocation set, an important problem that affects the allocational decision on the basis of historical data will always tend to overweight the assets that have performed well over the sample period.[3] For instance, Schneeweis and Spurgin [1998] provide an analysis of the risk and return benefits of hedge fund and managed futures investments, along with other principal "traditional" alternative investment assets (e.g., real estate, private equity, private debt, high-yield debt, commodities), when they are considered as part of an investor's overall portfolio. In their study, alternative investments (e.g., hedge funds and managed futures) make up approximately 20% of the optimal portfolio under all of the expected return scenarios. The severity of this problem will grow with the number of assets in the investment universe. In the present context of managed futures investment, this overweighting, if unchecked, would result in "optimal" allocations in which the bulk of a portfolio will end up in a small number of CTAs that performed well. One could constrain allocations to be less than a certain percentage of total assets, but that would defeat the purpose of investigating the optimal contribution of CTAs as an asset class to portfolios containing traditional investment vehicles. One may wish instead, to examine the value of CTAs as an asset class without optimizing on the deviations of individual CTA historical returns from their expected returns. To do this, a procedurally simple process is proposed that involves randomizing over candidate CTA and then optimizing via a traditional quadratic programming algorithm over the sampled CTAs. The sample distributions of the resulting weights are used as a basis for drawing inferences about the value of CTAs. Through this procedure (explained more fully later), it is shown that the addition of CTAs provides substantial improvement in the risk/return properties of an optimized portfolio, and that these results are not replicated or superseded when compared against the addition of traditional assets, *viz.* individual equities. These results are robust because they do not depend on the returns of any particular CTA, but on the distributional properties of CTAs as an asset class.

With this framework, a test of the impact of increasing the number of CTAs on optimal quadratic optimization is conducted. The results are consistent with the observable practices of institutional investors with managed futures programs; they are also consistent with previous results for traditional diversification among stock sectors or stock and bond portfolios. Likewise, the limitations associated with CTA investment decisions based on historical data are consistent with the limitations for stock and bond investment from historical data.

EXHIBIT 1 NUMBER OF CTAS IN DIFFERENT SECTORS

Sector	Number
Agriculture	7
Currency	25
Diversified	84
Financial	32
Energy	4
Metal	1
Stocks	8
All	161

DATA AND METHODOLOGY

The time period of the analysis is January 1991 to December 1995. All CTAs with continuously reported monthly performance included in the LaPorte (MAR) database are included in this study. The sample contains 161 CTAs for a period of sixty months. CTA performance is self-reported after typical account fees and expenses. Exhibit 1 shows how the CTAs in our sample are grouped into sectors by LaPorte. Portfolios of

EXHIBIT 2 ASSET INDICES AND BENCHMARKS USED IN THIS STUDY

Asset Class	Index Name
Stocks	S&P 500 total return
	MSCI world dollar den.
	Fidelity Magellan
Bond	US Salomon Bros. Govt. Bond
	World Sal. Bros. Govt. Bond
Commodities	JPMCI all (ofcl.)
	GSCI Commodity total return
CTA	Mt. Lucas
	MAR CTA equal weighted
	MAR CTA $ weighted
	Barclay CTA Index
	Barclay Diversified
	Barclay Currency
	Barclay Financials/Metals
	Barclay Discretionary
	Barclay Systematic
	Barclay Energy
	Barclay Agriculture

traditional assets are approximated by different bond and stock indexes. These indexes as well as additional CTA indexes are used as benchmarks for various tests. Conventional asset indexes are obtained from DATASTREAM while CTA indexes are taken from *Managed Account Reports* (MAR) and Barclay. All indexes used in this study are summarized in Exhibit 2. Additionally, we compute an equally weighted portfolio from all individual CTAs in the data set.

An analysis is done of the risk/return characteristics of CTAs as additions to conventional asset indexes and portfolios using two basic approaches which are termed "naive" (i.e., random) and "planned" (i.e. the result of some optimization procedure) diversification. The first set of analyses involves random selection of CTAs, according to CTA sector, and then computation of the statistics which indicate the impact of random CTA selection (sampling without replacement) on the risk reduction within the CTA sector and as additions to traditional as well as non-traditional benchmarks. These tests are similar to those conducted by Billingsley and Chance [1996] and Oberuc [1993]. However, Billingsley and Chance as well as Oberuc limited their analysis to traditional stock and bond benchmarks. This analysis extends their analyses to a wide range of potential indexes given in Exhibit 2. In addition, the paper offers a closer focus on the impact of the number of CTAs required within a CTA sector and across alternative investment indexes to achieve both a stable correlation pattern with the corresponding benchmark investment and the number of CTAs required to reduce the tracking error of the benchmark (in order to reduce uncertainty about estimated correlation or variance-covariance matrices). It is shown in the next section that, similar to previous studies on stocks (Statman [1987]) and bonds (Hill and Schneeweis [1981]), the number of CTAs required to lower tracking error to a lower bound is greater than that required to lower variance (correlation) to the lower (higher) bound. It is also shown that the number of CTAs required to achieve these bounds is CTA-sector and benchmark dependent.

In the second set of analyses, a version of an optimal portfolio selection is implemented in which:

1) A sequence of potential portfolios of individual CTAs is selected via Monte Carlo simulation.
2) A quadratic programming routine is used to choose the actual weightings for each of these portfolios.
3) The resulting weightings are then analyzed to obtain inferences on the optimal weightings.

The general motivation behind this analytical technique is that the computation of the global solution to the mixed integer-quadratic programming problem of optimal weights for an arbitrary subset of securities of fixed size often results in inconsistent results since a large number of assets with non-zero variation will tend to generate ex-post selections of "optimal" portfolios whose composition is determined primarily by random forecast errors rather than the underlying economic return generating process. The statistics resulting from the proposed selection process are more robust since they are a function not of the extreme values of the distribution of CTA returns, but the general structure of the return generating process for CTAs (or a selected subgroup) — which is far more stable than the realized tail properties. This method also represents a compromise on the issue of return/covariance forecastability in that a standard deterministic formulation of the portfolio selection problem assumes not only that the covariance matrix and expected returns are known with certainty but that they fully characterize future returns and covariances. Furthermore, the method allows for the introduction of a substantial stochastic element into the portfolio choice problem since one is randomizing the parameter values in a manner determined by the empirical distribution function of observed returns.

CTA Portfolio Selection

Portfolios of CTAs are formed by randomly selecting CTAs from the data set. The CTAs are chosen from the data set without replacement. (Results were also obtained allowing replacement which results in portfolios of fewer CTAs with unequal weighting. The results are similar to random drawing without replacement.) Since the portfolio optimization algorithm in the later section does not allow a singular matrix as an input we chose to report only the results without replacement.

EMPIRICAL RESULTS

Descriptive Statistics

Descriptive statistics of the data set are summarized in Exhibit 3. The first four rows give the first four moments where excess kurtosis can be obtained by subtracting three from the kurtosis number given in Table 3. Most notable is the low average correlation between the individual CTAs, where average correlation refers to the average of the

EXHIBIT 3 DESCRIPTIVE STATISTICS FOR INDIVIDUAL CTAs FROM JAN-1991 TO DEC-1995

	CTAall	AG	CUR	DIV	FIN	EN	MET	STX
Average	1.084751	0.601833	1.293667	0.988486	1.127917	1.220698	0.998000	0.573375
Std. dev.	7.683999	6.077679	8.205811	8.119442	5.794808	7.280401	4.671313	4.952340
Skewness	1.079687	5.694206	1.234426	0.835667	0.587117	1.252655	1.582101	0.143694
Kurtosis	7.851965	89.000670	6.401076	5.913532	1.489107	7.019485	7.221267	3.989226
Correlation	0.164489	0.000376	0.231910	0.223177	0.293423	0.027440	—	0.016557

EXHIBIT 4 MONTHLY RETURN DISTRIBUTION OF THE CTA DATASET WITH FITTED NORMAL DISTRIBUTION

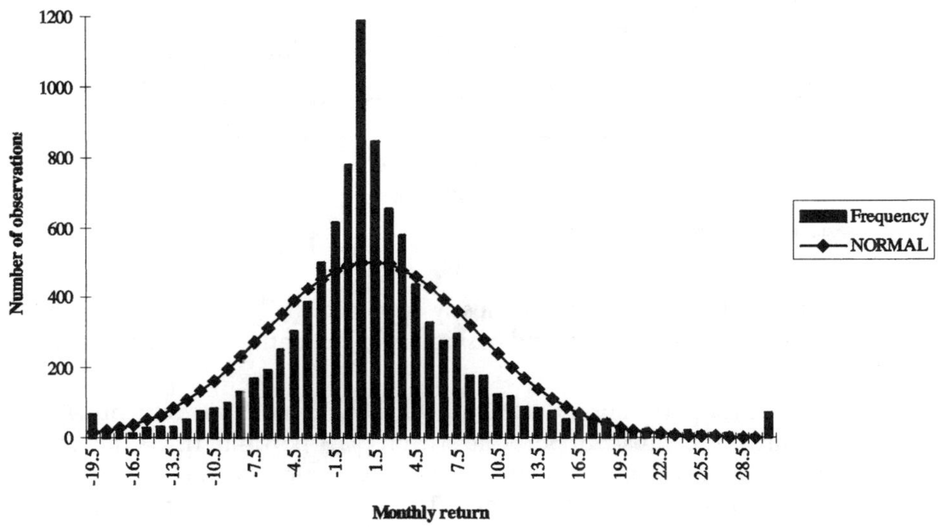

correlations of all possible pairs within the designated sector. Even within any given sector the average correlation among individual CTAs is below 0.30. The distribution of monthly CTA returns for the whole data set is shown in Exhibit 4. A normal distribution with the matching first two moments is fitted to the empirical return distribution. The distribution of returns is not unlike that of other asset classes, that is, it is more peaked than the normal distribution with leptokurtokic tails. Most importantly, the return distribution is approximately symmetric which justifies the use of variance and standard deviation as measures of investment risk.

Benefits of Naive Random CTAs Diversification: Full Sample

Exhibit 5 provide a description of the impact of increasing the number of CTAs in the portfolio on portfolio standard deviation. The correlation of the CTA portfolio with alternative benchmarks is given in Exhibit 6. For Exhibit 5, CTAs are drawn randomly from the population of all CTAs while for Exhibits 6a-d, CTAs are drawn randomly with replacement from the whole CTA sample and for three CTA subsets, Diversified (multiple markets), Currency, and Financial (e.g., interest rate) CTAs. The results shown in Exhibits 5 are as expected, the impact of random diversification is greatest (a 40% reduction in standard deviation) for the entire CTA sample (e.g., lowest intersample correlation) and is lowest (20% reduction in standard deviation) for the Currency CTA subsample (highest intersample correlation). Results also show that the

EXHIBIT 5 STANDARD DEVIATIONS OF RETURNS FOR CTA PORTFOLIO OF INCREASING SIZE

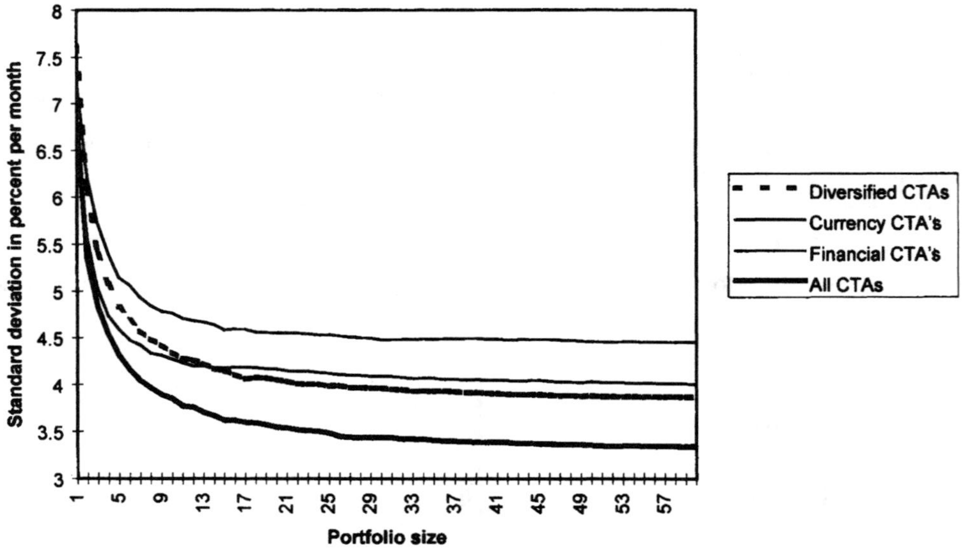

Sampling with replacement 300 repetitions.

number of CTAs required to closely approach the lower bound on portfolio standard deviation is about 10-15 and is similar for the entire CTA sample and the CTA subgroups.

CTA portfolios are seldom held as stand-alone investments. As a result, as important as the impact of portfolio size on CTA portfolio risk is the impact of portfolio size on the relationship between the CTA portfolio and alternate investment benchmarks, including CTAs themselves. In Exhibit 6, the impact between portfolio size for the full CTA sample and correlation with alternative traditional and nontraditional investments is given. Of special interest is that CTA portfolios of approximately 15-20 CTAs are required before the CTA portfolio/CTA benchmark correlation approaches its upper boundary. However, at that level, the correlation between the CTA portfolio and the CTA benchmark is almost 0.90. Thus the use of a CTA benchmark such as the MAR CTA$ or the Barclay CTA index will produce similar asset allocation impacts as a naively determined CTA portfolio of approximately twenty CTAs. As important is that as few as 5-10 CTAs raises the average correlation from about 0.4 to 0.8. Thus the impact on CTA benchmark correlation is, as we would expect, nonlinear and determined mostly by the initial diversification of the benchmark index. The correlation of a CTA portfolio with a benchmark are measures describing how well a CTA portfolio tracks a respective benchmark.

In contrast to the high correlation of the CTA portfolios with general CTA benchmarks (e.g., MAR$ and Barclay CTA), the average correlation falls as the characteristics of the CTA portfolio differ from that of the benchmark. For instance, the average correlation of the full CTA portfolio with that of the Barclay CTA energy subindex is less than 0.20. Thus for the diversified investor, investment in a CTA based on the characteristics of the sample and weighted away from smaller subgroups may require additional investment in CTA subgroups in order to reduce overall portfolio risk. Similarly, as the characteristics of the benchmark differs from that of the CTA portfolio, the correlation between the two approximates zero. Correlations with some very different benchmarks are even negative and are further reduced as the CTA portfolio size in-

EXHIBIT 6 CORRELATIONS OF CTA PORTFOLIOS WITH BENCHMARKS

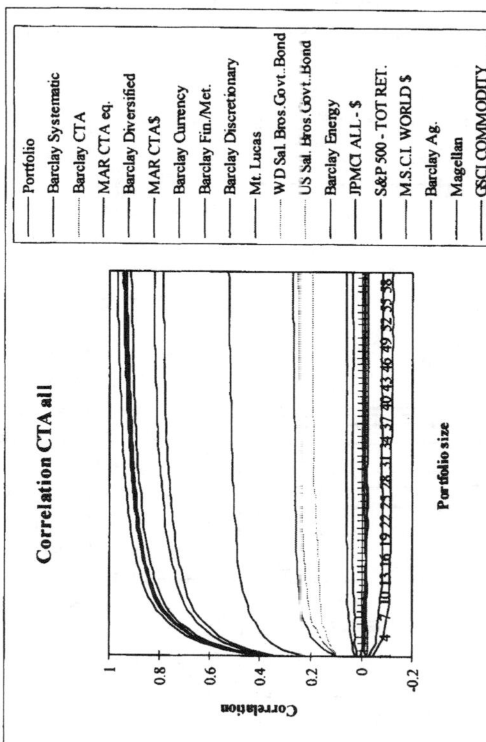

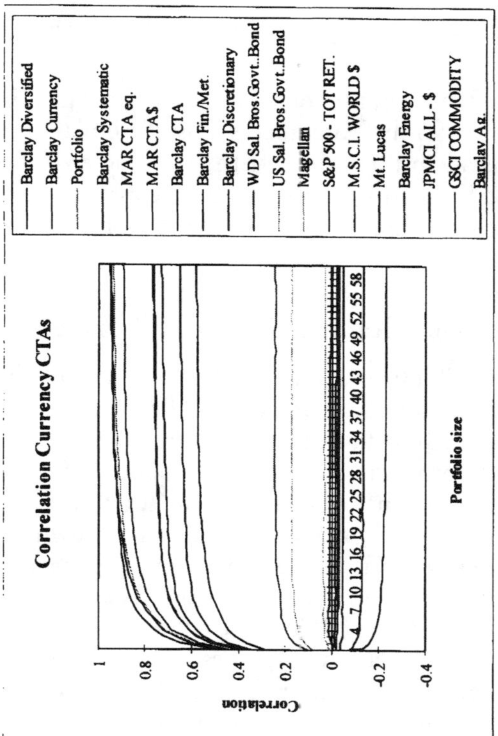

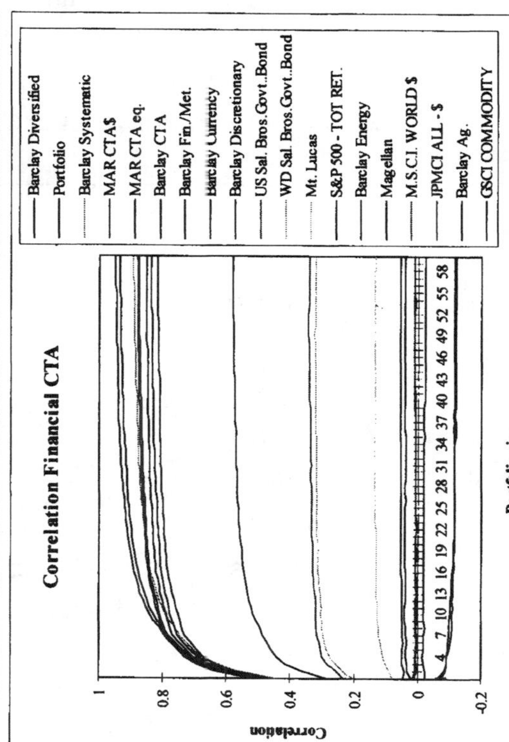

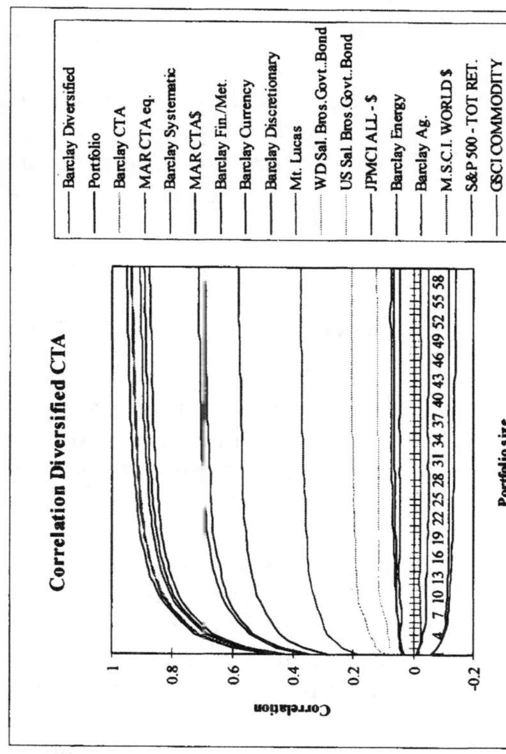

The order of indexes in the legends corresponds to the order of the lines in the figures.

creases. For these benchmarks, however, the limit of the impact of CTA portfolio size on the level of correlation is reached at a lower level (approximately 5-10 CTAs) than that of the limit of the impact of CTA portfolio size on CTA based benchmark standard deviation (15-20 CTAs).

Similar to the results presented in Exhibit 6, as shown in Exhibit 7 the tracking error (e.g. root mean squared error) is highest for the benchmarks most dissimilar to the CTA portfolio and the reduction in the standard deviation of the tracking error is less for these benchmarks as the size of the CTA portfolio is increased. In contrast, the tracking errors of alternative investment indexes are much smaller than those of traditional asset benchmarks.

Benefits of Naive Random CTAs Diversification: Segmented Sample

The low correlation exhibited in Exhibit 6 between the CTA portfolio and dissimilar benchmarks such as the S&P 500, Magellan fund, or Salomon Brothers Bond indexes reflects the differential markets and trading strategies of CTAs. However, while the correlation between managed futures products and stock and bond portfolios is approximately zero, recent research has shown that when returns are segmented according to whether the stock/bond market rose or fell, managed futures are shown to have a negative correlation with these markets when these cash market portfolios posted significant negative returns and are positively correlated when these cash portfolios reported significant positive returns [Schneeweis 1996, and Schneeweis et al., 1996]. Thus managed futures offer unique asset allocation properties and differing correlation patterns in differing market environments. In Exhibit 8a, the relative impact of CTA portfolio size on the correlation of the full CTA portfolio with stock and bond benchmarks during up (top 25 months) and down (worst 25 months) stock and bond performance is given. As in previous research [Schneeweis et al., 1996], CTAs portfolio re-

EXHIBIT 7 AVERAGE TRACKING ERROR OF CTA PORTFOLIOS WITH BENCHMARKS

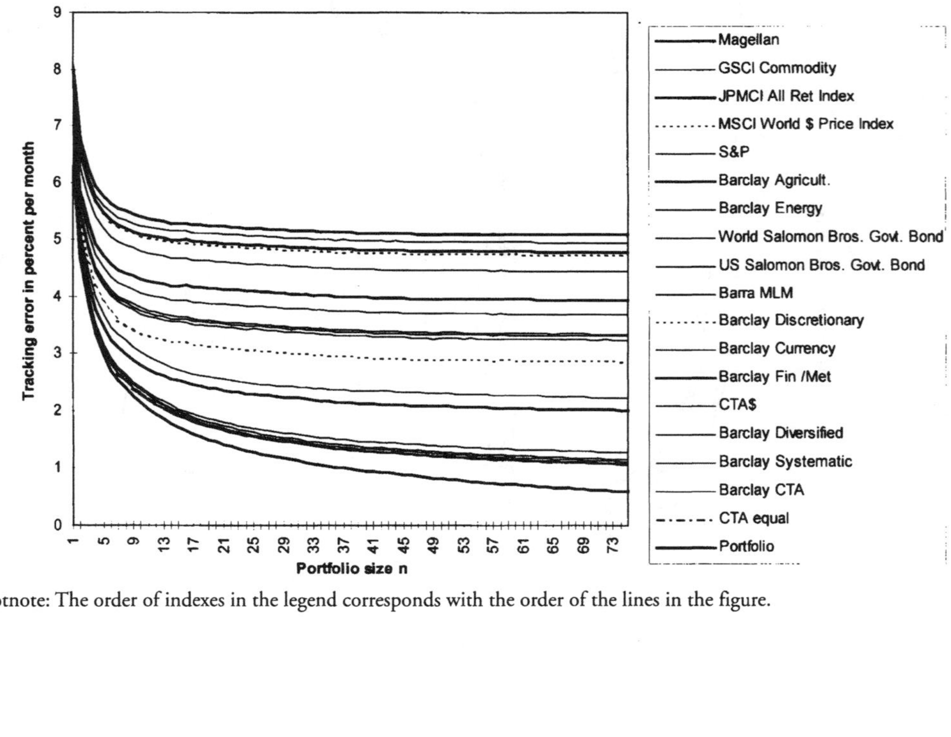

Footnote: The order of indexes in the legend corresponds with the order of the lines in the figure.

turns are shown to have a positive correlation with the S&P 500 as well as the Magellan fund in the top twenty-five months and a negative correlation in the bottom twenty-five return months.[4] However, results also show that a randomly selected portfolio of about 10 CTAs is required to reach the upper or lower correlation bound. Similar results are shown for the CTA portfolio and bond indexes in Exhibit 8b.

While results show that random selection of about 10 CTAs produces correlation results similar to that of the benchmark CTAs used in previous analysis, the correlation patterns of CTAs with the other benchmarks is also impacted by segmentation of the two primary investment markets (stock and bonds) into their high and low return months. Results in Exhibits 9 and 10 show that, for the most part, the correlation patterns and average standard error with other non-stock/bond benchmarks remain stable during periods of high/low stock/bond return months.

Benefits of CTA Portfolio Size in Optimal Return/Risk Diversification

EXHIBIT 8A CORRELATION OF CTA PORTFOLIOS WITH BENCHMARK IF THE BENCHMARK PERFORMS WELL/POORLY

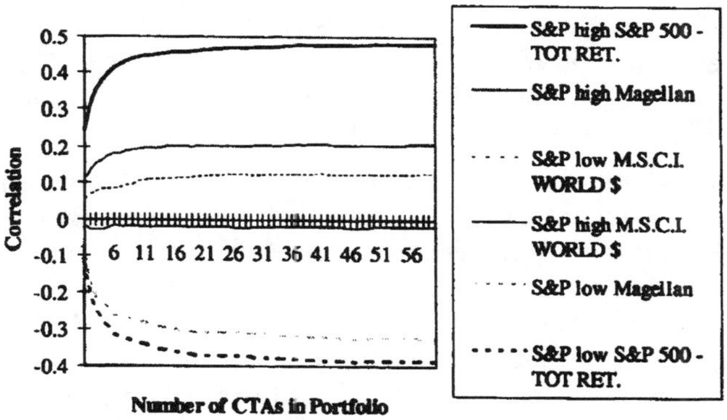

EXHIBIT 8B CORRELATION OF CTA PORTFOLIOS WITH BENCHMARK IF THE BENCHMARK PERFORMS WELL/POORLY

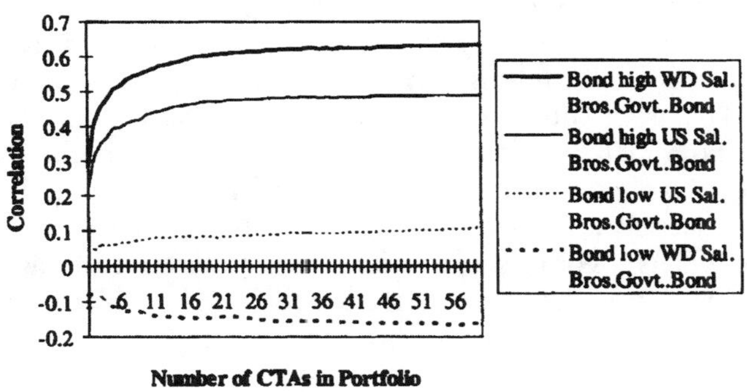

(B)

In optimal risk/return efficient frontier determination, the inclusion of an asset into an existing portfolio is a tradeoff between the relative returns of the existing portfolio and the alternative assets and their correlations with the existing portfolio. Previous research [Billingsley and Chance, 1996] has shown that the reduction in variance achieved by adding CTAs to a portfolio of stocks and bonds is less than the impact of adding CTAs to a stock portfolio due to the already low correlation between stocks and bonds. However, despite the lessening impact, other research [Schneeweis, 1996] has shown in various periods, adding CTAs to an existing stock/bond or stock/bond/commodity index portfolio still results in an improved Sharpe ratio, a measure for risk adjusted return.

Results in Exhibit 11 show the impact of differing CTA portfolio sizes on the percentage of CTAs in the optimal portfolio given a stated target return is traced. Sampling of CTAs is conducted without replacement. In Exhibit 11, the average optimal weight of a naively-selected CTA portfolio (full sample and subgroups) increases as the number of CTAs in the portfolio increases when this CTA portfolio is added to a stock/bond portfolio. This is not unexpected since as the number of CTAs increases, the variability of the CTA portfolio returns decreases and the correlation with stocks/bonds in down months for these asset decreases. However, as shown in Exhibit 11, the impact on optimal CTA weight is most significant for initial changes in the number of CTAs. For the planned diversification case this is examined slightly differently since we want to be alerted to tendencies of the optimization process to weight a small number of CTAs most heavily even in a portfolio with a large number of CTAs. This is done by examining not only the total weight to CTAs, but the sum of squared weights—which will be larger if the portfolio overweights individual CTAs.

Exhibit 12 shows a chart of the distribution of weights for CTA overall and in subgroupings for increasing numbers of CTAs included in the respective portfolio. The indicated upper and lower bounds represent respectively the values that would be obtained if the entire weighting were in one CTA or equally divided amongst all CTAs in the portfolio. The results indicate that for less than four or five CTAs the optimizer tends to heavily weight only one asset, thus suggesting that the benefits of diversification do not start to accrue properly in until at least five CTAs are held in the CTA portfolio. Moreover, the results also suggest that once one has reached the level of four or five CTAs in a portfolio, the increasing weights are due not to optimizing biases due to ex-post selection but the bona fide reduction in inter-asset correlations. Were it to the contrary, then we would see substantial growth in the sum of squared weights as the increase in the number of candidate CTAs would provide the optimizer with more opportunities to select and weight abnormally high asset returns (outliers) with intrinsically high variance.

Since the target return in this section remains the S&P 500, the inclusion of CTAs in the optimal portfolio is derived exclusively from their contribution to risk reduction. As shown in Exhibit 13, as CTA portfolio size increases, the expected risk of the optimal portfolio decreases. This is, of course, consistent with the lowering correlation as the weight of CTAs in the optimal portfolio increases. Note further that the reduction in variability generally occurs after more than three or four CTAs are held in the portfolio. The portfolios in this section are ex-post optimal allocations between different asset classes (stocks, bonds, CTAs). For this reason the monthly standard deviation of portfolio returns is much lower than the return variability that can be achieved with ex-ante portfolio allocations.

EXHIBIT 9 CORRELATION OF CTA PORTFOLIO WITH BENCHMARK DURING 25 MONTHS WITH HIGH/LOW BENCHMARK RETURNS

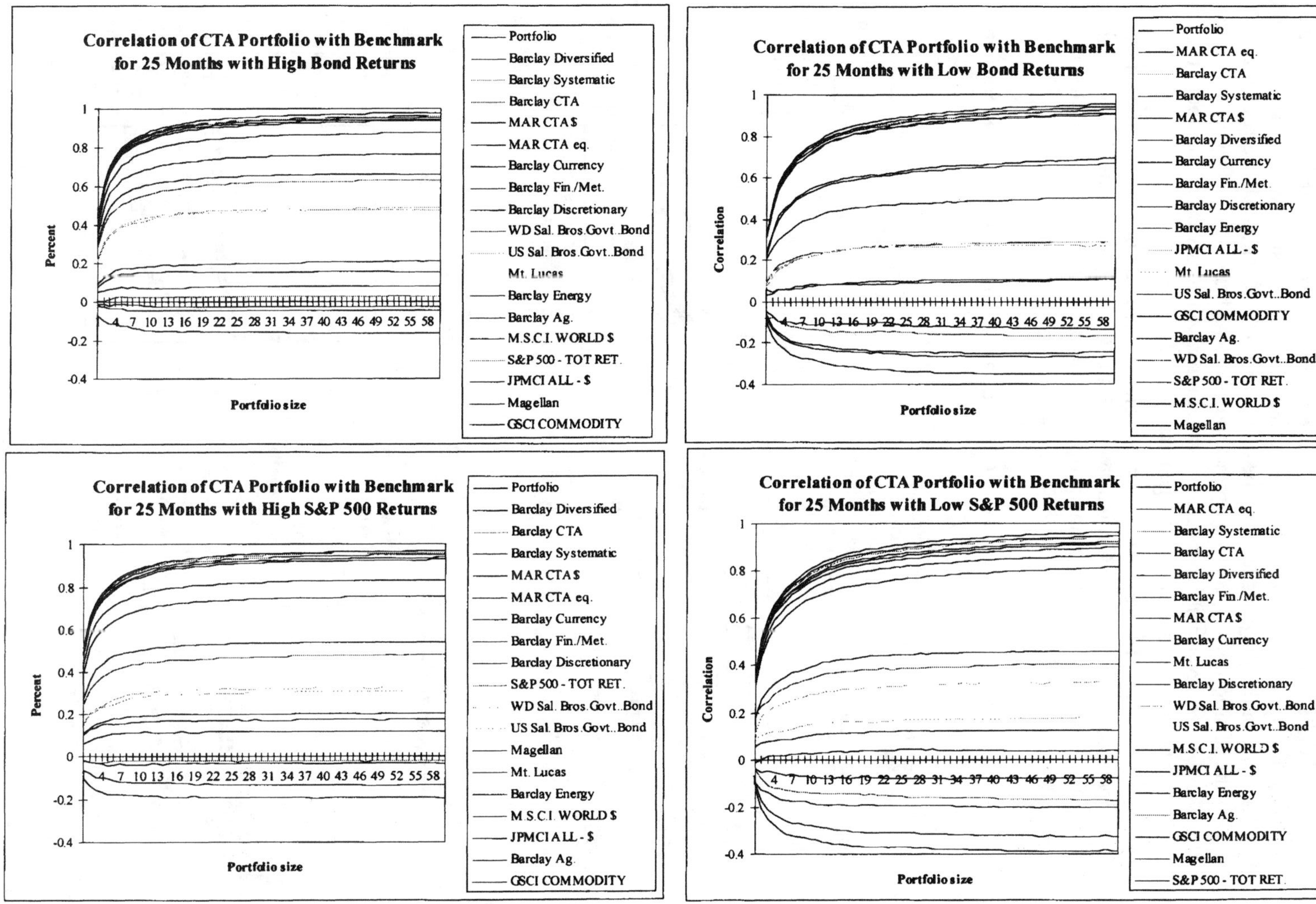

The order of indexes in the legend corresponds to the order of the lines in the figure.

Properties of the Efficient Frontier for Adding Individual CTAs to a Stock/Bond Portfolio

While increasing CTA portfolio size results in increasing portfolio allocation to CTAs in the optimal portfolio, the relative degree of the impact may be measured in different ways. In the previous section, the examination was by necessity restricted the effects of the addition of CTAs to an optimal portfolio with a particular target return (e.g. S&P 500). However, this is a rather narrow comparison, as investors care about the character of the entire efficient frontier generated.

In Exhibit 14, we show the impact on expected rate of return, standard deviation as well as the slope of the Capital Market Line (CML) (i.e. Sharpe Ratio) and for a given slope of the CML, the distance between the risk free rate point and the point of tan-

EXHIBIT 10 MEAN TRACKING ERROR OF CTA PORTFOLIOS WITH BENCHMARKS IN 25 MONTHS WITH HIGH/LOW BOND AND S&P 500 RETURNS

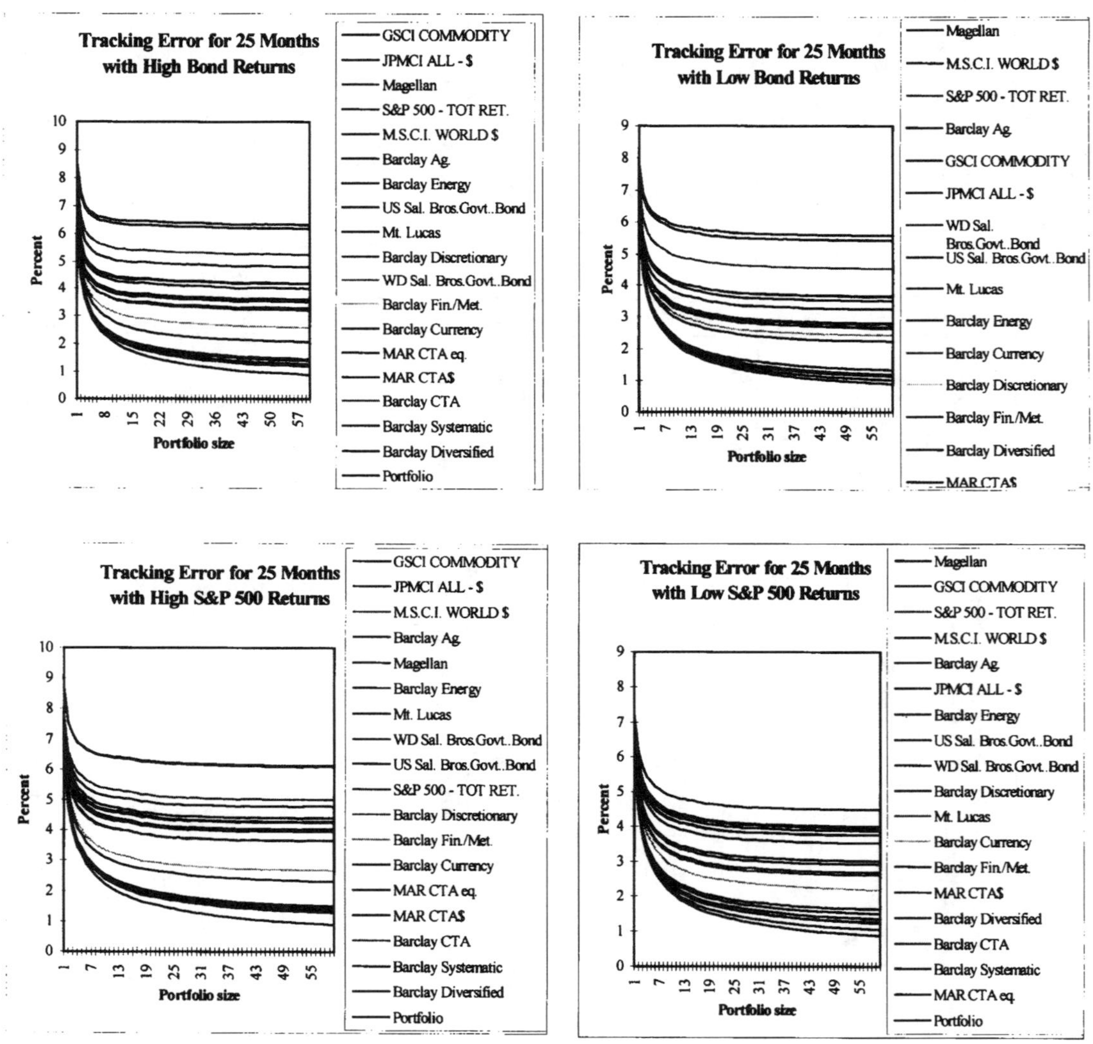

The order of indexes in the legends corresponds to the order of the lines in the figures.

EXHIBIT 11 PLANNED DIVERSIFICATION FOR CTAS: WEIGHT TO CTAS IN OPTIMAL PORTFOLIO WITH S&P 500 AND SB BOND INDICES WHEN TARGET RETURN IS EQUAL TO S&P 500 RETURN

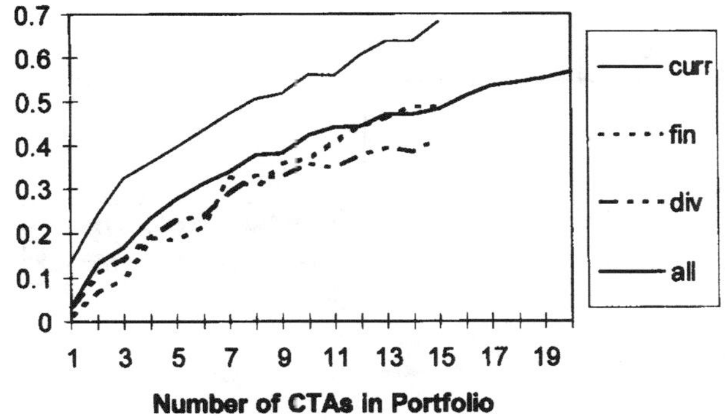

EXHIBIT 12 SUM OF SQUARED WEIGHTS FOR CTAS IN OPTIMAL PORTFOLIO (WITH S&P 500 AND SB, TARGET S&P 500)

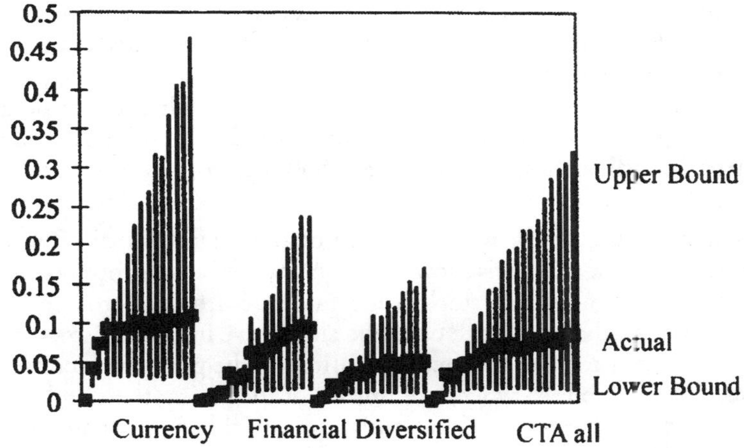

gency between the CML and the efficient frontier.[5] Recalling basic mean-variance analysis, we wish to have an efficient frontier with the steepest CML. In brief, the results on the slope of the tangency line and the length of the CML to the tangency line reflects the decreasing portfolio variance of adding an increasing number of CTAs. An improving efficient frontier is characterized by a steeper slope of the CML and a shorter length of the CML (for Sharpe ratios less than one) to the tangency point.

Stocks versus CTAs in Optimal Asset Allocation

In the previous section, an analysis was provided on the impact of adding an increasing number of CTAs to a CTA portfolio and its impact on the optimal portfolio (with a target return equal to the S&P 500). The reader will no doubt wonder whether the results are due to the fact that the quadratic optimization routine will include some non-zero weight in all available assets—provided these assets have less than perfect cor-

EXHIBIT 13 PLANNED DIVERSIFICATION FOR CTAS: PROPERTIES OF RISK REDUCTION FOR ADDING INDIVIDUAL CTAS FROM ENTIRE SAMPLE TO A PORTFOLIO OF S&P 500 AND SB US BOND INDICES AT A TARGET RETURN EQUAL TO THE S&P 500 RETURN

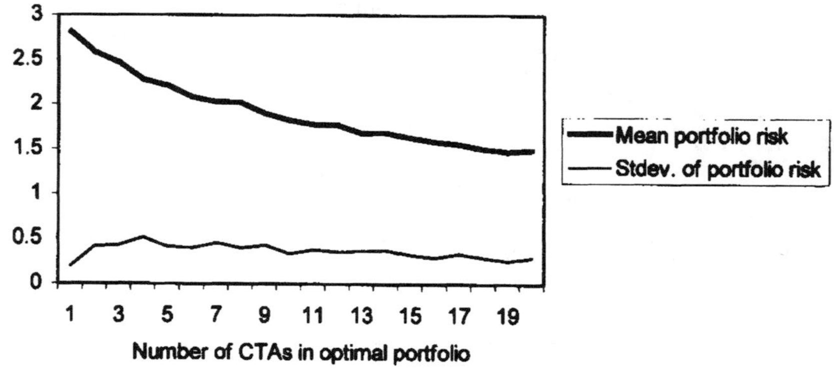

relation with each. Obviously, this would suggest that the more CTAs are made available for the candidate portfolio, the greater must be the total weight to CTAs. (This is in addition to the previously discussed tendency of the optimizer to select assets with the greatest relative deviation of realized returns from expected returns—a tendency whose consequentiality is increasing with the number of assets in the candidate portfolio.) One can evaluate the relative contribution of individual CTAs on average if one compares the portfolio results to those in which another set of individual assets is available. All of the individual stocks in the S&P 500 with continuous record for the sample period are chosen to be that set of assets.

In Exhibits 15 and 16 the relative impact of adding individual CTAs to our benchmark bond and stock indexes is shown when compared against our bond index and our CTAeq index plus individual stocks for a target return equal to the CTAeq index.[6] Results are similar, that is in both cases the alternative individual stock and CTA portfolio weights increase as the number of securities in the portfolio increase. The primary difference is in Exhibit 16 where the impact of increasing the number of CTAs in a stock/bond portfolio results in greater diversification benefits than adding additional stocks to a bond/CTA portfolio. This is expected since stocks tend to have a higher within-group correlation.

CONCLUSIONS AND PORTFOLIO IMPLICATIONS

The results of this research find benefits of diversifying within managed futures investments as well as benefits of the addition of managed futures to classical "Markowitz" mean/variance optimized stock and bond portfolios. However, to the degree that investors use "popular" asset allocation programs based on traditional passive or active manager indexes to determine investment allocations, investors must ensure that their stock, bond, or managed futures portfolios reflect the performance of the underlying indexes or portfolios used to construct the expected performance benchmark. Thus for managed futures, as for stock and bond investments, a greater effort must be devoted to determining the underlying distributional factors of the portfolio return and its performance under economic conditions expected to exist over the planned investment horizon.

EXHIBIT 14 PLANNED DIVERSIFICATION FOR CTAs: WEIGHT OF CTAs IN OPTIMAL PORTFOLIO WITH S&P 500 AND SB BOND INDICES WHEN TARGET RETURN IS EQUAL TO S&P 500 RETURN

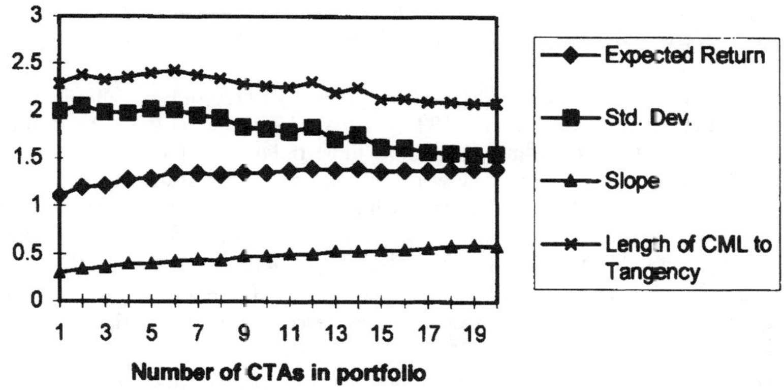

EXHIBIT 15 COMPARISON OF INDIVIDUAL CTAs VS. STOCKS IN OPTIMAL PORTFOLIO WEIGHTINGS: SB BOND AND EITHER S&P 500 AND INDIVIDUAL CTAs FOR CTAEQ. AND INDIVIDUAL STOCKS FOR TARGET RETURN EQUAL TO CTAEQ. RETURN

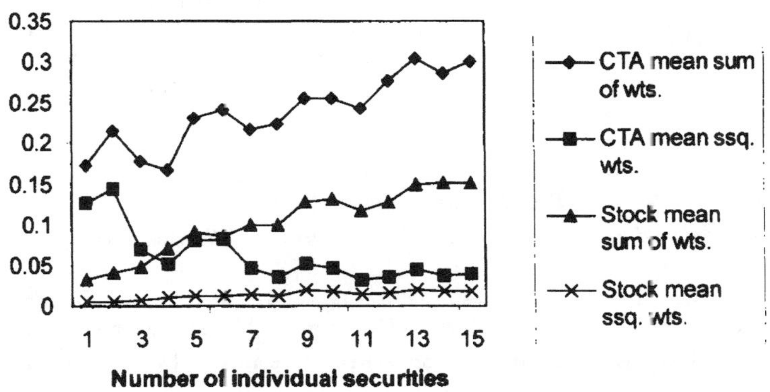

EXHIBIT 16 COMPARISON OF RISK FOR INDIVIDUAL CTAs VS. STOCKS: SB BOND AND EITHER S&P 500 AND INDIVIDUAL CTAs OR CTA EQUAL AND INDIVIDUAL STOCKS FOR TARGET RETURN EQUAL TO CTAEQ.

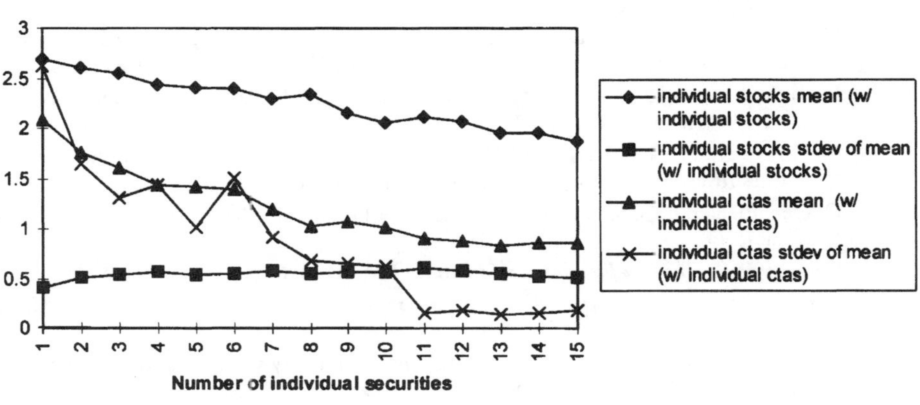

ENDNOTES

This article was published in *The Journal of Alternative Investments* [Fall 1998], pp. 25-49

[1] For a full description and discussion of the distributional characteristics of various futures based commodity indexes and manager based CTA or hedge fund performance indexes, see Schneeweis and Spurgin [1996, 1997].

[2] Within the past several years, research has been presented on return persistence in managed futures returns (Irwin [1994]; Schneeweis et al. [1997]), survivor bias (Elton et al. [1993]; Schneeweis et al. [1996]), the potential benefits of managed futures in portfolio creation (Chance [1994], McCarthy et al. [1996]); Schneeweis et al. [1996]; Schneeweis [1996]), single and multi-factor analysis of CTA and hedge fund return (Irwin [1994]; Fung and Hsieh [1997]; Schneeweis and Spurgin [1998]) as well as risk and return comparisons of commonly used passive commodity and active and passive managed futures and hedge fund benchmarks (Schneeweis and Spurgin [1996] and [1997]).

[3] This is because the optimization procedure optimizes on deviations of historically realized returns from expected future returns. For an analysis of the impact of return forecasting on efficient frontier estimation see Chopra and Ziemba [1994].

[4] The tables indicate the correlation of CTAs with particular benchmarks (such as MSCI or SBI World Bond returns) when stratified according to S&P 500 or SBI US Bond returns.

[5] The length of the CML gives us a useful index of whether our Sharpe ratio is due to the ratio of very small numbers, very large numbers or some intermediate values.

[6] The average CTAeq return is selected as the target rate of return since choosing the (higher) S&P 500 rate of return for the case of individual stocks and the CTA index may generate samples in which achieving the S&P 500 rate of return is infeasible with the available assets. Here it is guaranteed that the target return is feasible since the optimizer can always load our portfolio into the CTA index. In the case of individual CTAs and the S&P 500 index, the optimizer can always achieve the target return since the S&P 500 return is greater than CTAeq.

REFERENCES

Billingsley R., and D. Chance "Benefits and Limitations of Diversification Among Commodity Trading Advisors," *The Journal of Portfolio Management*, Fall, 1996, pp. 65-80.

Chance, D. *Managed Futures and Their Role in Investment Portfolios* (Institute of Chartered Financial Analysts, 1994).

Chopra, V. K. W.T. Ziemba, "The Effect of Errors in Means, Variances, and Covariances on Optimal Portfolio Choice," *The Journal of Portfolio Management*, Winter 1993, pp. 6-11.

Elton, E. "Efficiency with costly information: A Reinterpretation of Evidence from Managed Portfolios," *Review of Financial Studies* 6, 1993, pp. 1-22.

Elton, E. and M. Gruber "Risk Reduction and Portfolio Size: An Analytical Solution," *Journal of Business*, October, 1977, pp. 415-437.

Elton, E., M. Gruber, and J. Rentzler "The Arbitrage pricing Model and and Returns on Assets under Uncertain Inflation," *Journal of Finance* 38, 1983, pp. 525-537.

Fung, W. and D. Hsieh "Performance Attribution and Style Analysis: From Mutual Funds to Hedge Funds," Working Paper # 9609 (Duke University, 1996).

Hill, J. and T. Schneeweis "Diversification and Portfolio Size for Fixed Income Securities," *The Journal of Economics and Business* 33, Winter, 1981, pp. 115-121.

Irwin, S., C. R. Zulaf and Barry Ward "The Predictability of Managed Futures Returns" *The Journal of Derivatives*, Winter, 1994, pp.20-27.

McCarthy, D., T. Schneeweis, and R. Spurgin "Investment Through CTAs: An Alternative Managed Futures Investment," *The Journal of Derivatives*, Summer 1996, pp. 36-47.

Oberuc, Richard E. "Comparative Performance of Bond, Equity and FuturesAdvisors," *The MFA Journal* (June 1993), 19-29.

Schneeweis, T. *The Benefits of Managed Futures*. EMFA, 1996.

Schneeweis, T. and R. Spurgin. *Alternative Investments in the Institutional Portoflio*, AIMA, London, 1998.

Schneeweis, T. and R. Spurgin. "Comparisons of Commodity and Managed Futures Benchmark Indexes," *The Journal of Derivatives*, Summer 1997, pp. 317-340.

Schneeweis, T., R. Spurgin, and D. McCarthy. "Informational Content in Historical CTA Performance" *Journal of Futures Markets*, May 1997, pp. 317-340.

Schneeweis, T., R. Spurgin, and D. McCarthy. "Survivor Bias in Commodity Trading Advisor Performance" *Journal of Futures Markets*, October, 1996, pp.757-772.

Statman, M. "How Many Stocks Make a Diversified Portfolio," *The Journal of Financial and Quantitative Analysis* 22, 1987, pp. 353-363.

6 THE BENEFITS OF MANAGED FUTURES

THOMAS SCHNEEWEIS
University of Massachusetts

INTRODUCTION

During the past decades, the investment management industry has undergone numerous changes. New forms of investment products have come into existence to meet the needs of changing financial regulation, information technology, and investor demands. Today, while most investors concentrate on traditional investment vehicles such as stocks, bonds, and currencies, an increasing number of alternative investment products, such as managed futures (investment funds which use international futures and options markets as their primary investment vehicle), are becoming available which offer the investor new means of increasing return while reducing risk through diversification.

Many investors, however, are uncertain as to the value of many of these new investment vehicles. This is not unexpected. Financial instruments such as stocks, foreign securities, and mortgage-back bonds existed for years before they were regarded as 'suitable' investments. Today, every reasonable investor would have a portion of their wealth in such financial instruments. Similarly, while managed futures products have existed for over thirty years, they remain unfamiliar to some investors. Today, managed futures may be viewed as a 'new alternative investment' for professional money managers as well as individual investors. Managed futures offer investors a means of investing in all major international markets and financial instruments through investment vehicles offered by commodity trading advisors (CTAs) who use global futures/option markets as their primary investment universe. There are three common methods of investment in managed futures products: publicly traded commodity pools (funds), private commodity pools (pools), and individually managed single or multi-advisor commodity trading accounts (CTAs). Another alternative investment is hedge funds, for which investment managers use futures and options markets as well as direct investment in traditional securities and physical commodities.

The benefits of investing in derivative-based investment products (e.g., exotic swaps and options) have been widely debated in the popular financial press. Unfortunately, much of this publicity, while good theater, is often bad economics.[1] These discussions often focus on a few isolated cases in which investors misunderstood the risks of the investment, and rarely focus on the broader question of whether a diversified portfolio can benefit from properly managed exposure to futures and options markets. This study shows that:

- Academic and practitioner literature has shown that profitable trading strategies based on market trends and unexpected changes in information can be achieved in traditional security markets. Managed futures can replicate many of these investment strategies and enable one to do much of what is available in the spot market more cheaply (e.g., replication of cash indexes) and some things that cannot be easily achieved in spot markets (e.g., ability to short). As a result, managed futures may offer risk/return patterns that differ from underlying cash markets. Specifically, the differing investment styles and investment areas of CTAs enable investors to create asset allocated portfolios which offer expected positive returns in various market cycles and market conditions not available through traditional stock or bond market investment.

- Results indicate that direct CTA investment as a standalone investment offers the risk/return tradeoff similar to other investment assets, and that when added to existing stock and bond portfolios they offer unique relative risk return enhancement opportunities. For other managed futures products (e.g., public commodity funds), the benefits of managed futures are primarily from their addition to existing traditional assets or asset portfolios.
- Correlation tests comparing managed futures indices with traditional assets reveals an interesting property of the relationship between managed futures returns (MAR$CTA) and returns to traditional asset classes. Overall, the correlation between managed futures and stock portfolios is approximately zero. However, when the data are segmented according to whether the stock market rose or fell, results indicate that managed futures are negatively correlated with traditional asset classes (e.g., stock and stock and bond portfolio) when these cash market portfolios posted significant negative returns and are positively correlated when these portfolios report significant positive returns. Thus managed futures may offer unique asset allocation properties.
- Managed futures may offer risk/return benefits when compared to a partially hedged position in the stock market. For instance, it is shown that an equal weighted investment in the MAR$CTA index and the S&P 500 outperformed investment in the S&P 500 plus a simulated at-the-money put under most market conditions. These results indicate that managed futures may offer some of the hedging properties of a put option at a lower cost.
- Hedge funds, which invest directly in futures and options as well as direct investment in traditional securities and physical commodities, may offer an additional investment alternative. Unfortunately, historical index data on various hedge fund investment styles and trading strategies only exist for the past two years. Even over this time period, which corresponds to a historically poor risk/return period for managed futures, managed futures offer potential for risk/return improvement when considered as additions to existing hedge funds.

It is important to note that neither this nor any study can capture or review all possible questions relating to the future or past performance of various investment products. Over the past two years, for instance, the S&P 500 as well as the Salomon Brothers US government bond index have generally outperformed managed futures on a stand alone basis. Moreover, results show that, over this very recent time period, some managed futures investment styles or trading strategies failed to improve the risk/return tradeoff when added to existing traditional asset portfolios. However, investors must realize the uniqueness of the recent time period. Returns to the S&P 500 in 1995 (annualized returns over 35%) have not been repeated in any of the past eleven years while the annualized returns to the MAR$CTA index (14.1%) were similar to the eleven-year average (15.8%).

In the following sections, the history of managed futures is reviewed along with the bases for the economic benefits of futures and option markets and investments created by trading in these markets. Previous research in the managed futures area is also reviewed and results updated and extended. Tests are conducted on both the relative performance of managed futures products on a standalone basis and as additions to existing traditional asset portfolios. Test results show that investors must come to ap-

EXHIBIT 1 MANAGED FUTURES ASSETS UNDER MANAGEMENT 1980 TO 1994

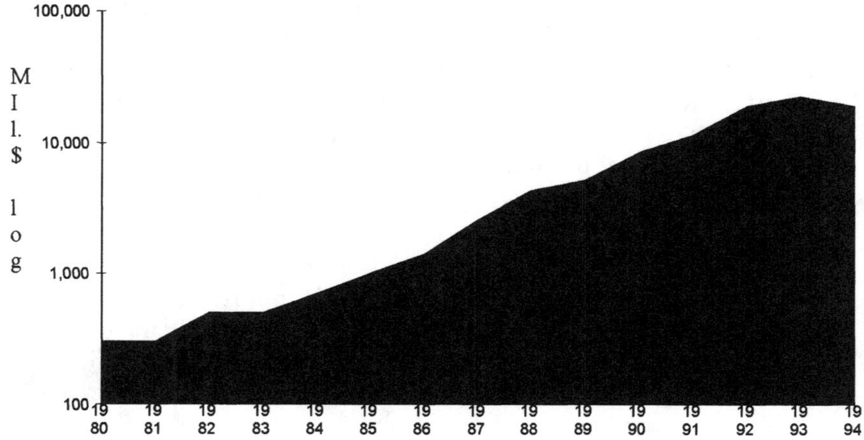

preciate that both theory and past empirical results support the choice of managed futures as an additional investment area and that, moreover, failure to invest in this area may, in fact, result in foregone returns and increased portfolio risk.

HISTORY OF MANAGED FUTURES

Futures and options have been used for centuries both as a risk management tool and return enhancement vehicle. Managed futures have been used as an investment alternative since the late 1960s.[2] More recently, institutional investors such as corporate and public pension funds, endowments and trusts, and bank trust departments have been including managed futures as one segment of a well-diversified portfolio. As shown in Exhibit 1, the dollars under management in the managed futures industry has grown from less than $1 billion under management in 1980 to approximately $20 billion in 1994.

Despite the long history of futures and options as investment and risk management vehicles, managed futures have only recently begun to gain acceptance as investment vehicles. This is not surprising. Studies on individual behavior have shown the reluctance of individuals to accept new products or ideas. Despite the acceptance of equity securities today as investment vehicles, stocks were not always regarded as suitable investment vehicles. Only after the bull market of the early 1980s were stocks regarded as a suitable investment alternative for many investor clientele. Likewise, despite years of financial theory and empirical evidence that indicated the importance of international investment in reducing risk and increasing potential investor return, international investment has only recently become regarded as a central part of an overall investment portfolio. Behavioral research and market structure explain this seeming lag in investor acceptance of new investment products. While investors have witnessed greater losses in cash bond and stock markets than in futures and options markets, those losses were also felt by most market participants. Since 1985, stock and long-term bond markets have both reported negative annualized returns. The S&P 500 achieves negative returns in excess of -3% as recently as 1990 while long-term government bonds had negative returns in excess of -2.5% in 1987. Many mutual funds and equity markets experienced monthly declines in excess of -30% during the equity market crashes of 1987, while managed futures indices have been able to keep their maximum monthly losses far below that level. However, individuals have been shown to accept risk if they believe that risk is also shared by other individuals. Individual risk not shared by others is viewed as unacceptable. Moreover, since individuals are not accustomed to the risk and return structure of managed futures products, the very differences in investment structure increases reluctance to invest in these assets. In short, individuals need to increase their comfort level with managed futures. In order for this to be accomplished, investors must come to appreciate that investment in managed futures is well founded in financial theory and empirical evidence.

What are the benefits of managed futures as part of an investor's overall asset portfolio? Basically, as investors have increased their portfolio exposure to international investments and nonfinancial sectors such as commodities in order to increase return or to reduce risk, managed futures likewise offer an means to gain exposure to risk and return patterns not easily accessible with investment in traditional stock and bond portfolios. In short, the question should not be: "why include managed futures as part of an overall investment strategy?" but instead, "why not?"

ECONOMIC BENEFITS OF FUTURES/OPTIONS MARKETS

The economic benefits of futures and options markets have been well documented in practitioner and academic literature.[3] Futures and option markets provide market participants with the means to hedge the value of inventories (e.g., futures markets) as well as providing insurance against unexpected price changes and increasing price volatility(e.g., options). In addition futures and option markets provide an implicit method of borrowing and lending commodities.

In fact, financial markets, as they exist today, would not have their present form if not for the existence of investment media which permit risk transfer and asset management. In most markets, there is often no natural equality between those wishing to manage the risk of long cash positions and those wishing the risk of short cash positions. In short, non-hedgers are required to make markets work. In the futures and options market, many managed futures traders, as other market participants, take part in this beneficial speculative role. It is in the very act of providing offsetting positions to those desiring risk transfer, that managed futures investors may obtain an expected positive return for providing necessary liquidity (convenience yield).[4]

RISK/RETURN BENEFITS OF MANAGED FUTURES

While futures and options markets may provide economic benefits to the underlying users of their markets, traders in futures and options markets are often viewed as operating in a zero sum game; that is, where investor losses equal investor gains on any given day and the long term return to a managed futures position is simply the risk-free return on invested capital. However, the existence of a zero sum game does not restrict futures and options investors from holding positions which directly mimic the return of the underlying contract. In fact, for futures and options markets, cost of carry and put/call parity models insure that futures and options can be used to create similar if not identical investment positions to the underlying cash instruments. Moreover, given the lower transaction costs of trading in futures and options markets, managed futures returns may be superior to the underlying cash markets for comparable long (short) positions. Secondly, institutional characteristics and differential carry costs among investors, may permit managed futures traders from taking advantage of short-term pricing differences between theoretically identical futures, options and cash market positions. Thus, managed futures traders, in contrast to a large number of traditional security traders, have opportunities for arbitrage profits under a number of varying market conditions.

Arbitrage profits and risk/return positions which replicate the underlying cash markets, however, are not the only potential risk/return benefits of managed futures. Speculative positions are often required as a means of meeting the hedging demands of cash market participants. This hedging demand may create investment situations were hedgers are required to offer speculators a 'risk' premia for holding open long or short positions even in a world of arbitrage traders. This positive return to holding futures positions which are opposite that of the desired hedgers, may result positive rates of return in the underlying futures and options markets. This return to traders for offering liquidity to hedgers desiring to limit losses may exist not only in futures markets but may exist in a wide range of derivative products. For instance, option traders may be able to create positions which offer a 'risk premium' for holding various options contracts when cash market participants increase purchases of options to protect themselves in markets with trending prices or volatility. This return (e.g., convenience yield) can be earned simply by buying and holding a derivative portfolio and is, arguably, the basis for the positive long term return in various futures markets based publicly available commodity index products (e.g., JPMorgan or Goldman Sachs commodity indices).

The return to managed futures can also stem from the ability of managers to exploit 'imperfections' in the markets for futures and options as well as the market for the underlying cash instrument. Research on traditional investment vehicles (e.g., stocks, bonds, and currency) indicates that investors underreact to information and consequently trends are present in security prices. Trading techniques based on capturing these trends may be profitable.[5] In addition, research on traditional security markets also has shown that market prices react to unexpected changes in micro (e.g., earnings) or macro (e.g., interest rates, GNP) information. Unlike many traditional money managers, there are no restrictions on taking short positions or ability to sell short unless the asset market first moves up (uptick rule). Therefore, managed futures traders may take both long and short positions depending on market environments. Because of the ability of futures traders to take unrestricted short positions, it is not necessary for markets to trend upward (e.g., 1995) or gap upward to make money. In fact, some of the most impressive periods of return for trading advisors have been during periods of poor performance in the equity markets (e.g., October, 1987).

While the existence of market trends (upward or downward) has been questioned in academic literature, evidence exists that due to institutional factors (e.g., end of month window dressing, portfolio rebalancing, specialist risk positions, government actions), markets may trend for varying time periods in various markets. While security returns resulting from various technical trading rules have been questioned, part of this inability to capture trend patterns is due to high transaction costs in cash markets. The low transaction costs combined with the ability to go short may permit the use of technical trading rules by managed futures to obtain positive returns in markets which, for short time periods, may be overvalued. In fact, these market cycles embedded in cash market trading styles has been used to explain some portion of the return to a technically based commodity futures trading system (MLM reports). The ability to take short positions in futures and option markets also permit manage futures traders to create positions which offer potential returns due to changes, not in market trends, but in market volatility. At present, unique financial instruments do not exist that permit individuals to trade market volatility directly. As a result, investors must create investment positions which allow them to take advantage of forecasts in changing market volatility (e.g., straddle positions or option based contracts).

Despite the potential for managed futures to obtain positive rates of return above the risk free rate, the primary benefit of adding a managed futures component to a diversified investment portfolio is that it may decrease a portfolio's return volatility. Managed futures reduce overall portfolio risk because of the low to slightly negative correlation of managed futures with equities and bonds. For example, managed futures accounts can participate in different markets worldwide. Thus, managed futures have the opportunity for profit potential and risk reduction across a broad number of noncorrelated markets. As indicated previously, various traditional asset classes all have time varying risk/return patterns. For many traditional assets (even stock and bonds), returns and risk are positively correlated during various parts of the market cycle. Stocks from different sectors of the economy are influenced by similar macro-economic factors (e.g., GNP). Thus, lowering inflation may effect bonds and stocks both positively, however if the lowering inflation is accompanied with declining GNP bonds may rally and stocks fall. Thus both historically and in terms of expected risk/return tradeoffs, the inclusion of managed futures improves expected portfolio returns by either reducing risk at a given level of return, or by increasing returns at a level of risk, or a combination of both.

MANAGED FUTURES: RISK AND RETURN PERFORMANCE

Both practitioner and academic research has addressed the importance of futures and options in global asset management as well as the potential return from holding active positions in global futures and options markets. Ultimately, however, the question of whether managed futures can obtain these benefits for their investors is an empirical one. Previous analyses of the benefits of managed futures in asset management have principally focused on the benefits of public commodity funds [Elton et al., 1987, 1990, 1992; Irwin et al., 1992, 1994]. Some of these studies have often concluded that publicly traded commodity funds may provide poor investments as standalone vehicles and may only provide marginal value as additions to alternative asset classes. However, as indicated in this study, these results may be time period specific, may not reflect either the current structure of these funds (e.g., single manager versus multiple manager forms) or the availability of new managed futures products (such as an individually managed single or multi-advisor trading account available for institutional investors).

Today, fund management in the derivative products area includes not only investment through public commodity funds but investment directly with commodity trading advisors for which the management fees charged by certain public commodity funds do not reflect the negotiated fees applicable to large investors or portfolio managers.[6] Moreover, academic research results based on fund performance during the early to mid 1980s (during which many managed futures funds were single manager or invested primarily in commodity markets) may not fully represent the risk/return tradeoffs available today through managed futures, which can trade in a widening variety of financial and commodity markets throughout the world and are primarily multi-manager in form. Lastly, results which concentrate on managed futures fund and pool performance may be based on a select set of commodity trading advisors and not on the larger CTA universe which prefer not to offer their investment services through funds or pools.

In fact, a number of previous studies on managed futures has supported the benefits of managed futures investment. For instance, Schneeweis et al., [1992] tested the benefits of CTA, pool or funds as standalone investments, as additions to existing stock and bond portfolios, or as inclusion in optimal portfolio management. Their analysis concludes that direct CTA investment, commodity pools and commodity funds may even offer a profitable addition to a portfolio of stocks or bonds a indices on a standalone when alternative performance measures (e.g., skewness, minimum and maximum returns) are considered. Similarly, Peters [1992] suggests that the benefits of managed futures may be seen most dramatically in reducing downside risk for a mixed asset portfolio such that traditional mean/variance comparisons may not reflect the true benefits of managed futures products.[7]

DATA AND METHODOLOGY

Risk/Return Performance

In the final analysis, the ability of managed futures to offer benefits not available in underlying cash markets remains an empirical question. Moreover, from the viewpoint of a potential investor in manage futures, the question is simply put, 'Do manage futures provide an increased benefit relative to the risks involved?" Issues of risk assessment must therefore be addressed.

To paraphrase, an oft quoted remark, 'It is always precarious to say anything about risk and people's perception of risk'. How do people perceive risky things? Are people's perceptions of risk consistent over different judgments? Unfortunately, the area of financial decision making needs to be concerned with the meaning of risk and how risk is measured. Thus some central view of risk is required if one is to appreciate investors' decision choices. The predominant model for decision making under uncertainty in finance is expected utility theory; that is, if investors' actions are consistent with a certain set of assumptions (e.g., prefer more to less, exhibit overall risk aversion) then their preferences over a set of outcomes can be expressed by a decision model relating required return to expected risk. For finance, in a classical sense, risk is described in terms of offering estimates of the probability of obtaining a certain level of return. For most investment assets, the first two moments (mean and variance) of the asset's distribution of outcomes provides this information; that is, for instance, an asset with a 15% expected return and a standard deviation of 15% has a 60% probability that investor return will be between zero and 30%. purposes one often uses historical measures of risk (variance or standard deviation) and return (change in asset value) as a surrogate for future expected risk and return

Moreover, in models of risky choice, the assumption is made that, all else equal (e.g., risk), investors prefer increased expected return and that they prefer smaller risk given equal expected return. This is the essence of the mean/variance analysis proposed by Markowitz and is the fundamental view of risk held by financial economists. Thus in the simple case, two assets should be compared by their relative return/risk tradeoff; or expected return divided by expected risk. For the investor who holds more than a single asset, the real risk of investment is the return and risk tradeoff at the portfolio level. For these investors, modern investment theory focuses not on an individual asset's return and risk tradeoff, but on the relative return and risk of investors' alternative portfolios of investment assets. In short, by adding or leaving out a particular investment can the overall return/risk ratio of an investor's portfolio increase. For a given investor's existing portfolio, the impact of adding or subtracting an asset from a portfolio is determined by both the standard deviation of an asset and how it correlates; that is, moves with the returns of other assets held in the portfolio. In the perfect case, one may desire an asset which is negatively correlated (returns move up and other assets return falls; however, this reduced risk is often met with reduced return). The question is, do assets exist which provide reduced risk and equal return or increased return with similar risk?

For many asset comparisons, the Sharpe Ratio (see Appendix II) has been used as a basis for relative performance comparison. Sharpe [1994] has pointed out that the above Sharpe Ratio can be considered a special case of the more general ratio of the mean of any distribution to its standard deviation. For ease of representation in the direct comparison of investment choice, in this paper the Sharpe Ratio is reported as the annual rate of return/annualized standard deviation. This simple ratio of return/risk is often called a return information ratio and while described by Sharpe as a useful statistic it may lead, in certain circumstances, to wrong decisions for investors who can leverage their portfolios in a zero investment strategy. In this paper, for ease of simplicity, we have reported on the simple ratio of the mean return divided by the standard deviation. Actual Sharpe Ratios which assume a zero investment strategy can be determined by readers after subtracting out the risk-free rate over that time period.[8]

Various models have been proposed to measure the possible impact of adding a security onto an existing portfolio and its impact on that portfolios risk and return. For instance, for stocks, the effect on diversification of adding additional randomly selected securities to an existing portfolio has shown that a portfolio of approximately 8-10 equally weighted randomly selected securities results in a reduction of approximately 50% of the average variance of an individual stock.[9] However, for most investors, assets are not held individually and have already been formed into requisite portfolios. Simple break-even models have been suggested which indicate whether adding an asset or a portfolio of individual assets to an existing portfolio increases its Sharpe ratio. As in earlier studies, the break-even (Rc) and excess break-even rate of return(EBK) is computed as follows:

$$R_c = \left(\frac{R_P - R_F}{\sigma_P}\right)(P_{CP})\sigma_C + R_F \tag{1}$$

$$EBK = R_c - \left(\left(\frac{R_P - R_F}{\sigma_P}\right)(P_{CP})\sigma_C + R_F\right) \tag{2}$$

where,

R_c = Break-even rate of return required for CTA to improve Sharpe Ratio of the index

R_f = Riskless rate of return

R_p = Rate of return on index p

P_{cp} = Correlation coefficient between CTA c and index p

σ_c = Standard deviation of CTA c

σ_p = Standard deviation of index p

In short, investors should consider including an investment vehicle in their portfolio if they believe it constitutes a separate asset classes; that is, increases ones potential return/risk tradeoff relative to all other existing assets.[10] Thus for managed futures to be regarded as an asset class, they must provide either increased return relative to other equally risky assets or reduce portfolio risk (all else equal) relative to other existing assets. In fact, managed futures by investing in options and futures markets which have been shown to provide unique risk/return opportunities may, in fact, offer investors return enhancement opportunities and portfolio risk reduction opportunities not easily found in other assets.

EXHIBIT 2 AVERAGE MONTHLY STANDARD DEVIATION PORTFOLIO CTAs

		Average CTAs Stdev	Stdev of Stdev	Portfolio CTAs Equal Wgt. Stdev	MAR CTA Index Equal Wgt. Stdev	Equity Stdev	Stdev of Stdev	Portfolio Equity Equal Wgt Stdev
Period	1987-1995	10.51	4.26	5.95	4.75	8.36	2.60	6.17
	1987-1991	12.22	5.46	7.20	6.00	9.31	2.90	6.51
	1992-1995	7.45	3.07	3.72	2.33	6.98	2.52	5.67

* CTAs drawn from a sample of 68 CTAs with consistent data from 1987-1995 (see EMFA Study)
** Equities are drawn from a sample of 250 equity issues drawn from the S&P 500

Even on a standalone basis, CTAs may also be held in portfolio form. In Exhibit 2, results are presented on the impact of creating multi-manager CTA portfolios. For the creation of various size CTA portfolios created from randomly selected CTAs, the period of analysis is 1987-1995 and returns are expressed as simply monthly arithmetic returns. This period is used to permit analysis of a necessary number of individual CTAs for tests of random diversification on portfolio risk. For this period all CTAs from the LaPorte data set with continuous data were obtained. Sixty-eight CTAs were used (5 Agriculture; 6 Currency; 46 Diversified; 9 Financial; 2 Stock). For portfolio sizes 1 through 68, 30 samples were drawn with replacement. Confidence intervals were established according to a 95% T-Distribution with 29 degrees of freedom. Portfolios are formed by equally weighting the CTAs in the portfolio. For comparison purposes at the individual security level and at the portfolio level, 250 individual stocks were drawn from the S&P 500 for the similar time periods.

For results presented in the Exhibits, the primary period of analysis is January 1985 through December 1995 and returns are expressed as the logarithmic monthly holding period returns or annualized logarithmic returns. Managed Accounts Reports dollar weighted and equal weighted indices and subindices for both CTA and fund/pool performance, JPMorgan commodity indices, and the MLM commodity trading index, Salomon Brothers US and World government bond index, and the S&P 500 are used as the primary asset class comparisons. Hedge fund returns from Hedge fund Research are also used for relevant time comparisons. MSCI regional and country stock indices denominated in US dollars were used for international comparisons.

RESULTS

Managed Futures Stand-Alone and Multi-CTA Risk Analysis

The term managed futures represents an industry comprised of professional money managers known as commodity trading advisors (CTAs) who manage client assets on a discretionary basis, using global futures markets as an investment medium. CTAs have often been regarded as a high risk investment. However, as shown in Exhibit 2 for the period 1987-1995, the average monthly standard deviation of a sample of over 60 CTAs with complete data over the time period was not significantly different from the average monthly standard deviation derived from a random sample of over 250 stocks taken from the S&P 500. Thus, CTAs are on average not more risky than an equity security listed in the S&P 500.

Exhibit 2 reflects the similarity of the risk pattern between the risk of the sample CTA portfolio and that of the MAR equal weighted CTA index. Results indicate that as for stocks, over 50% of the average CTA standard deviation is reduced if held as part of a relatively large multi-CTA portfolio. This is similar to that reported for the sample of 250 stocks taken from the S&P 500, although the impact on risk reduction is greater for combining CTAs than equity issues. It is important to remember that while the impact on standard deviation of creating CTA portfolios is similar to that of creating portfolios of stocks, the variability of standard deviation around the average standard deviation is greater for CTA than stocks, such that individuals choosing individual CTA should be aware of the greater heterogeneity of risk for individual CTAs as compared to individual stocks.

Multi-CTA Portfolio Risk

Modern portfolio theory points out that the true measure of risk for investors who hold portfolios of assets, is the expected standard of a portfolio of investments. Past

EXHIBIT 3 STANDARD DEVIATION OF RETURNS

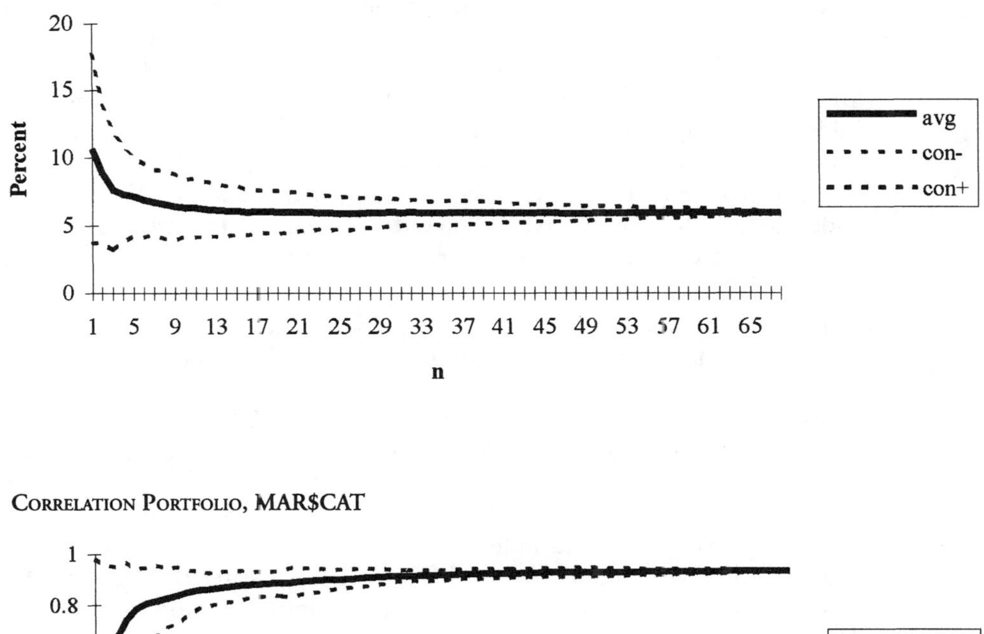

CORRELATION PORTFOLIO, MAR$CAT

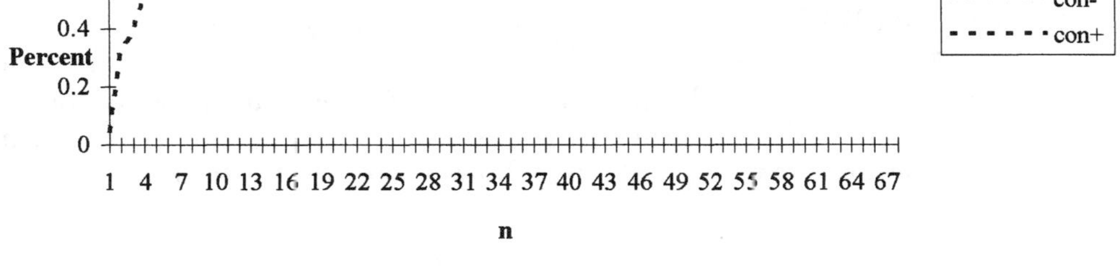

research has shown that an equally weighted diversified portfolio of 8-10 randomly selected equity securities will result in a portfolio standard deviation similar to that of the population from which it is drawn. As shown in Exhibit 3, similarly for managed futures, a randomly equal weighted portfolio of 8-10 CTAs has a standard deviation similar to that of the population from which it is drawn. Thus, as for multi-firm equity portfolios, multi-manager CTA portfolios may have risk levels similar to that of a larger population of CTAs. As important, as shown in Exhibit 3 a portfolio of randomly selected CTAs may likewise have a correlation in excess of .90 with that of a typical benchmark for managed futures returns; that is, the dollar weighted MAR CTA portfolio. Confidence intervals around the respective standard deviations and correlations are also given in Exhibit 3. Thus, the use of the MAR$CTA can represent the performance of smaller subset (e.g., multi-CTA portfolios) of CTAs.

In Exhibit 3 the impact of adding randomly selected CTAs on portfolio risk and its correlation with a sample benchmark is given as well as the confidence interval around that estimation. While results may differ for CTA portfolios which are not equal weighted and which do not reflect the composition of the benchmark, these results indicate that, as for traditional assets, the management of managed futures may add an additional benefit to the benefits of managed futures.

CTA Performance

Over the past eleven years (1985-1995), investment in a portfolio of commodity trading advisors (e.g., MAR$CTA) provides risk and return benefits when considered as an addition to existing passive and actively managed stock and bond portfolios (e.g., S&P 500, Salomon Brothers U.S. Government bond indices (USBI), Salomon Brothers World Government bond indices (WGBI), Fidelity Magellan Fund and Fidelity Intermediate bond fund, and MSCI world, regional and domestic stock indices). In addition, managed futures offer increased investor return with reduced risk even when considered as an addition to widely diversified asset portfolios which include investment in passive and actively traded commodity indices (e.g., JPMorgan commodity index, MLM). Similar results are achieved when managed futures are compared to stock and bond indices in individual countries and to U.S. stock and bond fund indices based on Morningstar classifications.

In Exhibit 4, the key risk and return performance statistics (e.g., annualized return standard deviation, return/risk ratios, return correlations, and excess break-even return) for MAR$CTA, JPMorgan commodity indices, the MLM commodity trading index, Salomon US Government bond index (USBI), the S&P 500 index, Fidelity Magellan and Intermediate bond fund, MSCI equity and Salomon Brothers World bond index (WGBI) are presented for the period 1985-1995. For the full period analyzed (1985-1995), the MAR$CTA (15.81%) is greater than the S&P 500 (15.11%), Salomon Brothers government bond index (9.89%), and the Fidelity Intermediate bond fund (9.03%). Similarly, the return of MAR$CTA was greater than that of the measured passive commodity and active (technical trading) commodity indices (JPMorgan (10.34%), MLM (9.83%)) as well as the MSCI world equity index (14.86%) and Salomon World Government Bond Index (12.17%). Of the comparison benchmarks, only the Fidelity Magellan fund had a higher average rate of return (17.96%).[11]

The results in Exhibit 4 also indicate that for traditional measures of adjusted risk-return (e.g., return/risk ratios), the MAR$CTA index had superior performance to several traditional investment alternatives. For instance, for the 1985-1995 period, the return/risk ratio for MAR$CTA (1.08) was above the return/risk ratios for the various

EXHIBIT 4 PERFORMANCE MEASURES FOR MANAGED FUTURES AND OTHER ASSET CLASSES
11-YEAR PERFORMANCE: JANUARY 1985 TO DECEMBER 1995

1/85 to 12/95	MAR$CTA	MLM	JPMCI	SP500	Salomon US Bond	MSCI	Salomon World Bnd	Fidelity Magellan	Intermed. US Bond
Average Annual Return	15.81	9.83	10.34	15.11	9.89	14.86	12.17	17.96	9.03
Annual Standard Deviation	14.58	6.33	17.88	15.06	5.12	14.85	7.22	17.20	4.28
Avg. Ret./Std. Dev.	1.08	1.55	0.58	1.00	1.93	1.00	1.68	1.04	2.11
Minimum Monthly Return	-5.37	-4.12	-14.53	-24.31	-2.42	-18.59	-4.07	-29.85	-2.67
Maximum Monthly Return	17.83	6.41	19.81	12.66	4.75	11.13	6.52	12.22	5.46
Correlation with MAR	1.00	0.43	-0.06	0.12	0.18	0.08	0.17	0.10	0.18
Excess Annual Breakeven	0.00	6.01	10.02	8.79	7.76	9.14	7.69	8.75	7.96

U.S. and world equity comparisons such as the S&P 500 (1.00), MSCI (1.00), and Fidelity Magellan fund (1.04). In contrast the measured return/risk ratio for MAR$CTA (1.08) was below that for the Salomon Brothers' US and World Government bond indices, and Fidelity Intermediate bond fund (return/risk ratios of 1.93, 1.63 and 2.11 respectively).[12]

As important, however, is that while managed futures (MAR$CTA) underperform certain comparison benchmarks when the return/risk ratio is used the means of comparison, they outperform the traditional asset classes when alternative measures of risk and return are considered. For instance, over the 1985-1995 period the MAR$CTA monthly minimum return (-6.37%) was less negative than any of the equity benchmark comparisons (e.g., S&P 500 (-24.31%), MSCI (-18.59%), Fidelity Magellan (-29.85%)) while the MAR$CTA monthly maximum returns (17.83%) were greater than these equity benchmark comparisons. This may be partly caused by the unique structure of the CTA funds and their active management (e.g., managed drawdown) as compared to a passive or fully invested active equity portfolios.

Lastly, in Exhibit 5, comparisons are made with the MAR$CTA index and portfolios of the single asset benchmarks. In Exhibit 5, the key risk and return performance statistics for MAR$CTA and a U.S. multi-asset portfolio(equal weighted stock, bond, and active (BARRA) and passive (JPMorgan commodity index - Portfolio II), a stock (55%) and bond (45%) portfolio (Portfolio III), and similarly created Fidelity multi-asset portfolio (Portfolio V) and Fidelity stock and bond portfolio (Portfolio VI) and international multi-asset portfolio (Portfolio VIII) and stock and bond portfolio (Portfolio IX) are also presented for the period 1985-1995. For the full period analyzed (1985-1995), the annual MAR$CTA return (15.81%) is greater than that for any of the comparison portfolios. However, on a risk adjusted basis (e.g., return/risk ratio), the results in Exhibit 5 also indicate that for the period 1985-1995, the MAR$CTA index had return/risk ratios below the U.S. passive (Portfolio II and Portfolio III,), World passive (Portfolio VIII and Portfolio IX), and the Fidelity based managed portfolios (Portfolio VI and Portfolio VII).

EXHIBIT 5 11-YEAR PERFORMANCE OF MANAGED FUTURES AND ASSET PORTFOLIOS:
JANUARY 1985 TO DECEMBER 1995

1/85 to 12/95	MAR$CTA	*Port I* US Equal Weighted	*Port II* US Equal No CTA	*Port III* US Stock and Bond	*Port IV* Fidelity Equal	*Port V* Fidelity No CTA	*Port VI* Fidellity Stock/Bond	*Port VII* World Equal	*Port VIII* World No CTA	*Port IX* World Stock/Bond
Average Annual Return	15.81	12.85	11.91	13.02	13.31	12.47	14.28	13.26	12.40	13.88
Annual Standard Deviation	14.58	5.79	5.50	9.17	5.81	5.55	10.06	6.20	6.20	9.89
Avg. Ret./Std. Dev.	1.08	2.22	2.17	1.42	2.29	2.25	1.42	2.14	2.00	1.40
Minimum Monthly Return	-6.37	-2.88	-4.19	-10.76	-3.95	-5.66	-14.10	-2.38	-3.19	-6.51
Maximum Monthly Return	17.83	6.54	7.34	7.58	6.21	6.93	7.68	6.71	7.55	7.95
Correlation with MAR	1.00		0.21	0.15		0.20	0.14		0.17	0.12
Excess Annual Breakeven			6.54	8.09		6.36	8.18		7.22	8.40

As important, however, and as noted in Exhibit 5 when managed futures are added to the No CTA multi-asset portfolios (Port 1, Port IV, Port VII), the return/risk ratio for the portfolios which includes managed futures (MAR$CTA) are greater than the comparison No CTA or stock and bond portfolios which do not include managed futures. As important, even when managed futures are compared on a standalone basis, they often outperform traditional asset classes when alternative measures of risk and return are considered. For instance, over the 1985-1995 period, the MAR$CTA monthly maximum return (17.83%)) were greater than that of the cited stock/bond portfolios or multi-asset portfolios.

Modern investment theory shows that investments should be considered from the perspective of their attractiveness as additions to existing portfolios of alternative investment media (e.g., stocks and bonds) and not on a strict stand alone comparison basis. Break-even analysis can be used to determine if managed futures could be added at some level to improve the potential Sharpe ratio of an existing portfolio. As noted previously, the relative break-even comparisons, depends on the relative standard deviations and correlations. In Exhibits 2 and 3 correlation coefficients and the relevant excess break-even ratios for alternative time periods and for the alternative assets are also shown. For the eleven year period, 1985-1995 MAR$CTA were found to have a very low correlation with stocks (.12), bonds (.18), the published commodity indices (i.e., JPMorgan (-.06)) as well as active stock and bond funds and international equity and bond indices. Only for the MLM commodity trading index (.43) was the correlation significantly positive. These results are consistent with analyses of earlier time periods (e.g., Schneeweis et al., 1991, 1992).

In general, correlations with traditional asset classes remain below .25. As noted in an earlier analyses [Schneeweis et al., 1991, 1992], when the correlation is zero, the break-even rate is equal to the risk-free rate. In periods of high ex post interest rates, ex post

EXHIBIT 6 RETURN/RISK RATIO OF STOCK, BOND AND MANAGED FUTURES PORTFOLIO

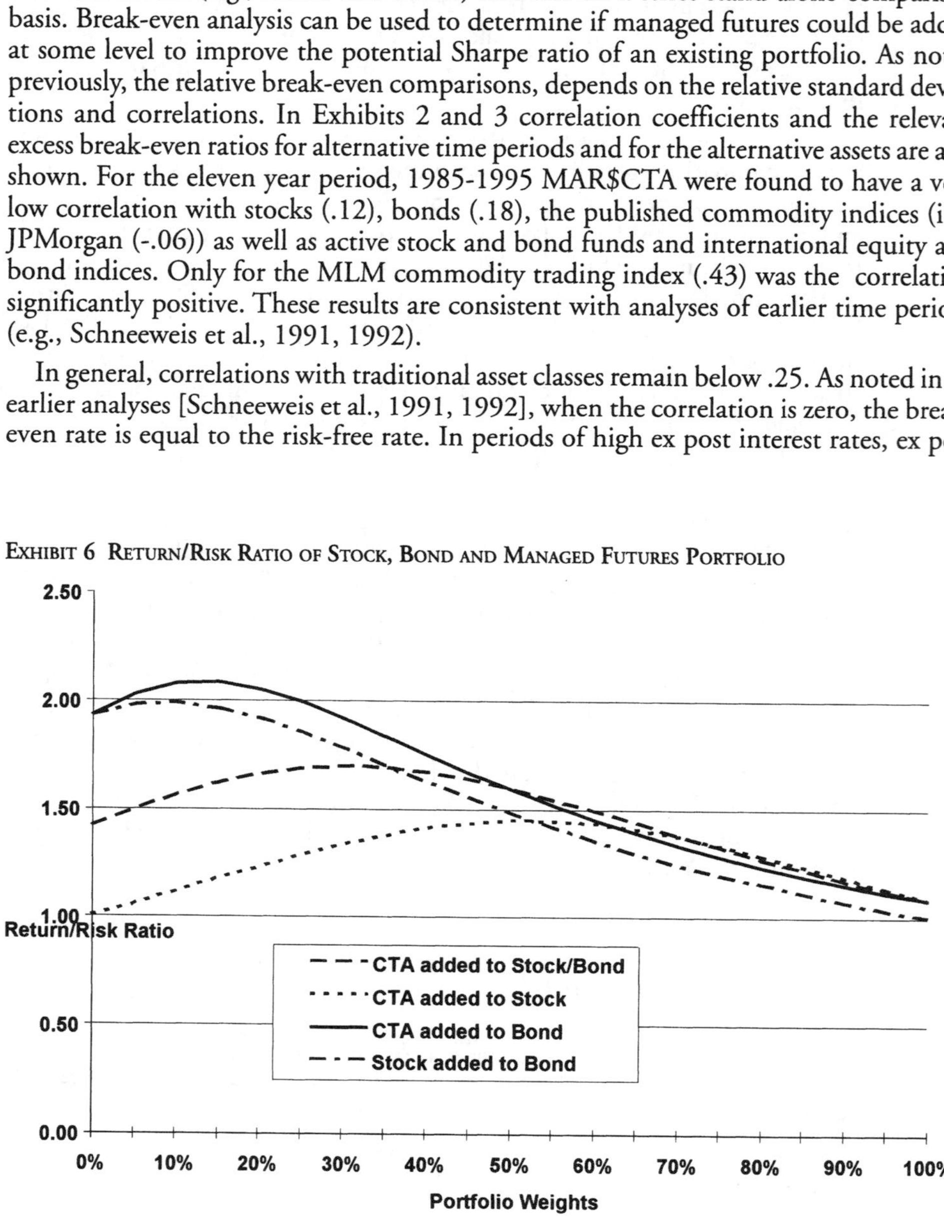

managed futures returns (as many other asset classes) may fail even to outperform a riskless return. In this study, we have assumed an annual risk free rate of 6% which for this period is above the actual but may better represent true investor 'low risk return' comparison. In Exhibits 4 and 5, the annualized excess break-even rate of return for MAR$CTA and comparison assets are given. Results show that the average monthly return of the MAR$CTA exceeded the required break-even level for inclusion in all portfolios of U.S. and non-U.S. stocks and bonds for the full time period, 1985 to 1995. For instance, against the S&P 500, MAR$CTA exceeded its required break-even rate of return by 8.79% for the full time period. Against the MSCI, MAR$CTA exceeded its required return by 9.14% and against Fidelity Magellan, it exceeded its required return by 8.75%. While against the comparison U.S., world, and country bond

EXHIBIT 7 RISK AND RETURN OF STOCK, BOND AND MANAGED FUTURES PORTFOLIOS

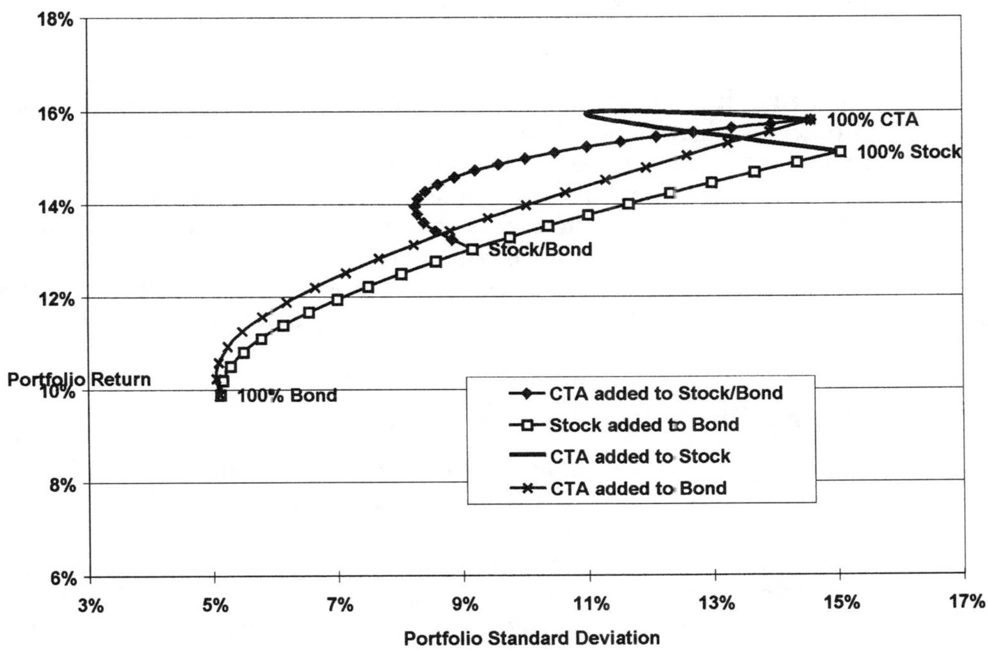

indices or combined stock and bond portfolios, the excess break-even returns were less positive than against the comparisons U.S. equity benchmarks, in all cases the excess break-even return was positive. It should be noted that the MAR$CTA exceeded its required rate of return relative to the comparison stock, bond, or stock/bond portfolios by more than the estimated annual cost of creating multi-advisor CTA portfolios (approximately 1 - 2% p.a.).

The ability of managed futures as additions to existing stock and bond portfolio to improve the relative return/risk tradeoff is shown in exibit 6. Results are presented which indicate the actual return and risk performance of including CTAs with alternative asset over a wide range of CTA weights for the period 1985-1995.

The improvement in return/standard deviation ratios from adding managed futures to existing stock, bond, and stock and bond positions as shown in Exhibit 6 is further

EXHIBIT 8 FUND/POOL SUBINDEX PERFORMANCE, JANUARY 1985 TO DECEMBER 1995

FP Index Performance	Dollar Weight	Equal Weight	Public	Single Advisor
Average Return	10.35	9.11	8.02	11.54
Standard Deviation	15.07	15.17	16.61	14.81
Avg. Ret./Std	0.69	0.60	0.48	0.78
Excess Breakeven Return				
SP500 Composite	2.72	1.68	0.16	3.75
US Govt. Bond Index	1.92	1.09	-0.69	3.05
MSCI	2.88	1.89	0.40	3.85
SB World Govt Bond	1.62	1.09	-1.08	2.74
Fidelity Magellan	2.56	1.65	-0.11	3.57
Fid. Intermed. Bond	2.29	1.44	-0.29	3.44
US - NoCTA Equal	0.51	-0.62	-2.30	1.87
US Stock/Bond Port.	1.85	0.95	-0.81	2.84
World - NoCTA Equal	0.96	-0.01	-1.75	2.23
MSCI/World Bond Port.	1.87	1.12	-0.73	2.80
Fidelity - NoCTA Equal	0.19	-0.76	-2.77	1.56
Magellan/Intermed Bond	1.86	1.09	-0.89	2.85

reflected in Exhibit 7 which shows the risk and return frontier of S&P 500, Salomon Brothers U.S. government bond index and portfolios containing the stock (55%) and bond (45%) indices as managed futures are added to the existing asset portfolios. Results show that adding managed futures to these existing traditional asset positions results in risk and return alternatives not easily found in individual stock or bond portfolios or in combined stock and bond portfolios. In addition, for various borrowing/lending rates, the projected tangency points of the combined CTA/traditional asset portfolios dominate the non-CTA traditional single asset or combined stock and bond portfolios.

Managed Futures Fund/Pool Performance

For retail investors, who may not be able to invest directly with commodity trading advisors, alternative managed futures products such as commodity funds and pools, which may carry higher investor fees than direct CTA investment, also offer the potential to improve the return of a portfolio for a given level of risk. As increased competition and a wider market for managed futures products reduces fees for managed futures products to levels similar to actively managed investment in traditional asset classes, the potential benefits of retail managed futures products will increase further.

In Exhibit 8, the key risk and return performance statistics for MAR commodity fund and pool indices and subindices are reported as well as the excess break-even returns compared to alternative investment vehicles; the S&P 500, Salomon US Government bond index, The MSCI equity index, the Salomon Brothers World government bond index, the Fidelity Magellan and Intermediate bond fund, and the corresponding equal weighted no-CTA portfolio and stock and bond portfolio created for each of these asset for the period 1985-1995.

In contrast, to direct investment in CTAs, results in Exhibit 4 indicate that the return/risk ratios of the commodity fund and pool indices and subindices fail to outperform traditional asset vehicles on a standalone basis. These results are consistent with earlier research [Elton et al. 1987; Irwin et al., 1992, and Schneeweis et al., 1992]. However, in Exhibit 8 results are also presented on benefits of commodity pools and funds as additions to existing alternative investment vehicles. For the period 1985-1995, results show that the MAR$FP had positive excess break-even ratios when compared to alternative investment vehicles (e.g., S&P 500, USBI, Fidelity Magellan and

Intermediate bond fund, MSCI and WGBI, as well as bond and stock portfolios and multi-asset portfolios constructed from these single asset classes). Similar results are reported for the 1985-1995 time period for the MAREQFP (MAR equal weighted fund and pool); that is, return/risk ratios below that of the MAR$CTA and traditional asset classes, however, positive excess break-even returns when compared to most alternative asset classes.

It is important to point out that for the period, 1985-1995, the performance of the MARFPUB (MAR public commodity funds) was generally below that of the MAR$FP or MAREQFP. Given the traditionally higher cost structure of public commodity funds to private pools, these results are not unexpected. However, results also show that for the period, 1985-1995, MARFPUB had positive excess break-even returns when compared to domestic and international equity indices, although negative excess break-even ratios were reported for additions to bond and several multi-fund portfolios which contain passive or active commodity trading based products). Thus, for the investor of public commodity funds, managed futures may not be regarded as standalone investments or as additions to mixed asset portfolios unless alternative risk/return benefits (e.g., minimum and maximum returns) are considered.

While using traditional performance comparisons, managed futures public pools failed to provide investments benefits to many mix asset portfolios in the periods measures, as management fees and performance fees continue to decline, their overall performance will improve relative to the comparison portfolios. Lastly, to the degree that individual commodity pool or fund managers may show consistent superior performance, individual funds and pools may provide risk/return benefits to a wider variety of existing portfolio composition.

Bases for CTA/Fund/Pool Risk/Return Benefits

Managed futures may be difficult if not impossible to achieve through other investment media. Managed futures may enable an investor to capture those returns available

EXHIBIT 9 MONTHLY STANDARD DEVIATION FOR MAR$CTA AND S&P 500

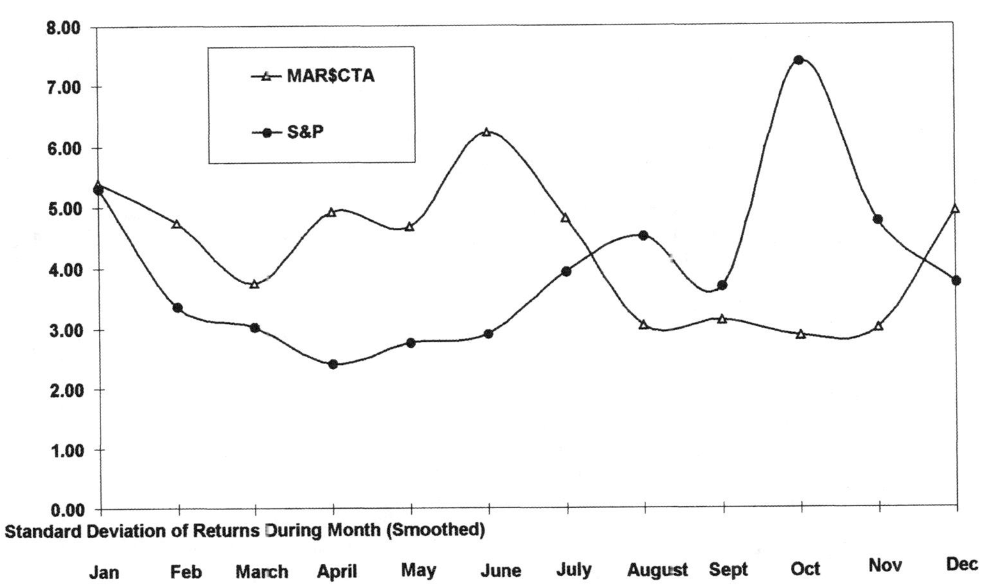

in the spot market more cheaply (e.g., replicate cash indices with lower transactions costs) and capture opportunities not easily achieved in spot markets (e.g., the ability to sell short and the ability to alter the degree of leverage in an asset position).

The differing investment styles and sector specialization of CTAs enable investors to create portfolios that offer higher expected returns in market cycles and market conditions when traditional stock or bond market investment have low expected returns. For instance, analysis of seasonal patterns of managed futures and various futures and options based products as well as traditional investment media show that managed futures products have the potential for return patterns not available in traditional asset investment. Managed futures products may better capture seasonal returns due to liquidity problems in energy and other commodity markets (e.g., convenience yield), trending markets due to unexpected informational releases in markets with low liquidity (e.g., currency markets), or changes in expected volatility in months with historically high informational uncertainty (e.g., summer agricultural markets).

The primary basis for the benefits of CTA addition to an existing portfolio may be due to the reported low correlation in security return movements. For instance, infor-

EXHIBIT 10 RELATIVE PERFORMANCE OF CTA INDEX AND US ASSET INDICES

Panel 5A. MAR CTA Index and SP500 Index

Group Rank	Avg. Return SP500	Avg. Return MAR$CTA	Number of Months MAR$>SP500
1	-7.06	2.65	12
2	-2.53	-0.34	8
3	-1.19	0.81	9
4	-0.09	1.12	7
5	0.91	1.36	7
6	1.59	0.09	4
7	2.40	0.69	3
8	3.21	0.35	1
9	4.13	1.31	3
10	5.12	2.62	3
11	8.47	4.84	1

Group 1 Correlation: -0.12
Group 11 Correlation: 0.46

Panel 5B. MAR CTA Index and SB Bond Index

Group Rank	Avg. Return US Bond Idx	Avg. Return MAR$CTA	Number of Months MAR$>USBI
1	-1.82	0.87	11
2	-0.91	-0.50	9
3	-0.26	2.57	11
4	0.18	-0.54	4
5	0.56	2.17	7
6	0.90	1.16	5
7	1.19	1.22	4
8	1.53	0.36	2
9	1.91	2.78	4
10	2.30	2.38	2
11	3.64	3.03	1

Group 1 Correlation: 0.20
Group 11 Correlation: 0.39

Panel 5C. MAR CTA Index and Portfolio II

Group Rank	Avg. Return Port II	Avg. Return MAR$CTA	Number of Months MAR$>Port II
1	-2.03	0.34	12
2	-0.58	0.20	8
3	0.02	1.16	9
4	0.41	1.79	9
5	0.76	0.22	4
6	1.05	0.17	3
7	1.31	1.44	5
8	1.66	0.70	2
9	2.03	3.33	4
10	2.60	2.06	3
11	3.89	4.08	0

Group 1 Correlation: -0.12
Group 11 Correlation: 0.14

Panel 5D. MAR CTA Index and Portfolio III

Group Rank	Avg. Return Port III	Avg. Return MAR$CTA	Number of Months MAR$>Port III
1	-3.95	2.18	12
2	-1.66	-0.57	9
3	-0.52	2.21	8
4	0.26	0.96	6
5	0.78	0.58	7
6	1.26	-0.05	2
7	1.62	1.74	5
8	2.19	-0.55	1
9	2.88	0.62	2
10	3.75	2.51	3
11	5.78	5.88	2

Group 1 Correlation: -0.17
Group 11 Correlation: 0.39

mation pattern and seasonal return patterns for CTAs may differ form that of the underlying stock and bond markets resulting in low return correlations between CTAs and alternative assets. Considerable academic research exists which indicates that stock, bond, and currency markets contain seasonal risk and return patterns. Similarly, considerable research exists which indicates the existence of abnormal rate of return in stock, bond, and commodity, and currency markets due to liquidity or market imperfections that may be seasonal in nature. To the degree that CTAs are not constrained to take positions in such markets, in contrast to traditional stock and bond managers, CTA investors may provide expected months in which traditional assets may not be expected to offer similar return patterns. For instance, managed futures which have the opportunity of trading in markets that have return and risk patterns that may differ from traditional investment classes. For instance, in Exhibit 9, for the U.S. stock markets a U-shaped yearly risk and return pattern exists. In contrast, the MAR$CTA index follows the reverse pattern which reflects return\risk opportunities existing in months in which the underlying S&P 500 offers lower rates of return and risk[13].

Pattern of Managed Futures Returns

Managed futures indiexes (e.g., MAR$CTA index) produced consistently higher returns in those months in which the S&P 500, Fidelity Magellan, or MSCI world equity indices; the Fidelity Intermediate bond fund, the Salomon Brothers U.S. and World Government bond indices, and U.S. and world active and passive stock/bond portfolios as well as combined stock, bond, and commodity portfolios had the highest negative returns. Managed futures also achieve superior returns in months when various traditional asset classes and created stock, bond, and stock, bond, and commodity portfolios had their highest positive returns. Correlation tests comparing managed futures indices with traditional assets reveal an interesting property of the relationship between managed futures returns (MAR$CTA) and returns to traditional asset classes.

EXHIBIT 11 PERFORMANCE OF MAR$CTA INDEX RELATIVE TO S&P 500

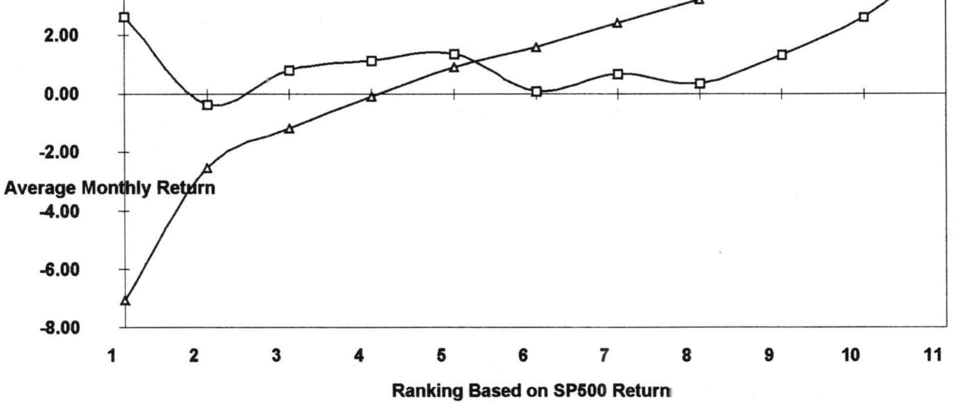

Overall, the correlation between managed futures and stock portfolios is approximately zero. However, when the data are segmented according to whether the stock market rose or fell, results indicate that managed futures are negatively correlated with traditional asset class products (e.g., stock and stock and bond portfolio) when these cash market portfolios posted significant negative returns and are positively correlated when these portfolios report significant positive returns. Thus managed futures may offer unique asset allocation properties.

As important, relative return patterns between managed futures products and traditional financial investments may reflect the ability of various managed futures traders to obtain return in markets in which long positions in the underlying assets provide negative returns. As shown in Exhibit 10, when stock, bond, stock and bond portfolios or stock, bond and commodity portfolios returns are ranked from low to high and divided into 11 twelve month subperiods, the number of months in which the MAR$CTA index provides superior returns to the alternative asset or portfolio is given. [14]

In Exhibit 10, for instance, results show that for 12 of the 12 worst S&P 500 return months and that for 11 of the 12 worst USBI months, the MAR$CTA outperformed the alternative index. Similar results are evident for the combined stock, bond, and commodity portfolio (portfolio II) and for the combined stock and bond portfolio (portfolio III). For instance, the graphical representations of the monthly return patterns for each of the comparison MAR$CTA and the S&P 500 are given in Exhibit 11.[15]

Lastly, for each of the single asset or portfolio comparisons, the Pearson correlation for the high and low twelve return months are given in Exhibit 10 between the MAR$CTA and the corresponding asset group. In general, the correlation patterns indicate that within the low return months, the lower the monthly asset return, the greater the MAR$CTA return; while in the high return months, the higher the monthly asset return, the greater the MAR$CTA return.[16]

EXHIBIT 12 COMPARISON OF MAR CTA PERFORMANCE WITH PROTECTIVE PUT STRATEGY ON S&P 500 INDEX

Group Rank	Average Return SP500	Average Return MAR CTA	Portfolio SP500/ MAR CTA	Portfolio SP500/ Put Option
1	-7.46	2.57	-2.45	-2.20
2	-2.57	-0.40	-1.49	-1.60
3	-1.20	0.70	-0.25	-1.70
4	-0.10	1.04	0.47	-1.63
5	0.91	1.31	1.11	-1.22
6	1.58	0.01	0.79	-0.25
7	2.37	0.66	1.52	0.53
8	3.16	0.31	1.74	1.39
9	4.04	1.33	2.69	1.87
10	5.00	2.39	3.69	2.82
11	8.11	4.58	6.34	5.83
Average	15.11	15.81	15.46	4.20
Std. Dev.	15.06	14.88	11.07	8.82
Avg. Ret./Std. Dev.	1.00	1.06	1.40	0.48

EXHIBIT 13 PERFORMANCE OF MAR$CAT AND S&P 500 PROTECTIVE PUT STRATEGY

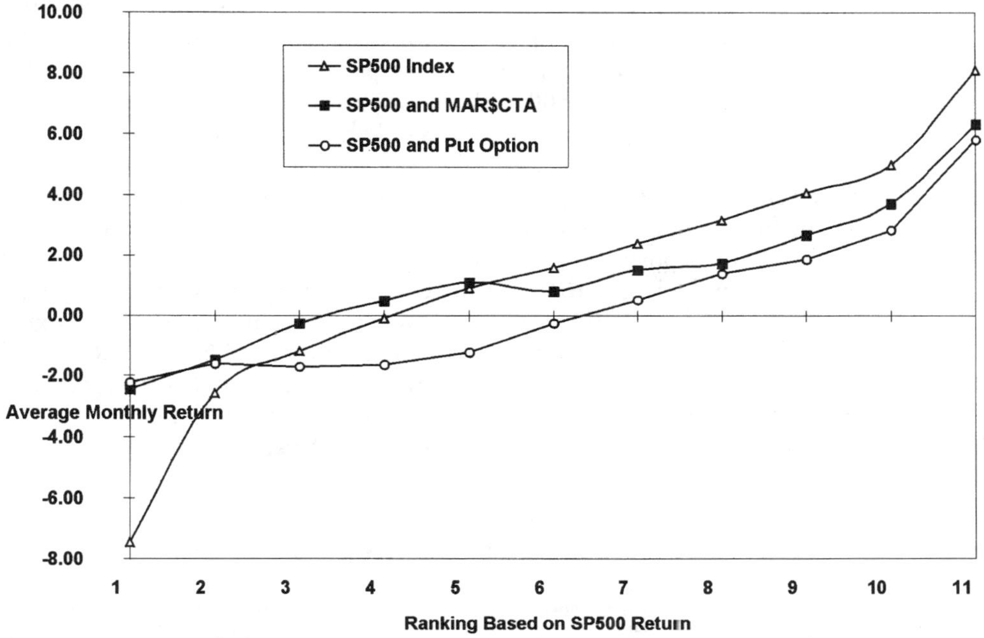

Alternative Risk/Return Opportunities

While historical data indicates that including managed futures in a stock and bond and/or combined equity and commodity portfolio would have increased the return for a given level of risk, it is possible that similar benefits could be obtained using other investment media (e.g., options, hedge funds). Results also show that managed futures may offer risk/return benefits when compared to a partially hedged position in the stock market. For instance, it is shown that an equal weighted investment in the MAR$CTA index and the S&P 500 outperformed investment in the S&P 500 plus a simulated at-the-money put under most market conditions. These results indicate that managed futures may offer some of the hedging properties of a put option at a lower cost.

In the previous section, results indicated that the differential markets as well as trading style (ability to short) may allow managed futures to provide diversification benefits or return benefits in trending markets that are not easily available in alternative cash markets. Specifically, in markets with negative market conditions, managed futures have shown the ability to offer positive returns. Non-managed futures alternative investment strategies have been given to provide similar risk/return performance in such markets. For instance, the purchase of portfolio insurance (e.g., puts) also provide downside risk protection. The question remains however, as to the cost of this alternative and its relative performance. In Exhibit 12, we show the relative performance in S&P 500 markets of 1) a combination S&P 500 portfolio and MAR$CTA portfolio and 2) an at the money protective put strategy. As shown in Exhibit 6, the return/risk ratio for the S&P 500 and MAR$CTA portfolio are greater than that of the S&P 500 plus the protective put.

For the at-the-money protective put strategy, an at-the-money put value was derived with a rolling 35 day maturity with an 35 day implied volatility estimates from Goldman Sachs and the Black-Scholes model. Previous results (Exhibit 5) show that MAR$CTA index is negatively correlated with the S&P in the down months and positive correlated in the up months. As important, the results for the MAR$CTA may not reflect the actual relationship between the S&P 500 and CTAs who trade the S&P 500. If traders follow the equity markets and take short positions during negative markets, then a combination of the S&P 500 plus the MAR$CTA index may outperform an at the money put protected portfolio[17]. Results in Exhibit 12 show that in down S&P months, the combination S&P 500 portfolio and MAR$CTA outperformed the S&P 500. However, results also show that the protective put strategy also outperformed the S&P 500 in down months. Of interest is the performance difference between the S&P 500 and MAR$CTA portfolio and the protective put and S&P 500 portfolio. Results show that in down S&P months the protective put portfolio at times outperformed the MAR$CTA and S&P 500 portfolio, however, results in Exhibit 12 and Exhibit 13 also show that a combination of 50% S&P 500 portfolio and 50% MAR$CTA dominates on average the protective put portfolio under all ranked months when months are group into 11 twelve month groups after ranking on the S&P 500. It is, of course, important to point out that the performance of the equity/protective put and the equity/managed

EXHIBIT 14A HEDGE FUND SUBINDEX PERFORMANCE, JANUARY 1994 TO DECEMBER 1995

Hedge Performance	**Convertable**	**Distress**	**Emerging Market**	**Fixed Income**	**Growth**	**Macro**	**Market Netural**	**Market Timing**	**Merger/ Arb**	**Multi Strategy**	**Opportunity**	**Sector**	**Short Selling**
Average Return	7.54	10.86	1.97	8.29	14.94	9.87	10.00	6.04	12.00	8.38	11.52	17.10	-5.52
Standard Deviation	3.15	5.08	13.49	1.71	7.28	12.80	2.72	5.70	3.23	2.83	4.17	9.03	26.28
Avg. Ret./Std.	2.40	2.14	0.15	4.86	2.05	0.77	3.68	1.06	3.71	2.96	2.76	1.89	-0.21
Excess Breakeven Return													
SP500 Composite	-0.40	1.73	-6.71	2.18	2.61	-3.55	2.90	-5.32	4.11	1.14	2.12	5.82	6.12
US Govt. Bond Index	1.28	4.58	-4.03	2.20	8.56	2.97	3.94	-0.42	5.90	2.24	5.19	10.60	-10.66
MSCI	0.88	3.37	-6.68	2.20	5.64	0.60	2.98	-2.49	5.29	1.75	3.98	9.53	-3.28
SB World Govt Bond	0.82	4.24	-2.46	2.03	7.84	3.87	3.31	-1.22	5.77	2.20	5.03	11.83	-10.60
Fidelity Magellan	0.54	2.62	-6.76	2.34	4.72	0.64	3.11	-3.31	4.75	1.49	3.55	7.71	3.92
Fid. Intermed. Bond	2.12	5.52	-3.89	2.49	9.82	6.13	4.16	1.02	6.23	2.74	6.22	12.20	-13.17
US - NoCTA Equal	-1.05	1.40	-5.03	1.86	2.78	-7.23	2.66	-4.40	4.79	-0.04	0.71	5.84	-8.79
US Stock/Bond Port.	-0.17	2.40	-5.65	2.03	4.34	-2.44	3.22	-4.14	4.66	1.34	2.80	6.89	0.87
World - NoCTA Equal	0.32	2.86	-5.13	2.02	4.80	-0.91	2.19	-2.46	5.56	0.93	2.92	10.60	-12.25
MSCI/World Bond Port.	0.63	3.24	-5.75	2.10	5.48	0.92	2.78	-2.79	5.26	1.73	3.92	10.00	-3.68
Fidelity - NoCTA Equal	-1.17	-0.26	-8.41	2.17	-0.04	-7.05	1.79	-6.03	3.96	-0.77	-0.07	4.00	5.68
Magellan/Intermed Bond	0.53	2.85	-6.20	2.25	5.30	0.44	3.24	-2.95	4.93	1.55	3.71	8.03	1.15

EXHIBIT 14B CTA INDEX PERFORMANCE, JANUARY 1994 TO DECEMBER 1995

CTA Index Performance	Dollar Weight	Equal Weight	Currency	Discretionary	Diversified	Energy	Europe	Financial	Stock	Trend Follow
Average Return	6.68	7.22	-0.13	4.11	9.59	7.91	1.23	7.07	-2.77	6.34
Standard Deviation	9.47	7.05	11.11	5.44	12.53	7.20	4.75	9.37	14.08	13.67
Avg Ret./Std.	0.70	1.02	-0.01	0.75	0.77	1.10	0.26	0.75	-0.20	0.46
Excess Break-even										
Convertible	0.96	1.18	-7.78	-2.93	3.54	2.88	-4.57	2.36	-6.49	1.24
Distressed	1.37	1.26	-8.38	-2.29	5.25	2.63	-3.44	0.92	-2.29	0.86
Emerging Market	0.02	0.85	-6.80	-1.82	3.05	1.47	-4.96	0.40	-10.51	-0.57
Fixed Income	-2.93	-1.97	-7.86	-2.56	-0.64	2.30	-6.80	-2.92	-6.00	-4.87
Growth	1.75	2.09	-8.50	-3.31	5.97	3.96	-3.45	1.28	2.37	1.53
Macro	0.41	1.11	-6.84	-2.81	3.31	2.63	-4.72	0.80	-6.38	0.12
Market Neutral	-1.30	-0.77	-13.07	-2.51	3.41	2.93	-4.03	-2.02	-0.41	-3.35
Market Timing	0.68	1.23	-6.13	-1.90	3.60	1.94	-4.77	1.08	-8.69	0.35
Merger Arbitrage	2.45	3.21	-5.82	-3.03	4.28	7.24	-3.68	4.06	3.47	2.25
Multi-strategies	-1.23	-0.40	-9.55	-3.62	1.63	1.85	-5.04	-0.68	-4.25	-2.55
Opportunitic	-0.27	0.38	-7.75	-4.30	2.36	2.71	-4.17	-0.29	2.21	-1.64
Sector	1.53	1.64	-8.65	-4.22	5.58	4.17	-4.67	1.36	-1.24	1.11
Shortselling	2.64	2.60	-5.28	-1.31	6.22	3.35	-3.85	2.67	-5.00	2.72

futures position are not strictly comparable since the performance of the managed futures position is stochastic. The individual investor must determine whether the potential relative return compensates for the expected risk.

EXHIBIT 15A CTA SUBINDEX PERFORMANCE, JANUARY 1990 TO DECEMBER 1995

CTA Index Performance	Dollar Weight	Equal Weight	Currency	Discretionary	Diversified	Energy	Financial	Trend Follow
Average Return	13.43	9.46	13.09	14.31	10.30	7.32	13.38	12.19
Standard Deviation	11.49	10.12	16.60	8.19	12.87	10.75	13.85	18.09
Avg. Ret./Std.	1.17	0.93	0.79	1.75	0.80	0.68	0.97	0.67
***Excess Breakeven** Return*								
SP500 Composite	8.39	4.58	7.46	9.28	5.41	2.91	7.65	7.45
US Govt. Bond Index	6.41	2.99	5.33	7.51	3.28	2.97	5.24	4.49
MSCI	7.52	3.54	7.09	8.35	4.36	1.40	7.39	6.31
SB World Govt Bond	5.65	2.37	4.58	7.83	2.12	2.85	4.06	3.25
Fidelity Magellan	8.82	5.07	7.85	9.69	6.18	2.99	7.82	8.01
Fid. Intermed. Bond	6.07	2.75	5.12	7.36	2.95	2.79	4.90	4.01
US - NoCTA Equal	6.27	2.53	6.15	7.47	2.95	0.50	6.34	4.34
US Stock/Bond Port.	8.11	4.45	7.01	9.07	5.14	3.30	7.10	7.00
World - NoCTA Equal	6.85	2.92	6.40	7.81	3.42	0.79	6.70	5.25
MSCI/World Bond Port.	7.64	3.70	6.80	8.45	4.34	1.85	7.08	6.41
Fidelity - NoCTA Equal	6.29	2.66	6.24	7.60	3.19	0.29	6.20	4.28
Magellan/Intermed Bond	8.49	4.89	7.38	9.46	5.84	3.31	7.24	7.48

EXHIBIT 15B EXCESS BREAKEVEN RETURN FOR MAR CTA AND FUND/POOL SUBINDEXES, 1994-1995

CTA Subindex Performance, January, 1994 to December, 1995

CTA Index Performance	Dollar Weight	Equal Weight	Currency	Discretionary	Diversified	Energy	Europe	Financial	Stock	Trend Follow
Average Return	6.68	7.22	-0.13	4.11	9.59	7.91	1.23	7.07	-2.77	6.34
Standard Deviation	9.47	7.05	11.11	5.44	12.53	7.20	4.75	9.37	14.08	13.67
Avg. Ret./Std.	0.70	1.02	-0.01	0.75	0.77	1.10	0.26	0.75	-0.20	0.46
Excess Breakeven										
SP500 Composite	2.75	3.17	-5.68	-3.55	6.43	4.07	-3.10	2.60	3.18	3.06
US Govt. Bond Index	0.63	1.18	-6.11	-2.11	3.47	2.07	-4.70	1.09	-7.59	0.24
MSCI	1.32	1.76	-6.45	-2.40	4.71	2.38	-3.63	0.98	-2.82	1.29
SB World Govt Bond	-1.68	-0.20	-8.91	-2.67	1.05	1.64	-5.32	-1.14	-5.55	-3.26
Fidelity Magellan	2.45	2.78	-6.57	-1.66	6.58	3.57	-3.52	2.08	-1.99	2.26
Fid. Intermed. Bond	0.93	1.42	-5.88	-1.31	4.04	1.52	-4.97	1.17	-11.23	0.75
US - NoCTA Equal	-3.00	-1.57	-7.78	-6.64	-2.89	-1.34	-3.56	-1.33	1.73	-3.79
US Stock/Bond Port.	1.84	2.32	-5.83	-3.34	5.06	3.54	-3.60	2.02	0.85	1.78
World - NoCTA Equal.	-3.96	-2.21	-9.97	-4.78	-2.84	-1.75	-4.17	-3.27	-2.49	-5.38
MSCI/World Bond Port.	0.25	1.10	-7.61	-2.68	3.51	2.22	-3.97	0.04	-2.00	-0.35
Fidelity - NoCTA	-1.63	-0.41	-9.61	-4.74	0.19	-0.13	-2.52	-0.94	3.76	-2.70
Magellan/Intermed Bond	1.95	2.35	-6.58	-1.95	5.73	3.37	-3.72	1.82	-2.51	1.67

Managed Futures: Alternative Product Forms

The benefits of hedge funds, which invest directly in futures and options as well as direct investment in traditional securities and physical commodities may offer an additional investment alternative. Unfortunately, historical index data on various hedge fund investment styles and trading strategies only exist for the past two years. Even over this time period, which corresponds to a historically poor risk/return period for managed futures, managed futures offer potential for risk/return improvement when considered as additions to existing hedge funds.

The investment universe is constantly evolving. While results in previous sections indicate the benefits of managed futures over both ex post investment periods as well as ex ante investment periods. In Exhibit 14a, the risk and return performance of measured hedge fund indices over the 1994-1995 are given. As noted in the following section, generalizations from a two year performance period are difficult. Results do indicate, however, that the return/risk ratios of many of the reporting hedge fund subindices were greater than that of the S&P 500 or the USBI. Moreover, various subindices also provided historical benefits as additions to existing cash stock or bond portfolios. This is especially true for hedge funds which concentrated in fixed income or distressed securities which had relatively strong markets over this time period. In contrast, hedge funds which concentrated in short-selling (especially short-selling domestic stock indices) had poor performance on a standalone basis and as additions to existing cash portfolios. Even in this case, however, the short-selling hedge fund subindex had a positive excess break-even return compared to the S&P 500 index.

Unfortunately, historical index data on various hedge fund investment styles and trading strategies only exist for the past two years. As shown in Exhibit 14b, even over this time period, which corresponds to a historically poor risk/return period for managed futures, managed futures offer potential for risk/return improvement even when considered as additions to existing hedge funds.

Recent Performance

It is important to note that neither this nor any study can capture or review all possible questions relating to the future or past performance of various investment products. Over the past two years, for instance, the S&P 500 as well as the Salomon Brothers U.S. government bond index have generally outperformed managed futures on a stand alone basis. However, investors must realize the uniqueness of the recent time period. Returns to the S&P 500 in 1995 (annualized returns over 35%) have not been repeated in any of the past eleven years while the annualized returns to the MAR$CTA index (14.1%) were similar to the eleven-year average (15.8%).

It must be noted however, that while over the most recent six year period (1990-1995), the MAR$CTA indices provided benefits as additions to existing stock, bond and stock/bond portfolios (Exhibit 15a), over the most recent two year subperiod, (1994-1995), that several of the MAR$CTA subindexes a (e.g., Europe, stock) failed to provide risk/return benefits when compared to traditional stock and bond investments.

Over the past two years, for instance, the S&P 500 as well as the Salomon Brothers U.S. government bond index have generally outperformed managed futures on a standalone basis. Moreover, while results show that, over this very recent time period, some managed futures investment products failed to improve the risk/return tradeoff when added to existing traditional asset portfolios, investors must realize the uniqueness of the recent time period. Returns to the S&P 500 in 1995 (annualized returns over 35%) have not been repeated in any of the past eleven years while the annualized returns to the MAR$CTA index (14.1%) were similar to the eleven-year average (15.8%).[18]

Conclusion

Recent analyses of the benefits of managed futures have focused on both the potential benefits of managed futures in return enhancement and portfolio diversification. As noted in these studies, the ability of managed futures traders to trade in a wide variety of international futures and options markets which are often more liquid than traditional cash markets and for which the transaction costs and market impact of trading are less than traditional cash markets result in relative benefits to managed futures traders who can benefit from the structural efficiencies of the futures/options markets. In addition, the ability of managed futures traders to trade primarily in regulated exchanges helps insure investor safety. Lastly, the ability of managed futures traders to take unique leverage positions in both rising and falling markets results in unique return opportunities not easily found in either traditional stock and bond markets or commodity investments.

The failure of managed futures to grow in the recent market environment may be due to several factors. First, public perception of the risk of futures and option markets as standalone investments does not correspond to the actual risks of investing in managed futures products - especially when the risk is considered at the investor's portfolio level. Second, the unexpected recent performance of stock and bond markets may lead certain investors to expect similar returns in the near future. In fact, research has shown that for many individuals, future risk and return expectations are based on recent experience. Lastly, it is possible that, for many investors, the concerns over benefits of managed futures leads them to avoid managed futures. However, investors must realize that these concerns are not unique to managed futures. As shown in the studies listed in Appendix IV, concerns over the use of managed futures benchmarks as indicators of actual investor performance also exist for more traditional benchmarks. As in all investment markets, investors must take time to analyze the actual performance of their potential investment with their existing or potential portfolio. However, as managed futures, traditional stock indices also have problems over survival bias and style or asset class consistency (note only one firm of the original Dow Jones listing is still part of the index).

It is hoped that the results of this study will put to rest many of these concerns. Simply put, most traditional asset managers presently use futures and options markets in numerous ways (e.g., rebalance portfolios, manage currency risk, trade bonds with option features such as convertibility or callability). Most traditional money managers, however, are restricted by regulation or convention from using more actively traded futures and option contracts. Moreover, as new financial products come into existence, such as futures contracts traded on S&P 500 value or growth stocks, managed futures may provide the most logical means of quickly taking advantage of the potential returns from such new products. The logical extension of using investment managers with specialized knowledge of traditional markets to obtain maximum return/risk tradeoffs is to add specialized managers who can obtain the unique returns in market conditions and types of securities not generally available to traditional asset managers; that is, managed futures.

ENDNOTES

This article was published by AIMA, 1996 and is reprinted with permission from AIMA.

[1] In fact, direct losses to investors due to what may be considered 'improper' industry practices may be regarded as small compared to recent investor losses in traditionally safe securities (e.g., savings and loans collapse). Similarly, public perception of the risk of derivative products may be exaggerated due to the public presses attempts to 'educate' investors on the risks of derivative investing while failing to stress the possible benefits or risks of alternative cash market securities. See " T. Schneeweis, "Derivatives and the Public Trust: What Have We Learned From 'Front Page' Highly Levered Derivative Transactions" [1994 Financial Risk Management Congress, N.Y.] and "Dealing with Myths About Derivatives" Chicago Mercantile Exchange [Summer, 1995].

[2] Books which include information on the history of managed futures and hedge funds include Chandler [1994], Fox-Andrews and Meaden [1995], and Epstein [1994]. Books which include discussions on the history of futures and options markets and the economic benefits of derivative products see Peck [1985, Vols. 1-5].

[3] See Peck [1985].

[4] For currency markets see McCallum, "A reconsideration of the Uncovered Interest Rate Parity, " [1992, NBER Working Paper # 4113] and Clardia and Taylor, "The Term Structure of Forward Premium and the Forecastability of Spot Exchange Rates," [1993, NBER Working Paper # 4442]. For the existence of convenience yields in energy markets see Litzenberger and Rabinowitz, "Backwardation in Oil Futures Markets: Theory and Empirical Evidence," *Journal of Finance* [December, 1995], pp 1517-1545.

[5] Evidence that investors under react to information and consequently trends are present in security prices is found in Jagdeesh, "Evidence of predictable behavior of security returns," *Journal of Finance*, [1990, pp 881-898]. and Chan, Jagdeesh, and Lakonishok, "Momentum Strategies," [1995, NBER Working Paper # 5375].

[6] The previous results were given net of expenses, such that the impact of manager fees are directly considered in the empirical results. At the same time, concern has been raised as to the level of fees in the managed futures industry. Several basis exist for the relative fee differential between managed futures and other investment media. First, as indicated in previous sections, to the degree that investment managers control downside risk, the fee paid to managers may in part be seen as a payment for a protective put. However, compensation costs due affect relative performance. Investors must compared the after fee payment return structure to evaluate the comparison returns. Likewise, other relative cost considerations should be considered in more detailed analyses including tax, liquidity and personal timing of investment needs.

[7] Peters [1995] argues that portfolio diversification with managed futures provides partial stochastic dominance in the lower return ranges and produces long term effects similar to insurance, that is, reduction to upside performance (cost) with protection in down markets. As the use of alternative risk measures capturing semi-variance (e.g., downside risk) gain popularity, these benefits of managed futures may become more apparent.

[8] Sharpe [1994] also points out that risk/return comparisons based on mean and variance do not take into consideration differences in portfolios in other moments or differences in distributions over various states of natures that may affect investor utility differently. Thus to the degree that managed futures returns may be described by higher moments than traditional stock and bond portfolios the Sharpe ratio may not provide a suitable return/risk comparison. Lastly, while not addressed directly in this study, many CTAs also offer 'overlay' strategies which do no directly require additional investment. For these strategies more complex performance measures have been suggested (Yau, Savanayana, and Schneeweis, "Alternative Performance Models in Interest rate Futures," in B. Goss Rational Expectations and Efficiency in Futures Markets [Routledge, 1992].

[9] For a discussion of random diversification on portfolio risk and return see Elton and Gruber, Modern Portfolio Theory and Investment Analysis [John Wiley, 1995]. For random security selection there is no impact on return, however, the impact on risk reduction is dependent upon the heterogeneity of the sample.

[10] For instance, Kapadia , "The Price of Volatility Risk", [NYU, N.Y., 1995] points out that options are not redundant securities by playing an important role in allowing market participants to hold volatility. Similarly, manage futures are not redundant securities if they play an important role in allowing market participants to more easily hold futures and options positions which take advantage of the benefits (e.g., convenience yield, downside risk control) of these nonredundant securities.

[11] Similar tests were conducted for MSCI regional and country specific equity and Salomon Brothers World government bond indices and country specific bond indices as well as stock and bond portfolios and stock, bond, and commodity portfolios formed from these international investment vehicles. Results are similar to those presented here [See EMFA, "The Benefits of Managed Futures, Technical Report, 1996].

[12] However, it is important to point out that the Sharpe ratios for the bond benchmarks were also superior to the equity based Sharpe ratios for the entire period. In fact, their is no ten year period from 1926 to 1985 in which the fixed income annualized return for a ten year period was over ten percent. Thus given present levels of return, it is unlikely that the return scenario for fixed-income securities achieved over the past ten years will ever be achieved again.

[13] Results in "Benefits of Managed Futures", [EMFA, 1996] show that the return and risk patterns of

using various technical trading techniques to trade various underlying markets such as grains and energy are consistent with seasonal informational uncertainties existing in these markets. For instance, as shown in EMFA [1996] returns to the MLM trading index is higher for grains in summer months and for energy in the fall and winter months. This is not unexpected. Since asset return has been shown theoretically to be directly related to return sensitivity to macro economic information (e.g. APT), periods which contain greater information uncertainty may also contain greater expected rates of return. Results from other studies (P. Clarke, Managed Futures [Ph.D. Dissertation, University of Massachusetts, 1995] shows that for CTAs whose trading style is more fundamental in nature (e.g., information based), seasonal return patterns differ from those CTAs with technical trading styles.

[14] Similar tests were conducted for cited world stock, bond, multi-asset. and stock/bond portfolio and Fidelity stock, bond, multi-asset, and stock/bond portfolio. Results are similar to those presented here [See EMFA, "The Benefits of Managed Futures", Technical Report, 1996].

[15] Similar tests were conducted for Fidelity Magellan and Intermediate bond fund, and MSCI equity and Salomon Brothers World government bond indices as well as stock and bond portfolios and stock, bond, and commodity portfolios formed from these active U.S. investment vehicles and international investment vehicles. Results are similar to those presented here [See EMFA, "The Benefits of Managed Futures", Technical Report, 1996].

[16] Similar figures were created for Fidelity Magellan and Intermediate bond fund, and MSCI equity and Salomon Brothers World government bond indices as well as stock and bond portfolios and stock, bond, and commodity portfolios formed from these active U.S. investment vehicles and international investment vehicles. Results are similar to those presented here [See EMFA, "The Benefits of Managed Futures", Technical Report, 1996].

[17] For a parallel discussion on the benefits of managed futures as portfolio insurance see Peters [1995]. Preliminary results indicate that a greater positive correlation exists between the performance of the CTA equity traders and a straddle position than between CTA equity traders and the S&P 500. This is consistent with CTA equity traders who take short positions in down markets and long positions in up markets.

[18] Probable investment scenarios which assume that the next ten years will reflect the past are created using a shuffling routine. Historical returns are sampled randomly rather than in sequence. Results indicate, as expected, that managed futures offer positive risk/return benefits especially when considered as additions to traditional stock, bond, or stock and bond portfolios. Results are available from author.

REFERENCES

Bodie, Z., A. Kane, and A. Marcus, *Investments* (Irwin, Chicago, 1995).

Chance, Don. *Managed futures and Their Role in Investment Portfolios.* Charlottesville, AIMR, 1994.

Chandler, B. *Managed futures: An Investor's Guide.* New York: John Wiley & Sons, 1994.

Edwards, F. and J. Park, "Do Managed Futures Make Good Investments." *The Journal of Futures Markets* (August, 1996), pp 475-517

Elton, E.J., M.J. Gruber, and J.C. Rentzler. "Professionally Managed, Publicly Traded Commodity Funds," *Journal of Business* (April 1987), pp 177-199.

Elton, E.J., M.J. Gruber, and J.C. Rentzler. "New Public Offerings, Information, and Investor Rationality: The Case of Publicly Offered Commodity Funds," *Journal of Business*, Vol. 6, No. 1, (1989) pp 1-15.

Elton, E.J., M.J. Gruber, and J. Rentzler, "The Performance of Publicly Offered Commodity Funds," *Financial Analysts Journal* (July-August, 1990), pp 23-30.

Elton, E.J., M.J. Gruber, and J. Rentzler, "The Performance of Publicly Offered Commodity Funds " in C. Peters ed. *Managed futures* (Probus Publishing, 1992), pp 387-401.

Fox-Andrews, M. and Nicola Meaden. *Derivative Markets and Investment Management* (Prentice Hall, Hertfordshire, G.B., 1995)

Irwin, S., T. Krukemyer, and C. R. Zulauf, " Are Public Commodity Pools a Good Investment, " in Peters, C.C. ed. *Managed futures*: Performance Evaluation and Analysis of Commodity Funds, Pools and Accounts (Probus Publishing, 1992), pp 405-433.

McCarthy, D.., T. Schneeweis, and R. Spurgin, "Investment in CTAs: An Alternative Managed Futures Investment," *The Journal of Derivatives* (Forthcoming, 1996).

Peck, A.E. ed., *Selected Writings on Futures Markets.* Vol. 1-5 (Chicago Board of Trade., 1995).

Peters, C.C. ed. *Managed futures: Performance Evaluation and Analysis of Commodity Funds, Pools and Accounts* (Probus Publishing, 1992).

Schneeweis, T., U. Savanayana, and D. McCarthy, "Alternative Commodity Trading Vehicles: A Performance Analysis," *The Journal of Futures Markets* (August, 1991), pp 475-490.

Schneeweis, T., U. Savanayana and D. McCarthy. "Multi-Manager Commodity Portfolios: A Risk/ Return Analysis," in C. Epstein ed. *Managed Futures* (Wiley, 1992), pp 81-102.

Sharpe, W. "The Sharpe Ratio," *The Journal of Portfolio Management*," (Fall, 1994).

Thaler R, *The Winners Curse: Paradoxes and Anomalies of Economic Life*, (The Free Press, 1992).

APPENDIX I

Individual Accounts represent about 30 percent of all managed accounts. They are usually opened by institutional investors or high-net-worth individuals. These funds usually require a substantial capital investment so that the advisor is able to diversify his trading among a large number of market positions. An individual account enables the institutional investor to customize the account to his own specifications.

Private Pools currently represent about 55 percent of all managed futures accounts. This type of account commingles money from several investors, usually into a limited partnership. Most of these pools have minimum investments ranging from approximately $25,000 to $250,000. These futures partnerships usually allow for admission/ redemption on a monthly or quarterly basis. The main advantage of private pools is the economy of scale that can be achieved for middle-sized investors. A pool also may be structured with multiple trading advisors and trading approaches, providing the investor with maximum diversification. Because of the lower administrative and marketing costs, private pools have historically performed better than public funds.

Public Funds or Pools currently represent about 15 percent of all managed accounts. The advantage of public funds is that they provide a way for small investors to participate in an investment vehicle.

Commodity Trading Advisors (CTAs) are responsible for the actual trading of the managed account. The two major types of advisors are technical traders and fundamental traders. Technical traders may use computer software programs to follow pricing trends and perform quantitative analysis. Fundamental traders forecast prices by analysis of supply and demand factors and other market information.

Futures Commission Merchants (FCMs) are the brokerage firms that execute, clear, and carry CTA directed trades on the various exchanges. Many of these firms also act as CPOs and trading managers, providing administrative reports on investment performance. Additionally, they may offer managed future funds as an alternative investment opportunity to their customers.

Commodity Pool Operators (CPOs) assemble public funds or private pools. There are approximately 1,215 registered with the NFA. In the United States, this is usually in the form of limited partnerships. Most commodity pool operators hire independent CTAs to make the daily trading decisions. The CPO may distribute the product directly or act as a wholesaler to the broker/dealer community.

Investment Consultants can be a valuable institutional investor resource for learning about managed futures alternatives and in helping to implement the managed fund program.

Trading Managers or 'Manager of Managers" are available to assist institutional investors in selecting CTAs from the more than 2,500 registered with the National Futures Association (NFA). These managers have developed sophisticated methods of analyzing CTA performance records so that they can recommend and structure a portfolio of trading advisors.

* These descriptions are from the CBOT "Managed Futures an Alternative Investment Opportunity" [1994].

APPENDIX II

ALTERNATIVE COMMODITY AND MANAGED FUTURES INDICES

Dow Jones Futures and Spot Commodity Index is comprised of twelve commodities: cattle, coffee, copper, corn, cotton, gold, hogs, lumber, silver, soybeans, sugar, and wheat. The weightings of the indices is neutral; that is, each commodity's price on a given day is divided by its price on the base date and the results are totaled. The total is divided by twelve and multiplied by 100 to yield the index. To estimate the price of a commodity five months in the future, two contract months are used, one expiring in fewer than 150 days and one expiring in more than 150 days. It is assumed that each contract expires on the 15th of its delivery month. For each commodity, weights are assigned to the two contracts, based on the number of days between the 150th and the theoretical expiration date of the contract. Then the price of each contract is multiplied by its weight, the results are added, and the sum is divided by the number of days between the expiration dates of the two contracts. The result is the estimated price of the commodity for delivery in exactly five months, or 150 days.

Commodity Research Bureau Index (CRB) futures price index represents an unweighted geometric average of 21 component commodity prices. Each of these 21 commodity prices has been arithmetically averaged for all actively traded contracts expiring on or before the end of the ninth calendar month from the current date, excluding noncycle months. After these two averaging techniques have been performed, the resulting value is converted to a percentage of the base year value.

Goldman Sachs Commodity Index (GSCI) is an arithmetic measure of the performance of actively traded, dollar-denominated nearby commodity futures contracts. As of January 9, 1995, there were 22 commodities in the index.

The weights assigned to individual commodities are based on a five-year moving average of world production. Weights are determined each July and are made effective the following January. All contracts are rolled on the fifth business day of the month prior to the expiration month of the contract. Subindices are calculated for agricultural, energy, industrial, livestock, and precious metals contracts. Two versions of the indices are available: a total return version, which assumes that capital sufficient to purchase the basket of commodities is invested at the risk-free rate, and a spot version, which only tracks movements in the futures prices. This study uses the total return measure.

JPMorgan Commodity Index (JPMCI) is comprised of 11 highly liquid industrial commodity futures contracts. It excludes "softs," relying exclusively on energy, precious metals, and industrial metals. The two nearby contracts for each commodity are used, and rolls are conducted over a five-day period from the fifth to the ninth business day of the month. Component weights are rebalanced monthly according to a scoring system that seeks to maximize risk-return performance, track unexpected changes in inflation, provide a hedge against stock and bond investments, and correlate with economic growth measures. Sub-indices for energy, precious metals, and industrial metals are also available. The JPMCI is published in both spot and total return formats. This study uses the total return measure. The JPMCI was officially launched on September 21, 1994.

Bankers Trust Commodity Index (BTCI) is based on spot rather than futures prices. It assumes ownership of a basket of five physical commodities: crude oil, gold, aluminum, heating oil, and silver. 55% of the weight is given to energy components, and the remaining 45% to the three metals. The basket is priced daily using spot quotes such as the London gold fix. Front-month futures quotes, which are equivalent to cash market quotes, are used for energy prices. BTCI thus reproduces the price changes of a basket of physical assets without the storage and holding costs. The BTCI was launched on July 18, 1994.

Mount Lucas (MLM) Index differs from other indices in two important ways. First, it allows both long and short positions in the underlying futures contracts. Second, it incorporates financial and currency futures (but not stock index futures) into the index, along with the commodities tracked by other indices. The index is an equally weighted average of the monthly returns from 25 separate futures contracts. Within each market (e.g., corn futures), the index will be long or short depending on whether the contract is above or below its trailing 12-month moving average. MLM is a total-return index. It was launched in May, 1989.

Managed Account Reports (MAR) tracks the performance of individual CTAs as well as CTA Funds and Pools that invest in individual CTAs. MAR produces several performance indices, the dominant being the CTA equal-weighted and dollar-weighted indices. MAR classifies CTAs into a number of different groups, and publishes each group's performance index. These groups are currency, energy, financial, diversified, discretionary, and trend-following. MAR also reports the following subindices for fund and pool performance: guaranteed, multi-advisor, single-advisor, private pools, and public pools.

Barclay Trading Group, publisher of the Barclay Managed Futures Report, also creates CTA performance indices. Indices are based on monthly returns of CTAs with established track records. Barclay publishes an equal weighted index of all CTAs as well as the following subindices: agricultural, currency, diversified, energy, financial/metal, discretionary, and systematic.

TASS offers historical managed futures performance similar to MAR or Barclays. It publishes a dollar weighted CTA index and one subindex of currency CTAs. Additional indices and subindices will be available in the future.

Hedge Fund Research, EACM, Van Hedge and MAR offers historical managed futures/hedge fund performance on an array of indices and subindices designed to capture the return to unique managed futures/hedge fund strategies. These indices include relative value, event-driven, equity hedge funds, global asset allocators and short selling. Subindices include long/short equity, convertible hedge, bond hedge, rotational, deal arbitrage, bankruptcy, and multi-event. For managed futures, the principal subindices include discretionary and systematic groups.

APPENDIX III. RISK AND RETURN MEASURES

The risk and return measures used in this analysis are consistent industry definitions for investment analysis for traditional and alternative investment media. The following return and risk measures are used to identify the risk factor for evaluating the risk/return benefit of managed futures performance:

Measure of Return:

Returns: Determined as the logarithmic monthly holding period returns and are presented on as annualized logarithmic returns. For multi-asset CTA portfolio, efficient frontier and relative return after ranking on traditional asset, arithmetic returns are used.

Measure of Volatility:

Standard Deviation: A measure of the dispersion (distance) of the observations (return performance) from the mean (or average) observation. This measure is expressed as a percentage on an annualized basis.

Sharpe Ratio: A ratio that represents a rate of return adjusted for risk (standard deviation), as is generally calculated as ((Annual rate of return - Risk free rate of return)/ Annualized Standard Deviation). In this paper, except for excess break-even ratios, the Sharpe ratio is given as a "return information ratio" that is, the Annualized rate of return/Annualized Standard Deviation. For a complete discussion of the Sharpe ratio see Sharpe (1994).

Minimum Monthly Return: The lowest return observed in any month over the time period analyzed and is expressed on a annualized basis.

Maximum Monthly Return: The highest return observed in any month over the time period analyzed and is expressed on a annualized basis.

Correlation: The standardized comovement of managed futures benchmark (e.g., MAR$CTA) and an alternative investment benchmark measured from their respective historical averages.

Excess Annual Break-even: Various models have been proposed to measure the possible impact of adding a security onto an existing portfolio and its impact on that portfolios risk and return. For instance, simple break-even models have been suggested which indicate whether adding an asset to an existing portfolio increases its Sharpe ratio. The break-even (Rc) and excess break-even rate of return (EBK) is computed as follows:

$$R_c = \left(\frac{R_p - R_F}{\sigma_P}\right)(P_{CP})\sigma_C + R_F \qquad EBK = R_c - \left(\left(\frac{R_p - R_F}{\sigma_P}\right)(P_{CP})\sigma_C + R_F\right)$$

where, R_c = Break-even rate of return required for CTA index to improve Sharpe ratio of index p

R_f = Riskless rate of return

R_p = Rate of return on alternative index p

P_{cp} = Correlation coefficient between CTA index c and alternative benchmark index p

σ_c = Standard deviation of CTA index c

σ_p = Standard deviation of alternative index p

APPENDIX IV

PERFORMANCE MEASURES FOR MANAGED FUTURES, REGIONAL, COUNTRY AND U.S. MUTUAL FUND PERFORMANCE

PERFORMANCE MEASURES FOR MANAGED FUTURES AND INDIVIDUAL COUNTRIES

ELEVEN YEAR PERFORMANCE: JANUARY, 1985 TO DECEMBER, 1995

MSCI Country Stock Indices

	MAR$CTA	MSFRNC$	MSWGRM$	MSJPAN$	MSSWIT$	MSUTDK$	MSUSAM$
Average Annual Return	15.81%	18.45%	17.03%	14.24%	20.95%	16.59%	15.14%
Annual Standard Deviation	14.58%	22.57%	23.12%	26.25%	18.71%	20.82%	14.94%
Avg.Ret/Std. Dev.	1.08	0.82	0.74	0.54	1.12	0.80	1.01
Minimum Monthly Return	-6.37%	-20.33%	-19.40%	-21.55%	-19.40%	-24.25%	-23.85%
Maximum Monthly Return	17.83%	19.09%	18.43%	21.72%	15.43%	14.81%	12.47%
Correlation with MAR	1.00	0.16	-0.05	0.06	-0.04	0.02	0.12
Excess Annual Breakeven	0.00%	8.49%	10.16%	9.53%	10.29%	9.68%	8.74%

Salomon Brothers Country Government Bond Indices

	MAR$CTA	FRSBGVT$	BDSBGVT$	JPSBGVT$	SWSBGVT$	UKSBGVT$	USSBGOVT
Average Annual Return	15.81%	16.57%	14.65%	15.01%	12.85%	13.60%	9.89%
Annual Standard Deviation	14.58%	12.27%	13.35%	14.60%	13.77%	15.22%	5.12%
Avg.Ret/Std. Dev.	1.08	1.35	1.10	1.03	0.93	0.89	1.93
Minimum Monthly Return	-6.37%	-10.36%	-10.79%	-11.90%	-8.47%	-10.01%	-2.42%
Maximum Monthly Return	18%	11%	10%	15%	11%	15%	5%
Correlation with MAR	1.00	0.17	0.13	0.12	0.15	0.04	0.18
Excess Annual Breakeven	0.00%	7.67%	8.59%	8.69%	8.68%	9.53%	7.76%

Stock and Bond Portfolio

	MAR$CTA	FRANCE$	WEST GERMANY	JAPAN$	SWITZER-LAND$	UNITED KING-DOM$	USA
Average Annual Return	15.81%	18.08%	16.51%	15.20%	17.72%	15.61%	13.03%
Annual Standard Deviation	14.58%	15.87%	16.17%	18.72%	13.93%	16.34%	9.13%
Avg.Ret/Std. Dev.	1.08	1.14	1.02	0.81	1.27	0.96	1.43
Minimum Monthly Return	-6.37%	-10.83%	-13.12%	-14.87%	-8.79%	-9.32%	-10.54%
Maximum Monthly Return	18%	14%	13%	17%	11%	15%	8%
Correlation with MAR	1.00	0.19	0.01	0.09	0.04	0.03	0.16
Excess Annual Breakeven	0.00%	7.72%	9.70%	9.15%	9.32%	9.55%	8.04%

Regional MSCI Stock Indices and Salomon Brothers World Government Bond Index

	MAR$CTA	MSWRLD$	MSEAFE$	MSEROP$	MSPACF$	MSFARE$	WDSBGVT$
Average Annual Return	15.81%	14.86%	15.96%	17.62%	14.59%	14.66%	12.17%
Annual Standard Deviation	14.58%	14.85%	18.76%	17.42%	23.95%	24.83%	7.22%
Avg.Ret/Std. Dev.	1.08	1.00	0.85	1.01	0.61	0.59	1.68
Minimum Monthly Return	-6.37%	-18.59%	-15.07%	-21.05%	-19.84%	-20.61%	-4.07%
Maximum Monthly Return	17.83%	11.13%	14.51%	11.26%	19.58%	21.09%	6.52%
Correlation with MAR	1.00	0.08	0.04	0.02	0.05	0.06	0.17
Excess Annual Breakeven	0.00%	9.14%	9.48%	9.59%	9.53%	9.51%	7.69%

Regional Stock and World Bond Portfolio

	MAR$CTA	World$	EAFE$	EUROPE$	PACFIC$	FAR EAST$
Average Annual Return	15.81%	13.88%	14.58%	15.47%	14.08%	14.16%
Annual Standard Deviation	14.58%	9.89%	12.29%	11.37%	14.90%	15.41%
Avg.Ret/Std. Dev.	1.08	1.40	1.19	1.36	0.94	0.92
Minimum Monthly Return	-6.37%	-6.51%	-7.41%	-7.70%	-10.92%	-11.30%
Maximum Monthly Return	17.83%	7.95%	10.07%	8.92%	13.02%	13.91%
Correlation with MAR	1.00	0.12	0.08	0.07	0.08	0.09
Excess Annual Breakeven	0.00%	8.40%	8.98%	8.97%	9.14%	9.12%

SIX YEAR PERFORMANCE: JANUARY, 1990 TO DECEMBER, 1995

MSCI Country Stock Indices

	MAR$CTA	MSFRNC$	MSWGRM$	MSJPAN$	MSSWIT$	MSUTDK$	MSUSAM$
Average Annual Return	13.43%	5.75%	6.76%	-2.77%	17.71%	10.07%	12.69%
Annual Standard Deviation	11.49%	18.08%	19.73%	28.20%	16.69%	17.27%	11.64%
Avg.Ret/Std. Dev.	1.17	0.32	0.34	(0.10)	1.06	0.58	1.09
Minimum Monthly Return	-6.19%	-13.61%	-19.40%	-21.55%	-12.44%	-9.30%	-9.59%
Maximum Monthly Return	13.51%	12.42%	12.19%	21.72%	15.43%	13.89%	10.82%
Correlation with MAR	1.00	-0.06	-0.16	-0.04	-0.21	-0.26	-0.16
Excess Annual Breakeven	0.00%	7.42%	7.50%	7.29%	9.10%	8.14%	8.49%

Salomon Brothers Country Government Bond Indices

	MAR$CTA	FRSBGVT$	BDSBGVT$	JPSBGVT$	SWSBGVT$	UKSBGVT$	USSBGOVT
Average Annual Return	13.43%	13.03%	11.54%	13.35%	12.17%	10.90%	8.85%
Annual Standard Deviation	11.49%	10.99%	11.38%	13.24%	11.96%	12.61%	4.37%
Avg.Ret/Std. Dev.	1.17	1.18	1.01	1.01	1.02	0.86	2.03
Minimum Monthly Return	-6.19%	-10.36%	-10.79%	-11.90%	-8.47%	-8.49%	-2.34%
Maximum Monthly Return	13.51%	8.69%	8.72%	15.21%	11.17%	8.23%	3.99%
Correlation with MAR	1.00	0.21	0.23	0.20	0.25	-0.03	0.14
Excess Annual Breakeven	0.00%	5.88%	6.13%	6.14%	5.97%	7.57%	6.41%

Stock and Bond Portfolio

	MAR$CTA	FRANCE$	WEST GERMANY	JAPAN$	SWITZER-LAND$	UNITED KING-DOM$	USA
Average Annual Return	13.43%	9.33%	9.29%	5.27%	15.50%	10.61%	11.09%
Annual Standard Deviation	11.49%	13.17%	13.88%	18.98%	12.61%	14.20%	7.64%
Avg.Ret/Std. Dev.	1.17	0.71	0.67	0.28	1.23	0.75	1.45
Minimum Monthly Return	-6.19%	-8.81%	-12.73%	-14.87%	-8.79%	-8.00%	-5.86%
Maximum Monthly Return	13.51%	10.48%	8.95%	16.85%	10.49%	11.38%	7.55%
Correlation with MAR	1.00	0.04	-0.03	0.03	-0.05	-0.19	-0.10
Excess Annual Breakeven	0.00%	7.32%	7.52%	7.44%	7.83%	8.13%	8.17%

Regional MSCI Stock Indices and Salomon Brothers World Government Bond Index

	MAR$CTA	MSWRLD$	MSEAFE$	MSEROP$	MSPACF$	MSFARE$	WDSBGVT$
Average Annual Return	13.43%	6.68%	3.32%	8.96%	-0.87%	-1.35%	10.60%
Annual Standard Deviation	11.49%	14.05%	18.74%	15.06%	25.35%	26.39%	6.24%
Avg.Ret/Std. Dev.	1.17	0.48	0.18	0.59	-0.03	-0.05	1.70
Minimum Monthly Return	-6.19%	-11.12%	-14.97%	-12.48%	-19.84%	-20.61%	-3.70%
Maximum Monthly Return	13.51%	10.03%	14.51%	8.44%	19.58%	21.09%	5.77%
Correlation with MAR	1.00	-0.16	-0.13	-0.23	-0.05	-0.05	0.21
Excess Annual Breakeven	0.00%	7.52%	7.22%	7.95%	7.26%	7.29%	5.65%

Regional Stock and World Bond Portfolio

	MAR$CTA	World$	EAFE$	EUROPE$	PACFIC$	FAR EAST$
Average Annual Return	13.43%	8.62%	6.93%	9.89%	4.96%	4.76%
Annual Standard Deviation	11.49%	9.48%	11.99%	10.05%	15.32%	15.90%
Avg.Ret/Std. Dev.	1.17	0.91	0.58	0.98	0.32	0.30
Minimum Monthly Return	-6.19%	-5.65%	-7.41%	-6.14%	-10.92%	-11.30%
Maximum Monthly Return	13.51%	7.04%	10.07%	6.46%	13.02%	13.91%
Correlation with MAR	1.00	-0.07	-0.06	-0.13	-0.01	0.00
Excess Annual Breakeven	0.00%	7.64%	7.49%	8.01%	7.42%	7.43%

Eleven Year Performance: January, 1985 to December, 1995

	MAR$CTA	Growth & Income	Growth	Equity Income	Aggressive	Small Company	Section Finance	Section Metals	Section Nat.Res.	Section Tech.	Section Utilities
Average Annual Return	15.8%	12.9%	13.8%	12.4%	14.8%	14.6%	16.4%	5.1%	9.4%	16.7%	11.6%
Annual Standard Deviation	14.6%	12.9%	15.1%	10.5%	19.6%	17.3%	16.6%	27.4%	16.5%	21.9%	9.3%
Avg.Ret/Std. Dev.	1.08	1.00	0.92	1.18	0.76	0.85	0.99	0.19	0.57	0.76	1.24
Minimum Monthly Return	-6.4%	-21.3%	-25.6%	-16.4%	-33.7%	-29.2%	-22.9%	-34.8%	-33.5%	-33.1%	-7.5%
Maximum Monthly Return	17.8%	9.9%	11.2%	7.4%	13.5%	11.0%	11.2%	24.3%	12.8%	16.9%	7.4%
Correlation with MAR	1.00	0.11	0.10	0.10	0.07	0.05	0.05	0.10	0.10	0.05	0.10
Excess Annual Breakeven	0.0%	9.0%	9.1%	8.9%	9.3%	9.4%	9.4%	9.9%	9.5%	9.5%	8.9%

	MAR$CTA	Government Bond	Corporate Bond	Multi-Sector	Asset Allocator	Balanced	Convert. Bond	Corporate High Yield	Multi-Asset Global
Average Annual Return	13.4%	8.6%	9.2%	9.6%	10.9%	11.9%	10.8%	10.1%	12.1%
Annual Standard Deviation	11.5%	4.4%	4.1%	6.0%	7.3%	9.0%	10.0%	6.1%	8.6%
Avg.Ret/Std. Dev.	1.17	1.99	2.21	1.59	1.49	1.32	1.08	1.66	1.42
Minimum Monthly Return	-6.2%	-3.3%	-2.6%	-4.8%	-6.8%	-13.0%	-17.7%	-5.1%	-16.0%
Maximum Monthly Return	13.5%	3.9%	4.5%	5.8%	6.9%	7.1%	6.9%	6.8%	7.0%
Correlation with MAR	1.00	0.14	0.17	0.21	0.16	0.13	0.08	0.04	0.19
Excess Annual Breakeven	0.0%	8.6%	7.9%	8.0%	8.2%	8.6%	9.3%	9.4%	7.8%

Six Year Performance: January, 1990 to December, 1995

	MAR$CTA	Growth & Income	Growth	Equity Income	Aggressive	Small Company	Section Finance	Section Metals	Section Nat.Res.	Section Tech.	Section Utilities
Average Annual Return	13.4%	10.9%	11.8%	10.6%	14.8%	14.1%	17.7%	0.2%	5.4%	21.2%	9.2%
Annual Standard Deviation	11.5%	10.6%	12.3%	8.9%	16.5%	15.1%	15.3%	24.0%	12.2%	19.5%	8.1%
Avg.Ret/Std. Dev.	1.17	1.02	0.96	1.19	0.89	0.93	1.16	0.01	0.44	1.09	1.14
Minimum Monthly Return	-6.2%	-8.4%	-9.5%	-7.0%	-12.6%	-12.8%	-10.7%	-14.7%	-7.3%	-14.2%	-5.5%
Maximum Monthly Return	13.5%	9.6%	10.8%	7.2%	12.0%	10.0%	11.2%	13.3%	8.2%	13.3%	4.7%
Correlation with MAR	1.00	-0.18	-0.21	-0.16	-0.25	-0.27	-0.20	0.11	-0.08	-0.31	-0.01
Excess Annual Breakeven	0.0%	8.4%	8.6%	8.4%	9.0%	9.1%	9.2%	7.7%	7.4%	10.2%	7.5%

	MAR$CTA	Government Bond	Corporate Bond	Multi-Sector	Asset Allocator	Balanced	Convert. Bond	Corporate High Yield	Multi-Asset Global
Average Annual Return	13.4%	7.3%	8.0%	9.2%	10.0%	10.0%	10.4%	10.8%	8.1%
Annual Standard Deviation	11.5%	3.6%	3.6%	4.6%	6.4%	7.6%	8.1%	6.6%	6.0%
Avg.Ret/Std. Dev.	1.17	2.02	2.22	1.99	1.55	1.32	1.29	1.63	1.34
Minimum Monthly Return	-6.2%	-1.9%	-2.0%	-3.0%	-4.2%	-5.7%	-6.1%	-5.1%	-3.8%
Maximum Monthly Return	13.5%	3.0%	3.2%	3.9%	6.9%	7.1%	6.2%	6.8%	4.4%
Correlation with MAR	1.00	0.11	0.12	-0.02	-0.09	-0.13	-0.21	-0.16	-0.07
Excess Annual Breakeven	0.0%	7.0%	6.6%	7.6%	8.1%	8.2%	8.8%	8.7%	7.7%

* Fund descriptions are detailed in Morningstar Mutual Fund Guides. Indices are equal weighted and are derived from data from Morningstar Ondisc.

7 MANAGED FUTURES AND HEDGE FUND INVESTMENT FOR DOWNSIDE EQUITY RISK MANAGEMENT

THOMAS SCHNEEWEIS
University of Massachusetts

RICHARD SPURGIN
Clark University

MARK POTTER
Babson University

INTRODUCTION

During the past decades, the investment management industry has undergone numerous changes. New forms of investment products have come into existence to meet the needs of changing financial regulation, information technology, and investor demands. Today, most investors concentrate on traditional investment vehicles such as stocks, bonds, and currencies. However, an increasing number of investors use managed futures[1] investment vehicles such as direct investment with commodity trading advisors (CTAs), or purchase of commodity funds and pools[2] and hedge funds. Commodity trading advisors use global futures and options markets as their investment universe. Hedge funds trade in these markets as well as the underlying security and physical commodity markets.

While academic and practitioner literature has shown that investment in managed futures\hedge funds offers investment benefits (e.g., increased Sharpe ratio) both as stand-alone investments and as additions to existing traditional assets or asset portfolios, managed futures and hedge funds investment may also offer unique risk and return opportunities in 'downside' risk control. [3] Specifically, in contrast to passive equity index investment, the differing managed futures/hedge fund investment styles enable investors to create managed futures/hedge fund and equity portfolios which offer positive returns in upside equity market cycles while offering positive returns or limiting losses in downside equity markets. Results presented in this paper indicate that, while managed futures returns are uncorrelated with the equity market on an overall basis, they are negatively correlated when the stock market posts their largest declines and positively correlated when equities have their largest gains. Since this pattern is similar to the payoff of many equity risk management strategies, the return of a mixed equity and managed futures portfolio is compared to a traditional protective put equity strategy. Results show that, for the period studied, an equity/CTA portfolio outperforms an equity/at-the-money put portfolio, such that a CTA investment may offer downside equity protection at lower cost than a protective put.[4]

ECONOMIC BASIS FOR MANAGED FUTURES RETURNS

While futures and options markets provide economic benefits to the underlying users of their markets, traders in futures and options markets are often viewed as operating in a zero sum game; that is, where investor losses equal investor gains on any given day and the long term return to a managed futures position is simply the risk-free return on invested capital. However, the existence of a zero sum game does not restrict commodity trading advisors from obtaining superior risk and return tradeoffs relative to the assets which underlying the traded futures and options markets. First, cost of carry and put/call parity models insure that CTAs can create futures and options positions similar if not identical investment positions to the deliverable cash instruments. Given the lower transaction costs of trading in futures and options markets, these 'synthetic' cash position returns may be superior to the returns of underlying cash markets for comparable long (short) positions. Secondly, institutional characteristics and differential carry costs among investors may permit CTAs to take advantage of short-term pricing differences between theoretically identical futures, options and cash market positions. Thus, for CTAs, in contrast to a large number of traditional security traders, opportunities exist for arbitrage profits to be made under varying market conditions.

Arbitrage profits and risk/return positions which replicate the underlying cash markets, however, are not the only potential benefits of managed futures. Speculative positions are often required as a means of meeting the hedging demands of cash market participants. This hedging demand may create investment situations were hedgers are required to offer speculators a 'risk' premia for holding open long(short) positions even in a world of arbitrage traders. This positive return to holding open futures positions which are opposite that of the desired hedgers may result positive rates of return in the underlying futures and options markets. This return to traders for offering liquidity to hedgers desiring to limit losses may exist not only in futures markets but may exist in a wide range of derivative products. Lastly evidence exists in academic literature [Chan et al. 1996; Jagadeesh, 1990] that due to institutional factors (e.g., end of month window dressing, portfolio rebalancing, specialist risk positions, government actions), markets may trend for varying time periods in various markets. Low transaction costs combined with the ability to go short may permit the use of technical trading rules by managed futures to obtain positive returns in markets which, for short time periods, may be overvalued. In fact, these market cycles, embedded in cash market trading styles, has been used to explain some portion of the return to a technically based commodity futures trading system (BARRA/MLM reports).

PATTERN OF MANAGED FUTURES RETURNS

Academic and practitioner literature [Schneeweis, 1996] has shown that investment in managed futures may offers investment benefits both as stand-alone investments and as additions to existing traditional assets or asset portfolios. Traditional analysis of managed futures performance, however, is concentrated in comparing managed futures in terms of return and standard deviation[5], and measuring the risk/return contribution of managed futures indices to a portfolio of traditional assets. Exhibit 1 shows the relative performance of Managed Accounts Reports dollar-weighted CTA index, the S&P 500, the Morgan Stanley Capital International equity index (MSCI), and Fidelity Magellan fund for the period 1985-1995. Managed futures, represented by a dollar weighted portfolio of commodity trading advisors compiled by Managed Accounts Reports (MAR$CTA index), has a stand-alone performance similar to that of traditional equity investment vehicles (SP500, MSCI, and the Fidelity Magellan fund) while having less negative minimum and higher maximum returns. For the period 1985-1995 MAR$CTA had an annualized Sharpe ratio of 1.08 while the Sharpe ratios for the SP500, MSCI, and Magellan fund were 1.00, 1.00 and 1.04 respectively. The minimum (maximum) monthly return for the MAR$CTA was -6.37% (17.83%) while the minimum (maximum) returns were more negative and less positive for the SP500 (-24.31% and 12.66%), the MSCI (-18.59% and 11.13%), and Magellan fund (-29.85% and 12.22%).

EXHIBIT 1 PERFORMANCE MEASURES FOR MANAGED FUTURES AND OTHER U.S. INDEXES
JANUARY 1985 TO DECEMBER 1995

1/85 to 12/95	MAR$CTA	SP500	MSCI	Fidelity Magellan
Average Annual Return	15.81	15.11	14.86	17.96
Annual Standard Deviation	14.58	15.06	14.85	17.20
Sharpe Ratio	1.08	1.00	1.00	1.04
Minimum Monthly Return	-6.37	-24.31	-18.59	-29.85
Maximum Monthly Return	17.83	12.66	11.13	12.22
Correlation with MAR	1.00	0.12	0.08	0.10
Excess Annual Breakeven	0.00	8.79	9.14	8.75

In addition, using traditional excess break-even analysis, results in Exhibit 1 also show that the MAR$CTA increases the Sharpe ratio of comparison stand-alone investments when considered as an as addition to existing equity portfolios.[6] In all cases, the excess annualized break-even rate was greater than 8%. This is greater than the cost generally charged by multi-advisor CTA portfolio managers for creating a multi-advisor CTA portfolio (i.e., 1-2%). As mentioned previously, a reason for the diversification benefits of managed futures is the low correlation of managed futures products with many traditional asset vehicles. This is also supported in Exhibit 1, where the correlation of MAR$CTA with the comparison assets is approximately zero (S&P500 (.12), MSCI (.08), and Magellan fund (.10)). This low correlation is due in part to the diversity of markets which managed futures can trade as well as the variety of trades available (e.g., short positions and option positions). The wide variety of markets and styles is indicated by the number of indices compiled by Managed Accounts Reports (MAR). MAR classifies CTAs into a number of different subclasses. These groups are currency, energy, financial, diversified, stock, and trend-following. For hedge funds, firms such as Managed Accounts Reports and Hedge Fund Advisors also produce performance indices for hedge funds specializing in financial, diversified, discretionary, and short-selling investments or trading styles.[7]

COMMODITY TRADING ADVISORS AS DOWNSIDE RISK PROTECTION

While the correlation between managed account performance and traditional asset classes is low when measured over the entire periods, the greatest investor benefit to managed account investment may be their ability in unique investment periods to offer positive returns when the underlying cash markets experience negative returns. In Exhibit 2, for instance, results for the period 1985-1995 show that the MAR$CTA index outperformed the S&P500 index in each of the 12 worst S&P500 return months.[8] Moreover, the negative correlation (-.12) in Group 1, which contains the 12 lowest equity return months, indicates that lower returns in this group for the SP500 are offset by higher returns for the MAR$CTA index. In contrast, the positive correlation (.46) in Group 11, the highest 12 return months, means the higher the S&P500 return in the group, the higher the MAR$CTA index return. This result, which covers the period 1985-1995, indicates that a diversified portfolio of managed futures traders who trade over a large range of alternative styles and products may provide potential for downside risk protection for equity products such as the S&P500 while offering upside potential in months with high S&P500 returns.[9]

EXHIBIT 2 PERFORMANCE OF MANAGED FUTURES RELATIVE TO PROTECTIVE PUT

	Portfolio Performance by Group				*Relative Portfolio Performance by Group*							
					MAR > SP500		SP/MAR > SP/Put		SP/Put > SP		SP/MAR > SP500	
Group	**SP500**	**MAR**	**SP/MAR**	**SP/Put**	**Months**	**%**	**Months**	**%**	**Months**	**%**	**Months**	**%**
1	-7.46	2.57	-2.45	-2.23	12	100	8	67	12	100	12	100
2	-2.57	-0.40	-1.49	-1.62	8	67	7	58	11	92	8	67
3	-1.20	0.70	-0.25	-1.71	9	75	10	83	4	33	9	75
4	-0.10	1.04	0.47	-1.64	7	58	11	92	0	0	7	58
5	0.91	1.31	1.11	-1.23	7	58	12	100	0	0	7	58
6	1.58	0.01	0.79	-0.25	4	33	9	75	0	0	4	33
7	2.37	0.66	1.52	0.52	3	25	9	75	0	0	3	25
8	3.16	0.31	1.74	1.38	1	8	6	50	0	0	1	8
9	4.04	1.33	2.69	1.85	3	25	8	67	0	0	3	25
10	5.00	2.39	3.69	2.78	3	25	7	58	0	0	3	25
11	8.11	4.58	6.34	5.64	1	8	9	75	0	0	1	8

Correlation between SP500 and MAR	
Group 1	-0.12
Group 11	0.46

Group: Group of 12 months ranked by SP500 Return. Group 1 contains lowest returns, Group 11 the highest
SP500: Standard and Poors 500 Total Return Index
MAR: MAR Dollar-Weighted CTA Index
SP/Put: SP500 index combined with 1-month at-the money put option on index
SP/MAR: Portfolio with equal weights in SP500 and MAR

Results in Exhibit 2 also indicate that managed futures provide returns similar to those obtained through traditional downside risk protection strategies such as purchasing put options. Specifically, the performance of a combination S&P500 (50%) and MAR$CTA (50%) portfolio is similar to that of an S&P500 at-the-money protective put strategy. For the protective put strategy, an at-the-money put value was derived with a rolling 35 day maturity using implied volatility estimates from Salomon Brothers. The pricing model used is the Black-Scholes dividend-adjusted option pricing model.[10]

EXHIBIT 3 COMPARISON OF MANAGED FUTURES AND PROTECTIVE PUT STRATEGIES

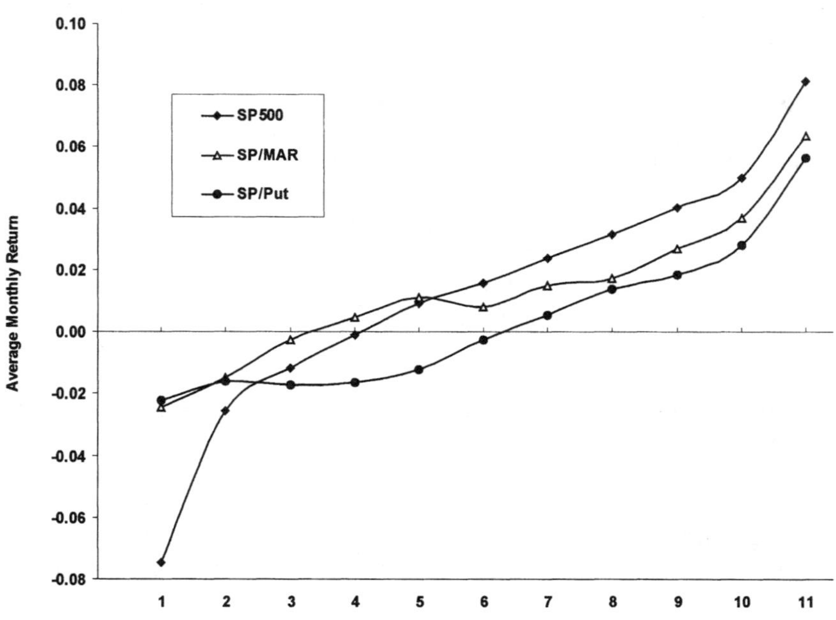

Results in Exhibit 2 show the number and percentage of months in each group that the MAR$CTA (MAR), the S&P500 plus MAR$CTA portfolio (SP/MAR), and the protective put strategy (S&P/Put) outperform the S&P500 index. As expected, the SP/Put portfolio strictly dominates the S&P500 in the lowest return group while it fails to outperform in any months in the high return group. Similarly, the S&P/MAR portfolio dominates the S&P500 in the lowest S&P500 return group and, in contrast to the S&P/Put portfolio, also provides higher returns than the S&P500 in some of the months when S&P500 posts its highest returns. Thus the S&P/MAR portfolio may provide both downside protection as well as upside return potential during periods in which the S&P500 performs well. Of special note is that the S&P/MAR portfolio strictly dominates the S&P/Put portfolio in group 5 for which the return for the S&P500 reflects its average monthly return. If, as reported in Exhibit 1, the mean return of the S&P500 is similar to the mean return of the MAR$CTA index, then a portfolio comprised of the S&P500 and the MAR$CTA will have a similar return to an all-equity portfolio. Moreover, this portfolio will always dominate a SP/Put portfolio, whose expected return is about half the expected return of the S&P500 (because the put delta of -1/2 means the instantaneous rate of return of the portfolio is 1/2 the return of the underlying security). For the entire period, the Sharpe ratio of the SP/MAR strategy was the highest (1.39) of any of the comparison benchmarks (S&P500, 1.00; MAR$CTA, 1.08; S&P/Put, .47).[11]

The pattern of relative return dominance is shown in Exhibit 3. After ranking on S&P500 returns in ascending order and separating the data into eleven 12 month periods, average returns in each group for the S&P500, the MAR$CTA, the S&P/Put and the S&P/MAR portfolio are illustrated. For the period, 1985-1995, the S&P/MAR

EXHIBIT 4A PERFORMANCE OF MANAGED FUTURES RELATIVE TO PROTECTIVE PUT STRATEGY, 1994-1995

	Portfolio Performance by Group				*Relative Portfolio Performance by Group*							
					MAR > SP500		SP/MAR > SP/Put		SP/Put > SP		SP/MAR > SP500	
Group	**SP500**	**MAR**	**SP/MAR**	**SP/Put**	**Months**	**%**	**Months**	**%**	**Months**	**%**	**Months**	**%**
1	-2.72	1.25	-0.73	-1.23	6	100	5	83	5	83	6	100
2	1.45	0.95	1.20	-0.26	3	50	6	100	0	0	3	50
3	2.92	0.34	1.63	1.37	1	17	2	33	0	0	1	17
4	3.88	-0.35	1.76	2.46	1	17	2	33	0	0	1	17

Correlation between SP500 and MAR	
Group 1	-0.14
Group 4	-0.08

EXHIBIT 4B PERFORMANCE OF MAR STOCK SUBINDEX RELATIVE TO PROTECTIVE PUT STRATEGY, 1994-1995

	Portfolio Performance by Group				*Relative Portfolio Performance by Group*							
					MSTK > SP500		SP/MSK > SP/Put		SP/Put > SP		SP/MSK > SP500	
Group	**SP500**	**MSTK**	**SP/MSK**	**SP/Put**	**Months**	**%**	**Months**	**%**	**Months**	**%**	**Months**	**%**
1	-2.72	4.19	0.73	-1.23	6	100	6	100	5	83	6	100
2	1.45	1.32	1.39	-0.26	4	67	6	100	0	0	4	67
3	2.92	-2.81	0.06	1.37	0	0	1	17	0	0	0	0
4	3.88	-3.62	0.13	2.46	0	0	1	17	0	0	0	0

Correlation between SP500 and MSTK	
Group 1	-0.68
Group 4	-0.05

EXHIBIT 4C PERFORMANCE OF HFR SHORT SELLERS INDEX AND PROTECTIVE PUT STRATEGY, 1994-1995

	Portfolio Performance by Group				*Relative Portfolio Performance by Group*							
					HDG > SP500		SP/HDG > SP/Put		SP/Put > SP		SP/HDG > SP500	
Group	SP500	HDG	SP/HDG	SP/Put	Months	%	Months	%	Months	%	Months	%
1	-2.72	6.58	1.93	-1.23	5	83	5	83	5	83	5	83
2	1.45	1.67	1.56	-0.26	4	67	5	83	0	0	4	67
3	2.92	-5.66	-1.37	1.37	1	17	1	17	0	0	1	17
4	3.88	-4.43	-0.27	2.46	0	0	0	0	0	0	0	0

Correlation between SP500 and HDG	
Group 1	-0.40
Group 4	0.19

Group: Group of 6 mos. ranked by SP500 Return. Group 1 contains lowest returns, Group 4
SP500: Standard and Poors 500 Total Return Index
MAR: MAR Dollar-Weighted CTA Index
STK: MAR Hedge Fund Short Sellers Index
HDG: Hedge Fund Research (HFR) Short Sellers Index
SP/Put: SP500 Index combined with 1-month at-the money put option on
SP/(MAR/STK/HDG): Portfolio with equal weights in SP500 and comparison

portfolio dominates the returns the S&P/Put strategy except marginally for the lowest return group. It is of course important to point out that the performance of the equity/protective put position and the equity/managed futures position are not strictly comparable since the performance of the managed futures position is stochastic. The individual investor must determine whether the potential relative return compensates for the expected risk.

The recent performance for the period 1994-1995 is also consistent with performance over the longer 1985-1995 period. For the period 1994-1995, tests similar to those presented in Exhibit 2 are conducted for MAR$CTA. In Exhibit 4A, S&P500 returns are ranked from low to high and divided into four six month subperiods.

The number of months in which the MAR$CTA provide returns superior to the comparative asset or portfolio is given. As in Exhibit 2, in the low S&P500 return group the CTA and hedge fund vehicles outperformed the S&P500 at least 50% of the time. In contrast to Exhibit 2, however, for the high return groups, the MAR$ had negative average returns and rarely outperformed the S&P500. One reason for this differential performance is that over the 1994-1995 period the S&P500 performed exceptionally well. For instance, in 1995 the annual return of the S&P500 was 37.11% in contrast to its average annualized return from 1985 through 1995 of only 15%. In contrast the 1995 annual return for the MAR$CTA was 16% which is in line with its annual average since 1985 (15.5%).

EQUITY BASED COMMODITY TRADING ADVISORS /HEDGE FUNDS AS DOWNSIDE RISK PROTECTION

The MAR$CTA index reflects the returns of numerous CTAs whose trading area (e.g., metals, commodities) does not correspond directly to the comparison equity benchmarks. For the period 1994-1995 tests, similar to those presented in Exhibit 4A for the MAR$CTA index, are conducted for the MAR stock index trading advisors (MARSTK) index and the Hedge Fund Research Short-Sellers index (HFRSTK). In Exhibit 4B and 4C, S&P500 returns are ranked from low to high and divided into four six month

EXHIBIT 5A TOTAL RETURN OF S&P/MAR PORTFOLIO AND PROTECTIVE PUT STRATEGIES, 1994-1995

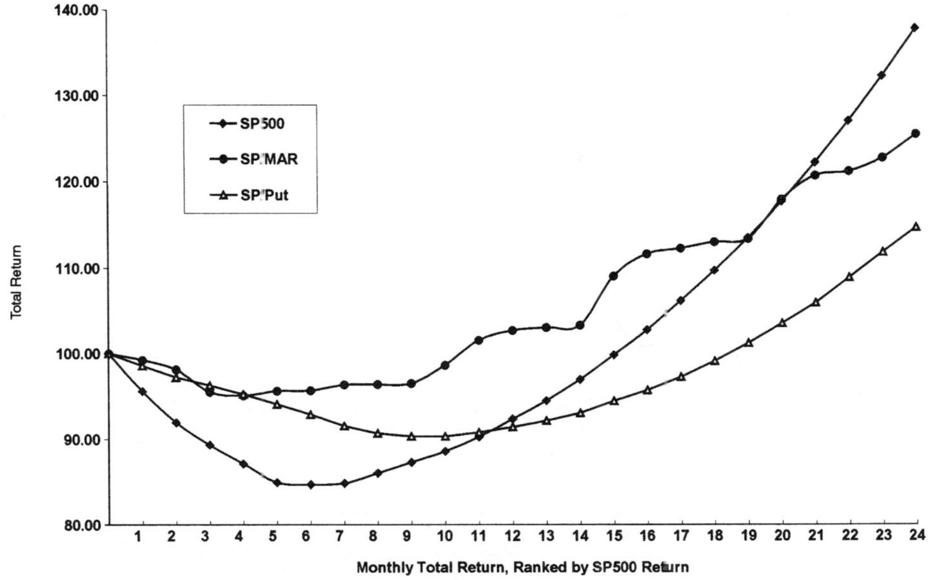

EXHIBIT 5B TOTAL RETURN OF MAR STOCK SUBINDEX AND PROTECTIVE PUT STRATEGIES, 1994-1995

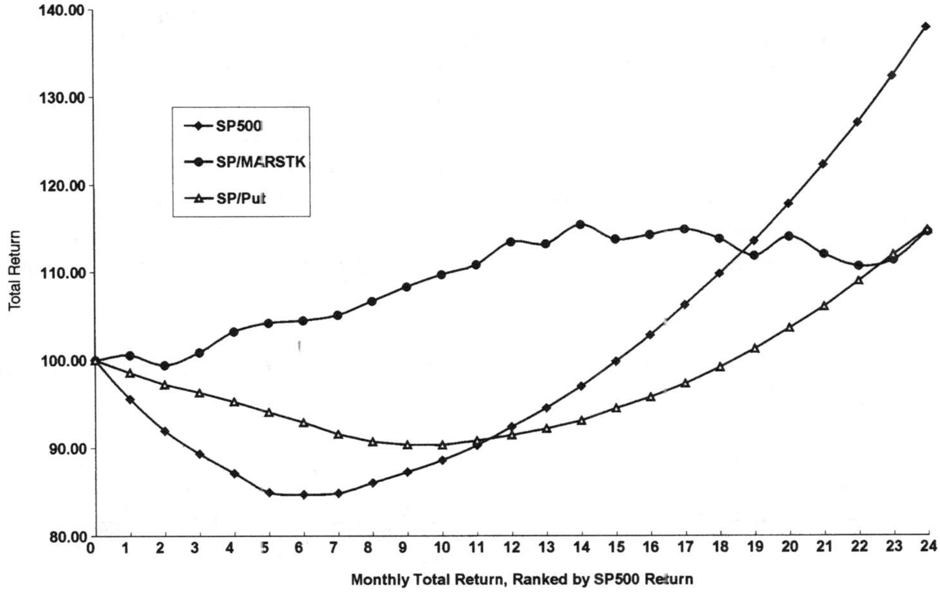

subperiods. The number of months in which the MARSTK (Exhibit 4B) and HFRSTK (Exhibit 4C) provide returns superior to the comparative index or portfolio is given.

Consistent with the MAR$CTA index in Exhibit 4A, both the MARSTK and HFRSTK have negative Pearson correlations with the S&P500 in the low return groups (MAR$CTA, -.14; MARSTK, -.68; HFRSTK, -.40). In the S&P500 high return months there is little evidence of correlation with the S&P500 for any of the comparison CTA or hedge fund indices (MAR$CTA, -.08; MARSTK, -.05; HFRSTK, .19). However,

EXHIBIT 5C TOTAL RETURN OF HFR SHORT SELLERS INDEX AND PROTECTIVE PUT STRATEGIES, 1994-1995

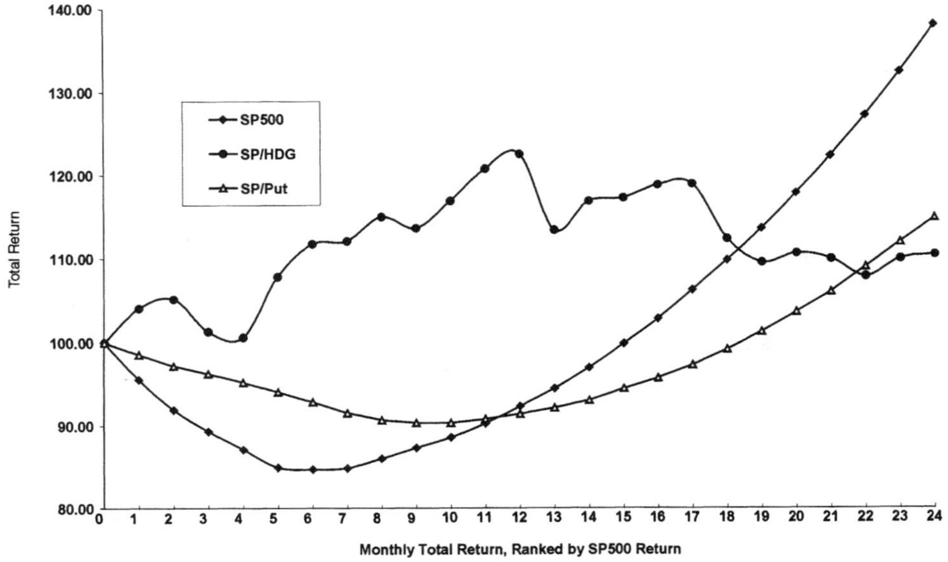

the two largest negative correlations (MARSTK and HFRSTK) are observed in the CTA and hedge fund indices with investment styles which are expected to provide returns based on equity performance. This is expected, since the MARSTK and HFRSTK represents traders who specialize in taking positions in corresponding equity markets while the MAR$CTA index is a broad index of all CTAs. In Exhibit 4C the relative performance of a 50% investment in the S&P500 and 50% investment in each of MAR$CTA, MARSTK, and HFRSTK is contrasted with the return to an at-the-money protective put strategy. Average returns to the S&P/MAR portfolio exceed the S&P/Put portfolio in three of the four periods, while the S&P/MARSTK and S&P/HFRSTK outperform this portfolio in only the two worst groups.

In Exhibits 5A-5C, the performance of the S&P500, S&P/Put, and combined S&P/(managed futures or hedge fund) indices is plotted. Total return is not calculated se-

EXHIBIT 6 PERFORMANCE OF HIGH-QUARTILE MEDIAN, BOTTOM-QUARTILE SHORT-SELLING HEDGE FUNDS, JUNE 1994- DEC 1995

	Portfolio Performance by Group						*Relative Portfolio Performance by Group*			
					HQ > SP500		Med > SP500		BQ > SP500	
Group	**SP500**	**HQ**	**Med**	**BQ**	**Months**	**%**	**Months**	**%**	**Months**	**%**
1	0.08	7.40	0.34	-6.03	9	90	5	50	1	10
2	3.57	7.77	0.01	-0.19	6	60	0	0	0	0

SP500 Correlation	HQ	Med	BQ
Group 1	-0.60	-0.46	-0.47
Group 2	0.12	0.04	0.11

Group: Group of 10 mos. ranked by SP500 Return. Group 1 contains lowest returns, Group 2
SP500: Standard and Poors 500 Total Return Index
HQ: Average of top quartile of short-selling hedge funds reported by
Med: Performance of the median short-selling hedge fund reported by
BQ: Average of bottom quartile of short-selling hedge funds reported by

quentially, but in order of lowest to highest S&P500 return. As returns for the S&P500 grow increasingly positive, the returns on MARSTK and HFRSTK grow increasingly negative.. In contrast, as the returns for the S&P500 grown increasingly positive, the returns on the MAR$CTA also experience positive returns such that when S&P500 has its highest return, the final return of S&P/MAR exceeds that of the S&P/Put.

MANAGER SELECTION

Empirical results for the eleven year period studied support the use of managed futures, as represented by the MAR$CTA, as a means of controlling downside equity risk while offering reasonable return potential in equity markets experiencing positive returns. Results for the most recent two year period indicate that, while various CTA and hedge fund products offered protection against equity losses, they often failed to offer comparable returns during stock market rallies. The fact that S&P500 performance was abnormally high during this period clearly contributed to the poor performance of CTAs and hedge funds that specialize in equity short sales (MARSTK and HFRSKT). However, not all of these funds performed poorly. For instance, many managers of short selling hedge funds posted positive or small negative returns despite the performance of the equity market in the past two years.

Exhibit 6 reports the performance of MAR hedge fund short-sellers divided into the high quartile (HFHQ), median (HFMED), and bottom quartile (HFBQ) index performance for the 20 months beginning June, 1994 and ending December 1995. Results indicate that during the 10 worst months for the S&P500 months there is a negative correlation between hedge fund returns and S&P500 returns (HFHQ, -.60; HFMED, -.46; HFBQ, -.47) and there is a positive correlation for the 10 best months (HFHQ, .12; HFMED, .04; HFBQ, .11).

In contrast to the HFRSTK results in Exhibit 4, as shown in Exhibit 6, the returns to high quartile hedge funds dominate the S&P500 index in both high and low return months. However, the HFMED outperforms the S&P500 only for the 10 months with the lowest S&P500 returns. The HFBQ underperforms the S&P500 in both up and down markets. Thus as for many other alternative investment choices such as mutual funds, the ability to obtain superior risk/return tradeoffs over all investment scenarios may be manager dependent.

CONCLUSION

Correlation tests comparing managed futures indices with traditional assets reveal an interesting property of the relationship between managed account returns and returns to traditional asset classes such as the S&P500. Overall, the correlation between managed asset returns and the S&P500 is approximately zero. However, when the data are segmented according to whether the stock market rose or fell, results indicate that managed futures and hedge funds were negatively correlated when the S&P500 posted significant negative returns and were positively correlated when the S&P500 reported significant positive returns. Thus managed futures may offer unique asset allocation properties.

Results also show that managed futures offer risk/return benefits when compared to a partially hedged position in the stock market. For instance, it is shown that an equal weighted investment in the MAR$CTA index and the S&P500 outperformed investment in the S&P500 plus a simulated at-the-money put under most market conditions. These results indicate that managed futures may offer some of the hedging properties of a put option at a lower cost. However, analysis of recent data on short-selling hedge funds indicates that earning positive returns in upmarkets requires the ability to select superior managers, and that the typical manager produces zero returns in this environment.

ENDNOTES

This article was published in *Derivatives Quarterly*, Fall 1996, pp 62-72.

[1] The term "managed futures" generally refers to investment vehicles based on returns to due direct investment in commodity trading advisors and/or commodity funds/pools. However, hedge funds are also often included under the term.

[2] On a relative basis, the performance of lower-cost direct investment in CTA products generally outperform the higher cost retail managed futures products such as commodity pools and funds. For studies analyzing the benefits of these products see Chance [1994] and Schneeweis [1996].

[3] Books which include information on the history of managed futures and hedge funds include Chandler [1994], Lederman and Klein [1995], and Fox-Andrews and Meaden [1995]. Books which include discussions on the history of futures and options markets and the economic benefits of derivative products include Peck [1985, Vols. 1-5].

[4] It is of course important to point out that the performance of the equity/ protective put position and the equity/managed futures position are not strictly comparable since the performance of the managed futures position is stochastic. The individual investor must determine whether the potential relative return compensates for the expected risk.

[5] The use of the Sharpe ratio as a measure of relative performance may be suboptimal to other measures of relative performance, such as semivariance, for investment strategies which are designed to truncate returns below a specified threshold level. While this study does not test for performance using alternative 'semivariance' performance measures, it should be noted that using mean-variance analysis to evaluate investment portfolios with skewed return distributions can lead to suboptimal portfolios (Bookstaber and Clarke [1985]; Marmer and Ng [1993].

[6] As in previous analysis (Elton, Gruber, and Rentzler [1987, 1990], Irwin, Krukemyer, and Zulauf [1992], Schneeweis, Savanayana, and McCarthy [1992]), excess break-even analysis is used to test for the contribution of CTAs to the risk/return profile of stocks, bonds, and other asset classes such as real estate. As in earlier studies, the excess break-even rate of return necessary for a security to enter a portfolio is computed as follows: $EBV = R_c - \left(\frac{R_p - R_f}{\sigma_p} \sigma_{cp} \sigma_c + R_f \right)$, where R_c = Return for CTA; R_f = Riskless rate of return; R_p = Rate of return on index p; σ_{cp} = Correlation coefficient between CTA c and index p; σ_c = Standard deviation of CTA c; σ_p = Standard deviation of index p.

[7] For a complete discussion of Managed Accounts Reports CTA and Hedge Fund indices, call MAR on the World Wide Web. For instance, the MAR Hedge Fund short-sellers indices track hedge fund managers who take positions that stock prices will go down. A hedge fund borrows stock and sells it, hoping to buy it back at a lower price. A hedge is for long-only portfolios and those who feel market is approaching a bearish trend. Similarly, the Hedge Fund Research indices for short-sellers simply defines the index and managers who go short securities.

[8] Other studies analyzing the downside risk potential of managed futures include Peters [1992] and Schneeweis [1996]. Peters [1992] argues that portfolio diversification with managed futures provides partial stochastic dominance in the lower return ranges and produces long term effects similar to insurance; that is, reduction to upside performance (cost) with protection in down markets. As the use of alternative risk measures capturing semi-variance gain popularity, these benefits of managed futures may become more apparent.

[9] Similar tests were conducted for world, regional, and country-specific equity and bond markets, as well as various portfolios of these assets, including and excluding commodities. Results are similar to those presented here (See Schneeweis [1996]).

[10] For individual managers, results may differ from indices used. For a study on the stability of CTA equity managers, see Potter and Schneeweis [1996].

[11] For a parallel discussion on the benefits of managed futures as portfolio insurance see Peters [1992].

Preliminary results indicate that a greater positive correlation exists between the performance of the CTA equity traders and a straddle position than between CTA equity traders and the S&P500. This is consistent with CTA equity traders who take short positions in down markets and long positions in up markets [Schneeweis and Spurgin 1995].

REFERENCES

Bookstaber, R. and R. Clarke, "Problems in Evaluating the Performance of Portfolios with Options," *Financial Analysts Journal*, (January/February, 1985), pp. 48-62.

Chan, A., N. Jagadeesh, and J. Lakonishok, (1995), Momentum Strategies, NBER Working Paper #5375.

Chance, Don. *Managed Futures and Their Role in Investment Portfolios.* Charlottesville, AIMR, (1994).

Chandler, B. *Managed Futures: An Investor's Guide.* New York: John Wiley & Sons, (1994).

Elton, Edwin J., Martin J. Gruber, and Joel C. Rentzler. "The Performance of Publicly Offered Commodity Funds", *Financial Analysts Journal*, (July-August 1990), pp. 23-30.

_______. "Professionally Managed, Publicly Traded Commodity Funds", *The Journal of Business*, Vol. 60, No. 2, (1987), pp. 175-200.

Fox-Andrews, M. and Nicola Meaden. *Derivative Markets and Investment Management* (Prentice Hall, Hertfordshire, G.B., (1995).

Irwin, Scott H., Terry Krukemyer, and Carl R. Zulauf. "The Investment Performance of Public Commodity Pools over 1979-1989", *The Journal of Futures Markets*, (October 1993), pp. 799-820.

Irwin, Scott H. and Diego Landa. "Real Estate, Futures, and Gold as Portfolio Assets," *The Journal of Portfolio Management*, (Fall 1987), pp. 29-34.

Jagadeesh, N. "Evidence of Predictable Behavior of Security Returns", *The Journal of Finance*, (1990(3)), pp. 881-898.

Lederman J. and Robert Klein, ed. *Hedge Funds* (Irwin, N.Y., 1995).

Lewis, A. "Semivariance and the Performance of Portfolios with Options," *Financial Analysts Journal*, (July-August, 1990), pp. 67-76.

Marmer, H. S. and F. K. Ng, "Mean-Semivariance Analysis of Option-Based Strategies: A Total Mix Perspective," *Financial Analysts Journal*, (May-June, 1993), pp. 47-54.

Peck, A.E. ed., *Selected Writings on Futures Markets.* Vol. 1-5 (Chicago Board of Trade., 1985).

Peters, C.C. ed. *Managed Futures: Performance Evaluation and Analysis of Commodity Funds, Pools and Accounts* (Probus Publishing, 1992).

Potter, M., and T. Schneeweis, 1996, "Equity CTAs as Asset Allocators". Working paper, Center for International Securities and Derivative Markets, University of Massachusetts, (March, 1996).

Schneeweis, T., 1996 (forthcoming), "The Benefits of Managed Futures", *Technical Report of the European Managed Futures Association.*

Schneeweis, T., U. Savanayana, and D. McCarthy, "Alternative Commodity Trading Vehicles: A Performance Analysis," *The Journal of Futures Markets* (August, 1991), 475-490.

Schneeweis, T., U. Savanayana and D. McCarthy. "Multi-Manager Commodity Portfolios: A Risk/Return Analysis," in C. Epstein ed. *Managed Futures* (Wiley, 1992), 81-102.

Schneeweis, T., and R. Spurgin, 1995, "Comparisons of Benchmark Indices in Futures Markets", Working paper, Center for International Securities and Derivative Markets, University of Massachusetts, (July, 1995).

8 SKEWNESS IN ASSET RETURNS: DOES IT MATTER?

GEORGE MARTIN
University of Massachusetts

RICHARD SPURGIN
Clark University

INTRODUCTION

In much of traditional asset return analysis, an asset's return distribution is assumed to be adequately described by its first two moments (expected return and variance) and its expected return by its relationship with the assumed market portfolio.[1] In fact, securities often exhibit additional return characteristics in which the probability of security's expected return in the extremes is often greater than that described by a simple normal distribution with equal expected return and variance. In short, an asset's return distribution is often better described not only by its expected return and variance but also by its higher moments of skewness or kurtosis.

Academics have attempted to explain the role of skewness in an asset's return distribution. In the early 1970's, academic literature contained theoretical models which described an asset's expected return in three moments; that is, return, variance and skewness [Jean, 1971]. In addition to simple skewness, academics have also attempted to explain an asset's return in terms of its co-skewness with the assumed market portfolio [Kraus and Litzenberger, 1976] in which individuals overprice assets and lower expected returns to obtain assets with high positive co-skewness with a market portfolio [Schweser and Schneeweis, 1980]. For traditional assets, however, research has indicated a low level of stability in an asset's skewness or co-skewness [Singleton, 1986]. Since, all else equal, an investor would prefer positively skewed returns, the ability to use various derivative products [e.g., options] to create such skewed distributions is often presented as a selling point for active versus passive asset management [Zurack, et al., 1997].

The foundation of modern portfolio theory and the two moment (i.e., capital asset pricing model) or three moment (multi-dimensional pricing models), however, is that investors should be only compensated for the non-diversifiable risk associated with an asset. Thus to obtain an downside truncated asset distributions (positive skewness) one must give up return either by paying directly to remove the downside returns (e.g., options, insurance) or by paying a higher price for assets that may have systematic positive co-skewness [Schweser and Schneeweis, 1980].

This does not mean that skewness has no consequences for portfolio management, since investors rarely hold a fully diversified portfolio. However, if the risk associated with skewness is fully diversifiable or is fully priced, then does skewness really add anything to a fully diversified investor's portfolio? In the area of alternative assets, considerable research has focused on the ability of alternative asset managers to adjust asset positions in various market environments in order to obtain positively skewed distributions in contrast to a traditional stock and bond portfolio [Peters and Warwich, 1997]. Even if there is little evidence of alternative investments having positively skewed return distributions, research has also shown that various alternative investment strategies [e.g., managed futures] may result in portfolios with option like characteristics [Schneeweis et al., 1996].

In this analysis, it is illustrated that while skewness generally does not exist in a randomly created alternative asset portfolio, there may still be a use for skewness in evaluating a manager's performance. In the next section, skewness is described as well as the expected benefits of positive skewness. It is then shown why for the diversified investor, the skewness of individual assets may not matter. On a positive note, it is concluded that for manager comparisons, tracking skewness may permit relative performance analysis of managers with similar trading styles.[2]

WHAT IS SKEWNESS?

Skewness is a statistical term that, along with the mean and standard deviation, helps describe a probability distribution.[3] The *mean (average)* of a random variable describes the *location,* the *standard deviation* describes the *spread* of the distribution, and the *skewness* helps describe the overall *shape.* In Exhibit 1, two distributions are plotted. The darker line is the Normal Distribution (the bell curve). This distribution is symmetric, and thus has no skewness. This particular Normal distribution has an average of 2 and a standard deviation of 2. The lighter line is a distribution with the same mean and standard deviation as the Normal curve, but a different shape. This distribution is *positively skewed,* meaning that the peak of the distribution (which occurs around zero) is to the left of the average value (which is 2). A *negatively skewed* distribution would have its peak to the right of the average.

A positively skewed distribution has several differences from the bell curve. Big losses occur less frequently. In the example below, the Normal has an 8% chance of a loss of more than 2%, while the skewed has no chance of a loss more than 2%. Small losses are more likely with the skewed distribution. Skewed has a 26% chance of a small

EXHIBIT 1 SKEWED AND SYMMETRIC DISTRIBUTIONS

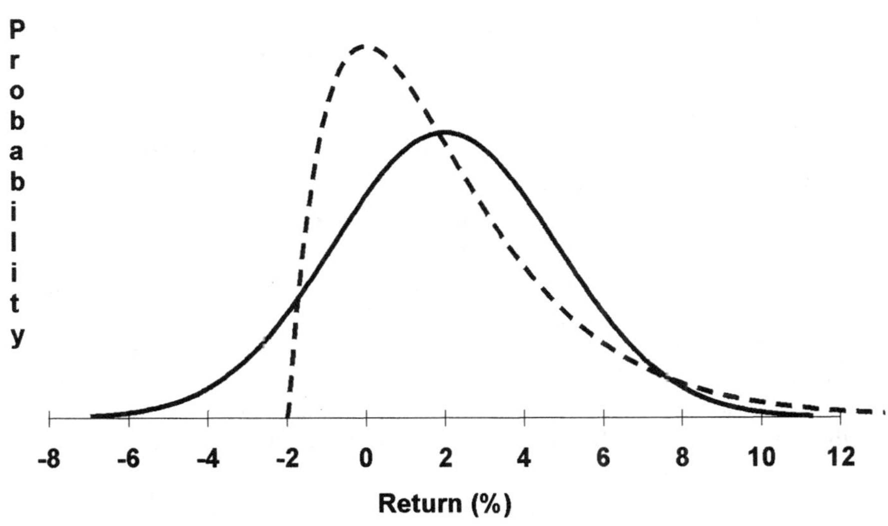

loss (between 0 and -2%), while Normal has a 16% chance of a loss in this range. Small gains are less frequent with a skewed distribution: 43% of Normal returns are gains between 2% and 6%, while 32% of Skewed returns are in this range. Big gains are more frequent with a skewed distribution: 2% of the gains to the skewed distribution are more than 10%, while only 0.2% of the Normal gains are more than 10%.

It is not hard to understand why investors might prefer skewed distributions: One can examine ones own preference with a simple test: Choose one of the following gambles: Each gamble has two possible outcomes: For example gamble *A* has a 90% chance of winning $2 and a 10% chance of an eight dollar loss.

	A		B		C	
Probability	*90%*	*10%*	*50%*	*50%*	*10%*	*90%*
Gain(Loss)	$2	($8)	$4	($2)	$10	$0

Most people prefer gamble *C* to both *A* and *B*, and would prefer *B* to *A*. However, all three have the same expected value, $1, and the same standard deviation, $3. The difference is in the skewness. *C* is positively skewed, *B* is symmetric, and *A* is negatively skewed.

Because investors are risk averse, they view losses differently than they view gains. Becoming $100 poorer causes more pain than becoming $100 richer gives pleasure. Symmetric return distributions give as many large losses as they give large gains, while positively skewed returns allow for the possibility of large gains while limiting large losses. Since investors are more concerned about large losses than large gains, positively skewed investment returns are preferred to either symmetric returns or negatively skewed returns.

MEASURED SKEWNESS FOR INDIVIDUAL ASSETS AND PORTFOLIOS

In order to estimate the actual impact or degree of skewness in an active asset strategy, it is necessary to use historical returns. Unexpected and nonrepeatable extreme values (random noise) may have major impacts on measured skewness. Calculating skewness requires cubing each observation, which places an emphasis on the extreme values in the data set. When you have one or two observations that are much higher (or lower) than the average, you are going to measure positive (or negative) skewness even if the underlying strategy has no inherent skewness. In order to conclude with any degree of statistical confidence that a particular strategy or fund has skewness, one would need numerous years of returns. Moreover, it is difficult to draw conclusions from skewness coefficients calculated using a few years of returns, since either the nature of market or the manager's strategy has likely changed over that time period.[4]

While it is clear that investors would prefer skewed investment returns to symmetric returns, a fully diversified portfolio may have no skewness.[5] The problem stems from a statistical property called the Central Limit Theorem (CLT). The CLT says that, under very weak assumptions, the sum (or average) of a large number of—possibly dependent, possibly time-varying— random variables will converge to the Normal distribution, no matter what distribution the variables have. So while a particular investment may be skewed, a well diversified portfolio will have so many small positions that the skewness of any investment or group of investments will be diversified away. The result will be a portfolio that has a mean and a standard deviation but no skewness.

Exhibit 2 shows an example of the CLT, where one adds up realizations from the same random process across time. The positively skewed gamble *C* was described ear-

EXHIBIT 2A DISTRIBUTION OF RETURNS FOR 4 REPETITIONS

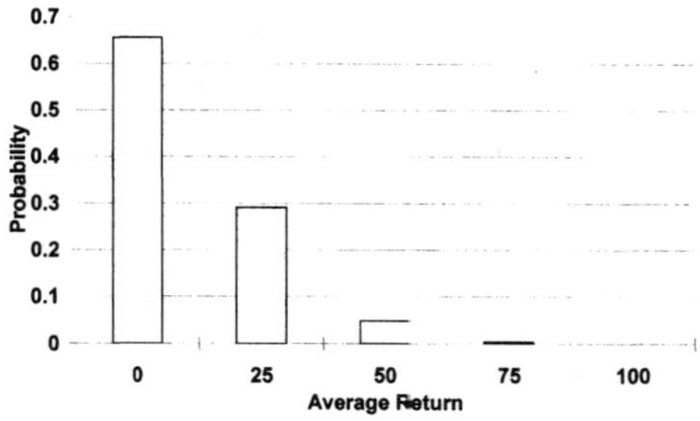

EXHIBIT 2B DISTRIBUTION OF RETURNS FOR 8 REPETITIONS

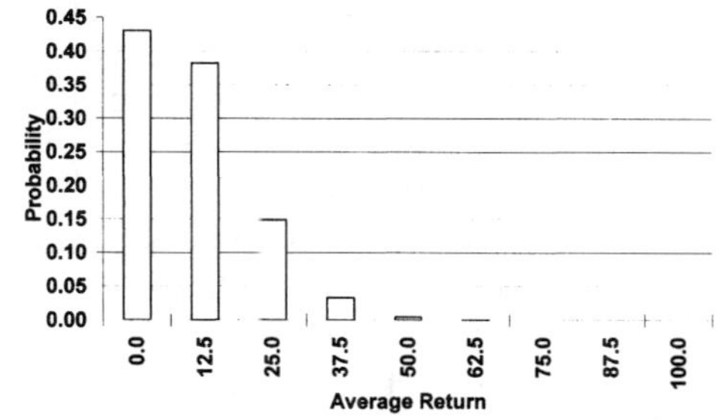

EXHIBIT 2C DISTRIBUTION OF RETURNS FOR 32 REPETITIONS

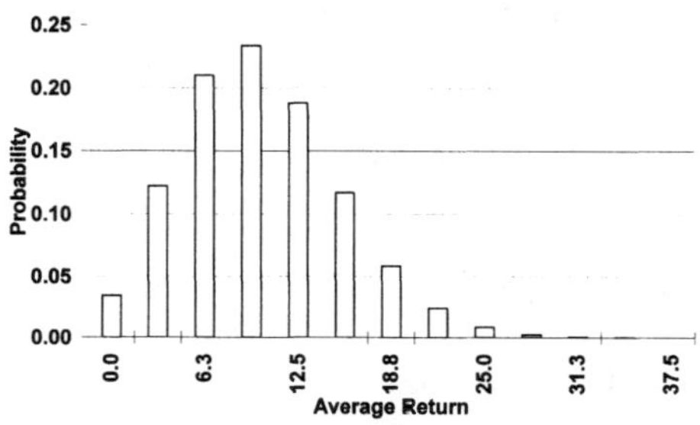

EXHIBIT 2D DISTRIBUTION OF RETURNS FOR 64 REPETITIONS

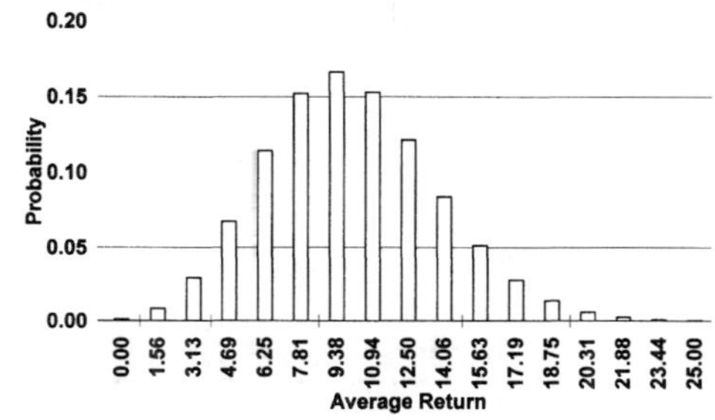

lier as having attractive properties. While that was true for a single gamble, if the gamble is repeated several times the investment loses its luster. The four panels of Exhibit 2 shows a simulation of the gamble if it were repeated 4 times, 8 times, 32 times, and 64 times. Thus in panel A, the payoffs are 0 (if all four gambles failed), 2.5 (if 1 was a success), 5 (2 successes), 7.5, or 10 (all successes). The returns to the gamble are still quite skewed. However, as more and more repetitions are averaged, the skewness disappears. The second and third panels, representing 8 and 32 repetitions still show some evidence of skew, but the final panel, with 64 repetitions is not distinguishable from the Normal Distribution.

Along with the temporal aggregation just described, adding together random returns from different strategies will have a similar 'Normalizing' effect on the returns of a portfolio. The CLT does not say that our random variables have to come from the same source. Individual investment returns are often highly skewed, but portfolios such as the S&P500 index or the MAR CTA index do not exhibit much skewness. The only way an investor can achieve a substantially skewed return is by limiting the number of assets in a portfolio to a few, highly skewed investments. However, the lack of diversification in this portfolio might outweigh the benefits of skewness.

Since transactions costs or other considerations may limit the ability of a portfolio manager to fully diversify her portfolio—recall that a fully diversified portfolio would require the portfolio manager to have exposure to *all* assets in the market, which are very large in number and may fall outside of the range of assets in which the investor is authorized to invest (e.g. real estate). As a result, one need to investigate the question of *how quickly* the central limit theorem brings our return distribution to that of a normal distribution.[6] There are many factors that will limit the dissipation of skewness as one add assets to a portfolio. These factors include the correlation between returns of each of the assets, as well as the mean of the distributions associated with each of the assets.

One can get a sense of how these factors affect the dissipation of skewness by looking at Exhibit 1. If the returns of the two distributions are positively correlated, adding them together will result in a distribution that still retains a substantial amount of the skewness of the originally skewed distribution. Were the returns from these two distributions highly negatively correlated, the skewness of the original distribution would be dissipated quickly. Similarly, if the distribution of the two return processes involve different means (for example, the skewed distribution in Exhibit 1 were shifted rightward), the amount of skewness that the combined returns would have would diminish slowly. In general, however, if one add returns from two distributions, each skewed, the distribution of the combined returns will have less skewness than the skew of the original distribution with the greatest magnitude of skew.

For traditional asset investment, one can investigate how fast skewness is dissipated using real market data. From daily returns from equity of all firms in the S&P500 with continuous records from 1/91-5/96 (465 firms), a sequence of portfolios with consecutive one month holding periods from returns a random subset of stocks is formed. The probability density functions associated with each of those sets of returns is estimated, and then one simulates returns from those density functions. The mean and standard deviation of skewness of portfolio returns with asset weightings are determined either

EXHIBIT 3 EXPECTED SKEWNESS IN PORTFOLIO RETURNS FOR DAILY S&P500 EQUITY RETURNS

Assets	Equal Weighted	Mean-Variance Optimal	Random Weighted
2	0.16	0.165	0.14
4	0.04	-0.03	0.08
6	-0.03	-0.18	0.02
8	-0.07	-0.25	-0.02
10	-0.09	-0.27	-0.04
12	0.01	-0.30	0.03
14	0.02	-0.32	0.04
16	0.05	-0.30	0.07
18	0.01	-0.24	0.03
20	-0.01	-0.19	0.013
22	0.05	-0.19	0.06
24	0.03	-0.19	0.05
26	0.02	-0.19	0.04
28	0.06	-0.21	0.08
30	0.13	-0.22	0.13

by equal weighting, random weighting or ex post mean-variance optimal weighting are estimated and shown in Exhibit 4.[7] While there is little skewness in returns to begin with, there is no readily observable decline in skewness as one increase the number of assets (to 30) using either equal weighted portfolios or randomly weighted portfolios, since factors other than diversification tend to swamp the diversification effect. What conclusion can be drawn from this empirical exercise? The results suggest that skewness is a relatively insignificant feature of portfolio returns constructed passively; however, using a mean-variance criterion one may even generate target portfolios that exhibit negative skewness.[8] In neither case, however, has one have diversified skewness away through broadening our portfolio.

EXHIBIT 4 EFFECT OF DIVERSIFICATION ON SKEWNESS OF PORTFOLIO RETURNS

Assets	Equal Weighted	Mean-Variance Optimal	Random Weighted
2	0.64	0.64	0.65
3	0.64	0.49	0.66
4	0.61	0.36	0.61
5	0.65	0.31	0.65
6	0.62	0.21	0.61
7	0.67	0.16	0.67
8	0.64	0.12	0.64
9	0.64	0.05	0.65
10	0.61	0.01	0.61
11	0.61	-0.03	0.61
12	0.66	-0.06	0.65
13	0.60	-0.10	0.61
14	0.61	-0.14	0.61
15	0.63	-0.16	0.64
16	0.59	-0.18	0.60
17	0.63	-0.21	0.63
18	0.63	-0.21	0.63
19	0.66	-0.23	0.65
20	0.62	-0.22	0.61
21	0.63	-0.19	0.63
22	0.63	-0.14	0.63
23	0.64	-0.22	0.64
24	0.64	-0.26	0.63
25	0.64	-0.30	0.63
26	0.63	-0.34	0.62
27	0.64	-0.37	0.65
28	0.63	-0.40	0.62
29	0.64	-0.41	0.64
30	0.63	-0.45	0.63
31	0.64	-0.48	0.64
32	0.62	-0.48	0.62
33	0.63	-0.49	0.63
34	0.63	-0.51	0.63
35	0.63	-0.53	0.63
36	0.62	-0.53	0.63
37	0.65	-0.55	0.64
38	0.62	-0.54	0.61
39	0.63	-0.56	0.63
40	0.64	-0.58	0.65
41	0.62	-0.59	0.61
42	0.64	-0.60	0.65
43	0.64	-0.61	0.64
44	0.63	-0.61	0.63
45	0.64	-0.62	0.64
46	0.65	-0.63	0.64
47	0.61	-0.63	0.61
48	0.62	-0.63	0.62
49	0.61	-0.65	0.62
50	0.61	-0.64	0.61

In order to investigate the extent to which a portfolio inherits the skewness of the underlying assets in a manner which is free from the confounding effects of temporal aggregation, time varying means, variances and skewness, and inter-asset correlations, one needs to resort to an artificial example. We conduct the same exercise as above, except that we substitute return data simulated from a multivariate 'stable' distribution with skewness for the stock data. (A stable distribution is characterized by two main features: it has 'tails' that are at least as thick as those a normal distribution, and the sum of two stable distributions is again a stable distribution. The normal distribution is a special case of the stable distribution. Most distributions are *not* stable; for example the sum of two lognormally distributed random variables is *not* lognormally distributed.) Our distribution is positively skewed, and assets are positively correlated. Our results are shown in Exhibit 4.

From Exhibits 3 and 4, one see that passive diversification does not substantially reduce our skewness as one includes more and more assets, and that our mean-variance selection process tends to push our portfolio into negatively skewed assets. A part of the reason so little trend in skewness is illustrated in Exhibit 5 is that the standard errors of our estimates are rather high, in part because of the phenomenon described above whereby a few large returns can have dramatic effects on the estimated skewness coefficient. The flip side to this observation is that it may be quite difficult to guarantee that portfolio returns will exhibit positive skewness, since a few comparatively large negative returns may substantially alter the sample distribution of an otherwise positively skewed portfolio.

In short, in portfolios that are not fully diversified, portfolio returns may exhibit (positive or negative) skewness. Managers and investors may have preferences regarding that skewness, and should adjust their valuation and asset allocation accordingly. In practice, the classical insights of modern portfolio theory may not offer clear prescriptions on these matters, since many of the assumptions that lie behind those insights may not match the portfolio management problems that managers and investors face.

A USE FOR SKEWNESS IN ALTERNATIVE INVESTMENTS

Many common alternative asset trading strategies result in skewed returns. The most common is "cut your losses and let profits run". This strategy results in lots of small losses and a few big gains. Strategies that use leverage, adding to winning trades and reducing losers, also yields skewed returns. Trend-following strategies such as moving averages also generally yield skewed returns, posting many small losses in choppy markets and a few large gains in trending markets. Buying options also results in skewed returns, as an option has built-in risk management characteristics.

Thus for alternative investment strategies, compared to long only traditional asset investments, an individual manager may create strategies that are inherently skewed. The results in the previous section relied on an important assumption — the average future return of the investment is assumed to be known. This is a standard assumption in finance, but is not particularly useful if there are questions about the expected return to a particular strategy or manager. Consider the following example: There are two managers, a "skilled" manager with an expected return of 2 and an "unskilled" manager with an expected return of -2. The investor's problem is to identify which is the skilled manager by observing their performance over time. If both managers follow skewed trading strategies (Exhibit 5B), it will become clear very quickly which is the skilled manager. The skilled manager cannot have a loss greater than -2, while fully 60% of the returns to the unskilled manager will be less than -2%. The investor's problem is simple:

EXHIBIT 5A COMPARISON OF NORMAL DISTRIBUTIONS

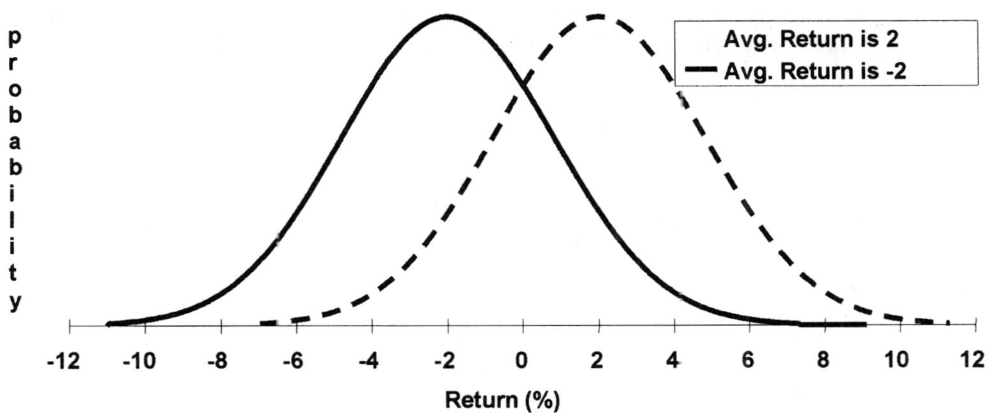

EXHIBIT 5B COMPARISON OF SKEWNESS DISTRIBUTIONS

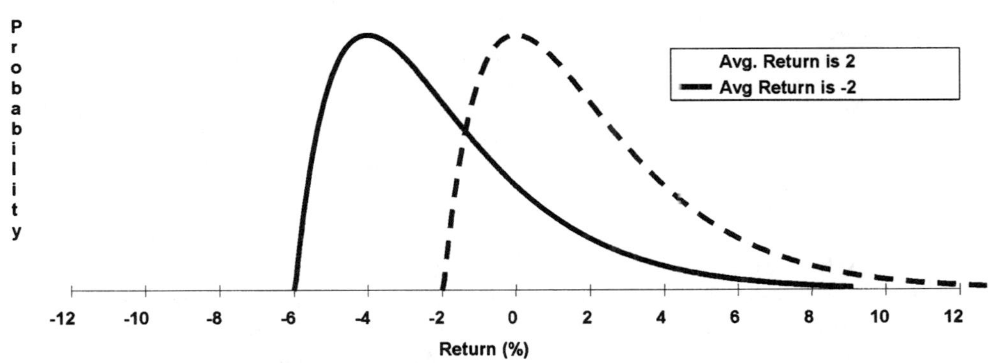

Wait until one of the managers posts a loss greater than -2 and then invest in the other. There is a 60% chance that this will happen the first period and an 84% chance this will happen by the second period. If both managers are following Normally distributed strategies (Exhibit 5A), however, the problem is much more complex. While on average the skilled manager will outperform the unskilled manager, in any period each manager's return could take on any value, so there is no simple rule that allows the investor to differentiate between the two. The investor will have to wait several periods before being able to gather enough data to make a decision, and even then cannot do so with certainty.

Thus, if managers have the ability to choose between a skewed or normal style (but cannot choose their skill level), then skilled managers will choose a skewed return distribution and unskilled managers will choose a normal distribution. This is because skilled managers want investors to be able to discern their skill level, but unskilled managers do not. Thus skewness in returns may be of value to investors, not for portfolio reasons, but in making it easier for them to identify a successful manager.

This is called *signaling*, because managers choose a strategy that best signals their skill level. An analogous argument can be applied to drawdown. The drawdown of a particular manager is a meaningless statistic from the perspective of a rational, well diversified investor's portfolio. However, it may be that skilled managers are able to minimize drawdown while unskilled managers are not. If so, then analyzing drawdown may be a

EXHIBIT 6 SUMMARY STATISTICS

	Average Return	Standard Deviation	Skewness	Kurtosis	Ln(observations)
Minimum	−0.054	0.000	−5.757	−2.000	0.693
First quartile	0.009	0.021	−0.166	−0.227	3.178
Mean	0.015	0.044	0.253	1.436	3.677
Median	0.013	0.037	0.259	0.561	3.829
Third quartile	0.019	0.058	0.703	1.858	4.363
Maximum	0.135	0.586	6.250	46.490	4.564
Standard deviation	0.013	0.037	0.902	3.567	0.788

EXHIBIT 7 REGRESSION OF AVERAGE MONTHLY RETURNS ON OTHER MOMENTS

	OLS Coef.	Rank Regression Coef.	OLS Std. Error	OLS t Value	OLS Pr(> |t|)
Intercept	0.014	N/A	0.0014	10.139	0.0000
Standard deviation	0.182	0.164	0.0082	21.978	0.0000
Skewness	0.002	0.001	0.0003	5.271	0.0000
Kurtosis	−0.000	−0.000	0.0000	−3.155	0.0016
Ln(observations)	−0.002	−0.002	0.0004	−5.266	0.0000

useful way of separating skilled from unskilled managers. If this signaling is actually occurring in the market, one would expect to see a positive association between mean returns and skewness. One can examine this hypothesis empirically, using a data set of 1355 commodity trading advisors (CTAs) and Hedge funds with more than $5 million under management as of December 1997. (The data are monthly, from MAR, and begin in January 1990 and end in December 1997).[9] From this data set one compute the monthly mean returns, standard deviations, skewness and kurtosis over the life of each fund, as well as the number of observations available (see Exhibit 6). The mean return of each fund is then regressed on the higher moments and number of observations (Exhibit 7).

Of note is the fact that the coefficient associated with the skewness of a fund's returns is positive and significant, as signaling theory predicts. Standard deviation is highly statistically significant, as would be expect in a world where risk (variance) is positively priced. When one adjusts for the different scales associated with the variables (t-values), one sees that standard deviation is the most important determinant of mean returns, followed by skewness and then kurtosis. The natural logarithm of the number of observations in our regression is included to determine whether there are any consequences of the potentially biased sampling used to construct the data set. From the significant (t-value) and negative sign on the term, there is some selection bias present, with funds

EXHIBIT 8A RANK CORRELATION COEFFICIENTS

	Avg. Ret 1997	Avg. Ret 1996	Std. Dev. 1997	Std. Dev. 1996	Skewness 1997	Skewness 1996
Avg. monthly return 1997		0.22	0.16	0.10	0.05	0.06
Avg. monthly return 1996			0.23	0.26	0.02	0.01
Std. dev. 1997				0.63	0.02	0.04
Std. dev. 1996					0.03	0.02
Skewness 1997						0.69
Skewness 1996						

EXHIBIT 8B RANK CORRELATION COEFFICIENT SIGNIFICANCE: PROBABILITY THAT COEFFICIENT IS ZERO

	Mean 1997	Mean 1996	Std. Dev. 1997	Std. Dev. 1996	Skewness 1997	Skewness 1996
Mean 1997		0.00	0.00	0.00	0.00	0.00
Mean 1996			0.00	0.00	0.22	0.42
Std. Dev. 1997				0.00	0.16	0.02
Std. Dev. 1996					0.06	0.28
Skewness 1997						0.00
Skewness 1996						

that have shorter life spans having higher returns. (Those funds with shorter life spans may generate significant returns from random successes of their investment strategies rather than reflecting any long term fundamental manager skill.) The results of a rank regression[10] is included and indicates the OLS results are, in fact, robust to outliers.

SKEWNESS PERSISTENCE

An important question remains: Can skewness be used to improve forecasts of future manager performance? To answer this question, the same data set is used but restricted to funds with complete data from the years 1996 and 1997 (963). The means, standard deviations and skewness of each fund's returns are computed for each year. We then compute the rank correlation coefficients across parameters and years. The rank correlation (Panel A) and its level of significance (Panel B) are reported in Exhibit 8.

The rank correlation coefficient between skewness in 1996 and mean returns in 1997 is positive, and statistically significant. However, with such a small correlation coefficient, it seems that lagged skewness alone is only of limited use in forecasting future manager performance. The moments associated with each fund tend to persist from 1996 to 1997 (for example skewness in 1996 is the best predictor of skewness in 1997), and that lagged standard deviation is, on average, a good indicator of future expected returns (reflecting the relationship between risk and return).

CONCLUSION

This paper examines the role of skewness in actively managed assets including that of alternative investment portfolios. While investors prefer skewed returns to symmetric returns, it is shown that a rational, *fully* diversified investor may not benefit from the skewness in individual investments, because the skewness will be diversified away. Under typical conditions faced by managers and investors, however, the diversification effects may not be sufficient to eliminate skewness from their valuation and allocation decisions. Moreover, it may be that skewness is useful in helping investors differentiate between good and bad investments. This applies to a variety of risk measures often proposed for assets, including semi-variance, drawdown, and recovery time. However, each of these measures is uninformative in a fully diversified portfolio. Only the mean, standard deviation, and correlation among assets are meaningful in a modern portfolio context. Thus it may be that skilled managers adopt strategies that minimize risk measures such as drawdown as a means of differentiating themselves from less skilled managers. Further research is, of course, required on using skewness to facilitate skill assessment of individual managers is clearly important as well as using measures of co-skewness to illustrate return benefits of alternative assets.

ENDNOTES

This article was published in *The Journal of Alternative Investments*, Fall 1998.

[1] One of the central premises of capital market theory is the existence of a linear relationship between risk and return. For the traditional capital asset pricing model risk is defined by a security's beta which measures the marginal impact on the variance of the investor's market portfolio [Bodie, Kane, and Marcus, 1996].

[2] A shortened summary version of this paper was presented in AIMA Newsletter.

[3] In this paper, the presentation of skewness as part of an asset's return properties is described in basic terms. For a more complete description, readers are directed to any advanced statistics book. However, readers are cautioned against the uncritical use of simple historical parameter estimates of an asset's skewness. Research has shown that, even if an asset's returns follows a normal distribution, changes over time in the mean or variance of that distribution will result in a measured distribution function that may show evidence of non-zero higher moments (e.g., skewness, kurtosis). That is, while asset returns may be conditionally normal, their kurtosis) unconditional distribution may be substantially nonnormal.

[4] See previous footnote.

[5] This article does not address the issue of co-skewness; that is, whether the strategy may have extreme high returns in positive market portfolio months without similar return movements in extreme negative market return months. In terms of co-skewness, the question is if the benefits in extreme markets results in higher prices (e.g., lower expected) returns to obtain the investment.

[6] The study of how quickly the distribution of averaged random variables converge to their limiting distribution called the theory of 'large deviations', and sees many obvious applications is insurance and risk management.

[7] Further details are available from the authors.

[8] This result comes from the fact that the optimizer heavily weights assets that have high returns and small variances; when these assets are combined with assets with lower means and higher variances, the mixture of returns has a larger probability mass just above the overall mean.

[9] The data is thus not free from survivorship bias, and so inferences drawn here should not be considered as conclusive.

[10] We thank Mike Osborne and Karen George for the software used to conduct the regressions.

REFERENCES

Bodie, Z., E. Kane, and A. Marcus. *Investments.* Irwin, (1996).

Das, S., S. Foresi, and R. Sundaram, "Taming The Skew, Kurtosis and Stochastic Processes for Asset Pricing." Harvard Business School, Working Paper: (December, 1996).

Kraus, A. and R. Litzenberger, "Skewness Preference and the Valuation of Risk Assets." *The Journal of Finance*, (September, 1976), pp. 1085-1100.

Lewis, A. "Semivaiance and the Performance of Portfolios with Options." *Financial Analyst Journal*, (July-August, 1990), pp. 67-76.

Marmer H. and F. K. Louis Ng, "Mean-Semivariance Analysis of Option-Based Strategies: A total Asset Mix Perspective." *Financial Analysts Journal*, (May-June, 1993), pp. 47-54.

Peters, C. and B. Warwick eds. *The Handbook of Managed Futures*, Irwin, (1997).

Schweser, C. and T. Schneeweis, "Risk Return and the Multi-Dimensional Security Pricing Market." *The Journal of Financial Research*, (Spring, 1980), pp. 23-32.

Schneeweis, T., R.Spurgin, and M. Potter. "Managed Futures and Hedge Fund Investment for Downside Equity Risk Management." *Derivatives Quarterly*, (Fall, 1996), pp. 62-72.

Singleton, J. C. and J. Wingender, "Skewness Persistence in Common Stock Returns." *Journal of Financial and Quantitative Analysis*, (September, 1986), pp. 335-341.

Sortino F., G. Miller, and J. Messina "Short Term Risk-adjusted Performance: A Style Based Analysis." *The Journal of Investing*, (Summer, 1997), pp. 19-28.

Zurack, M. E. Derman, J. Hill, and I. Kani, "Reshaping Equity Returns Using Options." *The Journal of Investing*, (Spring, 1997), pp. 34-40.

III HEDGE FUND INVESTMENT

INTRODUCTION

Recent events have focused interest on a relatively new investment entity, the hedge fund. While many definitions for hedge funds exist, they are basically loosely regulated private pools of investment capital that can invest in both cash and derivative markets on a leveraged basis for the benefit of investors. There are a number of myths surrounding hedge funds and the risk and return opportunities that hedge funds offer.[1] While both the number and size of hedge funds have grown in recent years, hedge funds have existed since the 1940s. It was not until the 1980s, however, that they began experiencing rapid growth. This growth was due in part to an increase in the number of new financial vehicles as well as a change in technology that permitted sophisticated investment strategies to be designed, implemented and offered to investors without the infrastructure of a large investment house.

Hedge funds can be viewed as the privatization of the trading floor. New technology has permitted investment professionals to leave investment banks and trade externally what for years was conducted only internally. The strategies are not new. Insurance companies, endowments, and other institutional investors have invested in alternative investments such as private debt, private equity and market-neutral strategies for years. What is new is that when these large, diversified investors took losses in a particular product, it often was hidden by their gains in other areas. For a single hedge fund, the lack of product diversification heightens firm risk, but does not necessarily increase the risk of the product to its investors, who should be well diversified across a number of hedge fund strategies and therefore a number of asset classes.

Both investors and regulators have recently raised concerns about the liquidity and transparency of many hedge fund strategies. These are legitimate concerns, as many hedge funds invest in relatively illiquid assets such as private equity, private debt, merger and acquisitions, and emerging markets. Furthermore, hedge funds have closely guarded their positions out of concern that making trades public would render them difficult to unwind, placing their investors at risk of loss. However, without the participation of hedge funds, many worthwhile projects could not find the necessary financing. The fact that hedge funds are willing to trade many exotic products offers liquidity to other investors in these assets, allowing banks, corporations and individuals to effectively raise capital, dispose of unwanted assets, and manage risk.

Not all hedge fund strategies carry significant levels of leverage. In fact, many of the hedge fund strategies that performed poorly in recent markets, such as funds that specialize in emerging markets, tend to carry little or no leverage. Other hedge fund strategies that offer a low return on assets, such as mortgage-backed securities lending, are leveraged to provide adequate return to investors. However, most other investors in these securities such as banks and insurance companies, also employ leverage for these assets for exactly the same reason.[2]

The articles reprinted in this section are included to address some of the myths of investment in hedge funds, as well as to address some of the important issues in implementing a hedge fund investment strategy. The first article focuses on the selection of a suitable set of benchmarks for use in evaluating manager performance. Next, the question of efficient approaches to designing hedge fund portfolios is addressed, using both passive diversification and active manager choice. Finally, the source of return to hedge funds is discussed in an article on the risk and return performance of hedge funds as well as traditional stock and bond investments.

ARTICLE REVIEW

Many performance indexes can be used as benchmarks for hedge fund performance. An appropriate benchmark will reflect the particular style of an investment manager, and will serve as a surrogate for the manager in studies of risk and return performance and asset allocation. In this section's first article, "A Review of Hedge Fund Performance Benchmarks," David McCarthy and Richard Spurgin compare the composition and performance of hedge fund performance indexes produced by Management Accounts Reports (MAR), Hedge Fund Research (HFR), and Evaluation Associates Capital Markets (EACM). Performance is analyzed in relation to passive performance indexes such as the S&P 500 and MSCI stock indexes as well as actively managed assets such as the Fidelity Magellan fund and Fidelity Intermediate bond Fund. Results demonstrate that, over the time period analyzed, hedge funds offered risk-adjusted returns greater than traditional stock and bond investments. However, results also demonstrate that there are considerable differences in the relative performance of these hedge fund indexes. These differences are sizeable enough that investors must realize that, as in the case for traditional stock and bond investment, the use of seemingly similar benchmark hedge fund indexes may result in different asset allocation decisions.

Benchmark indexes are important as investment benchmarks primarily if portfolios can be created which mimic their performance. In the second article, "Naive Diversification for Hedge Funds," Thomas Henker shows that, as for managed futures and traditional equity portfolios, naive diversification (random selection with equal weighting) in various hedge fund strategies requires approximately ten to fifteen hedge funds to exhaust the risk reduction from diversification. Results also show that as the number of funds increases to approximately 10, the correlation of the portfolio with the under-

EXHIBIT 1 PERCENTAGE OF ASSETS IN ALTERNATIVE HFR HEDGE FUND CLASSIFICATIONS (12/1998)

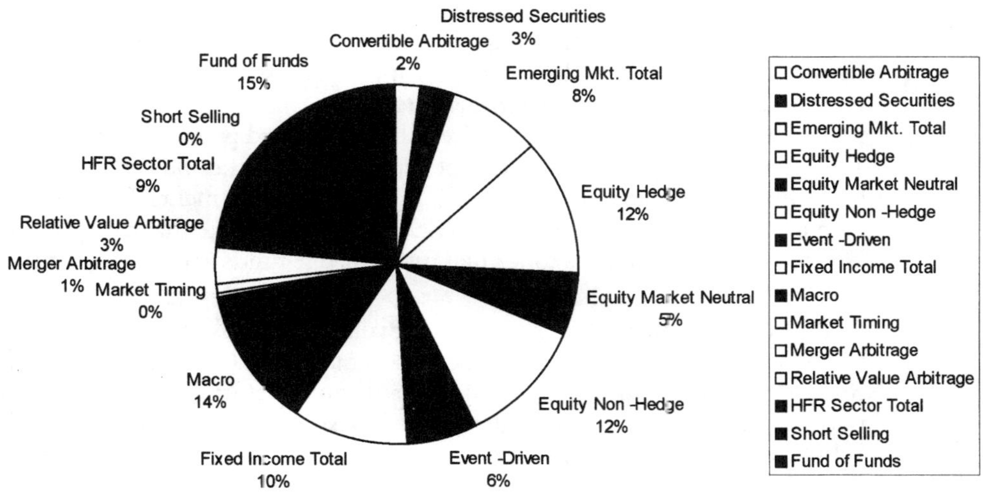

lying comparison active manager index approaches 0.90. However, the actual number of required hedge funds to mimic a particular benchmark index is dependent on the strategy index chosen.[3]

Market-neutral strategies are often viewed as the dominant, but by no means the only strategy followed by hedge funds. As can be seen in Exhibit 1, as of December 1998, the single largest strategy tracked by Hedge Fund Research (HFR) was equity hedge with 12% of hedge fund assets. Each of the various listed hedge fund strategies have their own unique source of return. Recent research [Sharpe, 1992; Elton et al., 1995] has shown that for stock and bond mutual fund investors, multi-factor models often provide improved explanatory power regarding the return structure of the investments. While the sources of return to actively managed assets in the mutual fund industry have been extensively studied, only recently [Ackermann, et al., 1999; Fung and Hsieh, 1997; Schneeweis and Spurgin, 1998] has academic research been conducted on the factors explaining the performance of alternative investments such as hedge funds or managed futures investment.[4]

This is important for several reasons. First, hedge funds often have different trading styles (e.g., long and short cash positions) and trading opportunities (e.g., private investments, commodity and currency markets) than traditional stock and bond mutual fund managers as well as commodity trading advisors. Thus, for hedge funds, theoretical and empirical models of return estimation must be based on the trading style of the hedge fund manager. For instance, hedge funds focusing on pure zero-risk arbitrage positions may have the risk free rate as a benchmark. If the hedge fund focuses on long international equity then international equity benchmarks similar to that used for traditional international mutual funds may be regarded as standard.

As for stocks and bonds, one needs to review the underlying strategies of various fund strategies and the benchmarks used to track that performance. Previous academic results have shown that stocks and bonds may not perform well in rising volatility markets which often are associated with an increase in risk premiums such as credit spreads. Stocks and bonds may be said to be short volatility in that they perform well when volatility is falling. In contrast, some traditional hedge fund strategies (e.g., option-based strategies, futures-based trading strategies, and some market-neutral strategies) may be long volatility in that they perform well in periods of increased market volatility or rapidly changing price trends. In the fourth article, "Multi-Factor Analysis of Hedge Funds, Managed Futures, and Mutual Fund Return and Risk Characteristics," Thomas Schneeweis and Richard Spurgin show that hedge funds and managed futures trading advisors have different trading styles and trading opportunities than traditional stock and bond mutual fund managers. As a result returns to managed futures and hedge funds are driven by factors (e.g., return drivers) that incorporate the possibility of returns to trending prices, short sales, and market volatility. In this study, a large set of factors is used to describe return movement of both traditional stock and bond funds and managed futures and hedge fund investments. Similar to other academic studies [Fung and Hiesh, 1997,1998] results indicate that a different set of market factors explains returns to mutual funds, hedge funds and managed futures investment.

To the degree that different factors explain the returns to managed futures, hedge funds, and stock and bond fund returns, each may provide investors exposure to unique sources of return, and provide an important source return to a diversified investment portfolio. In the fifth article, "Alternative Investments in the Institutional Portfolio," Schneeweis and Spurgin show that the optimal asset allocation to hedge funds is partly

EXHIBIT2 SUMMARY OF SELECTED RESEARCH REGARDING HEDGE FUND RESEARCH

Bibliography	Title	Topic	Major Results
Lake, R.ed. (Euromoney, 1998)	Evaluating and Implementing Hedge Fund Strategies	Series of articles dealing with the performance, evaluation and analysis of hedge fund strategies.	▪ Articles provides evidence of profitability in various hedge fund strategies.
Nicholas, J. (Bloomberg,1998)	Investing in Hedge Funds	Review of hedge fund industry and relative styles.	▪ Practitioner review of hedge fund industry and strategies.
Crerend, W. (McCRaw-Hill, 1997)	Fundamentals of Hedge Fund Investing	Review of hedge fund industry and relative styles.	▪ Practitioner review of hedge fund industry and strategies.
Lederman J. and R. Klien eds, (Irwin, 1996)	Market Neutral	Series of articles dealing with the performance, evaluation and analysis of hedge fund strategies.	▪ Articles provides evidence of profitability in various market neutral hedge fund strategies.
Fung, W. and D. Hiesh, RFS. (1997)	Empirical Characteristics of Dynamic Trading Strategies: The Case of Hedge Funds	Economic and market factors related to hedge fund performance.	▪ Academic based presentation of strategy groupings and differences in the market factors affecting the basis of relative groupings.
Fung, W. and D. Hsieh, FMDR (1998)	Price Trend Following Trading Strategies: Theory and Empirical Evidence	Reviews the performance of managed futures traders as lookback options.	▪ Lookback strategy can replicate key features of CTA performance.
Ackerman, C. and D. Ravenscraft, (JF) Forthcoming	A Comparative Study of Hedge Funds and Mutual Funds	Comparison of the Performance of Hedge funds and Mutual Funds.	▪ Presents evidence that the source of return difference between comparable hedge funds and mutual funds is due to performance fees and lockup periods (e.g., illiquidity premia).

Schneeweis, T., JAI (1998)	Evidence of Superior Performance Persistence in Hedge Funds: An Empirical Comment	Hedge fund manager performance Persistence.	▪ Result show the importance of using risk adjusted data in testing for relative return performance. While some managers show extreme relative risk/return performance, evidence of consistent outperformance is limited, indicating the importance of asset allocation in traditional and alternative investment management.
Schneeweis et al., JAI (Forthcoming)	Individual CTA/Hedge Fund Movement and Manager Indices	Review of manager based performance indices as surrogates for individual managers.	▪ Reviews consistency of return movement between individual managers and their underlying manager index. Shows a high degree of common directional return movement when the index moves into its upper or lower return quartile.
McCarthy, D. and R. Spurgin, JAI (1998)	A Review of Hedge Fund Performance Benchmarks	Hedge fund index Performance.	• Review the relative performance of a wide range of alternative manager based hedge fund indices.
Park, J. and J. Staum. (JAI, 1998)	"Performance Persistence in the Alternative Investment Industry"	Hedge fund and CTA performance Persistence	• Presents evidence that hedge funds and CTAs show a relationship between past and future risk adjusted performance
Schneeweis et al., JAI (1998)	"Dealing With Myths of Hedge Fund Investment"	Review of various questions related to hedge fund	▪ Reviews series of articles on questions of hedge fund performance and market impact (e.g., leverage, transparency).

Journal abbreviations: *JAI* — Journal of Alternative Investments; RFS — Review of Financial Studies; FMDR— Foundation of Managed Derivatives Research; *JF* — Journal of Finance;

EXHIBIT 3A PERFORMANCE MEASURES FOR HEDGE FUND INDICES

NineYear Performance of Indices: January, 1990 - December, 1998	EACM 100	MARCTA$	GSCI	S&P 500	Salomon US Treasury Bond	MSCI	Salomon US World Bond
Average Annual Return	13.9%	12.6%	0.4%	16.5%	8.3%	10.0%	9.1%
Standard Deviation	4.1%	10.8%	16.7%	13.5%	4.2%	14.2%	6.0%
Sharpe Ratio	2.19	0.71	-0.27	0.85	0.77	0.35	0.68
Minimum Monthly Return	-4.6%	-6.2%	-13.0%	-15.6%	-2.3%	-14.3%	-3.7%
Maximum Monthly Return	4.7%	13.5%	20.7%	10.8%	4.0%	10.0%	5.8%
Correlation With EACM 100		0.47	0.11	0.41	0.18	0.33	0.00
Excess Annual Breakeven		7.6%	9.1%	7.5%	8.4%	8.5%	9.0%

Nine Year Performance of Asset Portfilios: January, 1990 - December, 1998	Port I US Stock, Bond, Commodity and Hedge Funds	Port II US Stock, Bond, and Commodity	Port III US Stock and Bond	Port IV Wrld. Stock, Bond, Commodity and Hedge Funds	Port V Wrld. Stock, Bond, and Commodity	Port VI World Stock and Bond
Average Annual Return	11.7%	10.4%	12.6%	9.5%	8.2%	9.8%
Standard Deviation	6.4%	6.7%	7.7%	7.0%	7.3%	8.6%
Sharpe Ratio	104.4%	81.3%	98.0%	64.0%	44.4%	56.0%
Minimum Monthly Return	-5.9%	-6.1%	-6.1%	-5.4%	-5.6%	-5.4%
Maximum Monthly Return	5.6%	5.6%	7.2%	5.4%	5.3%	6.7%
Correlation With EACM 100		42.2%	39.9%		30.3%	26.9%
Excess Annual Breakeven		7.6%	7.4%		8.4%	8.3%

EXHIBIT 3B PERFORMANCE MEASURES FOR HEDGE FUND INDICES AND ASSET PERFORMANCE

Four Year Performance of Indices: January, 1995 - December, 1998	EACM 100	MARCTA$	GSCI	S&P 500	Salomon US Treasury Bond	MSCI	Salomon US World Bond
Average Annual Return	11.8%	11.4%	-2.9%	26.6%	9.6%	17.4%	8.9%
Standard Deviation	4.7%	9.4%	17.3%	14.4%	4.1%	13.3%	6.1%
Sharpe Ratio	2.49	1.20	-0.18	1.84	2.33	1.30	1.44
Minimum Monthly Return	-4.6%	-4.9%	-13.0%	-15.6%	-2.0%	-14.3%	-3.5%
Maximum Monthly Return	3.5%	7.9%	9.7%	7.9%	4.0%	8.7%	5.8%
Correlation With EACM 100		0.30	0.23	0.63	-0.02	0.61	-0.21
Excess Annual Breakeven		5.6%	7.1%	2.2%	6.6%	4.0%	7.2%

Four Year Performance of Asset Portfolios: January, 1995 - December, 1998	Port I US Stock, Bond, Commodity and Hedge Funds	Port II US Stock, Bond, and Commodity	Port III US Stock and Bond	Port IV Wrld. Stock, Bond, Commodity and Hedge Funds	Port V Wrld. Stock, Bond, and Commodity	Port VI World Stock and Bond
Average Annual Return	15.8%	14.4%	18.4%	11.8%	10.4%	13.4%
Standard Deviation	6.8%	7.3%	7.6%	6.6%	7.2%	7.4%
Sharpe Ratio	2.30	1.96	2.40	1.77	1.43	1.79
Minimum Monthly Return	-5.9%	-6.1%	-6.1%	-5.4%	-5.6%	-5.4%
Maximum Monthly Return	5.0%	5.6%	5.3%	4.6%	4.8%	5.8%
Correlation With EACM 100		0.59	0.58	0.00	0.47	0.44
Excess Annual Breakeven		3.1%	1.9%	0.0%	5.0%	4.3%

determined by the underlying investment strategy and partly by the approach used to determine the expected risk and return parameters of the assets. In their analysis, they show the benefits of diversifying across a range of alternative hedge fund strategies. They also show that allocation to hedge funds is not driven by the high returns earned in the past decade but by the low correlation with other assets. Lastly, they illustrate the relative performance of hedge fund portfolios in different market environments.

RESEARCH IN HEDGE FUNDS

Prior to 1995 there were almost no academic studies of hedge fund performance. However, academic interest in this area has grown rapidly in recent years, with a number of important articles published in 1997 and 1998. There are also a number of practitioner-oriented sources of information about the specific strategies employed by hedge funds and methods of selecting managers. A guide to these articles and books is given Exhibit 2.

EXHIBIT 4 RISK AND RETURN OF STOCK, BOND AND HEDGE FUNDS: 1990-1998

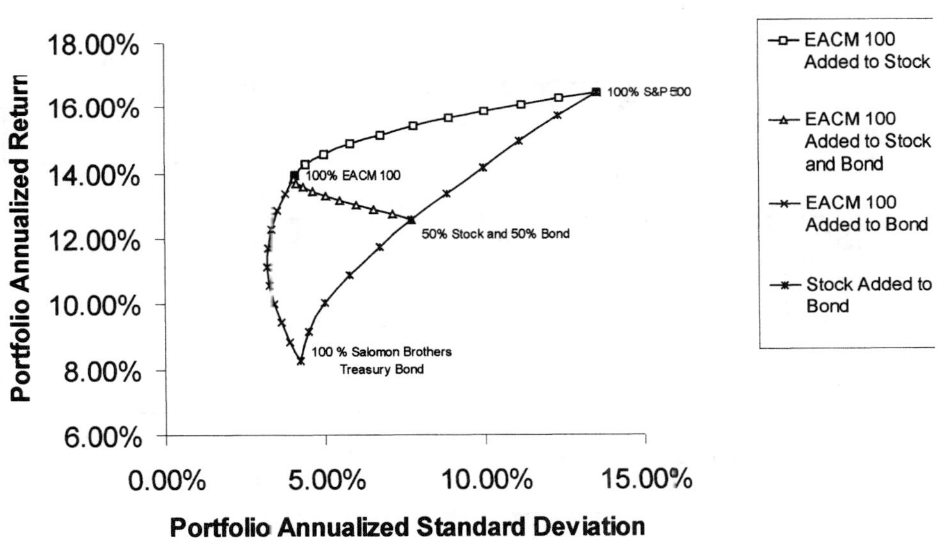

EXHIBIT 5 RISK AND RETURN OF STOCK, BOND AND HEDGE FUNDS: 1995-1998

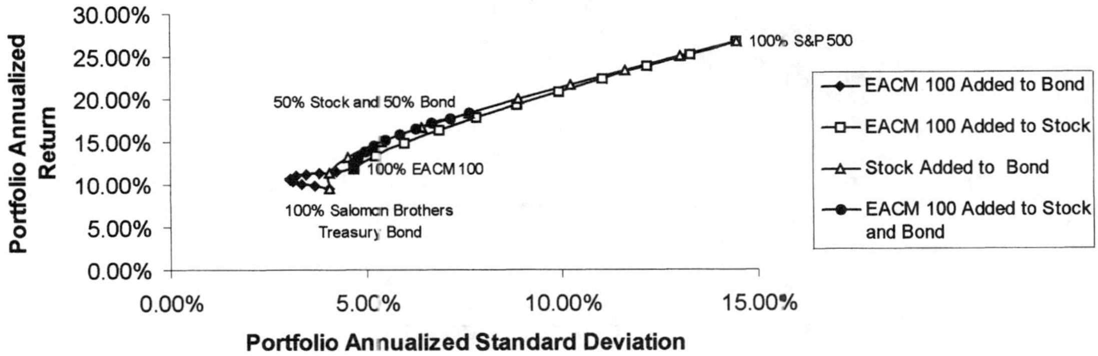

Updated Risk and Return Performance

Results in Exhibit 3a and 3b show that investment in a portfolio of hedge funds provided similar returns to stock and bond investments (e.g., S&P 500, Salomon Brothers U.S. Treasury bond indexes, Salomon Brothers World Government bond indexes and MSCI world stock indexes), but at a lower level of historical risk. As a result, a hedge fund portfolio may offer the investor an increased return-to-risk ratio when added to diversified portfolio.[5] The benefits of hedge funds in diversified portfolios are illustrated in Exhibit 4, which shows that the EACM hedge fund improves the risk/return tradeoff of a traditional asset portfolio. Similar results are shown in Exhibits 5, which uses just the most recent four-year period from 1995-1998, a period when hedge funds offered lower returns and higher volatility than during the entire period. Results in Exhibits 6a-6d also show the importance of hedge fund strategies in months when equity benchmarks have their worst performance. In fact, hedge fund strategies per-

EXHIBIT 6A PERFORMANCE OF STOCK AND BOND RETURNS IN 10 WORST S&P 500 MONTHS (1/90 TO 12/98)

	Aug-	Jan-90	Sep-	Jul-96	Nov-91
S&P 500	-14.5%	-6.6%	-4.8%	-4.4%	-4.2%
MSCI World	-13.3%	-4.7%	-10.5%	-3.5%	-4.3%
SB Treas. Bond	2.7%	-1.4%	1.0%	0.2%	1.0%

EXHIBIT 6B PERFORMANCE OF EQUITY HEDGE FUNDS IN 10 WORST S&P 500 MONTHS (1/90 TO 12/98)

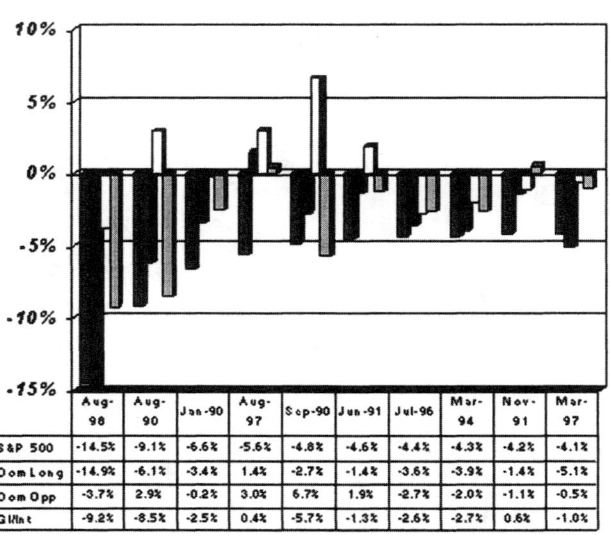

	Aug-98	Aug-90	Jan-90	Aug-97	Sep-90	Jun-91	Jul-96	Mar-94	Nov-91	Mar-97
S&P 500	-14.5%	-9.1%	-6.6%	-5.6%	-4.8%	-4.6%	-4.4%	-4.3%	-4.2%	-4.1%
Dom Long	-14.9%	-6.1%	-3.4%	1.4%	-2.7%	-1.4%	-3.6%	-3.9%	-1.4%	-5.1%
Dom Opp	-3.7%	2.9%	-0.2%	3.0%	6.7%	1.9%	-2.7%	-2.0%	-1.1%	-0.5%
Gl/Int	-9.2%	-8.5%	-2.5%	0.4%	-5.7%	-1.3%	-2.6%	-2.7%	0.6%	-1.0%

EXHIBIT 6C PERFORMANCE OF EVENT DRIVEN FUNDS IN 10 WORST S&P 500 MONTHS (1/90 TO 12/98)

	Aug-98	Aug-90	Jan-90	Aug-97	Sep-90	Jun-91	Jul-96	Mar-94	Nov-91	Mar-97
S&P 500	-14.5%	-9.1%	-6.6%	-5.6%	-4.8%	-4.6%	-4.4%	-4.3%	-4.2%	-4.1%
ARB	-6.0%	-5.7%	-11.1%	0.6%	-5.7%	0.3%	-0.4%	0.7%	1.0%	0.9%
BANK	-6.2%	-0.1%	-0.5%	0.2%	-2.7%	1.0%	-0.5%	-1.5%	1.2%	0.4%
MULTI	-8.5%	-0.2%	-2.7%	0.7%	-1.9%	1.1%	-0.1%	-0.7%	1.3%	0.2%

EXHIBIT 6D PERFORMANCE OF RELATIVE VALUE HEDGE FUNDS IN 10 WORST S&P 500 MONTHS (1/90 TO 12/98)

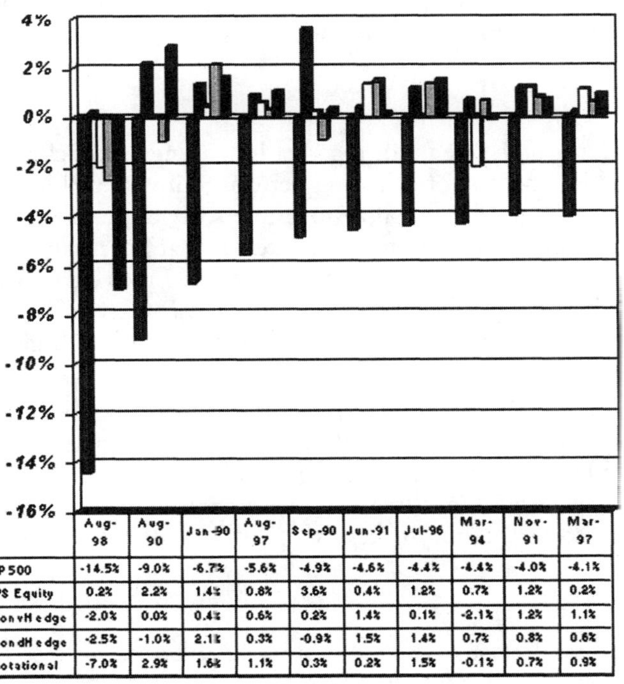

	Aug-98	Aug-90	Jan-90	Aug-97	Sep-90	Jun-91	Jul-96	Mar-94	Nov-91	Mar-97
SP500	-14.5%	-9.0%	-6.7%	-5.6%	-4.9%	-4.6%	-4.4%	-4.4%	-4.0%	-4.1%
L/S Equity	0.2%	2.2%	1.4%	0.8%	3.6%	0.4%	1.2%	0.7%	1.2%	0.2%
ConvHedge	-2.0%	0.0%	0.4%	0.6%	0.2%	1.4%	0.1%	-2.1%	1.2%	1.1%
BondHedge	-2.5%	-1.0%	2.1%	0.3%	-0.9%	1.5%	1.4%	0.7%	0.8%	0.6%
Rotational	-7.0%	2.9%	1.6%	1.1%	0.3%	0.2%	1.5%	-0.1%	0.7%	0.9%

formed as expected during the August 1998 global equity market decline. Strategies that have historically performed poorly when stock and bond markets perform poorly had negative returns during August, and those strategies that tend to be negatively correlated with the stock market in periods of stock market distress performed well.[6]

Performance Persistence

Investment choices are often based on past performance. The usefulness of historical hedge fund data is a topic of controversy. As is true for stock and bond analysis, Brown et al. [forthcoming] show that hedge funds with similar investment styles generate similar returns, and that there is little evidence of manager skill within a particular style group. Other researchers have noted that the volatility of returns is more persistent through time than the level of returns. This research [Schneeweis, 1998, Park and Staum, 1998] shows that the best forecast of future returns is one that is consistent with prior volatility, not one that is consistent with prior returns.[7]

Survivor Bias

Survivor bias is a major concern for investors in hedge funds. Survivor bias results when managers with poor track records exit the business, while managers with good records remain. If survivor bias is large, then the historical record of the average surviving manager is higher than the average return of all managers over the test period. Since a diversified portfolio would have likely consisted of funds that were destined to fail as well as funds destined to succeed, studying only survivors results in overestimation of historical return. Brown et al. [Forthcoming] estimated this bias to be in the range of 3% per year. One explanation for the proliferation of funds-of-funds is that managers of these funds may be able avoid managers destined to fail, thereby mitigating the survivor bias problem. Investors may be willing to bear an additional layer of management fees in order to reduce exposure to these funds.

CONCLUSION

It is difficult to lump all hedge funds together into a single asset class. Like a mutual fund, a hedge fund is a method of delivering returns to investors, but is not an investment in itself. Some hedge funds follow investment styles that are indistinguishable from equity mutual funds. Others follow strategies that are more consistent with a managed futures account. In recent years market-neutral funds have attracted the most investment. These funds come the closest to a unique asset class, as they have been able to deliver very attractive returns that are largely uncorrelated with global equity and debt markets.

The academic community has only just begun to study hedge funds in detail. The articles in this book represent a selection of the first group of articles to address some of the fundamental questions surrounding hedge fund investment. These questions include selection of appropriate benchmarks, construction of hedge fund portfolios, and the source of return to hedge fund strategies.

ENDNOTES

[1] One cannot cover in detail all of the misconceptions about the performance of hedge funds or other alternative investments. Journals such as *The Journal of Alternative Investments* have begun publication to permit a better long-term understanding of many of the new alternative investment forms.

[2] Banks for instance generally carry about 8 cents of equity capital for each dollar of assets, a leverage ratio of about 12 times. Very few hedge funds carry this degree of leverage.

[3] While benchmarks provide information about the performance of hedge funds, questions remain about the basis for this performance. The hedge fund industry encompasses a wide range of investment strategies. Each of these strategies has unique risk and return opportunities. Interested readers are directed to Goldman Sachs and Financial Risk Management "Hedge Funds Demystified: Their

Potential Role Institutional Portfolios," The Journal of Alternative Investments, [Winter, 1999] This article reviews the hedge fund industry, with a special emphasis on market-neutral strategies

[4] This chapter contains material more fully discussed in "Multi-Factor Analysis of Hedge Fund, Managed Futures, and Mutual Funds Return and Risk Characteristics [Schneeweis and Spurgin, 1998].

[5] Portfolio I is a portfolio comprised of the MAR$CTA (10%), GSCI (10%), S&P500 (40%), and Salomon TBond (40%) Indexes, Portfolio II is the GSCI (20%), S&P500 (40%), and SB TBond Index (40%), and Portfolio III is an equally weighted stock and bond portfolio. Portfolios IV though VI are similar to Portfolios I through III with the substitution of the MSCI World equity and Salomon Brothers World Bond Index for the S&P 500 and Salomon Treasury Bond Index. Excess Annual Breakeven is a measure of the difference between the actual return achieved and the return required for the investment to increase the Sharpe ratio of the portfolio.

SELECTED REFERENCES

Ackermann, Carl and David Ravenscraft, "The Impact of Regulatory Restrictions on Fund Performance: A Comparative Study of Hedge Funds and Mutual," Working Paper, University of Notre Dame and University of North Carolina, (July, 1998).

Brown, S. W. Goetsmann, R. Ibbotson "Offshore Hedge Funds:Survival and Performance, 1989—1995," Journal of Business (Forthcoming).

Crerend, W. Fundamentals of Hedge Fund Investing: McGraw Hill, (1998).

Fung, William and David A. Hsieh, "Empirical Characteristics of Dynamic Trading Strategies: The Case of Hedge Funds," *The Review of Financial Studies* Vol. 10 (1997), pp. 275-302.

Henker, T. and G. Martin, "Naive and Optimal Diversification For Managed Futures", *The Journal of Alternative Investments* (Fall, 1998), pp. 25-39.

Henker, T. "Naïve Diversification for Hedge Funds," *The Journal of Alternative Investments* (Winter, 1998), pp. 30-39.

Jaffer, Sohail ed., *Alternative Investment Strategies.* Euromoney, (1998).

Lederman, Jess. And Robert Klein. *Market Neutral.* Irwin, (1996).

Lake, R. ed. Evaluating and Implementing Hedge Fund Strategies. Euromoney, (1998).

McCarthy, D. and R. Spurgin. "A Review of Hedge Fund Performance Benchmarks," *The Journal of Alternative Investments* (Summer, 1998), pp. 18-28.

Nicholas, J. *Investing in Hedge Funds.* Bloomberg Press, (1998).

Park, James and J. Staum, "Performance persistence in Alternative Investment Industry," Paradigm Capital Management, (1998).

Schneeweis, T. *The Benefits of Managed Futures.* AIMA, (1996).

Schneeweis, T. "Evidence of Superior Performance Persistence in Hedge Funds: An Empirical Comment," *The Journal of Alternative Investments* (Fall, 1998), pp. 76-80.

Schneeweis, T. "Dealing with Myths of Hedge Fund Investments," *The Journal of Alternative Investments* (Winter, 1998), pp. 5-13.

Schneeweis, T. and R. Spurgin. "Alternative Investments in the Institutional Portfolio" AIMA, (1998).

Schneeweis, T. and R. Spurgin, "Managed Futures, Hedge Fund and Mutual Fund Return Estimation: A Multi-Factor Approach", *The Journal of Alternative Investments* (Fall, 1998). pp. 1-24.

9 A REVIEW OF HEDGE FUND PERFORMANCE BENCHMARKS

DAVID MCCARTHY
Global Asset Management

RICHARD SPURGIN
Clark University

A number of firms have created benchmark indexes that purport to mimic the performance of particular hedge fund strategies or styles. However, because the hedge fund industry is relatively young, until recently the amount of historical data available for analysis has not been sufficient to draw statistically meaningful conclusions about the relative performance of these indexes. This article compares the composition and performance of hedge fund performance indexes produced by Management Accounts Reports (MAR), Hedge Fund Research (HFR), and Evaluation Associates Capital Markets (EACM). Performance is analyzed in relation to passive performance indexes such as the S&P 500 stock index as well as actively managed assets such as the Fidelity Magellan fund and commodity trading advisors (CTAs). Results demonstrate that for the time period of analysis (1990-1997), hedge funds offered risk-adjusted returns greater than traditional stock and bond investments from 1990 through 1997. However, results also demonstrate that there are considerable differences in the relative performance of these indexes. These differences are sizeable enough that investors must realize that using seemingly similar benchmark hedge fund indexes from different firms may result in different asset allocation decisions.

Prior research on the relative performance of equity benchmarks (for example, see Reilly and Akhtar, 1995) and bond market benchmarks (Reilly, Kao, and Wright, 1992) has shown that seemingly similar equity benchmarks (e.g., S&P 500, Dow Jones) have significant differences in performance. Schneeweis and Spurgin (1997) have reported on the relative performance of commodity and managed futures benchmarks. Commodity indexes (e.g., Goldman Sachs commodity index, JP Morgan commodity index, Dow Jones Commodity Index) and managed futures indexes (Barclay, TASS, Managed Accounts Reports) are shown in Schneeweis and Spurgin (1997) to have unique features that result in differential return, correlation, and tracking error. Furthermore, despite the high correlation between commodity trading advisor (CTA) performance benchmarks, a month-to-month comparison of the index returns reveals considerable discrepancy in certain months. Given the wide differences in performance for seemingly similar stock, bond, commodity, and managed futures indices, it is reasonable to assume that hedge fund indexes exhibit considerable differences as well.

Relative hedge fund performance has been studied by Schneeweis and Spurgin (1998). However, their study was hampered by the limited time period analyzed. For example, Schneeweis and Spurgin (1998) only use 20 monthly observations in their analysis.[1] This article utilizes the methodology of Reilly, Kao, and Wright (1992) and Schneeweis and Spurgin (1997) to identify similarities and differences in benchmark performance and tracking error using monthly data covering an eight-year period from 1990 through 1997, a total of 96 observations. Results indicate that hedge fund benchmark indices differ from each other in important ways (e.g., return measurement and sector composition). Results also indicate that the differences between hedge fund indices are more pronounced than the differences between equity and managed futures benchmarks. This finding has implications for asset allocation recommendations, as the pro forma risk and return characteristics of a portfolio will differ depending on which benchmark is used in the analysis.

In the following section, the manager composition and return measurement structure of three widely disseminated hedge fund indices are discussed, as well as the implications of their alternative composition and return structures on risk and return performance and risk and return optimization is reviewed. The indexes are compiled by Managed Account Reports (MAR), Hedge Fund Research (HFR), and Evaluation Associates Capital Markets (EACM).[2] The next section reviews the data and methodology used in this study, followed by a section on results. The results include descriptive statistics, correlation, and tracking error for the indexes. Conclusions and areas of future research are discussed in the last section.

HEDGE FUND INDICES IN ASSET MANAGEMENT

Benchmarks are used for two main purposes. One is to serve as a proxy for the return to some asset class. This proxy can be used to decide how to allocate investments among broad asset classes. The other use is to provide a means of evaluating the performance of a particular manager. An index created primarily with the latter objective in mind will tend to include fewer managers and be focused on a particular strategy or investment style. The former calls for a greater sample of hedge fund managers, arranged in fewer classifications, in order to obtain a greater representative sample of the existing universe.

Hedge Fund Indices

There are many differences in the construction of the major hedge fund indexes. Indexes differ in

- *Selection Criteria,* the criteria used to decide which hedge funds are included in the index and which are excluded. Examples of selection criteria include length of service, assets under management, and restrictions on new investment.
- *Style Classification,* which determines how each hedge fund selected for inclusion is assigned to a style-specific sub-index.
- *Weighting Scheme,* or how much weight a particular fund's return is given in the index. Common weighting schemes are equally-weighted and dollar-weighted based on assets under management
- *Rebalancing Scheme,* which determines when assets are reallocated among the funds in a particular index. For example, some funds assume assets are rebalanced monthly, while others assume annual rebalancing

Among hedge fund indexes, MAR and HFR use fairly all-inclusive selection criteria. Their indexes are constructed from virtually all hedge fund managers who report their returns. In certain cases hedge funds whose performance not reported by the hedge fund manager is obtained from secondary sources. In contrast, EACM indexes are limited to 100 large funds selected by EACM management. As such, HFR and MAR indexes are directly comparable to broad measures of the stock market such as the Russell 3000, while EACM indexes are comparable to large-capitalization indexes such as the

S&P 100 index.

Sector classification is determined primarily from disclosure documents and from personal discussions with the hedge fund advisors. The principal difference between the various hedge fund indexes is in the number of classifications. EACM assigns each fund to one of five primary classes; relative value, event-driven, equity hedge, global asset allocators, and short selling. With the exception of short sellers, EACM also assigns each fund to one of 12 sub-groups. For example, event-driven funds are assigned to one of three sub-groups; deal arbitrage, bankruptcy/distressed, and multi-strategy. MAR classifies funds in a similar fashion to EACM. MAR identifies five primary classes (event driven, global, global macro, market neutral, and fund of funds) and ten sub-groups (for example, the MAR event driven class is broken into two sub-groups, risk arbitrage and distressed security). HFR, in contrast, classifies funds according to the underlying market sector traded as well as a style classification. This results in a sizeable increase in the number of classification. A total of 27 different strategies were tracked as of the end of 1997, the bulk of which were equity sector classifications (e.g., energy, financial, and health care/biotechnology) and fixed income classifications (e.g., mortgage, high yield, and convertible).

MAR does not use a weighting scheme, but instead reports the median of the returns in each sector. HFR uses equal-weighting. Equal-weighting assumes that assets are rebalanced monthly.[3] EACM recognizes that a lack of liquidity and fund investment rules makes it unrealistic to assume an investor can rebalance monthly. For EACM, the index composition is determined once each year. The index is assumed to be equal-weighted at the start of the year, but the investment is then maintained for the year. This means that top performing funds will have a higher weight towards the end of a calendar year, and poorly performing funds will implicitly have a lower weight in the index.

Survivor bias and selection bias are important factors to consider when using an index. These are particularly important problems when, as is true of the hedge fund indexes, the indexes were created retrospectively. MAR first began reporting results in May, 1994 and HFR and EACM began reporting indexes in 1996. However, all three report monthly performance back as far as 1990. When an index is created from historical results, there is the possibility for both selection bias and survivor bias.

Survivor bias results when failed funds are excluded from historical results. Selection bias occurs when the selection criteria used to create an index favors funds that performed well over the test period, while funds that performed poorly are left out. The degree of survivor/selection bias in the indexes cannot be analytically determined because the exact composition of all the indexes is proprietary. However, it is safe to assume that returns after May, 1994 for MAR and January, 1996 for HFR have low levels of survivor and selection bias.[4] Similarly for EACM, indexes should not exhibit survivor bias after, January, 1996, but selection bias may remain due to the subjective nature of the index composition.

Another difference between indexes is the lag in reporting and revisions to previously reported results. Since the index compilers must wait until month-end reports have been received, organized, and computed, there is a delay of from several days to a few weeks until the information is available for release. MAR and EACM do not revise their indexes, but HFR revises their indexes as many as three times until a final figure is set. Thus, as new information about funds and revisions made by funds to their historical performance are received, one must insure that one is using common data for comparison studies.

DATA AND METHODOLOGY

Monthly returns were obtained for the period from January, 1990 through December, 1997. Hedge fund returns were provided by HFR, MAR, and EACM. Returns for the Standard and Poors 500 Stock Index (S&P500), the Morgan Stanley Capital International Global Stock Index (MSCI), the Salomon Brothers U.S. Treasury Bond Index (US Bond), Salomon World Government Bond Index (World Bond) indexes, one-month Treasury bill yields (Tbill), the Mount Lucas Mgt. commodity index (MLM), and the Goldman Sachs Commodity Index (GSCI) were obtained from Datastream Inc. Data for an actively managed equity account, Fidelity Magellan, and an actively managed bond fund, Fidelity Intermediate Bond, were supplied by Morningstar. A dollar-weighted index of commodity trading advisor performance (CTA) was provided by MAR.[5]

Returns for all data series are expressed as monthly holding period returns. Statistical results include descriptive risk and return characteristics as well as correlation. For selected but comparable equity and hedge fund indices, the tracking error, which measures the degree that an index matches the performance of an alternative benchmark, is also studied. In determining the degree of tracking error, both the mean error and standard deviation of the monthly return differences as well as the mean error and standard deviation of the absolute monthly return differences are reported.

RESULTS

Principal Hedge Fund Indices as Stand Alone Investments

Exhibit 1 presents descriptive statistics (e.g., the average annualized returns, standard deviations) and the correlation with principal traditional and alternative asset benchmarks (e.g., S&P 500, US Bond, GSCI, MLM, MAR CTA, EACM 100, HFR Composite) over the 1/90-12/97 period. Results in Exhibit 1 indicate that, over the time period studied, US and global stock and bond indices performed considerably better than the risk-free rate. In addition, returns for actively managed traditional assets are comparable to their underlying stock or bond benchmarks. The Fidelity Intermediate bond fund underperformed the Salomon Treasury Index (7.36% annual return vs. 8.11%), but the fund also posted a lower standard deviation (3.37 vs. 4.32), resulting in a comparable Sharpe ratio. Fidelity Magellan had almost an identical return to the S&P 500 during the test period, and a slightly higher standard deviation.

Lastly, the performance of the MAR hedge fund-of-funds index, MAR CTA Index, HFR fund composite, and EACM 100 index are also given in Table 1. The returns for the two hedge fund universe indices (HFR and EACM) are similar (17.37% and 15.50% respectively). With roughly comparable standard deviations (5.58% and 3.46% respectively) the Sharpe ratios for the HFR (2.22) and the EACM (3.03) are also similar. In contrast, the MAR CTA index has both a lower return (12.79%) and a higher standard deviation (11.03%) than either of the HFR or EACM hedge fund composites. [6]

Exhibit 2 plots the performance of the measured indices in return/standard deviation space. Most of the hedge fund measures (open squares) are clustered in an area that represents an attractive risk/return relationship as compared to the line connecting the SP500 index performance and the average risk-free rate. This line represents the risk/return tradeoff available with traditional assets, and both the Salomon bond index and the MAR commodity trading advisor index are close to this line. These results suggest that a diversified portfolio of hedge fund advisors could have made an attractive stand-alone investment over the time period studied. However, certain hedge fund managers

EXHIBIT 1 BENCHMARK STOCK, BOND, AND COMMODITY DESCRIPTIVE STATISTICS AND CORRELATIONS, 1990-1997

	Descriptive Statistics					Correlation with Benchmark Indexes										
	Avg. Return	Annual St.Dev.	Sharpe Ratio	Min. Month	Max. Month	S&P 500	Fidelity Magellan	MSCI World Equity	Salomon Treasury Bond	Salomon World Bond	Fidelity Intermediate Bond	GSCI	MARCTA	MAR Hedge Fund Cmp.	EACM 100 Index	HFR Fund Cmp.
Equity Performance Measures																
S&P 500	15.38	12.16	0.85	−9.59	10.85	—	0.92**	0.73**	0.53**	0.52**	0.20*	−0.19	0.02	0.21*	0.31**	0.67**
Fidelity Magellan	15.34	13.36	0.77	−10.31	11.15	0.92**	—	0.74**	0.48**	0.49**	0.24*	−0.19	−0.04	0.20*	0.33**	0.74**
MSCI World Equity	8.53	13.40	0.26	11.12	10.03	0.73**	0.74**	—	0.40**	0.41**	0.43**	−0.16	−0.03	0.16	0.24*	0.57**
Fixed Income Performance Measures																
Salomon Treasury Bond	8.11	4.32	0.72	2.34	3.99	0.53**	0.48**	0.40**	—	0.97**	0.58**	−0.05	0.23*	0.24*	0.37**	0.28**
Salomon World Bond	8.42	5.96	0.57	3.70	5.77	0.52**	0.49**	0.41**	0.97**	—	0.59**	−0.04	0.28**	0.28**	0.43**	0.32**
Fidelity Intermediate Bond	7.36	3.37	0.70	−2.02	3.27	0.20*	0.24*	0.43**	0.58**	0.59**	—	−0.03	0.17	−0.03	0.14	0.03
Hedge Fund Performance Measures																
MAR Hedge Fund Composite	11.17	2.87	2.15	−1.47	3.30	0.20*	0.19	0.16	0.23*	0.28**	−0.04	0.15	0.25*	—	0.63**	0.51**
EACM 100 Index	15.50	3.46	3.03	−0.92	4.72	0.31**	0.33**	0.24*	0.37**	0.43**	0.14	0.03	0.67**	0.63**	—	0.58**
HFR Fund Composite	17.37	5.58	2.22	3.51	4.83	0.67**	0.74**	0.57**	0.28**	0.32**	0.03	−0.08	−0.01	0.51**	0.58**	—
T-Bill	5.01															

Confidence that correlation is not equal to zero: *is 95% confidence, **is 99% confidence.

have the ability to easily change investment areas and styles relative to the investment climate. It is important to measure the stationarity of the relative performance. While hedge funds have performed well in recent years, more data, covering more economic cycles, is needed before we can conclude that the risk/return tradeoff for hedge funds is superior to that of traditional assets.

Principal Hedge Fund Index Correlation with Stock and Bond Positions

The decision to add investment products to an existing portfolio depends on the relative average return and standard deviation of the investment vehicle, the properties of the existing portfolio, and the correlation between the investment vehicle and the portfolio. The correlation between each of the major comparison groups are given in Exhibit 1. As expected, the correlation between the equity benchmarks and other eq-

EXHIBIT 2 RISK AND RETURN FOR HFR HEDGE FUND INDEXES, 1990-1997

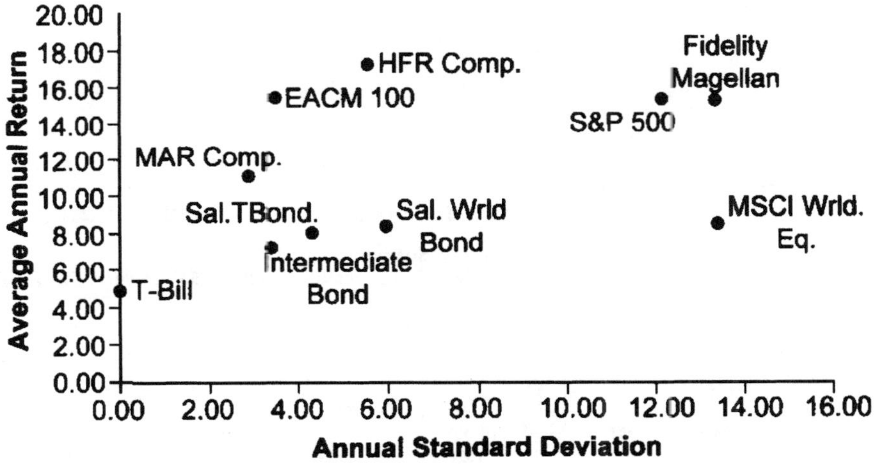

uity-based indexes is above .70. In addition, the correlation between the US bond index and equity indexes is likewise positive (above .40). In contrast, the correlation between the equity indexes and the GSCI, MLM, and CTA indices are generally negative. This is consistent with previous research (Schneeweis, 1996) which supports the notion that passive (GSCI), active (MAR CTA) and passive systematic (MLM) commodity strategies perform well when equity market returns are negative.

The stock indexes show a strong positive correlation with hedge fund indexes. The equity benchmark (e.g., SP500, Magellan, and MSCI) correlations with the EACM 100 were above .24 while the correlation with the HFR indices were all above .57. HFR indexes contain a greater proportion of long-only equity based hedge funds than EACM. The different composition of the EACM 100 and HFR composite index is also illustrated in correlations with GSCI, MLM, and MAR CTA indexes. For the EACM index, correlations with the GSCI and MLM are not significantly different from zero, but the HFR index has a significant negative correlation with the MLM. Also, the EACM has a correlation of .66 with the MAR CTA index, while the HFR has

EXHIBIT 3 HFR HEDGE FUND DESCRIPTIVE STATISTICS AND BENCHMARK CORRELATIONS

		Descriptive Statistics						Correlation with Benchmark Indexes			
Category	Performance Index	Num. Obs.	Avg. Return	Annual St. Dev.	Sharpe Ratio	Min. Month	Max. Month	SP500	USBond	GSCI	MAR CTA
	Convertible Arbitrage	96	11.08	3.23	1.88	2.83	2.29	0.36**	0.34**	0.04	0.02
	Distressed Securities	96	17.80	5.66	2.26	−3.65	6.82	0.32**	0.09	−0.03	-0.15
	Merger Arbitrage	96	12.64	4.49	1.70	−6.68	2.96	0.38**	0.24*	−0.26*	-0.06
	Relative-Value Arb	96	14.55	3.54	2.70	−1.20	5.56	0.22*	0.06	0.06	−0.23*
	Macro	96	20.56	9.34	1.67	−6.61	7.58	0.50**	0.46**	−0.06	0.31**
	Market Timing	96	14.15	7.71	1.19	−5.13	12.90	0.49**	0.17	−0.16	0.01
	Event-Driven	96	17.19	5.89	2.07	−5.86	4.89	0.59**	0.27**	−0.09	−0.14
Emerging Market	Asia	96	11.25	13.27	0.47	−12.86	12.49	0.41**	0.13	−0.23*	−0.06
Equity	Hedge	96	20.98	7.36	2.17	−3.40	6.97	0.58**	0.26*	0.08	−0.03
	Market-Neutral	96	11.45	2.75	2.34	−1.46	2.66	0.15	0.30**	0.13	0.15
	Non-Hedge	96	19.57	12.48	1.17	−11.27	9.15	0.75**	0.23*	−0.13	−0.12
Fixed Income	HighYield	96	12.76	7.17	1.08	−6.37	9.11	0.47**	0.24*	−0.13	−0.15
	Fixed Income Arbitrage	96	11.63	3.86	1.71	−2.61	4.59	−0.02	−0.38**	−0.09	−0.17
Short-Selling		96	1.27	18.74	-0.20	−17.72	11.37	−0.67**	0.14	0.11	0.23*

[2]Confidence that correlation is not equal to zero: *is 95% confidence, **is 99% confidence.

EXHIBIT 4 MAR HEDGE FUND DESCRIPTIVE STATISTICS AND BENCHMARK CORRELATIONS

		Descriptive Statistics						Correlation with Benchmark Indexes				
Category	Performance	Num. Obs.	Average Return	Annual St. Dev.	Sharpe Ratio	Min. Month	Max. Month	SP500	USBond	GSCI	MAR CTA	MAR Within-Category
Event Driven		96	13.78	4.30	2.04	−2.97	4.58	0.39**	0.19	0.00	−0.13	
	Distressed Security	96	16.96	7.20	1.66	−4.31	5.87	0.50**	0.18	0.05	−0.05	0.60**
	Risk Arbitrage	96	13.32	4.32	1.92	−4.28	4.63	0.39**	0.22*	−0.11	−0.11	0.88**
Global		96	12.84	7.80	1.00	−6.18	6.11	0.71**	0.26*	−0.17	−0.08	
	Emerging Market	96	18.74	14.35	0.96	−10.75	17.67	0.41**	0.16	−0.17	−0.10	0.64**
	Established Market	96	16.32	8.28	1.37	6.18	7.17	0.82**	0.30**	−0.17	−0.15	0.88**
	International Market	96	13.69	5.72	1.52	−3.47	4.96	0.40**	0.22*	0.17	−0.03	0.58**
Global Macro		96	15.79	7.58	1.42	−5.51	8.26	0.51**	0.33**	−0.07	0.22*	
Market Neutral		96	10.81	1.41	4.11	−0.13	2.31	0.34**	0.19	−0.05	−0.17	
	Arbitrage	96	11.79	2.48	2.74	−2.21	2.92	0.49**	0.20*	−0.24*	−0.26*	0.74**
	Long/Short	96	10.18	1.38	3.74	0.05	2.14	0.36**	0.38**	0.07	0.10	0.30**
Fund of Funds		96	11.15	4.05	1.52	−2.87	4.40	0.48**	0.35**	0.12	0.20*	
	Diversified	96	15.05	12.99	0.77	−2.77	35.98	0.15	0.09	−0.01	0.09	0.57**
	Niche	96	10.58	5.52	1.01	−4.04	5.76	0.41**	0.32**	0.01	0.25*	0.69**
Short-Selling	Short	96	0.85	15.54	−0.27	−12.86	11.85	0.65**	-0.19	0.25*	0.21*	

Confidence that correlation is not equal to zero: *is 95% confidence, **is 99% confidence.

a correlation close to zero. Again these results are consistent with the HFR having a larger proportion of long equity hedge funds, which have a low or negative correlation with various CTA, commodity, or active futures products. The EACM 100, in contrast, contains a sizeable investment in a strategy called global asset allocators. Global asset allocators are traders who trade primarily futures and option markets and thus have a strategy similar to that of many CTAs.

EXHIBIT 5 EACM HEDGE FUND DESCRIPTIVE STATISTICS AND BENCHMARK CORRELATIONS

		Descriptive Statistics						Correlation with Traditional Benchmark Indexes				
Category	Performance Index	Num. Obs.	Avg. Return	Annual St. Dev.	Sharpe Ratio	Min. Month	Max. Month	SP500	USBond	GSCI	MAR CTA	EACM Within Category
Relative-Value		96	11.67	2.12	3.14	–0.99	2.75	0.01	0.16	0.12	0.13	
	Long/Short Equity	96	10.85	2.76	2.12	–1.08	3.55	–0.20	0.18	0.33**	0.26*	0.26*
	Convertible Hedge	96	10.16	4.45	1.16	–5.09	4.91	0.05	0.14	0.05	0.03	0.76**
	Bond Hedge	96	10.62	2.04	2.75	–1.31	2.48	0.18	0.03	–0.11	–0.11	0.37**
	Multi-Strategy	96	14.86	4.52	2.18	–2.44	4.06	0.01	0.03	0.02	0.11	0.80**
Event-Driven		96	13.40	4.74	1.77	–4.88	4.89	0.46**	0.21*	–0.12	–0.10	
	Deal Arbitrage	96	9.60	6.69	0.69	–11.77	5.73	0.48**	0.21*	–0.27*	–0.18	0.84**
	Bankrupt/Distressed	96	15.86	6.28	1.73	–6.58	9.41	0.25*	0.10	0.11	–0.07	0.79**
	Multi-Strategy	96	14.54	4.27	2.23	–2.69	3.62	0.42**	0.21*	–0.13	0.03	0.86**
Equity		96	18.05	7.26	1.80	–3.98	6.17	0.66**	0.29**	0.00	–0.06	
	Domestic Long	96	17.70	9.21	1.38	–6.31	7.76	0.76**	0.33**	–0.06-	0.15	0.88**
	Domestic Opportunistic	96	16.35	7.74	1.46	–3.22	7.11	0.12	0.07	0.36**	0.06	0.63**
	Global/ International	96	19.61	10.52	1.39	–8.86	7.76	0.61**	0.27*	–0.21*	–0.04	0.83**
Global Asset Allocators		96	20.87	10.79	1.47	–5.59	11.30	0.02	0.24*	0.04	0.92**	
	Discretionary	96	19.97	8.13	1.84	–5.44	7.34	0.09	0.17	0.05	0.38**	0.63**
	Systematic	96	21.07	17.56	0.92	–10.37	19.12	–0.02	0.21*	0.03	0.95**	0.93**
Short-Selling		96	–3.78	22.78	–0.39	–13.92	16.13	0.72**	–0.17	0.05	0.20	

Confidence that correlation is not equal to zero: *is 95% confidence, **is 99% confidence.

Hedge Fund Subindices: Descriptive Statistics and Correlations

The descriptive statistics and correlation coefficients in the previous section emphasized the relationship between the hedge fund composite indices and various traditional stock, bond, and commodity indices. Composite indices are comprised up of a series of subindices, each representing a particular market or style. The differences in risk/return profile and correlation between the indexes discussed in the previous section should reflect differences in sub-index composition. However, one would also expect greater homogeniety among subindex performance, with similar return and correlation relationships for similar subindexes.

Descriptive statistics for hedge fund subindexes are given in Exhibits 3-5. Results are similar to those presented in the previous section. In general, subindex trading strategies which limit exposure to the systematic risks of stock and bond investment, such as relative arbitrage or relative value subindices, had lower returns and lower risk than fully exposed market sector strategies. For instance, for each of the index groups, the unhedged hedge equity subindices had higher returns than the market-neutral or long/short equity indexes, but also had higher risk. Similarly, unhedged equity subindices had the highest correlation with the S&P 500 (HFR Non-Hedge Equity, .75; MAR Global Established Market, .82; and EACM Domestic Long, .76). These correlations are similar to that reported for the Fidelity Magellan fund versus the S&P 500 (0.92). Market-neutral or arbitrage subindices have the lowest correlation across the measured benchmarks. For instance, for EACM Relative Arbitrage subindexes, the correlation with the stock, bond, commodity and CTA benchmarks were all insignificantly different from zero except in two minor exceptions (long/short equity with GSCI (.33) and long/short equity with MAR CTA (.26)).

In Exhibit 6, the descriptive statistics (average return, standard deviation, Sharpe ratio) as well as the intrasample correlations are given for a matched set of HFR, MAR, and EACM hedge fund subindices. Hedge fund subindices were grouped by name

EXHIBIT 6 EFFECTS OF DIVERSIFICATION WITHIN THE EQUITY HEDGE FUND CATEGORY

Panel A: Tracking Error for Traditional Assets and Broad-Based Hedge Fund Indices

Index 1:	S&P500	S&P500	MSCI	US Bond	HFR Comp	HFR Comp	EACM100
Index 2:	MSCI	FidMagln	FidMagln	FidBond	EACM100	MAR FoF	MAR FoF
Avg. Tracking Error	0.57	0.00	-0.57	0.06	0.14	0.52	0.38
StDev	2.72	1.52	2.80	0.38	1.32	0.99	0.84
Maximum	8.90	3.67	10.19	1.49	2.60	3.41	2.97
Minimum	-9.26	-5.02	-8.93	-0.91	-4.92	-3.08	-1.53
Avg. Absolute Tracking	2.00	1.19	2.08	0.30	1.04	0.85	0.71

Panel B: Tracking Error for Hedge Fund Sub-Indices

		Event			*Distressed*			*Equity*	
Index 1:	HFR	HFR	MAR	HFR	HFR	MAR	HFR	HFR	MAR
Index 2:	MAR	EACM	EACM	MAR	EACM	EACM	MAR	EACM	EACM
Avg. Tracking Error	0.33	0.33	0.00	0.06	0.16	0.10	0.63	0.02	-0.61
StDev	1.00	0.91	0.81	1.68	1.04	2.05	2.07	2.64	1.81
Maximum	2.78	3.00	1.83	5.35	3.51	5.14	6.32	6.41	4.07
Minimum	-3.65	-2.53	-2.78	-4.24	-4.53	-7.93	-5.11	-4.87	-5.29
Avg. Absolute Tracking	0.77	0.72	0.63	1.14	0.73	1.43	1.68	2.20	1.44
Correlation	0.82	0.85	0.81	0.62	0.83	0.47	0.85	0.70	0.81

		Relative Value			*Arbitrage*			*Short Selling*	
Index 1:	HFR	HFR	MAR	HFR	HFR	MAR	HFR	HFR	MAR
Index 2:	MAR	EACM	EACM	MAR	EACM	EACM	MAR	EACM	EACM
Avg. Tracking Error	0.32	0.25	-0.07	0.00	0.17	0.17	0.35	0.08	-0.27
StDev	0.89	0.88	0.60	0.44	1.48	1.52	2.69	2.72	4.04
Maximum	3.38	3.58	1.25	1.52	9.21	8.91	6.16	6.63	8.70
Minimum	-2.92	-2.61	-1.94	-0.98	-4.58	-5.48	-8.50	-8.80	-11.93
Avg. Absolute Tracking	0.69	0.68	0.47	0.33	0.86	0.92	2.12	1.99	3.11
Correlation	0.54	0.54	0.37	0.81	0.71	0.65	0.92	0.86	0.80

rather than historical correlations. In cases where no similar name could be found, a close substitute was chosen. In one case, arbitrage subindices, the HFR equity, fixed income, and merger arbitrage were combined in an equal weight to form a HFR arbitrage subindex. While the annualized returns for the sample indices within each subindex often differ substantially, the standard deviations within each subsector are similar. For instance, for the event driven subindex, the annualized return (standard deviation) varies from 17.78% (5.89%) for the HFR event subindex to 13.40% (4.74%) for the EACM subindex.

Not only do differences exist between measured return and risk of potentially comparable indices differences also exist between the correlation patterns of similar subindices. Again, while the correlations between the event and short selling subindices are above .80, the correlations among the relative value/market neutral subindex are generally in the .30 to .60 range. Differences also exist between paired sets within a subindex grouping. In the relative value subindex the correlation between the MAR and HFR arbitrage subindexes is above .80 while the correlation between the MAR and EACM is approximately .60. Again these results show that the use of alternative subindices may result in differing patterns of return movement. The actual relative return movement may be best measured by testing for relative tracking error.

Tracking Error

Tracking error is the difference between the return on two comparison portfolios or indexes. In Exhibit 6, Panel A, tracking error for the S&P 500, MSCI, and the Magellan fund are reported, along with the tracking error for the Salomon bond index and the

Fidelity Intermediate Bond fund. The standard deviation of the tracking error is 1.52 for the SP500 and Magellan, and 2.72 for MSCI and Magellan. Thus in a typical month, there is a 95% chance that the SP500 and Magellan return will be within about 3.04% of each other, while the confidence interval for the difference between MSCI and Magellan is much larger, about 5.6%. In contrast, the standard deviation of the tracking error between the US bond and Fidelity bond is only .38 Panel A also reports the standard deviation of the tracking error for the major hedge fund indices was 1.32 for HFR vs. EACM, 0.99 for EACM vs. MAR Fund of Funds, 0.84 for MAR Fund of Funds vs. EACM. Thus the tracking error for hedge fund indexes is smaller than that of the equity indexes studied, but larger than that of bond indexes.

In Panel B of Exhibit 6, tracking error is reported for the principal hedge fund subindexes. The standard deviation of the tracking error for the reported hedge fund sub indices differed widely depending on the style of investment. For example, Relative value indexes posted low tracking error, with standard deviations ranging from 0.6 (for MAR vs. EACM) to 0.89 (for MAR vs. HFR). However, considerable differences were noted for the distressed and short selling indexes, where, for example, the standard deviation of the short selling indexes ranged from 2.69 (for HFR vs MAR) up to 4.04 (EACM vs. MAR). The differences can be attributed to two factors: the volatility of the underlying funds and also the differences in the composition of the indexes. Relative value hedge funds have very low volatility (about 2% annualized) while short sellers have a much higher standard deviation (about 22% annualized). Thus, even if the relative value indexes had widely differing composition, we would not expect to see a large tracking error. However, the volatility of short sellers will tend to emphasize differences in index composition. In fact, the correlation among short selling indexes is between .80 and 92, much higher than the correlation among relative value indexes (ranges from .37 to .54).

CONCLUSIONS

This study reviewed the risk/return performance and relative tracking error of the various hedge fund benchmark indexes. Results indicate that, while commonalities exist, hedge fund benchmark indices each have unique risk/return patterns. More importantly, because each index differs both in composition and construction, there is considerable tracking error both among broad-based hedge fund indexes and among subindexes that purport to reflect the same investment style. These differences are significant enough to influence investment allocation decisions. However, the differences are not significant enough to call into question the overall risk/return performance of hedge funds during the 1990-1997 period. During this period all the hedge fund indexes report risk-adjusted returns greater the risk-adjusted returns to traditional assets such as stock and bond investment.

APPENDIX I
MANAGED ACCOUNT REPORTS (MAR)

Event Driven:

Distressed Securities: Manager focuses on securities of companies in reorganization and bankruptcy, ranging from senior secured debt (low risk) to common stock of the company (high-risk).

Risk arbitrage: Manager simultaneously buys stock in a company being acquired and sells stock in acquiring company. If the takeover plan fails, traders may be left with losses. Profitable if bidding war pushes up price of target relative to initial bidder.

Fund of Funds:

Diversified: Capital is allocated among a number of hedge funds, providing investors with access to managers they might not be able to discover or evaluate on their own. Diversified across a number of styles to reduce volatility.

Niche: Capital is allocated to a number of funds with a particular trading style or underlying market.

Global:

Emerging: Manager invests in less mature financial markets of the world e.g., Hong Kong, Singapore, Pakistan, and India. Because shorting is not permitted in many emerging markets, managers must go to cash or other markets when valuations make being long unattractive.

Established Market: Manager allocates capital primarily to G7 nations. Principally invests in equities and equity derivatives.

International: Manager studies economic change around the world (except US). Allocates primarily to equity markets, but may use fixed income and derivative markets.

Global Macro:

Opportunistic trading manager that profits from changes in global economics, typically based on major interest rate and currency shifts, using leverage and derivatives.

Market Neutral:

Long/short stocks: Takes equally sized short and long positions in various equities. Attempts to earn return from stock-picking skill while eliminating risk associated with changes in the broad stock market.

Arbitrage: One of the more conservative styles. Manager attempts to take advantage of mispricing. Examples include convertible bonds/stock, fixed income arbitrage, options and other derivative strategies.

Short-sellers: Manager focuses on selling short overvalued stocks. While not technically a market-neutral strategy, this fund can be combined with a long equity strategy to produce a market-neutral portfolio.

EVALUATION ASSOCIATES CAPITAL MARKETS (EACM)

Relative value:

Balanced, or hedged, long and short positions.

Long/short equity: Long undervalued equities/short overvalued equities usually on an equal dollar bases.

Convertible hedging: Long convertible bonds or preferred, short underlying common

Bond Hedge: Yield curve arbitrage or long/short debt positions.

Event-Driven:

Corporate transactions and special situations.

Deal arbitrage: Long/short equity securities of companies involved in corporate transactions.

Bankruptcy/distressed: Long undervalued securities of companies usually in financial distress or operating under Chapter 11.

Multi-Strategy: Includes deal funds dealing in both deal arbitrage and bankruptcy.

Equity Hedge Funds:

Long and Short securities with varying degrees of exposure and leverage.

Domestic long equity: Long undervalued US equities; short selling is used sparingly.

Domestic Opportunistic Equity: Long and short U.S. equity with ability to be net short overall

Global/international: Primarily long undervalued equities with the ability to use short selling opportunistically.

Global Asset Allocators:

(including CTAs) - opportunistically long and short multiple financial and/or non-financial assets.

Systematic: Long or short markets based on trend-following or other quantitative analysis.

Discretionary: Long or short markets based on qualitative/fundamental analysis often with technical input.

Short Selling:

short sale of U.S. equities with expectation of price declines.

HEDGE FUND RESEARCH (HFR)

Convertible Arbitrage:

Investment strategy that is long convertible securities and short the underlying equities.

Distressed Securities:

Invests long (and some short) securities of companies that are in reorganizations, bankruptcies, or some other corporate restructuring.

Merger Arbitrage:

Invests in event-driven situations of corporations, such as leveraged buy-outs, mergers, and hostile takeovers. Managers purchase stock in the firm being taken over and, in some situations, sell short the stock of the acquiring company.

Relative Value Arbitrage:

Attempts to take fully hedged positions that take advantage of mispricings in equity, fixed income, currency, and derivative markets.

Macro Funds:

The investment philosophy is based on shifts in global economies. Derivatives are often used to speculate on currency and interest rate moves.

Market Timing:

Allocation of assets among investments primarily switching between mutual funds and money markets.

Event Driven:

Invests in special corporate situations, including mergers, leveraged buyouts, and distressed securities.

Emerging Markets:
Investment in securities of companies in developing or emerging countries. Subindices include funds that specialize in Asia, Latin America, as well as funds that allocate among global emerging markets.

Equity:
Funds that follow equity investment strategies. Strategies include hedge, which use both long and short positions, Market Neutral, which attempts to hold equal sized long and short positions at all times, and non-hedge which takes primarily leveraged long positions in equities.

Fixed Income:
Investment strategies based on public and private debt instruments with fixed rates and maturities, and their derivatives. Includes *convertible bond, high yield, mortgage,* and *arbitrage* strategies.

Sector Funds:
Invests in corporate securities from specific industry sectors. Includes financial, health/biotech, and technology among others. These funds can take both long and short, and may use options and leverage.

Multi-strategies:
Specific portions are used for separate strategies, e.g., growth, convertible arbitrage, and market neutral.

Opportunistic:
Investment theme is dominated by events that are seen as special situations or opportunities to capitalize from price fluctuations or imbalances.

ENDNOTES

This article was published in *The Journal of Alternative Investments,* Summer 1998.

[1] Other recent analysis of hedge fund performance include Goetzmann et al. (1996) and Fung and Hsieh (1997). These analysis deals with various issues of hedge fund performance including survivor bias and return determination. However, none of theses studies deals directly with the statistical properties of alternative hedge fund indexes.

[2] Other popular set of hedge fund indices include Hennessey and Van Hedge Fund indices. Monthly data for these funds is available starting in 1994. For a common time period (1994-1997) relative comparisons were made with reported indices. Similar differences and benchmark error was reported. Results are available from authors.

[3] For example, assume that a portfolio consists of equal investments in two funds. If one fund returns 50% in one month and the other has a zero% return, then the actual weights in the portfolio at the start of next month are 60% and 40%. Equal-weighting assumes you shift 10% of assets to maintain an equal investment.

[4] Some degree of survivor bias and selection bias is unavoidable, as some funds do not report data and are thus not represented in the indexes, and some funds (especially firms that are having difficulty) stop reporting although they are still in business. Thus the indexes may not exactly represent the population from which they are drawn.

[5] For a description and discussion of the relative performance characteristics of the alternative CTA indices see Schneeweis and Spurgin (1997).

[6] The MAR hedge fund of fund index has a lower return (11.15%) than either of the HFR or EACM composite hedge fund returns. This may be in part to the different composition of fund of fund hedge funds relative to the overall indices. In addition, it is important to note that the lower absolute return of the MAR CTA index is not indicative of their importance in asset allocation. Research by Schneeweis (1996) and Schneeweis and Spurgin (1998) shows CTAs offer unique return opportunities not found in hedge funds and thus should be included in any diversified portfolio.

REFERENCES

Brown S., W. Geotzmann, and R. Ibbotson, "Offshore Hedge Funds: Survival and Performance, 1989-1995." Working Paper. NYU and Yale University, June 1997.

Fung, W. and D. Hsieh. "Empirical Characteristics of Dynamic Trading Strategies: The Case of Hedge Funds."The Review of Financial Studies, 10 (1997) pp. 275-302.

Lukac, Louis, B.W. Brorsen and S. Irwin. "Similarity of Computer Guided Technical Trading Systems," *The Journal of Futures Markets* (February 1988), pp. 1-14.

Reilly and Rashid A. Akhtar. "The Benchmark Error Problem with Global Capital Markets," *The Journal of Portfolio Management* (Fall, 1995), pp. 33-53.

Reilly, F., G.W. Kao, and D. Wright, "Alternative Bond Market Indices", *Financial Analyst Journal* (May-June, 1992), pp. 44-58.

Schneeweis, T. and Richard Spurgin."Comparisons of Commodity and Managed Futures Benchmark Indices." *The Journal of Derivatives* (Summer, 1997) pp. 33-50.

Schneeweis, T. and Richard Spurgin."A Comparison of Return Patterns in Traditional and Alternative Investments" in S. Jaffer, ed. Alternative Investment Strategies, Euromoney (1998) pp. 157-188.

Schneeweis, T. *The Benefits of Managed Futures.* European Managed Futures Association, (August, 1996).

10 NAÏVE DIVERSIFICATION FOR HEDGE FUNDS

THOMAS HENKER
University of New South Wales, Sydney

INTRODUCTION

Numerous studies (Henker and Martin [1998], Park [1998], and Billingsley and Chance [1996]) have focused on the advantages of holding commodity trading advisors (CTAs) or hedge funds as addition to traditional asset classes in a portfolio. Sources of these advantages are relatively high returns over commonly used time periods in the 1990s and a low correlation of hedge fund and CTA index returns with traditional stock and bond portfolios. Because hedge fund indexes are usually not tradable this paper evaluates the reduction of the considerable idiosyncratic risk of individual hedge funds when they are held in portfolios. This reduction of risk achieved in hedge fund portfolios is due to the heterogeneous return characteristics of the hedge funds comprising the hedge fund portfolio. This paper uses individual hedge fund performance of funds included in the EACM 100 index (Evaluation Associates Capital Markets) over 69 months to assess the diversification benefits. Monte Carlo simulation is used to randomly select funds from the fund sector population without replacement. The diversification results rely on the assumption that sample fund performances and covariances are representative for the larger population of hedge funds.

DATA

The data used for this study is a subset of the managers included in the EACM 100 (Evaluation Associates Capital Management) index. Short hedge funds and global asset allocation funds are not considered in this study. The remaining categories are equity, event, and relative value funds with 19,13, and 15 funds with a full performance history for the period of 1/1/92 to 9/30/97. The source for the hedge fund performance data is the LaPorte hedge fund data base. Although the EACM index is a relatively small index, it has the advantage that the funds included in the index are identifiable for researchers and the funds are constantly monitored for consistency in their strategies which facilitates the accurate classification of funds according to their trading strategies. As with other data sources, performance numbers are net of fees (management and performance fees) for a typical account. Lower negotiated fees may increase overall expected return, but the impact on diversification issues is minimal. The exact composition of the data set is described in Exhibit 1.

For the following simulations, strategy categories of the hedge funds are considered separately. This will diminish the anticipated diversification benefits because portfolios are formed only of funds with similar basic strategies. The basic strategy categories are relative value funds, event-driven funds and equity funds. Descriptive statistics for the three groups of funds are summarized in Exhibit 2. The performance of the different groups differs considerably over the time period investigated. Equity fund returns are more than twice as volatile as event and relative value funds. Average returns are subject to considerable calendar effects. Because of the limited amount of data it is not meaningful to draw any statistically significant conclusions from these observations. The

EXHIBIT 1 HEDGE FUND STRATEGY CLASSIFICATION AND NUMBER OF FUNDS

Equity funds	19	Domestic long equity	7
		Domestic opportunity	8
		Global international equity	4
Event driven funds	13	Risk arbitrage	4
		Bankrupty	5
		Multi strategy	4
Relative value funds	15	Balanced	3
		Convertible hedge	2
		Long-short equity	6
		Rotational	4

diversification results in the next section need to be seen in the context of the considerable variation in return and volatility of hedge funds over short time periods.

EXPERIMENTAL DESIGN

Over the three strategy sectors, a Monte Carlo simulation with 20 repetitions selects portfolios of size 1 to N where N is 19, 13, and 15, respectively. The number of repetitions is kept small because an increase would only result in somewhat smoother confidence intervals for portfolios of increasing size without otherwise improving the results. Sampling is conducted without replacement which insures equal weighting of the hedge funds in the portfolio. By contrast, sampling with replacement would result in portfolios with potentially unequal weights and fewer different assets in the portfolio than intended. In the companion paper on CTAs (Henker and Martin [1998]) we find that differences between the two methods are negligibly small, a result that is also supported by Billingsley and Chance [1996].

HEDGE FUND DIVERSIFICATION RESULTS

Exhibit 3 presents the expected monthly rate of return for equity hedge fund portfolios of different size and the confidence bounds of these averages. The average monthly rate of return for equity hedge funds is 1.43% and, as expected, the simulation yields about this average for portfolios of any size. The confidence intervals provided are nonparametric with a 95% level of confidence. The realized portfolio rate of return with randomly selected hedge funds varies widely around the average if the portfolio is small. Once about five or six equity hedge funds are held in a portfolio return variability is reduced considerably.

Similar results for relative value and event driven funds are provided in Exhibit 4. The results are similar for these other two groups as far as the range of the confidence interval is concerned. As mentioned before the average returns of the portfolios differ considerably depending on the fund category.

PORTFOLIO STANDARD DEVIATION

The average monthly standard deviation of returns is a measure of diversification that can be achieved by adding additional hedge funds to an existing portfolio. For

EXHIBIT 2 DESCRIPTIVE STATISTICS OF MONTHLY HEDGE FUND RETURNS BY STRATEGY

	Equity			Event			Relative Value		
	Mean Return (%)	Standard Deviation (%)	Number of Returns	Mean Return (%)	Standard Deviation (%)	Number of Returns	Mean Return (%)	Standard Deviation (%)	Number of Returns
All	1.43	4.02	1311	1.23	1.81	897	0.98	1.50	1035
1992	1.15	3.67	228	1.19	1.79	156	1.16	1.83	180
1993	2.16	3.52	228	1.96	1.81	156	1.07	1.45	180
1994	−0.09	4.14	228	0.56	1.89	156	0.08	1.74	180
1995	1.89	3.69	228	1.37	1.59	156	1.36	1.20	180
1996	1.50	4.03	228	1.20	1.62	156	1.20	1.02	180
1997	2.12	4.76	171	1.08	1.88	117	1.03	1.16	135
1	1.77	3.78	114	2.18	1.97	78	1.23	1.80	90
2	0.30	4.30	114	1.06	1.91	78	0.93	1.23	90
3	0.26	4.93	114	1.30	1.84	78	0.99	1.30	90
4	1.53	3.26	114	0.27	1.53	78	0.91	1.77	90
5	2.63	3.39	114	1.32	1.65	78	1.10	1.66	90
6	1.03	4.10	114	1.28	2.01	78	1.20	1.80	90
7	1.65	4.46	114	1.44	2.08	78	1.11	1.25	90
8	1.74	3.71	114	1.23	1.46	78	0.83	1.23	90
9	2.37	4.03	114	1.54	1.45	78	1.04	1.41	90
10	0.99	3.80	95	0.57	1.55	65	0.76	1.43	75
11	0.57	3.86	95	0.91	1.87	65	0.63	1.08	75
12	2.21	3.56	95	1.57	1.54	65	0.96	1.75	75

EXHIBIT 3 AVERAGE MONTHLY RATE OF RETURN OF EQUITY HEDGE FUND PORTFOLIOS

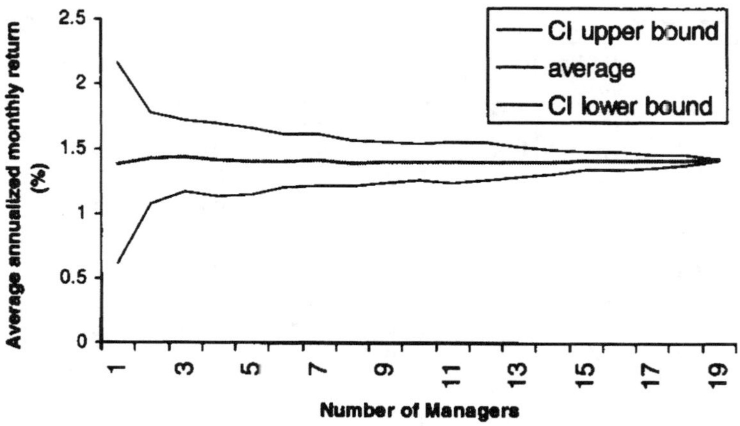

equities, a reduction in the standard deviation of 50% is achieved if an individual stock is compared to a fully diversified portfolio for the same time period. For equities it usually takes 15 to 30 securities to achieve full diversification. In a sample of the Dow 30 stocks for the same time period, 90% of the diversification benefits were obtained after 10 of the stocks were included in the portfolio. Hedge funds and CTAs as a group have a low correlation with traditional asset classes, but the inter-asset correlation between different hedge funds is not very different from that of individual stocks. For the dataset average inter-asset correlations of the strategy sectors are .32, .20, and .13 for the event, equity and realtive value category respectively while the individual Dow component stocks had a correlation of .21. As Exhibit 5 shows, the hedge fund portfolios show quite a similar reduction in risk as stocks do if assets are added, although we already consider funds with basic similar trading objectives. The low standard deviation of relative value and event driven funds compared to equity hedge funds reflects that many funds in the first two categories do not take directional positions. A portfolio of about five funds in each category captures most of the diversification benefits that can be achieved within that category.

Instead of relying on simulations, another approach to assess the standard deviation of a portfolio of securities is to consider the variance-covariance matrix of fund returns. Assuming that the average variances and covariances of the hedge funds considered in the sample are representative for the hedge fund population over the time period, Equation 1 is an unbiased estimate for portfolio standard deviation for a portfolio selected from that larger population. For a completely diversified portfolio the portfolio standard deviation is approaching the average covariance of the constituent assets.

$$\sigma_P = \sqrt{\frac{1}{N}\left(\bar{\sigma}_j^2 - \bar{\sigma}_{kj}\right) + \sigma_{kj}} \tag{1}$$

This approach to calculate portfolio standard deviations is taken to assess whether hedge fund strategies within the three categories differ markedly in their diversification properties. Exhibit 6 shows the result for the different trading strategies, domestic long, domestic opportunity, and global-international that constitute the equity hedge category.

Results for the subcategories within the equity hedge fund sector resemble those of the sector as a whole. This indicates that the diversification benefits within the equity

EXHIBIT 4 AVERAGE RATE OF RETURN RETRUN IN PERCENT PER MONTH FOR PORTFOLIOS OF DIFFERENT SIZE WITH 95% CONFIDENCE INTERVALS

Funds	CI upper bound	Equity avg. ret	CI lower bound	CI upper bound	Relative value avg. ret.	CI lower bound	CI upper bound	Event avg. ret.	CI lower bound
1	2.16	1.39	0.61	1.75	0.99	0.26	2.04	1.24	0.68
2	1.78	1.43	1.08	1.58	0.99	0.42	1.67	1.24	0.89
3	1.72	1.44	1.17	1.33	0.95	0.60	1.54	1.24	0.95
4	1.70	1.42	1.14	1.27	0.97	0.65	1.44	1.21	0.98
5	1.66	1.41	1.15	1.24	0.99	0.78	1.38	1.20	0.99
6	1.61	1.41	1.21	1.18	1.00	0.81	1.36	1.20	1.04
7	1.61	1.41	1.22	1.20	0.99	0.83	1.35	1.21	1.04
8	1.57	1.40	1.23	1.14	0.99	0.85	1.36	1.23	1.10
9	1.56	1.40	1.25	1.12	0.98	0.87	1.35	1.24	1.15
10	1.54	1.41	1.27	1.09	0.98	0.90	1.32	1.24	1.17
11	1.56	1.40	1.24	1.08	0.98	0.90	1.31	1.23	1.15
12	1.55	1.41	1.26	1.06	0.97	0.87	1.28	1.24	1.21
13	1.53	1.41	1.29	1.07	0.98	0.89	1.23	1.23	1.23
14	1.50	1.41	1.32	1.01	0.98	0.93			
15	1.49	1.42	1.34	0.98	0.98	0.98			
16	1.49	1.42	1.35						
17	1.47	1.42	1.36						
18	1.46	1.42	1.39						
19	1.44	1.43	1.42						

hedge fund sector are not a result of differences between the trading categories, but rather originate in fund specific differences. Purely idiosyncratic return volatility indicates that hedge funds should be held in portfolios of at least four or five funds regardless of how narrowly defined the trading strategies and objectives of the portfolio are.

BENCHMARK TRACKING

Hedge funds, even if held as a portfolio, are rarely used as a stand-alone investment. Indeed, probably the most attractive characteristic of CTAs and hedge funds are diversification benefits that result from the low correlation of these instruments with traditional asset classes. Schneeweis *et. al.* [1996] find low correlation between CTAs and traditional asset classes particularly in periods where traditional assets perform poorly. These findings about diversification benefits are usually based on CTA or hedge fund indexes. Unlike many equity indexes these indexes are often not tradable. Hence the ability to create hedge fund portfolios that are able to reliably track a benchmark is a crucial step in implementing a hedge fund based investment program. Exhibit 7 describes the correlation properties of portfolios of randomly selected hedge funds with the HFR composite fund weighted hedge index. The results show that composite index is not a particularly well suited benchmark for the event and relative value hedge fund categories, but portfolios chosen from the equity hedge fund category correlate highly with the index once the portfolio comprises 8-10 hedge funds. For all three fund categories, individual funds or small portfolios are unlikely to result in performances that are adequately described by the benchmark.

Because no tradable index exists for hedge funds, the tracking error, as measured by the standard deviation of the squared deviation between portfolio performance and

EXHIBIT 5 AVERAGE MONTHLY STANDARD DEVIATION FOR PORTFOLIOS OF SIZE N

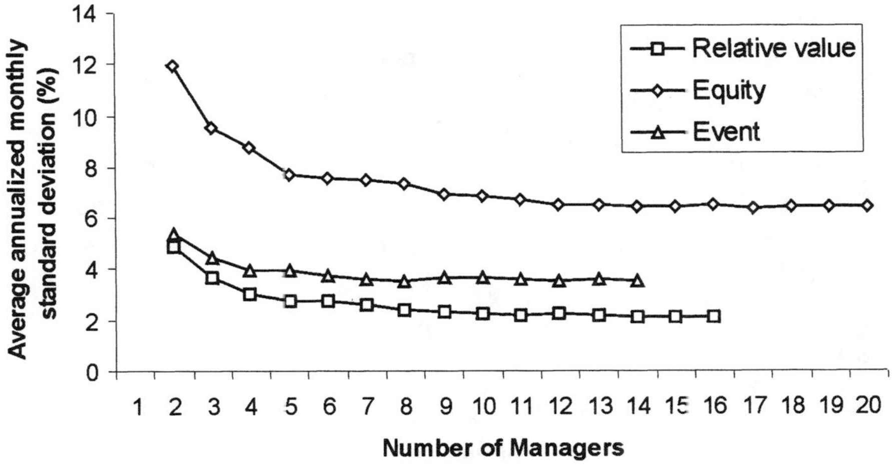

benchmark index, is of importance in measuring the ability of a portfolio to track the index. This measure of deviations of individual portfolios from the average deviation of returns from the benchmark is indicative of the heterogeneity of the portfolios generated by the simulation for any given portfolio size n [See Exhibit 8]. A large number indicates that average correlations and standard deviations are not particularly good indicators for any one particular portfolio realization. Again, random portfolios with fewer than five funds turn out to only poorly track the average characteristics of these portfolios and are hence inappropriate diversification tools. In smaller portfolios idiosyncratic fund characteristics overshadow the characteristics of hedge funds as a group.

EXHIBIT 6 EFFECT OF DIVERSIFICATION WITHIN THE EQUITY HEDGE FUND CATEGORY

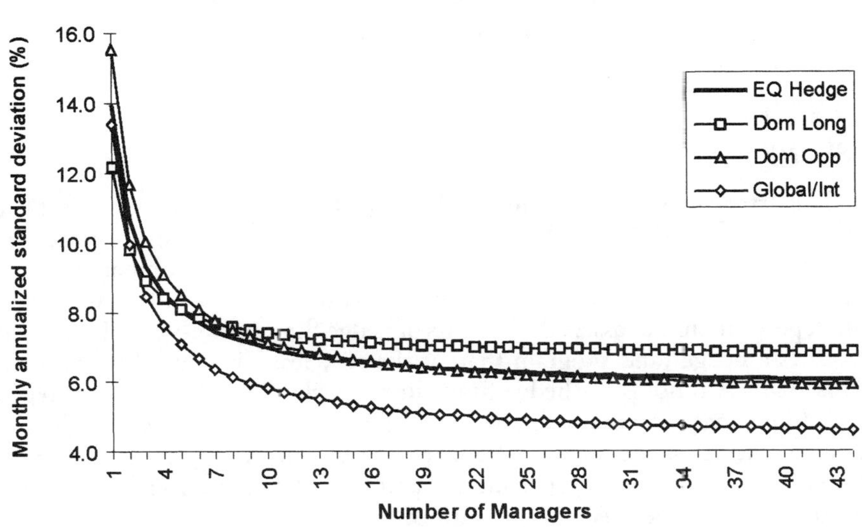

EXHIBIT 7 AVERAGE CORRELATION OF SIMULATED PORTFOLIOS WITH HFR INDEX BENCHMARK

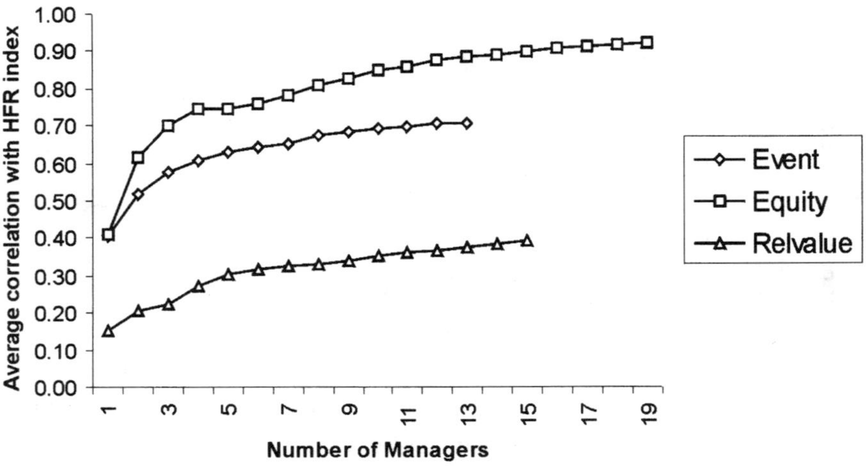

EXHIBIT 8 TRACKING ERROR OF RANDOMLY SELECTED PORTFOLIO WITH HFR BENCHMARK

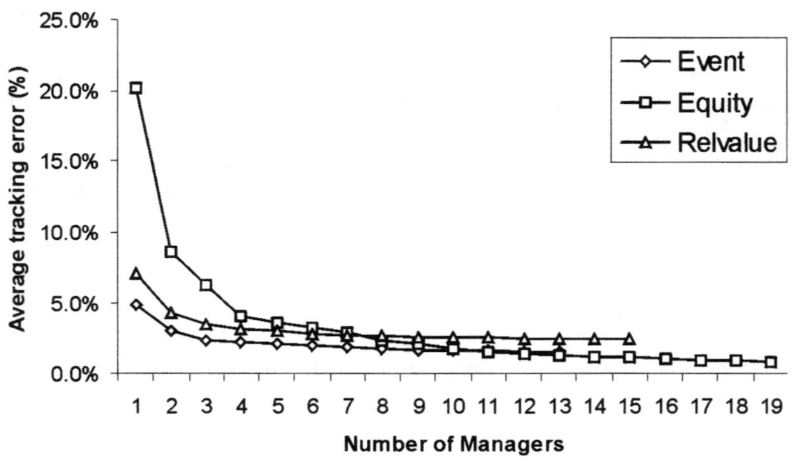

CONCLUSIONS

This article uses Monte Carlo simulation techniques to randomly select hedge funds from three sectors of the EACM 100 hedge fund index to form portfolios with these funds. The return performance of the resulting portfolios is compared to the expected performance and to the performance of the HFR composite index. Relying on benchmark performance to assess the benefits of hedge fund portfolios as diversification tools requires a hedge fund program that, at the very least, includes five individual funds. This result also holds for hedge funds in narrowly defined trading strategy segments with funds that supposedly follow similar strategies. Reasonably complete diversification requires about ten funds. Similar to results previously presented for CTAs, the simulation results in this paper show that if fewer funds are selected the portfolio performance cannot be adequately described by sector or broad index performance.

ENDNOTES

This article was published in *The Journal of Alternative Investments*, Winter 1998.

REFERENCES

Billingsley, R.S., and Chance, D.M., "Benefits and limitations of diversification among commodity trading advisors," *The Journal of Portfolio Management* v.23, (Fall, 1996) pp. 65-80.

Henker, T., and Martin, G., "Naïve and planned diversification for CTAs," *The Journal of Alternative Investments* (Fall, 1998), pp. 25-39.

Park, J.M, and Staum, J.C., "Fund of funds diversification: How much is enough," *The Journal of Alternative Investments*, (Winter, 1998), pp. 39-42.

Schneeweis, T., Spurgin, R., and Potter, M., "Managed futures and hedge fund investment for downside equity risk management," *Derivatives Quarterly* v.3 n1, (1996) pp. 62-72.

APPENDIX 1

Hedge Fund Indices (Evaluation Associates Capital Markets)

Relative value: Balanced, or hedged, long and short positions with subindices such as:

Long/Short Equity (Long undervalued equities/short overvalued equities usually on an equal dollar bases);

Convertible Hedging (Long convertible bonds or preferred, short underlying common);

Bond Hedging (Yield curve arbitrage or long/short debt positions);

Rotational (Multiple relative value strategies, including all of the above).

Event Driven: (Corporate transactions and special situations) subindices including:

Deal Arbitrage (Long/short equity securities of companies involved in corporate transactions; B*ankruptcy/Distressed* (Long undervalued securities of companies usually in financial distress or operating under Chapter 11).

Multi-strategy (Funds dealing in both deal arbitrage and bankruptcy.

Equity Hedge Funds: Long and short securities with varying degrees of exposure and leverage such as:

Domestic Long Equity (Long undervalued US equities; short selling is used sparingly);

Domestic Opportunistic Equity (Long and short U.S. equity with ability to be net short overall);

Global International (Primarily long undervalued equities with the ability to use short selling opportunistically).

11 MULTI-FACTOR ANALYSIS OF HEDGE FUND, MANAGED FUTURES, AND MUTUAL FUND RETURN AND RISK CHARACTERISTICS

THOMAS SCHNEEWEIS
University of Massachusetts

RICHARD SPURGIN
Clark University

INTRODUCTION

The past decade has witnessed a dramatic increase in the use of stock and bond mutual funds as stand-alone investments or as part of an investor's diversified portfolio.[1] Moreover, recent research [Sharpe, 1992; Elton et al., 1995] has shown that for stock and bond mutual fund investors, multi-factor models often provide improved explanatory power regarding the return structure of these investment vehicles. While the sources of return to actively managed assets in the mutual fund industry have been extensively studied, little research exists on the factors explaining the performance of alternative investments such as hedge funds[2] or managed futures investment[3].

This is important for several reasons. First, hedge funds and commodity trading advisors have different trading styles (e.g., long and short positions and leverage) and trading opportunities (e.g., commodity and currency markets) than traditional stock and bond mutual fund managers. As a result, factors which incorporate the possibility of trending prices (up or down) may better capture their relative return movement. Second, previous studies have focused on explanatory factors unique to a particular asset class. In this study the same set of factors is used to describe return movement across each of the asset classes studied. Previous research [Lintner, 1983; Schneeweis, 1996] has indicated the potential benefits to including alternative investments in stock and bond portfolios. However, the factors that explain the differences in the return of managed futures, hedge funds, and traditional stock and bond funds have not been fully explored.

SOURCES OF RETURN TO HEDGE FUND AND MANAGED DERIVATIVE INVESTMENTS

Much of the previous research on managed futures [Edwards and Ma, 1988; and McCarthy et al., 1996] compares historical CTA returns to the realized returns of public commodity funds or CTAs, with the goal of identifying the usefulness of historical returns in forecasting future performance. This study uses factors designed to capture the trading opportunities available to a CTA or hedge fund (e.g., arbitrage, overvalued markets) as a means of forecasting of return performance.

Previous research employs historical CTA performance as a proxy for the source of return. Irwin et al. [1994] use a simple managed futures benchmark as the best forecast of an individual CTA's return, while McCarthy et al. [1997] propose a single index benchmark with a Bayesian risk adjustment designed to capture differences in leverage relative to the underlying benchmark. While this research sheds light on how CTAs perform relative to one another, it does not address the underlying source of CTA return, Mitev [1996] suggests a five-factor model for CTAs that emphasizes the differential CTA trading strategies. Mitev concludes that the CTAs in his sample fall primarily into 1) trend following strategies, 2) surprise or stop-loss control models, 3) agricultural markets, 4) spread-strategies (primarily interest rate) and 5) fundamental economic factors or global markets.

Academic research on the sources of hedge fund returns is less well developed than for CTAs. Fung and Hsieh [1997] use factor-analytic approaches to determine the common factors that help explain hedge fund return patterns. Fung and Hsieh identify five general investment approaches (distressed, global/macro, systems, systems/opportunistic, and value) that are shown to explain most hedge fund return variation. Of these five groups, global/macro, systems, and systems/opportunistic were shown to have factors not easily explained by the factors common to stock funds, bond funds, distressed funds, or value funds. Fung and Hsieh do not determine if the difference is due primarily to differences in trading strategy or to differences in asset markets traded, but conclude that the differences occurred in time periods when rallies or severe declines were experienced. Like Mitev, Fung and Hsieh use factor analysis to identify funds with common factors, but do not conduct multi-factor regression aimed at determining what those factors are.[4]

CTAs and many hedged funds derive much of their return from derivatives. However, the derivatives market is, by definition, a zero-sum game. In order for these strategies to offer returns that exceed the cost of capital, the other players in these markets, principally hedgers, must experience returns on their derivative transactions that are less than the riskless rate of return. Empirical research [Schneeweis, 1996; Schneeweis and Spurgin, 1998] that studies the historical performance of CTAs and hedge funds clearly demonstrates that these assets have offered positive, risk-adjusted returns. Theoretical studies of derivative market structure have identified many potential sources of this risk premium in trading derivative-based products.

- Futures and options investors may simply hold positions that mimic the return of the underlying cash asset, which would yield a positive expected return if, as with stock index futures, the underlying asset had an expected return greater than the cost of financing.
- Speculative traders offer liquidity to hedgers. An imbalance between hedging demand from long hedgers and short hedgers may create opportunities to earn returns by purchasing (providing) the excess supply (demand) from the hedging community.
- Transaction costs in futures and options markets are generally lower than for comparable cash instruments. Low transactions costs may allow derivatives traders to exploit information about an asset's value that is too small for investors in cash instruments to utilize profitably.
- Many academic studies [Chan et al, 1996, Silber, 1994] have shown that momentum-based trading strategies are profitable over time. While most of these studies were conducted on equity markets, such that the momentum profits may not be large enough to cover the cost of transacting the trades, derivative markets may offer the opportunity to earn these returns because of their low transactions costs and high leverage.
- Options traders may be able to create positions that offer a risk premium in exchange for accepting exposure to certain portions of the return distribution of the underlying security.

- Options traders also have the ability to create positions that may profit from changes in expected volatility of the underlying asset. Investors in cash instruments can only profit from changes in the value of the underlying asset.

Thus, for the hedge funds and managed futures funds, theoretical and empirical models of return estimation may necessarily be based on the anticipated trading style of the hedge fund manager. For instance, hedge funds focusing on pure zero-risk arbitrage positions will have the risk free rate as a benchmark. If the hedge fund focuses on long international equity then international equity benchmarks similar to that used for traditional international mutual funds may be regarded as standard. Many factors have been proposed to explain the higher risk-adjusted returns earned by hedge funds in recent years as compared to mutual funds that trade similar assets.

- Hedge funds have a larger set of potential investments available to them than mutual funds. For instance, hedge funds can purchase restricted stock and debt, use short sales to profit from overvalued securities, and are better suited to influence the management of companies in which they hold debt or equity stakes.
- Hedge funds can use leverage to amplify returns to a particular strategy. If a mutual fund manager and a hedge fund manager identify the same mispriced security, the mutual fund can only allocate a portion of the available investment capital, while the mutual fund manger can allocate several times the invested capital base. Furthermore, if the mispriced security is overpriced, the mutual fund manager cannot take advantage because of short sale restrictions.
- Hedge funds are not required to offer daily liquidity, and often have lockup provisions longer than a year. This allows hedge funds to take illiquid positions that may be very difficult to mark to market, but will offer positive risk-adjusted returns.

Thus, to the degree that different factors explain the returns to managed futures, hedge funds, and stock and bond fund returns, each may provide investors exposure to unique sources of return, and, provide an important source return to a diversified investment portfolio.

DATA AND METHODOLOGY

Returns for all data series are expressed as monthly holding period returns. The test period, covering six years from January 1990 through December 1995, was chosen because several managed futures and hedge fund indexes started in 1/90. Monthly data are used because most CTAs and hedge funds report results monthly. See Appendix I for summary of hedge fund, managed futures, and mutual fund data.

Hedge fund indexes are supplied by Hedge Fund Research (HFR) and Evaluation Associates Capital Management (EACM). CTA indexes are provided by Managed Accounts Reports (MAR), Barclay Trading (Barclay), and EACM. Mutual fund returns are from Morningstar. The asset class benchmarks employed are the Standard & Poors 500 stock index (S&P500), the Salomon Brothers government bond index (SBBI), the Goldman Sachs Commodity Index (GSCI), and the US Dollar trade-weighted currency index (USDX). The Mount Lucas Management index (MLM) is used as a proxy for passive commodity futures timing skill. Other indexes employed in the study include the MSCI World Equity index, the Salomon World Government Bond index, the US producer price index (PPI) and the return on US 30-day Treasury bills. The source for the traditional benchmark data is Datastream.

To understand the differences between top performing, average, and bottom performing managers in each class, indexes were created from returns to individual managers. The top five, median, and bottom five CTA, hedge fund and Growth & Income mutual funds were selected. An equally weighted portfolio of their performance was computed. For CTAs and hedge funds, a subset was also selected. The CTA subset consists of all CTAs that identified themselves as Diversified (a total of 66 CTAs) and the hedge fund subset consists of funds that identified themselves as Opportunity funds (15 funds). Portfolios of the top five, median, and bottom five for each subset were constructed.

Statistical tests include descriptive risk and return characteristics and a number of return correlations. These correlations include each asset's correlation with nominal and absolute value of factor indexes, with the intramonth standard deviation of the indexes, and with the maximum intramonth drawdown and drawup as well. Multiple regression analysis is conducted using CTA, hedge fund, and stock and bond fund indexes as the dependent variables and the nominal, absolute value, and intramonth standard deviation of indexes as explanatory variables.

Returns to active management of stock, bond, CTA, and hedge fund investments are assumed to flow from four sources:

1. *A natural return to owning financial and real assets.* This is modeled by including the nominal value of stock (S&P500), bond (SBBI), commodity (GSCI), and currency (USDX) index returns.
2. *Flexibility to use both long and short positions to benefit from market timing skill.* This is captured with the absolute value of the monthly returns of the underlying asset markets.
3. *Intramonth volatility.* Managers can profit from intramonth volatility either by using option strategies or through intramonth timing strategies. Returns to this factor are modeled by the intramonth standard deviation of the indexes and by computing the maximum drawup and drawdown of the index for each month.
4. *Market inefficiencies that result in temporary trends in prices.* A proxy for this is the MLM index, which captures the return to a moving average strategy using 20 active commodity and financial futures.

This common set of factors is used to explain the returns to active management of hedge funds, stock and bond mutual funds, and CTAs.

RESULTS

Managed Futures, Hedge Fund, Stock and Bond Indices: Descriptive Statistics

Exhibit 1 gives descriptive statistics of the data used in this study. Included are the average annual return, standard deviation, maximum and minimum monthly return, the information ratio[5], and the Sharpe ratio for each of the CTA, hedge fund, and stock and bond fund indexes as well as the unmanaged indexes. Exhibit 2 shows a subset of the indexes plotted in return/standard deviation space.

Results in Exhibit 1 and the figure in Exhibit 2 are generally consistent with the hypothesis that stock and bond funds, hedge funds, and managed futures investments have different risk and return structures. For the period of analysis, fixed income and market-neutral hedge fund strategies dominate in terms of risk/return tradeoff, while hedge fund styles which concentrated primarily on equity short selling joined passive commodity investment (GCSI) and certain managed futures strategies in providing the

EXHIBIT 1 DESCRIPTIVE STATISTICS OF HEDGE FUND, CTA, MUTUAL FUND AND ASSET BENCHMARKS, 1991-1995

	Avg.	SD	Max	Min	Avg./SD	Sharpe
			Benchmarks			
MLM index	7.8	5.2	4.7	−4.0	1.50	0.58
GSCI	6.9	16.3	22.9	−9.4	0.43	0.13
S&P 500	13.0	11.8	11.5	−9.2	1.10	0.70
Treasury bond	9.0	4.4	4.1	−2.3	2.04	0.96
MSCI world	7.7	14.1	10.5	−11	0.55	0.21
World govt. bond	10.8	6.3	5.9	−3.6	1.72	0.97
U.S. dollar index	−1.6	9.1	8.5	−5.4	−0.17	−0.70
PPI	1.9	1.4	1.9	−0.8		
U.S. Treasury bill	4.8	0.5	0.7	0.2		
			Hedge Funds			
Hedge Fund Research Indexes						
Convertible arb.	13.2	4.4	4.3	−2.4	3.00	1.91
Distressed sec.	20.4	7.4	7.3	−5.5	2.74	2.10
Emerging	31.1	18.4	22.3	−8.8	1.69	1.43
Fixed income	19.1	7.0	12.0	−1.3	2.72	2.04
Foreign exch.	18.5	15.9	14.6	−8.2	1.17	0.87
Fund of funds	13.7	4.6	5.1	−1.9	2.98	1.95
Growth	19.9	8.9	8.2	−5.3	2.25	1.71
Macro	27.9	9.6	10.2	−6.0	2.90	2.40
Market neutral	13.7	3.1	3.5	−0.7	4.43	2.89
Market timing	16.1	6.6	8.9	−2.5	2.45	1.73
Merger arb.	12.0	5.1	4.2	−5.4	2.37	1.43
Sector	20.9	8.2	7.6	−4.6	2.53	1.95
Multistrategy	11.0	3.6	2.9	−1.8	3.10	1.76
Opportunistic	22.3	7.0	8.2	−2.3	3.18	2.50
Short selling	7.8	15.7	12.1	−11	0.50	0.19
Value	20.0	6.7	6.3	−4.5	3.00	2.29
Evaluation Associates Indexes						
EACM 100	15.9	3.4	4.8	−0.9	4.67	3.27
Relative value	11.6	2.3	2.5	−1.1	5.12	3.02
Long/short equity	11.7	3.1	3.5	−1.0	3.78	2.24
Convert hedge	9.7	5.0	5.0	−5.0	1.94	0.99
Bond hedge	10.2	1.5	2.0	−0.2	6.85	3.64
Rotational	14.9	5.1	4.3	−2.0	2.95	2.01
Event driven	13.8	5.3	5.1	−4.8	2.58	1.69
Arbitrage	8.9	7.4	5.9	−11	1.21	0.57
Bankruptcy	18.4	7.3	10.1	−6.4	2.53	1.88
Multistrategy	13.9	4.6	3.7	−2.7	3.05	2.01
Equity hedge	18.7	6.5	5.4	−3.4	2.90	2.16
DomLong	18.3	8.3	6.7	−4.6	2.19	1.62
DomOpp	16.7	7.1	6.7	−3.0	2.37	1.69
Global/int'l.	21.1	10.4	8.4	−8.5	2.03	1.57
Short	−1.1	19.8	12.7	−13	−0.05	−0.29

lowest return/risk ratios. The figure in Exhibit 2 shows that during the test period studied, most of the hedge fund categories offered higher risk-adjusted returns higher than that available by allocating assets to the S&P500 and cash. However, most mutual fund indexes are clustered very close to this line. CTA performance measures are more widely scattered, but are generally a bit below the line.

While the results in Exhibit 1 provide evidence that these assets have different historical risk/return tradeoffs, it does not explain what the determinants of that return are. The following section describes the results of multivariate analysis of the returns.

	Avg.	SD	Max	Min	Avg./SD	Sharpe
			Mutual Funds			
Managed Account Reports Indexes						
Dollar weight	14.2	11.8	14.5	−6.0	1.20	0.80
Equal weight	10.0	10.3	11.3	−5.4	0.97	0.51
Currency	14.6	17.2	16.4	−8.2	0.85	0.57
Discretionary	15.2	8.4	8.7	−4.6	1.82	1.25
Diversified	11.2	13.1	12.7	−7.5	0.85	0.49
Energy	7.9	10.9	10.0	−6.1	0.73	0.29
Financial	14.4	14.4	20.2	−8.6	1.00	0.67
Trend following	13.9	18.7	22.0	−10	0.74	0.49
Barclay Indexes						
CTA	7.4	9.9	10.0	−5.5	0.75	0.27
Currency	12.4	15.8	15.0	−7.7	0.79	0.49
Agriculture	8.1	6.9	5.8	−4.8	1.17	0.49
Fin/metal	8.0	8.5	7.0	−10	0.94	0.38
Energy	9.6	12.8	26.9	−4.4	0.75	0.38
Diversified	11.5	12.9	12.0	−6.6	0.89	0.52
Systematic	11.7	13.7	14.5	−7.6	0.86	0.51
Discretionary	6.5	5.3	8.5	−3.0	1.22	0.32
Evaluation Associates Indexes						
Global asset alloc.	24.0	12.1	16.6	−5.4	1.98	1.58
Discretionary	20.5	8.4	7.5	−5.2	2.43	1.87
Systematic	27.5	21.2	30.3	−10	1.30	1.07
			Mutual Funds			
Morningstar Indexes						
Growth & income	11.5	10.7	10.1	−8.0	1.07	0.63
Growth	12.6	12.4	11.4	−9.0	1.02	0.63
Equity income	11.1	9.0	7.5	−6.7	1.24	0.70
Aggressive growth	16.2	16.6	12.7	−12	0.98	0.69
Small company	15.3	15.1	10.6	−12	1.01	0.70
Govt. Bond	7.4	3.6	3.0	−1.9	2.03	0.73
Corporate bond	8.1	3.6	3.3	−2.0	2.23	0.93
Multisector bond	9.4	4.7	4.0	−3.0	2.01	0.99
Asset allocation	10.2	6.5	7.2	−4.1	1.57	0.84
Balanced	10.4	7.7	7.4	−5.6	1.35	0.73
Convertible bond	10.8	8.1	6.4	−5.9	1.33	0.74
Hybrid: HiYield	11.1	6.7	7.0	−5.0	1.66	0.95
Hybrid: Global	8.3	6.1	4.5	−3.8	1.37	0.58
			Absolute Values			
GSCI	35.5	12.7	22.9	0.1	2.80	2.42
S&P 500	33.8	7.6	11.5	0.2	4.45	3.82
Treasury bond	14.5	2.9	4.1	0.0	4.99	3.35
MSCI world	38.9	8.6	10.5	0.0	4.51	3.96
World govt. bond	19.3	4.3	5.9	0.0	4.54	3.42
U.S. dollar index	23.2	6.1	8.5	0.0	3.80	3.02

Results indicate that certain asset management strategies derive their return primarily from the nominal value of assets (e.g., mutual funds), while others derive their return primarily from the absolute value and intramonth volatility of the same indexes (e.g. hedge funds and managed derivative strategies).

Managed Futures, Hedge Fund, Stock and Bond Indices: Simple Correlations

Exhibits 3A-3C present the correlations among broad-based CTA indices and subindices from each of the three CTA index groupings (MAR, Barclay, and EACM)

EXHIBIT 2 RISK AND RETURN FOR SELECTED INDEXES, 1990-1995

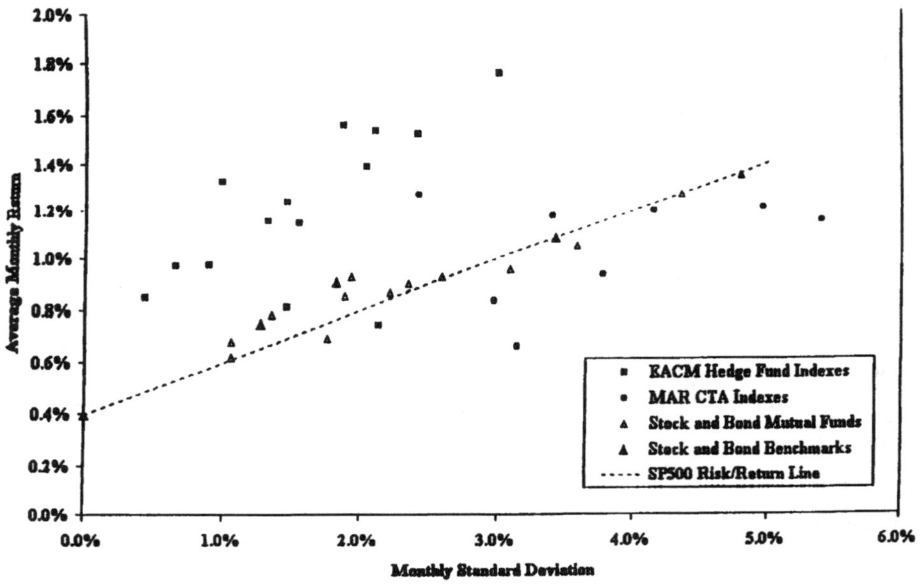

and between those indices and the nominal and absolute values of the primary indices (GSCI, SP500, Tbond, MSCI, World Bond, USDX) and the nominal values of the MLM, PPI, and Tbill. There is a highly significant (99% confidence) correlation between overall CTA indices (MAR CTA and Barclay CTA) and most CTA subindices. The only correlations that are not highly significant are the energy and agricultural CTA subindices. The correlation of systematic/trendfollowing CTAs with the broad-based indexes is higher than for discretionary CTAs. These results indicate that systematic/trendfollowing strategies are the dominant strategies followed by CTAs.

The potential impact of the explanatory variables is also shown in Exhibits 3A-3C. The MLM index had statistically significant positive correlations for most of the CTA indexes.[6] Two other variables show statistically significant correlations among broad-based indices, the absolute values of the Salomon World Bond and the US Dollar indexes. Among CTAs that focus on a particular market, financial CTAs are correlated with both the World Bond and USDX indexes, and energy CTAs are correlated with the energy-heavy GSCI index.

Hedge Fund Correlations with Commodity, Stock, Bond and Currency Indices

Exhibits 4A-4B show the correlation between each of the HFR and EACM hedge fund indexes and the set of explanatory factors. Of interest, are the differences, if any, in the correlations patterns of the HFR and EACM hedge fund performance indices given in Exhibits 4A and 4B compared to those in Exhibits 3A-3C. Three primary differences can be observed. First, in contrast to the CTA Exhibits, EACM subindexes are not highly correlated with the broad-based EACM 100 index. Second, there exists a relatively low correlation between hedge fund indices and the variable designed to capture trend-following strategies, the MLM index. Third, also in contrast to CTA indices, hedge fund indices are positively correlated with nominal stock and bond returns. None of the CTA indices had statistically significant correlations to the S&P500, but the majority of the EACM and HFR hedge fund indices had statistically significant corre-

EXHIBIT 3A MAR CTA CORRELATIONS

	Dollar	Equal	Curr.	Discret.	Divers.	Energy	Fin.	Trend
MAR CTA								
Dollar weight								
Equal weight	0.94**							
Currency	0.77**	0.79**						
Discretionary	0.62**	0.54**	0.47**					
Diversified	0.93**	0.82**	0.65**	0.55**				
Energy	0.11	0.11	0.01	0.32**	0.08			
Financial/metal	0.92**	0.87**	0.71**	0.47**	0.84**	−0.06		
Trend following	0.97**	0.96**	0.79**	0.51**	0.93**	0.02	0.94**	
Nominal Factors								
MLM	0.28*	0.30*	0.09	0.26*	0.37**	0.12	0.17	0.27*
GSCI	0.08	0.13	0.00	0.19	0.06	0.41**	−0.03	0.07
S&P 500	−0.13	−0.19	−0.03	−0.21	−0.15	−0.28*	−0.01	−0.10
Salomon bond	0.14	0.08	0.17	0.16	0.13	−0.23	0.25*	0.15
MSCI	−0.15	−0.15	0.01	−0.10	−0.09	−0.15	−0.01	−0.12
World bond	0.22	0.16	0.22	0.08	0.24*	−0.19	0.34**	0.24*
U.S. dollar	−0.21	−0.21	−0.16	0.09	−0.25*	0.29*	−0.35**	−0.26*
PPI	0.07	0.09	−0.01	0.00	0.10	−0.03	0.01	0.02
T-bill	0.01	0.05	0.07	−0.09	0.00	−0.12	0.00	0.02
Absolute Values								
GSCI	0.12	0.14	0.02	0.15	0.13	0.28*	0.05	0.08
S&P 500	0.14	0.12	0.04	−0.04	0.16	−0.15	0.21	0.19
Salomon bond	0.18	0.11	0.06	0.17	0.13	0.05	0.28*	0.17
MSCI	0.06	0.12	0.15	0.05	0.05	0.04	0.11	0.09
World bond	0.42**	0.38**	0.56**	0.23	0.35**	−0.12	0.47**	0.42**
U.S. dollar	0.41**	0.41**	0.60**	0.25**	0.30*	0.24*	0.34**	0.41**

*Significant with 95% confidence.
**Significant with 99% confidence.

EXHIBIT 3B BARCLAY CTA CORRELATIONS

	GAA	Discret.	System
EACM CTA			
Global asset all.			
Discretionary	0.51**		
Systematic	0.94**	0.19	
Nominal Factors			
MLM	0.28*	0.30*	0.09
GSCI	0.08	0.13	0.00
S&P 500	−0.13	−0.19	−0.03
Salomon bond	0.14	0.08	0.17
MSCI	−0.15	−0.15	0.01
World bond	0.22	0.16	0.22
U.S. dollar	−0.21	−0.21	−0.16
PPI	0.07	0.09	−0.01
T-bill	0.01	0.05	0.07
Absolute Values			
GSCI	0.12	0.14	0.02
S&P 500	0.14	0.12	0.04
Salomon bond	0.18	0.11	0.06
MSCI	0.06	0.12	0.15
World bond	0.42**	0.38**	0.56**
U.S. dollar	0.41**	0.41**	0.60**

*Significant with 95% confidence.
**Significant with 99% confidence.

EXHIBIT 3C EACM CTA CORRELATIONS

	CTA	Curr.	Agric.	Fin.	Energy	Divers.	System	Discret.
Barclay CTA								
CTA								
Currency	0.75**							
Agriculture	0.06	−0.17						
Financial/metal	0.77**	0.66**	−0.08					
Energy	0.28*	0.25*	−0.16	0.22				
Diversified	0.98**	0.74**	0.06	0.76**	0.30*			
Systematic	0.96**	0.83**	0.01	0.80**	0.26*	0.96**		
Discretionary	0.63**	0.45**	0.10	0.44**	0.68**	0.65**	0.54**	
Nominal Factors								
MLM	0.37**	0.08	0.23	0.27*	0.26*	0.40**	0.32**	0.38**
GSCI	0.15	0.07	0.00	0.12	0.50**	0.14	0.13	0.34**
S&P 500	−0.23	−0.16	0.12	−0.18	−0.25	−0.22	−0.17	−0.38**
Salomon bond	0.02	0.06	0.09	0.20	−0.12	0.02	0.09	−0.17
MSCI	−0.20	−0.07	0.04	−0.18	−0.23	−0.19	−0.17	−0.32
World bond	0.16	0.17	−0.08	0.28*	−0.02	0.13	0.18	−0.15
U.S. Dollar	−0.22	−0.25*	0.06	−0.23	−0.08	−0.20	−0.26*	0.08
PPI	0.11	0.10	0.01	0.11	0.22	0.13	0.08	0.30*
T-bill	0.05	0.18	0.06	0.11	0.29*	0.09	0.10	0.19
Absolute Values								
GSCI	0.16	0.11	−0.08	0.14	0.62**	0.15	0.12	0.46**
S&P 500	0.13	0.09	−0.23	0.17	0.34**	0.11	0.15	0.10
Salomon bond	0.06	0.04	0.04	0.27*	0.07	0.04	0.09	−0.02
MSCI	0.10	0.21	−0.33**	0.12	0.35**	0.10	0.09	0.24*
World bond	0.32**	0.55**	−0.20	0.51**	−0.02	0.29*	0.39**	0.03
U.S. Dollar	0.36**	0.51**	−0.25*	0.41**	−0.09	0.33**	0.39**	0.14

*Significant with 95% confidence.
**Significant with 99% confidence.

lations with this index. The principal similarity between CTA and hedge fund performance indices is that both groups are positively correlated with the absolute value of the USDX. Except for this, CTAs and hedge fund advisors seem to be capturing differing return patterns.

Stock and Bond Fund Correlations with Commodity, Stock, Bond and Currency Indices

In Exhibit 5, the correlation between each of the stock and bond fund performance indices and the nominal and absolute values of the set of explanatory variables is given. Again, of principal interest, is the differences, if any, in the correlation patterns of the CTA and hedge fund performance indices given in Exhibits 3 and 4 with those given in Exhibit 5. The buy-and-hold strategy employed by stock and bond mutual fund managers results in correlation patterns that are very different from broad hedge fund and CTA indices. First, the correlations among the equity-based indices are all above .80. Similar correlations are seen among the government and corporate bond mutual funds. As discussed in previous analysis [Fung and Hsieh (1996) and Schneeweis (1996)], the high intercorrelation among stock and bond mutual funds lessens the potential diversification benefits within those groups.

The MLM index is negatively correlated with stock funds and is uncorrelated with bond funds. This is in contrast to the pattern for CTA indices. Lastly, in contrast, to both hedge funds and CTAs, there is little evidence of the importance of the absolute values of the factors on stock or bond mutual fund performance.[7]

Different correlation patterns are evident in the three classes of assets studied. CTAs capture a trendfollowing component through their correlation with the MLM index,

EXHIBIT 4A HFR HEDGE FUND INDEX CORRELATIONS

	Cnvrt.	Distrs	Emrge.	FixInc	Forex	FoF	Growth	Macro	Neutral	Timing	Merger	Sector	Multi	Opprt.	Short	Value
HFR Index																
Convertible arb.																
Distressed sec.	0.58**															
Emerging	0.47**	0.44**														
Fixed income	0.20	0.28*	0.11													
Foreign exch.	0.05	−0.10	0.06	−0.06												
Fund of funds	0.27*	0.15	0.43**	0.07	0.38**											
Growth	0.65**	0.48**	0.47**	0.24*	−0.07	0.37**										
Macro	0.44**	0.17	0.43**	0.08	0.12	0.66**	0.55**									
Market neutral	0.03	0.16	−0.03	0.12	0.09	0.11	0.26*	0.05								
Market timing	0.45**	0.34**	0.54**	0.09	0.12	0.37**	0.62**	0.54**	−0.05							
Merger arb.	0.46**	0.68**	0.40**	0.17	−0.13	−0.10	0.47**	0.18	0.07	0.33**						
Sector	0.49**	0.52**	0.57**	0.28*	−0.12	0.32**	0.71**	0.44**	0.28*	0.59**	0.48**					
Multistrategy	0.29*	0.26*	0.16	0.08	0.13	0.47**	0.16	0.28*	0.13	0.21	0.15	0.30*				
Opportunistic	0.58**	0.62**	0.40**	0.24*	0.13	0.45**	0.70**	0.52**	0.22	0.48**	0.34**	0.58**	0.32**			
Short selling	−0.37**	−0.24*	−0.20	−0.11	0.07	0.00	−0.54**	−0.24*	0.13	−0.53**	−0.33**	−0.43**	−0.07	−0.31*		
Value	0.49**	0.46**	0.46**	0.43**	−0.14	0.25	0.69**	0.40**	0.19	0.42**	0.34**	0.68**	0.21	0.62**	−0.40**	
Nominal Factors																
MLM	−0.23	−0.35**	−0.15	−0.17	0.12	0.08	−0.42**	−0.08	−0.28*	−0.13	−0.40**	−0.41**	0.11	−0.23	0.20	−0.35**
GSCI	−0.18	−0.28*	−0.39**	−0.28*	0.10	0.17	−0.22	−0.11	0.01	−0.23	−0.34**	−0.36**	0.33**	−0.08	0.15	−0.22
SP500	0.51**	0.31*	0.43**	0.18	−0.04	0.08	0.74**	0.40**	0.05	0.61**	0.48**	0.51**	0.02	0.41**	−0.60**	0.56**
Salomon bond	0.44**	0.13	0.24*	−0.02	0.17	0.23	0.30*	0.39**	0.21	0.24*	0.18	0.14	0.15	0.27*	−0.14	0.26*
MSCI	0.37**	0.23	0.45**	−0.04	−0.04	0.06	0.56**	0.36**	0.07	0.58**	0.33**	0.54**	0.17	0.31*	−0.41**	0.54**
World bond	0.24*	−0.06	0.14	−0.06	0.23	0.04	0.10	0.07	0.10	0.18	−0.03	0.05	0.08	−0.04	0.03	0.12
U.S. dollar	0.06	0.23	0.08	0.06	−0.23	0.15	0.19	0.23	0.02	0.01	0.23	0.20	0.06	0.24*	−0.16	0.10
PPI	−0.34**	−0.47**	−0.27*	−0.05	0.00	0.01	−0.41**	−0.16	0.00	−0.26*	−0.63**	−0.23	0.00	−0.33**	0.24*	−0.28*
T-bill	−0.03	−0.09	−0.07	0.22	0.09	0.00	−0.01	−0.02	0.21	−0.02	−0.17	0.01	0.28*	−0.06	−0.04	−0.08
Absolute Values																
GSCI	−0.21	−0.35**	−0.16	0.06	0.09	0.28*	−0.13	−0.06	0.02	−0.07	−0.38**	−0.20	0.14	−0.15	0.08	−0.11
S&P 500	0.12	−0.14	0.17	0.18	0.17	0.03	0.13	0.01	−0.23	0.23	−0.22	−0.13	−0.06	0.01	−0.31*	0.11
Salomon bond	0.21	−0.07	0.19	0.04	0.13	0.07	−0.01	0.07	−0.06	0.03	−0.09	−0.04	−0.08	0.01	−0.02	0.16
MSCI	−0.10	−0.22	0.12	−0.04	0.14	0.19	−0.04	0.08	−0.02	0.12	−0.20	−0.06	0.28*	−0.15	−0.07	−0.16
World bond	0.28*	−0.03	0.19	0.03	0.54**	0.31*	0.24*	0.32**	0.21	0.14	−0.05	0.20	0.15	0.15	0.04	0.15
U.S. dollar	0.15	0.08	0.06	−0.07	0.49**	0.36**	0.21	0.31*	0.14	0.04	0.02	0.07	0.02	0.26*	0.13	0.08

*Significant with 95% confidence.
**Significant with 99% confidence.

Exhibit 4b EACM Hedge Fund Index Correlations

	100	RerVal	L/S Eq.	Conv	Bond	Rotat.	Event	Arb.	Bnkrpt.	Multi	Equity	Domlong	DomOpp	Gl/int.	Short
EACM Index															
EACM 100															
Relative value	0.50**														
Long/short equity	0.26*	0.25*													
Convert hedge	0.32**	0.78**	−0.06												
Bond hedge	0.01	0.19	−0.16	0.00											
Rotational	0.42**	0.81**	−0.06	0.45**	0.15										
Event driven	0.34**	0.23	−0.24	0.34**	0.15	0.18									
Arbitrage	0.18	−0.03	−0.32**	0.09	0.08	0.03	0.84**								
Bankruptcy	0.31*	0.42**	−0.11	0.47**	0.16	0.30*	0.81**	0.40**							
Multistrategy	0.38**	0.19	−0.15	0.29*	0.15	0.11	0.86**	0.68**	0.58**						
Equity hedge	0.50**	0.25*	−0.08	0.30*	0.08	0.18	0.59**	0.52**	0.45**	0.50**					
DomLong	0.27*	0.15	−0.18	0.25*	0.12	0.11	0.57**	0.49**	0.47**	0.45**	0.85**				
DomOpp	0.40**	0.27*	0.26*	0.20	−0.07	0.15	0.07	0.01	0.04	0.17	0.50**	0.19			
Global/int'l	0.44**	0.16	−0.19	0.22	0.10	0.15	0.59**	0.56**	0.44**	0.44**	0.85**	0.64**	0.09		
Short	−0.03	−0.09	0.30*	−0.26*	−0.07	−0.06	−0.57**	−0.53**	−0.42**	−0.46**	−0.70**	−0.82**	−0.13	−0.56**	
Nominal Factors															
MLM	0.06	−0.01	0.09	−0.12	−0.01	0.05	−0.29*	−0.32**	−0.23	−0.15	−0.33**	−0.36**	0.07	−0.37**	0.43**
GSCI	0.00	0.13	0.37**	0.03	−0.16	0.03	−0.17	−0.33**	0.09	−0.18	−0.14	0.22	0.38**	−0.34**	0.29*
S&P 500	0.22	−0.02	−0.23	0.05	0.10	0.02	0.46**	0.53**	0.24*	0.36**	0.69**	0.79**	0.04	0.63**	−0.77**
Salomon bond	0.35**	0.19	0.18	0.17	0.08	0.04	0.23	0.27*	0.09	0.22	0.38**	0.37**	0.16	0.30*	−0.26*
MSCI	0.16	0.00	−0.12	0.04	0.12	0.00	0.27*	0.33**	0.16	0.18	0.57**	0.59**	0.08	0.54**	−0.53**
World bond	0.20	0.10	0.20	0.05	0.03	0.00	−0.02	0.05	−0.09	−0.01	0.11	0.10	0.05	0.09	−0.08
U.S. dollar	−0.02	0.03	−0.19	0.15	0.03	0.01	0.23	0.13	0.24*	0.20	0.17	0.17	0.09	0.12	−0.17
PPI	−0.22	−0.05	0.25*	−0.12	−0.18	−0.07	−0.65**	−0.68**	−0.42**	−0.52**	−0.44**	−0.40**	−0.09	−0.43**	0.44**
T-bill	0.07	0.02	0.28*	−0.20	−0.08	0.09	−0.19	−0.11	−0.20	−0.18	0.02	0.05	0.16	−0.12	0.07
Absolute Values															
GSCI	0.05	0.03	0.33**	−0.12	−0.17	0.03	−0.34**	−0.39**	−0.20	−0.24*	−0.14	−0.22	0.21	−0.23	0.24*
SP500	0.07	0.02	−0.08	−0.04	−0.09	0.14	−0.25*	−0.26*	−0.12	−0.26*	0.06	0.14	−0.02	0.03	−0.11
Salomon bond	0.12	0.15	0.15	0.12	−0.05	0.07	−0.11	−0.06	−0.11	−0.12	0.01	0.02	−0.04	0.04	−0.02
MSCI	0.10	0.09	0.15	−0.11	−0.07	0.20	−0.27*	−0.23	−0.20	−0.23	0.02	−0.10	0.17	0.01	0.11
World bond	0.48**	0.31*	0.28*	0.26*	−0.13	0.16	−0.06	−0.03	−0.05	−0.08	0.21	0.17	0.19	0.12	−0.05
U.S. dollar	0.44**	0.31*	0.17	0.33**	−0.04	0.14	0.05	−0.02	0.12	0.03	0.13	0.04	0.12	0.13	0.00

*Significant with 95% confidence.
**Significant with 99% confidence.

EXHIBIT 5 MORNINGSTAR MUTUAL FUND INDEX CORRELATIONS

	G&I	Growth	Equity Income	Aggress. Growth	Small Co.	Govt. Bond	Corp. Bond	Multi Bond	Asset Alloc.	Bal-anced	Conv. Bond	High Yield
Index												
Growth & Income												
Growth	0.98**											
Equity income	0.98**	0.93**										
Aggressive growth	0.90**	0.97**	0.85**									
Small company	0.89**	0.95**	0.84**	0.99**								
Govt. bond	0.58**	0.51**	0.63**	0.40**	0.37**							
Corporate bond	0.58**	0.51**	0.64**	0.40**	0.38	0.98**						
Multisector bond	0.67**	0.62**	0.73**	0.55**	0.56**	0.77**	0.82**					
Asset allocation	0.98**	0.95**	0.97**	0.88**	0.86**	0.69**	0.70**	0.73**				
Balanced	0.98**	0.96**	0.98**	0.88**	0.87**	0.70**	0.71**	0.75**	0.99**			
Convertible bond	0.93**	0.95**	0.92**	0.93**	0.94**	0.54**	0.56**	0.73**	0.93**	0.93**		
High yield	0.51**	0.49**	0.55**	0.49**	0.53**	0.36**	0.45**	0.82**	0.52**	0.53**	0.64**	
Global	0.82**	0.79**	0.85**	0.73**	0.72**	0.60**	0.63**	0.80**	0.84**	0.84**	0.84**	0.60**
Nominal Factors												
MLM	−0.36**	−0.40**	−0.34**	−0.44**	−0.45**	0.01	0.00	−0.15	−0.29*	−0.32**	−0.39**	−0.27*
GSCI	−0.29*	−0.33**	−0.24*	−0.36**	−0.36**	−0.08	−0.07	−0.18	−0.24*	−0.26*	−0.31*	−0.14
S&P 500	0.99**	0.95**	0.97**	0.86**	0.84**	0.60**	0.60**	0.66**	0.96**	0.97**	0.89**	0.47**
Salomon bond	0.52**	0.45**	0.58**	0.33**	0.30*	0.98**	0.99**	0.74**	0.65**	0.65**	0.48**	0.33**
MSCI	0.68**	0.64**	0.70**	0.58**	0.56**	0.44**	0.44**	0.59**	0.67**	0.68**	0.65**	0.40**
World bond	0.29*	0.23	0.32**	0.13	0.09	0.63**	0.60**	0.48**	0.36**	0.37**	0.25*	0.08
U.S. dollar	0.02	0.05	0.00	0.12	0.16	−0.23	−0.19	−0.10	−0.02	−0.02	0.07	0.18
PPI	−0.43**	−0.45**	−0.42**	−0.47**	−0.50**	−0.10	−0.16	−0.42**	−0.39**	−0.40**	−0.47**	−0.55**
T-bill	0.04	0.05	0.00	0.03	0.01	0.20	0.16	0.07	0.06	0.07	−0.05	−0.13
Absolute Values												
GSCI	−0.19	−0.19	−0.20	−0.23	−0.25*	0.01	−0.05	−0.23	−0.14	−0.16	−0.27*	−0.36**
S&P 500	0.27*	0.26*	0.22	0.20	0.16	0.12	0.10	0.02	0.27*	0.24*	0.18	−0.08
Salomon bond	0.18	0.14	0.19	0.07	0.05	0.53**	0.52**	0.26*	0.27*	0.26*	0.17	0.02
MSCI	−0.04	−0.03	−0.06	−0.06	−0.11	−0.06	−0.10	−0.14	−0.05	−0.05	−0.12	−0.24*
World bond	0.22	0.20	0.22	0.16	0.13	0.47**	0.44**	0.30**	0.28*	0.28*	0.21	0.06
U.S. dollar	−0.04	−0.01	−0.04	0.05	0.06	−0.01	0.00	0.04	−0.02	−0.02	0.03	0.14

*Significant with 95% confidence.
**Significant with 99% confidence.

while hedge funds and mutual funds are negatively correlated with this index. CTAs also correlate more strongly with the absolute values of asset benchmarks than with nominal values, reflecting the ability to sell short and to engage in option strategies. Pairwise correlation patterns suggest CTA investment would provide diversification benefits to a portfolio of stocks, bonds, and hedge funds. Hedge funds, on the other hand, share some explanatory factors with stocks and bonds. A close examination of the strategy employed by the fund is necessary before determining the diversification benefits of a hedge fund relative to a stock and bond portfolio.

Factors Determining CTA, Hedge and Mutual Fund Returns: Regression Analysis

Correlation results suggest the factors determining CTA and hedge fund performance differ considerably from the factors that drive stock and bond fund returns, although hedge funds share some factors with CTAs and some factors with traditional stock and bond fund managers. In this section, regression analysis is used to fit an explicit multi-factor model. Exhibits 6 and 7 give a correlation matrix for the full set of explanatory variables. These results show few pairwise correlations above .5. While low pairwise regressions do not prevent high levels of multi-collinearity among the explanatory variables, the relatively low correlations allow the assumption of stable coefficients.

Regression Analysis of CTA, Hedge, and Mutual Fund Returns

Exhibits 8-10 report the regression results. Exhibit 8 shows the coefficients using the MAR CTA indexes. Exhibit 9 gives the EACM hedge fund regression results, and Exhibit 10 reports the Morningstar stock and bond mutual fund regressions. In each instance, the independent variables are the nominal and absolute values of the S&P500, GSCI, SBBI, and USDX, the intramonth standard deviation of the S&P500, GSCI, bond, and USDX, and the nominal value of the MLM index. For each regression, the *r*-square, *f*-statistic, intercept, and thirteen slope coefficients are reported. Significance of coefficients is reported at the 5% and 1% significance levels.

In Exhibit 8A, the regression results for the CTA dollar-weighted index are given. For the overall sample, the most significant variables are the MLM trendfollowing index, and the absolute value of the USDX. The sign for the MLM factor is positive, as is the sign for the absolute value of the USDX. The sign is negative for the intra-month standard deviation of the USDX. This is as expected. The MLM variable captures various long-term trendfollowing models used by many CTAs. The absolute value of the USDX may also capture returns to CTAs who were long or short foreign currencies during the period of analysis for which currency trends existed. The MAR Diversified index, also on Exhibit 8A, has the same two significant coefficients and also the intramonth standard deviation of the USDX. The negative coefficient for the intra-month standard deviation of the USDX confirms the expectation that, to the degree that many CTAs are trendfollowers, high intra-month standard deviation may result in traders being 'whipsawed' in a volatile market. While these variables are generally significant across all of the various sub-indices, the relative significance is a function of the CTA trading style or market. For instance, the highest significance for the absolute value of the USDX is reported for CTA currency managers. The significance of the USDX variable is lowest for Discretionary CTA managers, whose investment opportunities and trading style are not fixed on a single market or trendfollowing system.

In Exhibits 8B and 8C, regression results for the top five, median, and bottom five CTAs are presented. Exhibit 8B covers all CTAs who reported results for the full 1990-

Exhibit 6 Traditional Asset Correlations

Index	MLM	GSCI	S&P 500	T-Bond	MSCI	W-Bond	USDX	PPI	T-Bill
MLM									
GSCI total return	0.19								
S&P 500	−0.33**	−0.28*							
Salomon treasury bond	0.03	−0.05	0.54**						
MSCI world	−0.23	−0.24*	0.69**	0.41**					
Salomon world govt. bond	0.11	−0.07	0.33**	0.63**	0.53**				
U.S. dollar index	−0.21	−0.04	−0.02	−0.21	−0.28	−0.78**			
PPI	0.33**	0.23	−0.41**	−0.10	−0.27*	0.03	−0.15		
U.S. Treasury bill	0.15	0.17	0.07	0.15	−0.11	0.09	−0.12	0.23	

	Nominal Index Values									Absolute Index Values				
Index	MLM	GSCI	S&P 500	T-Bond	MSCI	W-Bond	USDX	PPI	T-Bill	GSCI	S&P 500	T-Bond	MSCI	W-Bond
GSCI	0.29*	0.56**	−0.17	0.00	−0.23	0.03	−0.10	0.47**	0.30*					
S&P 500	0.10	0.03	0.28*	0.08	0.11	0.17	−0.18	0.17	0.31*	0.32**				
Salomon bond	0.04	−0.06	0.19	0.56**	0.11	0.44**	−0.18	0.06	0.04	0.04	0.27*			
MSCI	0.06	0.24*	−0.01	−0.09	0.12	0.11	−0.11	0.24*	0.26*	0.46**	0.55**	−0.05		
World bond	−0.20	−0.10	0.23	0.45**	0.27*	0.56**	−0.31*	0.03	0.15	0.00	0.13	0.39**	0.17	
U.S. dollar	−0.21	−0.10	−0.05	−0.01	−0.02	−0.07	0.24*	−0.20	−0.22	−0.04	−0.09	−0.05	−0.02	−0.54**

*Significant with 95% confidence.
**Significant with 99% confidence.

Exhibit 7 Correlation of Intramonth Standard Deviation Measures

Intramonth SD	Nominal Index Values					Absolute Values				Intramonth SD			
	MLM	GSCI	S&P 500	USSB	USDX	GSCI	S&P 500	USSB	USDX	S&P 500	JPBD	GSCI	USDX
S&P 500	0.16	0.14	−0.21	−0.12	−0.08	0.47**	0.36**	0.04	−0.06				
Salomon bond	−0.01	−0.05	0.09	−0.22	0.12	−0.12	−0.07	−0.14	−0.11	0.05			
GSCI	0.11	0.01	−0.08	−0.05	−0.10	0.55**	0.32**	0.06	−0.12	0.68**	0.06		
USDX	−0.24*	−0.06	0.04	0.19	0.19	−0.13	−0.10	0.18	0.24*	0.10	−0.05	−0.03	

*Significant with 95% confidence.
**Significant with 99% confidence.

Exhibit 8a Regression using MAR CTA Performance Indexes

Performance Index	Adj. R^2	F Stat	Intercept	Nominal Index Coefficients					Absolute Index Coefficients				Intramonth SD Coefficients			
				MLM	GSCI	S&P 500	SBBI	USDX	GSCI	S&P 500	SBBI	USDX	GSCI	S&P 500	SBBI	USDX
Dollar weight	0.32	3.57	−0.015	0.555*	0.027	−0.122	0.474	−0.265	−0.034	0.183	0.149	1.035**	3.074	−0.677	−1.079	−2.815
Diversified	0.30	3.39	−0.006	0.745*	−0.016	−0.216	0.736	−0.280	−0.029	0.307	−0.200	1.001**	1.670	1.484	−0.799	−4.754*
Equal weight	0.42	5.04	−0.001	0.427	0.048	−0.161	0.501	−0.211	−0.050	0.168	−0.030	0.974**	2.946	−0.103	−0.987	−5.431**
Energy	0.32	3.57	−0.015	0.555*	0.027	−0.122	0.474	−0.265	−0.034	0.183	0.149	1.035**	3.074	−0.677	−1.079	−2.815
Currency	0.53	7.22	−0.042	0.358	0.077	−0.092	1.312*	−0.439**	−0.231	0.102	−0.930	2.128**	7.401**	4.967	−1.203	−6.442**
Financial/metal	0.35	3.97	−0.003	0.231	−0.055	−0.182	0.792	−0.491**	−0.051	0.340	0.422	1.099**	3.321	−3.366	−1.323	−5.270*
Discretionary	0.14	1.88	−0.014	0.379	0.050	−0.173	0.557	0.124	0.022	0.001	0.156	0.339*	1.371	1.358	−0.490	0.882
Trend following	0.41	4.83	−0.018	0.756	0.039	−0.275	1.032	−0.486*	−0.116	0.537	−0.037	1.726**	4.322	0.844	−2.040	−7.338*

*Significant with 95% confidence.
**Significant with 99% confidence.

EXHIBIT 8B REGRESSION USING BEST PERFORMING, WORST PERFORMNING, AND MEDIAN CTAs

				Nominal Index Coefficients					Absolute Index Coefficients				Intramonth SD Coefficients			
Performance Index	Adj. R^2	F Stat	Intercept	MLM	GSCI	S&P 500	SBBI	USDX	GSCI	S&P 500	SBBI	USDX	GSCI	S&P 500	SBBI	USDX
All CTAs	0.38	4.34	0.002	0.976**	0.035	−0.124	0.405	−0.404*	−0.091	0.191	−0.149	1.366**	3.489	−1.986	−1.077	−6.219*
Best five	0.42	5.02	0.085	1.582*	0.300	−0.257	0.109	−0.980**	−0.132	0.584	0.287	3.256**	8.966	0.642	−0.933	−11.102*
Median	0.38	4.36	0.005	0.919**	0.029	−0.043	0.225	−0.443**	−0.069	0.173	−0.025	1.125**	2.844	−3.320	−1.273	−5.139*
Worst five	0.25	2.83	−0.081*	1.410**	−0.126	−0.136	0.790	−0.288	−0.133	−0.346	−0.319	0.814*	1.880	−2.337	−1.389	−8.502*

*Significant with 95% confidence.
**Significant with 99% confidence.

EXHIBIT 8C REGRESSION USING BEST PERFORMING, WORST PERFORMING, AND MEDIAN DIVERSIFIED CTAs

				Nominal Index Coefficients					Absolute Index Coefficients				Intramonth SD Coefficients			
Performance Index	Adj. R^2	F Stat	Intercept	MLM	GSCI	S&P 500	SBBI	USDX	GSCI	S&P 500	SBBI	USDX	GSCI	S&P 500	SBBI	USDX
All CTAs	0.31	3.48	0.004	1.256**	−0.010	−0.110	0.182	−0.367	0.000	0.206	−0.130	1.247**	3.111	−2.667	−1.553	−5.472
Best five	0.30	3.33	0.083	1.759*	0.038	0.034	−0.337	−0.768	0.267	0.430	0.776	2.449**	4.856	2.445	−2.454	−8.553
Median	0.29	3.24	0.007	1.163**	−0.010	−0.093	0.125	−0.415*	−0.064	0.253	−0.183	1.080**	2.348	−3.037	−1.201	−5.020
Worst five	0.31	3.44	−0.065*	1.560**	−0.105	−0.127	0.599	0.017	−0.028	−0.272	−0.610	0.684*	4.191	−11.356	−2.355*	−5.189

*Significant with 95% confidence.
**Significant with 99% confidence.

1995 period, and Exhibit 8C gives results for CTAs listed as Diversified by MAR. If relative investor skill is important (and not just differential leverage or risk factors), the top five should be sensitive to the same variables as the other groups, but have a positive alpha. The median CTAs should have an insignificant alpha while the bottom five CTAs should have a negative alpha. Results in Exhibit 8B are consistent with this hypothesis. The best 5 CTAs have a monthly alpha of 8.80%, the median CTA of .5% and the bottom 5 an alpha of -8.1%.

Similar results are reported for Diversified CTAs in Exhibit 8C. Moreover, the return model is consistent across alternative performing CTAs. For most regressions the MLM index and the absolute value and intra-month variance of the USDX are significant, and the coefficients have the same sign and similar magnitudes.

In Exhibit 9A, the regression results for the EACM hedge fund indexes are given. For the EACM 100 index (a broad index which tracks primarily hedge funds and has some exposure to managed futures strategies through the Global Asset Allocators sub-index), the most significant variable is the absolute value of the USDX. The MLM is almost significant at the 5% level (*p*-value is .062). The sign of both the USDX and the MLM are positive. This is expected because the index includes some CTAs and also some hedge funds that follow similar directional strategies. However, most hedge fund advisors have investment styles and trade in asset markets that differ from CTAs. The MLM index is not significant in any of the hedge fund index regressions[8]. As important, the signs are generally in line with expectations. For instance, the equity-based indexes (Event-driven, Equity Hedge, Domestic Long, Global/International, and Short Selling) are significantly correlated with the S&P 500 and have the expected signs. Similarly, for other hedge fund indices such as the Bond Hedge, there is little evidence of significant explanatory variables. This too is as expected, given that a pure hedge play should not be correlated directly with the long return of any of the underlying markets. Bond Hedge reports a statistically significant alpha of 1% per month. This suggests the source of the returns is not captured by the explanatory variables tested, and other variables are needed to fully explain this return. Many other hedge fund indexes report significantly positive alphas as well.

In Exhibits 9B and 9C, regression results for the top five, the median, and bottom five hedge funds are presented. Exhibit 9B covers all hedge funds that have reported data to MAR from 1990-1995, and Exhibit 9C analyzes the performance of those funds listed as US Opportunity funds. In Exhibit 9B, the best 5 hedge funds are shown to have a significant monthly alpha of 2.2%, the median hedge fund a significant monthly alpha of 1.5% and the bottom 5 a monthly alpha of -4.31% (this coefficient is significant at the 10% level, but not the 5% level). Results also indicate that the MLM index explains a portion of the lowest performers but not the median or best performers. This suggests that the worst performing funds in a given month were following directional strategies that, consistent with results in Exhibit 2, offered lower risk-adjusted returns during the sample period.

Exhibit 9C shows similar results for the US Opportunity hedge fund subsample. The return model is both consistent across varying performing hedge funds. For each group the S&P 500 index is significant, while for the median and bottom hedge funds the absolute value of the S&P 500 had a negative coefficient.

Exhibits 10A and 10B repeat this analysis for Morningstar stock and bond mutual fund indices and the best, median and bottom Growth & Income equity mutual funds. The results are consistent with results reported previously by Sharpe [1992], Blake et al., [1993], and Elton et al., [1995]. The major factor determining the return of a fund

EXHIBIT 9A REGRESSION USING EACM HEDGE FUND PERFORMANCE INDEXES

				Nominal Index Coefficients					Absolute Index Coefficients				Intramonth SD Coefficients			
Performance Index	Adj. R^2	F Stat	Intercept	MLM	GSCI	S&P 500	SBBI	USDX	GSCI	S&P 500	SBBI	USDX	GSCI	S&P 500	SBBI	USDX
EACM 100	0.27	3.03	0.010	0.150	0.031	0.075	0.207	−0.010	−0.036	−0.003	−0.142	0.299**	0.394	−2.336	0.114	−0.219
Long/short	0.29	3.25	0.007	−0.081	0.044	−0.061	0.239	−0.054	0.032	−0.084	0.053	0.110*	1.295*	−0.996	−0.165	−0.795
Relative value	0.07	1.40	0.011*	0.027	0.035	−0.005	0.075	0.005	−0.033	0.019	0.003	0.113*	−0.114	2.719	0.100	0.360
Convertible hedge	0.20	2.33	0.010	0.032	0.034	−0.021	0.098	0.040	−0.017	0.106	−0.039	0.182	−1.670	−4.131	−0.119	2.621**
Bond hedge	−0.10	0.51	0.010**	0.037	0.000	0.015	0.008	0.004	−0.029	−0.013	−0.055	−0.012	−0.209	−0.790	0.167	0.319
Event driven	0.33	3.72	0.028**	−0.033	0.012	0.211**	0.093	0.095	−0.031	−0.157	−0.274	−0.009	−0.748	−1.962	−0.205	0.135
Rotational	−0.09	0.55	0.019	0.122	0.062	0.047	−0.045	0.029	−0.119	0.065	0.053	0.172	0.127	−4.961	0.516	−0.706
Arbitrage	0.42	4.88	0.029*	−0.142	−0.077	0.286**	0.204	0.073	−0.004	−0.292*	−0.229	−0.075	−0.506	0.486	−0.335	−1.324
Bankruptcy	0.15	1.97	0.029*	0.004	0.134	0.225	−0.111	0.124	−0.099	−0.047	−0.300	0.058	−0.520	−5.836	−0.319	2.021
Equity hedge	0.50	6.50	0.015	0.008	0.052	0.390**	0.082	0.080	−0.028	−0.026	−0.360	0.122	−1.265	−2.174	0.425	1.727
Multi-index	0.21	2.46	0.027**	0.040	−0.021	0.123	0.185	0.088	0.010	−0.133	−0.292	−0.009	−1.220	−0.536	0.039	−0.293
Domestic long	0.67	11.9	0.005	0.047	0.070	0.585**	−0.044	0.106	−0.120	0.017	−0.408	0.059	−1.234	−0.987	0.751	2.771**
Dom. opportunity	0.11	1.67	0.003	0.137	0.198**	0.036	0.386	0.057	−0.019	0.038	−0.457	−0.192	−1.653	2.550	0.515	1.412
Short selling	0.64	10.6	0.022	0.307	0.063	−1.355**	0.852	−0.173	−0.087	0.040	0.185	0.156	3.350	−5.406	−0.054	−5.728*
Global/ internat'l.	0.39	4.50	0.036*	−0.161	−0.111	0.548**	−0.095	0.078	0.055	−0.132	−0.216	0.114	−0.908	−8.084	0.010	0.998

*Significant with 95% confidence.
**Significant with 99% confidence.

EXHIBIT 9B REGRESSION USING BEST PERFORMING, WORST PERFORMING, AND MEDIAN HEDGE FUNDS

				Nominal Index Coefficients					Absolute Index Coefficients				Intramonth SD Coefficients			
Performance Index	Adj. R^2	F Stat	Intercept	MLM	GSCI	S&P 500	SBBI	USDX	GSCI	S&P 500	SBBI	USDX	GSCI	S&P 500	SBBI	USDX
All funds	0.58	8.49	0.012	0.139	0.039	0.399**	−0.335*	0.097*	−0.108*	−0.130	−0.045	0.128	−0.425	−3.051	0.450	1.424*
Best five	0.53	7.20	0.022**	0.060	0.050	0.375**	−0.318	0.123*	−0.062	0.020	−0.041	0.170*	−0.365	−2.511	0.668*	1.403
Median	0.56	7.99	0.015**	0.065	0.056	0.303**	−0.169	0.075	−0.113*	−0.122*	−0.099	0.057	−0.382	−3.232	0.408	1.131
Worst five	0.22	2.53	−0.43	1.165**	−0.087	0.572**	−1.158	0.170	−0.315	−0.628*	−0.007	0.215	0.336	−10.950	0.217	4.125

*Significant with 95% confidence.
**Significant with 99% confidence.

EXHIBIT 9C REGRESSION USING BEST PERFORMING, WORST PERFORMING, AND MEDIAN OPPORTUNITY HEDGE FUNDS

				Nominal Index Coefficients					Absolute Index Coefficients				Intramonth SD Coefficients			
Performance Index	Adj. R^2	F Stat	Intercept	MLM	GSCI	S&P 500	SBBI	USDX	GSCI	S&P 500	SBBI	USDX	GSCI	S&P 500	SBBI	USDX
All funds	0.67	11.8	0.009	0.101	0.043	0.449**	−0.342*	0.073	−0.118*	−0.224**	−0.154	0.111	−0.964	−3.262	0.485	1.280
Best five	0.50	6.57	0.024**	0.054	0.056	0.352**	−0.219	0.130*	−0.070	0.039	−0.130	0.165*	−0.072	−2.499	0.552	1.261
Median	0.72	15.2	0.008	0.020	0.019	0.435**	−0.281	0.020	−0.063	−0.312**	−0.050	0.061	−1.216	−2.181	0.271	0.934
Worst five	0.58	8.51	−0.006	0.204	0.048	0.549**	−0.528*	0.062	−0.190*	−0.407**	−0.269	0.096	−1.733	−4.626	0.611	1.604

*Significant with 95% confidence.
**Significant with 99% confidence.

is the factor that reflects the primary market the fund is trading. For instance, all the mutual fund indexes have significantly positive S&P500 coefficients. Fixed income and asset allocation mutual funds also report significant coefficients with the Salmon Bond index (except Convertible bonds, which has no sensitivity to this index). For equity mutual funds, the intra-month standard deviation of the S&P 500 has a negative sign (significantly so for Growth & Income). Similarly, most bond funds have negative sensitivity to volatility in the bond index. This suggests that mutual fund returns are diminished by volatility in the underlying markets.

The average, best, median, and bottom Growth & Income funds all show significance at the 95% level to the SP500 (Exhibit 10B). The top Growth & Income managers have a significant positive sign with the absolute value of the S&P500 while reporting a lower overall fit (*r*-square of .88) with the model than the median manager (*r*-square of .98). The worst managers have a significantly negative coefficient with the absolute value of the S&P500. Interestingly, the best managers have a large, significant coefficient with the bond index, suggesting the managers who placed relatively more emphasis on income as opposed to growth performed best during the sample period.

Trading Style and CTA, Hedge Fund, and Mutual Fund Returns

Correlation Relationships

Results in the previous section show that CTA returns are positively related to factors such as market trends and currency movement, while hedge fund and mutual fund returns are best explained by the return to a buy-and-hold strategy in the markets the fund invests in. In this section, we further explore these sources of return by correlating the returns of the top five, median, and bottom five performers with other measures of intramonth price movement. Results are reported in Exhibit 11. Three measures of intramonth price movement are calculated: the standard deviation, the maximum drawdown, and the maximum drawup. For CTAs, results are consistent with results in section C that show a high positive correlation with the MLM index. There is a significant negative correlation with the maximum drawup of the SP500 and almost no correlation with the maximum drawup of the SP500. This is especially true for the top performers, and is consistent with the inclusion of CTAs to provide downside risk protection for equity portfolios [Schneeweis, Spurgin, and Porter, 1996].

Hedge fund performance is positively correlated with S&P500 drawups and drawdowns. Among top performers the coefficients are of the same magnitude, but for median and bottom performers the drawup coefficient is much lower than the drawdown. Hedge funds show significant correlation with the maximum drawup of USDX but not with the maximum drawdown, suggesting they are better able to time the currency market than the stock market. Growth and Income mutual fund performance is positively correlated with both S&P500 and JPM Bond index drawups and drawdowns. This is as expected, as mutual funds generally do not attempt to time entry and exit. Results for G&I funds also show a negative relationship with the standard deviation of the stock market. For the top performers, however, this relationship is less negative.

IMPLICATIONS OF RESULTS

Previous research on investment performance concentrates on single-factor models such as beta, standard deviation, and drawdown as an indicator of future risk/returns performance. In this paper, a number of factors are proposed to explain a broad range of managed assets. Results indicate that these factors may help explain the differences in

EXHIBIT 10A REGRESSION USING MORNINGSTAR MUTUAL FUND PERFORMNACE INDEXES

Performance Index	Adj. R^2	F Stat	Intercept	Nominal Index Coefficients MLM	GSCI	S&P 500	SBBI	USDX	Absolute Index Coefficients GSCI	S&P 500	SBBI	USDX	Intramonth SD Coefficients GSCI	S&P 500	SBBI	USDX
Growth & income	0.98	259.7	0.000	−0.017	0.012	0.895**	−0.062	0.029	−0.025	0.009	0.021	0.005	−0.719*	−0.134	0.295*	0.568
Equity income	0.95	101.6	0.005	0.008	0.052*	0.721**	0.149	0.027	−0.065	−0.024	−0.067	−0.003	−0.436	−1.458	0.238	0.468
Growth	0.91	59.34	−0.003	−0.101	−0.034	1.003**	−0.241	0.031	0.008	0.038	−0.055	0.030	−1.079	0.111	0.390	1.461
Aggress. growth	0.77	19.72	0.005	−0.234	−0.075	1.249**	−0.617	0.097	−0.006	0.032	−0.189	0.101	−2.382	−2.429	0.825	2.892
Small company	0.76	18.26	0.009	−0.147	−0.045	1.155**	−0.712	0.143	−0.052	−0.031	−0.075	0.108	−2.520	−3.348	0.937	2.863
Corporate bond	0.98	234.5	0.002	0.013	0.011	0.029**	0.784**	0.007	−0.025**	0.010	−0.034	0.006	0.101	−0.746*	0.009	0.051
Gov't. bond	0.97	190.9	0.001	0.002	−0.001	0.034**	0.767**	−0.009	−0.001	−0.005	−0.010	0.006	0.208	−0.612	0.012	−0.110
Multisect. bond	0.67	11.95	0.015**	0.050	0.032	0.190**	0.547**	−0.005	−0.101*	−0.069	−0.181	0.050	0.401	−4.888**	0.133	−0.042
Asset allocation	0.94	91.77	−0.002	0.034	0.016	0.482**	0.225**	0.018	−0.012	0.022	0.016	0.018	−0.452	−0.130	0.162	0.748*
Convertible bond	0.82	26.18	0.002	0.006	0.030	0.611**	−0.088	0.033	−0.098	0.007	−0.024	0.037	−1.356	−2.532	0.560*	2.447**
Balanced	0.97	152.5	−0.001	−0.019	0.009	0.562**	0.311**	0.019	−0.016	0.002	−0.025	0.015	−0.309	−0.496	0.172	0.598
High yield	0.34	3.76	0.027*	0.040	0.086	0.273**	0.198	0.120	−0.206*	−0.060	−0.265	0.113	0.331	−7.998*	−0.016	0.439
Global	0.65	11.31	0.012	0.167	0.047	0.437**	0.075	−0.088	−0.044	−0.047	−0.173	0.038	−0.867	−4.038	0.192	1.033

*Significant with 95% confidence.
**Significant with 99% confidence.

EXHIBIT 10B REGRESSION USING BEST PERFORMING, WORST PERFORMING, AND GROWTH & INCOME MUTUAL FUNDS

Performance Index	Adj. R^2	F Stat	Intercept	Nominal Index Coefficients MLM	GSCI	S&P 500	SBBI	USDX	Absolute Index Coefficients GSCI	S&P 500	SBBI	USDX	Intramonth SD Coefficients GSCI	S&P 500	SBBI	USDX
All funds	0.98	224.2	0.000	−0.021	0.015	0.882**	−0.046	0.035	−0.033	0.002	0.010	0.001	−0.731*	−0.256	0.340**	0.646
Best five	0.88	42.36	0.016	−0.185	0.019	0.843**	−0.120	0.163**	0.029	0.174*	0.242	0.040	−0.351	−1.593	0.815**	1.562
Median	0.98	296.2	0.000	−0.008	0.017	0.903**	−0.052	0.014	−0.025	0.001	0.015	0.003	−0.592*	−0.234	0.234*	0.560
Worst five	0.90	48.50	−0.023**	−0.097	0.005	0.818**	0.154	0.075	−0.107	−0.158*	−0.249	−0.006	−2.044**	0.976	0.334	1.365

*Significant with 95% confidence.
**Significant with 99% confidence.

EXHIBIT 11 TRADITIONAL ASSET CORRELATIONS

	CTA Performance Indexes					Hedge Fund Performance Indexes				Mutual Fund Performance Indexes			
	Average	Top 5	Median	Bottom 5	MLM	Average	Top 5	Median	Bottom 5	Average	Top 5	Median	Bottom 5
Top 5	0.88**					0.88**				0.93**			
Median	0.98**	0.81**				0.88**	0.85**			1.00**	0.93**		
Bottom 5	0.76**	0.52**	0.74**			0.54**	0.19	0.25*		0.94**	0.83**	0.93**	
MLM	0.37**	0.31*	0.38**	0.40**		−0.35**	−0.34**	−0.37**	0.04	−0.36**	−0.39**	−0.35**	−0.42**
S&P 500													
Return	−0.19	−0.24*	−0.15	−0.14	−0.34**	0.66**	0.63**	0.65**	0.11	0.99**	0.90**	0.99**	0.91**
Standard dev.	0.10	0.25*	0.05	−0.13	0.14	−0.24	−0.03	−0.27*	−0.20	−0.21	−0.03	−0.21	−0.38**
Max drawdown	−0.30*	−0.42**	−0.27*	−0.01	−0.35**	0.52**	0.32**	0.54**	0.26*	0.56**	0.37**	0.55**	0.69**
Max drawup	−0.02	−0.05	−0.01	−0.08	0.01	−0.06	−0.02	−0.08	−0.05	0.15	0.18	0.16	0.10
JPM Bond													
Return	0.04	−0.04	0.07	0.10	0.03	0.29*	0.29*	0.26*	0.21	0.53**	0.46**	0.54**	0.50**
Standard dev.	−0.14	−0.11	−0.16	−0.09	−0.01	0.23	0.22	0.24*	0.16	0.10	0.06	0.09	0.11
Max drawdown	0.08	−0.09	0.13	0.18	−0.08	0.06	0.06	0.12	0.04	0.37**	0.26*	0.38**	0.37**
Max drawup	0.09	0.02	0.10	0.10	0.01	0.28*	0.27*	0.25*	0.21	0.15	0.11	0.17	0.17
USDX													
Return	−0.26*	−0.25*	−0.32**	−0.20	−0.21	0.29*	0.29*	0.26*	0.21	0.02	0.11	0.00	0.10
Standard dev.	−0.23	−0.17	−0.23	−0.28*	−0.25	0.23	0.22	0.24*	0.16	0.08	0.15	0.07	0.14
Max drawdown	−0.15	−0.21	−0.18	0.06	0.08	0.06	0.06	0.12	0.04	−0.07	−0.08	−0.08	−0.03
Max drawup	−0.21	−0.16	−0.25*	−0.23	−0.20	0.28*	0.27*	0.25*	0.21	0.07	0.14	0.06	0.15
GSCI													
Return	0.08	0.18	0.07	−0.06	0.17	−0.27*	−0.18	−0.20	−0.30*	−0.29*	−0.23	−0.28*	−0.33**
Standard dev.	−0.04	0.11	−0.09	−0.19	0.12	−0.14	0.08	−0.18	−0.22	−0.07	0.11	−0.08	−0.22
Max drawdown	−0.02	−0.12	0.02	0.13	−0.25*	0.18	−0.03	0.25*	0.16	0.11	−0.06	0.12	0.26*
Max drawup	0.00	0.16	−0.05	−0.20	0.22	−0.30*	−0.12	−0.27*	−0.32**	−0.19	−0.05	−0.19	−0.33**

*Significant with 95% confidence.
**Significant with 99% confidence.

investment return, as well as some of the differences within each investment grouping. Adding managed futures and hedge fund products to traditional stock and bond portfolios only makes sense if these products derive return from sources unique from those that drive stock and bond return, and if, furthermore, the returns from those sources are positive. If this is the case, and results reported here support this, then alternative investments provide beneficial diversification to traditional stock and bond funds.

Future research is required to develop passive investment approaches that capture these unique factors more precisely. Unlike equity or bond mutual funds, the lack of a single factor that describes the return process means that alternative investments must be classified according to their style rather than a general return process. Alternatively, the fact that each position in a fund may draw from a unique return source means that a detailed breakdown of the individual positions in a fund may be required to understand the expected return. Results presented in this paper suggest both of these areas of research contain important information about the returns to actively managed assets in general, and managed futures and hedge funds, in particular.

ENDNOTES

This article was published in *The Journal of Alternative Investments*, Fall 1998, Vol. 1, No. 2.

[1] The authors would like to thank the Foundation for Managed Derivatives Research for their support in this research. The results of this study represent the conclusions of the authors and do not necessarily reflect the opinions of the foundation

[2] Hedge funds invest in futures and options as well as cash commodity, currency, and security markets.

[3] Investments managed by commodity trading advisors (CTAs), who trade primarily futures and options.

[4] The use of derived variables which attempt to replicate the factor loading in multi-factor regression models is consistent with research conducted in equity research [Chen and Jorden, 1993].

[5] The information ratio is the ratio of average return to standard deviation. It is similar to the Sharpe ratio, but does not adjust the return by the Treasury bill rate. We employ this measure in addition to the Sharpe ratio because the Sharpe ratio implicitly assumes a US investor whose risk-free rate is accurately described by the Tbill rate. The information ratio is a purely statistical measure of variability and assumes nothing about the behavior of investors.

[6] There is little evidence that the MLM index captures return patterns in the currency, energy, or financial return subindices. Similar results are seen in the Barclay currency subindex. This could in part be due to the small currency and energy weighting in the MLM index and the fact that financial markets, especially, the S&P 500 generally show little evidence of long-term trend following.

[7] The reported results, i.e., low correlation between commodity benchmarks and an equity index, may differ for subindices of the equity index that would be expected to be highly correlated with underlying commodity markets (e.g., mining, energy firms).

[8] Hedge funds that follow directional derivative strategies (EACM Global Asset Allocators) were grouped in the CTA category

REFERENCES

Chan, L., N. Jegadeesh, and J. Lakonishok. "Momentum Strategies." *Journal of Finance,* (December, 1996), pp.1681-1713.

Edwards, F. and Andy C. Ma. "Commodity Fund Performance: Is the Information Contained in Fund Prospectuses Useful?" *Journal of Futures Markets*, Vol. 8. No. 5 (1988), pp. 589-616.

Elton, E. .J., M. .J. Gruber, and C. Blake. "Fundamental Economic Variables, Expected Returns, and Bond Fund Performance." *Journal of Finance*, Vol. 50, No. 4, (September, 1995), pp. 1229-1256.

Fung, William and D. Hsieh. "Empirical Characteristics of Dynamic Trading Strategies: The Case of Hedge Funds." *The Review of Financial Studies*, 10 (1997), pp. 275-302.

Irwin, S. "Further Evidence on the Usefulness of CTA Performance Information in Public Commodity

Fund Prospectuses and a Proposal for Reform." *Advances in Futures and Options Research*, Vol. 7 (1994), pp. 251-265.

Lintner, J. "The Potential Role of Managed Commodity-Financial Futures Accounts in Portfolios of Stocks and Bonds." Annual Conference of the Financial Analysts Federation, Toronto, Canada, (1983).

Mitev, T. "Classification of Commodity Trading Advisors (CTAs) Using Maximum Likelihood Factor Analysis." Working Paper (CISDM/SOM, University of Massachusetts, 1996).

McCarthy D., Schneeweis, T., R. Spurgin and. "Informational Content in Historical CTA Performance." *The Journal of Futures Markets*, (May, 1997), pp. 317-340

Schneeweis, T. *The Benefits of Managed Futures*. European Managed Futures Association, (1996).

Schneeweis, T., R. Spurgin, and M. Potter. "Managed Futures and Hedge Fund Investment for Downside Equity Risk Management." *Derivatives Quarterly*, (Fall, 1996), pp. 62-72.

Silber, W. "Technical Trading - When it Works and When it Doesn't." *The Journal of Derivatives*, (Spring, 1994), pp. 39-44

Sharpe, W. "Asset Allocation: Management Style and Performance Measurement." *The Journal of Portfolio Management* Vol 18. No. 2 (1992), pp. 7-19.

Spurgin, R. "Managed Futures, Hedge Fund, and Mutual Fund Performance: An Equity Class Analysis." *The Journal of Alternative Investments*, (Summer, 1998), pp. 41-55.

APPENDIX I

Alternative Commodity, Hedge Fund, Managed Futures, and Mutual Fund Indices

Goldman Sachs Commodity Index (GSCI) is an arithmetic measure of the performance of actively traded, dollar-denominated nearby commodity futures contracts. As of January 9, 1995, there were 22 commodities in the index. The weights assigned to individual commodities are based on a five-year moving average of world production. Weights are determined each July and are made effective the following January. All contracts are rolled on the fifth business day of the month prior to the expiration month of the contract. Subindices are calculated for agricultural, energy, industrial, livestock, and precious metals contracts. Two versions of the indices are available: a total return version, which assumes that capital sufficient to purchase the basket of commodities is invested at the risk-free rate, and a spot version, which only tracks movements in the futures prices. This study uses the total return measure.

Mount Lucas (MLM) Index differs from other indices in two important ways. First, it allows both long and short positions in the underlying futures contracts. Second, it incorporates financial and currency futures (but not stock index futures) into the index, along with the commodities tracked by other indices. The index is an equally weighted average of the monthly returns from 25 separate futures contracts. Within each market (e.g., corn futures), the index will be long or short depending on whether the contract is above or below its trailing 12-month moving average. MLM is a total-return index. It was launched in May, 1989.

Managed Account Reports (MAR) tracks the performance of individual CTAs as well as CTA Funds and Pools that invest in individual CTAs. MAR produces several performance indices, the dominant being the CTA equal-weighted and dollar-weighted indices. MAR classifies CTAs into a number of different groups, and publishes each group's performance index. These groups are currency, energy, financial, diversified, discretionary, and trend-following. MAR also reports the following subindices for fund and pool performance: guaranteed, multi-advisor, single-advisor, private pools, and public pools.

Barclay Trading Group, publisher of the Barclay Managed Futures Report, also creates CTA performance indices. Indices are based on monthly returns of CTAs with established track records. Barclay publishes an equal weighted index of all CTAs as well as the following subindices: agricultural, currency, diversified, energy, financial/metal, discretionary, and systematic.

Hedge Fund Research and EACM offers historical managed futures/hedge fund performance on an array of indices and subindices designed to capture the return to unique managed futures/hedge fund strategies. These indices include relative value, event-driven, equity hedge funds, global asset allocators and short selling. Subindices include long/short equity, convertible hedge, bond hedge, rotational, deal arbitrage, bankruptcy, and multi-event. For managed futures, the principal subindices include discretionary and systematic groups.

Morningstar offers historical fund performance on an array of fund indices designed to capture the return to unique mutual fund stock and bond strategies including growth and income, growth equity income, aggressive growth, small company, government bond, corporate bond, multi-sector bond, asset allocation, balanced convertible bond, hybrid hi-yield, hybrid global.

12 ALTERNATIVE INVESTMENTS IN THE INSTITUTIONAL PORTFOLIO

THOMAS SCHNEEWEIS
University of Massachusetts

RICHARD SPURGIN
Clark University

In recent years, the flow of funds into alternative investments from pension funds, endowments, and foundations has experienced a dramatic increase. A Goldman Sachs and Frank Russell survey [1997] reported that alternative investments in 1997 comprises over 7% of the total asset mix among institutional investors who invest in that asset class. This is a 57% increase over 1995 commitments. For purposes of that study, alternative investments were defined as private, illiquid investments, including venture capital, leveraged buyout, distressed securities, private equity, oil and gas programs, and timber or farmland. Other alternative investment vehicles such as hedge funds and managed futures have also witnessed a dramatic increase in investment. Both academic and practitioner research have shown that managed futures and hedge funds each provide unique risk and return opportunities as stand-alone vehicles as well as additions to traditional stock and bond portfolios [Schneeweis, 1996]. However, a direct analysis of hedge funds and managed futures as surrogates for, or as additions to other alternative investment strategies, has not been conducted.

This summary review of a larger study by Schneeweis and Spurgin [1998][1] presents empirical evidence of the potential risk and return benefits of a wide range of alternative investments, including hedge fund and managed futures investments, real estate, private equity, private debt, high-yield debt, and commodities to an investor's core stock and bond portfolio. This analysis supports previous results that conclude managed futures, hedge funds, and traditional alternative investments such as REITs, commodities, and private equity should be added to stock and bond portfolios. This study also shows that hedge funds and managed futures belong in a diversified alternative investment portfolio. The Sharpe ratios of various efficient-frontier portfolios indicate that, depending on the choice of investment constraints (e.g., minimum levels of stock and bond investment, minimum allocation to traditional alternative investments such as risky debt), hedge funds and managed futures may improve the risk/return profile of the portfolio.

This study differs from prior research by considering a wide range of alternative assets, and by addressing an important issue that arises when using historical data to identify optimal portfolio allocations. Some assets have abnormally high (or low) historical returns that may be due to specific historical factors. Mean/variance optimization will generate a large (or small) allocation to this asset based on these historical returns. This study employs a return forecasting model that assumes all assets have the same risk-adjusted return (Sharpe ratio) but preserves the standard deviation of the asset and the correlation between assets. This reduces the risk of over- or under-allocating to an asset because of an anomalous return series. Results presented here show that optimal allocations to hedge funds and managed futures do not change considerably under the different return measure. This provides evidence that the primary benefit from adding these assets to a portfolio does not stem from unique or unusual historical returns.

METHODOLOGY

The principal method of investment analysis for stand-alone assets and portfolios involves analysis of Sharpe ratios (risk-adjusted returns). Mixed-asset portfolios are determined from Markowitz efficient frontiers. Since the benefits of adding traditional and alternative investments in efficient investment portfolios are typically presented using historical data, those results may be considered to be time-period specific. In this study, the Markowitz efficient frontier and incremental risk/return tradeoff is determined using historical returns, but the historical data are adjusted to reduce the impact of time-specific returns. This is accomplished by conducting a cross-sectional ordinary least squares (OLS) regression of historical return on historical variance for all the assets included in the study.[2] The monthly returns of each asset are then adjusted to give all assets the same risk-adjusted return. Since only the level of the return and not the other time series properties are adjusted, this approach preserves the variance of the asset as well as the correlation with all other assets.

Another methodology employed in this paper involves segmenting the historical data set into the highest, middle, and lowest months based on the performance of an equally weighted portfolio of U.S. stocks and bonds. This is done to analyze the potential portfolio properties of assets during periods of market extremes and relative calm. Correlation coefficients are calculated for each of the three subsets, and the implications of differing correlation for portfolio construction is discussed.[3]

DATA

A wide variety of indexes exist for managed futures, hedge funds, as well as private equity, private debt, or venture capital. For the purposes of this study, Evaluation Associates Capital Markets (EACM) is the source of hedge fund and managed futures returns. EACM indexes are briefly described in Appendix I.[4] Wilshire is the source of distressed, leveraged buyout, and venture capital indexes. The specifics of the Wilshire leveraged buyout and venture capital indexes are given in Nesbitt and Reynolds [1997]. Other methods of estimating LBO returns are studied in Philips [1995], who uses an internal rate of return based on vintage year comparisons from data made available from Venture Economics. The remainder of the data, including the REIT index, the SP500 index and the Salomon Corporate/Government bond index, are obtained from Datastream.

ALTERNATIVE INVESTMENTS: RISK AND RETURN PERFORMANCE

Investment theory has shown that assets should be compared on a risk-adjusted basis (e.g., Sharpe ratio) as well as on their relative impact on portfolio risk and return. Under past market environments (e.g., 1991-1996), managed futures, hedge fund products, and traditional alternative investment offer comparable risk and return opportunities when considered as stand-alone investments (Exhibit 1A). To examine the impact of adding alternative assets to an existing portfolio, eight representative portfolios are formed. The composition of these portfolios is outlined in Exhibit 1B, and the historical performance of these portfolios is given in Exhibit 1C. The Sharpe ratios of the portfolios that include alternative investments (Portfolios IV-VIII) dominate the Sharpe ratios of

EXHIBIT 1A DESCRIPTIVE STATISTICS OF INDEX PERFORMANCE, 1991-1996

	Average Annual Rtn	Standard Deviation	Monthly Minimum	Monthly Maximum	Rtn/Stdev
Traditional Assets					
S&P 500	16.2	10.0	-4.7	10.9	1.62
Russel 2000	18.4	13.3	-9.1	10.6	1.39
Sal. Broth. Corp/Govt.	8.3	4.4	-2.5	4.2	1.87
REIT	17.9	10.3	-4.8	9.5	1.73
T-Bill	5.0		0.3	0.6	
Traditional Alternative Assets					
Leveraged Buyout	22.3	25.6	-15.8	26.0	.87
Venture Capital	33.3	51.2	-41.5	34.4	.65
Distressed	24.0	15.1	-8.8	10.8	1.59
Trad. Alt. Portfolio**	28.7	26.9	-20.1	24.1	1.07
Hedge Fund Indexes					
EACM 100 Index	15.5	3.5	-0.9	4.7	4.41
Relative Value Index	12.0	2.1	-1.1	2.5	5.67
Long/Short Equity	10.3	2.4	-1.1	2.5	4.29
Convertible Bond	12.0	4.6	-5.1	4.9	2.62
Bond Hedge	11.1	1.3	0.3	2.0	8.24
Rotational	14.4	4.6	-2.1	4.2	3.09
Event Driven Index	15.9	3.7	-1.0	5.0	4.26
Arbitrage	12.1	3.1	-1.5	3.0	3.88
Bankruptcy	20.8	5.9	-1.6	9.6	3.49
MultiStrategy	15.2	3.9	-1.7	3.6	3.88
Equity Hedge Fund Index	19.8	6.1	-3.1	4.9	3.24
Domestic Long	20.7	7.7	-4.1	5.7	2.68
Domestic Opportunity	15.7	7.3	-3.3	5.8	2.14
Global International	22.7	8.4	-2.8	8.1	2.69
Global Asset Allocators	19.5	11.5	-5.8	15.3	1.69
Commodity Index					
GSCI	6.3	11.8	-9.9	9.7	.53

**Traditional Alternative is equal weights in Wilshire Venture Capital, Distressed, and Buyout

EXHIBIT 1B PORTFOLIO

Portfolio	US Equity*	Salomon Bond	REIT	GSCI	EACM 100	Traditional Alternative**
I	100%					
II		100%				
III	50%	50%				
IV	40%	40%	20%			
V	40%	40%	10%	10%		
VI	40%	40%	5%	5%	10%	
VII	40%	40%	5%	5%		10%
VIII	40%	40%	5%	5%	5%	5%

*US Equity is 80% SP500 Index, 20% Russell 2000

**Traditional Alternative is equal weights in Wilshire Venture Capital, Distressed, and Buyout

EXHIBIT 1C DESCRIPTIVE STATISTICS OF PORTFOLIO PERFORMANCE, 1991-1996

Portfolio	Average Annual Rtn	Standard Deviation	Monthly Minimum	Monthly Maximum	Rtn/Stdev	Sharpe Ratio
I	17.4	10.2	-5.3	10.8	.49	.35
II	8.4	4.5	-2.5	4.3	.54	.22
III	12.9	6.3	-3.5	7.1	.59	.36
IV	14.0	6.3	-3.6	6.6	.64	.41
V	12.9	5.9	-3.3	5.4	.63	.39
VI	13.2	5.6	-3.1	6.0	.68	.42
VII	14.9	7.8	-4.4	8.3	.55	.36
VIII	14.0	6.7	-3.7	7.1	.61	.39

the comparable U.S. stock (I), bond (II), or combined stock and bond portfolios (III).[5] Moreover, the portfolio with the highest hedge fund allocation (VI) is the one with the highest Sharpe ratio (1.46).

IMPROVING THE EFFICIENT FRONTIER BY ADDING ALTERNATIVE ASSETS TO AN EQUITY/FIXED INCOME PORTFOLIO

Exhibit 2 shows the historical performance that resulted from adding incremental amounts of an alternative investment index (EACM 100), a commodity portfolio (GSCI), real estate security investment (REIT), and a traditional alternative investment portfolio (LBO, venture capital, and distressed security) to an existing stock and bond portfolio. This figure indicates that adding the traditional alternative portfolio increases both

EXHIBIT 2 DIVERSIFICATION BENEFITS FROM ADDITION OF ALTERNATIVE ASSETS TO U.S. STOCK/BOND PORTFOLIO

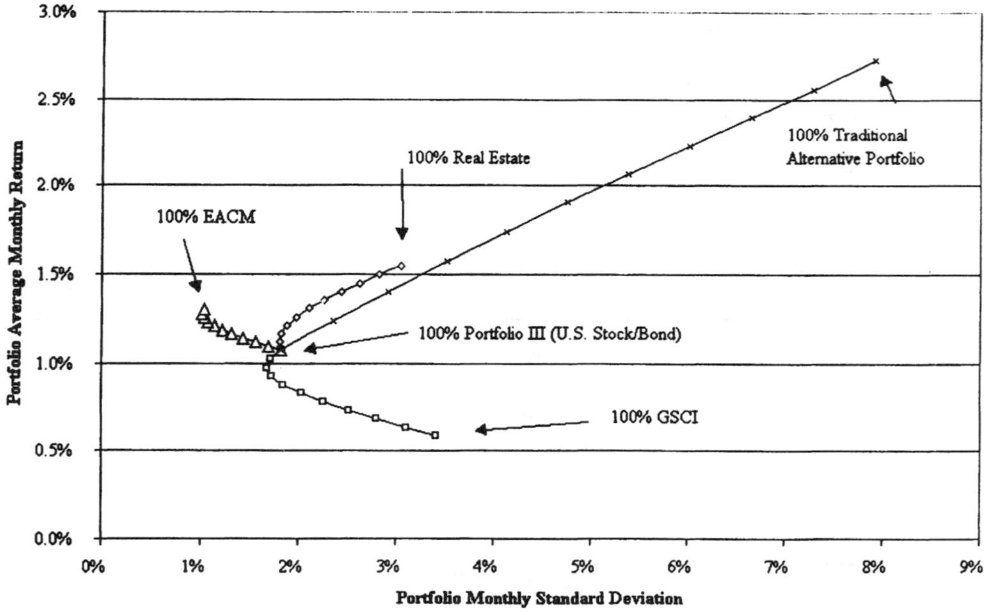

the risk and return of the portfolio. Furthermore, since the correlation between these two assets is quite high, there is very little variance reduction due to diversification. The low correlation between the Stock/Bond portfolio and the GSCI, REIT, and EACM indexes provide diversification benefits. However, only the EACM index provided the combination of return, standard deviation, and correlation so that allocations to this asset would have provided a considerable improvement in portfolio performance during the sample period.

OPTIMIZATION RESULTS FOR A PORTFOLIO CONSISTING EXCLUSIVELY OF ALTERNATIVE INVESTMENTS

Previous research on the role of managed futures and hedge fund products in asset allocation were based primarily on historical and risk and return parameters. The resulting asset allocations were shown to be very sensitive to changes to the average return of the assets during the sample period. In Exhibits 3 and 4 the optimal portfolio allocations are reported using two historical return measures: the actual historical return parameters as well as regression-based return forecast models.[6] Optimal allocations are determined using a constrained Markowitz optimization procedure.[7] Markowitz optimization involves finding the allocations that give the highest average return for a specified level of risk. Negative allocations (selling the asset short) are excluded in this model, as is borrowing or holding cash to increase or decrease leverage. As a result, all allocations are between zero and 100% and the total allocation is 100%. The exhibits report the variance constraint (the maximum allowable risk of the portfolio), monthly average return, standard deviation, and Sharpe ratio[8] of the resulting portfolio, and the optimal portfolio weights.

Exhibit 3 shows the results for a portfolio consisting only of alternative assets. The assets include a number of EACM hedge fund indexes, a managed futures index (EACM Asset Allocators, which consists of CTAs and hedge funds that make directional trades in exchange-traded and OTC derivative markets), and a number of other alternative assets. Panel A of Exhibit 3 shows the allocations using actual historical data. Investors with high risk tolerance found a maximum return by allocating only to venture capital and global international hedge funds.[9] This is because these assets offered the highest absolute return (see Exhibit 1A). For investors with the lowest risk tolerance, there is

EXHIBIT 3 OPTIMAL PORTFOLIO ALLOCATIONS FOR ALTERNATIVE ASSETS PORTFOLIO BASED ON RISK TOLERANCE CRITERIA

Panel A: Optimal Weights Using Historical Risk, Return, and Correlation Data

Variance Criteria	Monthly StDev	Monthly Return	Sharpe Ratio	Lng/Sht Equity	Convert. Hedge	Bond Hedge	Rotat-ional	Bank-ruptcy	Multi-Strategy	Domest. Long	Domest. Opport.	Global Int'l	Asset Allocat.	REIT	Lever'g Buyout	Venture Capital	GSCI
.80%	8.94%	3.02%	0.29									44%				56%	
.08%	2.85%	2.04%	0.58					31%				54%	4%			11%	
.04%	2.02%	1.87%	0.73					44%				38%	12%			5%	
.01%	1.05%	1.41%	0.97	23%		5%	3%	47%	3%	3%	2%	3%	10%	1%			

Panel B: Optimal Weights Using Historical Risk and Correlation Data, and with Regression-Based Return Forecasts

Variance Criteria	Monthly StDev	Monthly Return	Sharpe Ratio	Lng/Sht Equity	Convert. Hedge	Bond Hedge	Rotat-ional	Bank-ruptcy	Multi-Strategy	Domest. Long	Domest. Opport.	Global Int'l	Asset Allocat.	REIT	Lever'g Buyout	Venture Capital	GSCI
.80%	8.95%	2.94%	0.28										12%			60%	28%
.04%	2.02%	1.66%	0.62	7%		47%							17%			13%	16%
.02%	1.45%	1.55%	0.79	15%		53%							11%			9%	11%
.01%	1.05%	1.46%	1.01	26%		54%							8%			7%	6%

no allocation to these two assets because risk-adjusted returns, not absolute returns, dictate allocations to this portfolio. This portfolio is highly diversified, with 10 of the 14 assets receiving allocations. The largest allocations are to bankruptcy hedge funds (47%), long/short equity hedge funds (23%) and managed futures-based strategies (10%).

Panel B shows the results after modifying the risk-adjusted historical returns of the assets. The high-risk portfolio consists of allocations to venture capital (60%), GSCI (28%), and managed futures strategies (12%). The large allocation to the GSCI results because the regression-based return is considerably higher than the realized return over the period. The low-risk portfolio in Panel B consists of long/short equity (26%), bond hedge (54%), managed futures (8%), venture capital (7%), and GSCI (6%). Comparing low-risk portfolios from the actual (Panel A) and adjusted return (Panel B) exhibits, it is interesting to note that allocations to long/short equity and managed futures are quite stable, while the large allocation to bankruptcy hedge funds in Panel A disappears and is replaced by bond hedge funds in Panel B. This is because the long/short equity and managed futures allocations are driven primarily by their low correlation with other assets, while the fixed-income hedge fund allocations are driven primarily by their historical return.

OPTIMIZATION RESULTS FOR A PORTFOLIO OF TRADITIONAL AND ALTERNATIVE INVESTMENTS

EXHIBIT 4 OPTIONAL ALLOCATIONS FOR TRADITIONAL AND ALTERNATIVE ASSET PORTFOLIO BASED ON RISK TOLERANCE CRITERIA

Panel A: Optimal Weights with no Allocation Constraints: Historical Risk, Return, and Correlation Data

Variance Criteria	Monthly StDev	Monthly Return	Sharpe Ratio	SP500	Bond	LBO	Venture Capital	GSCI	REIT	EACM 100	HiYield
.50%	7.08%	2.56%	0.30			13%	40%		47%		
.08%	2.85%	1.77%	0.48			4%	14%		22%	46%	14%
.04%	2.02%	1.60%	0.59			2%	10%		12%	62%	15%
.01%	1.05%	1.36%	0.92				2%		2%	74%	22%

Panel B: Optimal Weights with Constraint of 40% SP500, 30% Salomon Bond, 10% HiYield Investment

Variance Criteria	Monthly StDev	Monthly Return	Sharpe Ratio	SP500	Bond	LBO	Venture Capital	GSCI	REIT	EACM 100	HiYield
.20%	3.45%	1.59%	0.35	40%	30%		16%		4%		10%
.08%	2.85%	1.48%	0.38	40%	30%		11%		9%		10%
.04%	2.02%	1.30%	0.44	40%	30%		5%		4%	11%	10%
.02%	1.56%	1.16%	0.49	40%	30%			1%		19%	10%

Panel C: Optimal Weights with Investment Constraints: Regression-Based Return Forecasts

Variance Criteria	Monthly StDev	Monthly Return	Sharpe Ratio	SP500	Bond	LBO	Venture Capital	GSCI	REIT	EACM 100	HiYield
.20%	3.96%	1.70%	0.33	40%	30%		20%				10%
.08%	2.81%	1.47%	0.38	40%	30%		12%	8%			10%
.04%	2.02%	1.28%	0.44	40%	30%		5%	11%		4%	10%
.02%	1.56%	1.13%	0.47	40%	30%			1%		19%	10%

EXHIBIT 5 CORRELATION WITH U.S. STOCK/BOND PORTFOLIO DURING BEST AND WORST MONTHS

	All Months	Bottom Third	Middle Third	Top Third
Portfolio III*	1.00	1.00	1.00	1.00
S&P 500	.96	.88	.66	.93
Salomon Bond	.68	.39	-.04	.47
Wilshire Leveraged Buyout	.95	.87	.72	.90
Wilshire Venture Capital	.60	.46	.12	.36
GSCI	.12	.58	.06	-.18
REIT	.46	.33	.24	.33
HighYield Bond	.50	.30	-.02	.18
Traditional Alternative	.83	.71	.30	.65
EACM 100	.41	.23	-.05	.54
Relative Value	.17	.13	-.05	.08
Event Driven	.34	.28	-.01	-.17
Equity Hedge	.62	.48	.13	.25
Asset Allocators	.29	.06	-.08	.70

*Portfolio III is 50% U.S. Equity and 50% U.S. Bond

Exhibit 4 shows the optimal allocations for a set of broad-based assets that includes both traditional and alternative assets. The EACM 100 index is considered for inclusion in the portfolio, along with traditional asset classes (SP500 and Salomon Corporate/Government Bond) and representative traditional alternatives (GSCI, venture capital, LBO, high yield debt, and REIT). Panel A shows the results of an unconstrained optimization. High-risk investors make no allocation to the EACM index because a higher absolute return can be achieved in traditional alternative assets. However, the low-risk portfolio allocates 74% to the EACM 100. The optimal portfolio has no allocation to either U.S. stocks or bonds. This result is clear from Exhibit 2. Exhibit 2 indicates that an investor interested solely in maximizing return would have done best in traditional alternatives, while on a risk-adjusted return basis the EACM dominated all the other assets during this period.

In Panel B, the portfolio is constrained to hold at least 40% in U.S. stocks, 30% in investment grade bonds, and 10% in high yield debt. Again, high-risk investors allocate the remaining 20% of their assets to traditional alternatives, while the optimal low-risk portfolio allocates 19% to the EACM 100 and 1% to GSCI. Panel C shows the same constrained portfolio using the regression-based return estimates. There is no difference in the low-risk allocations in Panels B and C, but the moderate-risk portfolios have a sizeable allocation to the GSCI and no allocation to REITs.

RELATIVE PERFORMANCE DURING MARKET EXTREMES

Markowitz optimization techniques are based on the assumption that correlation patterns are stable over time. However, the correlation between two assets may differ under varying market conditions. In particular, correlation may be different during periods when stock and bond markets are performing well than when those markets are doing poorly. Optimal diversification benefits would arise by adding an assets with a high, positive correlation during periods of peak performance, and a low (or negative) correlation during the worst months of the existing portfolio. This issue is addressed in Exhibit 5. A portfolio of stocks and bonds (Portfolio III) is taken as the benchmark portfolio. The returns to this portfolio are segmented into thirds, comprising the best, middle, and worst months for that portfolio. The correlation of various alternative assets with this portfolio is computed for the full data set as well as for each of the segments.[10]

Results in Exhibit 5 indicate that some alternative assets have similar correlation with the traditional portfolio in both the best months and the worst months (e.g., REITs). The GSCI shows a large discrepancy between the correlation in best and worst months. However, the correlation pattern works against the diversification goal — the GSCI has a high correlation (.58) during the worst months of the reference portfolio and a negative correlation during the best months (-.18). The EACM 100 is the only broad-based index that offers a beneficial differential correlation pattern. Its correlation is twice as high during the best months of the existing portfolio (.54) as during the worst months (.23).

Among EACM subindexes, the relative value index is essentially uncorrelated with the reference portfolio in both extremes. While the correlations for hedge fund subindexes are generally low, event-driven and equity hedge are more highly correlated during the worst months than the best months, which may be unattractive from a diversification perspective. The asset alloctators index provided the most attractive correlation pattern. It had a very low correlation (.06) during the worst months and a very high correlation (.70) during the best months. This pattern is consistent with Schneeweis, Spurgin, and Potter [1996] and Potter [1998], who show that CTAs have the lowest correlation with the SP500 when the SP500 experiences its largest losses, and the highest correlation when the SP500 has its largest monthly gains.

SUMMARY POINTS OF INTEREST:

1. Traditional approaches to determining asset allocation for investments such as stocks and bonds can also be used to determine suggested allocations to a wide range of alternative assets. Asset allocation methods based on return and covariance assume constant variance and covariances with other assets. Results presented in this paper suggest that alternative assets do not have constant covariances with traditional assets under various market conditions. This is shown to influence portfolio allocations to alternative investments.
2. Optimization techniques indicate that adding alternative investments to a balanced stock and bond portfolio improves the risk-adjusted return of the portfolio. This result holds even after historical returns are adjusted to eliminate the potential bias induced by the high returns these assets experienced during the 1991-1996 test period.
3. For portfolios consisting only of alternative assets, the highest risk-adjusted return was a balanced portfolio consisting of a broad range of equity, fixed-income, and bankruptcy hedge funds and managed futures. After adjusting for potential return bias, the optimal alternative portfolio consisted of equity and fixed-income hedge funds, as well as managed futures and an indexed commodity investment.
4. Benchmark indexes for traditional alternative investment vehicles such as venture capital and leveraged buyouts suggest these asset classes are characterized by both high risk and high returns. Hedge fund investments have a lower overall correlation

with a stock/bond portfolio than these assets, and have the added benefit that correlation has historically been the lowest during those months when the stock/bond portfolio performs poorest.

ENDNOTES

This article was published by AIMA, 1998, and is reprinted with permission from AIMA.

[1] Since this is a summary, much of the analysis presented in the larger paper is not published here. Specifically, the results for portfolios of international stocks (EAFE) and global bonds were not included in the summary. Also, a detailed analysis of the performance of sample portfolios during market extremes has been eliminated. Please refer to the full report for these analyses.

[2] For both the alternative investments set and for the full asset set, a linear regression was conducted using historical returns and historical variance for the period 1991-1996. The intercept and the slope parameters of that regression and the standard deviation for the period 1991-1996 were used to obtain the expected monthly returns of the various assets.

[3] In the larger study, the Markowitz optimization procedure is repeated on each of the three subsets. The resulting portfolio weights can be used to construct portfolios that performed optimally under specific market conditions.

[4] The full study uses hedge fund and managed futures benchmarks from Hedge Fund Research (HFR) and Managed Accounts Reports (MAR) in addition to EACM. Results are similar to those presented here.

[5] The venture capital and buyout indexes are based on a benchmark that provides monthly estimates of returns, but are not based on realized returns. If these asset classes are regarded as illiquid and held for longer time periods, a measure of their relative monthly sensitivity may not be required. Disinvestment of private equity or debt positions generally entails a heavy penalty depending on market conditions. These market conditions may be directly related to the performance of various equity indexes.

[6] A third return estimation method is employed in the full version of this paper. This return measure derives expected returns from surveys of institutional investors. Results are similar to those from the two return measures employed here.

[7] The Markowitz optimization is conducted using the "solver" routine in Microsoft Excel. Results are easily reproducible by readers. An example of the typical optimization input as well as the mean returns, variances, and covariances are given in Appendix II of the complete version of this report.

[8] The figures reported in Exhibits 3 and 4 are based on monthly returns, while Exhibit 1 shows annualized risk and return measures. While not exact, a rough comparison to the annualized figures can be made buy multiplying the monthly returns by 12 and the standard deviation and Sharpe ratios by the square root of 12.

[9] In practice, an investor can achieve higher returns by using leverage — either borrowing cash or selling low-return assets short. Since this was not permitted in the optimization procedure, the high-risk portfolios shown here are limited to those assets that offered the highest nominal return.

[10] Analysis of Exhibit 5 focuses on the similarities and differences among the bottom and top segments — the middle segment is basically statistical noise. The middle months of the reference portfolio are clustered very closely together. With such little variation, the correlation coefficient does not provide much useful information and will be dominated by a few outlier returns in the comparison asset.

REFERENCES

Chopra, V. and W. Ziemba, "The Effect of Error in Means, Variances, and Covariances on Optimal Portfolio Choice," *The Journal of Portfolio Management,* (Winter, 1993), pp. 6-11.

Connor, G., "Sensible Return Forecasting for Portfolio Management," *Financial Analysts Journal,* (September/October, 1997), pp. 44-51.

Goldman Sachs & Co., and Frank Russell Capital, *1997 Report on Alternative Investing,* (November, 1997).

Nesbitt, S. and H. Reynolds, "Benchmarks for Private Market Instruments," *The Journal of Portfolio Management* (Summer, 1997), pp. 85-90.

Philips, T., *A Portfolio Approach to Alternative Investing,* Rogers Casey Associates, (1995).

Potter, M., Équity-Based Commodity Trading Advisors: A Performance Appraisal, *The Journal of Alternative Investments,* (Summer, 1998), pp. 41-55.

Schneeweis, T. *The Benefits of Managed Futures.* AIMA (1996).

Schneeweis T., R. Spurgin and M. Potter, "Managed Futures and Hedge Fund Investment for Downside Equity Risk Management", *Derivatives Quarterly,* (Fall, 1996), pp. 62-72.

Schneeweis, T., and R. Spurgin, "Alternative Investments in Institutional Portfolios", CISDM Working Paper Series, University of Massachusetts, (1998).

APPENDIX I: SUMMARY OF ALTERNATIVE INVESTMENT BENCHMARKS

Traditional Alternative Investments

Distressed Securities: Investment in debt or trade claims of companies that are in financial distress, restructuring, or bankruptcy. Source - Wilshire Distressed Securities Index.

Private Equity: Illiquid or restricted equity investments in companies including leveraged buyout funds, venture capital, and other special situations. Source - Wilshire Venture Capital Index and Wilshire LBO.

High Yield Debt: Mezzanine financing or other non-senior private debt. Debtholder often participates in equity appreciation through direct conversion features or indirect equity stakes such as rights, warrants, or options. Index used - Salomon Extended High Yield Market index, which tracks the performance of sub-investment grade corporate bonds issued in the United States.

Real Estate: Investment in real estate properties via publicly traded securities (REITs) or private limited partnerships. Source of REIT data is Datastream.

Goldman Sachs Commodity Index The GSCI replicates the return to a passive, long-only commodity futures investment strategy.

Evaluation Associates Capital Markets (EACM) Hedge Fund Indexes:

Relative Value: Balanced, or hedged long and short positions, within various financial markets. Subindexes include *Long/Short equity* (long undervalued equities and short overvalued equities, usually on an equal-dollar basis); *Convertible hedging* (long convertible bonds or convertible preferred stock, short underlying common); *Bond hedging* (yield curve arbitrage or long/short debt positions); *Rotational* (multiple relative value strategies, including all of the above).

Event Driven: Corporate transactions and special situations including *Deal Arbitrage* (long/short equity securities of companies involved in corporate transactions); B*ankruptcy/Distressed* (long undervalued securities of companies in financial distress). *Multi-strategy* includes funds dealing in both deal arbitrage and bankruptcy.

Equity Hedge Funds: Long and short securities with varying degrees of exposure and leverage. Includes *Domestic Long Equity* (long undervalued US equities; short selling used sparingly); *Domestic Opportunistic Equity* (long and short U.S. equity with ability to be net short overall) and *Global International* (primarily long undervalued equities with the ability to use short selling opportunistically).

Global Asset Allocators: Long and short multiple financial and non-financial assets. Includes commodity trading advisors and hedge funds that follow directional strategies in exchange-traded and OTC derivative markets. Subindexes include *Systematic* (takes long or short positions using trend-following or other quantitative strategies) and *Discretionary* (long or short based on qualitative or fundamental analysis, often with technical input).

IV COMMODITY INVESTMENT

INTRODUCTION

The question of whether commodities represent a separate asset class has been extensively debated in both the academic and practitioner literature [Huberman, 1995, Strongin, 1995, Greer, 1994, Froot, 1996, Schneeweis et al., 1997(a)]. For many investors, the question no longer is whether commodity investment is an asset class, but whether this asset class is appropriate for a given investor, and if so what is the best approach to implementing the investment. Despite disappointing returns in 1997-1998, commodity investment remains an attractive investment for many institutional portfolios. This is particularly true for those institutions exposed to rapid increases in commodity based inflation or may wish to add assets that offer positive cash flows in market conditions that are expected to offer the lowest returns to the remainder of the portfolio.

The principal argument for investing in commodities is that investing in assets that rise in price with inflation provides a natural hedge against losses in equity and debt holdings that typically lose value during periods of unexpected inflation. While previous studies have concentrated on measuring commodity returns during high and low inflation periods, the real benefits of commodity investment may lie in periods of unexpected rises in inflation. Anticipated inflation, which results in high bond yields and high equity earnings growth, may result in positive real returns for stocks and bonds. It is the unexpected inflation that should cause concern to every serious investor. The importance of being exposed directly to commodity price movements is due to the possibility of obtaining natural sources of commodity return and inflation protection. Periods of financial and economic distress are often linked to increasing commodity prices. While present global economic conditions are weak, long term growth in world demand may also result in an increasing demand and prices for certain commodity products.

One of the most attractive aspects of commodity investment today is that there are now a number of passive indexes that are fully investible. Most alternative assets do not have a passive, investible index, requiring the investor to select and monitor active managers. In addition to providing a simple method to access these returns, commodity indexes have a number of other uses. Commodity indexes are a source of information on cash commodity and futures commodity market trends, used as performance benchmarks for evaluation of certain commodity trading advisors, and provide a historical track record useful in developing asset allocation strategies.

Direct commodity investment has been a small part of investors' asset allocation decision. Indirect commodity investment through ownership of equity in commodity producers has been the preferred strategy of obtaining claims on commodity investment. In recent years, a variety of passive investible commodity indexes or commodity-linked products have been created that provide direct access to commodity investment. These include exchange-traded commodity indexes such as the GSCI and CRB-Bridge, other commodity linked investments such as the Chase Manhattan Commodity Index, JPMorgan Commodity Index and the Dow Jones-AIG index, and market specific commodity indices such as the LME metals index, as well as more exotic futures-based products such as the MLM index. The LME index is a narrowly focused index that offers returns based on a basket of industrial metals, and the MLM index takes both long and short positions in a number of futures markets based on a technical trading rule.

ARTICLE REVIEW

In previous sections, investment benchmarks were shown to exist for hedge funds and managed futures that are similar in form to those available in traditional stock and bond markets. Likewise, in a previous article (Comparison of Managed Futures Benchmarks), the actual structure of commodity indexes was briefly discussed. As noted in that article, there are a variety of commodity indexes that attempt to replicate the return available to holding long positions in agricultural, metal, energy, or livestock markets. Since the cost of carry model insures that the return on a fully margined position in a futures contract should mimic the return on an underlying spot deliverable, futures contract returns are often used as a surrogate for cash market performance.

At present the CRB-Bridge and the GSCI are the only two commodity indexes that are exchange-traded. Futures contract-based commodity indexes have three separate sources of return: price, roll, and collateral return. Price return derives from changes in commodity futures prices. Roll return arises from rolling long futures positions forward through time and may capture a positive risk premium over time if rolling over a higher priced futures contract into a more distant lower priced contract (backwardation). Collateral return assumes the full value of the underlying the futures contracts are invested at a risk-free interest rate. This is equivalent to assuming an investor posts 100% margin with Treasury bills.

Commodity indexes, however, differ widely in purpose, composition, and weighting scheme. Commodity indexes use either arithmetic or geometric averaging to calculate the index return from the component returns. The GSCI uses an arithmetic average of the commodity returns. Investors attempting to replicate the index must rebalance their portfolios monthly to maintain constant dollar weights. The CRB-Bridge uses geometric averaging of the component returns (which are themselves calculated with arithmetic averaging). Each of the major indexes contains a different group of underlying assets. The CRB-Bridge and GSCI indexes include industrials, grains, and soft commodities, however, commodity indexes also differ in the relative emphasis placed on different commodities and the procedure used to determine the weightings in the index. Equal weighting is used in the CRB-Bridge index while world production weighting is used in the GSCI.

In the first article in this section, "Commodity Investing: Long-Run Returns and the Function of Passive Capital," Steve Strongin and Melanie Petsch illustrate the importance of commodity investing for the diversified investor. They offer arguments for the unique return properties of commodity investing and concentrate primarily on the ability of commodities to:

1. Diversify a portfolio against economic events such as unexpected inflation which favor commodities but harm stock, bonds and other investments.
2. Obtain "natural" sources of return over the long term which are available from commodity investing.
3. Exploit opportunistically through active management the pricing inefficiencies that may exist in the commodity markets.

In the second article, "GSCI Collateralized Futures as a Hedging and Diversification Tool for Institutional Portfolios," Paul Kaplan and Scott Lummer offer an update of their previous analysis [1994] and offer an analysis of returns of the GSCI commodity index through the 1990's. Their results show that the GSCI continues to be a long-run diversifier and inflation hedge although its performance may not offer similar diversification benefits over short time periods. Similarly, in the third article, "Hedging Portfolios with Real Assets," Ken Froot points out that commodity investing may offer unique returns not generally available though traditional alternative investments. Froot also concludes, however, that the argument is weak for holding individual commodities, such as gold, or other assets, such as real estate, on the bases of their hedging properties relative to traditional stock and bond investments.

The research, provided by Froot, raises an interesting question; that is, to obtain the benefits of commodity diversification, direct investment into energy related commodity products might offer the most effective diversification to traditional diversified portfolios. Extending this research, in the fourth article "Energy Futures and Alternative Energy Investments," Thomas Schneeweis and Richard Spurgin examine the correlations of oil-based futures contracts with energy-related and non-energy related stock, bond, real estate and commodity markets, and CPI. Their results confirm that, except in periods of extreme energy price movement, many traditional forms of indirect energy investment such as natural resource mutual funds or energy-based common stocks are not correlated with energy price movements. This is as expected. Given the risk management and firm diversification abilities of most corporate firms, unless the price change in the underlying commodity is structural and long lasting, short term changes in commodity prices may have little impact on a firm's equity performance. They also show that in addition to energy based passive long only commodity indices offering returns not available in traditional equity investments, active long/short energy traders offer returns (positive returns in markets with declining energy prices) not available in long only commodity indices or traditional commodity based equity investments.

RESEARCH IN COMMODITY INVESTMENT

In addition to the articles presented in this handbook, investors should be aware of a range of additional sources of information on recent research in the area of commodity investment. There are a number of that cover both practical management issues as well as academic/practitioner research in the area of managed futures. Investors are referred to a list of readings and books listed in the bibliography and reference section of this chapter. In these books and others, additional issues as to the performance of passive and active commodity based investment has been raised. A summary of selected articles and books is given in Exhibit 1.

Updated Risk and Return Performance

Risk and return analysis of commodity performance shows these assets have performed poorly as stand-along investments in recent years Results in Exhibit 2 show that using recent data, investment the CRB and the GSCI have significantly underperformed traditional investments. The CRB, however has a lower level of historical risk. In no case, however, did either commodity index offer the investor an increased return-to-risk ratio when considered as an addition to widely diversified asset portfolios. However, the potential benefits of both commodity indexes in diversified portfolios is illustrated in Exhibit 3 and Exhibit 4 in which the returns and risk estimates are derived from historical data for the period 1990-8/1998.

EXHIBIT 1 SUMMARY OF SELECTED RESEARCH REGARDING COMMODITY PERFORMANCE

Bibliography	Title	Topic	Major Results
Williams, J. and B. Wright (Cambridge, 1991)	"Storage and Commodity Markets"	Behavior of Markets for Storable Commodities	▪ Discusses possible return patterns for storable commodities and the interaction between storage and trade.
Huang, R., R. Masulis, and H. Stoll, (JFM, 1996)	"Energy Shocks and Financial Markets"	Oil Prices and Stock Markets	▪ Concludes Oil price movements not correlated with Stock price movements.
Blose, L. (JEB, 1996).	"Gold Price Risk and the Returns on Gold Mutual Funds"	Gold Price Risk and Equity Gold Investment	▪ Concludes that gold mutual funds and gold bullion do not bring identical risks to an investor's portfolio.
Schneeweis, T. and R. Spurgin (AIMA, 1997)	"Alternative Energy Investments and Asset Allocation"	Oil Prices and Alternative Oil Investment Markets	▪ Concludes that energy mutual funds and energy equity do not provide returns similar to oil investment.
Tufano, P. (JF, 1997)	" Gold Price Risk and the Returns on Gold Mutual Funds"	Gold Price Risk and Equity Gold Investment	▪ Firms which hedge gold risk have different risk components.

Froot, K. (JPM, 1997)	" Hedging Portfolios with Real Assets"	Relationships between Traditional and commodity investments	▪ Real estate and other traditional investments do not provide return properties of commodity investment.
Warsager, R. and P. Halpern (JAI, 1998)	"Performance of Energy and Non-Energy Based Commodity Vehicles in Periods of Inflation"	Relationships between traditional and commodity investments on periods of inflation	▪ Concludes that energy investment generally provides alternative return in periods of rapid inflation however, active energy traders provide returns in both rising and falling energy markets.

Journal abbreviations: *JAI* — Journal of Alternative Investments; *JPM* — Journal of Portfolio Management; *AIMA*- Alternative Investment Management Association; JFM — Journal of Futures Markets; *JEB*— Journal of Economcis and Business; *JF* — Journal of Finance

EXHIBIT 2 PERFORMANCE MEASURES FOR COMMODITY INDICES

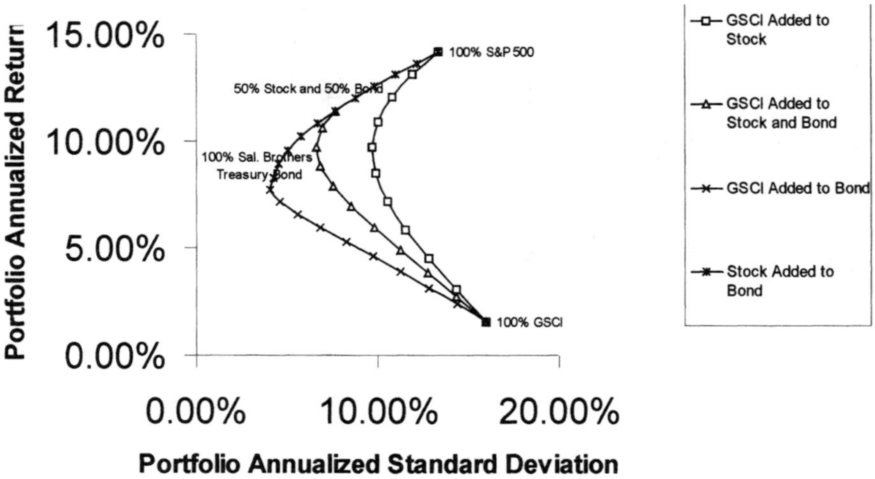

EXHIBIT 3 RISK AND RETURN OF STOCK, BOND AND GSCI: 1990-8/1998

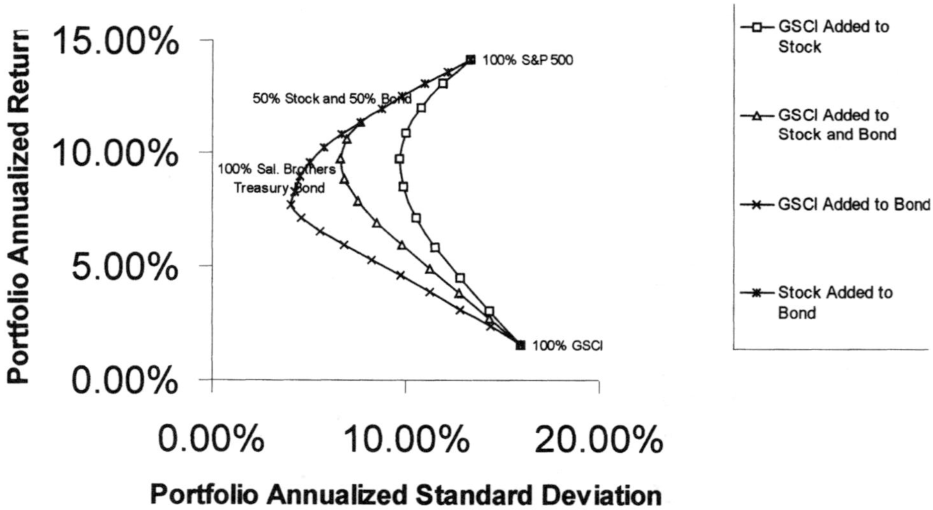

Performance Relationships

Prior research [Halpern and Warsager, 1998] has shown that most investible commodity indexes provide diversification advantages to stock and bond investment primarily during periods of unexpected changes in inflation. To the degree that inflation is already incorporated into the yield structure of bonds and the cash flow of firms, one may have periods of high commodity prices or price increases with positive stock and bond returns. However, during periods of unexpected changes in inflation Halpern and Warsager [1998] point out that commodity indexes provide their best hedge to traditional stock and bond portfolios.

EXHIBIT 4 RISK AND RETURN OF CRB, BOND AND STOCK: 1990-8/1998

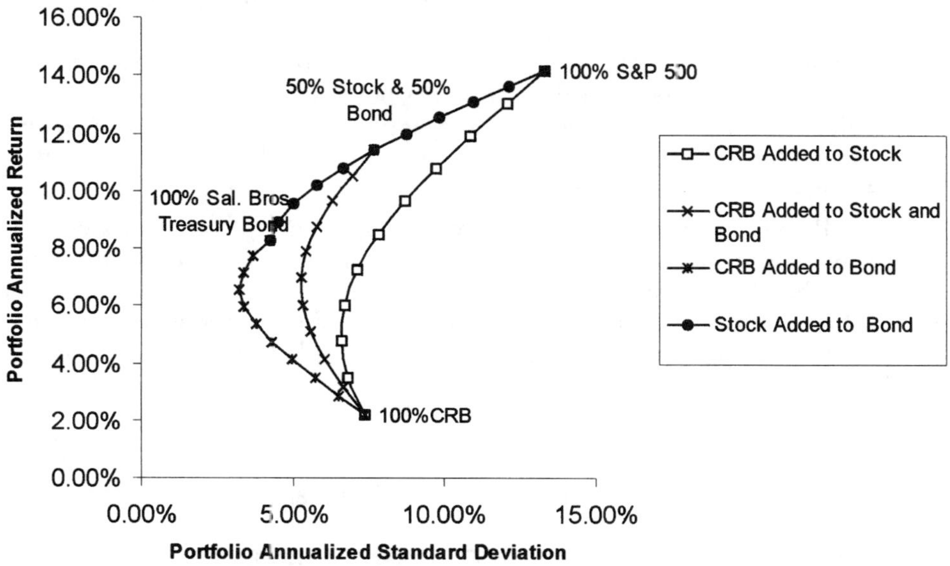

EXHIBIT 5 RANK BY MONTHLY STOCK AND BOND PORTFOLIO RETURNS (1990-8/1998)

Rank by Monthly Stock and Bond Portfolio Returns (1990-8/1998)

	CRB	GSCI	S&P 500	SB Treasury Bond	Stock/Bond Port	CPI%	Chg in CPI%
1	0.55%	2.61%	-4.53%	-0.95%	-2.74%	0.35%	0.05%
2	-0.46%	-0.82%	-1.79%	-0.20%	-0.99%	0.29%	0.04%
3	0.91%	0.77%	-0.09%	0.52%	0.22%	0.31%	0.00%
4	0.96%	0.69%	0.76%	0.85%	0.80%	0.25%	0.05%
5	0.52%	-0.69%	1.78%	0.76%	1.27%	0.19%	-0.06%
6	0.43%	1.37%	2.68%	0.80%	1.74%	0.25%	0.03%
7	-0.79%	-1.35%	3.67%	1.28%	2.48%	0.21%	-0.01%
8	0.05%	0.00%	5.24%	1.25%	3.25%	0.17%	-0.04%
9	0.17%	-0.07%	7.53%	2.62%	5.07%	0.21%	-0.13%

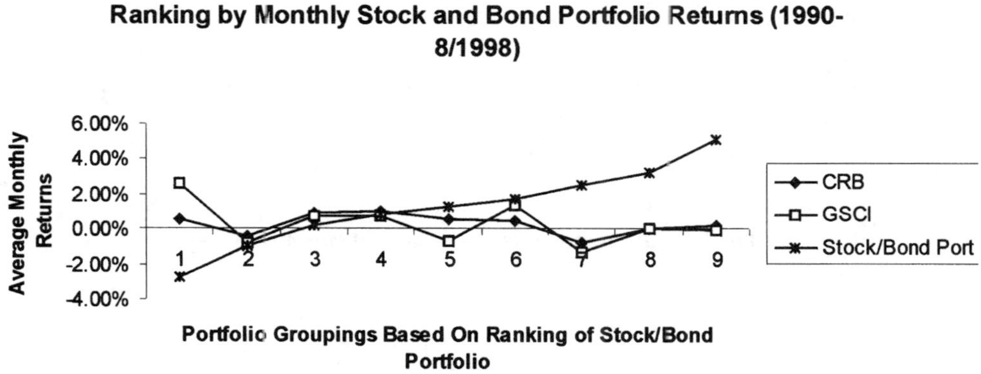

Halpern and Warsager also point out that long-only commodity investing limits the ability of investors to capture the underlying pricing process of commodity investing. To the degree that changes in technology and production may impact the fundamental price of commodities, strategies which can take long or short positions in commodity investing may offer return opportunities not available in long only investment strategies. For instance, Halpern and Warsager point out that active, energy-based commodity trading advisors have shown evidence of profitable return strategies both when oil prices are rising or falling.

Results in Exhibit 5 and 6 show the importance of various traditional long only commodity indexes in month of increasing inflation as well as in months of poor stock and bond performance.. Results in Exhibit 7 also show the importance of active long/short investment managers (e.g., energy commodity trading advisors) in offering return properties not available in energy investment or long only energy commodity investment.

EXHIBIT 6 RANKING BY MONTHLY CHANGE IN CPI% (1990-8/1998)

	CRB	GSCI	S&P 500	SB Treasury Bond	Stock/Bond Port	CPI%	Chg in CPI%
1	0.5%	2.6%	1.3%	0.4%	0.9%	0.2%	-0.2%
2	0.8%	0.7%	3.8%	1.2%	2.5%	0.2%	-0.1%
3	0.5%	0.6%	0.6%	0.4%	0.5%	0.2%	-0.1%
4	-0.2%	-1.0%	2.6%	0.9%	1.7%	0.2%	-0.1%
5	0.3%	0.5%	1.0%	1.2%	1.1%	0.3%	0.0%
6	0.7%	-0.3%	1.3%	0.5%	0.9%	0.2%	0.1%
7	-1.2%	-1.3%	0.2%	0.9%	0.5%	0.3%	0.1%
8	0.1%	-0.1%	1.1%	0.4%	0.8%	0.3%	0.2%
9	0.2%	0.6%	-2.0%	0.1%	-0.9%	0.6%	0.4%

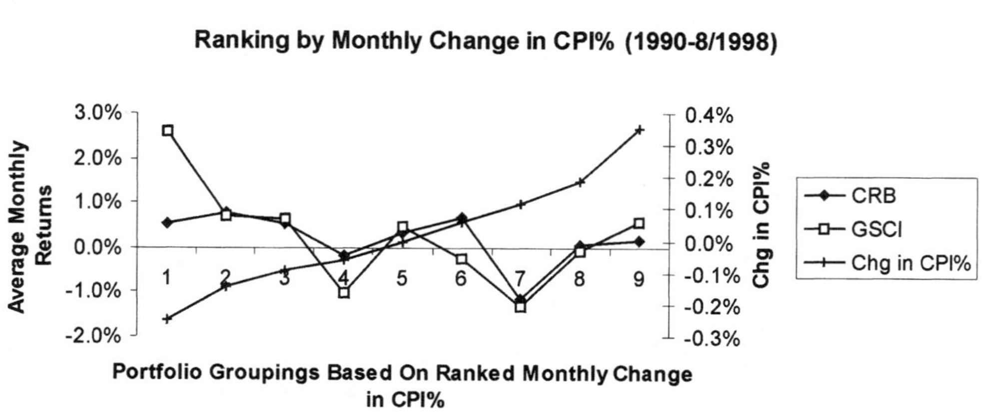

EXHIBIT 7 RANKING BY S&P 500 RETURNS (1990-8/1998)

	S&P Oil Comp.	S&P 500	SB Treasury Bond	Barclay CTA Energy	GSCI Energy
1	-3.38%	-5.77%	-0.07%	1.65%	-1.38%
2	-1.41%	-2.10%	-0.10%	-0.07%	0.20%
3	0.12%	-0.29%	1.04%	0.17%	-0.25%
4	0.19%	0.94%	0.29%	-1.17%	1.01%
5	2.23%	1.66%	0.52%	-0.52%	2.87%
6	2.12%	2.61%	0.92%	0.10%	-0.77%
7	2.11%	3.64%	1.15%	-1.12%	1.22%
8	3.33%	4.95%	1.22%	1.44%	-1.76%
9	5.29%	7.91%	1.63%	-0.36%	1.22%

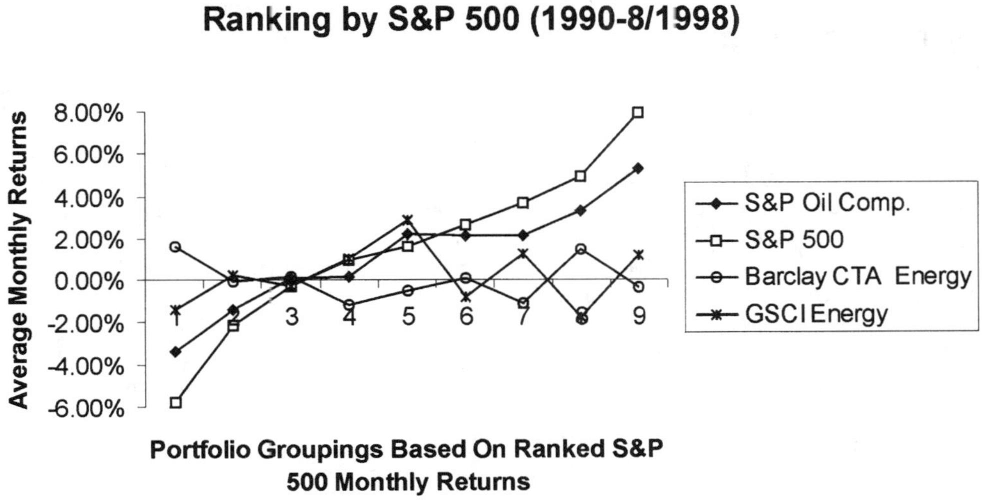

CONCLUSION:

One of the principal risks to a traditional stock and bond portfolio is unexpected inflation. These assets will lose value in the event of an unexpected rise in inflation, and will increase in value if inflation unexpectedly declines. The 1997-1998 period offered unexpectedly low inflation in the U.S., which is partly responsible for the rapid increase in equity and debt prices despite relatively modest increases in corporate earnings. Since commodity prices are positively correlated with unexpected inflation, it is not surprising that commodity indexes lost value during this period. However, inflation can have an unexpected rise just as easily as an unexpected decline. The argument for allocating some portion of investment assets to long only commodity investing rests on this simple notion. Moreover, to the degree that commodity prices revert to the underlying production costs active long/short commodity programs may also offer unique risk and return tradeoffs not found in traditional equity based passive index based commodity investment.

ENDNOTES

[1] Schneeweis T. and Spurgin R., "Energy Based Investment Products and Investor Asset Allocation," energy components include the NYMEX crude oil contract, MLM managed future oil investment,

actively managed CTA managed accounts, and the S&P 500 crude oil component. Original research paper detailing correlations and portfolio impacts can be provided by the New York Mercantile Exchange.

SECTION IV ARTICLES

Strongin, Steve, and Melanie. Petsch, "Commodity Investing: Long-Run Returns and the Function of Passive Capital," *Derivatives Quarterly* (Fall, 1995), pp. 56-64.

Kaplan, Paul and Scott. Lummer, Update: "GSCI Collateralized Futures as a Hedging and Diversification Tool for Institutional Portfolios," *Journal of Investing* (Winter, 1998), pp. 11-18.

Froot, K., "Hedging Portfolios with Real Assets," *Journal of Portfolio Management* (Summer 1995), pp. 60-77.

Schneeweis, Thomas and Richard Spurgin, "Energy Futures and Alternative Energy Investments," CISDM, 1997.

SELECT REFERENCES

Ankrim, E. and C. Hensel, "Commodities in Asset Allocation: A Real-Asset Alternative to Real Estate," *Financial Analysts Journal* (May/June, 1993), pp. 20-29.

Bodie, Zvi, and Victor Rosansky. "Risk and Return in Commodity Futures," *Financial Analysts Journal* 36 (May-June 1980), pp. 3-14.

Greer, R. "Methods for Institutional Investment in Commodity Futures," *Journal of Derivatives* (Winter, 1994), pp. 28-36.

Huberman, Gur. "The Desirability of Investment in Commodities via Commodity Futures," *Derivatives Quarterly* (Fall, 1995), pp. 65-67

Schneeweis, Thomas, Richard Spurgin, and Randy Warsager, "Commodity, Commodity Futures, Managed Commodity Futures and Inflation," AIMA Newsletter (December. 1997a).

Schneeweis, Thomas, and Richard Spurgin, "Energy Based Investment Products and Investor Asset Allocation," CIDSM/SOM, 1997.

APPENDIX I

Description of Exchange Traded Commodity Indexes

Commodity Research Bureau — Bridge Index (CRB-Bridge) futures price index represents an unweighted geometric average of 17 component commodity prices. The CRB futures and options contracts have been traded on the New York Futures Exchange since June 1986. The CRB futures contract has 6 expiration months per year (Jan-Feb-Apr-Jun-Aug-Nov).

Goldman Sachs Commodity Index (GSCI) is an arithmetic measure of the performance of actively traded, dollar-denominated nearby commodity futures contracts. As of January 9, 1995, there were 22 commodities in the index. The weights assigned to individual commodities are based on a five-year moving average of world production. Weights are determined each July and are made effective the following January. All contracts are rolled on the fifth business day of the month prior to the expiration month of the contract. Subindexes are calculated for agricultural, energy, industrial, livestock, and precious metals contracts. Two versions of the indexes are available: a total return version, which assumes that capital sufficient to purchase the basket of commodities is invested at the risk-free rate, and a spot version, which only tracks movements in the futures prices. This study uses the total return measure. The GSCI was officially launched in 1992.

13 COMMODITY INVESTING: LONG-RUN RETURNS AND THE FUNCTION OF PASSIVE CAPITAL

STEVEN STRONGIN
MELANIE PETSCH
Goldman, Sachs & Co.

There has been a recent significant increase in interest by balanced portfolio managers in long-term passive, long-only investing in the commodity markets through asset class benchmarks, such as the Goldman Sachs Commodity Index[sm] (GSCI). This interest has increased in order to take advantage of the substantial portfolio benefits that investing in the GSCI, with its strong historical negative correlations to equity and fixed-income markets, would have provided historically. However, the actual implementation of these programs has been hindered by a lack of understanding of the sources of long-run returns in these markets.

Commodity investments have historically been characterized as purely speculative investments with no intrinsic income generating properties. This portrayal confuses the modern form of commodity investing through a fully collateralized portfolio of a well-diversified index of futures contracts with the cliché of a speculative commodity position, which is typically a highly leveraged position in a single commodity. Even more confusing is the incorrect characterization of commodity investing as commodity hoarding, where returns are assumed to be equivalent to holding large piles of physical commodities, with a steady depreciation due to technological progress.

Investing in commodity futures through an index such as the GSCI is similar to investing in any other asset class. The returns from each type of investment can be separated into cash yield and risk yield. For fully collateralized futures investment, the cash yield component is the Treasury bill return on the held collateral, the same as that for any other futures investment, such as a synthetic S&P or government bond investment. The risk yield is the expected return needed to compensate the investor for bearing the futures risk.

EXHIBIT 1 COMMODITY RETURNS IN A DOWNWARD TRENDING MARKET

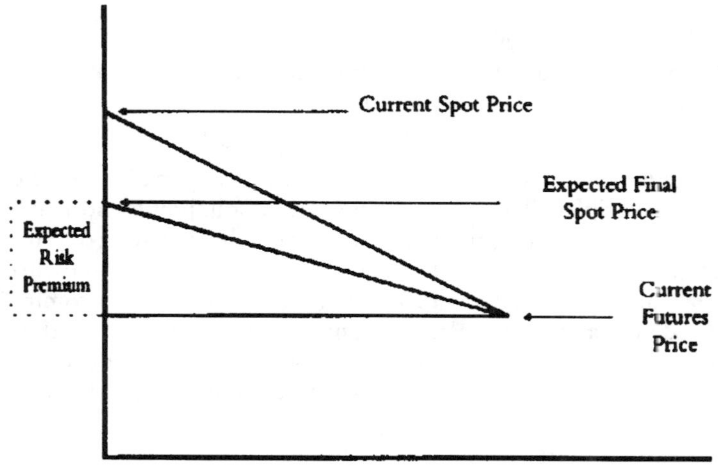

The key difference between commodity investing and financial futures investing is that the full carry arbitrage does not always hold, which breaks the normal equivalence between the synthetic spot investment and futures investing.

To emphasize the difference between holding the physical commodity and commodity futures, consider a partial carry market where the spot commodity price is expected to decline. A commodity market goes into partial carry, a common occurrence, when inventories of the commodity are not fully loanable. That is, when they are tight enough that holders receive current production benefits from surety of supply or ability to arbitrage potential locational shortages. Under these conditions, the holder of the physical commodity expects to lose money. He bears the cost of carry, experiences a capital loss, and has no collateral earning at the risk-free rate. The futures investor, on the other hand, still expects to earn the risk-free rate on the collateral and the risk premium for bearing the price risk in the contract.

In a phenomenon called backwardation, the futures price is set sufficiently below the expected spot price to build the necessary risk premium into the expected futures return. Exhibit 1 presents a diagram of the relationship between the futures and spot prices.

The key difference between commodities and other asset classes is not that commodities fail to provide income. They do provide income, in exactly the same way as any risky investment. The difference is that commodities are valued primarily on the basis of current economic conditions instead of anticipated future conditions — the source of their negative correlations with equity and fixed income investments. Commodities can provide the investor with valuable protection against an economy that grows too fast, much as bonds provide the investor with protection against an economy that grows too slowly, without having to sacrifice expected long-run returns.

ECONOMIC BASIS FOR LONG-RUN COMMODITY RETURNS

The economic basis for which long-run returns from commodity investing can be traced to four economic observations:

- Commodity producers can conserve on equity capital by shifting commodity risk from their balance sheet to the commodity markets.
- The value to producers of shifting their commodity risk to the markets is sufficient to cause them to be willing to sell output forward into the commodity markets at discounts sufficient to approximate their cost of capital.
- Although commodity consumers are willing to absorb some of this risk without requiring compensation, they are not willing to bear all or even most of it. As a result, investor capital is required in these markets to balance supply and demand.
- Investors are willing to supply the necessary capital on these markets only at rates of return that are comparable to equity returns.

The exact magnitude of these returns will, of course, vary by market risk and with investor willingness to participate. This article examines these four points and analyzes the likely forces that will determine the long-run returns on commodity investing over the next five to ten years. In the end, we conclude that the long-run returns on commodity investments are likely to approximate equity returns much as they have in the past. As commodity investments also provide valuable negative correlations to equity and bond portfolios, such expected returns indicate that modest exposure to commodities in the 5%-10% range can provide investors concerned with the risk/return trade-off in their portfolios with superior overall value.

THE ECONOMIC WORK DONE BY COMMODITY MARKETS

Academics, citing the Modigliani-Miller theorems, used to argue that corporate hedging activities should not generate any shareholder value, based on the notion that any shifts in a firm's balance sheet can be replicated by the investor. Recently, however, there is a growing awareness that firms can and do manage various risks (currency, capital, and commodities) in order to improve performance. In the case of commodity risk, the reasons why firms are able to do better by hedging internal risks on their own instead of leaving such risks to investors to manage are simple. Commodity hedging depends critically on such private information as the firm's current order book, inventory position, and undisclosed contract terms. The information advantage makes the firm the only entity in a position to evaluate and execute effective hedging strategies.

WHY FIRMS HEDGE

To better understand the role and potential returns of futures investing in commodities, it is useful to make a few points about the process of managing working capital and commodity risk. Working capital is the capital associated with the current flow of production. The risks associated are primarily price risks, resulting from timing differences between production and delivery.

There are a number of ways in which this risk can be addressed. The firm can bear the price risk and allocate some of its equity against that risk. The firm can also contract with purchasers at a fixed price, thus shifting the price risk to the consumer. Or the firm can sell the output forward into the futures market. Comparing selling forward by contact sale and selling forward into the futures market is straightforward — the better price prevails. The more interesting decision is whether it is cheaper to sell forward or hold additional equity capital.

WHY FIRMS SELL FORWARD AT DISCOUNT

The key to understanding why the producer would be willing to sell forward at discount either by contract or through the futures market is understanding the difference between capital raised for funding activity and equity held to bear risk. True risk capital does not fund specific projects; it is held by the firm as a cushion against adverse shocks. It is the most expensive capital in the firm in that it represents the highest-value project that the firm has either had to forgo or postpone. Keeping working capital risk internal to the firm by not hedging commodity prices requires costly equity capital to bear the risk.

By managing parts of the risk through external hedging programs, the firm is able to segment off those risks that can be managed more cheaply in the open market than by allocating the firm's own equity capital. Further, the firm is then able to more easily vary the amount of capital applied to those risks, achieving greater efficiencies in the use of capital over time. In particular, by shifting commodity price risk to the futures market, the producer firm can reduce its true capital costs significantly. These savings provide the economic basis for long-run commodity returns.

WHY INVESTOR CAPITAL IS NECESSARY IN THE COMMODITY MARKETS

The role for long-term investor capital in the commodity markets arises from a natural mismatch between the natural shorts and the natural longs in the commodity markets. This discrepancy has two broad causes. First, there is a temporal mismatch. Producers must purchase their inputs before they can produce and before buyers must commit to purchasing the resulting product. Thus, producers want to sell their product before consumers want to buy it.

EXHIBIT 2 HISTORICAL RETURNS AND VARIABILITY

	Annualized Returns	Standard Deviations	Excess Return Sharpe Ratio*
	December 31, 1969 to December 31, 1994		
GSCI Total	14.10	18.50	0.37
S&P 500	11.94	16.68	0.28
Government Bonds	9.30	12.26	0.17
Gold	6.64	21.80	–0.03
Cash	7.26	1.45	0.00
	December 31, 1969 to December 31, 1982		
GSCI Total	16.40	18.20	0.48
S&P 500	9.20	18.20	0.09
Government Bonds	7.20	13.20	–0.03
Gold	23.60	32.00	0.50
Cash	7.60	1.60	0.00
	December 31, 1982 to December 31, 1994		
GSCI Total	11.20	18.60	0.26
S&P 500	14.40	14.60	0.55
Government Bonds	11.20	11.00	0.44
Gold	–0.40	14.40	–0.47
Cash	6.40	1.00	0.00

***Total return less cash return divided by standard deviation.**

Second, there is a size mismatch. The producer is a natural seller of the bulk of its production forward because, with the exception of agricultural products, the producer knows what it will produce and has already paid, or committed to pay, for almost all the necessary input. Thus, for a commodity producer, selling forward locks in profit margins and reduces margin volatility.

On the other hand, the commodity consumer, in general, knows neither how much of a commodity it will need to buy nor at what price it will sell its own products. The consumer only wants to purchase forward commodities in sufficient quantity to cover production already committed for both in terms of quantity and price. Forward commodity purchases beyond this point can actually add to earnings volatility. This gap between the producer's desire to lock in margins and the consumer's desire to retain flexibility is fundamental to the underlying economics of these markets and provides the foundation for the investor's long-term role in the commodity markets.

FORECASTING LONG-RUN RETURNS

The return profile for long-term commodity investing follows the determinants of expected returns in most financial markets. Returns are determined by the need for capital, the value of that capital to the purchasing firms, the risk that the investor bears, and the investor's willingness to take on that risk.

Expected returns vary up with

- the size of the gap between producer and consumer hedging,
- volatility, and
- the cost of capital in hedging firms.

Expected returns vary down with

- the comfort level of investors in the market,
- government price stabilization or income protection programs, and
- price-stabilizing programs among producers.

The question of what type of returns are required to get investors to fill the gap between producers and consumers in the commodity markets is not subject to direct analysis. Rather, we need to infer the answer from prior behavior and likely changes. Historically, it appears that investors have required large returns. Using the GSCI as a benchmark, since 1970 investors have earned returns of 14.1%, 6.8% above cash, on commodity investments.

Exhibit 2 shows the historical returns, variability, and Sharpe ratios of a number of assets. The GSCI returns are quite comparable to equities and substantially higher than cash. Even in the two subsamples, 1970-1982, one of the strongest commodity markets in history, and 1983-1994, the subsequent period during which there was a major downturn in the energy market, commodity returns remain fairly high. Commodities earn 16.4% in the early period and 11.2% in the later period with a 14.4% average. These returns are 7.2% higher than equities in the first period and 3.2% below in the later period, for an average of 2.2 % higher overall.

On a risk/return basis, as measured by the Sharpe ratio, the relationship between commodities and equities is similar to that for returns. The evidence seems to indicate that investors have not required excessive premiums to enter these markets, nor have they been willing to supply capital in sufficient amounts to saturate the market.

This attitude on the part of investors could also have been inferred from the relatively low amount of producer hedging that is still moving through these markets. Exhibit 3 shows the open interest and trading volume in the GSCI commodities over the last twenty years in comparison to total production. Three things stand out:

- how young these markets are,
- how fast they have been growing, and
- how much growth is still possible, since total open interest is still only a fraction of total production.

To get a better feel for the required investor returns, it is interesting to break the GSCI down into the individual components and examine the returns and Sharpe ratios of the subindexes. In Exhibit 4, we see the results for each subindex of the GSCI. Concentrating on the 1984-1994 period, which is the only period with data across all commodity groups, we first note that greater volatility does correlate with greater returns. Second, the crops have had low returns (as we suggest is implied by the existence of extensive government risk programs). Third, precious metals, the only commodities with extensive investor interest well beyond the requirements of producers to hedge all of current production, have the lowest returns, especially on a risk-adjusted basis.

EXHIBIT 3 TRADING VOLUME AND OPEN INTEREST VERSUS TOTAL PRODUCTION IN GSCI COMMODITIES

	Total Number of Contracts Traded During the Year					1984 Average Daily Open Interest	1994 Total Dollar Contract Volume	Average Daily Open Interest in Dollars	Total Dollar Value** of Production	Open Interest as % of Production
	1980	1985	1990	1993	1994					
Energy										
Crude Oil	*	3,973,360	23,641,000	24,943,100	26,811,820	103,251,410	$458,777,052,020	$7,038,784,382	$372,624,402,458	1.89
Unleaded Gas	*	132,611	5,205,995	7,446,600	7,470,837	23,330,377	$158,855,727,188	$1,976,431,046	$141,036,860,439	1.40
Heating Oil	237,327	2,202,930	6,375,590	8,688,810	8,968,834	40,046,021	$182,371,573,635	$3,237,695,996	$126,141,220,583	2.57
Natural Gas	*	*	132,820*	4,686,410	6,347,529	32,433,644	$126,301,163,512	$2,591,785,550	$119,449,284,476	2.17
Industrial Metals										
Aluminum	71,439	1,018,508	3,990,429	10,001,500	14,428,627	61,087,287	$541,901,706,300	$9,975,129,012	$45,417,531,150	21.96
Copper	232,475	1,266,631	5,668,847	14,405,800	17,557,181	51,068,916	$1,016,540,147,317	$13,025,683,936	$32,665,791,200	39.88
Nickel	17,855	135,551	572,970	1,221,750	3,355,892	13,233,683	$129,566,089,508	$2,240,935,141	$7,078,852,339	31.66
Zinc	70,469	306,197	1,417,384	4,194,140	5,384,761	23,185,702	$137,486,680,747	$2,642,812,972	$7,785,171,800	33.95
Precious Metals										
Gold	8,001,410	7,773,830	9,688,410	8,911,500	8,512,888	39,022,819	$329,788,274,682	$6,022,865,900	$24,541,582,476	24.54
Platinum	429,663	693,256	820,934	653,298	895,805	5,836,405	$18,306,042,772	$475,174,061	$3,937,152,501	12.07
Silver	1,058,730	4,821,210	3,873,800	4,851,130	6,000,070	30,114,127	$159,890,276,305	$3,197,144,835	$2,315,502,391	138.08
Agriculture										
Wheat	27,140,800	10,639,800	14,381,400	15,105,800	18,072,296	73,720,500	$325,513,766,399	$5,311,342,338	$89,152,341,544	5.96
Corn	59,567,000	31,964,100	57,115,100	57,254,900	57,731,537	337,070,160	$725,808,097,092	$16,816,222,958	$43,687,877,908	38.49
Soybeans	58,841,000	36,960,600	51,509,500	58,088,300	53,755,884	182,964,550	$1,668,096,148,610	$22,530,015,041	$22,590,862,316	99.73
Cotton	2,494,860	634,168	1,525,440	1,600,180	2,274,042	13,381,658	$85,323,633,598	$2,000,355,070	$36,544,876,280	5.47
Sugar	3,576,310	3,013,130	5,424,810	4,286,820	4,706,486	33,445,474	$64,463,133,950	$1,825,064,772	$35,797,993,439	5.10
Coffee	906,944	650,768	1,774,050	2,489,080	2,661,328	11,265,545	$145,525,168,696	$2,454,246,699	$24,078,487,824	10.19
Cocoa	389,002	801,569	1,635,910	2,128,380	2,419,431	19,728,91	$30,930,537,118	$1,004,849,408	$3,159,214,000	31.81
Livestock										
Live Cattle	5,997,050	4,437,330	3,796,580	3,308,650	3,624,410	19,144,359	$102,523,039,005	$2,148,940,967	$84,457,486,371	2.54
Live Hogs	2,153,870	1,719,860	2,240,710	1,400,540	1,561,043	7,704,930	$27,417,615,658	$537,010,768	$31,145,559,855	1.72
Totals	**171,186,204**	**113,145,409**	**200,658,859**	**235,666,688**	**252,540,701**	**1,121,036,358**	**$6,435,385,874,114**	**$107,052,490,852**	**$1,253,608,051,890**	

***Incomplete or no data available.*

****Based on 1990 production, the last date for which complete data is available.*

EXHIBIT 4 RETURNS FOR GSCI SUBINDEXES

	Annualized Returns	Standard Deviations	Total Return Sharpe Ratio	Annualized Returns	Standard Deviations	Total Return Sharpe Ratio
	December 31, 1969 to December 31, 1994			*December 31, 1972 to December 31, 1994*		
GSCI Total	14.10	18.50	0.76	12.82	19.35	0.66
Energy	NA	NA	NA	NA	NA	NA
Industrial Metals	NA	NA	NA	NA	NA	NA
Precious Metals	NA	NA	NA	10.09	27.55	0.37
Agriculture	11.87	24.04	0.49	10.04	23.98	0.42
Livestock	16.09	19.59	0.82	15.03	20.32	0.74
	December 31, 1976 to December 31, 1994			*December 31, 1984 to December 31, 1994*		
GSCI Total	11.61	17.59	0.66	11.52	18.74	0.61
Energy	NA	NA	NA	15.59	40.02	0.39
Industrial Metals	14.53	29.51	0.49	19.92	31.06	0.64
Precious Metals	6.96	24.34	0.29	–0.80	14.83	(0.05)
Agriculture	5.63	16.01	0.35	7.17	14.00	0.51
Livestock	16.67	18.12	0.92	13.98	15.64	0.89

The pattern of returns is almost in perfect congruence with the patterns suggested by earlier arguments. It should be noted, however, that as with any other description of investor returns, the lack of sufficient historical data to do full statistical testing makes it impossible to do more than assess the reasonableness of the arguments.

It is also useful to point out, how little information about returns is provided by spot price trends in individual commodities, as seen in Exhibit 5. The price of oil fell at an annualized rate of 0.3% a year from the beginning of 1987 to the end of 1994. Over that time, rolling the futures contract monthly in the same fashion as the GSCI benchmark investment provided returns of 7.7%, and the collateral provided an additional 6.3%, for a total annualized return of 14% over the period.

Gold, on the other hand, had a price trend from 1978 to 1994 of 4.9% per year and only provided a return of -3.3% on the rolling futures plus 7.9% on the collateral for a total return of 4.6% on an annualized basis. Copper, with a spot return very similar to that of gold at 4.4%, outperformed gold with a total return of 1.2% on an annualized basis. Finally, live hogs had a price decline of 1.2% per year and an annualized total return of 13.2%. The conclusion is that spot price changes have no predictive power for the total return on a futures investment.

The full force of this argument across the entire GSCI can be seen in Exhibit 6, which shows the total return index for the GSCI divided by a spot price index that eliminates the effect of spot price movements over the lifespan of the GSCI. The index has a steady upward movement, occasionally flattening or dipping very slightly, but on the whole it marches upward at a significant pace of 12% over this period. While expected returns do not depend on expected spot price movements, which are included in the slope of the forward price curve, the realized returns do. The realized returns equal the spot price trend plus the yield from collateral plus whatever bias is built into the futures price to generate the necessary capital inflows into these markets.

THE OUTLOOK FOR RETURNS ON COMMODITY INVESTMENTS

The outlook for commodity returns does not depend on the long-term outlook for commodity prices, which would be fully capitalized into the futures forward curve. As with any other asset class, it depends on the supply and demand for risk capital in these markets. To analyze how returns are likely to differ from historical returns, we need to assess how different the supply and demand balance is likely to be.

Factors likely to cause the demand for capital to increase are

- Increased acceptance of the role of hedging in lowering volatility,
- Increased demands by debtholders for hedging programs to reduce their risk,
- Increased privatization, which increases the number of producers needing risk capital, and
- Increased demand for hedging from fast-growing producers in the emerging markets, where capital costs are higher and consumers less able to commit to long-term contracts.

Factors likely to reduce the supply of capital are

- Reduced willingness of consumers to bear unnecessary balance sheet risk in long-term contracts,
- Reduction in government-supplied risk capital in agriculture as a result of treaties and budget difficulties,
- Reduced willingness of governments to subsidize money-losing industries, and

EXHIBIT 5 INDIVIDUAL HISTORICAL COMMODITY RETURNS

		Annualized Percentage Change Start Date Through 1994		
	Start Date	Spot Price Index	Excess Return Index	Total Return Index
Energy				
Crude Oil	1987	–0.30%	7.70%	14.00%
Heating Oil	1983	–3.90	3.00	9.90
Unleaded Gas	1988	2.30	10.40	16.80
Natural Gas	1994	–19.20	–48.80	–46.60
Industrial Metals				
Aluminum	1991	5.80	–2.60	1.50
Copper	1977	4.40	3.90	12.20
Nickel	1993	19.60	13.70	18.00
Zinc	1991	–2.50	–6.50	–2.60
Precious Metals				
Gold	1978	4.90	–3.30	4.60
Platinum	1984	1.00	–2.50	3.80
Silver	1973	4.10	–4.50	2.90
Agriculture				
Wheat	1970	4.10	1.90	9.50
Corn	1970	2.60	–2.70	4.60
Soybeans	1970	3.30	1.80	9.40
Cotton	1977	1.40	4.40	12.70
Sugar	1973	2.20	–6.90	0.40
Coffee	1981	1.90	–0.80	6.80
Cocoa	1984	–6.10	–15.00	–9.50
Livestock				
Cattle	1970	3.70	7.60	15.60
Hogs	1976	–1.20	4.90	13.20

EXHIBIT 6 RATIO OF GSCI TOTAL RETURN INDEX TO GSCI SPOT PRICE INDEX

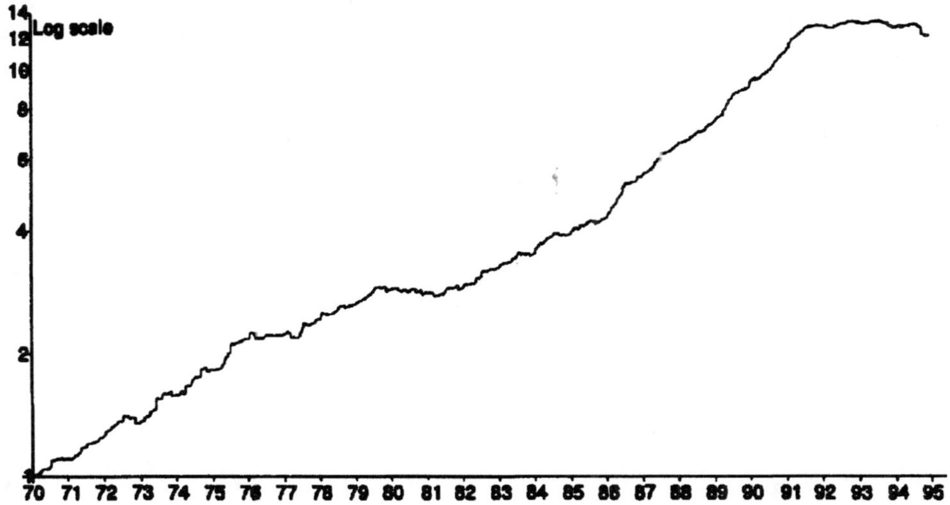

- Reduced willingness of major OPEC members to serve as swing producers due to tighter fiscal situations.

Factors likely to change the willingness of investors to supply capital to commodity markets are

- Increased liquidity of futures and increased recognition of the legitimacy of commodity investing, and
- Increased willingness of major investor groups to diversify risk across markets and to take advantage of the portfolio benefits of passive commodity investing.

CONCLUSIONS

It is hard to assess what the eventual equilibrium returns to commodity investing might be. Clearly, real economic work is being done by the capital in commodity markets. This will continue to supply a foundation for continued economic returns from these investments. Nevertheless, it is possible that the covariance properties of commodities, which have often been cited as the primary justification for long-term commodity investments, could cause investors to bid down these returns. How fast and how far remain to be seen.

We would suggest that even if commodities become widely accepted as a mainstream investment, investor willingness to accept subpar returns is quite limited. And although investors will trade off some reduced returns for reduced portfolio variance, we expect the extent of this trade-off to be limited. Positing an equivalence between expected equity and commodity returns would not be unreasonable and positing an equivalence with bond returns would be conservative. In the medium term, higher returns would be more likely as commodity investments continue to benefit from insufficient mainstream acceptance. In the longer term, this effect is less likely.

It should also be pointed out that if other investments, either derivative-based or fundamental, are developed that offer similar covariance properties, the value of those covariance properties should decrease. Hence, the expected returns on commodity investments should rise.

For the foreseeable future, however, commodity investments appear to offer highly competitive returns, even without considering the value of their negative covariances to equity and bond returns. Under these conditions, commodities offer very high value to investors who have a need or desire for negative covariance investments to manage overall portfolio risk.

ENDNOTES

This article was published in *Derivatives Quarterly*, Fall 1995.

14 GSCI COLLATERALIZED FUTURES AS A HEDGING AND DIVERSIFICATION TOOL FOR INSTITUTIONAL PORTFOLIOS: AN UPDATE

PAUL D. KAPLAN
Ibbotson Associates

SCOTT L. LUMMER
401K Forum

INTRODUCTION

Both bonds and stocks are contingent claims on the wealth of firms. Bonds, the senior claims, are promises to make payments denominated in money, and perform very poorly when the real (purchasing-power) value of money declines in an inflationary environment. Stocks, as claims to the real economic assets of firms once bondholders have been satisfied, provide a greater measure of purchasing power protection than bonds over the long run, although their short-run performance during periods of inflation has been poor. (A review of the literature on equity returns and inflation is in Ibbotson and Brinson [1993].)

By holding real economic assets directly in the portfolio, investors can hedge against inflation much more effectively than with stocks. Real assets also tend to diversify away some of the risk of equities, with which they have surprisingly low correlations. Real assets include real estate, precious metals, commodities, and a variety of other items that have value independent of the monetary units in which they are denominated. All of these can be used to achieve the goals of diversification and inflation protection (see Ankrim and Hensel [1993]).

WHAT IS A GSCI COLLATERALIZED FUTURES POSITION?

This article focuses on one particular real asset, a collateralized position in the Goldman Sachs Commodity Index (GSCI) futures contract. The GSCI itself is diversified among commodities, and represents a cross section of the principal raw and semi-finished goods used by producers and consumers.[2]

A collateralized position in the GSCI futures contract consists of the full dollar value of an unleveraged long GSCI position held over a period of time, using U.S. Treasury bills for 100% collateral. The dollar value of the GSCI futures position is based upon the futures contract's $250 multiplier (e.g., if the Index is at 200.00, the dollar value of the futures contract would be $50,000).

The analysis reported here is based on a simulation of historical returns to a fully collateralized long position in the GSCI futures contract as represented by the GSCI Total Return Index.

The GSCI futures contract trades at the Chicago Mercantile Exchange with a contract for every month of the calendar year. The simulation assumes that when a futures contract matures the position is liquidated, and the funds are fully reinvested in a long position in the next lead month contract. This "roll" would take place twelve times per year.

EXHIBIT 1 GROWTH OF $100: 12/31/69-2/28/97

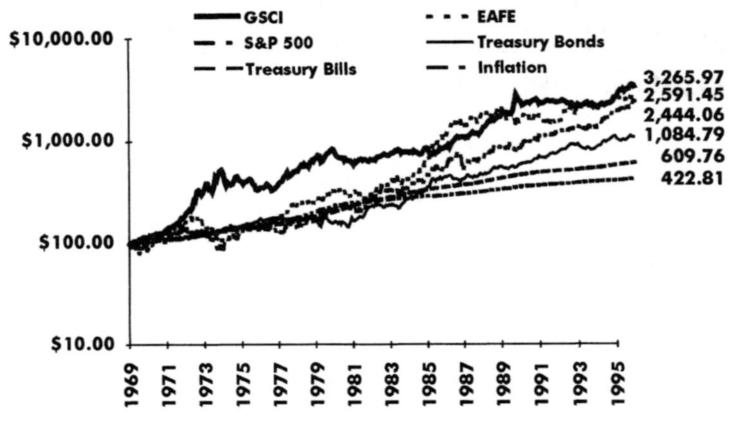

EXHIBIT 2 COMPOUND ANNUAL RETURNS: 12/31/69-2/28/97

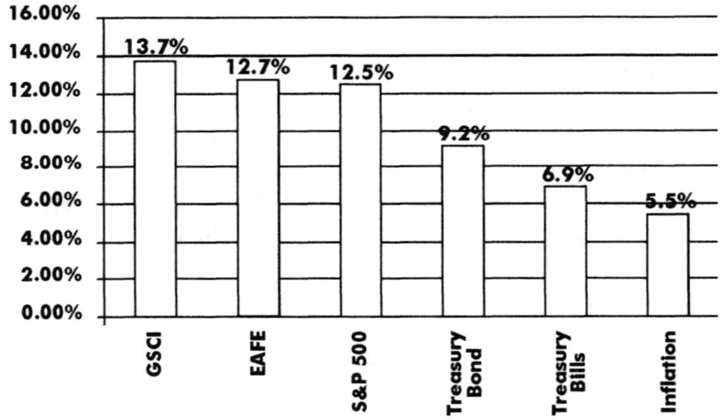

EXHIBIT 3 ANNUALIZED MONTHLY STANDARD DEVIATIONS: 12/31/69-2/28/97

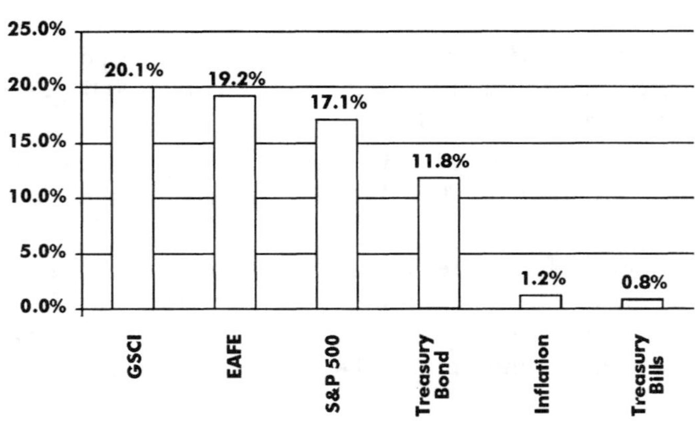

Returns are then derived from three sources: 1) change in the market value of the GSCI futures contract (related to changes in the component commodity prices), 2) interest from the Treasury bills held as collateral, and 3) any systematic bias between the prices of different contract months.

PERFORMANCE OF THE GSCI TOTAL RETURN INDEX COMPARED WITH OTHER INVESTMENTS

Exhibit 1 shows the growth of a $100 investment made on December 31, 1969, in various asset classes including the GSCI Total Return Index.[3] The GSCI Total Return Index has the best performance over the ensuing twenty-seven years and two months, growing almost thirty-three-fold for a compound annual total return of 13.7%.

The two stock market indexes shown, the MSCI EAFE and the S&P 500, also have high returns. Bonds and bills do not perform as well, despite record-high bill yields and a vigorous bull market in bonds in the second half of the period.

All the asset classes beat inflation. Exhibit 2 shows the compound annual returns on each of the asset classes graphed in Exhibit 1.

As Exhibit 3 shows, the higher-returning asset classes generally have higher risk. The GSCI Total Return Index is roughly as risky as stocks, with a standard deviation of 20.1%.[4] The S&P 500 and EAFE stock market indexes have standard deviations of 17.1% and 19.2%, respectively. Bonds exhibit moderate risk over the period taken as a whole, although they fluctuate wildly during the late 1970s and early 1980s. Treasury bills, which have no default risk and negligible price risk, show variability due to the drift in their yields over time, which indicates their reinvestment risk.

DIVERSIFICATION BENEFITS: CORRELATION OF THE GSCI TOTAL RETURN INDEX WITH OTHER ASSETS

The GSCI Total Return Index has significant negative correlations with stocks and bonds. Exhibit 4 shows the correlations of annual returns over 1970-1996. The large negative correlation of the GSCI Total Return Index with bonds is expected, because theory suggests that the prices of real asset claims and money claims (bonds) will move in opposite directions.

EXHIBIT 4 ANNUAL CORRELATIONS OF GSCI WITH OTHER ASSETS: 1970-1996

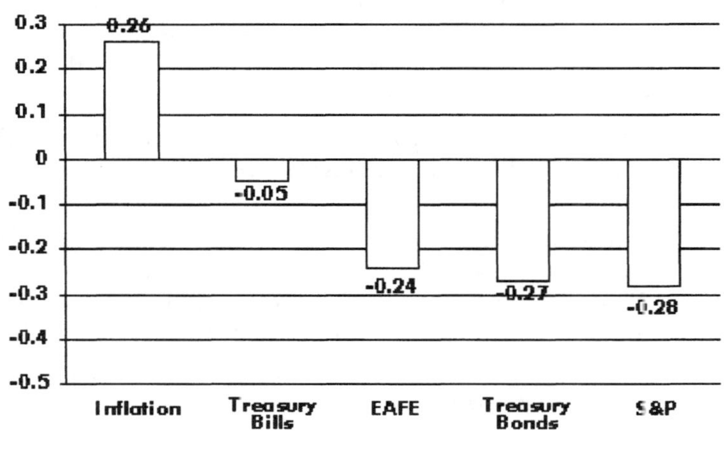

The GSCI Total Return Index is also negatively correlated with stocks. These findings are noteworthy given the acceptance of stocks as a long-run inflation hedge. Not only is the GSCI Total Return Index negatively correlated with bonds, but it appears to hedge the risks of stocks as well.

Correlations of *monthly* returns on the GSCI Total Return Index with other assets are close to zero when computed over the whole period. Over the latest five years studied, March 1992 to February 1997, the GSCI Total Return Index has a monthly correlation of 0.12 with bonds, 0.28 with S&P 500 stocks, 0.39 with EAFE stocks, 0.25 with Treasury bills, and -0.06 with inflation. Every one of these correlations is opposite in sign to the long-term annual correlations.

These results are in sharp contrast with those in Lummer and Siegel [1993] who found that over the five-year period of their study (May 1987 to April 1992) with the exception of Treasury bills, the monthly correlations were similar to the long-run annual correlations.

The recent change in monthly correlations is at least partly attributable to the composition of the GSCI. While the recent increases in commodity prices have been reflected in the GSCI and the Producer Price Index, they have not yet had an impact on consumer prices and the Consumer Price Index. While producer and consumer prices must be tied together in the long-run, over the short-run they can move differently.

To see the effectiveness of GSCI collateralized futures as a portfolio diversifier, consider a portfolio consisting of 60% in U.S. stocks, 30% in bonds, and 10% in bills, and a portfolio that is 57% in U.S. stocks, 28.5% in bonds, 9.5% in bills, and 5% in the GSCI Total Return Index. Both portfolios are rebalanced monthly.

The portfolio without the GSCI Total Return Index returns 11.1% annually with a standard deviation of 11.8% over 1970-1996. Over the same period, the portfolio with the GSCI Total Return Index returns 11.4% annually with a standard deviation of 11.0%, exhibiting a higher return with less risk.

Over the long run, the GSCI Total Return Index is also an inflation hedge, as shown by the positive (0.26) correlation of the annual GSCI with inflation. Consumer prices, producer prices, and commodity futures prices moved upward together, at first rapidly, over the period of generally accelerating inflation from 1970 to mid-1981, then less quickly during the disinflation that followed.

PERFORMANCE OF THE GSCI TOTAL RETURN INDEX BY SUBPERIOD

Inflation rates, and yields on both long- and short-term bonds, tended to rise during the entire decade of the 1970s, except for the brief 1975-1976 period — and reached their peak in mid-1981. In order to divide the study period into inflationary and disinflationary parts, the date September 30, 1981 is used. This is the month-end with the highest long-term U.S. Treasury bond yield ever recorded (14.82%).

Exhibit 5 shows the growth of $100 invested over the period from December 31, 1969 to September 30, 1981 in various assets. This figure replicates, in magnified form, the left half of Exhibit 1.

The GSCI Total Return Index is the winner by a large margin, growing to $649 (representing a 17.26% compound annual return). Foreign stocks outperform U.S. stocks, with $100 growing to $288 and $208, respectively. The long-suffering bond market, which grew to only $146, was at the bottom, far below the inflation rate.

This environment, which included two oil price shocks as well as a large secular increase in the inflation rate, was ideal for the commodity investor. The GSCI Total

Exhibit 5 Growth of $100 from 12/31/69-9/30/81

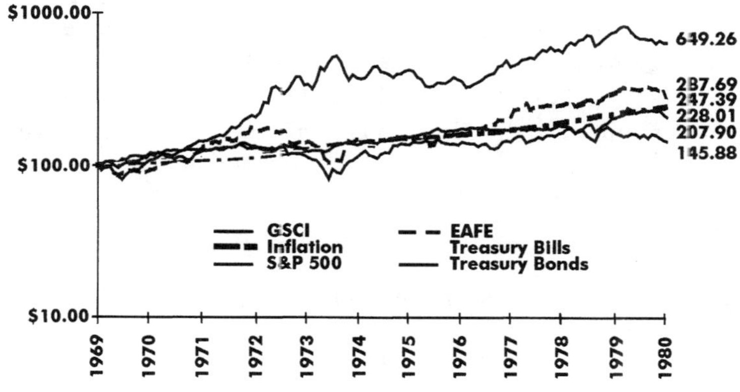

Return Index rose by 75% in 1973 (the year of the first oil price shock) and nearly 40% in 1974, mitigating the sharp declines of the stock market in those two years. In fact, the GSCI Total Return Index was practically a mirror image of the S&P 500 during the crash-and-recovery cycle of 1973-1976, illustrating the gain from diversification.

It is noteworthy that oil futures were not in the GSCI during this period because no heavily traded oil futures existed at the time; the rise in the price of oil was hedged by increases in the prices of other kinds of commodities that were represented in the GSCI.

In 1979, the year of the second oil price shock, the GSCI Total Return Index rose by almost 34%. While the U.S. and foreign stock markets both rose in 1979, bonds declined, their high income returns more than overshadowed by the capital losses due to rising yields over the year. Once again, the diversification benefits of a position in GSCI collateralized futures are illustrated.

An abrupt shift in the course of the U.S. economy took place in the fall of 1981, as bond yields and inflation rates tumbled, in what proved to be the greatest bond market rally in history. (The stock market reacted later, in mid-1982, with a huge rally, and real GNP finally began to rise in late 1982 after declines in twelve of the previous fifteen quarters.)

Exhibit 6 Growth of $100 from 9/30/81-2/28/97

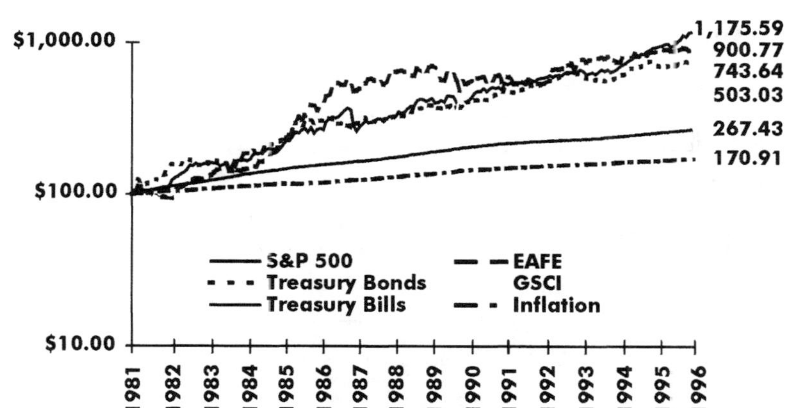

Exhibit 6 shows the growth of $100 invested in various assets on September 30, 1981, and held to February 28, 1997. Stocks are the big winner over this period, with the S&P 500 and EAFE growing to $1,176 and $901 respectively. A $100 investment in bonds grew to $744. During this period, the GSCI Total Return Index grew to $503, easily outdistancing Treasury bills and inflation.

In summary, the GSCI Total Return Index performed well in periods of both accelerating and decelerating inflation. One can expect, however, a GSCI collateralized futures position to perform significantly better when the inflation rate is rising. It is precisely during these periods that assets traditionally held in portfolios experience low or negative returns.

EXHIBIT 7 YEAR-BY-YEAR TOTAL RETURNS ON GSCI COLLATERALIZED FUTURES, S&P 500 STOCKS & EAFE

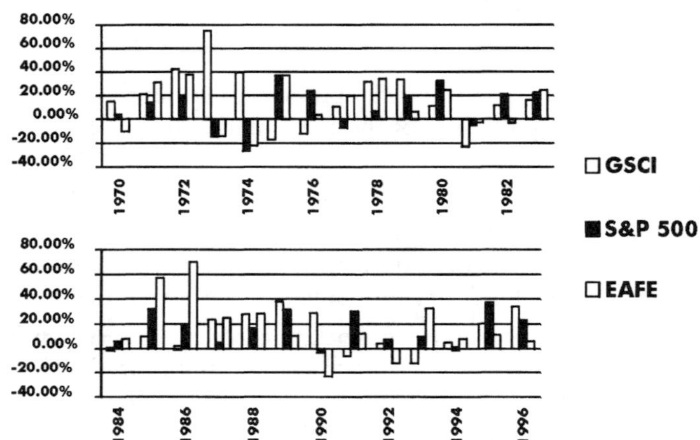

YEAR-BY-YEAR PERFORMANCE OF THE GSCI TOTAL RETURN INDEX

An examination of the performance of the GSCI Total Return Index relative to other assets on a year-to-year basis shows the diversification potential of the GSCI. Exhibit 7 compares the yearly total returns on the GSCI Total Return Index, U.S. stocks (the S&P 500), and foreign stocks (the EAFE index).

EXHIBIT 8 YEAR-BY-YEAR TOTAL RETURNS ON GSCI COLLATERALIZED FUTURES & LONG-TERM TREASURY BONDS

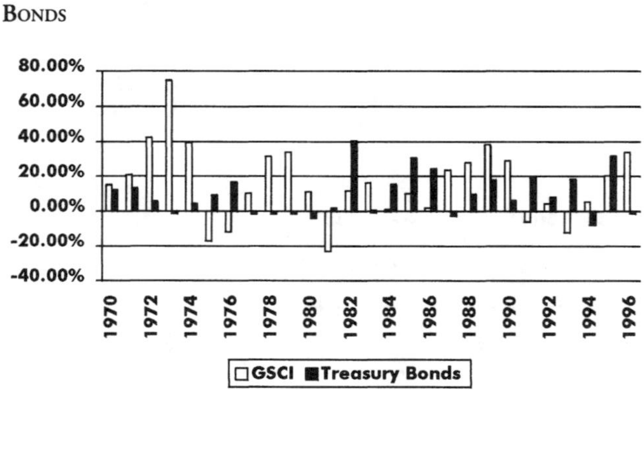

Note that of the twenty-seven full years shown, only one (1981) had negative returns on both the GSCI Total Return Index and either of the stock market indexes. Stock market declines tended to be canceled out by rises in the GSCI Total Return Index for an investor holding both types of assets.

Exhibit 8 shows a similar analysis for bonds. None of the twenty-seven years had negative returns for both the GSCI Total Return Index and long-term U.S. Treasury bonds. This record should be considered in light of the miserable bond performance over 1973-1980, when total returns were negative in five of the eight years. The results displayed in Exhibits 7 and 8 suggest that GSCI collateralized futures are an even better diversifier for bonds than for stocks.

EXHIBIT 9 YEAR-BY-YEAR TOTAL RETURNS ON GSCI COLLATERALIZED FUTURES & INFLATION

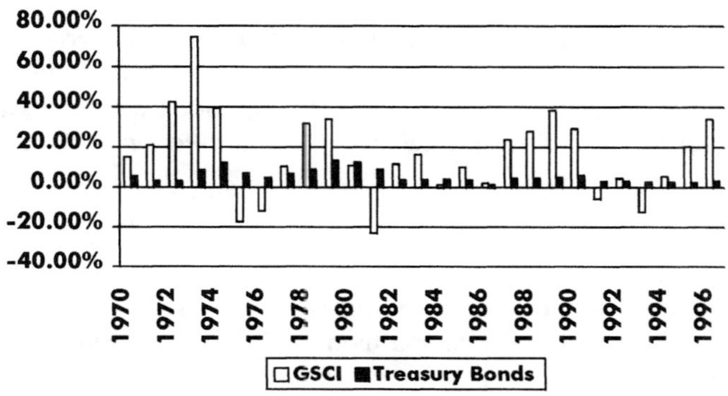

THE GSCI TOTAL RETURN INDEX IN A HIGH-INFLATION ENVIRONMENT

Exhibit 9 compares the GSCI Total Return Index with inflation as measured by the Consumer Price Index (CPI). The high-inflation years are those with inflation rates above 8%.

Note that in the four years with the largest increases in inflation, 1973-1974 and 1978-1979, the GSCI Total Return Index rose by over 30%. In contrast, in 1980, which had one of the highest inflation rates on record but not an increase from the previous year, the GSCI Total Return Index rose by less than the rate of inflation.

The only high-inflation year in which the GSCI Total Return Index declined was 1981, but that year showed a sharp inflation *decline* from the previous year. Thus, returns on collateralized long positions in GSCI futures tend to be high in periods of high inflation, but they are even more closely related to *changes* in the inflation rate.

WHY HOLD GSCI COLLATERALIZED FUTURES?

Although the GSCI Total Return Index has done spectacularly well over the period studied, from January 1970 to February 1997, the expected return does not necessarily mirror this segment of recent history. More likely, its long-run expected return is closer to that of Treasury bills. Why, then, should investors hold GSCI collateralized futures?

GSCI collateralized futures are essentially a diversification asset. They do well when other assets do poorly. Most investors do not expect or hope for a return to the high inflation rates of the 1970s, when stocks and bonds did poorly, and the GSCI Total

Return Index performed well. There is some possibility, however, that such an environment will reoccur. GSCI collateralized futures should provide protection against declining stock and bond values in a future period of rising inflation or rising commodity prices.

If inflation rates are stable or decline further, GSCI collateralized futures may have flat or negative returns, even though they did well in the disinflation that began in 1981. Such an outcome would be acceptable to most investors, who would be likely to experience further gains in their primary wealth-generating assets — stocks and bonds.

GSCI collateralized futures present investors with the opportunity to hold positions that move with the prices of real assets in the economy. Real estate is sometimes held for this purpose, but GSCI collateralized futures and real estate are quite different asset classes. Differences in their characteristics, such as liquidity, can give a place to both in a diversified portfolio.

GSCI collateralized futures provide exposure to the prices of real assets in roughly the proportions in which they are used for production. The real estate market, in contrast, consists of wealth-generating businesses that provide exposure to an important real asset (buildings), but it does not track a broad cross section of real asset prices.

CONCLUSION

GSCI collateralized futures can be held by risk-averse investors who seek diversification and protection against poor returns in other asset classes. These instruments are especially valuable to investors who attach a high probability to rising inflation and interest rates and who want to hedge their stock and bond positions against such changes.

Such investors, however, are not the only ones who should consider GSCI collateralized futures as an investment. If an investor believes there is any realistic possibility of another inflationary or commodity spasm over the investment horizon, a position in GSCI collateralized futures would serve as a diversifier. Investors who want to hold a more complete cross section of the assets in the economy should consider GSCI collateralized futures for their exposure to real assets.

ENDNOTES

This article was published in *The Journal of Investing*, Winter 1998.

Scott Lummer was a managing director of Ibbotson Associates when this article was written.

The authors thank Laurence B. Siegel of the Ford Foundation who co-authored the first version of this article (Lummer and Siegel [1993]). With his permission, we have continued to use many of his contributions in this revised version.

The authors appreciate the financial support of the Chicago Mercantile Exchange. They thank Richard Redding and Brett Vietmeier, both of the Chicago Mercantile Exchange, and Mark Riepe for their helpful comments. At Ibbotson Associates, Sheryl Cohen made substantial contributions to the research.

1. Lummer and Siegel [1993] used a preliminary version of the GSCI Total Return Index.
2. The GSCI is described in The *GSCI Manual: A Guide to the Goldman Sachs Commodity Index* [1997]. The GSCI futures contract, traded on the Chicago Mercantile Exchange, is described in the *GSCI Futures and Options 1997 Information Guide* [1997].
3. For all figures and appendixes in this article, results for the GSCI Total Return Index (abbreviated "GSCI" where space necessitates) are constructed by Goldman, Sachs & Co.

The Standard & Poor's 500 Stock Composite Index (S&P 500) is used to represent the U.S. stock market. Returns shown for the S&P 500 are total returns as calculated by Ibbotson Associates.

Morgan Stanley Capital International (MSCI)'s Europe, Australia, Far East (EAFE™) index is a capitalization-weighted, total return index of the principal developed-country stock markets outside North America. EAFE returns are in U.S. dollars with gross dividends reinvested.

Bonds are represented by Ibbotson Associates' index of U.S. Treasury bond total returns, constructed by holding a one-bond portfolio with a maturity as close to twenty years as the data permit. Treasury bills are represented by Ibbotson Associates' Treasury bill index, which reports the total return from rolling over each month a one-bill portfolio containing, at the beginning of each month, the shortest bill with not less than one month to maturity.

The Consumer Price Index , constructed by the Bureau of Labor Statistics (BLS), represents inflation over 1970-1978; thereafter, we use the BLS' Consumer Price Index for All Urban Consumers (CPI-U). The inflation indexes are not seasonally adjusted.

4. Monthly standard deviations were annualized by treating an annual return as a compound return of twelve independent monthly returns. See the *Stock, Bonds, Bills, and Inflation 1997 Yearbook*[1997], p. 106 for details.

All derived statistical data, such as standard deviations and correlations, are calculated by Ibbotson Associates from the data described in note 3.

REFERENCES

Ankrim, Ernest M., and Chris R. Hensel. "Commodities in Asset Allocation: A Real-Asset Alternative to Real Estate?" *Financial Analysts Journal.* May/June 1993.

GSCI Futures and Options 1997 Information Guide. Chicago Mercantile Exchange, 1997.

GSCI Manual: A Guide to the Goldman Sach Commodity Index. Goldman, Sachs & Co., 1997.

Ibbotson, Roger G., and Gary P. Brinson. *Global Investing.* New York: McGraw-Hill, 1993, Chapter 12.

Lummer, Scott L. and Laurence B. Siegel, "GSCI Collaterized Futures: A Hedging and Diversification Tool for Institutional Investors, *The Journal of Investing.* Summer 1993.

Stock, Bonds, Bills, and Inflation 1997 Yearbook. Ibbotson Associates, 1997.

APPENDIX A YEAR-BY-YEAR TOTAL RETURNS ON GSCI COLLATERALIZED FUTURES AND OTHER PRINCIPAL ASSET CLASSES (%)

Year	GSCI Collateralized Futures	S&P 500 Stocks	EAFE Stocks	Long-Term Treasury Bonds	Treasury Bills	Inflation
1970	15.10	4.01	-10.51	12.11	6.52	5.49
1971	21.08	14.31	31.21	13.23	4.39	3.36
1972	42.43	18.98	37.60	5.69	3.84	3.41
1973	74.96	-14.66	-14.17	-1.11	6.93	8.80
1974	39.51	-26.47	-22.15	4.35	8.00	12.20
1975	-17.22	37.20	37.10	9.20	5.80	7.01
1976	-11.92	23.84	3.74	16.75	5.08	4.81
1977	10.37	-7.18	19.42	-0.69	5.12	6.77
1978	31.61	6.56	34.30	-1.18	7.18	9.03
1979	33.81	18.44	6.18	-1.23	10.38	13.31
1980	11.08	32.42	24.43	-3.95	11.24	12.40
1981	-23.01	-4.91	-1.03	1.86	14.71	8.94
1982	11.56	21.41	-0.86	40.36	10.54	3.87
1983	16.26	22.51	24.61	0.65	8.80	3.80
1984	1.05	6.27	7.86	15.48	9.85	3.95
1985	10.01	32.16	56.72	30.97	7.72	3.77
1986	2.04	18.47	69.94	24.53	6.16	1.13
1987	23.77	5.23	24.93	-2.71	5.47	4.41
1988	27.93	16.81	28.59	9.67	6.35	4.42
1989	38.28	31.49	10.80	18.11	8.37	4.65
1990	29.08	-3.17	-23.19	6.18	7.81	6.11
1991	-6.13	30.55	12.49	19.30	5.60	3.06
1992	4.42	7.67	-11.85	8.05	3.51	2.90
1993	-12.33	9.99	32.94	18.24	2.90	2.75
1994	5.29	1.31	8.06	-7.77	3.90	2.67
1995	20.33	37.43	11.55	31.67	5.60	2.54
1996	33.92	23.07	6.36	-0.93	5.21	3.32
Jan - Feb 1997	-8.26	7.07	-1.87	-0.74	0.84	0.47

Appendix B Decade-By-Decade and Whole Period (January 1970 to February 1997) Summary Statistics of Monthly Return on GSCI Collateralized Futures and Other Principal Asset Classes

		Compound Annual Return (%)	Annualized Arithmetic Mean of Monthly Return (%)	Annualized Standard Deviation of Monthly Return (%)
1970-1979	GSCI	21.25	23.87	26.19
	S&P 500	5.86	7.18	17.07
	EAFE	10.09	11.42	17.43
	Treasury Bonds	5.52	5.87	8.25
	Treasury Bills	6.31	6.31	0.58
	Inflation	7.37	7.38	1.19
1980-1989	GSCI	10.67	11.71	15.30
	S&P 500	17.55	19.13	19.39
	EAFE	22.77	24.61	21.57
	Treasury Bonds	12.62	13.71	16.04
	Treasury Bills	8.89	8.89	0.89
	Inflation	5.09	5.10	1.26
1989-1997 (Feb)	GSCI	7.92	9.22	17.45
	S&P 500	15.14	15.91	13.44
	EAFE	3.44	4.99	18.35
	Treasury Bonds	9.63	10.00	9.05
	Treasury Bills	4.92	4.93	0.46
	Inflation	3.32	3.32	0.72
1970-1997 (Feb)	GSCI	13.69	15.36	20.05
	S&P 500	12.49	13.77	17.13
	EAFE	12.73	14.32	19.24
	Treasury Bonds	9.17	9.80	11.84
	Treasury Bills	6.88	6.88	0.83
	Inflation	5.45	5.46	1.21

15 HEDGING PORTFOLIOS WITH REAL ASSETS

KENNETH A. FROOT
Harvard Business School, Harvard University

Investors are always searching for assets that are negatively correlated with common portfolios of stocks and bonds and that provide reasonable average returns. One broad group of such assets might be termed real assets — assets that are at least partially hedged against inflation, in that they tend to increase in price in response to an inflation shock.

Real assets ought to be valuable for portfolio diversification because widely diversified portfolios of stocks and bonds are strongly negatively correlated with inflation.[1] Thus, real assets are important partly because they might provide a kind of inflation insurance for other assets in the portfolio.

Although this is conventional wisdom, there is surprisingly little evidence on how investors ought to choose among real assets and how effectively different real assets protect financial portfolios.[2] For example, it is often argued that real estate helps protect returns on financial portfolios, but the properties of real estate are rarely compared with those of other real assets, such as commodity-linked equities or CPI-linked bonds. Commodities themselves are also often thought of as potential hedges, yet there is little discussion of whether commodity futures and commodity-linked equities are more appropriate.

This article examines the properties of a variety of asset classes that might broadly be thought of as "real" assets. It looks at how closely correlated these classes are with inflation, as well as how effectively they help insure major financial asset classes against adverse shocks. It also examines how inflation hedges might be combined in a portfolio.

For example, can holdings of real estate fully insure a stock/bond portfolio against inflation and other adverse shocks? Can holdings of commodities do a better job? What combinations of commodities, commodity-based equities, real estate, and CPI-linked bills are best for reducing the risk of equity and bond portfolios? As we will see, the answers to these questions can help guide the use of real assets as hedging vehicles.

We find evidence that oil and production-weighted indexes of commodity futures are the most potent hedges of financial portfolios. Direct investments in real estate are themselves hedged against inflation, but they are generally not good at hedging the rest of a portfolio. Moreover, certain commodity indexes and oil actually appear to be more powerful hedging vehicles than even inflation itself. For example, stocks and bonds respond negatively to commodity price increases even when such shocks are not related to measures of CPI inflation (an example would be the behavior of asset and consumer prices around the Kuwait war).

These results suggest two main conclusions. First, risk-averse investors will wish to bear a positive amount of commodity risk even when commodity futures pay expected returns that are lower than returns of other major asset classes. Indeed, to the extent that producers sell off oil exposures in futures and forward markets, equilibrium reasoning suggests that investors will want to buy those oil exposures as part of their diversified portfolios.

Second, the argument is weak for holding individual commodities, such as gold, or other real assets, such as real estate, on the basis of their hedging properties. A sounder argument would be that gold and real estate provide little hedging potential, but have attractive expected returns.

WHAT ARE REAL ASSETS?

Real assets are those that tend to increase in nominal value in the face of inflation. One easy way to identify such assets is by process of elimination. For example, the nominal payment stream from domestic fixed-income instruments (e.g., bonds) cannot rise with unexpected inflation. It follows that bonds cannot be real assets.

Foreign bonds (both hedged and unhedged against currency fluctuations) are also unlikely to retain their real value when there is domestic inflation. This is because inflation shocks in the major industrialized countries are highly positively correlated with one another.

Assets such as stocks are more complex. On the one hand, diversified stock portfolios are claims against real physical and intangible assets, so it might seem that stock returns ought to be positively related to measures of unexpected inflation. Inflation surprises, however, can be bad news for stocks if they are correlated with adverse "real" shocks, such as declines in factor productivity or usage.

The empirical reality seems to favor the latter explanation: Not only do domestic stocks fail to keep up with inflation at horizons up to one year, but their nominal prices also actually fall when inflation unexpectedly rises. The negative response of domestic stocks to inflation carries over to foreign stocks as well; that is, foreign stock returns (regardless of whether they are hedged against unexpected currency movements) are negatively correlated with U.S. inflation.[3]

Even though broad portfolios of stocks may not behave as real assets, it seems reasonable to think that targeted industry stocks might do better. For example, the stocks of companies that own and/or manage primarily real estate assets might be expected to help hedge against inflation, according to the logic that real estate is itself a real asset. Thus, an investor looking to hedge inflation might consider direct holdings of real estate or the securitized equivalent, Real Estate Investment Trusts (REITs), which trade in the stock market. A second group of stocks that might behave more like real assets are commodity-producing firms, again on the logic that the values of the commodities they produce respond sharply to inflation. Thus, we might expect stocks of real estate-holding and commodity-producing firms to behave like real assets.

Of course, for hedging inflation the best hedge would be a CPI-linked bill or bond. The federal governments of the U.K. and Canada issue such bonds, as do those of a number of developing countries. While no such instrument exists in the U.S., its unexpected returns can be simulated by estimating unexpected U.S. inflation.

That is, unexpected inflation approximates the unexpected return on a zero-coupon CPI-linked instrument, with duration equal to the horizon over which unexpected inflation is measured. We therefore use unexpected inflation as a proxy for the returns on a hypothetical CPI-linked bill. This will give us a benchmark against which to compare the performance of other hedging vehicles.

HEDGING EXPOSURES TO REAL ASSETS

Underlying any discussion of hedging policy is the notion of exposure. The exposure of an asset class to a real asset is the expected percent change in value of the asset per 1%

change in the value of the real asset.[4] For example, if a stock has an exposure of -0.5 to commodity inflation, then an unexpected 1% increase in commodity prices will on average decrease the value of the stock by 0.5%.

Conveniently, exposures are additive: The exposure of a portfolio of assets is just the weighted average of the exposures of the individual portfolio components. Thus, if stocks and bonds have inflation exposures of -0.1 and -0.7, respectively, the inflation exposure of an equally weighted stock/bond portfolio will be -0.4.

How does one optimally hedge a portfolio using real assets? Suppose that an investor holds a preexisting portfolio of risky stocks and/or bonds, and wishes to acquire exposure to real assets. To do so without selling any part of the preexisting portfolio, the investor can sell T-bills to purchase real assets. (A swap or futures contract linked to the real asset accomplishes the same in one step.) The size of the hedge is the amount of exposure to the real asset acquired in this way. The amount of hedge that is optimal will obviously depend on the properties of the fixed, preexisting portfolio.

We can think of the optimal hedge, expressed as a fraction of portfolio value, as having two components.[5] The first is what we might call the target exposure — the level of exposure to a real asset that an investor ultimately wants to have. The second component is the exposure of the initial portfolio, or the preexisting exposure. The hedge is just the difference between the target of preexisting exposures.

Expressed in equations, this can be written:

Optimal Hedge Ratio = Target Exposure - Preexisting Exposure

Standard mean-variance portfolio theory tells us that the target exposure depends on risk tolerance and the Sharpe ratio of an asset:

Target Exposure = Risk Tolerance x Expected Excess Return of Hedge Asset ÷ Variance of Hedge Asset

where the excess return is the return in excess of the riskless rate.

Mean-variance analysis also tells us that preexisting exposure depends on the initial portfolio:

Preexisting Exposure = Exposure of Preexisting Portfolio to Hedge Asset

Notice that target exposure depends only on the investor's risk tolerance and the risk/return ratio of the hedge asset. It has nothing to do with covariances of the hedge asset with other assets. On the other hand, the preexisting exposure has nothing to do with investor preferences or expected returns; it depends only on the covariance of the hedge with assets in the preexisting portfolio and the variance of hedge returns. Transaction costs are ignored here, but can easily be incorporated into the formulas (see Froot and Pérold [1993]).

Such decomposition of the optimal hedge is useful because it separates out the speculative versus diversification motives for exposures to real assets. The risk-tolerant investor takes on hedging positions that are very sensitive to changes in expected returns, and relatively insensitive to preexisting exposures. The investor with little risk tolerance, on the other hand, generally has little desire to hold speculative exposures. Such an investor therefore hedges out the portfolio's preexisting exposure, to arrive at a near-zero target exposure. Since most real assets inherit inflation's negative correlation with broad portfolios, this hedge would imply diversifying — taking a long position to hedge portfolio risk.

EXHIBIT 1 DESCRIPTIVE STATISTICS FOR TOTAL RETURNS ON REAL ASSETS (QUARTERLY DATA 1970-1993)

	Mean (%)	Variance (%)[a]	ρ_1[b]	Number of Observations
unxpi	0.00	0.01	0.12	94
infla	5.75	0.03	0.89	94
gsci	4.86	2.06	0.11	94
crb	3.01	1.09	0.19	94
gold	10.09	5.39	0.22	94
oil	7.35	11.34	0.01	94
cmeq	8.71	1.75	0.22	94
reit	−8.88	8.47	0.24	88
eval	8.44	0.15	0.78	90
cpihouse	5.94	0.05	0.83	94
adj	7.47	1.17	0.60	85

[a]Annualized return variance.
[b]ρ_1 indicates the first-order autocorrelation coefficient.

DATA

We use three broad categories of real asset returns: inflation (in order to approximate the returns on a "real" inflation-linked bond), commodity price changes, and real estate returns. Exhibits 1 and 2 present summary statistics for these data during the entire 1970-1993 and 1983-1993 sample periods.

The specific data for inflation are:

unxpi— unexpected inflation, measured as the unpredictable element of monthly percentage changes in the U.S. consumer price index using past CPI changes and U.S. Treasury bill rates; and

infla— U.S. inflation, measured as the percentage change in the CPI.

Alternative models of unexpected inflation produce very similar results, so are not reported here.

It should be noted that total inflation, *infla*, is perfectly correlated with the return on a CPI-linked bill only if the real interest rate is constant. This is a very restrictive assumption; we nevertheless include *infla* in the results below because the excess return on *infla* — inflation less the T-bill rate — is the most commonly used measure of unexpected inflation.

For commodity-related investments we use several measures (end-of-period prices):

gsci— percentage changes in the Goldman Sachs Commodity Index, a world production-weighted index of liquid exchange-traded commodity spot-market prices. This index is chosen because its weights approximate those of the PPI;[6]

crb— percentage changes in the Commodities Research Bureau Spot Index, an equally weighted average of the spot prices of traded commodities;

gold— percentage changes in the spot price of gold; and

oil— percentage changes in the spot price of crude oil (near-end-of-month prices from wellhead transactions in Brent crude).

EXHIBIT 2 DESCRIPTIVE STATISTICS FOR TOTAL RETURNS ON REAL ASSETS (QUARTERLY DATA 1983-1993)

	Mean (%)	Variance (%)[a]	ρ_1[b]	Number of Observations
unxpi	0.00	0.00	–0.17	42
infla	3.76	0.01	0.80	42
gsci: spot	–2.92	2.93	–0.19	42
gsci: futures	12.09	3.35	–0.13	42
crb: spot	0.24	0.76	0.03	42
crb: futures	5.10	0.90	–0.29	28
gold: spot	–1.53	1.77	–0.14	42
gold: futures	–1.90	1.76	–0.07	42
oil: spot	–5.04	15.56	–0.20	42
oil: futures	9.85	22.12	–0.18	41
cmeq	14.00	1.36	0.20	42
reit	–8.29	3.38	0.11	36
eval	5.19	0.17	0.71	42
cpihouse	3.53	0.00	0.93	42
adj	0.68	1.04	0.55	42

[a]Annualized return variance.
[b]ρ_1 indicates the first-order autocorrelation coefficient.

The commodity prices are measured using spot (rather than rolled futures) prices. Investments in spot inventories are somewhat impractical, though, so most investors prefer to use futures markets to gain commodity exposure. Because futures markets were not functioning for several of these commodities over the entire sample period — most notably, oil futures were not very actively traded until 1983 — we use spot prices in much of the analysis instead.

It is worth noting that substituting spot for futures return data is not completely innocuous. Spot returns differ from those of collateralized futures. (To see the empirical importance of this difference, compare the total returns on spot and futures investments reported in Exhibit 2; also see Exhibit 11 below.)

Specifically, the return on the collateralized futures position is equal to the spot return plus two additional components: the short-term interest rate (from the financial collateral) plus the futures' roll yield. This sum is positive when futures prices fall below carry-adjusted spot prices. In such a case, "rolling" — i.e., following a strategy of buying the future, selling it as it approaches maturity, and then purchasing a new longer-dated future — generates a positive "roll" yield.

For some commodities, such as gold, the sum of the interest rate and roll yield approximately net out, so that the return from buying and rolling (collateralized) gold futures is about equal to the return on holding inventories of gold. For other commodities, however — particularly oil — the interest rate plus roll yield has been considerably greater than zero.

Exhibit 3 presents data on the Treasury bill rate plus the roll yield for most major liquid commodities over the 1970-1993 period. It demonstrates that, historically, the return differential between collateralized futures and spot investments is positive and large: Across individual commodities, collateralized futures have outperformed spot investments by an average of 6.30% per year.

For crude oil, the corresponding number (calculated from 1983 to 1993) is 13.57%. Because the estimates below use spot returns, they ignore this return increment. Wherever this component may have an impact on the results, we provide commentary and additional estimates for the shorter period over which futures returns are available.

The last commodity-related investment alternative is to buy the equity of commodity-producing companies. To analyze the properties of this alternative we include the series:

> *cmeq*— return on an index of primarily commodity-producing companies' stocks. The index is composed of S&P sector-specific stock return indexes for: oil, aluminum, steel, miscellaneous metals, and foods. These sectors are then combined into a single index, using approximate relative GNP weights of the commodities they are intended to represent: 0.5, 0.03, 0.03, 0.03, and 0.4, respectively.

Measuring the returns on real estate investments is, of course, even more problematic than for commodities. First, real estate is a diverse class of assets, including commercial, residential, industrial, and retail investments, each driven in part by geographic factors.

Second, as is well known, most indexes of real estate returns are of poor quality, in the sense that they do not accurately measure actual holding-period returns. Real estate properties trade infrequently, so most indexes estimate value using appraisals or other estimates in lieu of transaction prices. Because appraisals are conducted infrequently, and because even a current appraisal may not incorporate all recent market developments, appraisal-based indexes include predominantly "stale" prices. Staleness tends to

EXHIBIT 3 SUM OF ROLL AND T-BILL YIELD

Date	Crude	Heating	Gasoline	Cattle	Hogs	Wheat	Corn	Soy	Coffee	Cocoa	Cotton	Sugar	Gold	Silver	Platinum	Copper
1970	N/A	N/A	N/A	8.50	26.84	8.4%	4.79	4.81	N/A	0.40	−4.04	9.43	N/A	−4.49	−0.73	9.33
1971	N/A	N/A	N/A	18.85	−9.67	10.28	1.12	2.03	N/A	1.59	−8.21	0.72	N/A	−3.54	0.95	−0.23
1972	N/A	N/A	N/A	5.11	1.97	13.32	−6.10	7.88	N/A	−2.34	33.95	−5.64	N/A	−2.30	−0.09	−3.78
1973	N/A	N/A	N/A	−6.96	14.58	26.69	27.60	67.69	−8.27	41.14	19.05	20.36	N/A	−0.33	−4.16	25.44
1974	N/A	N/A	N/A	−5.54	−10.90	11.83	11.95	7.00	3.12	53.83	16.63	65.09	N/A	−1.44	−3.25	18.09
1975	N/A	N/A	N/A	28.63	16.84	1.85	11.32	3.26	4.04	37.68	−4.69	18.99	−1.02	−3.69	−2.22	−5.68
1976	N/A	N/A	N/A	−9.52	39.30	−8.81	6.06	−2.36	15.25	32.84	2.27	−14.30	0.18	−0.52	−1.85	−3.51
1977	N/A	N/A	N/A	12.41	24.80	−10.74	−8.27	24.18	40.22	42.06	8.25	−18.38	0.53	−1.32	−1.17	−4.08
1978	N/A	N/A	N/A	2.48	17.68	4.84	−1.48	10.37	45.87	25.01	−5.96	−14.51	−1.22	−1.13	3.15	−3.59
1979	N/A	1.78	N/A	5.46	18.17	13.53	−1.49	3.82	20.77	−1.32	1.73	−14.44	−0.82	0.82	10.12	5.32
1980	N/A	−11.44	N/A	2.93	−9.67	−3.48	−5.46	−6.53	−3.09	5.32	15.30	−1.81	−3.52	−1.60	−0.39	2.80
1981	N/A	3.29	N/A	16.12	−3.67	−4.58	−1.16	0.60	20.32	−4.17	14.96	7.98	−0.54	−2.22	0.59	−2.28
1982	N/A	26.53	N/A	25.66	7.84	−9.21	−5.07	0.88	40.02	−7.13	−5.79	−15.57	−2.92	−1.44	1.91	−2.02
1983	N/A	11.94	N/A	14.00	18.18	−7.15	7.14	−2.36	15.15	0.87	2.79	−14.11	0.87	−1.16	3.44	−2.69
1984	10.29	21.75	N/A	13.93	−6.52	5.87	19.41	15.26	23.06	10.87	17.76	−30.81	−0.86	−1.04	0.41	−1.90
1985	30.77	19.05	37.40	0.61	0.75	10.92	8.81	1.57	7.30	10.67	8.21	−19.99	−0.07	−0.38	3.16	0.85
1986	9.85	18.81	18.10	23.09	28.08	40.17	16.62	5.56	0.30	−7.73	71.74	−20.44	0.42	−0.73	3.55	2.17
1987	17.95	5.83	2.81	20.30	44.35	6.89	−8.21	2.51	−5.75	−3.19	11.68	−18.21	−0.72	−1.44	1.20	13.66
1988	10.37	17.40	39.72	9.96	−3.90	−4.04	−7.71	−0.44	0.82	2.95	15.68	9.72	0.18	−1.58	4.80	49.29
1989	39.77	25.65	30.78	11.50	5.44	8.10	12.77	13.92	14.51	10.23	1.45	13.95	1.38	−1.36	6.39	−49.78
1990	−0.65	25.96	29.26	20.32	23.74	2.50	3.98	−4.07	−6.31	−3.16	21.03	8.88	0.43	−1.40	3.23	29.78
1991	18.55	16.68	28.37	3.32	19.11	−7.39	−5.37	−4.24	−10.98	−13.23	17.39	19.64	0.31	−1.35	1.26	12.19
1992	2.20	−5.87	−1.10	16.97	14.41	9.64	−8.38	−3.17	−14.67	−19.28	−6.65	14.23	0.19	−0.76	4.24	3.52
1993	−0.40	0.39	−8.35	13.75	10.93	19.44	−6.24	0.90	−13.61	−8.31	2.51	−9.07	−0.32	−0.22	2.46	−0.14
Average	13.57	11.85	19.67	10.50	12.15	5.79	2.78	6.21	8.96	8.57	10.29	0.03	−0.40	−1.44	1.55	3.87
Standard Deviation	12.96	11.71	16.70	9.97	14.87	11.91	9.79	14.55	17.51	19.22	16.68	20.60	1.18	1.14	3.12	17.07
T-Bill Average	6.32	7.99	5.93	7.25	7.25	7.25	7.25	7.25	7.57	7.25	7.25	7.25	7.50	7.25	7.25	7.25
Roll Yield Average	7.25	3.86	13.74	3.24	4.90	−1.46	−4.48	−1.04	1.39	1.32	3.04	−7.22	−7.96	−8.69	−5.71	−3.39

make return data appear "smoothed" and of low volatility. One implication is that only a small component of each period's index return is related to current changes in the properties' market value — much of the "news" in the current index return is the predictable result of past changes in market conditions.[7]

Fortunately, there are several ways of eliminating or mitigating these data problems. One way is to use statistical procedures that intend to isolate the portion of appraisal-based returns that is related to contemporaneous changes in market prices, although there is no guarantee that these methods produce accurate measures of true holding-period returns, particularly in samples limited to post-war data (see Ankrim and Hensel [1992]).

A second way to mitigate these data problems is to avoid appraisal-based series altogether. One can, for example, assume the return on real estate properties is equal to the return on the stocks of companies that hold primarily real estate assets, such as REITs. The quality of these returns is much higher, as they are based on actual transaction prices.

Yet an investment in the stock of a REIT is not exactly the same as an outright purchase of real estate: REITs are managed by someone else, and often use a large amount of debt finance (on average over 50%). High levels of debt finance imply that, even if the value of the properties remains constant, the REIT stock price can change with changes in the value of the debt (due, say, to interest rate movements). Nevertheless, a large component of REIT returns will still reflect real estate itself.[8]

Our strategy is to use both original and statistically adjusted appraisal-based series, as well as an index of REIT returns. The specific series are:

reit — the S&P subindex of REIT stock returns.

eval — quarterly appraisal-based return index from Evaluation Associates, Inc. (a real estate analysis group located in Westport, Connecticut). These returns are on a diversified portfolio of open-ended real estate equity funds, and run from the second quarter of 1970 to the second quarter of 1993.[9]

house — monthly survey series of the value of residential properties, conducted by the U.S. Bureau of Labor Statistics.

adj — an equally weighted average of the statistically adjusted versions of eval and house. Adjustments to remove the effects of "staleness" are made using a method similar to that in Ross and Zisler [1991]. To make these adjustments, we first specify an ad hoc model of the predictable component of index returns.

For both *eval* and *house* simple univariate autoregressive specifications are estimated:

eval: $$r_{i,t} = \alpha + \underset{(2.8)}{0.22}\, r_{i,t-1} + \underset{(8.2)}{0.69}\, r_{i,t-4} + \varepsilon_t;$$

$R^2 = 0.63$; DW = 1.97;

housel: $$r_{i,t} = \alpha + \underset{(3.6)}{0.37}\, r_{i,t-1} + \underset{(2.9)}{0.30}\, r_{i,t-4} + \varepsilon_t;$$

$R^2 = 0.34$; DW = 1.88;

where $r_{i,t}$ is the time t return on index i, and t-statistics are in parentheses. The residual, ε_t, is proportional to the adjusted return, with a coefficient of proportionality derived using Ross and Zisler [1991]. This adjustment process increases the return variance of the unadjusted series by a factor of about 10.

MEASURING PREEXISTING EXPOSURES OF STANDARD PORTFOLIOS

Measuring the preexisting exposures of portfolios to real assets is straightforward. Exposure is equal to the coefficient in a regression of the portfolio excess return on the excess return of the real asset:

$$r_{p,t} = \alpha + \beta r_{ra,t} + \varepsilon_t$$

where $r_{p,t}$ is the time t excess return on some preexisting portfolio, β is the negative of the preexisting exposure of the portfolio, and $r_{ra,t}$ is the excess return on the real asset hedge.

To see this, suppose that for a given real asset, say, gold, we measure a regression β of -0.5. That implies that a 1% up-move in the price of gold is on average associated with a 0.5% decline in the value of the preexisting portfolio. If the value of the preexisting portfolio is, say, $100 million, then this level of exposure implies that the portfolio has an exposure to gold of -0.5 x $100 = -$50 million. To offset this exposure, one would need to go long the equivalent of $50 million of gold.

The coefficient β is also equal to the minimum-variance hedge ratio, i.e., the hedge ratio that strips out the real assets' risks, and therefore minimizes total portfolio volatility. The amount by which the portfolio's risk falls is just the R^2 from the regression. We can also use the regression framework to test whether the exposure, β, is statistically significant.

EXHIBIT 4 EXPOSURES OF PRE-EXISTING PORTFOLIOS TO REAL ASSET RETURNS (QUARTERLY RETURNS 1973:1-1993:2)

Exposures Portfolio					Real Assets					
	unxpi	*infla*	*gsci*	*crb*	*gold*	*oil*	*cmeq*	*reit*	*eval*	*adj*
Domestic Stocks	**−2.54**	−1.98	**−0.32**	−0.24	−0.04	**−0.14**	1.09	0.35	−0.15	−0.27
Domestic Bonds	**−2.52**	**−2.64**	**−0.30**	**−0.42**	−0.03	**−0.09**	0.21	0.09	−0.25	−0.19
Foreign Stocks	**−3.61**	−1.99	**−0.32**	−0.08	0.14	**−0.17**	0.88	0.32	1.14	−0.02
Foreign Bonds	**−1.41**	**−0.70**	**−0.11**	**−0.09**	−0.02	**−0.04**	0.08	0.03	−0.21	**−0.11**
Currencies	**−5.33**	1.73	−0.09	0.08	0.21	−0.03	0.24	−0.05	**−1.75**	−0.30
Diversified Portfolio	**−2.79**	**−2.07**	**−0.30**	−0.24	0.01	**−0.12**	0.78	0.26	0.07	−0.22

T-Statistics Portfolio					Real Assets					
	unxpi	*infla*	*gsci*	*crb*	*gold*	*oil*	*cmeq*	*reit*	*eval*	*adj*
Domestic Stocks	**−2.68**	−1.84	**−2.63**	−1.44	−0.51	**−2.65**	15.09	6.37	−0.28	−1.60
Domestic Bonds	**−3.88**	**−3.63**	**−3.63**	**−3.84**	−0.59	**−2.35**	2.27	1.92	−0.64	−1.47
Foreign Stocks	**−3.65**	−1.74	**−2.49**	−0.44	1.73	**−3.26**	8.12	5.56	2.05	−0.08
Foreign Bonds	**−7.06**	**−2.66**	**−3.71**	**−2.12**	−0.88	**−2.83**	2.37	1.95	−1.55	**−2.38**
Currencies	**−5.78**	1.46	−0.67	0.43	2.53	−0.49	1.67	−0.70	**−3.08**	−1.54
Diversified Portfolio	**−3.92**	**−2.54**	**−3.32**	−1.91	0.10	**−3.22**	12.68	6.25	0.16	−1.63

R^2s Portfolio					Real Assets					
	unxpi	*infla*	*gsci*	*crb*	*gold*	*oil*	*cmeq*	*reit*	*eval*	*adj*
Domestic Stocks	**0.07**	0.04	**0.07**	0.02	0.00	**0.07**	0.71	0.32	0.00	0.03
Domestic Bonds	**0.14**	**0.13**	**0.13**	**0.14**	0.00	**0.06**	0.05	0.04	0.00	0.03
Foreign Stocks	**0.13**	0.03	**0.06**	0.00	0.03	**0.11**	0.42	0.26	0.05	0.00
Foreign Bonds	**0.36**	**0.07**	**0.13**	**0.05**	0.01	**0.08**	0.06	0.04	0.03	**0.07**
Currencies	**0.27**	0.02	0.00	0.00	0.07	0.00	0.03	0.01	**0.10**	0.03
Diversified Portfolio	**0.15**	**0.07**	**0.11**	0.04	0.00	**0.10**	0.54	0.31	0.00	0.03

It should be noted that standard portfolio theory provides no explicit means of incorporating uncertainty about exposures and correlations. If an exposure estimate is statistically insignificant, it is an indication only that the data cannot rule out a zero correlation, not a statement that a zero correlation is likely. Such statistical testing, however, is a way of asking the data to convince us that certain hedging properties do actually exist. Thus, a lack of statistical significance provides evidence consistent with those who argue that the true correlation is zero.

The top panel of Exhibit 4 reports estimates of the exposures of major asset classes to real asset returns on a quarterly basis from 1970 through 1993. (Annual return horizons were also estimated, and yield broadly similar results. Monthly return horizons yield slightly lower exposures, but similar qualitative results otherwise.)

The middle panel reports t-statistics of the coefficients. The bottom panel contains the associated R^2 values. Boldfacing indicates the coefficient estimates are statistically negative — i.e., that purchases of the real asset help reduce the volatility of the preexisting portfolio. Each column in the Exhibit corresponds to a particular real asset hedge, and each row corresponds to a particular preexisting portfolio.

The "preexisting portfolios" are: domestic stocks (measured by the returns on the S&P 500 from Ibbotson Associates); domestic bonds (measured by the Ibbotson series for total returns on medium-term U.S. government bonds); foreign stock returns (measured by the dollar return of the currency-unhedged EAFE index); foreign bond returns (measured as the average of dollar returns on medium-term currency-hedged government bonds in Japan, Germany, France, the U.K., Switzerland, and Canada); returns on currency hedges (measured as the dollar return of short-term currency forward contracts on the Canadian dollar, French franc, deutschemark, Japanese yen, and British pound); the returns on real estate portfolios (measured by the three real estate series mentioned above: *reit, eval,* and *adj*); and the returns on a broadly diversified portfolio (a 70/30 portfolio of stocks and government bonds, and a domestic/foreign mix of 75/25 in both stocks and bonds).

There are a number of noteworthy points to emerge from Exhibit 4. First, long positions in most of the real assets help hedge the diversified portfolios. The last line of the Exhibit shows a negative exposure of the diversified portfolio to most real assets. (A negative exposure to a real asset implies that a long position is needed to offset that exposure. In this sense, long positions in real assets are "hedges.")

The exceptions are two of the real estate series, *reit* and *eval,* and the commodity-based equities series, *cmeq*. Indeed, the portfolio exposures to *reit* and *cmeq* are highly statistically positive in both the quarterly and annual return data, suggesting that long positions in these assets actually *add* to portfolio risk, rather than reduce it. In fact, most equity and bond investments show positive exposures that are similar to those of *reit* and *cmeq*.

In this sense, these investments — which are both traded on stock exchanges — appear to trade more like stocks than they do like real assets. (The resemblance of REIT returns to those of stocks has been noted by Gyourko and Keim [1992] among others.)

It is not clear how to interpret these positive exposure estimates, particularly the estimate for the exchange-traded real estate series, *reit*. Some observers have argued that returns of exchange-traded real estate are "excessively" correlated with other stocks, the result of noise traders who drive all stock exchange prices temporarily up and down relative to true value. The underlying true values, the argument goes, are much less positively (and probably negatively) correlated.

A second explanation of the positive correlations is that *true* underlying stock market and real estate values are, in fact, highly positively related in the first place. The reasoning here is that very similar factors — e.g., domestic productivity of capital and labor — ought to drive both stock prices and real estate values, and that, in any case, approximately 25% of the corporate assets are real estate in the first place. This alternative argument supports the view that REIT values are reasonably accurate measures of underlying real estate values.

This brings us to the second point to emerge from Exhibit 4: There is only weak evidence at best that real estate is a useful hedging tool. REITs do not appear to be candidates for hedges, and both the unadjusted and adjusted appraisal-based series, *eval* and *adj*, show statistically insignificant hedging properties in diversified portfolios.

It should be noted that other authors have, in contrast, concluded that real estate can help hedge broad portfolios — particularly those of domestic bonds.[10] Like these other studies, our data also provide evidence that real estate returns are positively correlated with both inflation and unexpected inflation. (For example, the exposure of *adj* to inflation is the highest among all three real estate series, at a statistically significant 2.08; the *reit* series is, like other stocks, negatively exposed to inflation.)

Nevertheless, in our data the exposures of stocks to *eval* and *adj* are not sufficiently negative to provide much evidence of hedging potential in diversified portfolios. Indeed, when these near-zero exposures are combined with the evidence from the *reit*

EXHIBIT 5 EXPOSURES OF PRE-EXISTING PORTFOLIOS TO REAL ASSET RETURNS (QUARTERLY RETURNS 1983:1-1993:2, USING ROLLED FUTURES FOR COMMODITY RETURNS)

Exposures Portfolio	Real Assets									
	unxpi	*infla*	*gsci*	*crb*	*gold*	*oil*	*cmeq*	*reit*	*eval*	*adj*
Domestic Stocks	−0.89	−1.25	**−0.25**	−0.34	**−0.34**	**−0.11**	1.00	0.26	−0.37	−0.24
Domestic Bonds	**−2.56**	**−2.81**	**−0.25**	−0.23	−0.07	**−0.11**	0.03	0.02	−0.38	−0.11
Foreign Stocks	−2.70	−4.39	0.07	0.18	0.20	−0.08	0.95	0.38	1.32	0.12
Foreign Bonds	**−1.77**	−0.80	**−0.09**	**−0.15**	−0.01	**−0.04**	0.05	0.00	−0.27	−0.07
Currencies	**−7.57**	3.53	0.06	−0.23	0.65	0.01	−0.20	**−0.40**	**−2.37**	−0.52
Diversified Portfolio	−1.86	−2.46	**−0.21**	−0.23	−0.15	**−0.10**	0.70	0.19	−0.09	−0.21

T-Statistics Portfolio	Real Assets									
	unxpi	*infla*	*gsci*	*crb*	*gold*	*oil*	*cmeq*	*reit*	*eval*	*adj*
Domestic Stocks	−0.49	−0.64	**−2.01**	−1.06	**−2.03**	**−2.21**	7.44	1.80	−0.57	−1.04
Domestic Bonds	**−2.07**	**−2.08**	**−2.89**	−1.31	−0.59	**−3.23**	0.23	0.23	−0.81	−0.67
Foreign Stocks	−1.25	−1.91	−0.44	0.49	0.96	−1.39	5.10	2.56	1.84	0.40
Foreign Bonds	**−3.88**	−1.39	**−2.43**	**−2.04**	−0.23	**−2.32**	0.82	0.08	−1.48	−1.03
Currencies	**−4.09**	1.51	0.41	−0.62	3.41	0.18	−0.79	**−2.68**	**−3.38**	−1.90
Diversified Portfolio	−1.34	−1.64	**−2.21**	−1.02	−1.09	**−2.72**	6.65	1.83	−0.19	−1.10

R^2s Portfolio	Real Assets									
	unxpi	*infla*	*gsci*	*crb*	*gold*	*oil*	*cmeq*	*reit*	*eval*	*adj*
Domestic Stocks	0.01	0.01	**0.09**	0.04	**0.09**	**0.11**	0.58	0.09	0.01	0.03
Domestic Bonds	**0.10**	**0.10**	**0.17**	0.06	0.01	**0.21**	0.00	0.00	0.02	0.01
Foreign Stocks	0.04	0.09	0.01	0.01	0.02	0.05	0.41	0.16	0.08	0.00
Foreign Bonds	**0.28**	0.05	**0.13**	**0.10**	0.00	**0.12**	0.02	0.00	0.05	0.03
Currencies	**0.29**	0.05	0.00	0.01	0.22	0.00	0.02	**0.17**	**0.22**	0.08
Diversified Portfolio	0.05	0.07	**0.11**	0.04	0.03	**0.17**	0.54	0.09	0.00	0.03

Boldface numbers represent statistically significant negative exposures at the 5% level.

EXHIBIT 6 EXPOSURES OF PRE-EXISTING PORTFOLIOS TO REAL ASSET RETURNS (ANNUAL RETURNS 1947-1992)

Exposures Portfolio	Real Assets				
	unxpi	*infla*	*gsci*	*crb*	*gold*
Domestic Stocks	**−1.11**	**−1.41**	**−0.38**	−0.15	−0.13
Domestic Bonds	0.02	−0.49	**−0.28**	**−0.20**	−0.11
Diversified Portfolio*	**−0.77**	**−1.14**	**−0.35**	−0.16	−0.12

T-Statistics Portfolio	Real Assets				
	unxpi	*infla*	*gsci*	*crb*	*gold*
Domestic Stocks	**−2.30**	**−2.11**	**−2.51**	−0.87	−1.12
Domestic Bonds	0.08	−1.28	**−3.51**	**−2.22**	−1.90
Diversified Portfolio*	**−2.10**	**−2.27**	**−3.18**	−1.29	−1.47

R^2s Portfolio	Real Assets				
	unxpi	*infla*	*gsci*	*crb*	*gold*
Domestic Stocks	**0.11**	**0.09**	**0.12**	0.02	0.03
Domestic Bonds	0.06	0.04	**0.22**	**0.10**	0.08
Diversified Portfolio*	**0.09**	**0.10**	**0.19**	0.04	0.05

*This is a 70/30 weighted portfolio of domestic stocks (S&P 500) and domestic bonds (U.S. government bonds).

Boldface numbers represent statistically significant negative exposures at the 5% level.

data, it appears that real estate is at best marginally helpful in hedging diversified portfolios, even though real estate itself may be adequately hedged against inflation.

The third point to take from Exhibit 4 is that the most effective hedges (in terms of statistically significant negative exposures and high R^2 values) are unexpected inflation, GSCI returns, and oil price changes. Gold and the CRB index are not themselves good hedges — both are negatively correlated with the returns on diversified portfolios, but have low and statistically insignificant R^2 values.

The negative exposures of diversified portfolios to *unxpi, gsci,* and *oil* are fairly evenly distributed across stocks and bonds, both domestic and foreign (see Exhibit 4, columns 1, 3, and 9, and rows 1 through 4). Note that the exposure of the diversified portfolio to unexpected inflation is particularly large in magnitude (at approximately -2.8; see line 6, column 1 in the top panel). This implies that the minimum-variance hedge ratio requires a long CPI-linked bond position equal to almost three times the value of the preexisting portfolio. The exposures of the broad portfolio to the GSCI and oil are much more modest, at about -0.30 and -0.12, respectively.

Exhibit 5 reports an analogous set of estimates, but with only the most recent ten years of data. Besides singling out more recent data, the late starting date permits the use of futures commodity data. This comparison gives us a sense of the reliability of the spot commodity correlations in the longer time series samples above.

The estimates show that there is, in fact, little difference in the hedging properties of spot versus futures positions in commodities. GSCI and oil futures appear to offer hedging properties that are as effective as those of comparable spot investments.[11]

Perhaps the most striking result in Exhibit 5 is the effectiveness of the GSCI and oil hedges in comparison with other, non-commodity hedging vehicles. In particular, it appears that unexpected inflation has become a much less effective hedge during the recent period — the magnitude and statistical significance of portfolio exposures to both *unxpi* and *infla* have declined substantially.

At the same time, the R^2s of the GSCI and oil appear to have increased during the recent period. This suggests that during periods of relatively low inflation, broad portfolios are less exposed to inflation risk, but remain highly exposed to commodity price risks.

EXHIBIT 7 CO-EXPOSURES OF PRE-EXISTING PORTFOLIOS TO REAL ASSET RETURNS (QUARTERLY RETURNS 1970-1993)

Initial Hedge Regressions of $r_{p,t} = \alpha_1 + \beta_1 r_{ra1,t} + \varepsilon_{t1}$;

Secondary Hedge Regressions of $\varepsilon_{t1} = \alpha_2 + \beta_{1,2} r_{ra2,t} + \varepsilon_{t2}$

Exposures to Secondary Hedge $\beta_{1,2}$

Initial Hedge	Secondary Hedge									
	unxpi	*infla*	*gsci*	*crb*	*gold*	*oil*	*cmeq*	*reit*	*eval*	*adj*
unxpi		**−1.57**	**−0.22**	**0.31**	−0.01	**−0.09**	0.72	0.23	0.38	−0.12
infla	**−2.48**		−0.17	−0.14	0.06	**−0.09**	0.77	0.23	0.06	−0.12
gsci	**−2.25**	−0.64		−0.04	0.06	−0.02	0.77	0.23	0.23	−0.12
crb	**−3.00**	**−1.59**	**−0.21**		0.04	**−0.11**	0.78	0.26	0.18	−0.17
gold	**−2.78**	**−2.10**	**−0.31**	−0.24		**−0.13**	0.78	0.26	0.06	−0.23
oil	**−2.29**	−1.17	−0.06	−0.18	0.03		0.77	0.24	0.20	−0.12
cmeq	**−1.76**	**−1.78**	**−0.28**	**−0.21**	−0.02	**−0.11**		0.05	0.07	−0.15
reit	**−2.34**	−0.92	**−0.20**	**−0.23**	0.01	**−0.09**	0.47		−0.53	**−0.32**
eval	**−2.79**	**−2.00**	**−0.31**	**−0.25**	0.00	**−0.13**	0.77	0.24		−0.24
adj	**−2.53**	**−1.59**	**−0.29**	−0.22	0.02	**−0.11**	0.76	0.26	0.45	

T–Statistics of Secondary Hedge

Initial Hedge	Secondary Hedge									
	unxpi	*infla*	*gsci*	*crb*	*gold*	*oil*	*cmeq*	*reit*	*eval*	*adj*
unxpi		**−2.07**	**−2.61**	**−2.68**	−0.11	**−2.56**	12.38	5.97	1.04	−0.97
infla	**−3.57**		−1.90	−1.16	1.12	**−2.34**	13.43	5.51	0.15	−0.88
gsci	**−3.28**	−0.81		−0.37	1.12	−0.56	14.54	5.69	0.59	−0.91
crb	**−4.37**	**−1.96**	**−2.34**		0.71	**−2.95**	13.14	6.39	0.46	−1.24
gold	**−3.91**	**−2.59**	**−3.35**	−1.94		**−3.24**	12.65	6.26	0.15	−1.65
oil	**−3.34**	−1.48	−0.70	−1.49	0.53		14.01	5.95	0.53	−0.92
cmeq	**−4.18**	**−3.80**	**−5.62**	**−2.86**	−0.67	**−5.02**		1.68	0.29	−1.83
reit	**−3.71**	−1.31	**−2.53**	**−2.16**	−0.13	**−2.79**	6.66		−1.43	**−2.77**
eval	**−4.02**	**−2.50**	**−3.51**	**−2.00**	0.04	**−3.40**	11.88	5.65		−1.74
adj	**−3.42**	**−1.95**	**−3.15**	−1.76	0.27	**−2.89**	11.79	6.06	1.08	

R^2s of Secondary Hedge

Initial Hedge	Secondary Hedge									
	unxpi	*infla*	*gsci*	*crb*	*gold*	*oil*	*cmeq*	*reit*	*eval*	*adj*
unxpi		**0.05**	**0.07**	**0.07**	0.00	**0.07**	0.63	0.29	0.01	0.01
infla	**0.12**		0.04	0.01	0.01	**0.06**	0.67	0.26	0.00	0.01
gsci	**0.11**	0.01		0.00	0.01	0.00	0.70	0.27	0.00	0.01
crb	**0.18**	**0.04**	**0.06**		0.01	**0.09**	0.66	0.32	0.00	0.02
gold	**0.15**	**0.07**	**0.11**	0.04		**0.10**	0.64	0.31	0.00	0.03
oil	**0.11**	0.02	0.01	0.02	0.00		0.69	0.29	0.00	0.01
cmeq	**0.16**	**0.14**	**0.26**	**0.08**	0.00	**0.22**		0.03	0.00	0.04
reit	**0.14**	0.02	**0.07**	**0.05**	0.00	**0.08**	0.34		0.02	**0.09**
eval	**0.16**	0.07	**0.13**	**0.04**	0.00	**0.12**	0.52	0.28		0.04
adj	**0.13**	**0.04**	**0.11**	0.04	0.00	**0.09**	0.53	0.32	0.01	

Boldface numbers represent statistically significant negative exposures at the 5% level.

The same finding — that commodity prices can be better hedges than unexpected inflation — also emerges from much longer time series data. Using annual returns from 1947 through 1992, Exhibit 6 shows that the preexisting exposure of a U.S. domestic stock/bond portfolio to the GSCI is -0.35, with an R^2 of 0.19. By comparison, the exposure to unexpected inflation is -0.77 (with an R^2 of only 0.09), and the exposure to inflation itself is -1.14 (with an R^2 of 0.10).

Like the previous two exhibits, the results of Exhibit 6 suggest that almost any combination of commodities does at least reasonably well in protecting bond portfolios against inflation. Oil, however (with or without other energy prices), is needed to hedge stock portfolios effectively.

Is it possible that commodities futures positions can reduce as much or even more risk than unexpected inflation hedges? The answer is yes, especially if stocks respond negatively to commodity price movements when inflation remains unchanged. That is, if the relative price of industrial inputs to outputs is more important to businesses than overall inflation, then commodity inflation will be more effective than CPI inflation for hedging stocks. Indeed, it is even plausible that the well-known negative correlation between stock prices and inflation is actually driven by changes in relative input prices, which, after all, are highly correlated with inflation.[12]

An alternative explanation for these results is that they understate actual exposures to unexpected inflation. This can occur because unexpected inflation is unobservable, so that *unxpi* is likely to measure it with error.

At the same time, there is evidence that measurement error is not a serious problem. First, we estimated a number of different models for unexpected inflation, all of which yielded results similar to those reported. Second, actively traded CPI-linked bonds exist in several countries, such as Canada and the U.K. Wadhwani and Shah [1993] find that the GSCI index appears to be a better hedge for U.K. portfolios than are British long-maturity CPI-linked bonds.

COMPARING AND COMBINING REAL ASSET HEDGES

It would be rare for a portfolio manager to rely on a single real asset to hedge a portfolio of bonds and stocks. If real asset returns were uncorrelated with one another, then exposures to each could be adjusted separately, and one could rely on the regressions for guidance on the efficacy of each hedge. Most real asset returns are positively correlated, however, creating more of an either/or decision when choosing hedges. We need to examine how real hedges interact with one another, in order to understand better how they might be combined.

The method we use is just an extension of the exposure measurement above. Now we want to measure the exposures of a preexisting portfolio to combinations of real asset hedges. To do this, we first implement the minimum-variance hedge for each of the real assets individually. Then we ask whether other real assets can provide evidence of further hedging the portfolio.

This involves regressing the diversified portfolio's return, $r_{p,t}$, on one of the real asset returns, $r_{ra1,t}$, taking the residuals, ε_{t1}, and then regressing them on other real asset returns, $r_{ra2,t}$:

Initial Hedge Regression: $$r_{p,t} = \alpha_1 + \beta_1 r_{ra1,t} + \varepsilon_{t1};$$

Secondary Hedge Regression: $$\varepsilon_{t1} = \alpha_{1,2} + \beta_{1,2} r_{ra2,t}, + \varepsilon_{t2}$$

The resulting secondary exposure, $\beta_{1,2}$, applies to the preexisting portfolio inclusive of the initial hedge's returns. The statistical significance of $\beta_{1,2}$ reveals whether the secondary minimum-variance hedge reduces portfolio variance.[13] The coefficient of determination of the secondary regression, ρ^2, indicates the amount of portfolio variance reduction offered by the secondary hedge.

In this setup, the most potent hedges will exhibit two properties. First, they should still be useful for reducing portfolio volatility even after a minimum-variance hedge in another real asset has been executed; and second, once a minimum-variance hedge in a

EXHIBIT 8 CO-EXPOSURES OF PRE-EXISTING PORTFOLIOS TO REAL ASSET RETURNS (QUARTERLY RETURNS 1983-1993)

Initial Hedge Regressions of $r_{p,t} = \alpha_1 + \beta_1 r_{ra1,t} + \varepsilon_{t1}$;

Secondary Hedge Regressions of $\varepsilon_{t1} = \alpha_2 + \beta_{1,2} r_{ra2,t} + \varepsilon_{t2}$

Exposures to Secondary Hedge $\beta_{1,2}$

Initial Hedge	Secondary Hedge									
	unxpi	*infla*	*gsci*	*crb*	*gold*	*oil*	*cmeq*	*reit*	*eval*	*adj*
unxpi		−2.44	−0.17	−0.23	−0.18	**−0.08**	0.73	0.18	0.17	−0.16
infla	−1.84		−0.15	−0.20	−0.11	**−0.07**	0.71	0.17	−0.27	−0.19
gsci	−1.00	−1.35		−0.08	−0.02	−0.03	0.76	0.18	0.07	−0.14
crb	−1.53	−2.27	−0.12		−0.19	−0.07	0.65	0.13	−0.30	−0.19
gold	−2.11	−2.16	−0.16	−0.17		**−0.08**	0.71	0.16	−0.13	−0.24
oil	−0.59	−0.87	0.00	−0.16	−0.01		0.75	0.16	−0.01	−0.15
cmeq	**−2.58**	**−2.64**	**−0.28**	−0.23	−0.16	**−0.12**		−0.01	−0.39	−0.23
reit	−3.01	−1.81	**−0.21**	−0.27	−0.10	**−0.09**	0.57		−0.61	−0.36
eval	−1.76	−2.53	**−0.20**	−0.22	−0.15	**−0.10**	0.71	0.20		−0.18
adj	−1.56	−2.35	**−0.19**	−0.18	−0.17	**−0.09**	0.71	0.23	0.29	

T–Statistics of Secondary Hedge

Initial Hedge	Secondary Hedge									
	unxpi	*infla*	*gsci*	*crb*	*gold*	*oil*	*cmeq*	*reit*	*eval*	*adj*
unxpi		−1.66	−1.82	−1.02	−1.35	**−2.21**	7.56	1.88	0.36	−0.85
infla	−1.37		−1.65	−0.89	−0.83	**−2.06**	7.34	1.64	−0.58	−1.03
gsci	−0.76	−0.93		−0.36	−0.16	−0.79	9.52	1.901	0.16	−0.76
crb	−0.89	−0.98	−1.21		−1.25	−1.40	6.79	1.04	−0.55	−0.93
gold	−1.56	−1.45	−1.70	−0.76		**−2.25**	6.93	1.58	−0.27	−1.28
oil	−0.45	−0.59	0.03	−0.75	−0.05		10.02	1.67	−0.02	−0.85
cmeq	**−2.96**	**−2.73**	**−5.68**	−1.71	−1.73	**−6.41**		−0.12	−1.19	−1.87
reit	−1.91	−1.13	**−2.26**	−1.13	−0.74	**−2.62**	4.65		−1.21	−1.88
eval	−1.26	−1.69	**−2.18**	−0.99	−1.11	**−2.70**	6.74	1.93		−0.96
adj	−1.13	−1.59	**−2.02**	−0.81	−1.27	**−2.61**	6.99	2.33	0.60	

R^2s of Secondary Hedge

Initial Hedge	Secondary Hedge									
	unxpi	*infla*	*gsci*	*crb*	*gold*	*oil*	*cmeq*	*reit*	*eval*	*adj*
unxpi		0.07	0.08	0.04	0.05	**0.12**	0.60	0.09	0.00	0.02
infla	0.05		0.07	0.03	0.02	**0.10**	0.59	0.07	0.01	0.03
gsci	0.01	0.02		0.01	0.00	0.02	0.70	0.10	0.00	0.01
crb	0.03	0.04	0.06		0.06	0.08	0.66	0.05	0.01	0.03
gold	0.06	0.05	0.07	0.02		**0.12**	0.56	0.07	0.00	0.04
oil	0.01	0.01	0.00	0.02	0.00		0.73	0.08	0.00	0.02
cmeq	**0.19**	**0.16**	**0.46**	0.11	0.07	**0.53**		0.00	0.04	0.08
reit	0.10	0.04	**0.13**	0.06	0.02	**0.17**	0.39		0.04	0.09
eval	0.04	0.07	**0.11**	0.04	0.03	**0.17**	0.54	0.10		0.02
adj	0.03	0.06	**0.10**	0.03	0.04	**0.16**	0.56	0.14	0.01	

Boldface numbers represent statistically significant negative exposures at the 5% level.

potent hedge has been executed, other additional hedges should have little additional impact on return volatility. Weaker hedging vehicles will lack one or both of these properties.

Exhibit 7 allows us to assess these properties in the group of real assets over 1970-1993. To conserve on space, we report the secondary exposures for only one preexisting portfolio — the stock/bond diversified portfolio. In addition, we report the t-statistics testing the likelihood that the secondary exposures are equal to zero, plus the overall R^2s of the regression.

The results show that unexpected inflation, the GSCI, and crude oil all basically satisfy both of the properties above. They basically retain their stand-alone exposures (and their statistical significance as volatility-reducing hedges) when they are combined with other real assets, such as gold, the CRB index, or real estate.

For example, when the GSCI is the initial minimum-variance hedge, it renders the other hedge assets ineffective (except for *cmeq* and *reit*, which are positively correlated with the diversified portfolio). To see this, note that the GSCI row of Exhibit 7's t-statistic panel shows that few of the secondary hedges are statistically useful in reducing what remains of portfolio variance after the GSCI minimum-variance hedge has been implemented. On the other hand, when the GSCI is the follow-on or secondary hedge, it remains statistically significant (see the GSCI column of the t-statistics panel).

The same cannot be said for real estate. Exhibit 7 shows that once the real estate hedges have been implemented, exposures to other real assets (such as unexpected inflation, the GSCI, and oil) remain just as large. On the other hand, real estate does little to reduce portfolio volatility once most other hedges have already been put in place.

Exhibit 8 reports analogous results for the most recent decade only, again showing futures data for the commodities. (The results for spot data over the same sample period are very similar, and therefore are omitted.) Here, unexpected inflation loses much of its negative correlation with the stock/bond portfolio, so that the most potent hedging combination is that of the GSCI and oil, which together can reduce as much as about 25% of preexisting portfolio variance.

The results are similar for the longer time series sample, estimates of which are shown in Exhibit 9. The main difference in Exhibit 9 is that the time sample is large enough to give considerable statistical significance to the GSCI exposure estimates in all cases.

SUMMARY

To sum up so far, the evidence above suggests that broad portfolios have large negative preexisting exposures to some commodities (such as the GSCI and oil) and to unexpected inflation. We find little evidence of a strong negative exposure to real estate or to commodity-based equities. Data problems notwithstanding, this raises questions about the usefulness of real estate for hedging diversified stock and bond portfolios.

Furthermore, there is even less evidence that real estate or commodity-based equity investments can help reduce portfolio variance once unexpected inflation, the GSCI, or oil are included in the preexisting portfolio. In effect, these latter assets appear to strip out most of the portfolio risks that one looks to real assets to protect against.

Finally, there is some evidence that even if the perfect CPI-inflation hedge were available in the U.S. (i.e., U.S. CPI-linked government bills and bonds), its use would not crowd out a hedging role for commodities such as the GSCI and oil.

EXHIBIT 9 CO-EXPOSURES OF PRE-EXISTING PORTFOLIOS TO REAL ASSET RETURNS (ANNUAL RETURNS 1947-1992)

Initial Hedge Regressions of $r_{p,t} = \alpha_1 + \beta_1 r_{ra1,t} + \varepsilon_{t1}$;

Secondary Hedge Regressions of $\varepsilon_{t1} = \alpha_2 + \beta_{1,2} r_{ra2,t} + \varepsilon_{t2}$

Exposures to Secondary Hedge $\beta_{1,2}$

Initial Hedge	Secondary Hedge *unxpi*	*infla*	*gsci*	*crb*	*gold*
unxpi		–0.28	**–0.23**	–0.06	–0.06
infla	–0.11		–0.18	–0.09	–0.04
gsci	–0.22	–0.15		0.03	0.03
crb	–0.62	–0.94	**–0.27**		–0.07
gold	–0.57	–0.79	**–0.24**	–0.07	

T–Statistics of Secondary Hedge

Initial Hedge	Secondary Hedge *unxpi*	*infla*	*gsci*	*crb*	*gold*
unxpi		–0.56	**–2.04**	–0.53	–0.74
infla	–0.29		–1.59	–0.70	–0.47
gsci	–0.63	–0.31		0.23	0.36
crb	–1.64	–1.83	**–2.33**		–0.83
gold	–1.55	–1.56	**–2.13**	–0.58	

R^2s of Secondary Hedge

Initial Hedge	Secondary Hedge *unxpi*	*infla*	*gsci*	*crb*	*gold*
unxpi		0.01	**0.09**	0.01	0.01
infla	0.00		0.05	0.01	0.00
gsci	0.01	0.00		0.00	0.00
crb	0.06	0.07	**0.11**		0.02
gold	0.05	0.05	**0.09**	0.01	

Boldface numbers represent statistically significant negative exposures at the 5% level.

TARGET EXPOSURES

Optimal target exposure is more difficult to determine than preexisting exposure. That is because target exposures depend on investor risk tolerance and future expected returns, both of which are unobservable. Nevertheless, we can discuss what different assumptions about these quantities have to say about optimal target exposures.

INVESTOR RISK TOLERANCE

Investor risk tolerance reflects the investor's trade-off between expected return and risk (expressed in the framework we have been using as the variance of excess returns). In order to give a rough sense of scale, we calibrate the figures so that a risk tolerance of 0.5 applies to an investor who is willing to accept an increased portfolio variance of 1% in order to increase expected return by 100 basis points.

Using the average returns and volatility of stock and bond portfolios over the last

EXHIBIT 10 INVESTOR RISK TOLERANCE IMPLIED BY HISTORICAL RETURN

	Domestic Stocks	Domestic Bonds	Foreign Stocks	Foreign Bonds	Diversified Portfolio
Historical Return	5.10%	2.40%	1.70%	3.00%	3.70%
Historical Volatility	16.10	11.20	17.00	9.80	11.40
Implied Risk Tolerance*	0.51	0.52	1.74	0.32	0.35

*Implied risk tolerance for each portfolio is calculated as the historical return variance divided by the historical average return.

twenty years, Exhibit 10 gives the implied risk tolerance of an investor whose preexisting portfolio consists entirely of: domestic stocks; domestic bonds; foreign stocks; foreign bonds; and a 70/30 stock/bond diversified portfolio with a 75/25 domestic/foreign mix.

Exhibit 10 shows that an investor who holds only U.S. domestic stocks would have an implied risk tolerance of 0.51. Alternatively, an investor who holds the diversified portfolio has a risk tolerance of 0.35. Assuming that today's excess expected return on the diversified portfolio is 3.0%, the implied risk tolerance of an investor who holds that portfolio rises to 0.43. Alternatively, if one expects a future excess return of 5.0%, implied risk tolerance drops to 0.26.

Given these rough computations, a generous range for risk tolerance might be between 0.25 and 0.50.

EXPECTED EXCESS RETURNS

Expected returns are also difficult to gauge. While historical data tend to provide relatively accurate estimates of future portfolio variance, the same data provide only imprecise estimates of future expected returns. Exhibit 11 reports the historical average excess returns.

The imprecision of estimated expected returns is a problem for all these real assets. For the inflation measures, one must recall that unexpected inflation is not a traded security. If CPI-linked bills were in fact traded, their expected excess return over T-bills would probably be negative.

Expected returns on commodities and real estate are also problematic. First, for commodities — particularly oil — low frequency price movements make it risky to extrapolate out past average returns. For example, it is likely that the average return on oil over 1970-1993, which includes little net change in OPEC's market power, is more representative of future returns than the return from the past decade.

Second, as discussed above, spot and futures positions in commodities have historically resulted in very different excess returns. One might assume that the past excess returns on commodity futures will be sustained in the future, although improved commodity market efficiency is unlikely to raise roll yields, and very likely to lower them. Thus, the statistical imprecision of our estimates is amplified in the case of commodities, where it is not clear which benchmark — past spot or futures returns — is more relevant.

There is a similar problem with expected returns on real estate. For example, the *eval* and *adj* series total return indexes show declines of only about 5% and 14%, respectively, since their peaks in the late 1980s. It is unclear whether this decline reflects the full downturn in commercial real estate markets. Here, the unadjusted data appear smooth and unvolatile, but the degree to which average returns can be estimated is

EXHIBIT 11 HISTORICAL EXCESS RETURNS ON REAL ASSETS (ASSETS ABOVE THE U.S. TREASURY BILL RATE, IN PERCENT PER YEAR)

Real Asset		Historical Excess Returns: 1970-1993	Historical Excess Returns: 1983-1993
unxpi		0.0[a]	0.0
infla		−1.3	−2.8
gsci:	spot	−2.1	−9.5
	futures	6.3[b]	5.5
crb:	spot	−4.0	−6.3
	futures	1.0[c]	0.6[c]
gold:	spot	3.1	−8.1
	futures	−3.3[d]	−8.5
oil:	spot	0.3	−11.6
	futures	3.3[e]	3.3
cmeq		1.7	7.4
reit		−7.0	−7.0[f]
eval		1.4	−1.4
adj		0.3	−5.9

nevertheless imprecise. Furthermore, transaction costs (including costs of illiquidity) should also factor into the expected return on real estate, even though such considerations are not reflected in Exhibit 11.

CALCULATING TARGET EXPOSURES AND OPTIMAL HEDGE RATIOS

We have looked at all the inputs into the target exposure and optimal hedge ratio decisions. We now combine them using the framework laid out above to gain a sense for the magnitudes and sensitivity of optimal real asset hedge ratios.

As indicated above, the calculation of hedge ratios requires three main inputs: investor risk tolerance; expected future excess returns; and preexisting portfolio exposures. In the calculations presented below, we assume investor risk tolerance is 0.5. We also discuss the sensitivity of the results to different assumptions about risk tolerance.

For expected returns, we try several different assumptions for each hedging vehicle. First, we calculate target exposures and optimal hedge ratios under the assumption that the expected excess return on the real asset is zero.

Second, we try an expected excess return of 10 basis points. This latter assumption is not meant to capture realistic return expectations. Instead, it is used to identify the sensitivity of the optimal hedge ratio to changes in expected return. Because this sensitivity is constant across different levels of expected return, we can use the change in the hedge ratio induced by a 10-basis point increase in expected return to compute easily the optimal hedge ratio for any expected return.

For example, suppose that the optimal hedge ratio is 10% with zero expected return and 12% with a 10-basis point expected return. Then an investor who expects an excess return of 50 basis points would have an optimal hedge ratio of 10% + [(12% - 10%) x 50 bp/10 bp] = 20%.

Finally, we try a third assumption about expected excess returns: that they are equal to whatever amount is needed to induce an investor to hold a real asset hedge of zero. In

EXHIBIT 12 OPTIMAL REAL ASSET HEDGE RATIOS FOR A DIVERSIFIED PORTFOLIO OF STOCKS AND BONDS (AS A FRACTION OF PRE-EXISTING PORTFOLIO VALUE)

		Expected Return (basis points)	Target Exposure	Preexisting Exposure	Optimal Hedge Ratio
unxpi	1	0	0.00	−2.78	2.78
	2	10	9.49	−2.78	12.27
	3	−3	2.78	−2.78	0.00
gsci	1	0	0.00	−0.30	0.30
	2	10	0.03	−0.30	0.33
	3	−93	−0.30	−0.30	0.00
oil	1	0	0.00	−0.12	0.12
	2	10	0.01	−0.12	0.13
	3	−189	−0.12	−0.12	0.00
reit	1	0	0.00	0.26	−0.26
	2	10	0.02	0.26	−0.24
	3	107	0.26	0.26	0.00
eval	1	0	0.00	0.07	−0.07
	2	10	0.25	0.07	0.18
	3	3	0.07	0.07	0.00
adj	1	0	0.00	−0.22	0.22
	2	10	0.08	−0.22	0.30
	3	−26	−0.22	−0.22	0.00

other words, the third assumption reports the expected return of an investor who chooses not to hedge at all. This return level is therefore a kind of threshold: Investors of similar risk tolerance who are more bullish than the reported expected return should be long; those more bearish should be short.

The results of these computations are reported in Exhibit 12.[14] There are several points to note. First, *unxpi's* hedge ratios are extremely sensitive to changes in expected returns — a single basis point of additional expected return increases the optimal hedge ratio by almost 100% of the value of the preexisting portfolio. This is a result of the very low volatility of unexpected inflation, which makes optimizing investors very responsive to expected excess returns on hypothetical CPI-linked bills. A slightly negative excess return of -3 bp (to reflect the small amount of inflation insurance that CPI-linked bills would add to T-bills) is the threshold return that results in a hedge ratio of zero.

Second, note that an investor who has a zero hedge ratio expects strongly negative excess returns for both the GSCI and oil. This reflects the commodities' negative correlations with diversified portfolios as well as their relatively high volatilities.

Third, as one would expect, the hedge ratios for REITs are negative (unless expected excess returns are over 107 basis points). This implies that a short position in REITs is the optimal hedge when expected excess returns are under 107 basis points. Hedge ratios for the appraisal-based real estate returns are usually positive, although required returns for holding such hedges are considerable higher than those for the GSCI and oil.

CONCLUSION

In our examination of the hedging properties of real assets for a variety of diversified portfolios, we find that long exposures to a number of real assets — gold, the CRB index, commodity-linked equities, and, particularly, broad real estate indexes — provide relatively weak hedges for broadly diversified portfolios. Levered long positions in equity-based real estate and commodity stocks, even those of oil companies, do not reduce portfolio variance; on the contrary, such exposures actually tend to increase portfolio variance strongly.

By contrast, leveraged positions in commodities with a high energy component — such as oil and the GSCI — exhibit strong hedging properties, as such positions are able to reduce total portfolio variance significantly. The same is true for levered long positions in a hypothetical CPI-linked bond, which can be used to insulate stock and bond portfolios.

It appears that commodity hedges are, at least for stocks, more potent hedges than even CPI-linked bonds. The reason appears to be a negative correlation between stock (and to some extent bond) returns and commodity prices, even when holding inflation fixed.

We combine these correlation results with several measures of expected return in order to calculate optimal hedge ratios for a fixed-weight portfolio of stocks and bonds. Our results suggest that, for this portfolio, diversification provides a powerful rationale for holding energy-weighted commodities.

The same cannot be said for gold, real estate, and equities in commodity and real estate businesses. With respect to a widely diversified portfolio of stocks and bonds, the rationale for holding gold, real estate, or industry equities must rely almost entirely on expected return relative to own volatility.

ENDNOTES

This article was published in *The Journal of Portfolio Management*, Summer 1995.

The author thanks Ernie Ankrim, Zvi Bodie, Jim Crimmins, Chris Hensel, Jay Light, André Pérold, Phil Scott, and Larry Siegel for useful comments and help in obtaining data, and the J. Aron Division of Goldman Sachs and the Department of Research at Harvard Business School for research support.

[1] On the correlations of asset classes with inflation see Bodie [1976, 1979, 1982, 1983, 1990], Fama [1981, 1982], Gay and Manaster [1982], Geske and Roll [1983], Nelson [1976], and Stulz [1986].

[2] Important exceptions include Bodie [1976, 1979] and Ankrim and Hensel [1992, 1993].

[3] While real stock returns are negatively correlated with inflation at shorter horizons, the correlation appears to shrink toward zero at longer horizons. Empirical work suggests that it takes roughly five years before stock prices catch up with inflation shocks (see Boudoukh and Richardson [1993]). Nevertheless, many investors will find it optimal to hedge stocks against inflation shocks.

[4] For the purposes of hedging, one should use the unexpected percentage change in the value of the real asset to determine the exposure. Over reasonably short horizons, however, the variation over time in expected return is dwarfed by that of the actual return.

[5] See Froot and Pérold [1993] for a more formal derivation of what follows.

[6] For a description of the GSCI and its properties, see Ankrim and Hensel [1993] and Lummer and Siegel [1993].

[7] On the problems of measuring real estate returns, see, for example, Gyourko and Keim [1992].

[8] Yet another means of avoiding appraisal-based indexed is to use transaction-based indexes. Because the mix of properties that trade tends to vary with market conditions, transaction-based indexes are also problematic. Case and Shiller [1987] have developed a transaction-based index based on repeat sales in order to attenuate this problem of shifting mix. Their data seem to exhibit similar properties to adj (see the results reported by Goetzmann [1993]) but they include only residential real estate, and therefore the

real estate is unlikely to be owned primarily by investors (as opposed to homeowners).

[9] We do not use the popular Russell-NCREIF Property Index because it begins only in 1978; its statistical properties appear very similar to those of the Evaluation Associates Index.

[10] Goetzmann and Ibbotson [1990] and Goetzmann [1993] find that both residential and commercial real estate have negative correlations with domestic bonds and smaller (probably insignificant) correlations with domestic stocks. Their results suggest that commercial real estate returns are positively correlated with the S&P 500, but that residential and farmland appraisal-based returns are negatively correlated. The differences between our results and theirs may be partly attributable to differing sample periods and partly to differences between residential returns and those of other real estate classes.

[11] Estimates for the same 1983-1993 sample period using spot commodity returns produce very similar results, and so are omitted. The CRB futures and spot indexes have similar hedging properties, but these indexes differ somewhat in their composition. See the notes to Exhibit 11.

[12] There is other evidence consistent with this view. For example, Ball and Mankiw [1992] argue that larger relative price shocks are associated with higher overall inflation; and Benabou [1992] finds inflation to be empirically associated with lower markups, a finding that can be interpreted as evidence that input price increases both cause inflation and are costly to industry.

[13] The estimated standard errors of the coefficient b1,2 are correct only under the assumption that the hedge ratio for the initial real asset is known with certainty.

[14] Exhibit 12 assumes a risk tolerance coefficient of 0.5. If a smaller coefficient is used instead, the sensitivity of optimal hedge ratios to changes in expected returns is reduced proportionately.

REFERENCES

Ankrim, Ernest M., and Chris R. Hensel. "Exchange-Traded Real Assets: Commodities in Asset Allocation." *The Journal of Portfolio Management*, 1993.

——. "Real Estate in Mean-Variance Asset Allocation." *Russell Research Commentary*, December 1992.

Ball, L., and G. Mankiw. "Relative Price Changes as Aggregate Supply Shocks." *NBER Working Paper* No. 4168, September 1992.

Benabou, Roland. "Markups and Aggregate Price Shocks." *European Economic Review*, 1992.

Bodie, Zvi. "Commodity Futures as a Hedge Against Inflation." *The Journal of Portfolio Management*, Spring 1983.

——. "Common Stocks as a Hedge Against Inflation." *The Journal of Finance*, Vol. 31, No. 2 (May 1976).

——. "Hedging Against Inflation." *Sloan Management Review*, Fall 1979.

——. "Inflation, Index-Linked Bonds, and Asset Allocation." *The Journal of Portfolio Management*, Winter 1990.

——. "Inflation Risk and Capital Market Equilibrium." *The Financial Review*, May 1982.

Boudoukh, Jacob, and Matthew Richardson. "Stocks Are a Good Hedge for Inflation (In the Long Run)." *American Economic Review*, 1993.

Case, Karl E., Jr., and Robert J. Shiller. "Prices of Single Family Homes Since 1970: New Indexes for Four Cities." *New England Economic Review*, September/October 1987, pp. 45-56.

Fama, Eugene F. "Inflation, Output, and Money." *Journal of Business*, Vol. 55, No. 2 (1982).

——. "Stock Returns, Real Activity, Inflation, and Money." *American Economic Review*, September 1981.

Froot, Kenneth A., and André Pérold. "Determinants of Optimal Currency Hedging." Harvard University, October 1993.

Geske, Robert, and Richard Roll. "The Fiscal and Monetary Linkage Between Stock Returns and Inflation." *The Journal of Finance*, Vol. 38, No. 1 (March 1983).

Goetzmann, William Nelson. "The Single Family Home in the Investment Portfolio." *Journal of Real Estate Finance and Economics*, 6 (1993).

Goetzmann, William Nelson, and Roger G. Ibbotson. "The Performance of Real Estate as an Asset Class." *Journal of Applied Corporate Finance*, Fall 1990.

Gyourko, Joseph, and Donald B. Keim. "What Does the Stock Market Tell Us About Real Estate Returns?" *Journal of the American Real Estate and Urban Economics Association*, Vol. 20, No. 3 (1992).

Lummer, Scott L., and Laurence B. Siegel. "GSCI Collateralized Futures: A Hedging and Diversification Tool for Institutional Investors." *The Journal of Investing*, Summer 1993, pp. 75-82.

Nelson, Charles R. "Inflation and Rates of Return on Common Stocks." *The Journal of Finance*, Vol. 31, No. 2 (May 1976).

Ross, Stephen A., and Randall C. Zisler. "Risk and Return in Real Estate." *Journal of Real Estate Finance and Economics*, Vol. 4 (1991).

Stulz, René M. "Asset Pricing and Expected Inflation." *The Journal of Finance*, Vol. 41, No. 1 (March 1986).

Wadhwani, Sushil, and Mushtaq Shah. "Commodities and Portfolio Performance." Goldman Sachs International Limited, September 1993.

16 ENERGY BASED INVESTMENT PRODUCTS AND INVESTOR ASSET ALLOCATION

THOMAS SCHNEEWEIS
University of Massachusetts

RICHARD SPURGIN
Clark University

INTRODUCTION

Until recently, commodity investments have been a minor part of most individuals' or institutional investors' investment portfolios. In recent years, however, investible commodity indices and commodity linked assets have increased the number of available commodity based investment products. A number of these investment vehicles permit investors to obtain exposure to price movements of energy based futures contracts. In a recent study commissioned by the New York Mercantile Exchange [Schneeweis and Spurgin, 1997], the impact of various energy based investments on the risk and return performance of individual stocks and bonds, as well as portfolios of stocks, bonds, real estate, and commodity positions was presented. Results of this study show that energy-based futures contracts not only have a low correlation with both energy related and non-energy related stock and bond markets, but various long-short and long-only energy futures products have low correlation with each other and thus all may be part of an investor's fully diversified portfolio. Results also show that certain asset classes such as real estate, which are often regarded as inflation hedges, not only fail to provide that protection but offer limited risk and return benefits to a portfolio which contains even simple long-only energy based products. In contrast, various energy-based products improve a portfolios risk and return tradeoffs when added to a portfolio which contains an investment in real estate equity positions.

Energy investment vehicles provide alternative risk/return opportunities to traditional investments. Past research has shown that the long-term returns to direct crude oil or futures investment must be based largely on (1) returns to an exhaustible resource [Hotelling, 1931], (2) returns to a producer's call option on crude oil [Litzenberger and Rabinowitz, 1995], or (3) speculative returns based on unusual shocks to supply or demand and a market timing model which exploits those shocks [Schneeweis and Spurgin, 1997]. For oil and energy-based investments, the following vehicles were used to reflect alternative investment opportunities.

Passive Cash Commodity Investment

Direct asset investment return: Long term returns approximate zero except in case of the asset becoming a nonrenewable resource. Short-term returns may be positive in periods of unusual supply and demand contraction. E.g., *Oil Investment Vehicle*: West Texas Crude.

Passive Futures Based Return

Long term returns are positive as a function of cash price movement, storage, cost of carry, rollover, and convenience yield returns. E.g,. *Oil Investment Vehicle*: GSCI Energy Index.

Long term return to unlevered futures position. Return is a function convenience yield and of expected risk. E.g., *Oil Passive Investment Vehicle*: NYMEX Crude.

Manager Based 'Long Only' Futures Based Investment

Long term return to risk capital invested in storage and production process. E.g., *Investment Vehicle*: Oil Based Firms.

Passive Futures Based 'Long/Short' Futures Based Investment

Long term returns to passive nonlevered long/short Commodity futures position which captures primarily market pressures as found in autoregressive price trends. E.g,. *Oil Investment Vehicle*: MLM oil index.

Manager Based 'Long/Short' Futures Investment

Long term returns reflective of active speculative return to providing liquidity in futures markets as a function of timing model of information and/or technical trading models. E.g., *Oil Investment Vehicle*: Barclays CTA Energy Index.

Returns for all data series (see Exhibit 1) are expressed as monthly holding period returns. The test period is January, 1987 - December, 1996. For NYMEX crude oil

EXHIBIT 1 DESCRIPTIVE STATISTICS OF INDEX (MONTHLY RETURNS, JANUARY 1987 TO DECEMBER 1996)

Index	Average	StDev	Min	Max	Ret/SD
SP	1.28	4.16	-21.58	13.50	0.31
BD	0.69	1.80	-3.52	5.36	0.39
SP&BD	0.99	2.49	-8.44	8.06	0.40
CTA	1.10	4.65	-8.23	27.40	0.24
MLM	0.81	1.62	-4.04	6.62	0.50
SP OIL	1.17	4.23	-21.12	16.15	0.28
CRUDE	0.66	8.67	-23.21	44.98	0.08
GSCI	1.28	4.35	-9.39	22.94	0.29
GS EXEN	0.91	2.49	-5.24	8.60	0.36
GS ENE	1.74	8.42	-17.54	37.71	0.21
NYM CRU	1.90	8.76	-22.00	46.61	0.22
MLM OIL	1.40	7.97	-22.00	44.79	0.18
CTA ENE	1.18	3.95	-5.00	26.90	0.30
MAR CTA	1.44	4.11	-6.00	19.52	0.35

SP	*Standard & Poors 500 Total Return Index*
BD	*Salomon Bros. 7-10 Year Govt. Bond Index*
SP&BD	*Equally weighted portfolio of SP and BD*
CTA	*Barclay CTA index*
MLM	*Mount Lucas Commodity Index*
SP OIL	*Standard & Poors Oil Company Total Return Index*
CRUDE	*West Texas Intermediate Spot Crude (Datastream)*
GSCI	*Goldman Sachs Commodity Index - Total Return*
GS EXEN	*GSCI Ex-energy - Total Return*
GS ENE	*GSCE Energy Index = Total Return*
NYM CRU	*NYMEX Crude Oil - 2nd Nearby Contract - Total Return*
MLM OIL	*Mount Lucas Oil Index (Passive)*
CTA ENE	*Barclay CTA Energy Index*
MAR CTA	*Managed Account Reports Equal Weighted CTA Index*

based futures, end-of-month prices were used on the near term contract and were rolled over to the next contract the month before the delivery month. Thus returns were determined from separate price series and no overlapping contracts were used. In the full study by Schneeweis and Spurgin, 1997, statistical tests include:

(1) Presentation of descriptive risk and return characteristics,

(2) Return correlations between each of the primary and sub-indices indices,

(3) Return and excess return correlations of both U.S. and non-U.S. energy based firms (source: FT/S&P Actuaries World Indices), U.S. natural resource based mutual funds (Morning star), and the returns of the NYMEX crude oil futures contracts,

(4) Return and excess return correlations (equity security returns adjusted for own country's stock index return) of both U.S. and non-U.S. energy based firms U.S. natural resource based mutual funds and the returns of the NYMEX crude oil futures contract

(5) Relative decile performance comparisons and months of similar directional return (average and excess) of both U.S. and non-U.S. energy firms U.S. natural resource based mutual funds when ranked by NYMEX crude oil futures returns,

(6) Relative performance impact of various energy based investment instruments when considered as part of traditional stock, bond, and real estate investments and

(7) The benefits of various futures based energy based investments as overlays to traditional investments.

Results from the full study [Scheneweis and Spurgin, 1997] indicate that except in months of extreme oil price movement, equity based oil investment does not provide

EXHIBIT 2 RISK/RETURN RELATIONSHIP FOR STAND-ALONE INVESTMENTS (MONTHLY DATA, 1987 TO 1996)

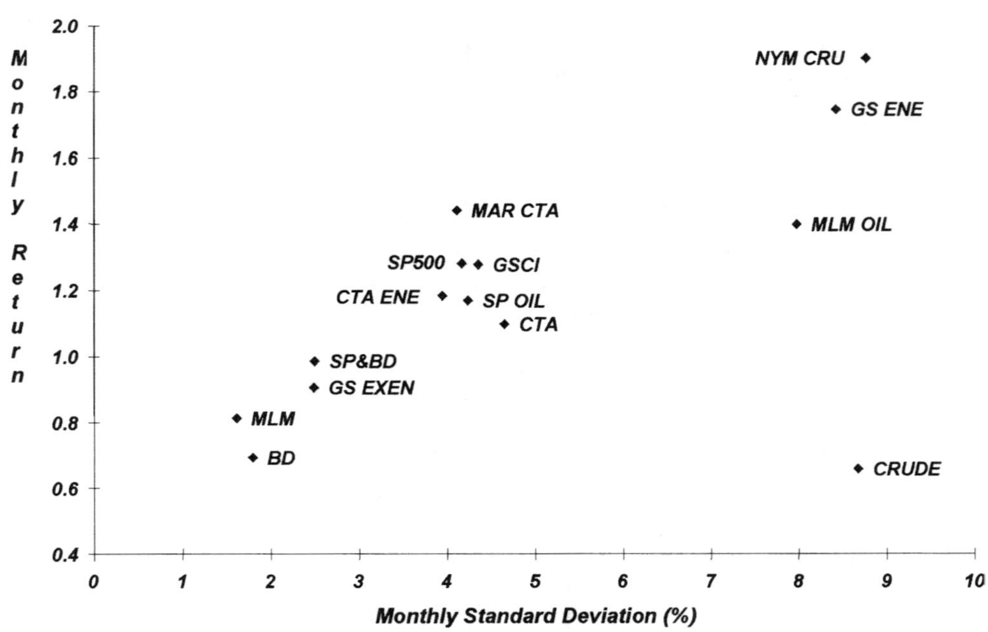

similar return patterns as that of long only passive oil or energy investment. Results from the full study also indicate that active (long/short) trading in energy futures markets provides unique return opportunities not found in passive long only investment in that active long/short trading provides positive returns not only when energy prices are rising but also when energy prices have their largest declines.

RESULTS

Stand-Alone Asset Class Comparisons

As shown in Exhibit 1 and Exhibit 2, for the various asset classes measured, a linear relationship between return and risk (measured as standard deviation) is reflected. For energy based investment products, as well as traditional stocks and bonds and managed futures investments, higher returns were generally obtained from investments with higher measured risk (standard deviation). Lastly, passive energy (GSCI energy), managed futures oil investment (MLM oil), or direct oil investment (NYMEX crude oil futures) are located in the upper right quadrant (e.g., highest return/risk). This is as expected. Passive, energy-only and oil-only based investments represent a less diversified, unmanaged asset investment. In contrast, the other asset classes are more diversified (e.g., portfolios of individual stocks (S&P 500), multiple commodities (GSCI)) than other trading-based futures contracts (MLM) or actively managed investments (CTAs), and thus may be expected to offer a less volatile investment.

In Exhibit 3, the simple correlation patterns are indicative of the possible risk diversification benefits of NYMEX crude oil futures contracts as additions to existing portfolios of traditional stocks and bonds and/or portfolios consisting both of traditional investment vehicles as well as commodity and or managed futures based invest-

EXHIBIT 3 CORRELATION ANALYSIS: TRADITIONAL INVESTMENTS, MANAGED FUTURES, AND COMMODITY INDICES

	SP	*BD*	*SP&BD*	*CTA*	*MLM*	*SP OIL*	*GSCI*	*GS EXEN*	*GS ENE*	*NY CRU*	*MLM OIL*
SP											
BD	.29***										
SP&BD	.94***	.60***									
CTA	.04	.07	.05								
MLM	-.07	.03	-.05	.46***							
SP OIL	.64***	.12	.58***	.06	.07						
GSCI	-.12	-.17*	-.17*	.08	.18*	.34***					
GS EXEN	.11	-.13	.04	.25**	.10	.09	.19*				
GS ENE	-.15*	-.15	-.18*	-.01	.12	.33***	.95***	-.10			
NYM CRU	-.23**	-.19*	-.26**	-.04	.15	.25**	.87***	-.14	.91***		
MLM OIL	-.14	-.05	-.14	.16*	.52***	.08	.49***	.01	.43***	.46***	
CTA ENE	-.06	-.01	-.06	.12	.19*	.16*	.40***	-.15*	.46***	.35***	.31***

** 5% significance, ** 1% significance, *** 0.1% significance*

SP	*Standard & Poors 500 Total Return Index*
BD	*Salomon Bros. 7-10 Year Govt. Bond Index*
SP&BD	*Equally weighted portfolio of SP and BD*
CTA	*Barclay CTA index*
MLM	*Mount Lucas Commodity Index*
SP OIL	*Standard & Poors Oil Company Total Return Index*
GSCI	*Goldman Sachs Commodity Index - Total Return*
GS EXEN	*GSCI Ex-energy - Total Return*
GS ENE	*GSCE Energy Index = Total Return*
NYM CRU	*NYMEX Crude Oil - 2nd Nearby Contract - Total Return*
MLM OIL	*Mount Lucas Oil Index (Passive)*
CTA ENE	*Barclay CTA Energy Index*
MAR CTA	*Managed Account Reports Equal Weighted CTA Index*

ment products. In contrast, the high correlation between NYMEX crude oil futures contract returns and various crude oil based investments (e.g., spot crude) is indicative of the possible use of NYMEX crude oil futures not only as diversification vehicles but as vehicles for direct risk management or risk minimization (e.g., hedging) investments. In Schneeweis and Spurgin [1997], additional empirical results on use of NYMEX crude oil futures contracts both for hedging opportunities for traditional oil-based corporate users and as an investment opportunity for institutional investors are presented. Results, on return and excess return correlations (equity security returns adjusted for own country's stock index return) of both U.S. and non-U.S. energy based firms (source: FT/S&P Actuaries World Indices) and U.S. natural resource based mutual funds and the returns of the NYMEX crude oil futures contract, show that except in periods of extreme NYMEX crude oil futures price movements, and then only for specific energy based equity firms, that traditional 'long only' equity energy based investments do not provide similar return opportunities to direct investment in 'long only' NYMEX crude oil futures contracts.

Portfolio Benefits

To the degree that no consistent relationship can be shown between energy based equity firms and underlying NYMEX crude oil futures markets, futures and/or options-based energy contracts may be used as an alternative asset class that represents a fundamental return pattern which should be included in a diversified investment portfolio. Moreover, for hedge funds or managed futures, the ability to derive more exotic trading strategies may lead to additional investment benefits from futures based energy products. In Exhibit 4, the impact of adding a ten percent position of alternative energy products (GSCI energy index, MLM oil sensitive index, Barclay CTA energy index) to an existing stock portfolio is presented. Adding various forms of energy 'long only' investments such as the GSCI or oil futures improved the return/risk tradeoff. In addition, the addition of more active 'oil based long and short' trading positions (MLM and

EXHIBIT 4 PORTFOLIO RISK/RETURN ANALYSIS: COMBINING ALTERNATIVE ASSETS WITH S&P 500 (1987-1996)

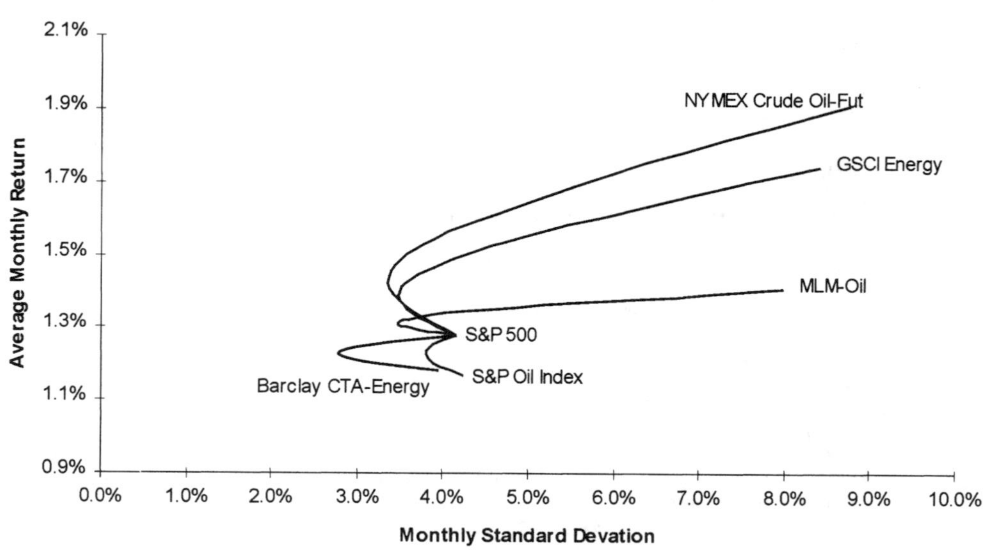

EXHIBIT 5A PERFORMANCE OF LONG ONLY ENERGY FUTURES BASED INVESTMENTS RELATIVE TO RANKED S&P 500 RETURN (1987-1996)

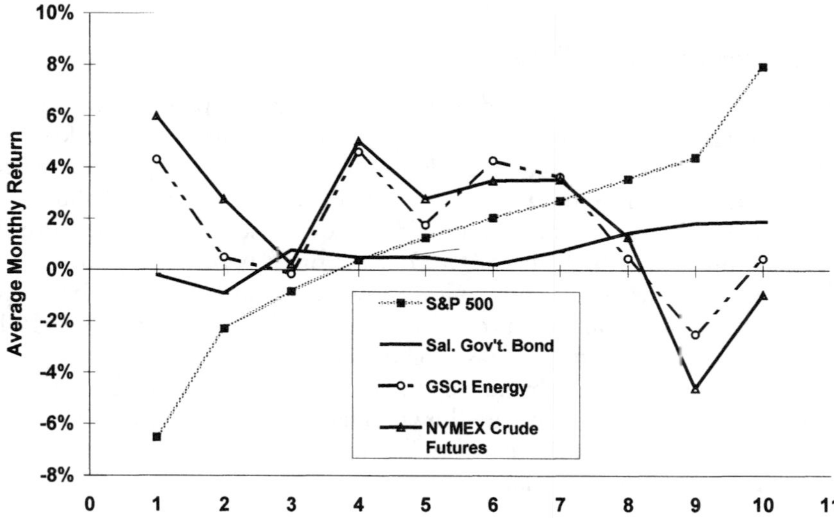

EXHIBIT 5B PERFORMANCE OF NYMEX CRUDE OIL AND S&P OIL INDEX RELATIVE TO RANKED S&P 500 RETURN (1987-1996)

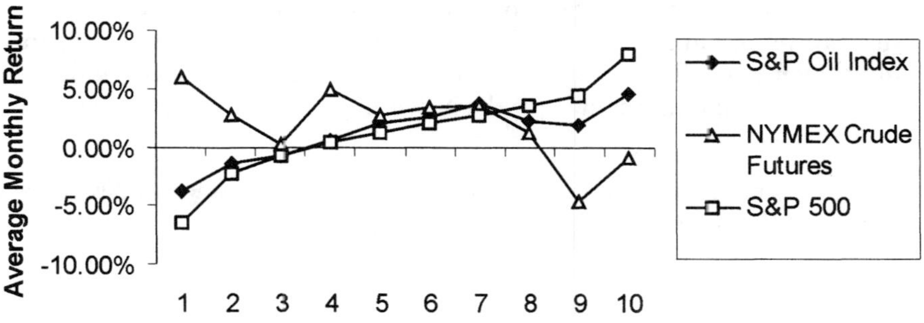

EXHIBIT 5C PERFORMANCE OF ACTIVE LONG/SHORT ENERGY RELATIVE TO RANKED NYMEX CRUDE OIL (1987-1996)

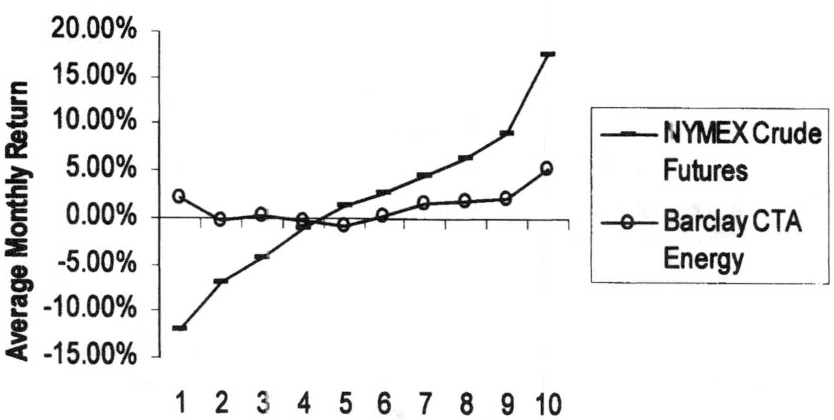

Barclay) also provided opportunities for return/risk improvement. In contrast, the S&P oil sector investment does not effectively lower the risk of the relevant S&P 500 index.

Upside/Downside Risk/Return Impacts

Previous research has indicated that assets' correlation patterns may differ between periods of large market movements and periods of relatively low market volatility. As shown in Exhibit 5a, for instance, S&P 500 and long only energy based futures investments did not have the same average return in the twelve worst S&P 500 months. Thus futures-based oil investment may provide unique risk reduction opportunities especially in months in which the S& P 500 performs poorly. Moreover, as shown in Exhibit 5b, S&P listed oil companies do not necessarily provide the diversification benefits given by long only crude oil futures in months in which the S&P 500 performs poorly. Lastly, long only futures based oil investments does not necessarily offer the risk and return benefits offered by active energy traders. In Exhibit 5c, active long/short managed futures energy traders are shown to have made positive returns not only when NYMEX crude oil returns have had their worst months but when the NYMEX crude oil returns have performed relatively well.

Portfolio Risk and Return Impacts of Real Estate and Oil based Investment

In Exhibit 6, results are presented on the impact of adding various percentages of alternative oil based investments to an existing stock and bond, and real estate portfolio. For most comparable risk positions, an energy based futures contract provided a superior return and risk tradeoff to that of the combined stock, bond, and real estate multi-asset portfolio. As important, the active managed oil based products offered risk reduction beyond that shown for the NYMEX crude oil futures contract. These results

EXHIBIT 6 PORTFOLIO RISK/RETURN ANALYSIS COMBINING INVESTMENTS WITH A PORTFOLIO OF STOCKS, BONDS, AND REAL ESTATE (1987-1996)

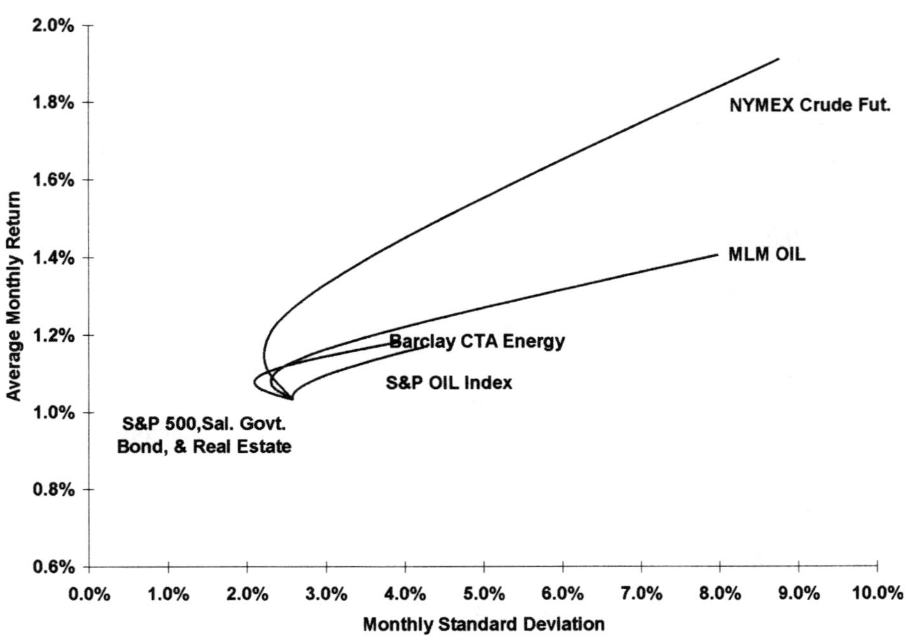

are consistent with the ability of various strategies to obtain returns in various market environments in which 'long only' oil positions may not offer positive returns. It is also important to point out, that the impact of adding long only as well as a 'long/short' oil based investment to various financial assets also indicated the risk/return benefits of alternative oil investments as an overlay strategy.

CONCLUSION AND AREAS OF FUTURE RESEARCH

Oil and other alternative energy based futures have often been used as hedge vehicles or as a tactical means to manage the risk of oil or energy sensitive commodity positions. Rarely have oil and other alternative energy based futures or active energy based futures investment vehicles been viewed as a means to manage the risk of an investor's diversified portfolio or energy specific firm or portfolio investment. Results of this analysis show that NYMEX crude oil futures can be used to hedge oil price movements both firm- and oil-sensitive portfolios but only with caution and during periods of extreme market movements. In contrast, for the diversified investor, oil and energy-based investments are shown to provide a wide range of 'potential' diversification benefits when added to a traditional stock, bond, or stock/bond/commodity portfolio such that oil or energy based-futures products should be more readily considered as additions to existing individual investor and institutional investor portfolios.

ENDNOTES

This article was published by CISDM/SOM, 1997, and is reprinted with permission.

SELECTED REFERENCES

Froot, K. "Hedging Portfolios with Real Assets," *The Journal of Portfolio Management* (Summer, 1995), pp. 60-77.

Hotelling H. "The Economics of Exhaustible Resources," *Journal of Political Economy* 39 (1931), pp. 137-175.

Litzenberger, R. and N. Rabinowitz. "Backwardation in Oil Futures Markets: Theory and Empirical Evidence," *The Journal of Finance* (December, 1995), pp. 1517-1546.

Schneeweis, T. The Benefits of Managed Futures. European Managed Futures Association, (August, 1996).

Schneeweis, T. and Richard Spurgin. "Energy Based Investment Products and Investor Asset Allocation." CISDM (1997).

V TRADITIONAL ALTERNATIVES

INTRODUCTION

For many investors traditional alternative (TradAls) investments such as private equity, private debt, venture capital, real estate, and other direct 'long term' investments are synonymous with alternative investment. A recent reports by Goldman Sachs/Frank Russell [1997] stressed the continued increase of institutional investment into TradAls. The basis for investment returns to traditional alternatives is similar to that for traditional stock and bond investment: that is, a claim on longterm earnings, a return to risk (e.g., positive risk premia for risk capital) and lastly, a return premia for providing capital to an illiquid investment as well as positive alpha generated from unique trading strategies or private information.

Inflows of capital to traditional alternative investments have witnessed substantial increases over the past decades. For instance, funds flowing into the venture industry and the number of active venture organizations increased dramatically during the late 1970s and early 1980s. An important factor accounting for the increase in money flowing into the venture capital sector was the 1979 amendment to the "prudent man" rule governing pension fund investments, as well as lowering of capital gains taxes in 1978.[1] Prior to 1979, the Employee Retirement Income Security Act of 1974 limited pension funds from investing substantial amount of money into venture capital or other high-risk asset classes. The Department of Labor's clarification of the rule explicitly allowed pension managers to invest in high-risk assets including venture capital. [2] Somewhat as a result, the capital under management in the private equity market in the US has grown from $4 billion in 1978 to $150 billion in 1995. Exhibit 1 illustrates the wide range of asset areas generally listed under private equity. Similarly, the private debt market is currently estimated to be about $250 billion, and is an important source of finance to medium sized firms.[3]

The actual risk and return performance of the differing sections of TradAls reflect the differing economic functions of the underlying investment. For instance, venture capitalists are active investors. They monitor the progress of firms, sit on boards of directors and mete out financing. Venture capitalists retain the right to appoint key managers and remove members of the entrepreneurial team. In addition, venture capitalists provide entrepreneurs with access to consultants, investment bankers, and lawyers. Typically, all funds that the firm needs are not provided at once: rather the funds are disbursed in a series of financing rounds based on attainment of milestones. Venture capitalists typically exit their successful investments by taking them public. While they rarely sell their shares at the time of the IPO, they frequently sell the shares or distribute them to their investors within two years of going public. Given that one of the sources of returns to this investment class is based on access to non-public information, it is not surprising that little information is available about the actual return performance of a wide variety of investments in the traditional alternative return area. Moreover, due to the lack of information on the performance of various alternative investments it is expected that, as for managed futures, hedge funds, and commodity investments, a number of myths may exist regarding traditional alternatives.

EXHIBIT 1 PRIVATE EQUITY INVESTMENT UNIVERSE

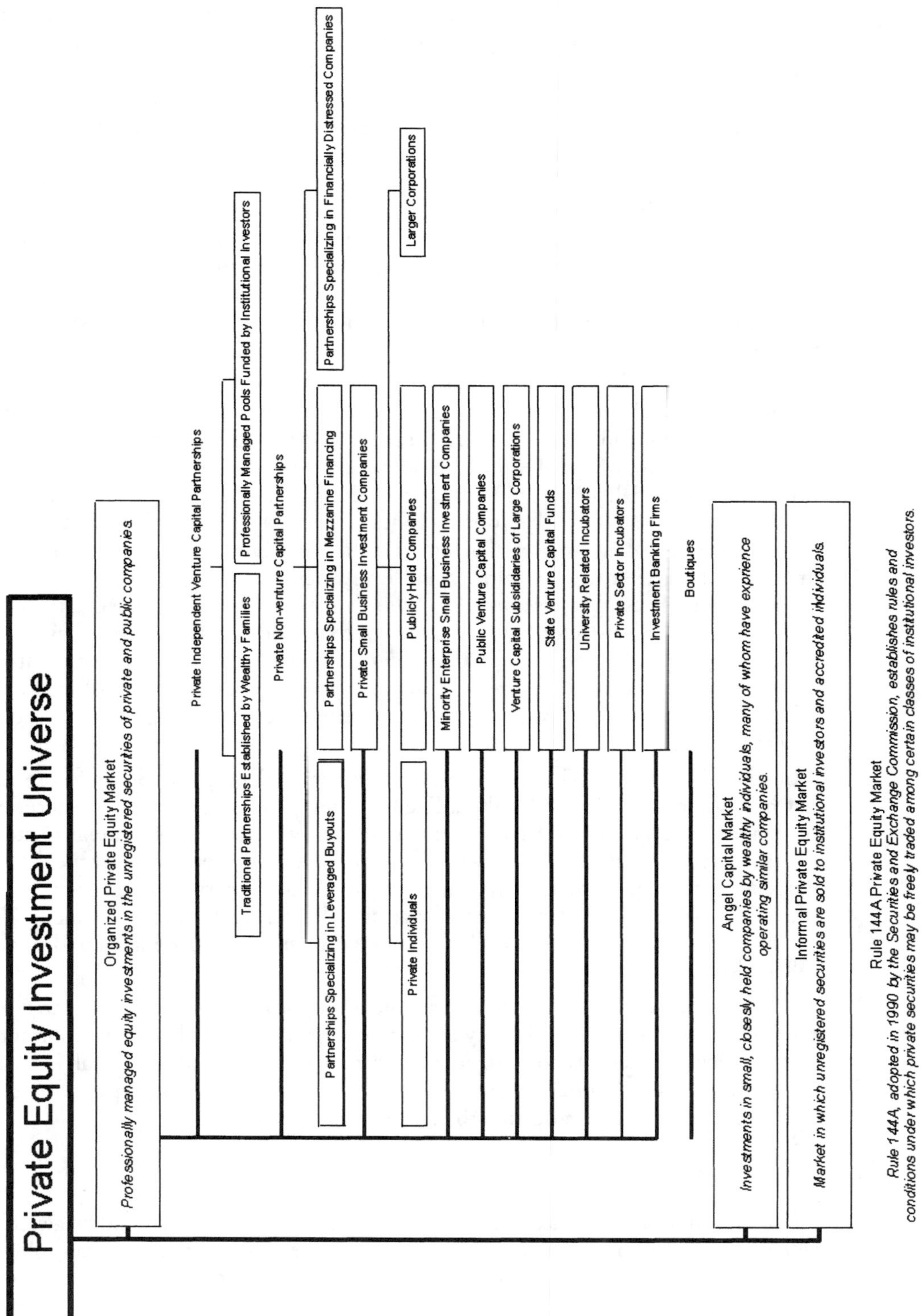

ARTICLE REVIEW

As in the previous sections on managed futures, hedge funds, and commodities, the articles included in this section remove some of the myths of investment in traditional assets. First, while investment benchmarks have been shown to exist for hedge funds, managed futures, and commodity investment, performance indices for various traditional asset investments are less developed. In the first article, "Risk and Reward in Private Equity Investments: The Challenge of Performance Assessment", Paul Gompers and Josh Lerner describe various efforts in creating investment indices which accurately reflect changes in the value of various venture capital and buyout indices. Gompers and Lerner stress the importance of attempting to create an index, which tracks the actual 'market-based' performance of the investment in contrast to the traditional cash flow return estimate. This alternative form of benchmark determination is especially critical as secondary markets for various private equity and debt positions evolve and institutional investors are increasingly required to provide 'market based' estimates of the value of their entire portfolio, liquid and illiquid alike.

Problems of benchmark determination and measuring return performance also exits in other traditional alternative investments such as real estate. In the second article, "A Transaction-Based Index of Commercial Property and its Comparison to the NCREIF Index," Dean Gatzlaff and David Geltner discuss the creation of a transaction based index of commercial property in contrast to the alternative appraisal approach commonly used in the NCREIF Property Index. Thus Gatslaff and Geltner attempt to address for the real estate area the same central question that Gompers and Lerner attempt to address in the venture capital investment area. In both of the first two articles, the authors have attempted to address the use of market-based estimates of value change or multi-factor based methods of return determination that may be used as a 'surrogate' return forecast for the underlying investment. Thus, as presented in earlier articles on managed futures and hedge funds, researchers in traditional alternatives are concern with determining the actual return factors driving the returns of the underlying strategy.

In the third article, "Timberland Return Drivers and Investing Styles for an Asset that has Come of Age", Jon Caulfied likewise stresses the importance of determining the fundamental economic factors which drive timberland returns. Similar to studies on other alternative asset classes discussed in this handbook, he shows that the determinants of timber investment value may be driven by factors (timber growth, land value . . .). which are independent of traditional stock and bond investment. Thus timber investment may provide both return and diversification benefits to traditional as well as alternative investments.

While estimates of market performance are of importance to any investor, an understanding of the structure and history of the investment vehicle is likewise important. In the last article, W. Keith Schilit provides a summary review of venture capital. In "Structure of the Venture Capital Industry," Schlit describes the different types of investors and recent developments affecting their investment practices.

RESEARCH IN TRADALS

In addition to the articles presented in this handbook, investors should be aware of a wide range of additional sources of information and recent research in the area of traditional alternatives. A variety of materials exists which cover both practical management issues as well as academic/practitioner research in the area of traditional alternatives. Investors are referred to Exhibits 2 and 3 for a summary of selected research.

EXHIBIT 2 SUMMARY OF KEY RESEARCH REGARDING PRIVATE EQUITY MARKETS AND INVESTMENTS

Bibliography	Title	Topic	Major Results
** Schilit, W. K. *JI* (1996)	"Venture catalysts or vulture capitalists?"	The nature of entrepreneur-venture capitalist relationship; their typical roles.	Describes venture capital as the catalyst for entrepreneurial activity -- not merely in furnishing financial resources, but also in providing management assistance and strategic guidance to emerging growth ventures.
** Schilit, W. K. *JPE* (1998)	"Structure of the venture capital industry"	Classification and discussion of venture capital investors.	Proposes and explores the following classification of VC industry: ▪ Private independent venture capital partnerships ▪ Private Small Business Investment Companies ▪ Public venture capital companies ▪ Venture capital subsidiaries of larger corporations ▪ State venture capital funds and University related incubators ▪ Private sector incubator ▪ Investment banking firms
Barry, C., Muscarella, C., Peavy, J., and Vetsuypens, M. *JFE* (1990)	"The role of venture capital in the creation of public companies: evidence from the going public process".	The nature of venture-capital investments explored through the analysis of more than 400 IPOs by venture-capital backed firms and 1120 IPOs by non-venture-capital backed firms.	The analysis suggests that venture capitalists: ▪ take significant equity positions in their investees, ▪ participate directly in their governance, ▪ hold about one third of the board seats ▪ typically have been associated to them for about half of their corporate lives before the IPO. And: ▪ Venture capitalists continue to hold nearly all of their equity and board positions through and for some time after the offering; ▪ The quality of venture capitalists monitoring skills reduces investor uncertainty
Brav, A. and Gompers, A. P. *JF* (1997).	"Myth or reality? The long-run under-performance of initial public offerings: evidence from venture capital and non-venture capital backed companies"	Investigation of long-run under-performance of recent initial public offering firms in a sample of 934 venture-backed IPOs from 1972 - 1992 and 3407 non-venture backed IPOs from 1975 - 1992.	▪ The results suggest that venture backed IPOs outperform non-venture backed IPOs using equal weighted returns. ▪ Value weighting significantly reduces under-performance for non-venture backed IPOs. ▪ Evidence suggests that under-performance is actually not an IPO issue as similar size and book-to-market firms that have not issued equity perform as poorly as IPOs during the sample period.
Chan, Y.S., *JF* (1983)	"On the positive role of financial intermediation in allocation of venture capital in market with imperfect information"	The first theoretic study of the rationale for the existence of venture capitalists as financial intermediaries.	Develops an optimization model, where venture capitalists serve as information agents in the market increasing investor welfare by forcing entrepreneurs to offer higher return projects.
Gompers, A. P., *JFE* (1996).	"Grandstanding in the venture capital industry"	Development and tests of the hypothesis that young venture capital firms take companies public earlier than older venture capital firms in order to establish a reputation and successively raise capital for new funds.	The analysis confirms that: ▪ Companies backed by young venture capital firms are younger and more under-priced at their IPO than those backed by established venture capital firms. ▪ Young venture capital firms have been on the board of directors a shorter period at the IPO and they hold smaller equity stakes.

Gompers, A. P., *JF* (1995).	"Optimal investment, monitoring, and the staging of venture capital"	Examination of the structure of venture capital investments when agency and monitoring costs exist based on a random sample of 794 venture capital backed firms.	▪ Venture capitalists concentrate investments in the early stage. ▪ Venture capitalists tend to invest high technology companies where informational asymmetries are the highest. ▪ Decreases in industry ratios of tangible assets to total assets, higher market-to-book ratios, and greater R&D intensities lead to more frequent monitoring. ▪ Venture capitalists periodically gather information and maintain the option to discontinue funding projects with little probability of going public.
Gompers, A. P., Lerner J. *JF* (1998)	"Venture capital distributions: short-run and long-run reactions"	Distribution of venture capital investments to the investors in venture capital funds by the fund's general partners; impact of these distributions on the stock value of the investee firms.	▪ The evidence demonstrates a 2 percent drop around the distribution; this is consistent with market reacting to the insider information of the venture capitalists. ▪ The price drop around the distributions is less profound for firms backed by higher quality underwriters.
Gompers, A. P., Lerner J., *forthcoming in the JFE*, (1999)	"Money chasing deals?: "the impact of fund inflows on private equity valuations"	Impact of the capital inflows into venture funds on the valuation of their investments in firms.	▪ Demonstrates that growth in venture capital commitments increase the valuation of new investments. ▪ Changes in valuations do not appear related to the ultimate success of the firms.
Gompers, A. P., Lerner, J., *JPE* (1997)	"Risk and reward in private equity investments: the challenge of performance assessment"	Measurement of risk and reward in private equity investments.	▪ Outline of a method for addressing the problem of measurement of risk and reward in private equity investments by "marking to market" returns of private equity groups.
Lerner J. *JF* (1993).	"Venture capitalists and the decision to go public"	Examination of the timing of initial public offerings and private financing by venture capitalists.	▪ Venture-capital backed companies are more likely to go public when equity valuations are high and more likely to employ private financing when equity market values are lower. ▪ Seasoned venture capitalists appear to be particularly proficient at taking companies public near market peaks.
Megginson, L., W., and Weiss, K., *JF* (1991).	"Venture capitalist certification in initial public offerings"	Certification role of venture capitalists in initial public offerings.	▪ The results indicate that venture capital backing results in significantly lower initial returns and gross spreads. ▪ The presence of venture capitalists in the issuing firms serves to lower the total costs of going public and to maximize the net proceeds to the offering firm.
Sahlman, W. A. *JFE* (1990)	"The structure and governance of venture-capital organizations"	Structure of venture capital firms.	The analysis is centered on the relationship between investors in venture capital firms and the venture capitalists and between venture capital firms and their investee firms. Discusses organizational structure adopted by the industry as well as the operating procedures and contracts that have been developed to deal with the specific features of venture capital operations such as agency and informational asymmetry issues.

Journal abbreviations: *JAR* — Journal of Accounting Research; *JAE* — Journal of Accounting and Economics; *AR* — The Accounting Review; *FAJ* — Financial Analysts Journal; *JF* — Journal of Finance; *JFE* — Journal of Financial Economics; *JPE* -- The Journal of Private Equity; *JI* - The Journal of Investing;

Performance of Venture Capital

Until now, most of the studies on venture capital operations and performance have not explicitly referred to any theoretical framework. Some exceptions include Chan [1983], which is the first theoretical study of the rationale for existence of venture capitalists as financial intermediaries. Under Chan's model, venture capitalists serve as information agents in the market. Through their actions, venture capitalists increase investor welfare by forcing entrepreneurs to offer higher return projects. In contrast, Sahlman [1990] focuses on the structure of venture capital, centering his analysis on the relationship between investors and venture capital firms and the venture capitalists and between venture capital firms and their investee firms.

Empirical work has also been conducted, though it is somewhat limited by the dearth of available information available to the non-investor.[4] Lerner [1993] examines the timing of initial public offerings and private financing by venture capitalists. Lerner uses a sample of 350 privately-held venture-backed biotechnology firms between 1978 and 1992. He shows that venture capital backed companies are more likely to go public when equity valuations are high and more likely to employ private financing when equity market values are lower. Brav and Gompers [1997] investigate the long-run under-performance of recent initial public offering firms in a sample of 934 venture-backed IPOs from 1972 – 1992 and 3407 non-venture backed IPOs from 1975 to 1992. The authors find that venture backed IPOs outperform non-venture backed IPOs using equal weighted returns. Nevertheless, Brav and Gompers note that value weighting significantly reduces performance differences and substantially reduces under-performance for non-venture backed IPOs. They also argue that under-performance is actually not an IPO issue as similar size and book-to-market firms that have not issued equity perform as poorly as IPOs during the sample period.

Gompers and Lerner [1999] study the determinants of flows of new funds to venture capital, and find, among other things, that fund performance is a significant predictor of capital inflows. Other factors that affect the demand for venture capital also play an important role in new flows of capital.

Additional information on the Private Equity market can be found in a broad study of the market issued by the Federal Reserve Board [Fenn et al. 1995].

Performance of Private Debt

Little empirical information exists on the total returns to investing in portfolios of privately placed bonds. Available information, such as that provided by Corcoran [1994] or Kwan and Carleton [1994], focuses on the portfolios of specific institutional investors. Corcoran finds that private placements returned more than 80bps more than comparable publics during the time period 1987-1992. Carey [1998] uses data—from the period 1986-92—from a Society of Actuaries study of private debt (covering a number of insurers' portfolios) to develop measures of the credit risk inherent in private debt, and suggests that the loss experience of private debt is about 75bps lower than public bonds. Martin [1999] investigates the effective return to the investor for assuming illiquid private debt over more liquid public debt with a theoretical model.

It is only recently, however, that actual index level data for private placement performance has become available. Lehman Bros and the American Council of Life Insurers has created an index of traditional (non-144a) investment grade private placements, which is comprised of about 70 billion dollars worth of securities. That performance data is given in Exhibit 4 for the period October 1996 to January 1999.

EXHIBIT 3 SUMMARY OF KEY RESEARCH REGARDING PRIVATE DEBT MARKETS AND INVESTMENTS

Bibliography	Title	Topic	Major Results
Arak, M. and Cocoran, P. JPM (1996)	"Yields on Privately Placed Debt"	An examination of the macroeconomic determinants of yield spreads on privately placed debt.	"Yield on privately placed debt do not closely follow comparable-quality public debt issues. For high-high quality issue, A-rated, there is more similarity in fluctuations, while for below-investment-grade issues, Ba-quality, there is little common movement." "Economic activity, and its direction of change, affects yields on private placements. High and/or expanding levels of economic activity generally reduce spreads, while low and/or contracting levels of economic activity tend to increase private placement yields relative to Treasury yields" "In late 1989 and the early 1990s, investment-grade private placement yields were about 30 bp-40 bp lower than would be expected, and below-investment-grade private placement yields were about 40 bp higher than expected, given the state of the economy. That is our data support the view that there was an important credit crunch for below-investment-grade borrowers in the private placement market, as life insurance companies preferences shifted toward investment-grade paper. "
Carey, M. et al.. (1994)	"The Economics of the Private Placement Market - A Federal Reserve Board *Staff Study*"	Surveys the various institutions and market dynamics that are a significant force in the private placement market.	Private placements are an important source of finance for medium sized firms. The reason for this is not due to some pure all-in cost advantage to issuing private debt, but because the private debt market and contracts are better poised to assess credit risks that require the intensive evaluation of information. Provides substantial institutional detail about the market.

Carey, M, W. K. *JI* (1998)	"Credit risk in private debt portfolios"	Quantification of the credit exposure associated with private placements and comparison with public instruments	Quantifies the credit risk of private vs. public bonds. While private debt is more likely than public debt to experience a "Credit Risk Event," the expected net losses to private debt are smaller than for public debt. Moreover, this superiority increases with steps down the credit rating ladder, indicating that the informational elements to the private placement contract has positive value.
Corcoran, P. (1994) JFI	"The Double-B Private Placement Market"	Outlines the experience of Prudential with junk-quality private placements	Low grade private placements exhibit superior returns to comparable quality publics during the period 1987-1992. The main source of this superior return is the covenants attached to private debt.
James, C. JFE, 1987	"Some evidence on the uniqueness of bank loans"	Measurement of the market value of news that a particular firm issues a particular type of security of note.	Shows that there is no statistically significant equity market reaction to the announcement of private placements, suggesting that the 'certification' value of private placements is more positive than equity, but less positive than bank debt.
Kahan, M, and Tuckman, B. (1996)	""Private vs. Public Lending"	Investigates the use of covenants in private debt, the incentive effects that such covenants have on investors.	Private debt covenants involve more monitoring and more frequent renegotiation than public debt securities. Such private covenants are structured so as to facilitate renegotiation of covenants, as well as to mitigate incentive conflicts between co-investors in the private issues. (Public bonds are stringently regulated by the Trust Indenture Act of 1940 and subsequent rulemaking.)

Journal abbreviations: *JAR* — Journal of Accounting Research; *JAE* — Journal of Accounting and Economics; *AR* — The Accounting Review; *FAJ* — Financial Analysts Journal; *JF* — Journal of Finance; *JFE* — Journal of Financial Economics; *JFI*—Journal of Fixed Income; *JI* - The Journal of Investing;

Given the absence of return data, most investment-oriented research has focused on the yield differential between public and private debt as the debt is first sold. Evidence provided by Arak and Cocoran [1996] suggests strong business cycle components to the spread between public and private debt. Other contract features that are characteristically found with greater intensity in private debt, such as call protection and stringent covenants, also result in differing risk profiles between the two classes of debt. Private debt is characteristically associated with more informationally "opaque" firms, and some of the returns to private debt are surely compensation for the increased credit assessment and monitoring costs.

Martin [1999] and Carey et al. [1994] discuss the role of covenants in actually securing that information. See Exhibit 5 for a comparison of these contract features with the features of other debt instruments. Martin [1999] provides a contingent claims model to value these differing contract features. Further discussion of the importance of such contractual features can also be found in Carey et al. [1994], though Martin's article offers criticism of Carey's findings. Martin [1999] also discusses the use of private placements in particular types of transactions, like M&A activity in the 1980's. (In more recent years 144a private placements have made their way in substantial quantities into collateralized bond and debt obligation structures). See also Emerick and White [1992], James [1987] and Kahan and Tuckman [1996]. Martin[1999] also includes an extensive bibliography of materials related to the private placement market.

CONCLUSIONS

For many investors traditional alternative (TradAls) investments such as private equity, private debt, venture capital, real estate, and other direct 'long-term' investments are synonymous with alternative investment. The basis for investment returns to TradAls is similar to that for traditional stock and bond investment, that is, a claim on long-term earnings, a return to risk (e.g., positive risk premia for risk capital), a return premia for providing capital to an illiquid investment, and, lastly, a positive alpha to returns generated from the costs of obtaining private information.

EXHIBIT 4 MONTHLY RETURNS FOR PRIVATELY PLACED DEBT
Source: ACLI-Lehman Bros.

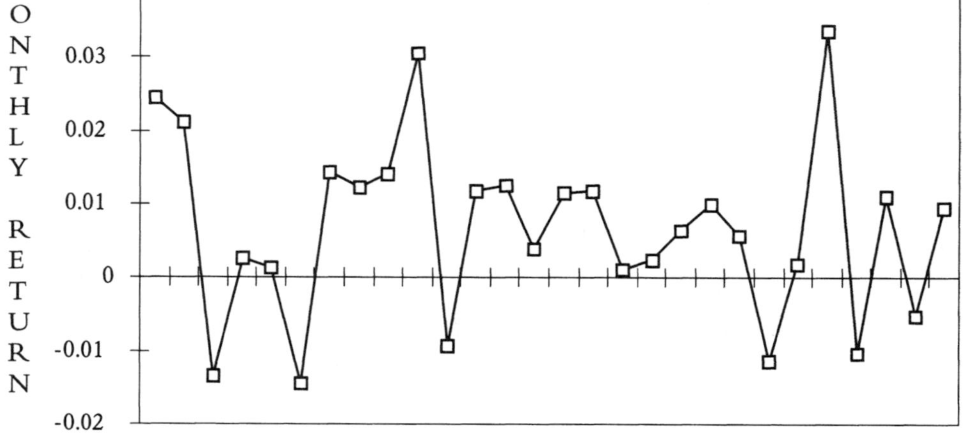

EXHIBIT 5 STYLIZED FACTS ABOUT VARIOUS CREDIT MARKET CONTRACTS

Contract Characteristic	Bank Loan	Private Placement	Public Bond Market
Maturity	Short (3 years)	Medium (7-10 years)	Long (10-15 years)
Rate	Floating	Fixed	Fixed
Callable	Yes, at anytime	no, except with substantial penalty	since 1990: no before 1990: almost always
Informational "opacity" of borrower	High	Medium	Low
Average Loan Size	Small	Medium to Large	Large
Average Credit Risk Level	Highest	Low to High	Lowest
Covenants	Most, and tightest, often concerned with the preservation of securing assets	Medium, with a focus on long term assets and liabilities	Fewest
Collateral	Usually	Occasionally	Rare
APR Seniority	Almost always	Usually	Almost never
Renegotiation	Frequent	Less Frequent	Rare (and expensive)
Lender Monitoring	Strong	Medium	Minimal (outside of NRSROs)
Liquidity of debt contract	Low	Low	Medium
Principal Lenders	Banks	Life Insurance Company	Institutional Investor (usually a Mutual Fund or a Life Insurance Company)
Regulatory Protection and/or Legal Recourse	Little, loans are not considered securities; UCC is primary code	Little outside of the antifraud provisions of the Securities Act; mostly a matter of contract law	Trust Indenture Act and amendments, as well as SEC rulemaking as well as contract law

Source: After Carey et. al. [1994]

ENDNOTES

[1] In a venture capital limited partnership, the venture capitalists are general partners and control the fund's activities. The investors serve as limited partners. Investors monitor the fund's progress and attend annual meetings, but cannot become involved in the fund's day-to-day management if they are to retain limited liability. Venture partnerships have a pre-determined, finite lifetime (usually ten years, though extensions are often allowed). Most venture organizations raise funds every two to five years. Partnerships have grown from 40 percent of the venture pool in 1980 to 80 percent in 1995.

[2] Initially publicly traded closed end funds and Small Business Investment Companies [federally guaranteed risk-capital pools that proliferated during 1960's] dominated the industry. During the 1970's, the limited partnership emerged as the dominant organizational form [one of the advantages

of the limited partnership is that capital gains taxes are not paid by the partnership but only at the investor level]. (Most early funds had been structured as publicly traded closed-end funds).

[3] In the discussion on private debt in this section, we consider only the private placements of domestic firms into the US capital markets.

[4] Recently, Wilshire has produced a private equity index. (See Nesbitt and Reynolds (1997)). Empirical examination of the returns to this index show that it is extremely highly correlated with the S&P500. This may not be very satsifactory, since it is unlikely that returns to a small number of private equity investments will actually be very high, as individual investments possess large amounts of ideosyncratic risk which may be difficult to diversify away.

SECTION V ARTICLES

Gompers, Paul and Josh Lerner, "Risk and Reward in Private Equity Investments: The Challenge of Performance Measurment", *The Journal of Private Equity* (Winter, 1997), pp. 5-12.

Gatzlaff, Dean and David Geltner, "A Transaction-Based Index of Commercial Property and its Comparison to the NCRIEF Index," *Real Estate Finance* (Spring, 1998), pp. 7-22.

Caulfield, Jon, "Timberland Return Drives and Investing Styles for an Asset that has come of Age," *Real Estate Finance* (Winter, 1988), pp. 65-78.

Schilit, W. Keith, "The Structure of the Venture Capital Industry", *The Journal of Private Equity* (Spring, 1998), pp. 60-67.

SELECTED REFERENCES

Arak, Marcelle and Corcoran, Patrick "Yields on Privately Placed Debt," *The Journal of Portfolio Management,* (Spring, 1996), pp. 88-96

Brav, A. and Gompers, A. P., "Myth or Reality? The Long-run Under-performance of Initial Public Offerings: Evidence from Venture Capital and Non-venture Capital-Backed Companies", *Journal of Finance,* (December, 1997), pp. 1791-1821.

Carey, Mark, Prowse, Stephen, Rea, John, and Udell, Gregory "The Economics of the Private Placement Market - A Federal Reserve Board *Staff Study,*" Washington, DC: Board of Governors of the Federal Reserve System. (1994).

Carey, Mark "Credit Risk in Private Debt Portfolios," *Journal of Finance,* (August,1998), pp. 1363-1387.

Corcoran, Patrick "The Double-B Private Placement Market," *The Journal of Fixed Income,* (June, 1994), pp. 42-51.

Emerick, D. and White, W., , "The Case for Private Placements: How Sophisticated Investors Can Add Value to Corporate Debt Issuers," *Journal of Applied Corporate Finance,* (1992), pp. 83-92.

Fenn, G. et al. "The Economics of the Private Equity Market," Board of Governors of the Federal Reserve. (1995).

Gompers, A. P. and Lerner, J., "What Drives Venture Capital Fund Raising?", Working Paper #6906, National Bureau of Economic Research. (1999).

James, Christopher "Some evidence on the uniqueness of bank loans," *Journal of Financial Economics* 19: (1987), pp. 217-235.

Kahan, Marcel and Tuckman, Bruce "Private vs. Public Lending," *Yearbook of Fixed Income Investing,* Irwin, M. Fridson and J. Finnerty (eds.) (1996)

Kwan, Simon and Carlton, Willard "The Structure and Pricing of Private Placement Corporate Loans," working paper, (1994).

Lerner, J., "Venture Capitalists and the decision to go public", *Journal of Finance.* (1993).

Martin, G., "Essays on the Private Placement Market," Dissertation (in progress), University of Massachusetts. (1999).

Martin, G., "Private Debt: Past, Present and Future, Part 1". *The Journal of Alternative Investments.* (Summer 1998), pp. 24-40.

Nesbitt, S. and Reynolds, H., "Benchmarks for Private Market Investments," *The Journal of Portfolio Management,* 23:4, (1997), pp. 85-90.

Schilit, W. K., "Venture Catalysts or Vulture Capitalists?" *The Journal of Investing,* (Fall 1996), pp. 86-95.

17 RISK AND REWARD IN PRIVATE EQUITY INVESTMENTS: THE CHALLENGE OF PERFORMANCE MEASUREMENT

PAUL A. GOMPERS
JOSH LERNER
Harvard Business School, Harvard University

Despite advances during the past decades in the pricing and risk adjustment of return in public markets, the measurement of risk and return in private equity has advanced relatively little. This is surprising, given the importance of return measurements for both fund managers and private equity investors.

The benchmark chosen to measure performance is critical in an institutional investor's decision to allocate funds across various asset classes, as well as the choice of individual managers within an asset class. Universities and foundations that spend a certain percentage of their endowments must be able to calculate the change in valuation of their private equity portfolios from year to year. Investment officers at pension funds whose bonuses are tied to the performance of their portfolios must similarly be able to accurately measure how well these funds are performing on a risk-adjusted basis in a timely manner. Private equity organizations need to document the performance of their earlier investments when raising new funds.

At the same time, the relatively slow pace of innovation in assessing riskiness and returns for private equity investments is understandable. Firms receiving capital from private equity funds very often remain privately held for a number of years after the initial investment. These firms have no observable market price. In order to present a conservative assessment of the portfolio valuation, private equity managers often refrain from marking portfolio firm values to market, preferring to maintain the investments at book value. Thus, the stated returns of private equity funds may not accurately reflect the true evolution of value. The problem is severe for both venture capital and buyout investments. In fact, current practices may substantially understate the true volatility of buyouts because they rarely have follow-on investments when the firm can be revalued.

This article describes our efforts to address this issue. In particular, we outline a method for addressing this problem by "marking to market" the returns of a private equity group. We next discuss the calculation of risk-adjusted returns. We then apply these concepts in an illustrative calculation of the returns of a private equity group that has been an active investor over the past three decades. The analysis and methodology used here represents a substantial improvement in the measurement of risk and return in private equity. The tool is potentially useful for addressing portfolio allocation and fund assessment in a rigorous and coherent manner.

THE PROBLEM

Two primary approaches have been taken in earlier efforts to assess the returns of private equity investments. The first has been to examine the change in the prices of firms backed by private equity investors that have recently gone public. A long-standing example of such an index is the "Venture Capital 100" reported each month in Venture Economics' *Venture Capital Journal*. Merrill Lynch has taken a similar approach in the construction of its private equity index: They use the prices of the least liquid public firms with the smallest market capitalization (Galante [1995]).

While such an index is relatively easy to construct in a timely manner (the prices of publicly traded firms can be obtained at the end of each trading day), it has several limitations. First, the valuation of private equity investments will be affected by a variety of factors that do not affect public firms. For instance, a considerable inflow of funds into venture funds may create an environment where "too many funds are chasing too few deals." It seems unlikely that such a problem will affect the pricing of public firms, as public investors can readily move their capital across industries and securities.

Second, the market for recently public firms has certain institutional features that affect the pricing of firms. For instance, smaller firms that go public frequently drop in value in their first several years, which may reflect overoptimism, at least by some subset of investors (Ritter [1991]; Brav and Gompers [1997]). These institutional features once again reduce the value of public firms as indicators of private valuations.

Finally, the public firms that make up these indexes may not be good proxies for the current mix of private equity-backed firms. Many of the new private firms may have no public comparables.

The second approach has been to calculate the internal rates of return of private equity funds. Among others, Venture Economics and Cambridge Associates collect data from institutional investors on the flow of capital into and out of private equity funds. These data are used to calculate annual and quarterly return series for private equity funds as a whole. These calculated returns are then used to compare the returns of private equity with small-capitalization stocks and other securities, as well as to determine the relative performance of particular private equity organizations.

Unfortunately, this methodology has two major problems as well, which limit its usefulness. The first is the inconsistency in how private equity groups value investments. Established private equity organizations are typically conservative in their approach to valuing their investments, often holding investments at cost until they are taken public. Less-established private equity organizations are often not as conservative in their valuation practices. Inexperienced private equity groups are often under tremendous pressures to raise follow-on funds (Gompers [1996]). Raising an initial private equity fund is frequently very difficult. Many institutional investors and investment advisors refuse, as a matter of principle, to invest in first-time funds, often on the grounds that they believe these funds have lower returns than other partnerships. As a result, many first-time funds are so small that the management fees generated can not cover the travel, office, and salary expenses that the partnerships incur.

Alternatively, the lead investor in the fund (and perhaps even the placement agent who helped in fundraising) may be given a substantial share of the management fees and carried interest. The general partners of the private equity fund are nonetheless willing to accept these terms, because they expect that subsequent funds will be raised on more attractive terms. A major focus of these organizations is consequently on raising such a follow-on fund.

It is not surprising, then, that these private equity organizations are very aggressive in presenting their investment results during fundraising. Among the behaviors encountered are:

- Aggressively valuing still-private firms in their portfolio above cost.
- Neglecting to discount firms in the portfolio that have encountered difficulties.

- Failing to discount for the illiquidity of the shares of publicly traded firms still held in the private equity group's portfolio.

These problems may not always be identified by institutional investors, who are often surprisingly willing to accept such claims at face value. Because a much larger fraction of established private equity organization investments are likely to have been liquidated, these problems are much less likely to have a material impact on their results. Differences in valuation methodology can give the appearance that certain groups have superior performance when interim returns are compared, while in actuality their long-run performance is no different (or even lower) than that of other organizations.

This inconsistency has been the subject of attention by institutional investors in both the U.S. and abroad. Efforts in this country — such as the initiative launched in 1989 by the Institutional Limited Partners Association (ILPA [1990]) — have made only modest progress. The persistence of such problems is discussed, for instance, in Mercer [1996] and Cain [1997].

The British Venture Capital Association (BVCA), in conjunction with a group of major limited partners, has taken an aggressive approach in addressing this problem. In 1991, it introduced a consistent set of valuation standards that its members must follow (summarized in BVCA [1993]). The effort seeks to standardize the valuation of privately held firms in private equity organization portfolios. In particular, it seeks to prevent incidents where private equity investors raise follow-on funds (often from retail investors) based on inflated valuations of still-private firms.

These standards were made more specific in 1993 in response to claims that private equity organizations were exploiting "loopholes" in the standards. Many observers have criticized the revised standards as well, arguing that they still allow too much room for maneuvering: e.g., the distinction between early- and late-stage firms is not precisely defined. Thus, despite the much greater progress made in Great Britain than in the U.S. or elsewhere, it is unclear whether the BVCA effort has succeeded in curbing many problematic instances of aggressive valuations by less-established private equity organizations.

Even if this problem can be addressed, however, there is a second issue. The practices of the established venture groups, as well as the reform efforts such as the BVCA initiative, emphasize the computation of returns using conservative assumptions. While these procedures allow investors to more readily compare the performance of different private equity funds and to avoid being misled by overly aggressive organizations, they make it difficult to compare private equity returns to those in other asset classes. Thus, while it may be possible for private equity organizations to demonstrate that their funds have outperformed other partnerships formed around the same time, it is very difficult for them to show that they have produced positive risk-adjusted returns for their investors relative to the equity market as a whole.

A key obstacle to such comparisons is what can be termed the "stale price" problem. While the movements of public market indexes can be observed on a daily basis, the increase in value of the private firms can only be observed by outsiders after a great deal of delay. Typically, there is a sudden jump in the valuation of a firm reported by the private equity group associated with its initial public offering or a third-party follow-on investment, rather than a gradual increase in value as the company builds up its sales and profitability.

As a result of this problem, it is very difficult to compare public and private equity prices. An illustration of this difficulty is to think about a hypothetical setting where 1) the valuation of private equity portfolios exactly mirrors the movement of the S&P

500, but 2) returns from private equity funds are observed with a one-day delay. If we try to relate the observed daily private and public equity returns, we would find virtually no correlation. (The S&P 500's movements on a given day have little predictive power for its movement on the following day.) This might lead us to falsely conclude that there is no relationship between these two asset classes.

This problem has been acknowledged by experienced observers of the private equity industry. To cite one discussion from the *Venture Capital Journal*:

> Venture Economics has often been asked in the past to comment on the performance of venture capital relative to other asset classes. It is imperative that any asset classes being compared be measured on the same basis [but] market prices for private venture capital partnerships don't exist.... Therefore, objective comparisons of risk and reward relative to other public markets are difficult to justify (Reyes [1990]).

Despite the widespread acknowledgment of this problem, few efforts have been made to date to address this concern. In the remainder of this article, we discuss an approach that we have developed and used to examine the returns of one private equity group.

A PROPOSED SOLUTION

A solution to the performance measurement problem is to "mark to market" the portfolio of the private equity organization. Rather than waiting until there is a "material" event (e.g., an initial public offering) to revalue the firm, we reexamine the valuations of all firms in the portfolio on a periodic basis. The quarterly or annual assessments can incorporate a wide variety of information about the changes over this period:

- The change in the public market valuations of comparable firms.
- The change in the relative market prices of private and public equity markets as a whole.
- The change in the profitability of the portfolio firm.
- The degree of leverage of the portfolio company.
- The change in any other firm characteristics commonly used for valuation purposes by equity market analysts to value similar publicly traded firms (e.g., for young biotechnology firms, the number of patents awarded).

By undertaking such a calculation, the "stale price" problem can be addressed: the entire portfolio has been revalued.

These revised valuations can be compared to the returns from the public market during the same time interval. A standard approach is to run a regression that seeks to explain the fund's returns using one or more measures of public market performance as well as a constant. The key item of performance measurement is the constant term. The analysis seeks to determine whether, once the movements in the market have been controlled for, the coefficient of the constant is positive, negative, or indistinguishable from zero (i.e., whether the market-adjusted performance is superior to the appropriate benchmark, inferior to that measure, or too close to the measure of market performance to discern).

A second feature of this analysis is that it yields a precise measure of the riskiness of the private equity portfolio. The coefficients on the public market return measures capture the level of riskiness of the portfolio. Risk, in modern theory and the practice of finance (at least in public markets), is measured by the correlation of an investment's return with the overall market return. The higher the level of correlation with the public market, the greater the riskiness of the portfolio. To put it another way, a large investor should only worry about how the investment affects the riskiness of their entire portfolio, not the riskiness of the individual investment.

In this way, analysts can avoid drawing false conclusions about the success of investment managers. For instance, consider two mutual funds, one that holds equities of small high-technology firms and one that holds securities issued by utilities. While the high-technology fund may have higher absolute returns over a given period, it may not be a superior performer once one controls the greater riskiness of its portfolio.[1]

The first model of risk-adjusting returns was the capital asset pricing model (CAPM). In measuring risk of an investment, and therefore its required return, investors should care about how the investment's returns covary (or move) with general market returns. For instance, while a highly variable stock that moves with the market (e.g., a designer clothing company) would need to have a high return, a highly volatile stock that does not move with the market (e.g., a gold mining firm) would not. In order to determine whether a given portfolio earns positive or negative risk-adjusted returns, a regression is run using the market return and a constant. In this context, the regression coefficient on the market return is the "beta" of the stock, its measure of riskiness. The coefficient on the constant (also known as the intercept), commonly referred to as Jensen's alpha,[2] is a measure of the abnormal return on the portfolio. A positive alpha implies positive excess risk-adjusted returns.

In recent years, there has been extensive discussion in the finance literature about what measures of market performance should be used as control variables in these regressions. A consensus has emerged around the view, first articulated by Fama and French [1992, 1993], that there are three crucial measures that should be used in such analyses. The Fama-French model is consistent with previous finance theory by Merton [1973] on what factors should affect the expected return on an investment. The intuition of the Fama-French model is that a firm's correlation with the market does not capture the full riskiness of a company. Fama and French propose using a size factor that will control for the fact that small firms are riskier than big firms, and a book-to-market factor that captures the differential riskiness between value and glamour stocks (Lakonishok, Shleifer, and Vishny [1994]).

In the regressions that follow, we use the Fama-French model as well as the CAPM. Their three factors are: RMRF, the return above Treasury bills on the value-weighted market portfolio; SMB, the return on an investment portfolio formed by subtracting the return on a large-firm portfolio from the return on a small-firm portfolio; and HML, the return on an investment portfolio calculated as the return on a portfolio of high book-to-market stocks minus the return on a portfolio of low book-to-market stocks. The intercept from the regressions is once again an indicator of risk-adjusted performance. The intercepts in these regressions have an interpretation analogous to Jensen's alpha in the CAPM framework. A positive intercept implies positive risk-adjusted performance. The three-factor model has been used by many researchers to explore investment performance (Barber and Lyon [1997]; Brav and Gompers [1997]; Kothari and Warner [1997]).

A REPRESENTATIVE CALCULATION

We now illustrate these calculations through an examination of the returns from a single private equity group, E.M. Warburg, Pincus & Co., one of the few firms that has more than twenty years of data. We obtain quarterly data on portfolio companies back to 1972 from this group. We proceed in two parts. First, we have taken the portfolio

EXHIBIT 1 CORRELATION OF UNADJUSTED WARBURG, PINCUS RETURNS WITH THE RETURNS ON OTHER ASSETS

Warburg, Pincus Private Equity Return Correlation with:	
Venture Capital	0.5182
Seed Stage	0.2585
Early Stage	0.7127
Balanced Fund	0.6900
Later Stage	0.4520
Buyouts	0.4201
Mezzanine	0.3154
S&P 500	0.5982
Small-Cap Stocks	0.6784
Corporate Bonds	0.1003
T-Bills	0.2214
T-Bonds	0.0683

values in the Warburg, Pincus data base as accurate reflections of the value of the underlying investments. In subsequent analyses, we "mark to market" investments that are held at cost to get a better assessment of the changes in portfolio value from quarter to quarter.

The quarterly return on the investment portfolio is calculated by taking the ending portfolio value less investments during the quarter plus any disbursements divided by the beginning portfolio value. (This is the manner in which returns are also calculated for public stocks.) In this way, we create a quarterly series of returns from the underlying data.

The return series provides a picture of the performance of Warburg, Pincus over the past twenty-five years. When we use the Warburg, Pincus data, starting with the first quarter of 1972 and ending with the third quarter of 1997, we find an arithmetic

EXHIBIT 2 RISK-ADJUSTED PERFORMANCE OF UNADJUSTED WARBURG, PINCUS PRIVATE EQUITY PORTFOLIO

Independent Variable	2.677	2.637
Intercept	[1.92]	[1.88]
Excess Market Return (RMRF)	1.0849	0.8950
	[6.06]	[4.11]
Excess Return on High Book-to-Market Firms (HML)		0.0237
		[0.08]
Excess Return on Small Firms (SMB)		0.7061
		[2.38]
Adjusted R^2	0.281	0.302
Number of Observations	96	96

average annual return (weighting each year equally and ignoring the amount of money invested) of 30.5%.[3]

In Exhibit 1, we examine the correlation of Warburg, Pincus' returns with other asset classes. The correlations of Warburg, Pincus's returns with both private and public market asset classes are relatively modest. Clearly, from the viewpoint of a large institutional investor, the diversification benefits of Warburg, Pincus are quite large. One caveat must, however, be kept in mind. We are only looking at the stated returns on the portfolio values, as recorded by Warburg, Pincus. To the extent that the valuations are not "marked to market," many of these correlations will be biased downward.

Exhibit 2 presents the calculation of risk-adjusted returns. As discussed earlier, we present the results from both a CAPM regression model and the Fama-French three-factor regression.[4] In these regressions, the intercept represents the quarterly excess return earned by Warburg, Pincus relative to the model. In the simple CAPM regression (first column), the intercept is 2.68, indicating that relative to the CAPM, Warburg, Pincus has earned an excess quarterly return of 2.68% on a risk-adjusted basis. This coefficient is significant at the 10% confidence level, i.e., we are 90% certain that the result is indeed positive.

It is also noteworthy that the Warburg, Pincus portfolio has a beta of slightly greater than 1 (1.08). This means that Warburg, Pincus's portfolio is only slightly riskier than the market. As a reference, most small-stock portfolios would have betas above 1.5. Again, we assess the impact of marking the portfolio to market on the risk adjustments in the next section.

The dependent variable is the quarterly returns on the private equity portfolio of Warburg, Pincus from the first quarter of 1972 through the fourth quarter of 1995. RMRF is the value-weighted market return on all NYSE/AMEX/Nasdaq firms (RM) minus the risk-free rate (RF), which is the one-month Treasury bill rate. SMB (small minus big) is the difference each month between the return on small firms and big firms. HML (high minus low) is the difference each month between the return on a portfolio of high book to market stocks and the return on a portfolio of low book to market stocks. (T-statistics are in brackets.)

The Fama-French results (second column) continue to show that the Warburg, Pincus returns are positive on a risk-adjusted basis. The magnitude of the excess returns is similar to the CAPM results, a positive 2.64% per quarter. On an annualized basis, the positive risk-adjusted performance of Warburg, Pincus is over 10%. It is also worth noting that the correction for small firms seems important. The Warburg, Pincus portfolio has a positive coefficient on the SMB portfolio, indicating that the portfolio returns move with the returns on small firms. This is not surprising, given the importance of venture investments in the Warburg, Pincus portfolio.

THE IMPACT OF MARKING TO MARKET

As discussed above, accounting conventions in private equity make portfolio evaluation and asset allocation difficult. The infrequency with which portfolio values are adjusted reduces calculated correlations and makes risk adjustment difficult. In this section, we explore one method of marking portfolio values to market that can aid in the evaluation of performance. In determining long-run performance, such an exercise is extremely valuable.

We undertake one methodology, although many others could be implemented in a similar manner. From the data on individual Warburg, Pincus investments, we match each portfolio company to a particular three-digit SIC industry. For each of the indus-

EXHIBIT 3 CORRELATIONS OF MARKED-TO-MARKET WARBURG, PINCUS ANNUAL RETURNS WITH PRIVATE EQUITY AND OTHER BENCHMARKS

Warburg, Pincus Private Equity Return Correlation with:	
Venture Capital	0.4846
Seed Stage	0.3240
Early Stage	0.6047
Balanced Fund	0.5985
Later Stage	0.5188
Buyouts	0.5709
Mezzanine	0.2262
S&P 500	0.7367
Small-Cap Stocks	0.7836
Corporate Bonds	0.1872
T-Bills	0.1319
T-Bonds	0.1449

tries, we calculate an equal-weighted industry index from the public market values of all firms in that industry. In this way, we know the relative public market values of firms in the same industry. We can calculate changes in the public market index from quarter to quarter and use these changes to adjust the portfolio value of each company.

In the quarter of any investment or distribution by Warburg, Pincus, we adjust the portfolio value to the stated value in the Warburg, Pincus data. If the company is written down by Warburg, Pincus, we similarly adjust the value to the marked-down value.

EXHIBIT 4 RISK ADJUSTED PERFORMANCE OF MARKED-TO-MARKET WARBURG, PINCUS PRIVATE EQUITY PORTFOLIO

Independent Variable	1.9731	1.714
Intercept	[1.82]	[1.77]
Excess Market Return (RMRF)	1.4399	1.2699
	[9.64]	[7.16]
Excess Return on High Book-to-Market		0.1393
Firms (HML)		[0.56]
Excess Return on Small Firms (SMB)		0.7557
		[3.14]
Adjusted R^2	0.492	0.536
Number of Observations	96	96

The dependent variable is the quarterly returns on the private equity portfolio of Warburg, Pincus from the first quarter of 1972 through the fourth quarter of 1995 marking the portfolio value to market. RMRF is the value-weighted market return on all NYSE/AMEX/Nasdaq firms (RM) minus the risk-free rate (RF), which is the one-month Treasury bill rate. SMB (small minus big) is the difference each month between the return on small firms and big firms. HML (high minus low) is the difference each month between the return on a portfolio of high book to market stocks and the return on a portfolio of low book to market stocks. (T-statistics are in brackets.)

In quarters in which there is neither an investment nor a write-down, we adjust the portfolio value by the change in the matched industry public market index. In this way, a computer hardware company that is in the private equity portfolio will increase in value by 10% if similar public computer hardware companies rise in value by 10%. We use the equal-weighted index to give more weight to small, public firms because of the nature of private equity investments.

In some ways, marking the portfolio value to changes in the public market will give the most conservative assessment of performance. By construction, we are maximizing the possible correlation with the public market returns. This will give the impression of riskier investments (because of the higher correlation), even though private equity valuations are not perfectly correlated with the public markets. (Work by Gompers and Lerner [1997] shows that while the valuations of public and private markets are correlated, the correlation is much less than one.) The estimated risk-adjusted performance should be seen as a lower bound on the true risk-adjusted performance.

In Exhibit 3, we reestimate the correlations of Warburg, Pincus's marked-to-market returns with various private equity and public market indexes. Notice that while correlation with most private markets declines from Exhibit 1, the correlation with public

EXHIBIT 5 BETA ESTIMATES FOR VARIOUS CLASSIFICATIONS OF VENTURE CAPITAL FUNDS

	Beta	Std. Dev.
Overall Venture Capital (1974-1989)	1.86	5.10
Overall Venture Capital (1983-1989)	3.82	5.68
Early Stage (1983-1989)	2.92	9.19
Balanced (1983-1989)	1.76	5.80
Later Stage (1983-1989)	1.07	3.73

The value of beta from CAPM regressions for the return of 175 mature venture capital funds compiled and reported by Venture Economics (Reyes [1990]).

market returns (e.g., the S&P 500 and small-cap stocks) increases. This is not unexpected given our adjustment to portfolio values.

We repeat the risk adjustment of returns using both the CAPM model and the Fama-French model in Exhibit 4. The regressions are run for Warburg, Pincus marked-to-market quarterly returns from the first quarter of 1972 through the fourth quarter of 1995.

The explanatory power of these regressions is much higher than in Exhibit 2. The adjusted R^2 is nearly twice as high in these new regressions. The CAPM regression in the first column shows that the beta on the Warburg, Pincus returns series has increased significantly, to 1.44. Clearly, marking the portfolio values to market using public indexes increases the correlation with the market. The intercept, however, is still positive and significant. The results indicate that relative to the CAPM, Warburg, Pincus earns positive risk-adjusted returns 2% per quarter, or roughly 8% per year.

As a comparison, Venture Economics has published the betas on 175 mature venture capital funds. Exhibit 5 reports these calculated betas for various types of venture capital funds. The betas calculated by Venture Economics suffer from the bias of not being marked to market (i.e., they are based on stated valuations), and therefore should probably be considered as analogous to the non-marked-to-market beta calculations that we have undertaken using the Warburg, Pincus data in Exhibit 2 (i.e., the estimate of 1.08 in the non-marked-to-market returns data).

Except for later-stage funds, the beta of Warburg, Pincus is substantially lower than all the other classifications of venture capital funds. In addition, because beta measures the level of risk that investors cannot diversify away, a combination of venture funds cannot have a lower beta than Venture Economics reports, i.e., the betas in Exhibit 5 represent a lower bound on the estimated beta of a portfolio of venture capital funds. The low beta on Warburg, Pincus's investments is likely the product of the flexible investment strategy practiced, which allows the organization to take advantage of investments across many industries and many stages of development.

The Fama-French results confirm the CAPM results. Once again, the coefficient on the market return has increased due to our marking to market. Similarly, the importance of small-firm risk has increased as well; i.e., the coefficient on SMB is significantly higher. Even after controlling for the three factors, however, Warburg, Pincus still earns significantly positive risk-adjusted returns. The magnitude in the Fama-French results is similar to the CAPM results; i.e., 1.7% excess return per quarter, or about 7% annual excess performance over a twenty-four-year period.

CONCLUSIONS

Our analysis has two goals. First, we explore the calculations for one private equity organization. The regression results from asset pricing models including the CAPM and Fama-French three-factor model indicate positive and significant abnormal returns. On an annualized basis, the excess risk-adjusted return is between 7% and 10%. In other words, Warburg, Pincus has earned 7% to 10% higher returns per year than a portfolio of similar-risk public stocks. These returns are not only significant, but they are large in economic terms as well. While these excess returns are calculated using the gross results of Warburg, Pincus, the size of the abnormal excess performance leaves a substantial return for limited partners, given current fund terms.

Second, we hope to encourage a more general discussion in the private equity industry about risk adjustment and benchmarking. We believe that the issues discussed here open the door to future work on improving the understanding of private equity returns. Innovations in this article are important for global asset allocation decisions across various asset classes, as well as the choice between individual portfolio managers. Our results indicate that these techniques can be fruitfully applied to the private equity arena.

ENDNOTES

This article was published in *The Journal of Private Equity*, Winter 1997.

The authors thank E.M. Warburg, Pincus & Co. and Venture Economics for access to data; Ken Froot, Jay Light, Andre Perold, and Jesse Reyes for helpful comments; and the Division of Research at the Harvard Business School for research support.

[1] One subtle issue associated with applying the "marked-to-market" approach to the private equity setting is that we are looking at the gross returns of the fund. Because investors (limited partners) frequently get their capital back before the general partners receive a share of the profits, the riskiness of the investors' investment is likely to be lower than that of the entire portfolio. Thus, our calculations are likely to overstate the riskiness of the portfolio.

[2] This type of regression was first introduced by Michael Jensen in 1968, and is now widely employed by fund evaluation services (e.g., Morningstar, Inc.) and others to evaluate mutual and hedge fund managers. Of course, because mutual funds calculate net asset value daily, they do not generally face

these types of valuation problems.

[3] The calculated returns in this article are the gross returns of Warburg, Pincus. The large positive performance of the gross returns on a risk-adjusted basis would indicate that net results still leave substantial performance premiums for investors. Other additional analyses might include looking at the time trend in excess returns, as well as weighting observations by fund size.

[4] The time period for the regression is the first quarter of 1972 through the fourth quarter of 1995. We did not have the factor returns for 1996 due to data availability.

REFERENCES

Barber, Brad M., and John D. Lyon. "Detecting Long-Run Abnormal Stock Returns: The Empirical Power and Specification of Test Statistics." *Journal of Financial Economics*, 43 (1997), pp. 401-432.

Brav, Alon, and Paul A. Gompers. "Myth or Reality? The Long-Run Underperformance of Initial Public Offerings: Evidence from Venture and Non-venture Capital-Backed Companies." *The Journal of Finance*, 52 (1997), pp. 1791-1821.

Cain, Walter M. "LBO Partnership Valuations Matter: A Presentation to the LBO Partnership Valuation Meeting." *Mimeo*, February 1997.

Fama, Eugene F., and Kenneth R. French. "Common Risk Factors in the Returns of Stocks and Bonds." *Journal of Financial Economics*, 33 (1993), pp. 3-55.

——. "The Cross-Section of Expected Stock Returns." *The Journal of Finance*, 47 (1992), pp. 427-465.

Galante, Steven. "Merrill Weighs In With Its Own Index for Private Equity." *Private Equity Analyst*, 5 (August 1993), pp. 1, 11-12

Gompers, Paul A. "Grandstanding in the Venture Capital Industry." *The Journal of Financial Economics*, 42 (1996), pp. 133-156.

Gompers, Paul A., and Josh Lerner. "Money Chasing Deals?: The Impact of Fund Inflows on the Valuation of Private Equity Investments." Working paper, Harvard University, 1997.

Guidelines for the Valuation and Disclosure of Venture Capital Portfolios. London: British Venture Capital Association, 1993.

Jensen, Michael C. "The Performance of Mutual Funds in the Period 1945-1964." *The Journal of Finance*, 23 (1968), pp. 389-416.

Key Terms and Conditions for Private Equity Investing. New York: William M. Mercer, Inc., 1996.

Kothari, S.P., and Jerry Warner. "Measuring Long-Horizon Security Price Performance." *Journal of Financial Economics*, 43 (1997), pp. 301-339.

Lakonishok, Josef, Andrei Shleifer, and Robert Vishny. "Contrarian Investment, Extrapolation, and Risk." *The Journal of Finance*, 49 (1994), pp. 1541-1578.

Merton, Robert. "An Intertemporal Capital Asset Pricing Model." *Econometrica*, 41 (1973), pp. 867-887.

"Proposal for a Standard Industry-Wide System for Measuring Interim Performance of Venture Capital Partnerships." Institutional Limited Partners Association, May 1990.

Reyes, Jesse E. "Industry Struggling to Forge Tools for Measuring Risk." *Venture Capital Journal*, 30 (September 1990), pp. 23-27.

Ritter, Jay R. "The Long-Run Performance of Initial Public Offerings." *The Journal of Finance*, 46 (1991), pp. 3-27.

18 A TRANSACTION-BASED INDEX OF COMMERCIAL PROPERTY AND ITS COMPARISON TO THE NCREIF INDEX

DEAN GATZLAFF
Florida State University

DAVID GELTNER
University of Cincinnati

BACKGROUND: WHY WE NEED A TRANSACTION-BASED PRICE INDEX[1]

Value indexes that map the periodic movements of asset prices provide valuable information not only to economists studying the market, but to practitioners and investors participating in the market. Understanding historical price volatility, correlations and autocorrelations, and identifying the timing and magnitudes of "peaks" and "troughs" in the market, allows investors to develop better price expectations and to make more-informed investment decisions.

Unlike stock and bond market prices, measuring asset price movements in property markets is particularly difficult, because the assets are highly heterogeneous and infrequently traded. In addition, property markets are dominated by private and negotiated transactions of whole assets, rather than public auctions of homogeneous shares as in the stock and bond markets.

Today, the most commonly used index of investment performance of income property is the NCREIF Property Index (NPI), which is based on the appraised values of properties held for tax-exempt institutions by members of the National Council of Real Estate Investment Fiduciaries (NCREIF). While the NPI provides much useful information, it has some problems. Perhaps most notably, both practitioners and academicians have wondered about the extent to which the NPI presents a "smoothed" or "lagged" representation of asset price changes in the commercial property market that the index is often assumed to represent. Such smoothing and lagging may be due to the nature of the appraisal process or to the nature of the aggregation in the index construction and reporting methodology.[2]

Another issue of interest is the nature of the possible differences in the investment returns performance to the so-called "institutional quality" properties held by NCREIF members compared to a broader sample of commercial properties. Institutional properties tend to be confined to the largest and highest quality commercial buildings in prime metropolitan locations. There is some evidence, for example, that the generally smaller commercial properties (in common with housing) may not have fared as badly as the institutional properties in the slump in property prices that occurred at the end of the 1980s and early 1990s.[3]

Both of these issues have obvious implications for the use of the NPI in portfolio analysis or as a benchmark of commercial property performance, and both of these issues are addressed in our study.[4] First, we explore a new type of data source and statistical methodology for estimating period-by-period capital return indexes for commercial property that is not dependent on appraisal valuations and that avoids temporal aggregation.[5] Specifically, we apply to a sample of historical commercial property transactions the time-weighted repeat-sale index construction methodology that has been pioneered in housing literature. Second, our data consist of the repeat sales occurring within the *entire population* of commercial properties within the metropolitan areas of the state of Florida. This population is dominated by the smaller, "non-institutional" properties. Thus, our index portrays the performance of this broader class of commercial properties during the market crash of the early 1990s, which can be compared with the NCREIF index of institutional property performance during the same period. In particular, our study compares the performance of our index with that of the relevant geographic and property type sub-indexes of the NPI.

A brief overview of the repeat-sales index estimation method is presented followed by a description of the data used to estimate the indexes. The characteristics of the transaction-based commercial property price movements are then compared with the NPI and also with the housing market. We end with a summary of our findings.

METHODOLOGY: HOW THE REPEAT-SALES INDEX WORKS

The repeat-sales regression (RSR) methodology was first proposed as a procedure for developing real estate price indexes thirty-five years ago by Bailey, Muth, and Nourse [1963]. Important advancements in the technique have been made in the past decade by Case-Shiller [1989], Clapp-Giacotto [1992], Gatzlaff-Haurin [1997], and Goetzmann [1992], and others. The RSR has been applied widely in both academic and industry studies of housing in the U.S. To date, however, no one has applied the RSR procedure to *commercial* property prices in this country.[6]

A different, but closely related, type of statistical procedure, the "hedonic regression" (HR), has been applied to commercial properties to estimate transaction-based price indexes in a few cases.[7] However, the hedonic procedure requires good data availability on a number of property characteristic variables, and from an econometric perspective the HR raises a number of specification issues and problems of omitted variables.[8] In practice, many of the HR indexes of commercial property developed so far appear rather "noisy."[9] A possible reason for the RSR procedure not yet being applied to commercial properties is that commercial properties are less numerous than houses (and transact less often) so data bases contain substantially fewer commercial property sales transactions than housing transactions. This is particularly critical for the RSR procedure, because it can only use a subset of all transactions, namely those where the same property transacts twice (or more) during the period covered by the data base. This usually greatly reduces the total number of observations on which the index can be estimated, especially when the property turnover rate is low, as is often the case with a commercial property. One of the methodological issues our study seeks to address is whether the RSR technique can be successfully applied to the commercial property market at a practical empirical level that can provide useful information for decision makers, in spite of the repeat-sales data restriction.

In this section of our article, a simple numerical example of the RSR is presented to clarify for readers how the basic procedure works to produce an index of the period-by-period capital returns (or percentage asset price changes) to the properties in a given population, using repeat-transaction price data from infrequently and irregularly traded individual properties.[10] In this example we posit a population consisting of four commercial properties whose "true periodic capital returns" were 5% in 1995, 3% in 1996, and 7% in 1997. We will shortly explain more specifically what we mean when we say that these were the "true" capital returns in this population. For now, however, suppose that these underlying true returns are not directly observable, because not every property in the population transacts every year. In particular, let us suppose that the only transactions among this population were those reported in Exhibit 1. For example,

Property #1 was sold at the end of 1994 for $1,000,000, and then sold again at the end of 1997 for $1,157,205.

Let us now clarify what we mean when we say that the "true" capital return in this population is 5%, 3% and 7% in the years 1995-1997. We mean that if we apply these periodic capital return rates to each property's first transaction price by growing that price at the given rate for each subsequent period, we will obtain the second transaction price for each property. This is seen as follows.

Prop.#1: 1,000,000 x 1.05 x 1.03 x 1.07 = 1,157,205
Prop.#2: 2,299,000 x 1.05 = 2,413,950
Prop.#3: 695,466 x 1.05 x 1.03 = 752,146
Prop.#4: 1,738,425 x 1.03 = 1,790,578 (1)

For example, the first property sold at the end of 1994 for $1,000,000. If that price grew by 5% during 1995, by another 3% during 1996, and by another 7% during 1997, then we would obtain the second transaction price of $1,157,205 at the end of 1997. Turning to the fourth property, we see that it had its first transaction later than the others, selling for $1,738,425 at the end of 1995, and its second transaction oc-

EXHIBIT 1 EXAMPLE PRICE DATA FOR FOUR PROPERTIES 1994-1997

Property\Year	1994	1995	1996	1997
Property #1	$1,000,000	NA	NA	$1,157,205
Property #2	$2,299,000	$2,413,950	NA	NA
Property #3	$695,466	NA	$752,146	NA
Property #4	NA	$1,738,425	$1,790,578	NA

Note: All transactions occurred at the end of the calendar year.

curred at the end of the following year, so its second price reflects only the 3% growth rate which prevailed during 1996. As the historical periodic growth rates of 5%, 3%, and 7% apply individually to all four properties in our example population, it seems apparent that these rates indeed accurately reflect the periodic capital returns in this population.

In this example, we assume that we already knew the true historical periodic capital returns in the population. Let us now see how the RSR procedure could be used in this population to estimate these returns simply from the transaction price data, if we did not already know what the returns were. Let "r_t" stand for the unknown value of the return in year "t," so that our equations include only the observable transaction price data and these unknowns:

Prop.#1: $1{,}000{,}000 \times (1 + r_{95}) \times (1 + r_{96}) \times (1 + r_{97}) = 1{,}157{,}205$
Prop.#2: $2{,}299{,}000 \times (1 + r_{95}) = 2{,}413{,}950$
Prop.#3: $695{,}466 \times (1 + r_{95}) \times (1 + r_{96}) = 752{,}146$
Prop.#4: $1{,}738{,}425 \times (1 + r_{96}) = 1{,}790{,}578$

Next, we divide both sides by the first transaction price, and switch the sides of the equals sign:

Prop.#1: $1{,}157{,}205/1{,}000{,}000 = (1 + r_{95}) \times (1 + r_{96}) \times (1 + r_{97})$
Prop.#2: $2{,}413{,}950/2{,}299{,}000 = (1 + r_{95})$
Prop.#3: $752{,}146/695{,}466 = (1 + r_{95}) \times (1 + r_{96})$
Prop.#4: $1{,}790{,}578/1{,}738{,}425 = (1 + r_{96})$

To linearize this system we need to make it additive rather than multiplicative, so we take the natural logarithm of both sides of each equation (and recall that the log of a product equals the sum of the logs):

Prop.#1: $LN(1{,}157{,}205/1{,}000{,}000) = LN(1 + r_{95}) + LN(1 + r_{96}) + LN(1 + r_{97})$
Prop.#2: $LN(2{,}413{,}950/2{,}299{,}000) = LN(1 + r_{95})$
Prop.#3: $LN(752{,}146/695{,}466) = LN(1 + r_{95}) + LN(1 + r_{96})$
Prop.#4: $LN(1{,}790{,}578/1{,}738{,}425) = LN(1 + r_{96})$

Now recall that $LN(1 + r_t)$ is the "continuously compounded" rate of return in period "t."[11] Note that the right-hand side (RHS) of the above equations can be equivalently expressed as the sum of a series of products defined as follows. Each product corresponds to one period of time. The product equals the continuously compounded return for that period multiplied by a dummy variable which equals one for time periods between the two transactions and zero otherwise:

Prop.#1: $LN(1{,}157{,}205 / 1{,}000{,}000) =$
$LN(1 + r_{95}) \times 1 + LN(1 + r_{96}) \times 1 + LN(1 + r_{97}) \times 1$
Prop.#2: $LN(2{,}413{,}950/2{,}299{,}000) =$
$LN(1 + r_{95}) \times 1 + LN(1 + r_{96}) \times 0 + LN(1 + r_{97}) \times 0$
Prop.#3: $LN(752{,}146/695{,}466) =$
$LN(1 + r_{95}) \times 1 + LN(1 + r_{96}) \times 1 + LN(1 + r_{97}) \times 0$
Prop.#4: $LN(1{,}790{,}578/1{,}738{,}425) =$
$LN(1 + r_{95}) \times 0 + LN(1 + r_{96}) \times 1 + LN(1 + r_{97}) \times 0$

It should now be obvious how we can use linear regression procedures to estimate the unknown periodic returns.[12] The observations on which the regression will be estimated consist of the repeat-sales transaction price pairs (the rows corresponding to the four properties above). The left-hand side (LHS), or dependent variable, in the regression is the log price relative for each observation: $LN(P_{is}/P_{if})$, where P_{it} is the transaction price observed for property (observation) "i" in time period "t," and t = f corresponds to the time period of the first sale while t = s corresponds to the time period of the second sale. The RHS variables of the regression consist purely of dummy variables corresponding to each time period, defined as above (1 if the time period is between the two transactions, 0 otherwise).[13] In this form, it is easy to see that the RHS regression parameters to be estimated, labeled "β_t," correspond to the continuously compounded returns each period: β_t, $LN(1 + r_t)$.

For our three-year example, the regression equation would be expressed as follows:

$Y = D\beta + e$

where: Y is a column vector of the log price relative observations, $Y_i \equiv LN(P_{is}/P_{if})$ for $i = 1, \ldots, n$ (where n is the number of repeat-sales pairs); β is a column vector of period-by-period capital returns; D is a dummy variable matrix whose rows correspond to the observations and columns correspond to the time periods; and e is a column vector of the regression "error" term.

The regression error results from "noise" in the property transaction prices. To understand what is meant by "noise," consider that the LHS variable is the log price relative of each observation. In other words, the LHS is the cumulative capital return for each observation across the calendar time between the two transactions. The regression error for each observation is the difference between what the regression *predicts* the cumulative return would be for that observation, versus what the cumulative return is actually observed to be for that observation.

For our three-period, four-observation numerical example the RSR regression would be estimated by the following system of four linear equations, where the β_t are the estimated parameter values (continuously compounded periodic capital returns), and the u_i are the residuals:

$$\begin{aligned}
LN(1{,}157{,}205 / 1{,}000{,}000) &= 0.1460 = \hat{\beta}_{95} \times 1 + \hat{\beta}_{96} \times 1 + \hat{\beta}_{97} \times 1 + u_1 \\
LN(2{,}413{,}950/2{,}299{,}000) &= 0.0488 = \hat{\beta}_{95} \times 1 + \hat{\beta}_{96} \times 0 + \hat{\beta}_{97} \times 0 + u_2 \\
LN(752{,}146/695{,}466) &= 0.0783 = \hat{\beta}_{95} \times 1 + \hat{\beta}_{96} \times 1 + \hat{\beta}_{97} \times 0 + u_3 \\
LN(1{,}790{,}578/1{,}738{,}425) &= 0.0296 = \hat{\beta}_{95} \times 0 + \hat{\beta}_{96} \times 1 + \hat{\beta}_{97} \times 0 + u_4 \quad (2)
\end{aligned}$$

The regression estimation must solve this system simultaneously. Note that if we ignore the residual terms there are three unknowns in this system, namely the three periodic-return parameters to be estimated. As there are more than three equations, there may not exist a single solution that solves all four equations (if the equations are not consistent). However, we can always find a solution for the parameter values that minimizes the sum of the squared residuals, that is, which minimizes the sum: $.u_1^2 + u_2^2 + u_3^2 + u_4^2$. Such a solution would correspond to "ordinary least squares" (OLS) estimation of the regression. In this numerical example, it is easy to see what the solution is, because in fact the four equations are consistent. The following solution will cause the sum of squared errors to equal exactly zero, which is certainly the minimum possible sum of squares:[14]

$$\hat{\beta}_{95} = 0.0488 = LN(1.05)$$

$$\hat{\beta}_{96} = 0.0295 = LN(1.03)$$

$$\hat{\beta}_{97} = 0.0677 = LN(1.07)$$

Furthermore, converting these estimated continuously compounded returns to annual wealth relatives with simple returns (by taking: $EXP(\hat{\beta}_t);(1+r_t)$), we can compare equation system (2) with equation system (1) and note that these two systems are identical with the above solution for equation (2) and all the residuals set equal to zero: $u_1 = u_2 = u_3 = u_4 = 0$. This reflects the fact that, in the previous solution to equation system (2), that is, in our OLS estimation of the RSR for our numerical example, we have recovered the exact true periodic capital returns for our four-property population. (Recall that the true returns for 1995, 1996, and 1997 are 5%, 3%, and 7%.) Thus, we see how the RSR procedure yields an estimate of the periodic capital returns in a population of properties for which we can only infrequently and irregularly observe transaction prices within the individual properties. All we require is that at least one transaction price must be observable in the population during each period for which we want to estimate a population return, and the total number of repeat-sale pair observations must at least equal the number of time periods for which we wish to estimate periodic returns.

The reason why the RSR obtained *exact* true returns in this example is that there was *no noise* in this case. That is, all the observed transaction prices of every property were exactly consistent with the true underlying population returns. This is why the four equations in the estimation system were consistent and the regression residuals were all zero. Of course, this will not generally be the case in the real world. However, in the real world there typically will be many more degrees of freedom in the regression estimation than were present in this example. (Here there was only one more observation than the number of periods of time for which we wished to estimate returns.) The more transaction observations per time period, the better the regression estimation can filter out the transaction noise. As noise is apparent in an estimated index by the presence of excess volatility and negative autocorrelation in the returns time series (a "spiky" or "sawtooth" appearance in the returns or the index levels), it should be possible in practice to judge whether the index has successfully filtered out most of the noise. This question is one of the focuses of this article.

In practice, it should be noted that the nature of transaction noise will cause a type of statistical problem known as "heteroskedasticity" in RSR index estimation.[15] For this reason, a three-stage "weighted least squares" (WLS) procedure is usually used in the housing literature to estimate RSR indexes, and this procedure will be applied in the present study as well.[16]

DATA: FLORIDA DOR TRANSACTION PRICES

The transaction data used for this study were obtained from the Florida Department of Revenue's (DOR) 1997 property tax records. These data are compiled each year by the DOR under a statutory provision requiring the auditing of each county's property assessments. The complete set of records includes information on every parcel in the state of Florida. Data were available to the authors that included transactions recorded through July 1997.

Property records were obtained for the twenty Metropolitan Statistical Areas (MSAs) located in the state of Florida. The MSAs represent all of the major urban areas in Florida, approximately 85% of the state's population, and over 6.7 million properties (residential and commercial). The information indicated for each parcel includes the lands-use code, the assessed property and land values, the most recent sale price and closing date (year and month), the second most recent sales price and closing date (year and month), and approximately forty other property- and owner-specific variables.[17] Commercial properties that sold twice between 1975 and 1997 were used to estimate annual RSR indexes for the aggregate market as well as five market sectors. However, their comparison with the NCREIF indexes is limited to later periods when sufficient

EXHIBIT 2 DESCRIPTIVE STATISTICS OF THE TRANSACTION DATA LISTED BY YEAR OF SALE, 1975 - 1997

Year	No. Obs.	Median Sale Price ($000)	Mean Sale Price ($000)	Std. Dev. Sale Price ($000)	Min. Sale Price ($000)	Max. Sale Price ($000)
1975	81	350	754	1,209	150	8,910
1976	113	300	516	537	150	3,210
1977	137	315	568	838	150	8,040
1978	147	300	715	1,093	150	8,493
1975	182	323	715	1,011	150	8,053
1980	226	421	1,233	2,026	150	9,250
1981	287	350	863	1,553	150	15,000
1982	268	415	1,090	2,964	150	42,200
1983	353	420	1,193	2,427	150	20,000
1984	414	398	1,194	2,115	150	20,735
1985	482	410	1,177	2,217	150	22,173
1986	573	425	1,278	3,174	150	35,400
1987	425	375	1,101	2,690	150	35,480
1988	506	447	1,333	2,595	150	20,734
1989	569	475	1,314	2,420	150	26,500
1990	471	450	1,096	1,774	150	16,800
1991	448	449	1,516	2,887	150	18,796
1992	470	448	1,371	3,089	150	32,550
1993	551	435	1,267	2,625	150	23,666
1994	496	460	1,224	2,701	150	24,200
1995	533	495	1,385	3,812	150	67,000
1996	765	572	1,843	4,058	150	35,200
1997	249	595	1,738	3,359	150	32,900

Note: The above statistics are calculated using sale price information from both the first and second sales of the 4,373 repeat-sale pairs. The statistics reported for 1997 are based on observations that extend through, and include, 1997:6 (July).

NCREIF properties were available for the NPI to be produced for Florida or the Southeast Region.

Properties were selected from the DOR data set that represented five sectors of the real estate market: 1) apartment, 2) retail, 3) office, 4) hotel, and 5) industrial.[18] A total of 124,871 properties were identified as having the appropriate land-use code for one of the five sectors (apartment, 11,280; retail, 36,232; office, 37,625; hotel, 4,548; and industrial, 35,186). Properties were then identified that reported both a most recent and second most recent sale price (and sale date) during the 1975 (January) to 1997 (July) period that had values greater than $150,000.[19]

Three steps were conducted to mitigate the effect that properties that experienced substantial capital improvements (renovations or demolition) during the study period would have on the RSR index estimates. First, properties were excluded that were identified as being a vacant parcel on either its first or second sale date. Second, those properties that indicated an effective-year-built after either its first or second sale date were

EXHIBIT 3 DESCRIPTIVE STATISTICS OF THE TRANSACTION DATA LISTED BY SECTOR FOR 1996 -1997

Sector	No. Obs.	Median Sale Price ($000)	Mean Sale Price ($000)	Std. Dev. Sale Price ($000)	Min. Sale Price ($000)	Max. Sale Price ($000)
Apartment	284	825	2,169	3,780	150	32,900
Retail	219	407	1,103	1,880	150	12,240
Office	235	365	1,371	3,271	150	34,000
Hotel	101	950	2,337	4,103	158	35,200
Industrial	175	450	2,442	5,916	153	27,580

Note: The statistics reported above are based on sales that occurred in 1996 through July of 1997.

deleted.[20] Finally, the repeat-sale data were limited to those properties with holding periods of at least three years between their transaction dates.[21] We believe that the resulting repeat-sales sample largely reflects the effects of no more than routine capital improvement expenditures on the properties between transaction dates.[22] The final data set includes 4,373 properties (apartment, 1,114; retail, 822; office, 979; hotel, 482; and industrial, 946) that were recorded as selling at least twice during the index construction period.

Descriptive summary statistics are reported for the repeat-sale data in Exhibit 2. This exhibit indicates that the data represent a wide range of property values ($150,000 to $67,000,000). In addition, the median sale prices of the properties that sold each year ranged from a low of $300,000 in 1976 (and 1978) to a high of $595,000 in 1997. The skewed nature of the sale price data is evidenced by the large differences in the yearly median and mean prices (and the large standard deviations).

Exhibit 3 reports the median, mean, standard deviations, minimum, and maximum sale price information by property type for the 1996 and 1997 periods. It is interesting to note that the apartment and hotel sectors were generally higher priced than the retail, office, and industrial sectors. However, the maximum sale prices in all sectors are reported to be similar, with the exception of the retail sector which was less than the others by a factor of two to three.[23] A comparison of these data, and data from previous periods, with those properties reporting only a single sale date indicates that the characteristics reported in Exhibits 2 and 3 are generally representative of the entire time series and population.

It is important to note that the vast majority of properties included in our repeat-sales data base are much smaller than the typical property included in the NCREIF index.[24] For example, the mean value of Florida properties in the NCREIF index during the second quarter of 1997 was $23,158,000, which is some thirteen times the mean 1997 sale price in our repeat-sales sample, and almost forty times our median sale price in that year.

RESULTS: "LOOK MIKE, NO SMOOTHING!" (OR IS THERE?)

Exhibit 4 shows the results of our RSR price index estimation for Florida commercial properties based on the aggregate sample of all 4,373 repeat-sales pair observations, including all property types. The estimated annual periodic capital returns, and the resulting index level (set arbitrarily to a value of 1.00 as of the end of 1975) are reported in Exhibit 4A, along with some basic summary statistics on the return time series.[25] Exhibit 4B charts the price level index across the 1975-1997 period.

EXHIBIT 4A THE RSR INDEX OF ALL FLORIDA COMMERCIAL PROPERTY

Annual Return Summary Statistics

GMEAN	4.23%
MEAN	4.44%
MEDIAN	3.56%
STDEV	6.99%

Return History

Year	End of Year Index Level	Capital Return
1975	1.00	
1976	1.18	18.11%
1977	1.16	–1.46%
1978	1.25	7.46%
1979	1.50	19.90%
1980	1.77	18.34%
1981	1.79	0.73%
1982	1.84	3.07%
1983	1.96	6.46%
1984	1.97	0.55%
1985	2.05	4.04%
1986	2.04	–0.71%
1987	2.17	6.65%
1988	2.09	–3.72%
1989	2.13	1.68%
1990	2.10	–1.07%
1991	2.03	–3.63%
1992	1.93	–4.62%
1993	2.03	5.17%
1994	2.19	7.58%
1995	2.18	–0.21%
1996	2.30	5.47%
1997	2.49	7.98%

The first conclusion suggested by these results is that the time-weighted RSR technique we employed here appears to be feasible for commercial property price index construction from a practical and statistical perspective, in this case with an average of about 200 repeat-sales observations per period. While there is some evidence of noise in this index during the first few years (possibly during 1976-1980), in general the all-property index appears free of serious noise problems. The overall annual volatility of 6.99% per year does not appear excessive, as it is considerably below the volatility typically observed in the stock market, for example. The overall first-order autocorrelation coefficient is +21%, which suggests a mildly sluggish asset market, but does not evidence a noise problem (which would be manifested by negative autocorrelation).[26]

In an extension of the work reported in this article, the authors have carried this question a bit farther, developing RSR price indexes without apparent excessive noise

EXHIBIT 4B RSR INDEX FLORIDA COMMERCIAL PROPERTY PRICE LEVEL

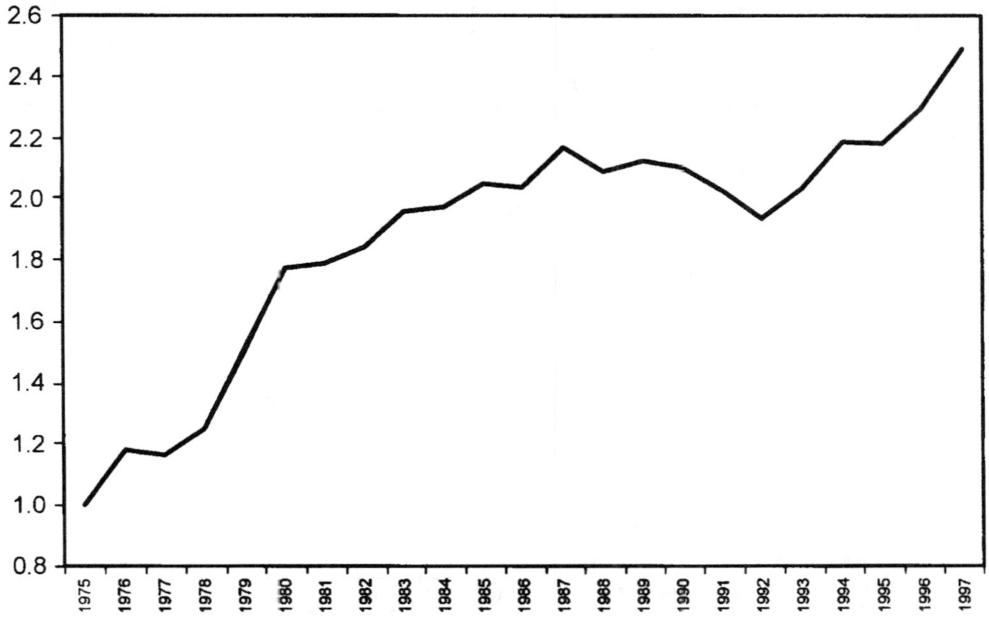

for the individual property type sectors within Florida, even though these indexes were estimated sometimes with as little as an average of only about twenty repeat-observations per period. This was done using a Bayesian/Method of Moments estimation technique developed by Goetzmann [1992], using the a priori assumption that the autocorrelation behavior in the capital returns of the individual property sectors would be similar to that observed in the overall commercial property index described here. (A description of the sectoral indexes is available in the RERI Working Paper by the authors, entitled: "A Repeat-Sales Transaction-Based Index of Commercial Property.")

The second major conclusion from this research regards the nature of the property price history revealed in the exhibits. The price history is dominated by a general growth trend, with strong growth periods notable in the late 1970s and again in the mid-1990s. The price slump of the early 1990s is also apparent, though not terribly deep. The cumulative price level loss is only about 9% during the 1990-1992 period, after which there is a strong recovery in 1993-1994 and 1996-1997.

COMPARISON WITH NCREIF

In order to gain some insight into the difference between transaction-based and appraisal-based price indexes, as well as the possible difference between the performance of a broader population of commercial properties as compared to "institutional quality" properties, we have conducted a comparison of our RSR index and the corresponding NCREIF index. In order to make the comparison in a most direct manner, the NCREIF index we use is the NCREIF Florida Index (NFI), which consists of all, and only, NCREIF properties in the state of Florida. Because NCREIF does not publish an index unless there are at least twenty properties in the index, the NFI only begins in late 1981, when there were twenty-three properties in the index (with an average value of $3.8 million per property at that time). By 1997 there were over 200 properties in the NFI (with an average individual property value over $23 million). Also, because the RSR is estimated on a calendar year basis and the NCREIF end of 1997 data are not yet available, our comparison extends only through 1996. Thus, we compare fifteen years of annual capital returns: 1982-1996.[27] The present analysis will not attempt to "unsmooth" the NFI, because our purpose is to compare our transaction-based index directly with the appraisal-based index to see how different the two appear. It is important, however, to make a different type of adjustment to the officially published NCREIF index for purposes of our comparison.

In breaking out the total return between the capital and income component, NCREIF

EXHIBIT 5A COMPARISON OF RSR VERSUS NCREIF ALL FLORIDA COMMERCIAL PROPERTY

Annual Return Summary Statistics (%)

	NFI	RSR
GMEAN	2.21	1.70
MEAN	2.28	1.78
MEDIAN	3.86	4.07
STDEV	50.59	

Return History

Year	NFI Price Level	Adj. NFI Return	RSR Price Level	RSR Return
1981	1.0000		1.0000	
1982	1.0263	2.63%	1.0307	3.07%
1983	1.1026	7.43%	1.0973	6.46%
1984	1.1875	7.70%	1.1033	0.55%
1985	1.2339	3.91%	1.1479	4.04%
1986	1.2722	3.10%	1.1397	–0.71%
1987	1.3354	4.97%	1.2155	6.65%
1988	1.4155	5.99%	1.1703	–3.72%
1989	1.4524	2.61%	1.1899	1.68%
1990	1.4573	0.34%	1.1771	–1.07%
1991	1.3931	–4.40%	1.1343	–3.63%
1992	1.3040	–6.39%	1.0819	–4.62%
1993	1.3278	1.83%	1.1379	5.17%
1994	1.3639	2.71%	1.2242	7.58%
1995	1.3684	0.33%	1.2216	–0.21%
1996	1.3887	1.48%	1.2884	5.47%

subtracts all capital improvement expenditures from the numerator (value change component) of the capital-return formula (and not from the numerator of the income-return formula). In this way, the NCREIF index income component represents an accrual-based accounting income return (akin to an "earnings/price" ratio in the stock market), and the NCREIF capital return reflects purely the effect of the property market on property values, without considering the effect of capital improvements made by the property owners. Because of this definition, when one constructs an accumulated index level from the NCREIF capital return index, the result is not the same thing as a chart of property price movements. To convert the NCREIF capital return into an index of property price change based on appraised value, one would have to add back the capital expenditures each quarter. This is what we have done in our comparison. This adjustment should make our version of the NFI more directly comparable to our RSR index, as both indexes will reflect property price changes, including the effect of capital improvements in the properties.[28]

The comparison between our RSR and the NFI is presented in Exhibit 5. The two indexes appear broadly similar, and are contemporaneously correlated at over +50% in the annual price changes. Both price indexes display a generally very gradual growth over the fifteen-year period, with the NFI exhibiting slightly greater growth overall (2.2% versus 1.7% per year).[29] The NFI also displays a slightly deeper drop in prices during the 1990-1992 property market recession. However, the difference in the degree to which institutional versus non-institutional property prices fell during the recession appears to be minimal in Florida (the RSR fell a total of 9.1% against the NFI fall of 10.5%.) In any case, both indexes agree in suggesting that the fall in commercial property prices in the early 1990s was less severe in Florida than it was in some other regions of the country.

Also there do not appear to be major differences between the two indexes regarding "smoothing," or the statistical effects of appraisal as opposed to transaction-based valuation. Both indexes display nearly identical annual volatility (4.1% for the RSR versus 3.9% for the NFI), which is quite low.[30] However, on closer inspection, there are some differences between the RSR and NFI that do reveal some of the expected differences between a transactions-based versus appraisals-based index. The RSR appears slightly more "rough" overall in Exhibit 5B, and the RSR exhibits some volatility in the late 1980s that the NFI does not show (e.g., a sharp rise in 1987 and fall in 1988). There is also some evidence that the RSR is slightly "leading" in time, and the NFI slightly "lagging." For example, the RSR registers the beginning of the major drop of the early 1990s a little earlier than the NFI (the RSR begins falling in 1990, the NFI not until 1991), and the RSR return is correlated +47% with the NFI return one year later.[31] The

Exhibit 5b RSR versus NFI Price Level

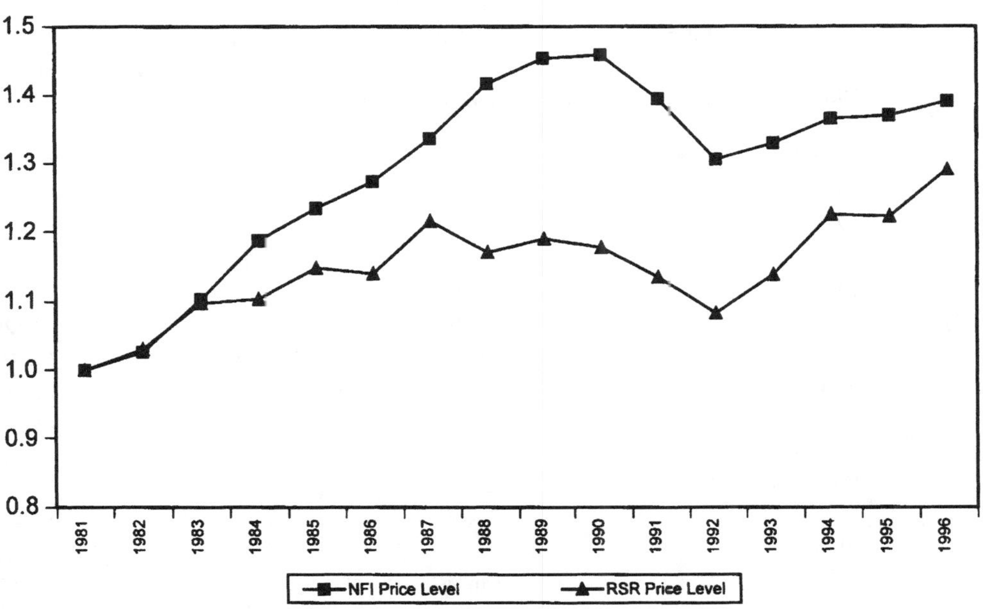

annual NFI returns display strong inertia with positive first-order autocorrelation of 61%, while the RSR returns do not show positive autocorrelation over the 1982-1996 period.

COMPARISON WITH HOUSING

In a separate report, Gatzlaff [1997] has developed an RSR based index of Florida single-family home prices that is quite comparable to the RSR commercial price index we have developed in the present study.[32] This enables, what is to the authors' knowledge, the first head-to-head comparison of housing and commercial property market prices in the same geographical region. The two price indexes are summarized and compared over the 1976-1997 period in Exhibit 6. Again, we see a striking similarity at the broad level. The overall twenty-two-year growth rate is almost identical (4.3% for houses versus 4.2% per year for commercial property), and the contemporaneous correlation is +63%. The housing index appears modestly less volatile, with 5.1% annual

EXHIBIT 6A COMPARISON OF RSR HOUSING VERSUS COMMERCIAL PROPERTY PRICE INDEX

Annual Return Summary Statistics (%)

	Houses	Comm.
GMEAN	4.28	4.23
MEAN	4.20	4.44
STDEV	5.07	6.99
CORREL	62.73	

Return History

Year	House Level	House Return	Comm.Level	Comm.Return
1975	1.00		1.00	
1976	1.02	2.10%	1.18	18.11%
1977	1.02	–0.07%	1.16	–1.46%
1978	1.20	17.38%	1.25	7.46%
1979	1.39	16.07%	1.50	19.90%
1980	1.60	15.00%	1.77	18.34%
1981	1.73	8.42%	1.79	0.73%
1982	1.77	1.96%	1.84	3.07%
1983	1.82	2.79%	1.96	6.46%
1984	1.86	2.59%	1.97	0.55%
1985	1.91	2.49%	2.05	4.04%
1986	1.95	1.85%	2.04	–0.71%
1987	2.01	3.17%	2.17	6.65%
1988	2.06	2.55%	2.09	–3.72%
1989	2.11	2.66%	2.13	1.68%
1990	2.16	2.20%	2.10	–1.07%
1991	2.17	0.33%	2.03	–3.63%
1992	2.17	0.37%	1.93	–4.62%
1993	2.22	2.26%	2.03	5.17%
1994	2.32	4.40%	2.19	7.58%
1995	2.37	2.13%	2.18	–0.21%
1996	2.46	3.83%	2.30	5.47%
1997	2.52	2.24%	2.49	7.98%

volatility compared to 7.0% in commercial property. Part of the housing index's lower volatility may reflect less noise due to a much larger property sample and use of the non-time-weighted RSR specification. It also seems likely, however, that housing prices really have been less volatile than commercial property in Florida during the historical period covered. Most notable is the fact that the property price slump of the early 1990s was much less pronounced in the housing sector. Indeed, Florida house prices appear to have experienced only a pause in their steady growth during the period when commercial prices were clearly falling.

SUMMARY: IT WORKS PRETTY WELL

This article reports the results of the development of the first repeat-sales transaction-based index of commercial property in the U.S., based on Florida's Department of Revenue data on all properties that sold twice during the last two decades. Based on this index-development work, we are encouraged that transaction-based commercial property index construction may be more feasible than previously thought. From a practical statistical perspective, the repeat-sales methodology appears to work well in filtering out transaction noise and producing return indexes that should be highly usable by decision-makers and academic analysts alike. Comparison of the RSR transaction-based index with the NCREIF Florida Index (appropriately adjusted) reveals interesting insights about the difference between appraisal and transaction returns and about the difference between "institutional quality" real estate performance as compared to a broader sample of commercial property.

The somewhat surprising finding is that there appears to be relatively little difference between the appraisal-based and transaction-based indexes in terms of overall performance and annual volatility. The RSR index does register, however, price movements that the NCREIF index does not exhibit, and the RSR index may slightly lead the

Exhibit 6b RSR Housing versus Commercial Price Level Indexes

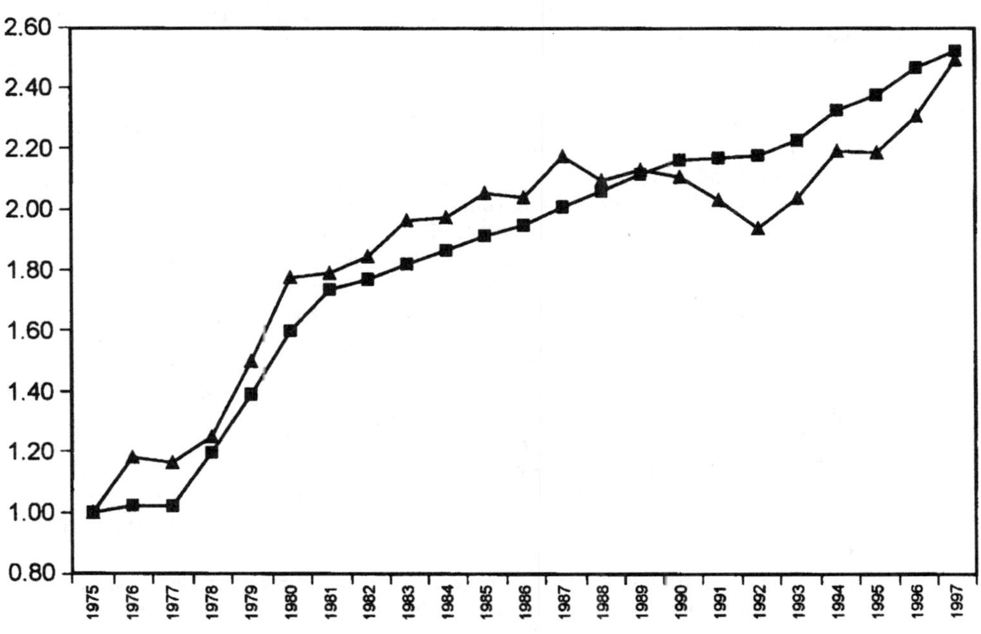

NCREIF index in time. Overall, the institutional quality properties represented by the NPI performed similarly to the broader population of Florida commercial properties regarding their price level history. Both indexes experienced only about a 10% drop in price level during the early 1990s.

ENDNOTES

This article was published in *Real Estate Finance*, Spring 1998.

[1] The authors thank the Real Estate Research Institute at the University of Indiana and the College of Business at Florida State University for the financial assistance they provided for this study.

[2] There has been a long-running (and good natured) debate between one of the humble co-authors of this article, and the esteemed and learned chief editor of *Real Estate Finance*, Mike Miles concerning the existence of "smoothing" in appraisal-based indexes. On the side of the existence of smoothing is a vast and impressive literature of great academic rigor and quality, including: Ross-Zisler [1991], Geltner [1989], Goetzmann [1990], Giacotto-Clapp [1992], Fisher-Geltner-Webb [1994], and Hendershott-Kane [1995], to name only a few of the most humble. On the other hand, weighing in on the side of "no-smoothing" are a paltry few seriously flawed articles and unpublished working papers, such as Webb-Miles-Guilkey [1992], Edelstein-Quan [1995], and Lai-Wang [1996]. Now, the low transactions-based price volatility we find has the chief editor crowing, but as the discerning reader will see in a subsequent footnote, Geltner has not admitted defeat! In any case, all parties to the debate agree that smoothing, if you define it only as reduced apparent volatility in real estate, makes relatively little difference to the real estate share in the optimal portfolio as long as real estate has low correlation with stocks and bonds.

[3] See, for example, Colwell-Munneke-Trafzger [1998]. It has also been pointed out that the other major source of commercial real estate investment performance data, publicly-traded REITs, may tend to hold different types of properties than NCREIF members, and manage them differently in terms of cash flow and capital improvements. Such differences may be less pronounced in recent years.

[4] This article is a condensation of a report for the Real Estate Research Institute (RERI), which partially funded this research. The full working paper is available from RERI at www.reri.org.

[5] Temporal aggregation occurs when asset value indications from specific points in time are aggregated across time, thereby reflecting an *average value across time*. For example, if different individual properties within a population are valued at various times throughout 1998, and the same properties are valued again each one a year later, and then we computed a capital return to the population by comparing the average 1999 value with the average 1998 value, that return would reflect "temporal aggregation."

[6] For example, FNMA and FHLMC regularly publish an RSR index of U.S. housing prices, and Florida State University regularly produces RSR house price indexes for the twenty Metropolitan Statistical Areas (MSAs) of Florida (published in "The State of Florida's Housing," University of Florida).

[7] Transaction-based price indexes of commercial property were developed by various academic researchers at least as early as the 1970s. A major attempt was by Gau [1985], using Vancouver apartments. Miles et al [1989] reviewed some of the early attempts, and concluded that a transactions-based index would not be practical for commercial property. A major issue was always how to control for quality differences between properties transacting in different time periods. It was recognized that, in principle, an hedonic model of property value could help with this problem. Early attempts to use hedonic models in this way, including Miles et al [1989], re-estimated purely cross-sectional hedonic models each period (or every few periods) using only the transactions occuring within those periods. With commercial property there are generally not enough transactions data for this approach to work very well. More recently, academic real estate researchers have begun to apply the classical Court-Griliches methodology. This approach uses a pooled time-series, cross-sectional database of transactions and derives the price index from the coefficients on time dummy variables. Such explicit time-dummy hedonic indexes of commercial properties have recently been developed by Fisher-Geltner-Webb [1994] which used properties sold from the NCREIF database; Colwell-Munneke-Trefzger [1998] which used a sample of Chicago properties; Downs-Slade [1996] which used nearly the entire population of all commercial property transactions in Phoenix, Arizona; and Goy-Londerville [1996] which used a sample of Vancouver properties.

[8] The "omitted variables" problem occurs when a variable that is important in determining property value (say, the prestige of the street address, or the percentage of the building encumbered under an unfavorable long-term lease) must be left out of the right-hand-side of the valuation regression because

the data is unavailable.

[9] The term "noise" in this context refers to spurious excess volatility in the estimated price index, caused by random statistical estimation error in the regression parameters. This will be discussed more fully shortly.

[10] In addition to the direct method presented here (which closely parallels the original development by Bailey-Muth-Nourse), the RSR can be derived indirectly from the hedonic model of property value, assuming that hedonic variables values and parameters remain constant across time within each property.

[11] This follows directly from the definition of the natural log: EXP(LN(1 + r)) ≡ 1 + r.

[12] Obviously, the type of periodic returns we are estimating are based only on the asset price change, and so represent only the capital or appreciation component of the total return. To be more precise, we should think of the returns we are measuring as price-change returns that may reflect typical levels of routine capital improvements in the properties. This issue will be discussed further in the data description section that follows.

[13] To eliminate temporal aggregation in the estimated returns index, one can define the dummy variable to equal the *fraction* of the time period that falls between the two sales in chronological time. Thus, for example, suppose that for a certain observation the first sale occurred at the end of September 1995 and the second sale occurred at the end of September 1997. Then for an annual return index the dummy variable values for that observation would be 0.25 for 1995, 1.0 for 1996, and 0.75 for 1997. This time-weighted specification was first proposed by Bryan and Colwell [1982], and we employ it in the present analysis.

[14] Equation #2 is directly solved for , $\hat{\beta}_{95}$, equation #4 is directly solved for $\hat{\beta}_{96}$, and then one can substitute into either equation #1 or #3 to observe: 0.1460 = 0.0488 + 0.0295+0.0677; and: 0.0783 = 0.0488 + 0.0295.

[15] Heteroskedasticity results when the likely magnitude of error differs for different observations. In this case, heteroskedasticity arises from the fact that there are two sources of transaction noise. First, each property may have an "idiosyncratic return component," that reflects the *true* difference between that specific property's capital return and the capital return of the population average during the interval between the two transactions. This component of noise would be a function of the amount of time that elapsed between the first and second transactions, because cumulative idiosyncratic returns accumulate over time. The second source of noise is a non-temporal component that could reflect "pricing error" which occurs at the time of each transaction, for example due to one party to the sale negotiating under financial duress.

[16] In WLS estimation, the observations that are likely to have larger errors (e.g., those with more time between the first and second sales) are given less weight in the regression estimation procedure. Another technical consideration is that the RSR specification described above and used in the present study estimates a geometric average index, equally weighted across properties. That is, the RSR estimated return each period is the *geometric* as opposed to *arithmetic* average across the individual property returns. This causes a minor downward bias in the estimated return, which we correct using an approximation suggested by Goetzmann [1991]. In applying this correction, we assume a cross-sectional standard deviation in transaction noise of 5% of the property price. (This is typical of the magnitude of non-temporal transaction noise found in studies of housing returns.)

[17] Note that our transaction dates are closing dates, not the date of price agreement between the parties. This may result in our index being slightly lagged behind the market.

[18] The Florida DOR categorizes properties using 100 land-use codes. The land uses selected for each sector were: apartment (multi-family, 03), retail (stores, 11; regional shopping centers, 15; and community shopping centers, 16), office (one-story offices, 17; multi-story offices, 18; professional service buildings, 19; and insurance company offices, 24), hotel (hotels and motels, 39), and industrial (light manufacturing and printing, 41; warehousing and storage, 48). Of the data initially identified, 26,541 properties having the required data characteristics were recorded as selling at least once during the index construction period (apartment, 4,468; retail, 6,617; office, 6,924; hotel, 1,963; and industrial, 6,569).

[19] In addition, a series of steps were conducted to delete invalid observations (e.g., property title transfers) and apparent data errors. We have, however, no way to know if a sale was conducted with below-market interest rate debt financing from the seller, so we are unable to adjust for that. Keep in mind, however, that the fundamental observations we are working with are repeat-sales pairs. Below-market financing from the seller (hence an apparent property transaction price higher than the true market value) will bias the capital return (price change) estimate downward, or upward, depending on whether it was the first or second sale that had the favorable financing. Therefore, on average this effect

may tend to largely cancel out across observations.

[20] In many most counties, the effective-year-built variable is updated when substantial capital improvements occur.

[21] In the RSR literature on housing price indexes, it has been noted that properties that are sold very quickly tend to come from a different population than those that are held longer. These differences may be due to nontemporal capital improvements at the time of purchase or other transaction-related characteristics.

[22] As we describe later in this article, we also adjust the NCREIF capital return to be comparable in this regard.

[23] Note that Exhibit 3 covers only sales during the last two years, during which there did not happen to be any repeat sales of very large properties, such as regional malls. During the entire history of our repeat-sales database, the largest single transaction observation included is $67 million.

[24] In addition, the database is dominated (72%) by the paired-sale observations of properties located in the four major metropolitan areas of Florida (i.e., Jacksonville, Miami, Orlando, and Tampa-St.Petersburg).

[25] The 1997 return is an annual figure estimated using the time-weighted RSR specification, but based only on data through July.

[26] Positive first-order autocorrelation in annual returns implies "inertia" in the returns: the return in one year tends to be followed by a similar return the next year. This suggests a partial response of market prices to the arrival of information, or lack of perfect "informational efficiency." Such a pattern is consistent with popular perceptions of how real estate markets function, and consistent with evidence from transaction-based housing price indexes.

[27] This period of comparison also has the advantage of being subsequent to the period when the RSR exhibits some evidence of possible noise.

[28] In the NCREIF Index capital improvements are generally for routine items, such as tenant improvements when a new lease is signed. Major property development or rehabilitation is rare in the NCREIF Index properties. However, we cannot rule out that some development may be present in our adjusted NFI, that would result in an overstatement of apparent property price growth. Similarly, however, in our RSR, while we have attempted to filter from our index estimation sample any properties that experienced major redevelopment, we may have missed some cases. Nevertheless, we feel confident that the RSR well-represents property price changes including only routine and small-scale capital improvements, similar to what is reflected in our adjusted NFI price index.

[29] Note that the greater price appreciation on the part of the NFI does not necessarily imply greater total return from an investment perspective. The greater price appreciation may reflect a generally higher rate of capital improvement expenditures in the NCREIF properties. Furthermore, if there are institutional and non-institutional clienteles that result in segmented asset markets, this would be reflected in the long-run in differences in the earnings/price ratio, or current yield, not in the price appreciation rate, as cointegration between the two market segments would prevent long-run permanent divergence in price growth rates.

[30] OK, so this is where the esteemed chief editor is gloating and claiming victory over Geltner in the debate about smoothing. Geltner, however, is far from admitting defeat, though he is calling a tactical (but well-ordered) retreat. In the first place, it should be noted that our comparison here is at the annual frequency, whereas the most serious smoothing problems in the NCREIF index clearly occur at the quarterly frequency. Furthermore, if you read on, you will see the picture here is not all bleak for the smoothing side of the debate. Indeed, we find that the transaction-based index has much less positive first-order autocorrelation than the appraisal-based index, and it has been in precisely this way (by reducing autocorrelation) that most of the unsmoothing techniques used by academicians and practitioners have worked. At a deeper, more conceptual level, it is important to note that much of the debate about smoothing has occurred in the context of comparing real estate returns with those of publicly traded stocks and bonds, to arrive at an "apples to apples" metric of risk. In this regard, an index based on transactions in the property market does not get us all the way there, because the property market is very different in its functioning from the stock and bond markets. In particular, when contrasted with the stock or bond market, the commercial property market (and the transaction prices that reflect that market) exhibits much less liquidity, and liquidity levels that vary greatly across time. The property market also displays much greater inertia than the stock market, which results in much greater predictability of returns. In comparing risk, or even just volatility, between property market transaction prices and stock market transaction prices, one is still comparing apples and oranges. (And we note that REIT volatility is much greater than the volatility we find in the present article.)

[31] In contrast, there is no positive correlation between the NFI returns and subsequent RSR returns. Nevertheless, from the formal statistical perspective of "Granger Causality," there is no significant leading or lagging relationship between the two indexes.

[32] The housing RSR was estimated at a quarterly frequency for the 1985 to 1997 period and annually for the 1975 to 1984 period, without the time-weighted specification described previously. As a result, it probably displays some temporal aggregation smoothing in the early years not present in the commercial index. The housing index also was not adjusted for the difference between arithmetic and geometric cross-sectional averaging of returns. However, it is unlikely that these differences would significantly affect the comparison, and the use of the non-time-weighted specification serves to further filter out transaction noise in the early years.

REFERENCES

Bailey, M., R. Muth, and H. Nourse. "A Regression Method for Real Estate Price Index Construction." *Journal of the American Statistical Association*, 58 (1963), pp. 933-942.

Bryan, T., and P. Colwell. "Housing Price Indexes." In C.F. Sirmans, ed., *Research in Real Estate*, Greenwich, CT: JAI Press, 2 (1982).

Case, K., and R. Shiller. "The Efficiency of the Market for Single-Family Homes." *American Economic Review*, 79 (1989), pp. 125-137.

Clapp, J., and C. Giacotto. "Estimating Price Indices for Residential Property: A Comparison of Repeat Sales and Assessed Value Methods." *Journal of the American Statistical Association*, 87 (1992), pp. 300-306.

Colwell, P., H. Munneke, and J. Trafzger. "The Stability of Office Property Values in the Post-TRA Period." *Real Estate Economics*, (forthcoming), 1998.

Court, A. "Hedonic Price Indexes with Automotive Examples." *The Dynamics of Automotive Demand*, General Motors Corporation, New York, 1939.

Downs, D.H., and B.A. Slade. "Characteristics of a Full-disclosure, Transaction-based Index of Commercial Real Estate." Working paper, College of Business, University of Georgia, 1996.

Edelstein, R., and D. Quan. "How Does Appraisal Smothing Bias Real Estate Returns Measurement?" Working paper #95-240, Haas School of Business, University of California — Berkeley, 1995.

Fisher, J., D. Geltner, and B. Webb. "Value Indices of Commercial Real Estate: A Comparison of Index Construction Methods." *Journal of Real Estate Finance and Economics* 9 (1994), pp. 137-164.

Gatzlaff, D. "House Price Appreciation." Ch. 5, in: The State of Florida's Housing, Real Estate Research Center, University of Florida, 1997.

Gatzlaff, D., and D. Haurin. "Sample Selection Bias and Repeat-Sales Index Estimates." *Journal of Real Estate Finance and Economics*, 14 (1997), pp. 33-50.

Gau, G. "Public Investment and Abnormal Returns in Real Estate Investment." *AREUEA Journal*, 13 (1985), pp.15-31.

Geltner, D. "Estimating Real Estate Systematic Risk from Aggregate Level Appraisal Based Returns." *AREUEA Journal*, 17 (1989), pp. 463-481.

Geltner, D., J. Hanson, and D. Loeb. "Land Investment in the Institutional Portfolio: Evidence from an Historical Return Index." *Real Estate Finance*, (forthcoming), 1997.

Giacotto, C., and J.Clapp. "Appraisal Based Real Estate Returns Under Alternative Market Regimes." *AREUEA Journal*, 20 (1992).

Goetzmann, W. "The Performance of Real Estate as an Asset Class." *Journal of Applied Corporate Finance*, 3 (1990), pp. 65-76.

Goetzmann, W. "The Accuracy of Real Estate Indices: Repeat Sale Estimators." *Journal of Real Estate Finance and Economics*, 5 (1992), pp. 5-54.

Goy, R., and J. Londerville. "Evaluation of Alternative Price Indices for Commercial & Investment Real Estate." Working paper, University of Guelph, 1996.

Griliches, Z., and I. Adelman. "On an Index of Quality Change." *Journal of the American Statistical Association*, 56 (1961), pp. 535-548.

Hendershott, P., and E. Kane. "U.S. Office Market Values During the Past Decade: How Distorted Have Appraisals Been?" *Real Estate Economics*, 23 (1995), pp. 101-116.

Lai, T., and K. Wang. "Appraisal Smoothing: The Other Side of the Story." California State University

— Fullerton Working paper presented at 1997 AREUEA Annual Meeting, 1996.

Miles, M., D. Hartzell, D. Guilkey, and D. Sears. "Is a True Transactions-Based Real Estate Index Possible?" *Salomon Brothers Research Report*, November 1989.

Webb, R.B., M. Miles, and D. Guilkey. "Transactions-Driven Commercial Real Estate Returns: The Panacea to Asset Allocation Models?" *AREUEA Journal*, 20 (1992).

Ross, S., and R. Zisler. "Risk and Return in Real Estate." *Journal of Real Estate Finance and Economics*, 4 (1991) pp. 175-190.

19 TIMBERLAND RETURN DRIVERS AND INVESTING STYLES FOR AN ASSET THAT HAS COME OF AGE

JON P. CAULFIELD
University of Georgia at Athens

Since the introduction of the first commingled timberland fund, this asset has "come of age," and now offers clear investing styles. While timberland is usually perceived as a non-core real estate category, its visibility as an institutional investment continues to increase rapidly during the 1990s.

In 1981, there existed a single timberland investment management company (TIMCO). By 1986, six firms had been established, and ran commingled funds with total assets of less than $100 million. This grew to $600 million by 1990 (Zinkhan [1990]). In 1992, five active TIMCOs remained —Forest Investment Associates, John Hancock, Prudential Timber, Resource Investments International and Wachovia Timberland Investment Management — and assets had risen to $2.04 billion. These remain the largest TIMCOs, but in 1997 the industry swelled to eleven companies, with total assets currently estimated at $5.6 billion.[1]

Despite this growth, the majority of real estate managers remain unfamiliar with timberland and the factors that drive its returns. We therefore begin with a description of timberland return drivers and how they interact. This sets the stage for a discussion of how TIMCOs have employed these drivers to develop the investing styles that exist today.

TIMBERLAND RETURN DRIVERS

Timberland investment returns are a function of three drivers: 1) biological tree growth, 2) timber product price changes, and 3) changes in the value of the underlying land asset (Caulfield [1994]). Biological growth is the unique feature of timberland that separates it from other types of real estate. It results in volume and value changes over time that are largely independent of economic or financial market conditions.

BIOLOGICAL GROWTH

TIMCOs invest the majority of client funds in even-aged softwood (pine or fir) forests in the U.S. south, west, north, or, in more recent years, overseas. Softwoods are by far the most commercially valuable timber type, accounting for two-thirds of industrial wood production on a global basis (FAO [1994]). The general relationship between tree growth and age for an even-aged forest is represented by the sigmoid curve in Exhibit 1.[2]

A typical forest's development is shown from planting to harvest, a period foresters refer to as the rotation length. When a new tree crop is planted, growth begins slowly. Once trees become established on a site, which takes several years, the growth rate increases. It eventually peaks, and from that point forward declines until the end of the rotation. Using plantation-grown pines in the U.S. South as an example, the inflection point in Exhibit 1 may be reached somewhere around age twelve to fourteen.

EXHIBIT 1 RELATIONSHIP BETWEEN BIOLOGICAL GROWTH, AGE, AND PRODUCTION OF A TYPICAL SOUTHERN PINE PLANTATION

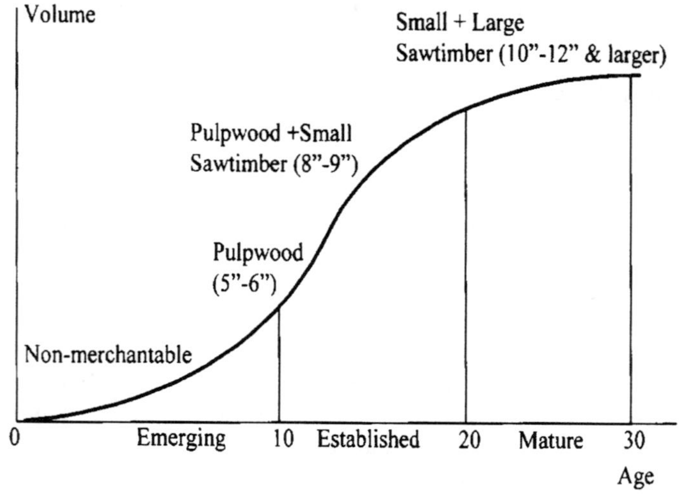

Numbers in parentheses are minimum threshold tree diameters for each product.

Timberland value growth, and, by extension, investment returns, are tied to volume growth. If 1) timber is merchantable from time of planting to rotation age, 2) prices received are constant per unit timber volume regardless of tree size, and 3) there is no product and land price volatility, investment returns would be completely defined by the biological growth rate.

Of course, these conditions do not hold in the real world. Newly planted trees are not merchantable, but must first reach various minimum threshold diameters before they can be sold for conversion to wood products.[3] Per unit timber product prices — or "stumpage prices" reflecting the value of timber on the stump — are positively related to tree size. And both stumpage and land prices vary over time.

The smallest merchantable trees are sold as pulpwood, which is used to make paper and has the lowest value per unit volume. Southern pines normally begin reaching this stage between ages ten and twelve, at a minimum diameter of five to six inches. As trees grow, they reach larger threshold diameters and can be sold for successively higher-value products.

Small sawtimber trees are used to manufacture commodity lumber grades like 2 x 4s and have a higher per unit value than pulpwood. Minimum threshold diameters of eight to nine inches for small sawtimber trees start being reached between ages thirteen and fifteen. When tree diameters reach ten to twelve inches starting at ages twenty-two to twenty-five, they are merchantable for the highest-value large sawtimber (used for large dimension lumber) or peeler logs (for plywood). The approximate ages at which trees enter the various product categories are shown in Exhibit 1.

A useful way to think of the development of a forest is to break it down into three stages. In Exhibit 1 these are denoted along the x-axis as "emerging growth," "established growth," and "mature growth." The emerging growth stage begins at the time of planting and ends when the forest first begins producing merchantable pulpwood. Growth occurs very rapidly as emerging growth transitions into established growth.

The growth rate peaks during the established growth stage, then begins to slow. But the volume of merchantable pulpwood continues to increase rapidly. Around the midpoint of this stage, trees begin to become large enough to be sold for higher-value small sawtimber. As the established growth stage progresses, the ratio of small sawtimber to pulpwood increases.

As the forest enters the mature growth stage, the biological growth rate slows markedly. But at this point trees also begin to become merchantable for even higher-value large sawtimber. Small sawtimber continues to be part of the product mix during this stage, as well as some pulpwood. The ratio of large sawtimber to small sawtimber continues to increase throughout the mature stage.

As biological growth increases tree diameters, the stumpage price differentials between pulpwood, small sawtimber, and large sawtimber means that the rates of volume and value growth diverge. But while a perfect correlation does not exist between biological growth and investment returns, they are positively linked. When forests are growing rapidly, they move more quickly into successively higher-value products. Therefore, young forests tend to grow faster in value. And, because periodic tree growth is always a positive quantity, growth and returns are related positively, ceteris paribus.

Exhibit 2 illustrates this concept using the example of a hypothetical pine plantation acquired in south Georgia in 1982 at age ten (end of the emerging growth stage) and

EXHIBIT 2 INFLUENCE OF BIOLOGICAL GROWTH DRIVER ON RETURNS* FOR A FIFTEEN-YEAR TIMBERLAND INVESTMENT WITH CONSTANT 1982 PRICES IN SOUTH GEORGIA, AND COMPARISON WITH ANNUAL RATE OF VOLUME CHANGE

(1)	(2)	(3)	(4)	(5)	(6)	(7)	(8)	(9)	(10)	(11)
		Volume (cords/acre)**			Constant 1982 Prices***				Annual Value Change	Annual Volume Change
Year	Age	Pulpwood	Small Sawtimber	Large Sawtimber	Pulpwood	Small Sawtimber	Large Sawtimber	Stumpage Value	(%)	(%)
1982	10	5.20	0.0	0.00	$30.00	$54.00	$60.48	$156.00		
1983	11	7.90	0.0	0.00	$30.00	$54.00	$60.48	$237.00	51.92	51.92
1984	12	10.80	0.1	0.00	$30.00	$54.00	$60.48	$329.40	38.99	37.97
1985	13	13.20	0.6	0.00	$30.00	$54.00	$60.48	$428.40	30.05	26.61
1986	14	14.90	1.6	0.00	$30.00	$54.00	$60.48	$533.40	24.51	19.57
1987	15	16.40	3.1	0.00	$30.00	$54.00	$60.48	$659.40	23.62	18.18
1988	16	17.10	5.2	0.00	$30.00	$54.00	$60.48	$793,80	20.38	14.36
1988	17	17.40	7.2	0.00	$30.00	$54.00	$60.48	$910.80	14.74	10.31
1990	18	17.50	9.5	0.00	$30.00	$54.00	$60.48	$1,038.00	13.97	9.76
1991	19	17.70	11.7	0.00	$30.00	$54.00	$60.48	$1,162.80	12.02	8.89
1992	20	18.30	13.5	0.00	$30.00	$54.00	$60.48	$1,278.00	9.91	8.16
1993	21	19.60	14.2	0.00	$30.00	$54.00	$60.48	$1,354.80	6.01	6.29
1994	22	21.10	14.5	0.00	$30.00	$54.00	$60.48	$1,416.00	4.52	5.33
1995	23	22.70	14.4	0.20	$30.00	$54.00	$60.48	$1,470.70	3.86	4.78
1996	24	24.20	14.2	0.40	$30.00	$54.00	$60.48	$1,516.99	3.15	4.02
1997	25	25.30	13.7	0.70	$30.00	$54.00	$60.48	$1,541.14	1.59	2.32

*Excludes land and operating costs and miscellaneous revenues.

**Generated using the North Carolina State Loblolly Pine Growth and Yield Simulator (Hafley [1989]), for Site Index 60 (Base 25), planted with 700 trees per acre.

***Georgia Region 2 (south Georgia) prices from Timber Mart South [1982].

held for fifteen years (into mature growth). The growth model used is representative of a typical institutional-grade property. To focus attention on the impact of biological growth, we begin by assuming that land is costless, there are no operating costs, and that stumpage prices remain constant over the investment period. Acquisition costs and final sale value therefore reflect only merchantable stumpage (these assumptions are relaxed later).

Columns (3) to (5) of Exhibit 2 show annual per acre timber volumes by product at ages ten to twenty-five.[4] In columns (6) to (9) are 1982 second-quarter prices per unit volume for pulpwood, small sawtimber, and large sawtimber for south Georgia.[5] Note the differences in magnitude of stumpage prices: The value of small sawtimber is 80% higher than pulpwood, and large sawtimber has a 12% premium over small sawtimber.

Assuming stumpage prices for each product stayed constant between 1982 and 1997, column (9) of Exhibit 2 shows total investment value at each age, the product of per acre volume times price. Column (10) shows annual value changes in percent,[6] and column (11) shows the annual rate of volume change. Both decline throughout the holding period. The differences in the annual rates differ because column (10) is based on dollar values aggregated over different products, while column (11) simply reflects total volume changes. But the relationship is clear: For constant prices, volume and value growth are higher when biological growth is fastest, and both decline over time.

TIMBER PRICE CHANGES

Timber price changes are the second return driver. A number of factors influence timber prices. At the macroeconomic level, housing starts, interest rates, and the overall level of economic activity play a role. But microeconomic variables are also important.

Trees are heavy and bulky, making them costly to transport to processing facilities. Operationally, this means that the wood procurement zone for a typical mill has a relatively fixed radius — usually 100 miles or less. Industrial processing capacity is also unevenly concentrated. In the south, for example, most papermaking capacity is concentrated close to either the Atlantic coast or the Gulf of Mexico. Greater competition

EXHIBIT 3 SOUTH GEORGIA TIMBER PRICES AND LONG-TERM TRENDS, 1977-1997

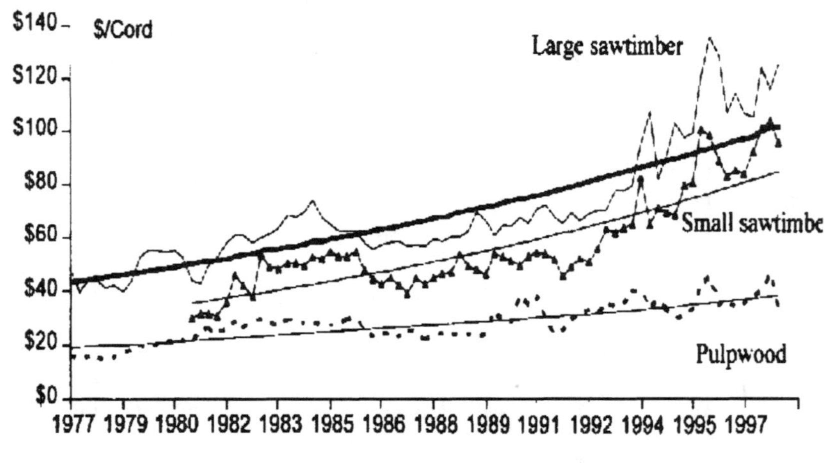

Source: Timber Mart South *(small sawtimber price series from 1980)*.

EXHIBIT 4 SECOND-QUARTER 1997 TIMBER PRICES AND TEN-YEAR CHANGES FOR SELECTED SOUTHERN MARKETS

Product*	South Georgia Price	Annual Change	South Arkansas Price	Annual Change	South Louisiana Price	Annual Change
Pulpwood	$35.04	3.7	$19.82	4.2	$26.00	9.5
Small Sawtimber	$96.87	7.9	$91.61	13.4	$77.50	11.9
Large Sawtimber	$126.09	7.7	$122.14	11.6	$113.97	14.0

*All prices are in dollar per cord, to facilitate comparison (sawtimber prices are normally reported in dollars per thousand board feet). One cord equals 128 cubic feet of wood.

Source: Timber Mart South.

exists for pulpwood stumpage in these areas, resulting in higher pulpwood prices. Prices for pulpwood generally decline as one moves from the Atlantic coast to the west, and from the Gulf toward the northern areas of the south.

Sawmilling capacity is similarly unevenly distributed. There also exist a variety of different types of such mills with respect to final product. Some require small sawtimber or large sawtimber exclusively as mill furnish. Others process a mix of large and small sawtimber, and still others produce plywood. The net result is that even within a single state there can exist numerous timber markets.

As a result of this fragmentation, stumpage price magnitudes and their rates of change are more random than biological growth. Period-to-period prices rise, fall, or sometimes stay flat. Exhibit 3 graphs historical stumpage prices for pulpwood, small sawtimber, and large sawtimber, superimposed on long-term price trends, for southern Georgia. While the slope is positive in each case, it is also apparent that prices will vary widely around their respective trends.

Similar relationships hold for other regions. In fact, the interrelationship between geographic location and the price formation process means that tremendous price variability can exist across timber market areas. The intensely competitive south Georgia pulpwood market means that pulpwood stumpage commands a far higher price there than in eastern Virginia, where there is less papermaking capacity and competition for small trees. 1997 stumpage price comparisons for three selected regions are shown in Exhibit 4, which also shows that the compound trend rates of price change since 1987 differ markedly across these market areas.

Exhibit 5 shows how stumpage price changes interact with biological growth to drive returns. It employs the annual prices from Exhibit 3 in the context of the pine plantation investment described previously. Columns (6) through (8) again begin with second-quarter 1982 prices for the ten-year-old plantation. Now, however, the prices in the table for each subsequent year are those that actually existed at each period. Column (10) shows annual returns for this situation, and column (11) shows annual returns from inception. The general price rise that occurred in south Georgia between 1982 and 1997 increased returns over the example that includes only biological growth.

Not surprisingly, periods of declining timber prices lower returns. In Exhibit 5 we see that in 1995 prices were down from 1994, and the annual return declined 16.5%. But since biological growth is an invariably positive quantity, it tends to dampen the impact of declines. This is seen in column (11), where the annualized return from inception, while down from the prior year, remains above 20%.

EXHIBIT 5 INTERACTIONS OF BIOLOGICAL GROWTH AND STUMPAGE PRICE DRIVERS ON INVESTMENT RETURNS*

(1)	(2)	(3)	(4)	(5)	(6)	(7)	(8)	(9)	(10)	(11)
		Volume (cords/acre)**			Actual Prices by Year***				Annual Value	Annual Return from
Year	Age	Pulpwood	Small Sawtimber	Large Sawtimber	Pulpwood	Small Sawtimber	Large Sawtimber	Stumpage Value	Change (%)	Inception (%)
1982	10	5.20	0.0	0.00	$30.00	$54.00	$60.48	$156.00		
1983	11	7.90	0.0	0.00	$29.33	$50.67	$67.86	$231.71	48.53	48.53
1984	12	10.80	0.1	0.00	$28.00	$55.00	$65.11	$307.90	32.88	40.49
1985	13	13.20	0.6	0.00	$26.00	$48.33	$58.33	$372.20	20.88	33.62
1986	14	14.90	1.6	0.00	$23.67	$43.00	$59.05	$421.48	13.24	28.21
1987	15	16.40	3.1	0.00	$24.43	$45.33	$60.00	$541.18	28.40	28.25
1988	16	17.10	5.2	0.00	$25.00	$49.80	$70.00	$686.46	26.85	28.01
1988	17	17.40	7.2	0.00	$30.00	$53.50	$64.64	$907.20	32.16	28.60
1990	18	17.50	9.5	0.00	$38.50	$55.00	$73.21	$1,196.25	31.86	29.00
1991	19	17.70	11.7	0.00	$30.50	$50.00	$67.14	$1,124.85	–5.97	24.55
1992	20	18.3	13.5	0.00	$36.74	$63.80	$78.57	$1,533.64	36.34	25.68
1993	21	19.60	14.2	0.00	$41.17	$83.00	$107.85	$1,985.53	29.47	26.02
1994	22	21.10	14.5	0.00	$31.03	$69.15	$98.57	$1,657.41	–16.53	21.77
1995	23	22.70	14.4	0.20	$46.25	$99.30	$129.64	$2,505.72	51.18	23.81
1996	24	24.20	14.2	0.40	$36.10	$85.06	$106.42	$2,124.04	–15.23	20.50
1997	25	25.30	13.7	0.70	$35.04	$96.87	$126.07	$2,301.88	8.37	19.65

*Excludes land and operating costs and miscellaneous revenues.
**Generated using the North Carolina State Loblolly Pine Growth and Yield Simulator (Hafley [1989]), for Site Index 60 (Base 35), planted with 70C trees per acre.
***Georgia Region 2 (south Georgia) prices from Timber Mart South [1982].

LAND PRICE CHANGES

Changes in the value of the underlying land asset is the third timberland investment return driver. Land values, like those of timber, are related to local supply and demand conditions and therefore vary spatially. Price is also partly a function of quality. Land capable of producing fast-growing plantations normally trades at a premium over average or poor land, which is similar to the situation found with agricultural property.

Washburn [1992] has shown that land prices are also correlated with the long-term average level of real stumpage prices on a regional basis. However, land value changes are much less volatile than for timber, and lag those of stumpage prices. This makes sense intuitively. Prices paid for bare forest land reflect the capitalized value of future timber crops (Faustmann [1968]). This is a function of anticipated timber prices, which reflect long-term aggregate trends.

The study by Washburn [1992] also demonstrates that the strongest indicators of the real value of land over time are the consumer price index and the nominal riskless rate of interest. During periods of low inflation and relative timber product price stability, timber land prices are expected to change slowly, which was the case during the 1980s. During periods of rapid inflation and/or when timber prices rise quickly, the rate of change in land prices will increase. This was observed during the 1970s, when inflation was at historically high levels (de Steiguer [1982]).

From the 1980s to the beginning of the 1990s, unpublished data suggest that, in the south, timberland prices increased at approximately the rate of inflation.[7] More recent

EXHIBIT 6 INTERACTIONS OF BIOLOGICAL GROWTH AND STUMPAGE PRICE AND LAND PRICE DRIVERS ON INVESTMENT RETURNS

(1)	(2)	(3)	(4)	(5)	(6)	(7)	(8)	(9)	(10)	(11)	(12)	(13)
		Volume (cords/acre)*			Actual Prices by Year**						Annual	Annual
			Small	Large		Small	Large	Stumpage	Land	Total	Value	Return from
Year	Age	Pulpwood	Sawtimber	Sawtimber	Pulpwood	Sawtimber	Sawtimber	Value	Value	Value***	Change (%)	Inception (%)
1982	10	5.20	0.0	0.00	$30.00	$54.00	$60.48	$156.00	$200.00	$355.00		
1983	11	7.90	0.0	0.00	$29.33	$50.67	$67.86	$231.71	$207.20	$437.91	23.35	23.35
1984	12	10.80	0.1	0.00	$28.00	$55.00	$65.11	$307.90	$214.66	$521.56	19.10	21.21
1985	13	13.20	0.6	0.00	$26.00	$48.33	$58.33	$372.20	$222.39	$593.58	13.81	18.69
1986	14	14.90	1.6	0.00	$23.67	$43.00	$59.05	$421.48	$230.39	$650.88	9.65	16.36
1987	15	16.40	3.1	0.00	$24.43	$45.33	$60.00	$541.18	$238.69	$778.86	19.66	17.02
1988	16	17.10	5.2	0.00	$25.00	$49.80	$70.00	$686.46	$247.28	$932.74	19.76	17.47
1988	17	17.40	7.2	0.00	$30.00	$53.50	$64.64	$907.20	$256.18	$1,162.38	24.62	18.46
1990	18	17.50	9.5	0.00	$38.50	$55.00	$73.21	$1,196.25	$265.40	$1,460.65	25.66	19.34
1991	19	17.70	11.7	0.00	$30.50	$50.00	$67.14	$1,124.85	$274.96	$1,398.81	-4.23	16.46
1992	20	18.30	13.5	0.00	$36.74	$63.80	$78.57	$1,533.64	$284.86	$1,817.50	29.93	17.74
1993	21	19.60	14.2	0.00	$41.17	$83.00	$107.85	$1,985.53	$295.11	$2,279.64	25.43	18.42
1994	22	21.10	14.5	0.00	$31.03	$69.15	$98.57	$1,657.41	$305.74	$1,962.14	-13.93	15.31
1995	23	22.70	14.4	0.20	$46.25	$99.30	$129.64	$2,505.72	$316.74	$2,821.47	43.80	17.29
1996	24	24.20	14.2	0.40	$36.10	$85.06	$106.42	$2,124.04	$328.15	$2,451.19	-13.12	14.80
1997	25	25.30	13.7	0.70	$35.04	$96.87	$126.07	$2,301.88	$339.96	$2,640.84	7.74	14.31

Generated using the North Carolina State Loblolly Pine Growth and Yield Simulator (Hafley [1989]), for Site Index 60 (Base 35), planted with 700 trees per acre.

**Georgia Region 2 (south Georgia) prices from Timber Mart South [1982-1997].

***Includes annual management costs and taxes of $2.50 and $3.50 per acre, and hunting lease revenue of $5 per acre.

anecdotal evidence provided by TIMCOs and forestland appraisers suggests that, from the mid-1990s, rapidly rising stumpage prices are currently leading to a faster increase in land values than observed over the previous decade.

Exhibit 6 incorporates land value changes into the example of the south Georgia pine plantation investment, along with the other return drivers. A 1982 bare land price for south Georgia of $200 per acre was representative of conditions at that time. A 1997 price of $340 per acre reflects a compound annual rate of change of 3.6%, about equivalent to the CPI over the period. Also included are the effects of annual property taxes and management costs, at $3.50 and $2.50 per acre, respectively, and miscellaneous income from a hunting lease at $5, which is average for Georgia (Caulfield [1996]).

Compared to the previous examples, including land costs decreases investment return both on a periodic annualized basis and from investment inception. This result is typical. The tendency of forest land prices to change slowly means that it also often tends to "buffer" returns. But land is obviously required to grow timber and fee ownership normally represents the most viable option.

Despite the impact of land value changes, the 14.3% annual return from inception for the example in Exhibit 6 implies timberland can compete strongly not only with other forms of real estate, but with most asset categories. Even though the example presented is hypothetical, its magnitude is consistent with the level of returns reported by TIMCOs using benchmarks based on actual properties.

The NCREIF Timberland Index reports an annualized return of 21.27% for the ten years since inception in 1987 (NCREIF [1997]). The complete index includes properties in the south, west, and northeast. But the southern component of the index by itself has achieved an annualized return of 14.18%. Another measure, the University of Georgia Timberland Performance Index (Caulfield [1994]), reports an annualized return of 12.2% for the fifteen-year period between 1982 and 1997. The latter measure consists primarily of southern timberland properties.

A CAVEAT

The examples in Exhibits 2, 5, and 6 demonstrate the impacts of and interactions between the three return drivers: biological growth, product price, and land price changes. But it should be stressed that they represent a truly hypothetical situation. Taken at face value, Exhibit 6 indicates that a plantation purchased at age ten should be sold at age eleven. But this rarely happens in the real world.

Young forests — those still in emerging or early in the established growth stage that contain little merchantable volume — have historically not traded actively because they are considered "illiquid." Many non-TIMCO timberland buyers, a group that includes paper companies, sawmillers, and private investors, attach a substantial liquidity value to timber that can be sold immediately. Emerging and young established growth plantations rarely possess this attribute.

Part of the reason for this comes from the operations side. Most loggers require a minimum of fifteen or more cords of merchantable wood per acre to justify the cost of moving equipment and personnel onto a site. This means young plantations, even if they contain some merchantable timber, are seldom candidates for harvest. As a result, although the actual wood and land value of the thirteen-year-old plantation in Exhibit 6 may be $600 per acre, this price may be unrealizable.

Put another way, the liquidation value of an emerging or young established growth plantation is often lower than its value from a discounted cash flow standpoint. This tendency for a "discount to discounted value" to exist in young plantations is widely

EXHIBIT 7 PERCENT OF TOTAL RETURN DISAGGREGATED BY RETURN DRIVER

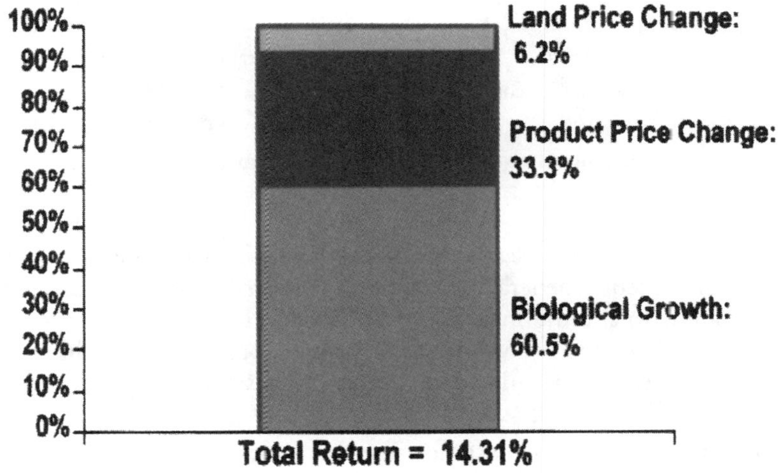

observed in the marketplace. As we discuss later, it has also offered a style opportunity that some TIMCOs have exploited.

RELATIVE IMPORTANCE OF RETURN DRIVERS

For the example in Exhibit 6, it is instructive to disaggregate returns to show the relative importance of each return driver. To adjust for annual management costs, taxes, and income from hunting leases, property taxes are charged against the returns from land, and management costs against biological growth returns. Hunting lease income is added back to land returns.

After accounting for these minor adjustments, the contributions of biological growth, product price changes, and land price changes to the 14.3% annual return are 60.5%, 33.3%, and 6.2%, respectively. These are shown in Exhibit 7. Biological growth accounts for the lion's share of total return.

Biological growth usually accounts for a significant share of total return. The example presented here is typical for the emerging or established stage. But this is not always the case. If instead we looked at an example where a twenty-year-old mature growth plantation were acquired, the proportion of total return accounted for by biological growth would be considerably lower. And during periods of rapid stumpage price increases, which happened from the beginning of the 1990s, product price changes would account for a higher proportion of the total.

TIMBERLAND INVESTING STYLES

TIMCOs have used these investment drivers alone and in combination to develop investing styles. In certain respects, they parallel the styles employed by equity managers. The following timberland investing styles (compared to their approximate equity style equivalent) have been used either in separate accounts or commingled funds since the introduction of the asset class in 1981:

Equity Investment Style	Equivalent Timberland Style
Growth	Established Growth
Growth and Income	Balanced Growth
Value	Mature Growth Value
Aggressive Growth	Emerging Growth

We describe timberland styles in terms of biological growth because of the important role it plays in the return generating process. The term "value" appended to the mature style corresponds to specific market conditions that have been exploited in that category. Styles are described below in the approximate order they were introduced to the institutional market. Bear in mind that the above list is not exhaustive, but includes the styles different TIMCOs have used to date.

In addition to the above, we also describe below a category called "large properties." This is not really a style in and of itself, because TIMCOs apply it when possible regardless of the investment style they happen to use. But it is included here for the sake of completeness.

ESTABLISHED GROWTH

With the first commingled timberland funds, TIMCOs emphasized the regular and consistent nature of biological growth, which was projected to provide returns competitive with fixed income. The original idea was to achieve what has been described by Caulfield [1997] as "biological growth and bond-like returns."

Synthetic timberland benchmarks developed during the 1980s suggest that timberland had a low correlation with traditional financial assets (see, for example, Mills and Hoover [1982], Redmond and Cubbage [1988], and Conroy and Miles [1989]). As a result, timberland was initially marketed partly for its diversifying effect. Timberland investment research during this period emphasized diversification benefits, rather than focusing on the asset's potential for achieving premium returns.[8]

A typical strategy was to purchase natural pine or pine plantation properties in the middle of the established growth stage. These were usually in the process of moving from consisting entirely of low-value pulpwood-sized trees to possessing a higher proportion of higher-value small and large sawtimber. With that move came a significant jump in asset value.

In general, the funds that followed this investing style performed in line with expectations. They offered investors an unusual diversification opportunity and provided returns comparable to bonds. The three earliest funds to use the style were introduced by First National Bank of Atlanta (now Wachovia), Travelers Insurance, and Equitable Insurance. All three funds have since been sold out. The Wachovia and Travelers funds had annualized returns averaging 10.3% over their common lives (1982 to 1992). While this is below the 12.2% annual return from the Lehman Brothers Government/Corporate Bond Index over the same period, note that during the 1980s bonds far outperformed historical norms.

BALANCED GROWTH

The balanced growth style refers to acquiring a combination of emerging, established, and mature growth forests. During the first few years of institutional timberland

Exhibit 8 Prices for Selected Regions, 1986-1996

Region*	VAEPW	VAESS	VAELS	GASPW	GASSS	GASLS	LASPW	LASSS
VAEPW	1.00							
VAESS	0.05	1.00						
VAELS	–0.08	–0.08	1.00					
GASPW	–0.07	–0.11	0.26	1.00				
GASSS	–0.02	0.26	0.23	0.40	1.00			
GASLS	–0.17	–0.07	0.46	0.43	0.47	1.00		
LASPW	0.03	0.18	–0.09	–0.21	–0.07	–0.02	1.00	
LASSS	0.00	–0.01	0.10	0.28	0.34	0.41	–0.06	1.00
LASLS	0.04	0.36	0.36	0.25	0.32	0.35	0.22	0.35

*VAEPW, VAESS, and VAELS = Eastern Virginia pulpwood, small sawtimber, and large sawtimber.
GASPW, GASSS, and GASLS = South Georgia pulpwood, small sawtimber, and large sawtimber.
LASPW, LASSS, and LASLS = South Louisiana pulpwood, small sawtimber, and large sawtimber.

investing, little explicit consideration was given to asset diversification, either geographically or with respect to the age classes of timberland held in portfolios. As a result, investments occasionally consisted of extremely concentrated holdings in a single market or state. Even when this was not the case, investments usually focused on timberland in a single age class, typically established growth.

Concentrated geographic ownership faces some increased risk from natural catastrophes such as hurricanes, ice storms, and insects in the eastern U.S., and fire in the west.[9] Purchasing timberland in a single age class and a single market area also increases investment risk.

As discussed earlier, stumpage prices in individual market areas are influenced by microeconomic factors. We saw in Exhibit 4 how annual trend rates of price change differ across three different markets and products. Consequently, stumpage price changes often are loosely correlated with one another. Exhibit 8 shows a correlation matrix for the same markets and stumpage categories. Correlations both across products and regions are low. Small and large sawtimber in eastern Virginia have a coefficient of –0.08. Louisiana and Georgia pulpwood prices have a coefficient of –0.21.

Another reason the balanced growth style developed is because institutional investors often require their timberland holdings to provide some level of current income from timber sales, as well as appreciation from biological growth. Emerging growth cannot do this, nor can young established growth. This means that at least some mixture of assets in each of the three growth stages has to be purchased.

TIMCOs found that the explicit use of Markowitz portfolio diversification (Markowitz [1959]) could lead to the construction of more risk-efficient portfolios, while providing required levels of current income. Low product price correlations within and across markets meant portfolios could be constructed by diversifying both geographically and across the three stages of growth.

Over time, TIMCOs have adopted individualized portfolio construction styles. John Hancock, for example, diversifies acquisitions by broad geographic region. Client holdings in their various commingled funds and separate accounts span the entire country. The core portfolio strategy they recommend consists of a 50% allocation in the south,

40% in the Pacific Northwest, and 10% in the northeast ("Timberland Investments" [1996]). Hancock also diversifies broadly across timber age classes.

Wachovia Timberland Investment Management primarily purchases timberland in the south. Their strategy is to acquire portfolios allocated across the emerging (40%), established (50%), and mature growth (10%) stages, diversified across market areas within the region. Acquisition and disposition decisions are based in part on a correlation analysis of timber product price changes similar to the one presented in Exhibit 6.[10]

Forest Investment Associates takes a different approach. They diversify client holdings across the south and mid-Atlantic states in different timber types. They are currently acquiring hardwood forests in New York and Pennsylvania, while simultaneously purchasing pine forests in the southeast. Unlike pines, which are used for commodity products such as paper and construction-grade lumber, northern hardwoods are ultimately destined for high-end uses such as furniture and appearance-grade veneer. The correlation between pine and hardwood timber prices consequently tends to be low.

MATURE GROWTH VALUE

The price of most timber products is cyclical. This is particularly true for sawtimber, which rises and falls with the expansion and contraction of housing construction. Evidence of cyclicality is apparent by referring back to Exhibit 3 for the south Georgia large and small sawtimber markets. Between 1977 and 1997, there were two periods during which sawtimber prices rose above trend and a sustained period of below-trend pricing. Similar relationships exist for other products and price regions.[11]

Price cyclicality is well-known to foresters, and most TIMCOs regularly use market timing in one form or another. Timber is unusual in that it can be "stored on the stump" when prices are low, an observation noted by Conroy and Miles [1989]. During these periods, investment managers tend to withhold supplies from market. Obviously, when premium prices are being paid, TIMCOs place greater volumes of timber out for bid.

Wachovia Timberland Investment Management employed market timing through a separate account that invested solely in mature growth properties, stocked with large sawtimber-size trees.[12] These were purchased during the 1989 to 1991 period, when prices were at a cyclical trough and property acquisition costs largely reflected the distressed value of the sawtimber assets. This superimposed a value component on the mature growth style.

The mature growth style was predicated partly on a forecast that timber prices would eventually move back to long-term trend levels as construction recovered. Sawtimber prices are volatile, particularly in rising markets. During sustained market downturns, sawmill woodyard inventories fall to very low levels because mills operate far below maximum capacity. When demand picks back up, mills must simultaneously purchase wood to meet immediate consumption needs and to replenish inventories to more normal levels. This normally results in a rapid price rise.

The account life was limited to seven years, which approximates the historical sawtimber cycle, providing the investment manager sufficient time to both acquire and dispose of properties in an orderly manner. As would be expected, a market timing strategy is not without risk. When sawtimber prices are depressed, there is no way to predict reliably when they will begin a period of sustained increase. Similarly, when prices are at levels far higher than the long-term trend — such as the prices in the period leading up to 1995 — there is no way to determine when they will begin to drop.[13]

EMERGING GROWTH

We saw in Exhibit 1 that near the end of the emerging growth stage forests enter a period of rapid volume and value growth. This has led to an emerging growth style for which at least two variations exist.

The first is to simply purchase existing pine plantations sometime near the end of the emerging growth stage. These are held until the growth rates slow, at which time they are merchantable for pulpwood and small sawtimber. This style was used for a fund introduced by Wachovia, which acquired eight- to ten-year-old southern pine plantations. The twelve-year fund life means that these assets will be disposed at about the time they begin to enter the mature growth stage.[14]

This strategy also takes advantage of a market inefficiency discussed previously — the "discount to discounted value" issue. Forest products companies and non-institutional buyers normally avoid purchasing premerchantable timberland because they do not want to hold it until it becomes merchantable.[15]

A second emerging growth strategy TIMCOs use is to purchase timber types that naturally grow quickly. Several varieties of eucalyptus achieve the fastest growth rates of any commercially grown species. As part of one investment, Prudential Timber is establishing 20,000 acres of eucalyptus plantations in Hawaii.[16] The expected rotation length is anticipated to be between seven and nine years — versus twenty or more for southern pines. The well-developed Pacific Rim market for eucalyptus pulpwood means that, despite relatively high front-end establishment and management costs, this short-rotation investment has the potential to realize annualized returns consistent with those expected by institutional investors.

Globally, the fastest growth rates for commercially valuable tree species occur in the southern hemisphere. UBS Resource Investments International (RII) uses an emerging growth style to capitalize on rapid biological growth by focusing on timberland investments in that region. In the early 1990s, they began buying radiata pine plantations in New Zealand, and then later in Chile. They have introduced three different funds based on this strategy ("Timber Talk" [1997]).

More recently, RII entered into a joint venture with Weyerhaeuser Company with the objective of acquiring an international portfolio of fast-growing pine and eucalyptus plantations. While the acquisition and management costs for these intensively managed plantations is higher than for domestic investments, the extremely rapid growth rates and high value-added products being grown may more than compensate for the incremental costs involved.

Timberland Investment Services (TIS) believes that planting and intensively managing pine plantations offers the same opportunity to achieve competitive returns that acquiring young plantations did in past years. In other words, they are pushing the emerging growth style to the left most portion of Exhibit 1, and employing this style for one of their separate accounts.

TIS' strategy is based on three observations. First, new forest management technology makes it possible to grow trees faster than in the past. Second, planting and management costs have actually declined in real terms over the past decade. This is because expensive, machinery-intensive preparation of planting sites is being replaced by cheaper, more environmentally-friendly chemical site preparation. Third, there has been a significant upward shift in timber prices since 1990 in most regions. Together these factors suggest it is possible to realize competitive returns from planting and growing trees, a departure from the usual TIMCO practice of purchasing existing plantations.

LARGE PROPERTIES

The earliest commingled timberland fund and separate accounts were characterized by an open-ended structure and very small pools of capital. Consequently, managers were constrained in the acquisition process, with typical fund purchases consisting of numerous tracts, some as small as 100 acres.

This situation began to change in 1987, when CALPERS, Ohio State Teachers Retirement System, and GTE placed investments with John Hancock totaling several hundred million dollars.[17] This had two effects. First, it signaled a visible and significant institutional acceptance of the asset class. Second, several acquisitions made by Hancock following these investments demonstrated to competing TIMCOs the advantage of being able to purchase large properties, for which there existed a wholesale discount on the underlying land asset.

Many of the properties acquired by TIMCOs for their clients are purchased from forest products companies, which frequently sell lands they no longer consider to be strategic supply sources for a specific mill. When these dispositions occur, selling firms often bundle together a large number of individual tracts and place the entire property package on the market. A 15,000-timberland sale, for example, might consist of 30 or 40 (or more) individual tracts, ranging from 200 to 1,000 acres each.

Exhibit 9 illustrates the relationship between property size and per acre land price on a southwide basis. There is a sharp decline in per acre price as property size increases up to about 2,000 acres, after which point it flattens out. This wholesale discount exists because the number of potential bidders declines with property size. For tracts in the 100 to 2,000 acre category, there is an active and competitive market for sales to hunt clubs, individual investors, and other buyers. Larger properties, however, are purchased almost exclusively by forest products firms or institutional investors.[18]

TIMCOs capitalize on the wholesale discount effect again when they later sell the property. In contrast to forest products firms, TIMCOs dispose of properties in much smaller pieces — ideally, a tract at a time — in order to realize a retail price on the land in each sale.

As a group, TIMCOs began packaging together larger commingled funds to capitalize on this wholesale discount effect. They also stopped offering the open-end fund structure, which encouraged small investments. Finally, they began marketing separate accounts with larger minimum investment requirements — usually between $15 to $25 million — much more aggressively than they had done previously. This had the predictable result of increasing the average size of acquired properties.

SUMMARY

The three timberland investment return drivers — biological growth, timber product prices, and land prices — influence investment characteristics alone and in combination. Each has also played a role in the development of individual TIMCO investing styles.

During the earliest years of the asset class, TIMCOs focused on an established growth style by acquiring mid-rotation softwood forests. As these moved from containing primarily pulpwood-sized trees to consisting of a combination of pulpwood and sawtimber, asset values increased significantly. Funds that followed this investment style provided returns competitive with fixed-income investments.

TIMCOs developed a balanced style to decrease portfolio risk and provide income returns to investors. The low correlations between timber price changes across product types and geographic regions mean diversified timberland portfolios can be constructed with desirable risk-adjusted return attributes. Each investment manager has developed its own balanced style. These include diversifying across broad geographic regions, subregions, timberland age classes, timber species, or some combination.

A mature growth value style takes advantage of the fact that timber prices tend to be cyclical. Most TIMCOs hold back timber supplies when prices are low. One TIMCO introduced a separate account in which sawtimber assets were acquired when prices were below the long-term price trend, and sold after they recovered to more normal levels.

At least two emerging growth styles exist. One is to buy timber assets immediately prior to their period of most rapid volume growth. The other is to purchase timber species that grow fast naturally, such as eucalyptus or pines in the southern hemisphere. Each makes use of the high correlation that exists between the rate of volume and value growth.

TIMCOs have capitalized on the wholesale discount effect that exists on the underlying land asset when large properties are acquired. They did this by ceasing to offer open-ended funds and instead bundling together larger commingled closed-end vehicles. They also began requiring higher minimum investments for separate accounts.

ENDNOTES

This article was published in *Real Estate Finance*, Winter 1988.

1 New TIMCOs since 1992 are: Forestland Group LLC, Timberland Investment Services LLC, Molpus Group, Harbinger Group, Strategic Timber Investments LLC, and Sustainable Forestry Systems. Assets under management include timberland and committed capital. This estimate is compiled from 1) Binkley et al. [1996] and UBS Resource Investments International [1997], 2) personal communication with Court Washburn, Hancock Timber Resource Group, James Webb, Wachovia Timberland Investment Management, and 3) Prudential Insurance Company as quoted on PRNewswire, World Wide Web.

2 The development of an even-aged forest is ultimately determined by tree species, site quality, management treatment, and other factors. This means that the curve for a specific forest can be higher or lower than the one in Exhibit 1 at each age greater than zero. The curve will, however, possess the general sigmoid shape (Clutter et al. [1992]).

3 It is not suggested that premerchantable forests do not have value. Typically, premerchantable forests are valued by appraisers based on the exchange value of the underlying land plus a proportion of the establishment cost of the forest; this proportion varies, but increases with forest age. As discussed later, the appraised values of very young forests often are less than the discounted value of the final timber crop.

4 Volumes are generated using the North Carolina State University loblolly pine growth and yield simulator, for Site Index 65 (Base 25) lower coastal plain sites planted with 700 trees per acre and 85% first-year survival.

5 Product prices are taken from Timber Mart South [1996], published quarterly, which reports on most major products sold in Alabama, Arkansas, Florida, Georgia, Louisiana, Mississippi, North Carolina, South Carolina, Tennessee, Texas, and Virginia. Each state consists of two pricing regions (either north-south or east-west).

6 Annual value change between ages ten and eleven is given by ($237/$156) – 1.

7 Marshall Thomas, F&W Forestry Services, personal communication.

8 More recent research using property-based indexes confirms timberland's tendency toward low correlations with other asset classes. This is documented for both a fund-based property benchmark

developed by Caulfield [1994] and an individual property index developed by NCREIF [1994].

[9] But even for undiversified timberland portfolios, this risk is much lower than accounts in the popular media would suggest. In the south, a typical forest plantation faces a risk of complete loss during the course of a rotation of less than 1% (Ebner et al. [1987]).

[10] James Webb, Wachovia Timberland Investment Management, personal communication.

[11] The very high and volatile pricing attained from the early 1990s to 1996 is also partly a function of timber harvest restrictions imposed on public lands, primarily in the U.S. west. As a consequence of these restrictions, western public harvests have declined almost 80% from the previous decade.

[12] The strategy therefore focused on the purchase of trees of the age and size represented by the rightmost portion of the sigmoid growth curve in Exhibit 1.

[13] As they did throughout much of 1996, for example (Timber Mart South [1996]).

[14] Referring to Exhibit 1, the strategy is implemented by acquiring forest plantations at about the point where they move from the premerchantable stage to the merchantable stage, and holding them until they contain a mix of both pulpwood and small sawtimber.

[15] Their rationale can also be considered from the standpoint of capital theory: Non-institutional investors, who tend to have a shorter timber horizon than institutional owners, implicitly place a higher capitalization rate on young trees, which declines as the trees grow into merchantable size classes.

[16] John Lord, Prudential Timber, personal communication.

[17] Court Washburn, Hancock Timber Resource Group, personal communication.

[18] The relationship in Exhibit 9 is fitted using property sales data provided by several large timberland appraisal firms. In the original proprietary study, data are disaggregated into smaller substate level regions.

REFERENCES

Binkley, C.S., C.F. Raper, and C.L. Washburn. "Institutional Ownership of U.S. Timberland." *Journal of Forestry*, 94 (9) (1996), pp. 21-28.

Caulfield, J.P. "Assessing Timberland Investment Performance." *Real Estate Review*, Spring 1994.

——. "Characteristics of Hunting Leases on Institutionally Owned Timberlands." In Proceedings, Symposium on the Economics of Wildlife Resources on Private Lands, Auburn, Alabama, August 1996 (in press).

——. "Evolution and Directions in Institutional Timberland Investment Strategy." In Proceedings of the 1997 Southern Forest Economics Workshop, Little Rock, Arkansas, April 1997.

Clutter, J.L., J.C. Fortson, L.V. Pienaar, G.H. Brister, and R.L. Bailey. *Timber Management: A Quantitative Approach*, 2nd edition. Malabar, FL: Krieger Publishing Co., 1992.

Conroy, R., and M. Miles. "Commercial Forestland in the Pension Portfolio: The Biological Beta." *Financial Analysts Journal*, September-October 1989.

de Steiguer, J.E. "Forestland Market Values." *Journal of Forestry*, 80, 4 (1982), pp. 214-216.

Ebner, T.J., M.I. Shearer, and J.F. Webb. "Risks Associated with Timberland Investments and the Timing of the Investment to Minimize the Risk." Presentation to Forest Products Research Society Conference, Milwaukee, Wisconsin April 1987.

Faustmann, M. "Calculation of the Value Which Forest Land and Immature Stands Possesses for Forestry." In Martin Faustmann and the Evolution of Discounted Cash Flow. Paper 42, Commonwealth Forestry Institute, Oxford, 1968 (translated by W. Linnard).

"FAO Forest Products Yearbook 1983-1994." Food and Agricultural Organization of the United Nations, Rome, 1994.

Markowitz, H.M. "Portfolio Selection." *Journal of Finance*, 7 (1959), pp. 77-91.

Mills, W.L., and W.L. Hoover. "Investment in Forest Land: Aspects of Risk and Diversification." *Land Economics*, 58 (1982), pp. 33-51.

National Council of Real Estate Investment Fiduciaries (NCREIF) and Frank Russell Company. "Special Report: The Russell-NCREIF Timberland Index. The Russell-NCREIF Real Estate Performance Report." 3rd Quarter, 1994.

NCREIF. "The NCREIF Real Estate Performance Report." 3rd Quarter, National Council of Real

Estate Investment Fiduciaries, 1997.

Redmond, C.H., and F.W. Cubbage. "Portfolio Risk and Returns from Timber Asset Investments." *Land Economics*, 64 (1988), pp. 326-337.

"Timber Mart South." D.B. Warnell School of Forest Resources, University of Georgia, Athens, 1996.

"Timber Talk." UBS Resource Investments International, Spring 1997.

"Timberland Investments, A Comprehensive Look at the Asset Class and Its Investment Characteristics." John Hancock Mutual Life Insurance Company, John Hancock Timber Resource Group, Boston, 1996.

Washburn, C.L. "The Determinants of Forest Value in the U.S. South." In Proceedings of the 1992 Southern Forest Economics Workshop, Mobile, Alabama, May 29, 1992.

Zinkhan, F.C. "Timberland as an Asset for Institutional Portfolios." *Real Estate Review*, Winter 1990.

20 STRUCTURE OF THE VENTURE CAPITAL INDUSTRY

W. KEITH SCHILIT
University of South Florida

We often use the terms "venture capital" and "venture capital firm" very loosely to describe any type of funding for privately held businesses. Actually, venture capital firms are just one source of such financing. There are several others, including large corporations as well as government and university supported programs, that provide investment capital and management assistance. The purpose of this article is to describe the different types of investors and to discuss the recent developments affecting their investment practices.

The "venture capital industry"[1] can be broken down into the following groups:

- Private independent venture capital partnerships
- Private Small Business Investment Companies (SBICs)
- Public venture capital companies
- Venture capital subsidiaries of large corporations
- State venture capital funds Universtiy related incubators
- Private sector incubator
- Investment banking firms

Let's explore these in detail.

PRIVATE INDEPENDENT VENTURE CAPITAL PARTNERSHIPS[2]

Private venture capital partnerships are either traditional partnerships established by wealthy families to aggressively manage a portion of their funds (for example, Venrock Associates, which is the fund established by the Rockefeller family) or professionally managed pools funded by institutional investors (such as Hambrecht & Quist, Kleiner Perkins Caufield & Byers, E. M. Warburg, Pincus & Co., etc.) Such partnerships represent the predominant type of venture investors in this country.

Some venture capital partnerships provide "seed capital" for start-up businesses. Others invest in turnaround or LBO situations. However, the majority of venture capital partnerships invest in growth companies. Investments are generally in the range of $2-$10 million.

Venture capital firms are generally organized as limited partnerships for tax purposes (i.e., to avoid corporate income tax) and other legal reasons. These partnerships have a general partner, usually the venture capital firm that manages the partnership's investment portfolio. The limited partners of the fund are the investors - usually passive - who each typically invest a minimum of $1 million, and often much more, in the larger funds. The investors include pension funds, foreign investors, corporations, banks, insurance companies, and wealthy individuals. Since a typical investment by a venture capital firm has a time horizon of three-seven years, most partnership funds establish an eight-ten year lifetime, whereby the general partner holds the option to extend this lifetime for up to two years. This ensures orderly dissolution of investments by a fund. The general partner is usually paid a management fee of approximately 2.5%!}f the committed capital plus an incentive bonus of 20% of the funds realized net gains. The limited partners (i.e., the investors) would receive the remainder.

PRIVATE SMALL BUSINESS INVESTMENT COMPANIES (SBICs)[3]

Small Business Investment Companies (SBICs), which were created by Congress in 1958, are licensed and regulated by the Small Business Administration (SBA). These government-backed (but privately owned) investment companies (that include such companies as Citicorp Venture Capital, Allied Investment Corp., and Clinton Capital, etc.), may provide management assistance as well as venture financing for such emerging businesses. Over the years, SBICs have provided financing for such entrepreneurial successes as Apple Computer, Cray Research, Intel Corp., ROLM Corp., and Federal Express. SBICs have also enabled several unprofitable or marginally profitable ventures to become profitable businesses. Typical success stories include: American Frozen Foods, NBI, Ault Inc., Lifeline Systems, and Pandick Press.

Due to SBA regulations, the investment policies for SBICs are much more restrictive than those for traditional venture capital firms. SBICs must uphold guidelines related to the size of the companies in which they invest and the portion of their portfolios that are invested in any particular company.

There are about 300 SBICs in this country, most of which are found in the states where entrepreneurial growth is highest i.e., New York, California, Massachusetts, Connecticut, and Texas. Some SBICs are primarily interested in equity positions in their investments; others serve as lenders.

American Commercial Capital Corp., of New York, for example, lends money on a secured basis. (Thus, there is less risk and, consequently, less potential return for the investor.) The company's clients, therefore, tend to be low-technology companies with fixed assets, rather than high-technology companies with merely ideas. If the borrower does not succeed, American Commercial will take ownership of the secured assets. Like many venture capital firms, some SBICs specialize in specific industry groups (for example, high-technology, health care, etc.), whereas others provide funding for all types of ventures. Although a few SBICs — notably, Clinton Capital Corp. (NYC), Edwards Capital Co. (NYC), Allied Capital Corp. (Washington, DC), Medallion Funding Corp. (NYC), and Transportation Capital Corp. (NYC) — are actively involved in funding start-ups, most of the SBICs engage in later stage investments.

SBICs are initially capitalized from private sources. They then become eligible to obtain loans at attractive interest rates from the government (or guaranteed by the government), thereby enabling the SBICs to leverage themselves by three times and, four times in the case of SBICs that fund minority owned businesses — (these are called Minority Enterprise Small Business Investment Companies [MESBICs]), — their paid-in capital. This financing ability allows SBICs to either make long term loans or equity investments to emerging growth companies.

SBICs can be either private individuals, publicly held corporations, or subsidiaries of larger companies. Many of the SBICs — such as Citicorp Venture Capital (NYC), First Chicago Venture Capital (Chicago, IL), Chemical Venture Partners (NYC), Chase Manhattan Capital Corp. (NYC), Manufacturers Hanover Venture Capital Corp. (NYC) — are subsidiaries of commercial banks, whose capital comes from clients of the bank.

MINORITY ENTERPRISE SMALL BUSINESS INVESTMENT COMPANIES (MESBLCs)[4]

As just mentioned in addition to SBICs, there are over 100 Minority Enterprise Small Business Investment Companies (MESBlCs) that provide funding to businesses owned by racial minorities. They operate in a manner similar to other venture capital companies and, therefore, evaluate proposals based on the owner's previous experience and on the company's business plan. Some of the larger MESBlCs in the country (in addition to Medallion Funding Corp. and Transportation Capital Corp., mentioned earlier as SBlCs that invest heavily in start-ups) they include: Columbia Capital Corp. (NYC), affiliated with Clinton Capital Corp; Allied Financial Corp. Washington D.C., affiliated with Allied Capital Corp); Fulcrum Venture Capital Corp. (Washington, DC), affiliated with Syndicated Communications, Inc; and Syncom Capital Corp. Pro-Med Investment Corp. (North Miami Beach, FL) affiliated with Pro-Med Capital and Western Financial Capital Corp.

One current controversial issue is a federal regulation which prohibits MESBlCs from having controlling interest in a minority business. According to some MESBIC investors, this has limited the returns to the MESBlCs.

PUBLIC VENTURE CAPITAL COMPANIES

Several of the large venture capital firms (as well as SBlCs) in this country are publicly held corporations, and are referred to as business development companies (BDCs). They have similar investment orientations as privately held venture capital firms. However, because they are public corporations, they differ from private venture capital firms in terms of: regulations placed upon them by the Securities and Exchange Commission (SEC), tax laws that may affect their investment activity, and the expectations of their investors. For example, unlike private venture capital limited partnerships, a BDC does not liquidate itself after a set period of time. In addition, because BDCs are public corporations, management must be concerned with the stock price of the corporation.

Some of the larger publicly held venture capital companies are Allied Capital Corp. (Washington, DC), Capital Southwest Corp. (Dallas), and Rand Capital (Buffalo). Publicly held SBlCs include First Connecticut SBIC (Bridgeport) and Greater Washington Investors (Chevy Chase).

VENTURE CAPITAL SUBSIDIARIES OF LARGE CORPORATIONS

Large corporations often invest in smaller companies to supplement their R & D programs as well as to keep abreast of technological and other innovations. This can be done by investing in the private venture capital limited partnerships discussed earlier. It can also be done by a direct investment in a smaller corporation. Furthermore, it can be accomplished by the formation of an internal venture within a company, i.e., an "intrapreneurial" venture. Or, this process can be formalized through the creation of a "venture capital subsidiary" (operates like a trust department in a bank or a separate, wholly owned company) of a large corporation. Some examples of the latter include: Xerox Venture Capital (Stamford), Amoco Venture Capital (Chicago), Lubrizol Enterprises (Wickliffe, OH), Hewlett-Packard Co. Corporate Investments (Palo Alto), Sears Investment Management Co. (Chicago), and Caterpillar Venture Capital (Peoria).

Such venture capital subsidiaries are often attractive sources of capital for entrepreneurial companies because they can invest $10 - $20 million in some ventures. Today, this multi-billion segment has about 100 non-financial corporations with venture capital subsidiaries, with many more doing some sort of ad hoc investing. These corporate subsidiaries not only have large pools of capital available for direct investments, but the parent corporations and their pension plans invest as limited partners of other venture capital partnerships. In addition, unlike typical venture capital funds, they have "deep pockets"; they can generally get additional capital from the parent company if attractive opportunities develop.

BENEFITS TO THE CORPORATE VENTURE CAPITAL SUBSIDIARY

There are several reasons why corporations have established venture capital subsidiaries. These include:

- deriving attractive financial returns;
- developing technology licenses, manufacturing rights, and marketing/supplier agreements;
- controlling supplier uncertainty;
- identifying and assess acquisition candidates;
- spinning off businesses;
- generating new products;
- learning the dynamics of a particular marketplace; and
- gaining exposure to new markets and technologies.

PRODUCT MARKETING RIGHTS

Because large corporations can provide marketing and distribution systems, small ventures are often happy to have large companies sell their products. For example, NCR and Burroughs secured marketing rights for Convergent Technology's products, which are manufactured for them on an OEM basis. Similarly, in the biotechnology area, several large pharmaceutical companies (in the U.S., Europe, and Japan) have secured marketing rights to various products developed by Genentech in return for development funds.

ACQUISITION CANDIDATES

A few years ago, General Electric had made a direct investment in Applicon, Inc., a computer-aided design/computer-aided manufacturing (CAD/CAM) company. Eventually, GE attempted to acquire Applicon. However, it was unsuccessful in its bid. Nonetheless, armed with the knowledge of the CAD/CAM industry, GE bid successfully for Calma, another company in that industry. (Similarly, Lubrizol acquired Agrigenetics, thanks in part to its venture capital involvement in related companies.)

A WINDOW ON TECHNOLOGY

Perhaps the most notable benefit that large corporations have derived from their investments in entrepreneurial companies is that they have gained a "window" on new technological developments without having to get directly involved with technologies that may deviate somewhat from their existing business mission. For example, when supercomputer genius Steve Chen, left Cray Research (which was, itself, formed by managers from the Control Data Corp. that, in turn, was an outgrowth of the Sperry Corp.), to start his own company, Supercomputer Systems, Inc. (Eau Claire, WI), IBM immediately invested in the new venture.

Technology and the desire to keep pace with technological developments has certainly been a driving force behind the emergence of corporate venture capital subsidiaries. This is evidenced by the fact that all of the ten largest electronics companies in the U.S. as well as several prominent foreign corporations have made direct venture investments over the last decade.

Numerous fledgling companies have derived the benefits of such investments by venture capital subsidiaries. Some examples of technology areas and companies that have received corporate venture capital include:

- *Artificial Intelligence*—Carnegie Group, Interference, Lisp Machines, Symbolics, Syntelligence, Teknowledge;
- *Biotechnology*—Advanced Genetic Systems, Amgen, Biogen, Calgene, Centocor, Cetus, Collaborative research, Cytogen, DNA Plant, Genetech, Genex, Genzyme, Hana, Ingene, Liposome, Molecular Genetics, Oncogene, Synergen, Syntro;
- *Computers*—Amdahl, Altos, Apple, Cray, Fortune Systems, Stratus, Sun Microsystems, Tandem, Trilogy, Wang;
- *Instruments*—Analog Devices, Nicolet, Waters Associates;
- *Medical Electronics*—ADAC, Cords, Kolff Medical, Orien Research;
- *Peripherals*—Centronics, Computer Memories, Decision Data, Seagate, Zitel;
- *Robotics*—Adept Technology, Advanced Robotics, Automatix, Robotic Vision Systems, Synthetic Vision Sytems, View Engineering;
- *Semiconductors*—Cypress, Intel, LSI Logic, Micron, Siliconix, VLSITechnology, Xicor, Zymos
- *Software*—Adobe, Comserve, Interleaf, Seattle Silicon, Synektron, Synercom;
- *Telecommunications*—Comdial, Intercom, MCI, Network Systems, Paradyne, Quotron, Rolm, Ungermann-Bass, VMX, Vodavi, Ztel;
- *Terminals*—Datapointe, Esprit, Lee Data, Ramtek, Syntrex, Wyse; and
- *Others*—Businessland, DataCard, Federal Express, Fibronics, Key Pharmaceutical, Siltec, Xidex.

BENEFITS TO THE EMERGING GROWTH COMPANY

There are numerous benefits that corporate venture subsidiaries bring to the companies in which they invest. In addition to the typical financial, resource, and strategic benefits that most venture capital firms provide, corporate venture subsidiaries have been able to provide:

- an established customer base;
- credibility with customers and suppliers;
- credibility with bankers and other financial resources;
- general assistance in managing the business;
- a merger partnership;
- additional capital; and
- a flexible financing package.

INVESTING IN EMPLOYEES

One way in which large corporations have funded emerging growth ventures has been through their own employees who wish to start companies of their own. For example, Tektronix provided financial support to Jim Hurd, a former manager of solid state engineering with the company, in order to form Planar Systems in exchange for 49.5% of the equity of the new business. Similarly, Campbell Soup provided William Sharp, a research director of the company, with the necessary financial, marketing, R&D, and personnel assistance (including a $5 million research laboratory) in return for a 30% equity position in the new venture. By providing employees with the necessary support to begin new ventures of their own, both the established companies and the new ventures have benefitted tremendously.

COLLABORATIVE ARRANGEMENTS

Another way by which corporations have invested in smaller companies has been through collaborative arrangements. For example, Immunex Corp., a genetic engineering company in Seattle, signed a collaborative research contract whereby Hoffman LaRoche paid Immunex $500,000 up-front (plus subsequent sales royalties) as well as monthly research payments so that it could manufacture and market Immunex drugs, pending regulatory approval. Several other biotechnology companies have entered into similar arrangements with larger corporations. This has been due to the scarcity of venture capital dollars and the high costs of developing and testing new products. For example, Collaborative Research Inc., of Boston, entered into an arrangement with American Hospital Supply Corp. for the funds needed to test and market its immunological products; Cetus Corp. received funding from Nabisco, Shell Oil, and Weyerhauser; Genetic Systems Corp. had assistance from Cutter Laboratories; and California Biotechnology, Inc., of Mountain View, California, created an alliance with Pfizer, Inc. to develop cures for diabetes and obesity.

SOME PROBLEMS ASSOCIATED WITH CORPORATE VENTURE CAPITAL

Despite the positive features noted, corporate venture capital programs have had their problems, generally arising from such reasons as the following:

- contradictory investment goals of the corporate venture subsidiary and the parent corporation (or division);
- unwillingness on the part of the corporate venture subsidiary to invest the seven-ten years necessary for venture capital commitments;
- conflicts of interests and legal problems, such as those involving fiduciary responsibility of the investing company; lack of skilled professional; and
- inconsistent goals of corporation (i.e., corporate venture subsidiary) and the entrepreneur.

A classic study from the Harvard Business Review reinforces some of the limitations of corporate venture capital. The authors found that, although there are positive features of corporate venture capital, such efforts have generally not been successful in promoting corporate diversification, primarily due to:

- limited investment opportunities;
- the difficulty of acquiring the funded company;
- the complications involved in obtaining technology from the funded company; and

- irreconcilable differences between organizational requirements for running a diversification program and those for building a healthy portfolio of investments.

Moreover, such ventures have not always worked out well for the entrepreneur, since the corporations often wound up owning these ventures. These factors many explain why, although approximately 30% of the "Fortune 500" companies established venture groups during the 1960s and 1970s, most of those are no longer in existence today. Consequently, such corporations as GTE, 3M, and Corning, which had traditionally invested directly in ventures, are now investing as limited partners through more traditional venture capital partnerships.

KEYS TO SUCCESSFUL CORPORATE VENTURE CAPITAL PROGRAMS

What makes corporate venture capital programs successful? It has been shown that, for corporate venture capital programs to succeed, the key elements of the corporation's operating environment and organizational structure should be adapted to its special characteristics. This would include:

- establishing realistic goals;
- providing for an opportunity for the corporation to utilize new technologies;
- establishing an appropriate system of controls; and
- selecting appropriate personnel.

Thus, there are mixed feelings regarding the advantages of organizing and maintaining the venture capital subsidiaries of established companies. Some efforts — such as the ones at Tektronix and Campbell Soup — have been successful; others have not fared as well. It is safe to conclude, however, that it is the manner in which such a program is implemented that is the best predictor of its success.

STATE VENTURE CAPITAL FUNDS

In 1975, Massachusetts and Connecticut established government-sponsored venture capital funds to provide financial assistance to emerging growth businesses. They were called, respectively, the Massachusetts Community Development Finance Corporation (CDFC) and the Connecticut Product Development Program. Since that time, several other states, including Georgia, Indiana, Michigan, Minnesota, New York, and Wyoming, have established similar programs, and Massachusetts has developed a second program, called the Massachusetts Technology Development Corp. (MTDC).

A COMPARISON OF THE PROGRAMS

Although the purposes of each program are essentially the same, the programs differ with regard to the sources of funding, investment parameters, and investment preferences. Specifically, funding for state-supported programs may come from either state sources exclusively (which is the case in Connecticut, New Mexico, and Utah), a combination of state and federal sources (as in, Massachusetts and New York), private sources exclusively (Minnesota and Wyoming), or a combination of state and private sources (Georgia and Michigan). Furthermore, investments can be targeted primarily for early-stage ventures (which is the case in Georgia, lowa, and Minnesota), for product development (Connecticut), or for high-tech businesses (Utah and New York). In addition, the funding can be in the form of royalty payments (as the case in Connecticut), or debt

(New Mexico), equity (Utah, Georgia, Indiana, lowa, Michigan, and Minnesota), or a combination of debt and equity (Massachusetts, New York, and Wyoming).

THE IMPACT OF STATE SUPPORTED PROGRAMS

What has been the impact of these programs on economic development? In Massachusetts, where the program was initiated, the results have been very positive. Massachusetts Community Development Finance Corp. (CDFC) has invested in such companies as: Automated Assemblies Corp., a "systems integrator" for industrial robots; and Runtal North America, which markets and distributes hydronic radiators. The other state-supported program in Massachusetts, the Massachusetts Technology Development Corp. (MTDC), has limited its funding to technology businesses such as Access Technology, a developer of business software and Zoom Telephonics, a telecommunications company.

Other state programs have had similar success stories. For example, Indiana's Corporation for Innovation Development has invested in such companies as Stratojac, and the Wholesale Club. New York's Corporation for Innovation Development, which, like MTDC, has geared its investments to technology start-ups, has invested in Applied Robotics and Xertronix. Nebraska's Enterprise Fund has invested in ICR Research Associates and Addax, Inc. The New Mexico R&D Institute has invested in RhoMed and Bacchus Industries.

UNIVERSITY-RELATED INCUBATORS

One of the more significant developments over the past decade, especially for technology oriented ventures, has been the emergence of the "incubator", a structure that enables entrepreneurs to develop their business skills in an environment conducive to fostering technical creativity. Incubators, that often university related, generally provide low-cost laboratory and office space, state-of-the-art technical thinking and equipment, administrative support, computer and library facilities, consultants, and contacts with bankers, venture capitalists, government officials, etc. to selected entrepreneurs for a nominal fee. Since the entrepreneurs are surrounded by others like themselves, there is often a sharing of ideas and contacts, thereby enhancing entrepreneurial growth. In addition, these incubators enhance public-private-industry-university relations, that often results in economic benefits for all parties involved.

Incubators, themselves, have been a growth industry. In 1984, there were forty incubators nationwide. Today, there are about ten times as many, with the greatest number found in Pennsylvania, Illinois, and New York.

The prototype university-related incubator/ research center is the University City Science Center (UCSC) in Philadelphia. UCSC it is affiliated with twenty-eight universities, colleges, and medical schools in the Philadelphia area (including the University of Pennsylvania, the Philadelphia General Hospital, the Philadelphia College of Pharmacy and Science, the Presbyterian University of Philadelphia Medical Center, Drexel University, and Villanova University), and is the only entirely urban research park in the country. UCSC has the capacity to house nearly 100 companies in its one-million square foot facility. Most of its current "tenants" are in high-tech industries.

Other similar but smaller university programs include: The Western Pennsylvania Advanced Technology Center in Pittsburgh, sponsored by the University of Pittsburgh and Carnegie-Mellon University; Georgia Advanced Technology Program in Atlanta; Rensselear Polytechnic Institute [RPI] in Troy, New York; Utah Innovation Center [UIC], in Salt Lake City, which has had a relationship with the University of Utah; and the Institute for Ventures in Technology [INVENT], which is sponsored by Texas A & M University.

THE ROLE OF PRIVATE VENTURE CAPITAL IN UNIVERSITY RESEARCH EFFORTS

A somewhat related structure is the Dallas Biomedical Corporation, a small venture capital firm which limits its investments to research projects at the University of Texas Southwestern Medical Center that have the potential for commercialization. The firm, started in 1986, serves as a bridge between other private venture capital firms and university research efforts. Dallas Biomedical invests only the interest on its capital — investments will, therefore, be in the range of $50,000 to $250,000 — and returns any profits plus the original principal to the outside investors in five years in return for half the interest in the twenty technology; the other half is split between the university and the scientist. The firm has established a low-risk, socially oriented concept that could serve as a prototype for public-private-university relationships. Similar to this program is BCM Technologies, Inc. (BCMT), a for-profit business development arm of Baylor College of Medicine, that establishes new commercial entities based on inventions from researchers at the college. In its first five years of operation, BCMT developed five companies in such fields as blood salvage in open heart surgery and cancer diagnostics. The funding for these projects comes from outside venture capital companies, rather than from the College or the University system.

PRIVATE SECTOR INCUBATORS

Private-sector incubators, like university-related incubators, provide office space, administrative support, an entrepreneurial atmosphere, etc. to entrepreneurs. However, they differ from university-related centers in that 1) the funding is strictly from private, rather than public, sources, and 2) the primary goal is profit-job creation and community economic development are not nearly as important as the profit motive.

Incubators are generally ideal for early stage ventures, i.e., pre-seed or seed-stage. Some examples of private incubators include The Technology Center (Montgomeryville, PA) and The Rubicon Group (Austin).

INVESTMENT BANKING FIRMS

Investment banking firms are usually involved in more established companies, but occasionally form investor syndicates for venture proposals. These firms are in business to arrange financing and structure deals for emerging growth-businesses. Many sophisticated entrepreneurs consider the use of investment bankers as the rule, rather than the exception, for raising capital, as they can do so more quickly and efficiently than can the managers of the venture themselves. Some of the larger investment banking firms in this country are: ABS Ventures Limited Partnership (Baltimore), Salomon Brothers (NYC), Morgan Stanley & Co. (NYC), and Montgomery Securities (NYC).

BOUTIQUES

Similar to the investment banking firms, but on a much smaller scale, are the "boutiques" that raise cash from banks, finance companies, and private individuals. Like investment banking firms, they will sometimes invest their own capital. Their clientele is generally local or regional, and they can usually arrange financing for companies in the $1 million to $10 million range.

The "boutiques" will generally charge 1/2% to 3% of the capital raised to arrange for a debt placement and 2% to 8% to arrange for an equity placement. A commonly used fee arrangement in equity transactions is the so-called "Lehman formula" of 5-4-3-2-1%, that translates into 5% of the first million dollars of capital raised, 4% of the next million, etc. Thus, for a $3 million deal, the fees would be equal to $120,000, or 4% of the total capital raised:

$50,000+	$40,000+	$30,000	= $120,000
(5% of the first million)	(4% of the next million)	(3% of the next million)	

SYNDICATION

In order to satisfy the risk/return concerns of venture capitalists, most venture capital firms co-invest or "syndicate"with one another. For example, Sierra Ventures, a technology-oriented venture capital firm based in Menlo Park, CA, was the "lead investor" in StrataCom, Inc., a Silicon Valley based manufacturer of high-speed telecommunications equipment. However, in addition to Sierra Ventures' $1.4 million investment in this start-up, Sierra arranged for an additional $3 million in funding from Venrock Associates, U.S. Venture Partners, and International Technology Ventures.

Syndication has become the norm in the venture capital industry, with probably more of the deals of independent and corporate venture capital firms being syndicated.

ENDNOTES

This article was published in *The Journal of Private Equity*, Spring 1998.

[1] In this article, 1) we're using the term "venture capital" very broadly to describe not only the investments of a traditional venture capital limited partnership, but to describe similar types of investments in private companies; and 2) we're referring to the "formal" venture capital industry, rather than to "informal" investors, often referred to as "angels."

[2] The trade association of the venture capital industry is the National Venture Capital Association (NVCA), located in Arlington, VA.

[3] The trade association for SBICs is the National Association of Small Business investments Companies (NASBIC), located in Washington, D.C.

[4] The trade association for MESBICs the National Association of Investment Companies (NAIC), located in Washington, D.C.

REFERENCE

Hardyman, G. F., Denino, M.J., and M.S. Salter. "When Corporate Venture Capital Doesn't Work." *Harvard Business Review*, May-June, 1983, pp. 114-120.

VI NEW PRODUCT DEVELOPMENT AND DESIGN

INTRODUCTION

Accompanying the growth in both traditional and alternative investments are innovations both in market structure and security design.[1] Security designs that are common in capital markets such as swaps, closed-end funds, and structure products are now commonly available for delivering the returns to alternative investments. Today the investment vehicles for alternative investments are not materially different from traditional stock and bond investments. The essential difference between alternative and traditional investments is not how they are marketed or how the performance is measured, but that each offers unique risk and return properties that are essential for a diversified portfolio.

The growth of new market structures and security design for traditional and alternative assets is expected. Both academic and practitioner literature address the motivations for innovation in security design [Allen et al., 1994]. First, new security or investment product forms consistent with economic and technology advances may be more consistent with investors' needs, than existing products as well as providing structurers with a "first movers" advantage. Second, changes in regulatory and market structure lead to new forms of oversight as well as product structures. These may offer increased efficiency, lower cost, and in some cases, offer access to unique sources of return.

Whatever the basis for the new security design or investment product form, behavioral research predicts there will generally be a lag between introduction and widespread acceptance. There are two kinds of risk associated with any investment. Financial risk deals with the riskiness of the investment's cash flows. Uncertainty risk stems from unfamiliarity with the investment structure itself. Since investors are averse to both risks, it is natural to experience a delayed response to the introduction of new investment vehicles, even when the economic fundamentals of the investment suggest it would be suitable to a wide range of portfolios.

The articles reprinted in this section offer information about approaches to structuring alternative investments, examples of new investment offerings, as well as the means to manage the risk of new investment vehicles. Investors are also referred to a list of readings and books listed in the bibliography and a summary of selected articles in Exhibit 1 of this chapter.

ARTICLE REVIEW

The breadth of new investment products such as weather derivatives, energy derivatives, credit derivatives, and new structures such as linked notes, options on manager performance, and guaranteed products prevents a fully comprehensive survey of this area. Many of these new structures are much simpler than they appear and can offer highly tailored exposure to unique sources of return. By reducing investor uncertainty associated with these structures, investors can concentrate on the economic fundamentals of each product form.

Regardless of the form of the product design, the economic basis for a new product is its access to a unique source of return opportunities. In the first article, "An Introduc-

EXHIBIT 1 SUMMARY OF SELECTED RESEARCH REGARDING PRODUCT DESIGN AND PRODUCT DEVELOPMENT

Bibliography	Title	Topic	Major Results
Finnerty, J (FM,1988)	"Financial Engineering in Corporate Finance,"	Alternative forms of corporate finance vehicles	▪ Articles provides a summary of a wide variety of then existing financial lproducts and the basis for their existence
Peng, S. and R. Dattatregy (Probus, 1995)	"The Structured Note Market," Investing in Hedge Funds,"	Structured Notes	▪ Practitioner review of structured note creation
Edited Book (Risk,1998)	"Credit Derivatives"	Credit Derivatives in Risk Management and Investment	▪ Series of practitioner articles on credit derivatives
Edited Book (Risk,1998)	"Equity Derivatives"	Equity Derivatives in Risk Management and Investment	▪ Series of practitioner articles on equity derivatives and products
Edited Book (Risk,1998)	"VAR:Understanding and Applying Value-at-Risk"	VaRin Risk Management and Investment	▪ Series of practitioner articles on VaR analysis
Jarrow, R. ed., (Risk, 1998)	"Volatility: New Estimation Techniques for Pricing Derivatives,"	Volatility Estimation and Risk/Investment Use	▪ Series of practitioner articles on credit derivatives
Talib, N. (1997)	""Dynamic Hedging of Risk"	VaR Analysis	▪ Presents evidence that the problems of traditional VaR analysis.).

Journal abbreviations: Risk — Risk Publications; FM — Financial Management Journal; Probus — Probus Publishing;

tion to Credit Derivatives," Kerrin Howard discusses the growth of the credit derivative markets. This field has become one of the fastest growing areas in new products. Howard points out that credit derivatives are, at their simplest, customized agreements between two counterparties on the transfer of credit exposure. Thus, as part of the movement towards the splitting and securitizing of various risk/return structures, credit risk is now understood to be an attribute that can be hedged, traded, and therefore, invested in.

By their very nature, many of these new vehicles are being created by the originators of the product, such as insurance companies. In the second article, "Alternative Risk Transfer: Investing Directly in Insurance Risk as an Alternative Investment Strategy," David Mordecai offers a review of many new product forms and opportunities made available by insurance companies. These securities are examples of the trend toward disintermediation of financial risk-securitizing sources of return transferring both the risk and potential return directly to investors.

For instance, insurers and reinsurers are capitalizing on the convergence of the insurance and capital markets by employing capital market solutions to reallocate underwriting capacity. Catastrophe bonds and other insurance-linked securities or financing arrangements are now joining previous insurance innovations like financial reinsurance, loss portfolio transfers, and captive insurance vehicles. Contingent financial instruments such as catastrophe equity puts and contingent surplus notes are becoming common sources of mezzanine capital for insurers. Exchange-traded and over-the-counter insurance derivatives, credit derivatives, political risk derivatives, and weather derivatives are proliferating as substitutes and complements to traditional insurance and reinsurance capacity. In addition, hedge funds are establishing specialty insurance companies in order to manage insurance funds as sources of long-term return on capital.

RESEARCH IN PRODUCT DEVELOPMENT AND PRODUCT DESIGN

Since many of the product structures discussed in this section are new, there is little or no historical return record that can be analyzed. Only through time will the ability of

EXHIBIT 2 PERFORMANCE OF MAR FUND/POOL (EQUAL WEIGHT) AND MAR GUARANTEED FUND RANKED BY MAR FUND/POOL (1990-1998)

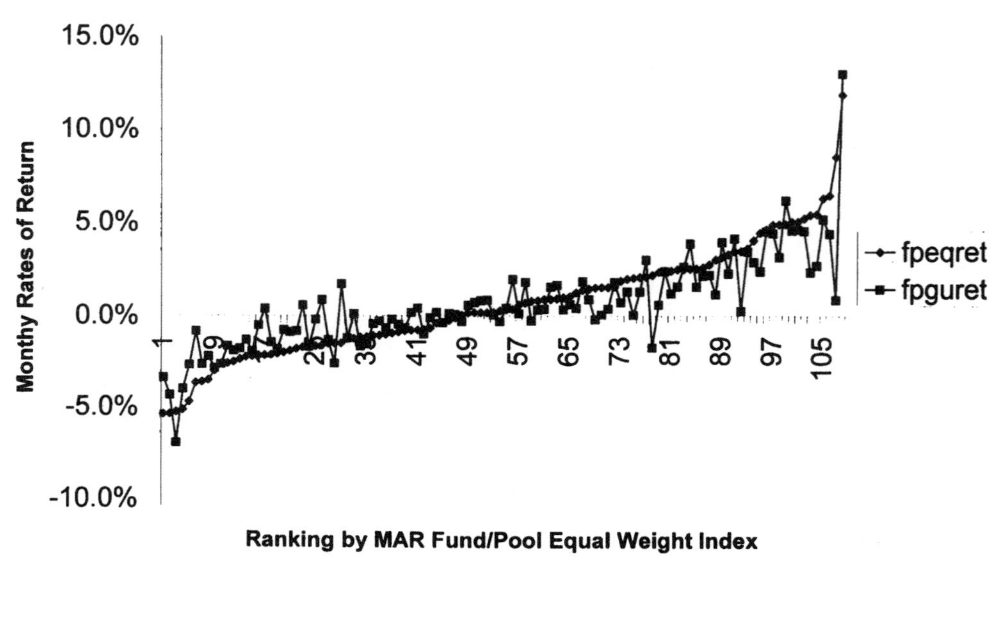

these new investment forms to offer efficient access to certain economic factors be evident. For instance, a guaranteed product is more than a simple insurance policy. It represents a complex contract between the investor, the guarantor, and the fund manager. In periods of poor manager performance, the investment is generally de-levered to protect the guarantor against a large loss. This reduction in leverage also reduces the expected return to the investor. The long-run success of these investment vehicles will depend on the willingness of investors to trade expected return for the certainty that the investment will not involve a loss of principal.

The same argument holds for the use of protective put options to hedge equity positions. The widespread use of protective puts suggests investors are willing to accept reduced returns in order to eliminate the chance of a large loss. These strategies may be particularly successful in alternative investments, where uncertainty about the underlying source of return may be deterring institutional investment even while the empirical evidence is clear that these assets belong in a diversified portfolio. Exhibit 2 describes the payoff to a managed futures based guaranteed fund relative to non-guaranteed funds over the period 1990-1998. While guaranteed fund design has changed over the time period (e.g., zero coupon, option based) and guaranteed funds on managed futures may be suitable to a small set of CTA strategies (e.g., managers who track volatility), in general, guaranteed fund returns (see Exhibit 2) consistent with lower leverage than non-guaranteed funds.

CONCLUSIONS

Economic change, governmental regulation, and a more informed investment community have triggered demand for new products and product design. These innovations reflect two ongoing trends. The first is a technological shift that has given investors the tools to analyze complex investment structures that until recently have been available only to dealers and insurers. The ability to independently assess the risk and return of an investment opportunity has allowed investors to overcome much of the uncertainty about these products.

The second innovation is the move towards disintermediation of investment strategies such as insurance, commercial banking, and relative value arbitrage that until recently have been the property of financial intermediaries. The articles in this section focus on a number of issues of importance to institutional investors. These articles provide insight into the design of alternative asset structures, the economic fundamentals of a number of new sources of return, and a comprehensive strategy for understanding and managing the risk of an entire investment portfolio.

SECTION VI ARTICLES

Howard, Kerrin, "An Introduction to Credit Derivatives," *Derivatives Quarterly* (Winter 1995), pp. 28-37.

Mordecai, David K. A., "Alternative Risk Transfer: Investing Directly in Insurance Risk as an Alternative Investment Strategy," *The Journal of Alternative Investments* (Spring 1999), pp. 43-57.

ENDNOTES

[1] For a critical look at some of the general concerns over financial innovation in the financial services industry see Allan [1994], Van Horne, [1985] and Dow [1998].

SELECTED REFERENCES

Allen, F. and D. Gale. Financial Innovation and Risk Sharing (MIT Press, 1994).

Angell, J., D. Chance, J.C. Francis, and G. Gastineau, "Comparison of Two Low-Cost S&P 500 Index Funds," *Derivatives Quarterly* (Spring, 1996), pp. 32-38.

Allen, Franklin and Douglas Gale. "Optimal Security Design," *Review of Financial Studies* (Fall, 1988), pp. 229-263.

Baubonis, C/ Gary Gastineau, and David Purcell, " The Bankers Guide to Equity-Linked Certificates of Deposit," *The Journal of Derivatives* (Winter, 1993), pp. 87-95.

Black, F. and M. Scholes, "From Theory to a New Financial Product," *Journal of Finance* (May, 1974), pp. 399-412.

Boot, Arnoud. and Anjan V. Thakor. "Security Design," *Journal of Finance* (September, 1993), pp. 1349-1378.

Dow, James, "Arbitrage, Hedging, and Financial Innovation," *The Review of Financial Studies*, Vol 11, No. 4 (Winter, 1998), pp. 739-757.

Gastineau, G. "An Introduction to Special -Purpose Derivatives: Roll Up Puts, Roll Down Calls, and Contingent Premium Options," *Journal of Derivatives* (Summer, 1994), pp. 40-43.

Gastineau, G., and M. Kritzman, *Dictionary of Financial Risk Management,* Fabozzi Associates, 1996

Figlewski, Steven. "The Birth of the AAA Derivatives Subsidiary," *The Journal of Derivatives* (Summer, 1994), pp. 80-84.

Finnerty, J. "Financial Engineering in Corporate Finance: An Overview" *Financial Management* (Winter, 1988), pp. 14-32.

Kane, E. "Technological and Regulatory Forces in the Developing Fusion of Financial-Services Competition," *Journal of Finance* (July, 1984), pp. 759-772.

McNeill, W. "Securitizing Future Generations Today," *The Journal of Derivatives* (Summer, 1996), pp. 90-95.

Merton, Robert. "Financial Innovation and Economic Performance," *Journal of Applied Corporate Finance,* Vol 4., No. 4 (Winter, 1992).

Miller, Merton. "Financial Innovation: Achievements and Prospects," *Journal of Applied Corporate Finance,* Vol. 4, No. 4 (Winter, 1992).

Peng, S. and R. Dattatreya. *The Structured Note Market.* Probus, 1995.

Silber, William L. *Financial Innovation* (Lexington, Books, 1975).

Silber, William L. "The Process of Financial Innovation," *American Economic Review* (May, 1983), pp. 89-95.

Tufano, P., "Financial Innovation and First-Mover Advantages," *Journal of Financial Economics,* 25 (December, 1989), pp 213-40.

Van Horne, J C. "Of Financial Innovations and Excesses," *The Journal of Finance,* Vol. 40, No. 3 (July, 1985), pp. 621-631

21 AN INTRODUCTION TO CREDIT DERIVATIVES

KERRIN HOWARD

Credit derivatives are, at their simplest, customized agreements between two counterparties on the transfer of credit exposures. The primary users are credit portfolio managers and this category includes corporate treasurers, portfolio and fund managers who invest in bonds and loans, and bank credit managers. The industry is attracting the notice of investors and regulators alike because credit is being perceived as an underlying security to be hedged and traded, the value of which can be enhanced.

A primary advantage of credit derivatives is that they are off-balance sheet items. As a result, credit portfolio managers can use credit derivatives to diversify and reduce credit risk, enhance yields, gain exposure to higher-yielding markets, or lock in lower credit spreads for financings, without booking additional transactions and exposures. Another advantage is that market risk is stripped out of the valuation because credit derivatives are traded purely on the value of the credit as assessed by the two counterparties. However, risks do exist when using credit derivatives, including liquidity, pricing, and counterparty risk.

The first section of this article discusses how credit portfolio managers can use swaps, options, and structured notes to manage their credit exposures. The mechanics, benefits, and various strategies of using credit derivatives are discussed in the second section of this article. Settlement and regulatory issues are discussed in the third and fourth sections. The risks of using credit derivatives is discussed in the final section.

CREDIT POSTURING

By definition, all credit-related instruments are traded at a spread relative to the coating-rate index; for example, credit spreads trade at, above, or below LIBOR in Europe. Depending on the quality of the credit or the likelihood that the company's debts will be repaid in full and on time, the spread can widen or narrow.

Credit can be perceived in two ways-as a risk or as an asset. Credit derivatives can be used to hedge against an increase in risk, as a method of gaining exposure to a market from which the portfolio manager is restricted, or as a method of diversification. As most credit portfolio managers are conditioned to viewing credit as a risk, this view will be addressed first.

Credit as a Risk

Credit derivatives can offer portfolio managers protection against default risk, downgrade risk, and credit spread risk. Default risk is the risk that a loan will not be paid in full, exposing the creditor to a loss of up to the full principal amount of the loan. Downgrade risk is the risk that a rating agency, such as Moody's or Standard & Poor's, will reduce the debtor's rating based on its perceived ability to repay the loan. If a debtor is downgraded, the value of the credit deteriorates, exposing the creditor to a decline in the market price of the debt. Credit spread risk is the risk that, if the credit deteriorates in value, the spread relative to the coating-rate index will increase or narrow.

Credit as an Asset

Secondly, credit can be viewed as an asset. For example, a portfolio of credits can be segregated into various baskets of loans on which the credit portfolio manager can use derivatives to enhance yields. Credit portfolio managers may also use credit derivatives to expand their capacity to take on exposure to a certain credit.

To diversify credit holdings as a means of offsetting risk, credit portfolio managers may use credit derivatives to diversify their credit holdings. In order to do this, they would exchange one risk for another with a counterparty. Credit portfolio managers can also use credit derivatives to gain exposure to, for example, Russian debt, which may be rated below the manager's criteria per his investment mandate. Plain vanilla, exotic swaps and options, and structured notes are used for all of these purposes.

HOW DO CREDIT DERIVATIVES WORK?

Using five entities alternatively as credit portfolio managers and counterparties, the mechanics of credit derivatives will be explained. The five are as follows: First Bank, Active Corporation, Building Corporation, Reach Funds, and Southern Securities.

Swaps

Swaps are used primarily to hedge and diversify risk profiles, enhance yields, and therefore gain exposure to a specific market, loan, or bond issuance. They are currently the most liquid credit derivative.

Single Risk Transfer

If a credit portfolio manager at First Bank wants to hedge the bank's exposure, through loans, bonds, or revolving credit lines, to Active Corporation against default risk, the manager could consider transferring the bank's Active exposure to Southern Securities via a credit swap. First Bank would enter a swap in which the bank would transfer its Active Corporation exposure to Southern Securities.

EXHIBIT 1

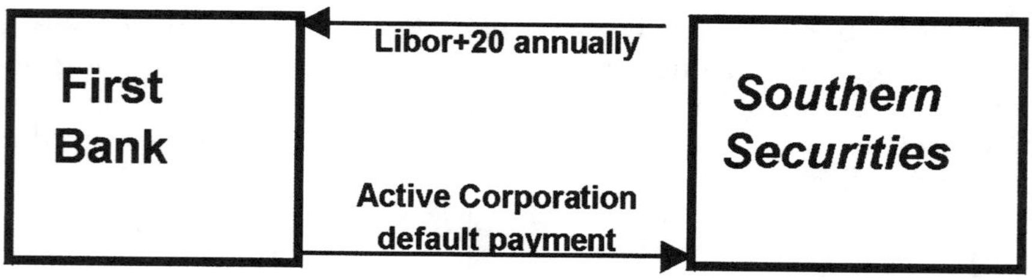

As shown in Exhibit 1, First Bank would pay Southern the performance of the credits and receive a spread, such as 20 basis points above the floating rate index (i.e., LIBOR + 20). If First Bank has transferred 100% of its Active exposure to Southern, it has effectively rid itself of its Active exposure. If it has transferred a portion of its exposure via the swap, it has partially hedged against default risk.

There are two primary reasons why First Bank would make this trade: to hedge against default risk and to diversify its portfolio, thereby reducing its exposure to Active.

Dual Risk Transfer

Suppose First Bank considers Active a high-quality debt and would like to take on more exposure but already holds the maximum exposure allowed by its investment criteria. It can achieve this exposure synthetically by entering a single risk transfer swap with Southern, as in the above example. If Southern Securities had Active exposure which it was able to transfer off its balance sheet, it could enter a swap with First Bank. Southern would synthetically provide First Bank additional exposure to Active by entering a swap in which First Bank would receive the performance of Active bonds and pay LIBOR + 20.

But suppose Southern has exposure to Building Corporation, another high-quality credit, in which Southern would like to simultaneously increase its exposure synthetically. The two can enter a dual risk transfer swap, where they exchange one credit for another. For example, First Bank could trade its exposure in Building Corp. loans to Southern Securities for exposure in Active loans, as shown in Exhibit 2.

EXHIBIT 2

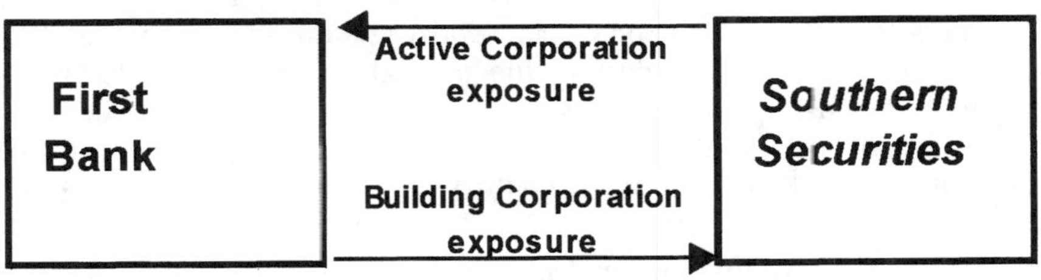

Yield Enhancement

If, in a routine audit of its credit portfolio, First Bank decides that a certain portion of its exposures will underperform the floating-rate index, but does not want to lose its exposure to the names, it can use a single or dual risk transfer credit swap to enhance yield, as shown in Exhibit 3. For example, First Bank can ask Southern Securities to enter a swap in which the bank would receive the Boating-rate and pay Southern the

EXHIBIT 3

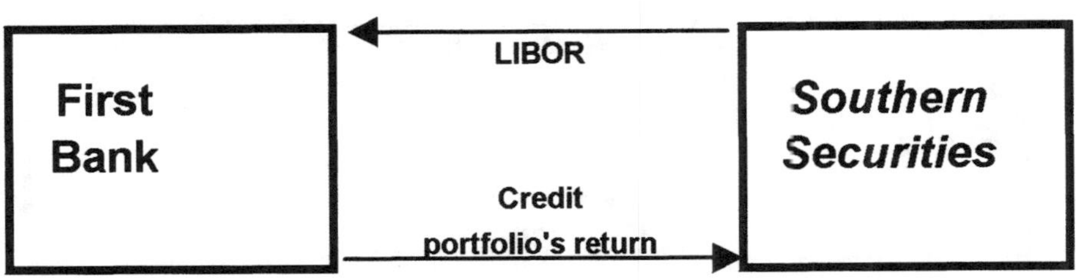

credit portfolio's return.

A dual transfer swap to enhance yields would operate as follows and is illustrated in Exhibit 4. Suppose Southern Securities holds an exposure to Active loans and First Bank believes that Active loans will outperform its own holding of loans to Building Corporation by 20%. First Bank could swap with Southern Securities and exchange the exposures via a dual swap. If Southern Securities is not inclined to take on the exposure to Building Corporation, First Bank would have to sweeten the deal, paying an additional coupon to Southern for doing the swap. First Bank, of course, would keep the coupon as low as possible, but high enough to be attractive, in order to keep its profits potential intact.

EXHIBIT 4

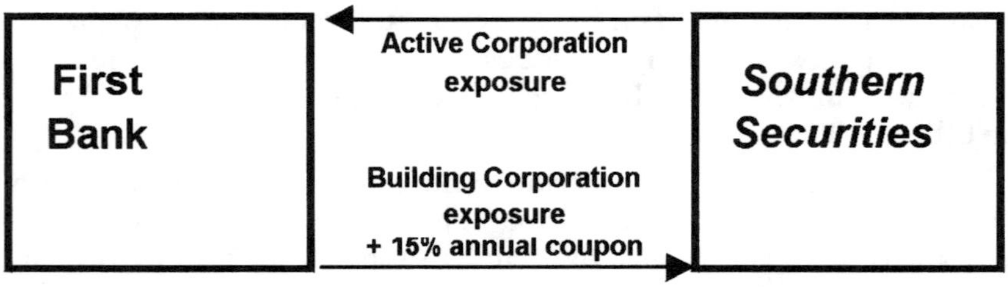

Gaining Exposure

Credit swaps offer a solution to the investment paradox of gaining exposure to high-yield markets without taking on the additional risk inherent to these markets. A manager may be restricted from dealing directly in the market for the following reasons: the fund's mandate prohibits investment in non-investment-grade debt; it does not have sufficient access to the cash bank loan market; or it might not have the monitoring ability to track changes in the country's political structure, interest rates or the position's performance.

For example, emerging market debts are becoming more attractive again, but many fund managers are still prohibited from investing in them. This prohibition occurs because these markets are perceived to be riskier since the Mexican peso crisis occurred in December 1994. Portfolio managers are attracted to emerging market debt, though, because it often offers higher yields than more established loan and bond markets.

Exhibit 5 showing a credit swap done in order to gain exposure follows. Suppose the credit portfolio manager at Reach Funds would like to invest in a specific loan syndicated by First Bank to the Korean government, but is restricted from doing so because it is BB+-rated debt. However, Reach Funds is required by its mandate to invest at least

EXHIBIT 5

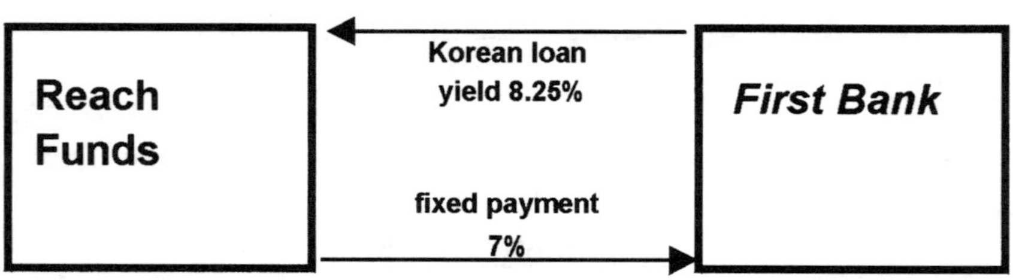

in single-A debt. It can go to First Bank and attain exposure through a total return credit swap.

Assume that Reach Funds decides to leverage the investment, because it is not investment grade, by pledging to First Bank US$1 million against a US$10 million underlying exposure. Assume also that the underlying loan yield paid to Reach Funds is 8.25%, while the fixed swap payment to First Bank is 7%. The 125-basis point spread is multiplied ten times the leverage factor, to 12.5%. Add this to the cash yield on the US$1 million of 6% and the swap generates current annual income of 18.5%.

The appeal of this transaction lies in the fact that, should the credit deteriorate, Reach Funds has now limited its potential loss to 10% by leveraging the transaction. However, it can attain all of the upside as the credit gains in value.

Options

Both plain vanilla and exotic call and put options can be used to hedge by trading credit spreads and options on loan portfolios, and to enhance yields.

Options are applied to credit exactly as they are on cash fixed income and equity-the credit portfolio manager purchases the right to buy or sell the credit at the strike price until expiration. For example, if a portfolio manager desires protection against a loan or credit falling in value, a credit spread put would be purchased. It is important to remember that, as long as the credit portfolio manager is purchasing an option, the manager only risks losing the premium, or cost, of the option.

Assume that Active has a floating-rate, less-developed country (LDC) debt and wants to protect against a fall in credit value. Active also wants to keep its underlying and its access to improvements in the credit.

To do this, Active would buy from Southern Securities a one-year put option on a five-year Latin American government bond, struck at 100 at maturity and paying a premium of 85 basis points. The duration of the five-year bond is 3.2. If the spread increases to 128, Active would then receive the spread above the strike, or 28 basis points, multiplied by the duration of the five-year bond, 3.2, for a total of 90 basis points.

Because Active hedged by buying the put minus the premium, it would receive about 5 basis points on the protection; it is subject to losing only the premium paid in the event the credit value plunges. A larger spread widening would increase the payoff commensurately and would go right to the manager's bottom line.

Exotic Options

Credit portfolio managers can also use exotic options to manage exposures in their portfolios. These options can be structured to restrict losses, via stop-loss limits or barriers, should the trade go against the credit portfolio manager, or to enhance the portfolio's performance if the manager would like to take a view on the credit. Premiums on exotic options tend to be less than on standard options because exotic options limit both profits and losses. Two common examples of credit options include barrier and digital options.

EXHIBIT 6

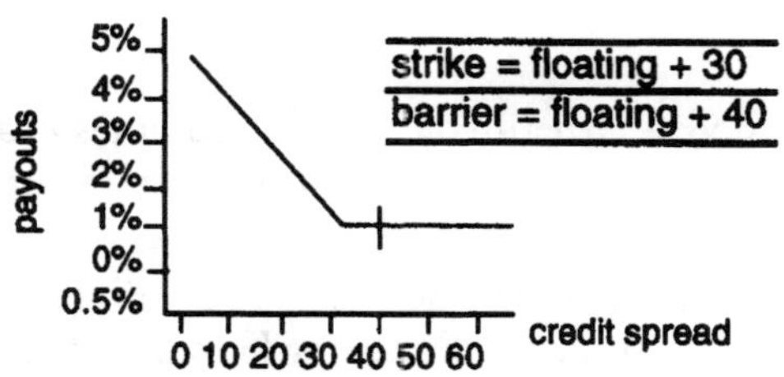

A barrier option is an option in which the contract is not activated until the underlying exceeds or falls below a preset level (Exhibit 6). Assume First Bank is bullish on the outlook for the credit value on Mexican par bonds rising. It seeks to profit from any narrowing of the credit spread relative to U.S. Treasury yields. First Bank could buy a knock-out put on the credit spread and profit as the credit spread narrows between Mexican par bonds and U.S. Treasury Notes below the strike.

If spreads are above the strike but below the barrier, the option has no intrinsic value. However, the potential remains that the option could expire in-the-money. If spreads ever rise above the barrier (i.e., First Bank picked the wrong direction and the trade goes horribly wrong), the knockout put ceases to exist and First Bank loses only the premium it paid to buy the put.

Barrier options also include three more variations in addition to the up-and-out structure described above: the up-and-in, where the option is not activated until the option rises above a preset strike; the down-and-out option, where the option is voided if the underlying falls below the preset strike; and the down-and-in option, where the option is not activated until it falls below the preset strike level.

Digital, or binary, options offer fixed payouts if the underlying security expires in-the-money based on a preset strike price. But the credit portfolio manager loses the opportunity to gain further on the investment if the option surpasses the strike by several hundred basis points because the payout is fixed. However, should the trade go against the manager, the manager ends up with a zero payout and loses the premium paid for the option.

Credit Spread Caps

In a rising interest rate environment, credit portfolio managers can also use credit spread caps to lock in lower credit spreads on future borrowing, such as project financings.

Assume Active is planning a project financing in one year's time and needs the funding over a period of five years. Assume also that Active believes that the credit spread on Active's debt is going to increase by 200 basis points above LIBOR during that time. However, Active would like to be exposed to a maximum rise of 175 basis points above LIBOR.

The credit portfolio manager at Active could purchase from First Bank a five-year credit spread cap, one year forward. The manager would buy a five-year cap with a strike of LIBOR + 175 that would not go into effect until the borrowing was completed, in one year. The cap would have a series of quarterly payouts during the life of the option based on the market spread above LIBOR at which Active's debt was trading and the LIBOR + 175 cap level. Premiums on these trades average between 3%-5%.

If Active's debt is trading at LIBOR + 200 at the time of the actual financing, First Bank would pay the 25-basis point difference between Active's cap of LIBOR + 175 and the market's credit spread of LIBOR + 200.

Structured Notes

Credit portfolio managers should view structured credit-linked notes as a combination of derivatives with an issuance (loan or bond) to provide protection against risk or to enhance the performance of an underlying note.

As can be expected, structured notes can only be described in relation to the specific investment objective or need being hedged. The forthcoming Handbook of Derivatives

Instruments outlines four types of notes commonly used: asset-backed; compound credit; full principal protection; and enhanced asset return."

Asset-Backed Notes

Asset-backed credit-linked notes are investment-grade debts or loans that provide high yields, leveraged upside, and limited downside returns relative to a diversified credit portfolio. This structure is the building block for the three other credit-linked structured notes.

This structure is similar to the example in Exhibit 5 where Reach Funds sought to gain exposure to a non-investment-grade credit via a credit swap with First Bank. In an asset-backed credit-linked note, First Bank would bundle a basket of non-investment-grade credits that it was currently holding into an underlying collateralized note. It would then offer this note to investors, (such as Reach Funds), seeking to diversify their credit exposures and enhance yields.

Once the note issue has been placed, First Bank would use the note proceeds to purchase Treasury securities which are then used to collateralize the basket of bank loans. Effectively, this makes note holders long the U.S. Treasuries as well as the underlying credits. The collateralization could be as low as 14.3%, allowing the investors to achieve an upside leverage of up to 7 to 1, with yields up to 20% per year. There are no margin calls on this structure, though, so the investor's loss exposure is limited to the initial investment amount. Exhibit 7 illustrates this point, as explained below.

EXHIBIT 7

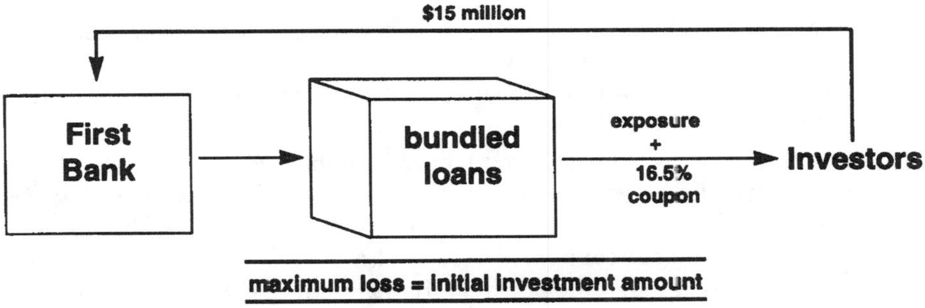

First Bank would issue $15 million in an asset-backed note. It would use the proceeds, the $15 million, to buy U.S. Treasury notes which will earn First Bank a 6% coupon. It then leverages by seven a purchase of $100 million in four non-investment-grade loans yielding an aggregate LIBOR + 250. The financing cost of buying the $100 million non-investment-grade loan portfolio is LIBOR + 150.

First Bank is earning the 150-basis point spread between the LIBOR + 150 financing cost of buying the loan portfolio and the LIBOR + 250 yield of the portfolio. This is multiplied by the leverage factor of seven and the resulting yield from the loan portfolio is 10.5%. Add to this number the 6% yield of the Treasuries and First Bank is able to pay note holders a coupon of 16.5%.

Asset-backed credit-linked notes offer investors the equivalent of purchasing a diversified portfolio of loans on margin, but, as mentioned earlier, without the risk of margin calls. Moreover, the note itself will carry an investment-grade rating even though the underlying portfolio is leveraged and has an average rating that is non-investment-grade.

From a risk management perspective, or the issuer's perspective, asset-backed credit-linked notes can be issued as a means of hedging the credit risk of an existing credit portfolio.

EXHIBIT 8

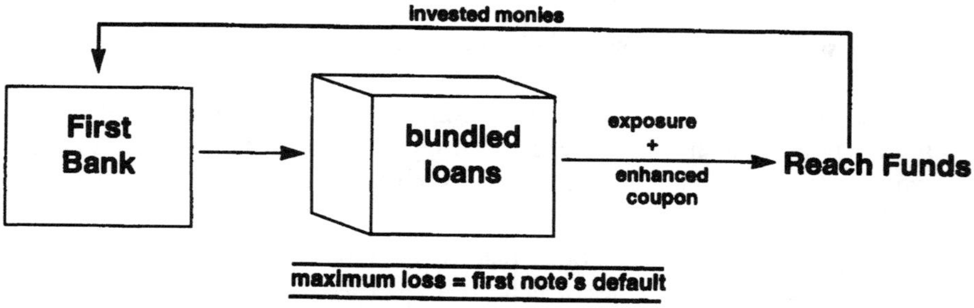

Compound Credit Notes

Compound credit notes are debt or loan obligations that pay investors an enhanced return for taking on compounded credit risk as shown in Exhibit 8. In this structure, First Bank typically would overcollateralize the note with a portfolio of underlying loans or credit-sensitive securities.

Reach Funds has a clear view on how each of the credits in the portfolio will perform and expects a high-yield coupon in return. Because it has a dear view, Reach Funds likely would have directly invested in the loan but may believe that the loan portfolio would bring a higher coupon. The fund also probably believes that its exposure to a default is lower through the portfolio. In the event of default, Reach Funds is exposed only to the first default of the first loan in the basket.

First Bank also has a clear view on how each of the notes will perform and likely expects that only one default will occur in the basket, at most. In the event of a default of any of the loans in the basket, First Bank terminates the note and puts, or transfers, the defaulted loan or security to the note holder. This equates taking physical delivery of the loan. Reach Funds then has exposure to the loan that defaulted. This also protects First Bank against the default risk of the first loan. First Bank could hold the view that not more than one of the credits will default, while Reach Funds hopes that none default.

For example, if Reach Funds invested $10 million in a non-investment-grade portfolio, it would receive LIBOR + 400 for the time during which the loans did not default. In the event of a default and remembering that Reach Funds was considering directly investing in the loans at the start, Reach Funds would receive the defaulted loan, which pays LIBOR + 250, versus the portfolio exposure it had bought initially that had paid LIBOR + 400. In the meantime, First Bank keeps the $10 million and transfers the underlying, defaulted loan to Reach Funds. First Bank would retain its exposure to the other three loans in the portfolio.

Cash settlement is another viable method of dealing with a default. Reach Funds can agree with First Bank to receive, in cash, the market value of the loan in the event of a default. For example, if the loan's market value at the time of default was $0.70 on the dollar, First Bank would pay Reach Funds the $7 million in cash from its initial $10 million investment and keep the exposure to the loans.

Full Principal Protection Notes

Full principal protection notes also allow Reach Funds to participate in appreciating price performance of a portfolio of bank loans or credit-sensitive securities, while offering full protection of the investors' principal. These notes are designed for risk-averse investors, looking to capitalize on the potential upside of riskier loans or securities.

Note holders trade reduced coupon payments, compared to the compound credit note's coupon, that is, for the principal protection and gain the increase in the underlying credits' value. Consequently, the note will outperform a direct investment in the underlying assets in a bear market and will achieve a mildly enhanced performance if the credits appreciate as expected. Overall, it has a more stable total payoff profile than the compound credit note profile, as shown in Exhibit 9.

EXHIBIT 9

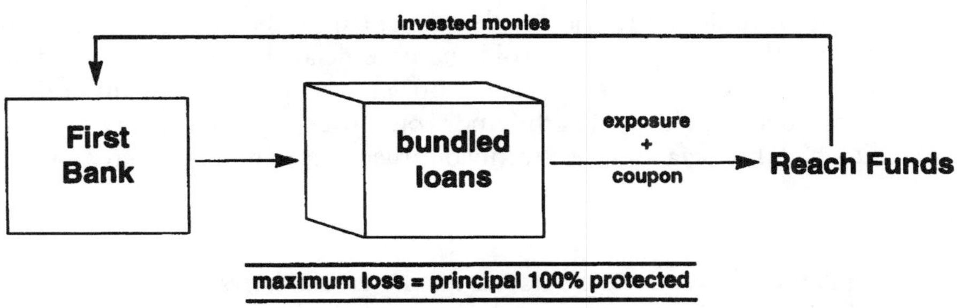

Enhanced Asset Return Notes

Enhanced asset return notes provide investors with enhanced returns relative to the portfolio of securities, but investors forfeit all or part of the recovery value in the event of a credit default. Investors would likely have a clear view that the probability of these credits defaulting is very low, and would be attracted to the high coupon, illustrated in Exhibit 10.

In the event of default of the underlying(s), the note is terminated at a pre-agreed-upon redemption value, which can be as low as zero, with no further recourse for either

EXHIBIT 10

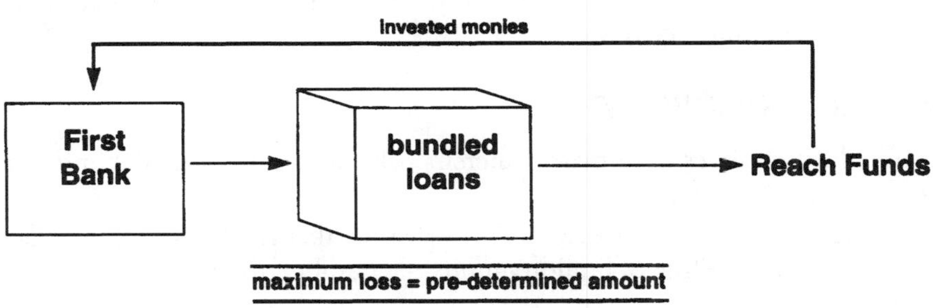

the issuer or the underlying borrower. Because the investor waives any further claim to the recovery value, the note's yield is significantly higher than that of the underlying assets.

SETTLEMENT

The most powerful impact on a credit derivative transaction will be a credit default. In the event of default, there are at least three different ways of settling the transaction, all of which must be agreed upon and documented at the outset of the deal.

First, if Reach Funds entered a credit swap which defaulted, it could opt for a cash setdement on the swap. This involves a time delay for Reach Funds, as it must wait for a dealer poll to be completed that assesses the value of the credit. The time delay could be extended longer than expected, as the issue of whether a default has occurred can sometimes be debated.

Second, it could opt for cash settlement at a multiple of the default payment calculated from the dealer poll. To avoid the time delay, Reach Funds could agree at the outset of the deal on a preset payout of 50% of the notional amount of the deal in the event of a default. Finally, Reach Funds could take physical delivery of the underlying credit which has defaulted, as described earlier in the compound credit note example.

REGULATORY ISSUES

Regulations have yet to be issued on the credit derivatives market. However, the Bank for International Settlement, the European Commission, the Federal Reserve Board, and the Office of the Comptroller of the Currency in the U.S. are all watching the market and its development closely. The main concern is monitoring the capital ratio of banks dealing in credit derivatives. The last thing regulators want is for a bank dealing credit derivatives to default because of its exposures from credit derivatives.

Under this umbrella comes the issue of how to classify credit derivatives. Should they be booked as letters of credit or as derivatives? What capital charge should the banks take per credit derivative transaction?

At the moment, regulators are leaning toward viewing credit derivatives as letters of credit, or guarantees. This means that when First Bank sells credit protection to Active Corporation, it takes 100% of the risk on its balance sheet, scaled according to the risk-weighting of the underlying credit.

Currently, however, if First Bank buys credit protection from a counterparty bank, the treatment is still determined on a per deal basis.

On the whole, regulators globally are watching how banks handle the current deal flow —hoping to learn from some banks' mistakes and to imitate other banks that effectively handle the exposures. As the industry continues to grow and deals become more voluminous, regulators intend to monitor the products and banks' treatment of the exposures more actively.

RISKS OF CREDIT DERIVATIVES

Credit derivatives have many inherent risks, including liquidity, information flow, and counterparty risk.

Currency liquidity in the credit derivatives market can be very thin, a fact that each dealer admits. The lack of liquidity limits the number of dealers pricing a credit option or swap and raises or lowers the unwind price. From the dealers' perspective, for example, in a total return swap, it is expensive to hold corporate bonds to maturity because the repo cost of the bonds exceeds the bond's redemption value as the bond ages. This cost is passed on to the investor via higher premiums on deals. In an option situation, an investor may find it hard to unwind before maturity because the market lacks the same amount of interest and liquidity as bond futures. Again, the investor pays for the counterparty to take on the risk of settling prior to expiration through higher premiums.

Additionally, information flow can be a risk as investors seek to determine whether a credit has actually defaulted. Defaults can be argued and dealer polls, as previously mentioned, take time and expose credit portfolio managers to unknown risk until the poll is completed. When a manager enters a swap to gain exposure to a remote market, it may be hard to get the information on how the debt is performing and what the credit spreads are.

Finally, as with any over-the-counter deal, investors are exposed to counterparty risk. This means that the counterparty could renege or default on the option, swap, or structured note, leaving the investor holding, in the worst cases, a worthless credit exposure. Research is especially important in making sure that counterparties on credit derivative deals have staying power to expiration or to pay the coupons promised and follow through on defaults. Even though the City and Wall Street are famous for having short memories, Baring Bank's demise as a result of losing futures trades will cast a long shadow. Were it not for ING Bank rescue, over-the-counter deals with Barings could have become worthless.

THE FUTURE OF CREDIT DERIVATIVES

Statistics show that in 1994 more than US$1 trillion was issued in new loans and bonds. That figure continues to grow. The credit derivatives market will grow parallel to and proportionally to the debt market's continued growth as credit portfolio managers continue to seek to achieve the "ideal" credit profile.

Traditionally, credit portfolio managers have sought to achieve the ideal risk return profile via trading directly in the underlying securities. Credit derivatives can help managers achieve this goal more easily for two main reasons. Credit derivatives are off-balance sheet items, allowing managers to avoid booking additional transactions or exposures. Also, the view being taken is on the assessed value of the credit, not the underlying's market value. By stripping out the market risk, credit portfolio managers are better able to define the risks being taken on or transferred in the transaction. As a result, credit derivatives are more flexible and efficient than buying or selling the underlying securities.

ENDNOTE

This article was published in *Derivatives Quarterly*, Winter 1995, when Kerrin Howard was at *Derivatives Week*.

[1] From the forthcoming *Handbook of Derivatives Instruments*, by Dattatreya and Konishi, 1995.

22 ALTERNATIVE RISK TRANSFER: INVESTING DIRECTLY IN INSURANCE RISK AS AN ALTERNATIVE INVESTMENT STRATEGY

DAVID K.A. MORDECAI
AIG Risk Finance

The markets for insurance-linked event risk and financial risks traded in the capital are converging. Insurance companies, in managing their investment portfolios, and developing tailored investment products for the marketplace, are also incorporating credit-risk management along with asset-liability management technology like Dynamic Financial Analysis (DFA). Financial guarantee insurers, in underwriting credit risks, are often subject to even more stringent regulatory and rating agency treatment than other sectors in the insurance industry. In other words, financial managers are thinking more like risk managers in their search for risk-adjusted return, and insurance companies are competing both in the capital market and increasingly in the reinsurance market against new entrants from the capital markets. Insurers and Reinsurers are capitalizing on the convergence of the insurance and capital markets by employing Alternative Risk Transfer, capital market solutions to reallocate underwriting capacity. Catastrophe bonds (indemnity or book-of-business, index-based, or parametric) and other insurance-linked securities or financing arrangements, are joining previous insurance innovations like finite risk, financial reinsurance, loss portfolio transfers, captive insurance vehicles. Contingent financial instruments such as catastrophe equity puts and contingent surplus notes are becoming common sources of mezzanine capital for insurers. Markets in exchange-traded and over-the-counter insurance derivatives, credit derivatives, political risk derivatives, and weather derivatives are proliferating as substitutes and complements to traditional insurance and reinsurance capacity. In addition, hedge funds are establishing specialty insurance companies in order to manage insurance funds as sources of long-term capital.

Insurance markets and credit markets both trade in discrete event risk, in contrast to the equity and commodity markets in which event risk (i.e., price changes) is more continuous in nature. Credit events are by their very nature extreme events (rare probabilistic events). Rating agencies and regulators mandate rigorous underwriting standards and capital requirements for financial guarantee insurers, based on perceived levels of underwriting risk. The result is that credit insurance tends to be a very capital-intensive sector of the insurance industry. Although analysts continue to utilize liability models, based on capital resources relative to underwriting exposures, a growing population of analysts are beginning to adopt models with a emphasis on assets in a credit insurer's portfolio, including the value of the assets that comprise unearned premiums. With the ongoing evolution of the credit-, insurance-, and asset-swap markets, even rating agencies are being required to price assets and estimate event likelihood in underlying or adjacent markets, in order to derive losses due to credit-risk (e.g. rating transitions and recovery values) and the ultimate probabilities of default. This trend towards arbitrage between credit-risk and event-risk is expected to persist, as the market risk approach and the statistical/actuarial risk approaches of the financial and insurance markets continue to converge.

THE ARBITRAGE BETWEEN ACTUARIAL- AND MARKET-PRICED RISK

Insurance- and reinsurance-linked derivative securities have emerged as a new asset class for portfolio managers. These instruments simultaneously provide the participants in the credit markets to gain exposure to insurance risks that are statistically uncorrelated with credit cycles, and insurance companies with direct access to risk capacity in the credit markets. Although the pricing in the traditional reinsurance market is currently soft, the cyclical dynamics of reinsurance market promises persistent periods of excess returns to the yield-hungry debt market. Insurance derivative securities issued in the debt markets attempt to arbitrage the difference in pricing between comparable debt market priced credit-risk, and "natural" event-risk priced in the reinsurance market. Event risk is priced in three markets: the insurance/reinsurance market, the debt markets and the equity and commodity markets. Each market prices comparable expectations of risk differently. Much as institutional, regulatory, tax and pricing conventions drive interest-rate and equity-price anomalies, similarly capital constraints, regulatory frictions (e.g. risk-based capital treatment) and risk-adjusted pricing (economic value at risk) disparities motivate arbitrage between the insurance and the capital markets.

APPROACHES TO RISK INTERMEDIATION

The intermediation of risk can be classified in three broad categories: risk pooling, risk sharing and risk transfer. Risk-pooling obtains benefits from diversification by optimally combining financial instruments with statistically independent or uncorrelated risks in a portfolio. The objective of pooling these instruments (loans, bonds, policies, etc.) is to reduce the relative weighting of any single risk exposure with respect to the average return of the portfolio. Examples of risk-pooling include not only insurance portfolios, but bank loan portfolios, CBOs, CLOs and commercial paper ("CP") conduits. Risk-sharing attempts to achieve benefits of diversification by contractually swapping risk exposures with uncorrelated risks in portfolios or instruments held by other parties. Examples of risk-sharing include derivative product companies ("DPCs" or "swapcos") and certain types of reinsurance (coinsurance). Risk-transfer attempts to immunize the returns of a portfolio or instrument from certain risks by paying a third-party to contractually assume exposure to those risks. Examples of risk-transfer are primary insurance policies, excess-of-loss reinsurance, financial guarantees, bond insurance, portfolio insurance, and hedging with options, forwards & futures. An extension of both the risk-sharing and risk-transfer concepts is risk-spreading, or the transfer of risk over among many parties, the fundamental principle of the financial markets.

In cases of extreme information asymmetry, Risk shifting arises as a market failure or negative externality in any of the risk intermediation activities, when risks are misplaced by the seller of protection (the buyer of a risky instrument). An insurance provider is essentially the writer of a deep out-of-the-money put option. Event risk as a bundle of deep out-the-money options can be either priced and hedged via dynamic trading, if sufficiently liquid and "transparent" (informationally inefficient), or alternatively event risk can be inventoried ("warehoused") and offset via diversified pools of investments, if illiquid and "opaque" (i.e., informationally inefficient). Ultimately, informational asymmetry and moral hazard (misaligned incentives) can lead to opportunistic behavior by buyers of insurance protection in the form of risk shifting. Risk shifting occurs when risks are mispriced, resulting in a risk being assumed at a inadequate risk premium (i.e., the expected return for assuming that risk is negative). In other words, the buyer of protection pays a premium that is too low and the insurance provider (the investor) is undercompensated for the risk assumed.

CAPITAL MARKET APPROACHES TO CATASTROPHIC RISK

Categories for capital market approaches to catastrophic reinsurance risk include: traditional reinsurance, contingent (bank) financing, and capital market securitizations (insurance-linked credit-swap financing, synthetic reinsurance, third-party event-risk swaps). In general, traditional reinsurance involves direct payment from a reinsurer to a ceding insurer if a defined event occurs. Contingent bank financing is a liquidity facility provided to an insurer in exchange for a facility fee and interest paid on the drawn amount. A credit-risk securitization or insurance-linked credit-swap financing involves investment-grade fixed income securities held by an SPV, where the securities may be called by the insurance company, in exchange for surplus notes or debt issued by the insurance company. A synthetic reinsurance issuance is commonly referred as a catastrophe-linked bond or simply a "catastrophe bond," i.e., a reinsurance treaty-linked structured note issued by an SPV. Third-party event-risk swaps are structured or "flow" trades between insurers and a counterparty that involve an exchange of cashflows or securities triggered by a catastrophic event.

EXHIBIT 1 CATASTROPHIC BOND EXAMPLE

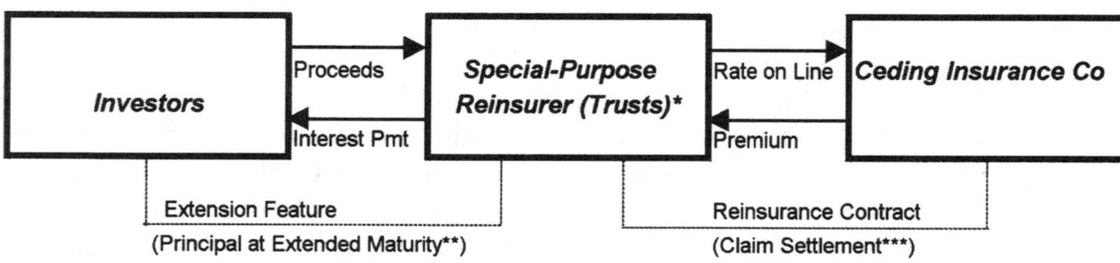

* May involve Collateral and Defeasance Accounts with Basis and/or Total Return Swaps
** If principal protected with zero-coupon treasury strips (or treasury-forward obligations)
*** Triggered by attachment point as specified in reinsurance contract terms

Insurance derivatives are in many ways analogous to credit derivatives, in particular, credit swaps, default options and total return swaps. In fact, default options and credit swaps could be described as simply a form of insurance, similar to bond insurance. Options are often used as market-event or price insurance, (i.e., financial hedging and portfolio insurance). Portfolio insurance is identical in principle to stop-loss reinsurance. Forms of principal protection, defeasance, e.g., guaranties, treasuries, forward obligations, etc., can be referred to as credit insurance. These instruments all serve as substitutes or complements for credit and portfolio insurance supplied by the monoline or specialty financial insurance companies. Insurance treaties as contingent claims are, in essence, derivative instruments. In other words, any derivatives market is in essence an insurance market.

There are essentially two kinds of reinsurance treaties: facultative treaties and event-trigger treaties. The former is a proportional reinsurance treaty, in which the reinsurer shares equally in the premiums written and claims incurred by the primary insurer. In this sense, the facultative treaty is like a blanket policy for the primary or "ceding" insurer. Catastrophe bonds are typically structured around an event-trigger treaty. Reinsurance treaties are essentially swaps, and credit-risk and default swaps employ a modeling approach that is similar to modeling catastrophe risk. The approach, adopted from extreme value theory, plays a particularly important role in the pricing of reinsurance contracts, especially those involving low-probability, high-severity events. The primary example is the Catastrophe Excess of Loss Cover per Event or CatXL reinsurance treaty, which is of the event-trigger type. The CatXL treaty corresponds in financial option theory to a bull spread with the market loss ratio as the reference asset.

There have been issued smaller, unrated Cat bond linked to aviation and shipping catastrophes, marine-drilling platform risks and oil spills, industrial accidents, satellite risk and a host of other insured risks. However, the rated catastrophe-linked bonds currently trading in the market all reference "acts of God" or natural disasters, specifically windstorm or seismic events. Also, at present, insurance regulators have restricted debt treatment (for risk-based capital purposes) on investments in cat bond by insurance companies to natural disaster-related bonds that are rated by one of the four Nationally Recognized Securities Rating Organizations (NRSROs). All of the rated transactions issued since May 1997 have been windstorm-related (hurricane, typhoon) and/or earthquake-related. Cat bond structures fall into three broad categories: book-of-business, index-based, and parametric-trigger structures.

Cat bond investors can experience losses to either principal or interest, depending on the covenants of the bond. The book-of-business structure securitizes a portion of a ceding insurer's policies. The index-based structure attaches to an index of claims as the reference asset. Losses to bondholders in both of these structures are triggered by the level of losses, from an event, above the referenced attachment point. A parametric trigger structure, however, triggers losses to the bond, based either on some inferred natural parameter, such as the magnitude and location of an earthquake, or by some other measure more directly related to the damage incurred in a region, e.g. by measured ground motion from an earthquake occurrence. Of the two parametric triggers, the latter although more complicated, presents fewer estimation problems and therefore provides more reliable model estimates. This would lead to more predictable expected cashflows for a parametric-trigger bond.

ACTUARIAL AND STOCHASTIC MODELING IN CATASTROPHE ANALYSIS

Rating agencies and sophisticated cat risk investors assess expected bond performance by first analyzing the data used to create a model for estimating long-run odds of occurrence of a catastrophic event. Second, they evaluate the model structure and implementation in using the data to estimate the event-risk. The model must adhere to standard practices. Third, they examine the structure of the bond. Not only must the structure be coherent, but the data must be accurate and complete. All three elements must be reasonable and consistent.

The growing interest in the capital markets for catastrophic risk securities is evident from recent accounts in the press. In addition to Property Claim Services (PCS) contracts already trading on the CBOT, rival indexes and futures are being introduced on other exchanges. In 1996, the CEA withdrew its $1.5 billion issue when Berkshire Hathaway bought the entire deal directly. Six months after the $68.5 million fully-principal protected Georgetown Re issue, heavy demand from investors more than doubled the at-risk portion of the USAA/Residential Re transaction. During that same period, the Swiss Re Earthquake Fund, an SPV issues a bond with a trigger that references losses as reported by the CBOT-traded PCS index. A few months later, in a yield-hungry environment, another investment bank managed to place a bond triggered by ten-year bet on the magnitude and location of an earthquake around Tokyo, Japan, the geographic region responsible for 6%-7% of the world's earthquakes. Security structures with contingent features generate interest as well, e.g., the 300 million SF Winterthur interest-at-risk convertible issue. Aon Capital market successfully placed an $80 million, five-year bond with a moving loss trigger, linked to losses from Japanese typhoons. Various issuers have announced plans for multi-year, multi-event, and/or index-based securitizations. Since that time, a number of over-the-counter swaps have been completed referencing these instruments as benchmark securities. During the past eighteen months, the over-the-counter weather swaps market has surpassed with $3 billion of notional outstanding.

These products offer enhanced yields for investors, and may provide both diversification opportunities and new capital for insurers. However, the need to assess the risk of this emerging asset class has resulted in a demand for stochastic models that can reliably and accurately represent the risk of loss from a catastrophic event. Insurance regulators are contemplating increasing their reliance on these models for setting rates. The question on everyone's mind is, "How to evaluate the performance of these models?" This article addresses the approach developed by the author for evaluating model performance from a due diligence and model validation perspective. As with any derivative transaction, the key to accurately and reliably verifying the expected performance of any catastrophe bond structure begins with assessing model robustness.

In the evaluation of stochastic or random event models, the robustness of a model can be described as the insensitivity or persistence of model outputs to changes in model inputs. This is the key feature of any statistical or probability estimation model that determines how well the model estimates perform on average as a best guess or approximation of the future losses from a catastrophic event.

A robust model minimizes model risk. Conceptually and in practice, we can discuss model risk as having two components: process risk and parameter risk. Process risk is minimized when hypothesized assumptions reasonably represent the true nature of actual events (the underlying process). This dimension of model risk is a function both of the selection of distribution assumptions and the estimation of parameters for those distributions. Parameter risk is minimized as the number of simulated draws from a distribution is increased. If process risk has been minimized (i.e., the hypothesized assumptions are reasonably accurate) as the number of iterations become sufficiently large, then the simulation estimates should converge to the long-run behavior actual physical phenomena being modeled (as parameter risk is minimized). This defines model robustness i.e., how reliable model estimates are as long-run averages of event occurrences and magnitudes.

An understanding of the following concepts is essential to evaluating the model and presenting its results in the context of rating catastrophic risk securities. The analyst must translate a model simulation of a random event (which is based on correlations derived from inferences of historical observed events), into an assignment of a rating. In turn, the rating is associated with the risk of loss from the potential realization of an actual event).

MODEL ROBUSTNESS: MINIMIZING PROCESS RISK

In addition to inspecting the underlying data for accuracy, consistency and completeness, the analyst must evaluate the underlying technical integrity of the model from the perspective of process risk minimization. The analyst should assess a random event model on the basis of (a) model structure (i.e., model design and procedural implementation), and (b) model specification (selection of distribution assumptions and parameter estimation).

In evaluating model structure, the analyst must review the mathematical functions used in the model to approximate the interactions between simulated storm values. The analyst compares them to current academic and industry practices to judge if they reasonably and adequately represent event characteristics. Some of these interactions are modeled as probability distributions, while others are functions measured or derived from current research.

The evaluation of the model specification includes an assessment both of the appropriateness of (a) the probability distribution assumptions selected, and (b) the estimation methods employed to fit the parameters of those distributions.

SENSITIVITY ANALYSIS: THE KEY TO EVALUATING MODEL ROBUSTNESS

In order to arrive at a level of comfort regarding process risk, the analyst will evaluate the robustness of model estimates in the following manner: (a) worst-case "what-if" scenarios (outlier analysis); (b) back-testing/out-of-sample tests; and (c) sensitivity analysis using alternative distributions.

Random event models and their resulting loss distribution estimates tend to be sensitive to tail specification (i.e., extreme value estimation). Tail specification is critical factor for the reliability or robustness of the model estimates as long-run averages of loss occurrence. In addition to data and error diagnostic tests (robust estimation techniques), the analyst should perform a simulation-sensitivity analysis of the model to simulations that employ alternate distribution assumptions for both frequency of event occurrence and magnitude of event occurrences. These alternate distributions should include distributions with fatter-tails and varied degrees of skewness.

Based on the above tests and other considerations, the analyst may decide to analytically modify the location of the attachment point or the shape of the curve to reflect bias in model estimates of loss (i.e. risk) based on the assessment model robustness or lack thereof. In other words, these adjustments will be based on the relative sensitivity of the model to modified assumptions.

Credit analysis and derivative pricing are both exercises in variance estimation. Quantifying uncertainty is always challenging, often problematic, and sometimes infeasible. As a general rule, rigorous robustness testing requires an estimate to be modeled as a probability distribution with a smooth, disperse surface, and finite variance. Models that generate point or spiked estimates tend to grossly understate uncertainty. In other words, these models are "infinitely" sensitive tail observations or "outliers." In addition, the distribution modeled must match the actual event process being modeled. These conditions dictate the kinds of parameters that can be used as triggers. Parameter triggers that employ loss-related damage functions are generally superior to parameter triggers that attempt to model predictive estimates of event locations and magnitudes.

Predictive estimates tend to have very large, nonlinear confidence bands (very large variance) and usually require a larger sample of reliable data than is feasibly available. In addition, the estimation and identification problems for some parameter triggers limit the effectiveness of most model calibration methods. Ironically, model diagnostics tend to be even more important for predictive parameter triggers, especially given common problems with autocorrelation and heteroskedasticity. Furthermore, confounding effects from measurement error in the data employed to specify estimates in the model, tend to result in estimation error and model misspecification that, under the circumstances, is extremely difficult, if not impossible to resolve or rectify.

However, damage-based parameter triggers tend to resolve many complications inherent to modeled event occurrence estimates. There are often natural physical relations approximated by damage functions that limit the effects of uncertainty around the model estimate of occurrence. In addition, loss and damage data, which tend to be more readily available and testable, can be used to independently calibrate the model and hence reduce model risk. Since damage parameters are conditioned upon the occurrence of an event, damage-based models employ a distribution of all feasible events for a region, resulting in a smoother, more robust distribution. Finally, knowledge about the structural relationships related to damage parameters tends to be more reliable and complete than knowledge about the physical processes related to occurrence parameters.

Other risks inherent to insurance-linked bonds include basis risk, moral hazard and adverse selection. As with many derivative instruments, insurance-linked securities can exhibit tracking error or "basis risk." Depending on the structure, basis risk can be retained by either the issuer (ceding insurer) or the investors. Issuers tend to prefer book-of-business triggers, because they minimize basis risk for the issuer, relative to changes in the risk profile of future policies or to the aggregate risk profile of an index. However, investors tend to prefer index-based triggers, unless the issuer has the ability to change the profile of the index. Issuers often like the level of confidentiality afforded to them by index-based triggers, but are averse to the exposure of their portfolio of policies to basis risk from an index trigger. Parametric triggers share some of the same issues as index-based triggers.

In the absence of adequate risk retention language in the reps & warranties regarding the ceding insurer, all of these bond types are subject to varying degrees of risk-shifting, e.g. moral hazard or adverse selection. For investors or issuers, predictive parameter triggers may exhibit the highest basis risk to either issuers or two investors, depending on several factors, including the composition of the insurance portfolio, the policy types written by the ceding insurer, the precise trigger mechanism, and the degree of model estimation error. The risk retention mechanism is a key feature of structure for these transactions that is explicitly absent from predictive parameter triggers. Even when loss data is limited, the incentives to improperly shift risk to bondholders may be mitigated with a damage-related trigger, correlated to loss retention-like covenants in a bond.

The rigorous application of these principles to the analysis of random event modeling is central to an accurate and reliable assessment of catastrophic risk transactions. If this emerging asset class is to grow and mature, model robustness is a timely and important issue to consider, not only for rating agencies, but also for regulators, bankers, issuers and investors.

Recent catastrophic events have resulted in both increased pricing and a funding gap in the reinsurance business. New entry has been stimulated by the demand for new sources of capital to fill that gap. Entry has occurred in the form of new reinsurers, new financial and risk management innovations. Financial and risk management innovations have included an insurance exchange, CBOT options contracts, contingent financing products for insurers & reinsurers, and catastrophe-linked derivative securities or "Cat Bonds." In addition to the direct placement of catastrophe bonds in the capital markets, and the investment in cat bonds by CBOs, credit swaps-linked contingent financing, CBO, and swapco structures are being explored as primary and secondary financing vehicles for standalone reinsurance portfolios.

A liquid market in these instruments should provide greater capacity and more robust, informationally-efficient pricing to the reinsurance market. In addition, "deadweight loss" or "market failure" might be eliminated, or at least mitigated. Deadweight loss arises from undersupply to sectors of a market, and results from undercapacity and/or "opportunistic" (i.e., inefficient) pricing.

EXHIBIT 2 INSURANCE SECURITIZATIONS: THE DEALS SO FAR

Date	Insurer	SPV Issuer/ Reinsurer	Value	Arranger	Risk
Feb-94	Hannover Re	Kover	$85m	Citibank	Worldwide catastrophe, excepting US, Japan
May-96	AIG	Guernsey SPV	$25m	AIG Capital Risks/ Benfield Ellinger	Porperty
Jan-97	Hannover Re	K2 (swap)	$100m	Citibank	US, Japan, northern Europe catastrophe,
Jan-97	St. Paul Re	George Town Re	$68.5m	Goldman Sachs	US, Caribbean, European cat risks, marine, aviation
Mar-97	Reliance National	SLF Re	Not disclosed	Sedgwick Lane Financial	Property, satellite launch, aviation, marine
Apr-97	Winterthur	Direct Issue	Sfr399.5m	CSFB	Hail-related motor
Jun-97	USAA	Residential Re (97)	$477m	Merrill Lynch/ Goldman Sachs/ Lehman Bros	East coast, gulf coast hurricane
Aug-97	Swiss Re	SR Earthquake Ltd	$137m	CSFB	California earthquake
Nov-97	Tokio Marine & Fire	Parametric Re	$100m	Goldman Sachs/ Swiss Re New Markets	Tokyo earthquake
Jan-98	Reliance National	SLF Re	Not disclosed	Sedgwick Lane Financial	Property, marine, aviation, satellite launch
Feb-98	Centre Solutions	Trinity Re	$83.5m	Goldman Sachs/ Chase/ DJL/ Zurich Capital Markets	Florida hurricane
Apr-98	Mitsui Marine & Fire	Swap	$30m	Goldman Sachs/ Swiss Re New Mexico	Tokyo earthquake
Apr-98	Hannover Re	LI	Dm100m	Rabobank	Life acquisition costs
Jun-98	Yasuda Fire & Marine	Munich Re (front)	$80m	Aon Capital Markets	Japan windstorm
Jun-98	USAA	Residential Re (98)	$450m	Merrill Lynch/ Goldman Sachs/ Lehman Bros	East coast, gulf coast hurricane
Jul-98	F&G Re	Mosaic Re	$54m	Goldman Sachs/ Blanch Capital Markets	US property
Aug-98	XL Mid Ocean Re	Swap	Not disclosed	Goldman Sachs/ Lehman Bros/ Merrill Lynch/ Aon Capital Markets/ Guy Carpenter Advisors	US, Caribbean hurricane and earthquake

N.B. The above is a list of the latest deals transacted chiefly in the public market and may not be comprehensive
Source: Euroweek/ Reactions

THE EMERGENCE OF WEATHER DERIVATIVES: TRADING THE VOLATILITY OF NATURAL EVENT PARAMETERS LIKE TEMPERATURE, WINDSPEED, OR PRECIPITATION

The potential demand and implications of a robust and liquid market in weather derivatives are staggering. Several transactions close each week ranging in size from $500,000 to over $25 million. Weather derivative-back bonds have been proposed and are being attempted by entities like Investor's Guaranty Fund of Bermuda. Prospective applications include event-, credit-, and price- risk management for both business lines and investment portfolios, financial engineering and alternative risk transfer, yield enhancement and total return management. The seeds of growth for demand and supply in this market reside in the existence of natural offsets between buyers and sellers of weather risk, and the correlation between weather variation and other dimensions of asset value, revenue and cost variation. As with other derivative transactions, weather derivatives are unfunded, credit sensitive contingent claims, which can contribute toward more efficient uses of funded capital, and reduce the cost of equity and debt funding. Weather derivatives can improve Sharpe ratios for investment portfolios by enhancing yield or minimizing portfolio variance, and thus contribute to excess portfolio returns, and obtaining a more efficient frontier. As volatility trades, weather derivatives are easily written and hence readily adapted to structured or synthetic instruments. Weather derivatives are also related to and can be used in conjunction with the PCS insurance contracts traded on the CBOT and the electricity and energy contracts traded on the NYMEX to structure exotic and complex hedges. In this way weather derivatives provide new avenues for reallocating and redistributing risk capital.

A weather derivative is a state-dependent, contingent contract in which parties exchange pre-specified payments based on the performance of some reference measure or index. Common examples of reference measures for weather derivatives include precipitation measures like monthly, seasonal, or annual rainfall for a particular city or region. Another example of a common weather derivative reference measure is the average heating degree-day over a period of time and for a city or region.

As with other derivative contracts, simple weather derivatives can take the form of forwards, swaps or options, and can be combined into more complex transactions like floors, caps, and collars. Weather swaps are often quoted in a manner consistent with volatility swaps, i.e., the incremental payout per unit above or below an agreed level or band. Weather options typically have a strike or trigger that references the relevant measure and a set amount or formula for payout at the strike. Since the weather is a highly chaotic and complex system, estimating the historical local volatility of weather in space and time is extremely data intensive, and should involve a more than passing familiarity with stochastic methods. Traditional regression methods and treating the local volatility around seasonal averages as a constant could ultimately lead to substantial model risk, and thereby result in significant mispricings due to systematic underestimation of tail events.

It is estimated that over 80% of all businesses are materially exposed to weather risk. The economic impact of weather risk manifests itself in any of three general ways:

a) the variability of a company's revenue (quantity and price risk, i.e. price elasticity of demand)
b) the variability of its cost structure (operating leverage)
c) negative shocks to the asset values and liabilities on its balance sheet (financial asset market values and/or total return, capacity, inventory, receivables, or payables - e.g. forward obligations).

Prior to the inception of the weather derivatives market, the equityholders in a company's capital structure have been subject to the adverse effects of these risks, and hence will have charged a premium for bearing these risks. In addition, with no liquid, traded market for weather volatility, price discovery for the composite risk premium in the equity market for combined business risks (i.e., product-market versus financial market risks) and weather risk might be either too expensive or too cheap. Whether the weather risk premium embedded either in the equity premium of a particular company is to too rich or too cheap is specific to the relative economic exposure of that particular company's portfolio of assets and liabilities, or revenues and costs to (seasonal and unseasonal) variation in the weather.

Business risk drives the motivation for managers to hedge price and quantity risk in their revenues, costs, and asset-liability mix. Revenue is a function of price and quantity. Discrete changes in revenue can result in excess supply or demand from the impact of weather risk to capacity or inventory levels. Demand and supply elasticity is represented by the slopes of the average revenue curve and marginal cost curve, respectively of a company, market or industry. The elasticities of supply express estimated or inferred relationships between shifts in prices or costs to shifts in unit quantity or volume. Traditional derivative contracts (forwards, futures, swaps, or options) written against underlying equity, commodity or interest-rate risk hedge only the price risk component of the revenue or cost structure of a firm. As such, these traditional derivative strategies, as useful as they may be, do not provide protection against the quantity dimension of cash flow or total return variability, or its impact on the market value of an asset (the present value of expected future flows). By compensating for shocks via estimates of correlations or elasticities of supply/demand, weather derivative contracts can help bridge the gap between price variation and revenue-cost margins.

Weather derivative transactions can be structured to match the terms and payout distribution of various pricing schedules and forward or take-pay supply contracts. This flexibility permits an entity to cover nonlinear effects of demand or supply shocks resulting capacity or storage constraints linked to weather risk, and to more effectively deliver on contracts or pricing schedules with both fixed and variable components. In combination with credit-derivatives, weather contracts can insure against counterparty credit risk on forward delivery contracts in weather sensitive product markets like natural gas and electricity.

By pricing and trading natural event volatility, weather derivatives contribute to the efficient pricing of physical and financial assets by redistributing risk in a more complete market for contingent claims. The relative value or utility of hedging weather risk is a function of the hedger's portfolio composition of assets and the volatility of cashflow associated with the assets in the portfolio, i.e., extent mix of the exposure mix of assets/liabilities of the particular company. On the other side of the weather derivative trade, the benefit of the premium to the hedge provider is a function of correlation with other risks in the hedge provider's portfolio. From a risk management perspective, the objective function in pricing either a weather swap or option is to minimize the all-in-cost (including net portfolio losses) subject to level of premium paid or received and the relevant correlation or "weather sensitivity." This sensitivity can also be computed as the utility of the weather hedge to the user.

In either case, depending on the portfolio of risks held by each, the counterparties on opposite sides of a weather trade can hence mirror each other, and thus the long and short positions can simultaneously play the role of both hedger and hedge provider. The existence of a natural offset in a weather derivative trade is a function of the correlation between each counterparty's risk profile and the referent weather measure. For the offset between counterparties is less than perfect (i.e. where the correlation between weather risks or revenue, cost, asset sensitivity to weather risk is less-than-perfectly negative between counterparties), residual weather risk might be placed with third parties via a derivative-linked structured note or traditional reinsurance contract.

The emerging field of alternative risk transfer applies the principles of portfolio theory (Markowitz-Sharpe), option theory (Black-Scholes), contingent claims analysis (Merton), and capital structure arbitrage (Miller-Modigliani) to the pricing and distribution of business and investment risk. Underlying much of the theory is the fundamental theorem of optimal risk bearing which prices risk by equating prices to the probability of obtaining the pre-specified states of the world that are being priced.

Derivatives supply synthetic capital to firms by substituting unfunded commitments for funded sources of capital. Synthetic capital in the form of unfunded commitments enable firms to reallocate funding from supporting unrealized and often ancillary risks to more immediate needs, and hence allow for higher returns to funded long-term equity capital. The oldest form of synthetic capital is traditional insurance and reinsurance. We are continuing to observe a convergence between derivative capital markets and insurance markets, and weather derivatives are just one more manifestation of this convergence.

As mentioned previously, weather derivatives can be employed to achieve a more optimal mean-variance efficient investment frontier, by either enhancing risk-adjusted portfolio returns or reducing portfolio variance. Since the premium from writing weather options can be more or less uncorrelated with market risks, these contracts can enhance portfolio a ("alpha"), i.e., excess returns uncorrelated with the market. Furthermore, as with other derivative contracts, weather derivatives allow for enhanced yield by implicitly levering contingent payouts as a nonlinear function of the reference measure.

Investment portfolios that are particularly sensitive to both the price and quantity impact of weather risk are Commodity Trading Advisors or CTAs. In addition, corporate debt and equity portfolios are comprised of numerous industries exposed to weather risk, including agriculture & grain conveyors, utilities & energy, travel, leisure & entertainment, retail, and insurance.

Much like credit risk, the causes and impacts of weather risk to capital, asset values (physical, financial, intangible), and cashflow streams are discrete, discontinuous, and heterogeneous. The spreads and premiums for bearing and transferring weather risk may never converge to match the premiums for interest rate or commodity price risk. At the same time, weather derivatives as a volatility trade employ standardized ISDA structures, documentation and practices comparable to those used in the equity and interest-rate derivatives market. In addition, temperature, precipitation, and storm run-off data for analysis of historical weather volatility is publicly available. The proprietary value added in weather trading will be in the design, structuring, pricing and placement of tailored solutions using weather derivatives in combination with other derivatives, and in the financing of residual weather risk.

Embedding weather derivatives in rated Medium Term Note or Commercial Paper Issuances can lower cost funding for working capital or short term investment costs. Synthetic note structures can also incorporate weather derivatives to form yield enhanced, zero cost investment portfolios by combining long and short weather positions. Insurance hedges can be structured around not only rainfall or degree-day measures, but around snow pack, runoff or overflow, and wind speed measures.

For this market to develop much further, the following risk modeling and informational issues need to be addressed:

- Reliable indexes (consistent and transparent disclosure, minimized measurement error).
- Robust analysis of volatility and sensitivity to regional cross- and auto- correlation.
- Analysis should extend beyond annual or seasonal variation, but to volatility (outliers) around seasonal averages. Rigorous error diagnostics on historical volatility measures.
- Market participants need to take into account the impact of stochastic volatility and correlation on intra-seasonal as well as inter-seasonal variation.

THE ENTRY OF CREDIT DERIVATIVES AND THE DISINTERMEDIATION OF THE TRADITIONAL CREDIT MARKETS

For the same capacity and capital availability reasons existing in the Property and Casualty markets, institutional investors with excess "off-the-run" credit analysis capacity will conceivably enter the credit-enhanced note market to compete with and potentially displace the traditional monoline portfolio insurers like Capmac, Ambac/MBIA, CGA, GCA, and FGIC. As the credit swaps market becomes broader, deeper, and more liquid, credit enhancement may become even more commonplace in the synthetics market place, especially for below investment grade issuers and counterparties. Rating agencies must continue to strive to consistently assign ratings to comparable levels of credit risk to events in different markets. To do so, rating analysts are being required to analytically compare the implied volatility of the default options embedded in these new debt instruments.

PARALLELS BETWEEN CREDIT AND INSURANCE DERIVATIVES

Credit derivatives in one form or another have enjoyed a long history in off-balance sheet and non-recourse structured financing as traditional contingent products. For example:

- back-to-back loans have facilitated cross-border corporate borrowing;
- backup lines of credit have contributed to securitization of corporate credit by supporting commercial paper issuance;
- other contingent credit issuances have served to guarantee project, equipment and trade financing;
- standby LOCs forward contracts;
- limited guarantees;
- defeasance/escrow.

Credit derivatives have traditionally existed, for at least twenty years, in the form of bond insurance, and in other forms of credit protection constructed from more conventional credit facilities, e.g., special-purpose or standby letters of credit. However, current credit derivative instruments are specifically designed to strip out and trade credit risk, to have a well-defined payoff and hence to be priced efficiently, based on the perceived risk of a specific credit event, such as a default. Increasingly, these traditional credit facilities are being replaced in special-purpose credit-enhanced structures, by over-the-counter, market-traded credit derivatives.

Similar development can be observed in the parallel histories of insurance risk management and commodity price-risk management, and the extension in to financial market-risk management, over the past twentyfive years. Alternative risk financing techniques, such as self-insurance, self-funding, financial reinsurance, and "captives," now common to the insurance industry, bear close resemblance to the structures now emerging in the synthetics and credit derivatives markets.

Much as synthetic securities maximize collateral efficiency for purposes of investment and market-risk allocation, market-based credit derivatives can potentially maximize collateral efficiency for credit enhancement purposes, relative to these traditional forms. For example, a total return swap provides off-market economic exposure to the credit-risk of the underlying asset for a synthetic financing cost significantly lower than the market rate, especially for a lower-rated buyer of the swap. As mentioned previously, from a contingent claims perspective, a reinsurance contract shares many of the same analytic features as a credit swap or a default option. As stated previously, extreme event risks, such as credit default risk and catastrophic insurance risk are traded in the market for intermediated event-risk. All risky debt claims (and insurance contracts as contingent claims) can be modeled "knockout" or "barrier" options. However, excess-of-loss reinsurance contracts and single-event catastrophe bonds tend to exhibit default behavior that is more discrete or "digital" in nature than a corporate credit instrument.

As illustrated throughout this chapter, insurance derivatives serve as economic alternatives for regulatory- and economic- risk-based capital relief, much as the economics of credit derivatives facilitate their use as substitutes or complements for more traditional credit enhancement approaches.

EXHIBIT 3 CREDIT EXCHANGE BOND

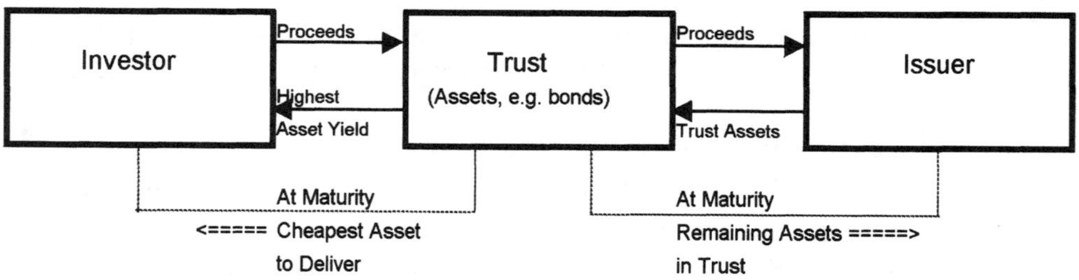

In short, interest-rate and credit-derivatives permit arbitrage of all of the following risk-adjusted credit premium relationships:

- default risk and credit sensitivity;
- preferences for fixed versus floating rate coupons;
- term structure risk (volatility i.e., duration and convexity), and
- term structure of credit risk (i.e., the correlation and integration of credit risk and market risk).

More complete contracting via insurance, credit (such as, equity) derivatives supplies investment opportunities to the marketplace that more efficiently capture the payoff distribution of an event, a specific pool of assets, particular industry structures, or the unique investment opportunity set of an individual firm. The potential of merchant banking and corporate finance using fundamental option and portfolio theory applications of credit derivative products is leading to further development of the contingent claims analysis of firm value and default risk. These approaches are leading to innovations in permanent financing for conventional and special-purpose insurance portfolios. Some of these contingent financing products (putable preferred, etc.) are based on derivative features that either segregate or combine both insurance event-risk and credit risk elements. Products in development include:

- basket Options;
- credit Spread Options, and
- correlation Products.

A credit exchange bond is one example of a complex credit derivative that allows an investor to earn excess returns relative to a traditional bond with comparable default risk. With this structure, the investor may achieve an enhanced return with assuming additional interest rate or call risk. A credit exchange bond is a basket trade, i.e. an obligation issued by a financial intermediary in which the reference asset is the credit

EXHIBIT 4 COVERED CALL

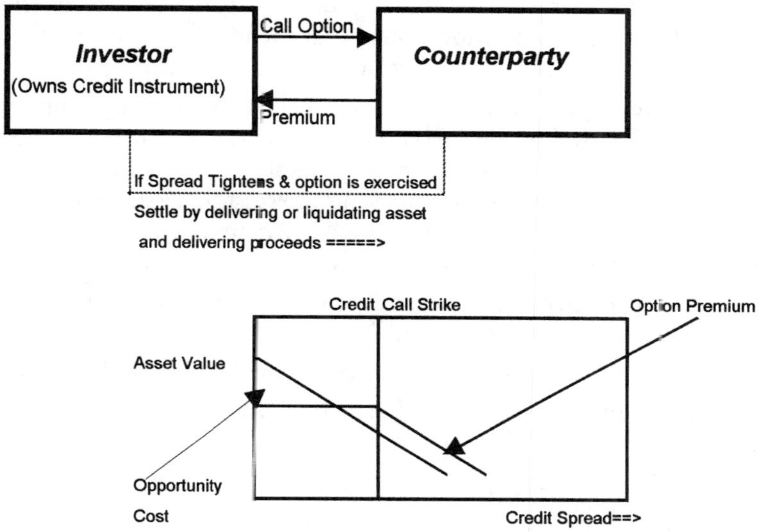

EXHIBIT 5 NAKED PUT

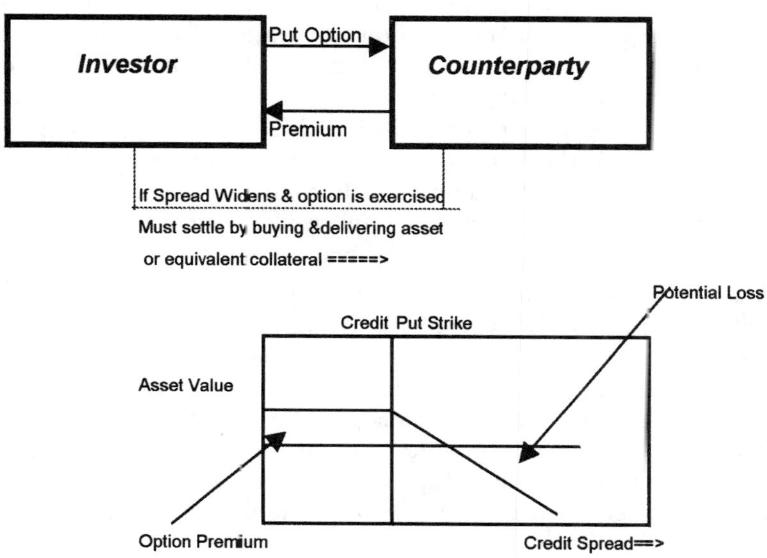

performance of a basket of underlying corporate bonds. In addition to an incremental spread paid during the option period, and a lower additional spread paid to the maturity of the bond, the investor will be delivered the cheapest of the underlying corporate bonds at option maturity.

Simple credit option strategies include: selling a covered call, selling a naked put, and hedging with credit puts. Selling a covered call is a yield enhancement strategy, where the risk is the opportunity cost if the credit spread tightens more than the amount of the yield enhancement (i.e. the premium received from the sale of the call).

Selling a naked put enhances yield and lowers the average cost of the portfolio by selling an obligation to purchase bonds at a predetermined spread-to-treasuries. Here, the risk is that the credit spread widens such that the loss from the exercised purchase obligation exceeds the yield enhancement (and funding cost savings).

Hedging with credit puts provides credit protection by purchasing options payable in future periods. These features are common in many, if not most, repackaged or synthetic notes, especially those where the originator of the structure also serves as the counterparty that guarantees the minimum return to trust that issues the notes. Whether these embedded features are priced as efficiently (i.e., competitively) as an implicit credit option by either the investor or the originator of the structure is an empirical question.

What's motivating these trades? The ability to build complex structures from simpler derivatives, by balancing cost, credit, and pricing considerations:

- The role of "implicit leverage" and "all-in-cost" concepts in pricing and structuring;
- Credit- or event- spread intermediation (i.e., the certainty-equivalent or "break-even" spread);
- Default substitution; and
- Capital Structure Arbitrage.

The breakeven spread on a risky debt instrument is the calculated yield-spread to treasuries at which an investor is indifferent between investing in an instrument with a given level of credit- or event- risk versus investing in a risk-free (e.g., a treasury) instrument. Market spreads tend to exceed break-even spreads for reasons related to regulation, risk aversion, liquidity or taxes.

As with other derivative instruments, constructing and valuing these structures involves the use of default or event estimation applications like the Stein estimator and volatility estimation and simulation methodologies, like Markov Chain Monte Carlo algorithms and stratified sampling techniques. The rating agencies are just beginning to conduct research incorporating elements of JP Morgan's Creditmetrics and CSFP's Creditrisk+ models into their rating analytics. Creditmetrics employs a value-at-risk approach to default and recovery estimation. In contrast, Creditrisk+ employs an actuarial approach similar to the methodology employed for insurance portfolios. McKinsey & Co. has subsequently unveiled their Creditview product.

Asset managers are increasingly focused on the spread between their Weighted Average Cost of Capital (WACC), i.e. the Weight Average Coupon (WAC) of their fixed obligations, and the Weighted Average Price (WAP) and Weighted Average Maturity (WAM) of assets in their portfolio. This further has further stimulated the other side of yield management, the modeling and managing of expected losses using credit derivatives. Bankers and portfolio managers are adopting more sophisticated credit modeling approaches based on VaR or actuarial approaches. Similar market pressures are driving credit and bond underwriters to adopt financial and derivative market vehicles to expand capacity and lower cost.

CONCLUSION

The risks underlying these new markets are informationally opaque, illiquid, discrete, heterogeneous, and nonstandardized. Hence the performance of these instruments can be expected to be both highly unpredictable and pricing may remain inefficient. This condition is a two-edged sword. On the one hand, the above-market yields on these investments can be expected to persist long after other comparable markets mature and hence become commoditized. On the other hand, the investor should be diligent in research and analysis. Prudence dictates that in markets for event-risk... *caveat emptor*!!!

ENDNOTES

This article was published in *The Journal of Alternative Investments*, Winter 1998.

REFERENCES

Allen, W. Robert. Integrating Credit and Risk Management. *Journal of Lending and Credit-Risk Management* (Robert Morris Associates), February 1996.

Das, Satyajit. Credit Derivatives: Products, Applications and Pricing. Wiley, New York 1997

International Risk Management, The Convergence of Financial and Insurance Markets, (EMAP) 1996

International Risk Management, The Practical Application of Financial Market Tools to Corporate Risk Management, (EMAP) 1997

Lamm, R. McFall. "The Catastrophe Reinsurance Market: Gyrations and Innovations Amid Major Structural Transformation." Bankers Trust, January 1997.

Lane, Morton. "The Year of Structuring Furiously." Sedgewick-Lane Financial, January 1997.

Litzenberger, Robert, David Beaglehole, and Craig Reynolds. "Assessing Catastrophe-Reinsurance-Linked Securities as a New Asset-Class." Goldman Sachs, July 1996.

Mordecai, David et al. "Emerging Market CBO Concentration Limits: Volatility, Business Cycle Correlation and the Diversification of Industry." Working paper, Fitch IBCA, October 1997.

Mordecai, David. "Credit Arbitrage Investment Opportunities in Credit-linked Synthetic & Structured Notes: Introduction and Overview." In *Alternative Investment Strategies*. Euromoney Books/AIMA. 1998.

————. "Employing Credit Derivatives to Credit Enhance Structured Notes." In *Credit Derivatives: Applications for Risk Management*. Euromoney Books/AIMA, 1998.

————. "Emerging Market Credit Derivatives and Default Estimation: Volatility, Business Cycle Correlation and the Diversification of Industry, Region & Country Risk in a Global Credit Portfolio." Chapter in *Credit Derivatives: Applications for Risk Management, Investment and Portfolio Optimization* (RISK). 1998.

Smithson, Charles. "Credit Derivatives." *RISK*, June 1996.

BIBLIOGRAPHY

GENERAL ARTICLE REFERENCES (MANAGED FUNDS)

Ackermann, Carl and David Ravenscraft, "The Impact of Regulatory Restrictions on Fund Performance: A Comparative Study of Hedge Funds and Mutual," Working Paper, University of Notre Dame and University of North Carolina, (July, 1998).

Brown, S., W. Goetsmann, R. Ibbotson "Offshore Hedge Funds: Survival and Performance, 1989—1995," *Journal of Business* Forthcoming.

Billingsley, R. and D. Chance. "Benefits and Limitations of Diversifcation Among Commodity Trading Advisors." *The Journal of Portfolio Management,* (Fall 1996), pp. 65-80.

Bodie, Zvi and Victor Rosansky. "Risk and Return in Commodity Futures." *Financial Analysts Journal* 36 (May-June, 1980), pp. 3-14.

Bodie,Zvi. "Commodity Futures as a Hedge Against Inflation." *The Journal of Portfolio Management* (Spring 1983), pp. 12-17.

Brorsen, B. Wade and Louis P. Lukac. "Optimal Portfolios for Commodity Futures Funds." *Journal of Futures Markets,* Vol. 10, No. 3 (1990), pp. 247-258.

"Commodity Futures As An Asset Class." *New York Futures Exchange.* Report by Powers Research Associates (January, 1990).

Conrad, Jennifer and Gautam Kaul. "An Anatomy of Trading Strategies, " *The Review of Financial Studies,* Vol. 11, No. 3 (Fall, 1998), pp. 489-520.

Diz, Fernando. "How Do CTA's Return Distribution Characteristics Affect Their Likelihood Of Survival?" Working Paper, Department of Management, Syracuse University.

Dow, James, "Arbitrage, Hedging, and Financial Innovation," *The Review of Financial Studies,* Vol 11, No. 4 (Winter, 1998), pp. 739-757.

Edwards, F. and Andy C. Ma. "Commodity Pool Performance: Is the Information Contained in Pool Prospectuses Useful?" *The Journal of Futures Markets,* Vol. 8, No. 5 (1988), pp. 589-616.

Edwards, Franklin and J. Park, " Do Managed Futures Make Good Investments," *The Journal of Futures Markets,* Vol. 16, No. 5, (1996), pp. 475-517.

Elton, E.J., M. Gruber and J.C. Rentzler, "New Public Offerings, Information, and Investor Rationality: The Case of Publicly Offered Commodity Funds." *Journal of Business,* Vol. 6, No. 1 (1988), pp. 1-15.

Elton, E.J., M. Gruber and J.C. Rentzler, "The Performance of Publicly Offered Commodity Futures." *Financial Analysts Journal,* (July/August, 1990), pp. 23-30.

Elton, E.J., M.J. Gruber and J.C. Rentzler. "Professionally Managed Publicly Offered Commodity Funds." *Journal of Business,* (1987), pp. 177-199.

Fenn, G., N. Liang and S. Prowse. "The Economics of the Private Equity Market". Washington, D.C. Board of Governors of the Federal Reserve System (1995).

Fishmar, D. and Carl C. Peters. "Portfolio of Stocks, Bonds and Managed Futures Using Compromise Stochastic Dominance." *The Journal of Futures Markets,* Vol. II, No. 3, (June 1991), pp. 259-270.

Froot, Kenneth A, David S. Scharfstein and Jeremy C. Stein. "A Framework For Risk Management." *Harvard Business Review,* (Nov-Dec, 1994), pp. 91-102.

Fung, William and David A. Hsieh, "Empirical Characteristics of Dynamic Trading Strategies: The Case of Hedge Funds," *The Review of Financial Studies* Vol. 10 (1977), pp. 275-302.

Fung, William and David Hsieh, "Survivor Bias and Invstment Style in the Returns of CTAs," *The Journal of Portfolio Management.* (Fall, 1997), pp. 30-41.

Goldman Sachs & Company/Frank Russell Russell Capital, Inc. Survey of Alternative Investing by Tax-Exempt Organizations. 1997.

Greer, R. "Methods for Institutional Investment in Commodity Futures, " *The Journal of Derivatives* (Winter, 1994), pp. 28-36.

Hartzmark, M. "Returns of Individual Traders of Futures: Aggregate Results." *Journal of Political Economy* 95 (1987), pp. 1292-1306.

Henker, T. and G. Martin, "Naive and Optimal Diversification For Managed Futures", *The Journal of Alternative Investments* (Fall, 1998), pp. 25-39.

Henker, T. "Naïve Diversification for Hedge Funds," *The Journal of Alternative Investments* (Winter, 1998, 1998), pp. 30-39.

Horn, Gregory S. "Enhanced Return, Less Volatility Make Managed Futures Attractive." *Trust and Estates,* (March, 1997).

Huberman, Gur. "The Desirability of Investment in Commodities via Commodity Futures," *Derivatives Quarterly* (Fall, 1995), pp. 65-67

Kaplan, Paul and S. Lummer, Update: GSCI Collateralized Futures as a Hedging and Diversification Tool for Institutional Portfolios," *The Journal of Investing* (Winter, 1998), pp. 11-18.

Irwin, S.H. "Further Evidence of the Usefulness of CTA Performance Information in Public Commodity Pool Prospectuses and a Proposal for Reform." In *Advances in Futures and Options Research,* Don M. Chance and Robert R. Trippi, Eds. Connecticut: JAI Press. 1994. pp. 251-265.

Irwin, S.H. and B.W. Brorsen. "Public Futures Funds." *Journal of Futures Markets* (Fall, 1985), pp. 463-485.

Irwin, S.H. and D. Landa. "Real Estate, Futures and Gold as Portfolio Assets." *The Journal of Portfolio Management* (Fall, 1987), pp. 29-34.

Irwin, Scott H., Terry Krukmeyer and Carl R. Zulaf. "The Investment Performance of Public Commodity Pools over 1979-1989." *The Journal of Futures,* 1992.

Kaplan, Paul and S. Lummer, Update: GSCI Collateralized Futures as a Hedging and Diversification Tool for Institutional Portfolios," *The Journal of Investing* (Winter, 1998), pp. 11-18.

Lee, Chung F., Raymond Leuthold and Jean Cordier. "The Stock Market and Commodities Futures Market: Diversification and Arbitrage Potential." *Financial Analysts Journal,* (July-August 1985).

Levy, H. "Futures, Spots, Stocks and Bonds: Multi-Asset Portfolio Analysis." *Journal of Futures Markets,* No. 4 (1987), pp. 383-395.

Lintner, J. "The Potential Role of Managed Commodity-Financial Futures Accounts (and/or funds) in Portfolios of Stocks and Bonds." Paper presented at the Annual Conference of the Financial Analyst Federation, Toronto, Canada, May 1983.

Lukac, L.P., B.W. Brorsen and S.H. Irwin. "A Comparison of Twelve Technical Trading Systems with Market Efficiency Implications." Station Bulletin No. 495, Department of Agricultural Economics, Agricultural Experiment Station, Purdue University, 1986.

Lukac, Louis, B.W. Brorsen, and S.H. Irwin. "Similarity of Computer Guided Technical Trading Systems," *The Journal of Futures Markets* (February, 1988), pp. 1-14.

Lummer, Scott and Lawrence B. Siegel. "GSCI Collateralized Futures: A Hedging and Diversification Tool for Institutional Investors," *The Journal of Investing* (Summer 1993), pp. 75-82.

McCarthy, D. and R. Spurgin. "A Review of Hedge Fund Performance Benchmarks," *The Journal of Alternative Investments* (Summer, 1998), pp. 18-28.

McCafferty, Thomas A. "Winning with Managed Futures: How to Select a Top Performing Commodity Trading Advisor." Chicago: Probus Publishing, 1994.

"Managed Futures Compared to Stocks and Bonds." *Managed Futures Association.* March, 1994.

"Managed Futures: A Resource Guide for Institutional Investors." *Chicago Mercantile Exchange.* Publication.

"Managed Futures: An Alternative Investment Opportunity." *Chicago Board of Trade.* Publication. 1993.

"Managed Futures: An Investment Alternative for the 1990's." *Family Office Exchange Newsletter.* 1 st Quarter, 1992.

Markowitz, H. "Portfolio Selection: Efficient Diversification of Investments. " New York: Wiley, 1959.

Murphy, J. Austin. "Futures Fund Performance: A Test of the Effectiveness of Technical Analysis." *The Journal of Futures Markets,* Vol. 6, No. 2, 1986, pp. 175-185.

Peters, Carl and Ben Warwick. The Handbook of Managed Futures-Performance, Evaluation and Analysis. Chicago: The McGraw-Hill Companies, Inc. 1997.

Peters, Carl C. (Ed.). "Managed Futures--Performance, Evaluation and Analysis of Commodity Funds, Pools and Accounts." Chicago: Probus Publishing, 1992.

Kaynauld, Jacques and Jacques Tessier. "Risk Premiums in Futures Markets: An Empirical Investigation." *The Journal of Futures Markets,* No. 2 (1984), pp. 189-211.

Schneeweis, Thomas, Uttama Savanayana and David McCarthy "Alternative Commodity Trading Vehicles: A Performance Analysis." *The Journal of Futures Markets* (1991).

Schneeweis, Thomas. "The Benefits of Managed Futures." EMFA Research. June, 1996.

Park, James and J. Staum, "Performance persistence in Alternative Investment Industry," Paradigm Capital Management, 1998.

Schneeweis, Thomas. *The Benefits of Managed Futures.* AIMA, 1996.

Schneeweis, Thomas. "Evidence of Superior Performance Persistence in Hedge Funds: An Empirical Comment," *The Journal of Alternative Investments* (Fall, 1998), pp. 76-80.

Schneeweis, Thomas. "Dealing with Myths of Hedge Fund Investments," *The Journal of Alternative Investments* (Winter, 1998), pp. 5-13.

Schneeweis, T. and R. Spurgin. "Alternative Investments in the Institutional Portfolio". AIMA, 1998.

Schneeweis, T. and R. Spurgin, "Managed Futures, Hedge Fund and Mutual Fund Return Estimation: A Multi-Factor Approach", *The Journal of Alternative Investments* (Fall, 1998). pp. 1-24.

Schneeweis, Thomas, Richard Spurgin, and Randy Warsager, "Commodity, Commodity Futures, Managed commodity Futures and inflation," *AIMA Newsletter* (December. 1997).

Schneeweis, Thomas, and Richard Spurgin, "Energy Based Investment Products and Investor Asset Allocation," CIDSM/SOM, 1997 (b).

Strongin, Steve, and M. Petsch, "Commodity Investing: Long-Run Returns and the Function of Passive Capital, " *Derivatives Quarterly* (Fall, 1995), pp. 56-64.

BOOKS (MANAGED FUNDS)

Chance, Don M. Managed Futures and Their Role in Investment Portfolios. The Research Foundation of the Institute of Chartered Financial Analysts: Charlottesville, 1994.

Chandler, Beverly. Managed Futures An Investor's Guide. New York: John Wiley and Sons, Inc. 1994.

Chandler, Beverly. Investing with the Hedge Fund Giants FT Pittman: United Kingdom, 1998.

Cottier, Philipp. Hedge Funds and Managed Futures. Paul Haupt Publishers: Berne, 1997.

Crerend, William. Fundamental of Hedge Fund Investing: A Professional Investor's Guide. McGraw-Hill, 1998.

Epstein, Charles B ed. Managed Futures In The Institutional Portfolio. New York: John Wiley and Sons, Inc. 1992.

Eichengreen, Barry and Donald Mathieson. *Hedge Funds and Financial Market Dynamics.* Occasional Paper 166. International Monetary Fund: Washington D.C., 1998.

Hammer, D. Dynamic Asset Allocation. John Wiley & Sons. 1991

Hills, Richard. Hedge Funds: An Introduction to Skill Based Investment Strategies. Rushmere Wynne: Harmill, 1996.

Investment Policy: Anatomy of Alternative Investing-Part One. Volume 1, Number 2. Cayuga, Press: Ithaca, 1997.

Investment Policy: Anatomy of Alternative Investing-Part Two. Volume 1, Number 3. Cayuga, Press: Ithaca, 1998.

Jaffer, Sohail, ed.. Alternative Investment Strategies. Euromoney Books: London, 1998.

Krieger, Andrew and Edward Claflin. The Money Bazaar: Inside the Trillion-Dollar World of Currency Trading. Times Books: New York, 1992.

Lang, Peter. Marketing of Hedge Funds: A key strategic variable in defining possible roles of an emerging investment force. St. Gallen University: Bern, 1995.

Lederman, Jess and Robert A. Klein. Hedge Funds: Investment and Portfolio Strategies for the Institutional Investor. Irwin Professional Publishing: Burr Ridge, 1995.

Lederman, Jess and Robert A. Klein. Market Neutral: State-of –the-Art Strategies for Every Market Environment. Irwin Professional Pub., 1996.

Lofthouse, S. Reading In Investments. John Wiley & Sons. 1994.

McCafferty, Thomas A. Winning with Managed Futures: How to Select a Top Performing Commodity Trading Advisors. Chicago: Probus Publishing, 1994.

Markowitz, H. Portfolio Selection: Efficient Diversification of Investments. New York: John Wiley & Sons, Inc. 1959.

Meaden, N. and M Fox-Andrews. Derivatives Markets and Investment Management. Prentice Hall Woodhead Faulkner. 1995.

Nicholas, J. Investing in Hedge Funds. Bloomberg Press, 1998.

Peters, Carl C. (Ed.). Managed Futures-Performance, Evaluation and Analysis of Commodity Funds, Pools and Accounts" Chicago; Probus Publishing, 1992.

Peters, Carl and Ben Warwick. The Handbook of Managed Futures: Performance, Evaluation & Analysis. Irwin: Chicago, 1997.

Schwager, Jack D. The New Market Wizards: Conversations with America's Top Traders. Harper Business: New York, 1992.

Schwager, Jack D. Managed Trading-Myths & Truths. New York: John Wiley and Sons, Inc. 1996.

Soros, George. Soros On Soros: Staying Ahead of the Curve. John Wiley & Sons: New York, 1995.

Soros, George. The Alchemy of Finance: Reading the Mind of the Market. Simon and Schuster: New York, 1987.

Staley, Katherine F. The Art of Selling Short. Probus Pub Co., 1995.

Train, John. The Money Masters. Harper & Row: New York, 1980.

Watsham, T. International Portfolio Management: A Modern Approach. Longman. 1990.

DICTIONARY OF TERMS[1]

Arbitrage: (1) Technically, the action of purchasing a commodity or security in one market for immediate sale in another market (deterministic arbitrage). (2) Popular usage has expanded the meaning to include any attempt to buy a relatively underpriced item and sell a similar, relatively overpriced item, expecting to profit when the prices resume a more appropriate theoretical or historical relationship (statistical arbitrage). (3) In trading options, convertible securities, and futures, arbitrage techniques can be applied whenever a strategy involves buying and selling packages of related instruments. (4) Risk arbitrage applies the principles of risk offset to mergers and other major corporate developments. The risk offsetting position(s) do not insulate the investor from certain event risks (such as termination of a merger agreement or the risk of delay in the completion of a transaction), so the arbitrage is incomplete. (5) Tax arbitrage transactions are undertaken to share the benefit of differential tax rates or circumstances of two or more parties to a transaction. (6) Regulatory arbitrage transactions are designed to provide indirect access to a market where one party is denied direct access by law or regulation. (7) Swap-driven arbitrage transactions are motivated by the comparative advantages that swap counterparties enjoy in different debt and currency markets. For example, one counterparty may borrow relatively cheaper in the intermediate- or long-term U.S. dollar market, while the other may have a comparative advantage in floating-rate sterling. A cross-currency swap can improve both of their positions.

Asset Class: An investment grouping or type of instrument with a positive expected return that is not conditional on the return of another grouping or type of instrument. More precisely, an investment grouping with risk and return characteristics that cannot be dynamically replicated in a continuous market with positions in another asset class and the risk-free asset. Recently, there has been a tendency to divide the world of investments into more asset classes than are warranted or useful.

Backwardation: (1) A futures/spot market relationship in which the futures price is lower than the spot price. Agricultural commodity markets with a harvest due before the settlement date of the futures contract and energy markets during winter months are often characterized by backwardation. In periods of backwardation, the owners of the underlying forego a riskless profit in exchange for the surety of having the commodity on hand to meet demand. John Maynard Keynes argued that backwardation was normal in speculative markets, but this position has few adherents today. (2) Crossed or inverted market: a market with the posted bid price higher than the offer.

Commoditization: A process of marketability enhancement in which illiquid financial contracts are modified for trading in more liquid and transparent markets. Securitization is a special case. Most observers consider this transformation desirable, but there are occasional references to commoditization as a cause of price fluctuations. In fact, prices do fluctuate in the less liquid market, but prices are harder to measure without liquidity.

Commodity Pool Operator (CPO): Section I a(4) of the Commodity Exchange Act defines Commodity Pool Operator as "any person engaged in a business that is of the nature of an investment trust, syndicate, or similar form of enterprise, and who, in connection therewith, solicits, accepts, or receives from others, funds, securities, or property, either directly or through capital contributions, the sale of stock or other forms of securities, or otherwise, for the purpose of trading in any commodity for future delivery on or subject to the rules of any contract market...." In short, the manager of a public or private futures fund.

Commodity Trading Advisor (CTA): In the U.S., any person (in the legal sense) registered with the Commodity Futures Trading Commission "who, for compensation or profit, engages in the business of advising others, either directly or through publications, writings or electronic media, as to the value of or the advisability of trading in any contract of sale of a commodity for future delivery made or to be made on or subject to the rules of any contract market; [or] any commodity option authorized under section 4 (c) [of the Commodity Exchange Act]...or who, for compensation or profit, and as part of a regular business, issues or promulgates analyses or reports concerning [any of the foregoing]." The approximate futures market equivalent of a rcgistered investment adviser in the securities market in the U.S.

Convergence: One of the tests of the quality of a derivatives market instrument is how closely the derivative's forward price converges to the cash market spot price at expiration. Some markets, such as the market in S&P 500 futures, are characterized by almost perfect convergence: An arbitrageur can be confident that a long stock index replicating portfolio sold at the opening on expiration day will match the value of the cash settlement on the related futures contract almost exactly. Where trading at the settlement price and therefore convergence, is less certain, the pricing relationship between the underlying and the futures contract is more tenuous. Other things equal, markets with good convergence and close spot/futures trading relationships tend to be more liquid markets.

Credit Derivative: A highly generic term often used to describe one or more of the following instruments or arrangements: (1) a put or a call with a payoff dependent on the interest rate spread between a specific corporate debt instrument and sovereign debt denominated in the same currency. The most common example is the Treasury EuroDollar, or TED spread. Alternately, an option with a payoff dependent on the spread between indexes of similar maturity debt instruments such as the five-year swap rate and a five-year government bond rate; (2) a swap or embedded swap with the payments on one side mirroring the interest and principal payments of a basket of bonds rated below investment grade. The payer of the bond return is the nominal holder of the low-rated bonds, but the receiver actually takes the credit risk. The payment on the other side can be a fixed or floating rate as the parties agree; (3) an asset swap in the form of a stand-alone swap or structured note where one party holds a below-investment-grade issue and pays the interest called for under the bond indenture, in exchange for a traditional fixed or floating rate. The fixed or floating rate is greater than usual in compensation for the acceptance of any losses from default by the holder of the below-investment-grade issue. (4) a total return swap with the "fixed" rate based on the total return of a corporate bond because the bond's issuer is overrepresented in the fixed-rate payer's credit portfolio.

Derivative Instrument or Product: (1) A contract or convertible security that changes in value in concert with and/or obtains much of its value from price movements in a related or underlying security, future, or other instrument or index. (2) A security or contract, such as an option, forward future, swap, warrant, or debt instrument with one or more options, forwards, swaps, or warrants embedded in it or attached to it. The value of the instrument is determined in whole or in part by the price of one or more underlying instruments or markets. (3) An instrument created by decomposing the return of a related underlying instrument or index. Examples include Americus Trust and Collateralized Mortgage Obligation (CMO) component instruments. (4) Occasionally limited to zero net supply contracts. This restrictive definition excludes warrants, convertibles, and CMO components. (5) In the financial press, any product that loses money.

Diversification: An approach to investment management analyzed and popularized by Harry Markowitz and encouraged by widespread acceptance of the usefulness of the capital asset pricing model (CAPM). With diversification, risk can be reduced relative to the average return of a portfolio by distributing assets among a variety of asset classes, such as stocks, bonds, money market instruments, and physical commodities as well as by diversifying within these categories and across international boundaries. Diversification usually reduces portfolio risk (measured by return variability) because the returns (both positive and negative) on various asset classes are not perfectly correlated.

Drawdown: Percentage loss measured from the high value of an account or fund. Many types of futures accounts and some general accounts are terminated if losses exceed a previously agreed upon drawdown from the initial investment or a recent high. In evaluating a commodity trading advisor's (CTA) performance, the maximum cumulative loss over a period of months is often cited as a measure of the risk the manager has taken.

Financial Engineering: The development and creative application of financial technology to solve financial problems and exploit financial opportunities. (The industry group is the International Association of Financial Engineers.) The art (with contributions from science) of creating desirable cash flow and/or market value patterns from existing instruments or new instruments to meet an investment or risk management need. The creations of financial engineers are typically based on traditional instruments such as bonds and notes with forward and futures contracts, options, and swap components added.

Global Hedge: A hedge covering the unwanted risks of a portfolio or an entire organization on an aggregate basis, taking advantage of any natural risk offsets and using broad spectrum hedging instruments. Global hedging is a low-cost approach to risk management available to large financial intermediaries, nonfinancial enterprises, and investors. A global hedge does not usually qualify for hedge accounting treatment.

Hedge Fund: A private pool of assets managed intensely and often aggressively. A wide variety of financial instruments may be used and the managers of the fund are typically paid a percentage of any profits. In spite of the name, many such funds do little or no hedging, and risk exposures vary greatly. Funds offered in the U.S. have a limited number of holders (usually limited partners), and partners must meet certain requirements in terms of net worth, minimum investment, etc.

Leveraged BuyOut (LBO): Any of a variety of techniques used to replace much of thc equity in a corporate capitalization with debt. LBOs in the 1980s led to opportunities (and need) for risk management and refinancing in the 1990s.

Market Neutral Investment Strategy: An approach to portfolio management that relies on the investment manager's ability to make money through relative valuation analysis, rather than through market direction forecasting. Although approaches vary, market neutral investment techniques usually generate gains in all or nearly all market scenarios. Market neutrality can be implemented with offsetting futures positions or with offsetting short and long positions. The offset is not necessarily measured in units of dollar exposure, but rather in relative variability units. Market neutrality does not insure non-volatile returns or positive returns.

Market Timing: Shifting in and out of asset groups and specific instruments on the basis of expectations that some are undervalued or overvalued relative to others, and that these discrepancies will soon be corrected.

Multi-factor Model: One of three types of models that try to explain risk/reward relationships based on two or more factors. Macroeconomic factor models use observable economic time series as measures of the factors correlated with security returns. Fundamental factor models use many of the measurements generated by securities analysts, such as price/earnings ratios, industry membership, company size, book-to-price, financial leverage, dividend yield etc. Statistical factor models generate statistical constructs that have no necessary fundamental or macroeconomic analogs, but that explain, in the statistical sense, many of the relationships of security returns from the security return data alone. Factor models are used to predict portfolio behavior, and in conjunction with other tools, to construct customized portfolios with certain desired characteristics, such as the ability to track the performance of indexes or other portfolios.

Optimal Portfolio: The portfolio that yields the highest level of expected utility. In portfolio theory, it is the portfolio located at the point on the efficient frontier where the investor's indifference curve is tangent to the efficient frontier.

Option: A stipulated privilege of buying or selling a stated property, security, or commodity at a given price (strike price) within a specified time (for an American-style option, at any time prior to or on the expiration date). A securities option is a negotiable contract in which the seller (writer), for a certain sum of money called the option premium, gives the buyer the right to demand within a specified time the purchase (call) or sale (put) by the option seller of a specified number of bonds, currency units, index units, or shares of stock, at a fixed price or rate, called the strike price or rate. Many options are settled for cash equal to the difference between spot value and the aggregate strike price rather than by delivery of the underlying. In the U.S. and many other countries, stock options are written for units of 100 shares. Other units of underlying coverage are standard in other option markets. Options are ordinarily issued for periods of less than one year, but longer-term options are increasingly common.

Passive Manager: An asset manager who invests assets in index portfolios or unmanaged baskets of securities and other instruments without attempting to select individual securities. Some passive managers, who made little or no effort to outperform an index in the past, now try to improve upon index returns with derivatives and return enhancement strategies, blurring the line between passive and active managers.

Private Equity: A reference to the frequently illiquid market for closely held, usually small companies. Transactions are often effected under an exemption from the laws and regulations covering the transfer of publicly traded securities.

R (Correlation Coefficient): A measure (ranging in value from -1 to 1) of the association between a dependent variable and one or more independent variables. If one variable's values are higher than its average value when another variable's values are higher than its average value, their correlation is positive. By contrast, if one variable's values are lower than its average value when another variable's values are higher than its average value, their correlation is negative. A correlation coefficient is not necessarily a measure of causality, but it does indicate the strength of a relationship. A correlation coefficient of 1 implies that the variables move perfectly in lockstep; a correlation coefficient of -1 implies that the variables move inversely in lockstep; a correlation coefficient of 0 implies that the variables, as calibrated, are uncorrelated.

R2 (Coefficient of Determination): In regression analysis, the fraction of variation in the dependent variable that is explained by variation in the independent variable or variables. R2 is calculated as the ratio of the sum of the squared differences between the predicted values for the dependent variable, and the average of the observed values for the dependent variable to the sum of the squared differences between the observed values for the dependent variable and the average of those values. R2 ranges in value from 0 to 1. A high value indicates a strong relationship between the dependent and independent variables, while a low value indicates a weak relationship.

Securitization: A process by which a loan (originally made by a bank or other financial intermediary) or some other non-traded instrument is converted into a security to increase its liquidity as a financial instrument and to reduce the financial intermediary's capital requirements (disintermediation). Securitization may involve the sale of loans (with or without recourse to the originating lender) or issuance of stand-by letters of credit and loan commitments. While securitization increases the liquidity of relatively standardized loans, it may increase the intermediary's role as a depository or holder of last resort for illiquid and relatively risky loans.

Sharpe Ratio: A risk-adjusted measure of return that divides a portfolio's return in excess of the riskless return by the portfolio's standard deviation. Because it adjusts return for total portfolio risk, an implicit assumption of the Sharpe ratio is that the portfolio will not be combined with other risky portfolios. It is relevant for performance evaluation when comparing mutually exclusive portfolios.

Speculation: (1) A term of opprobrium applied to any financial instrument or transaction of which the speaker or writer disapproves. (2) A financial transaction characterized by the acceptance of greater exposure to price change than might be usual or appropriate for the individual or entity taking the position. (3) A technical term characterizing certain transactions on a futures or commodity exchange in which the entity taking the position is increasing rather than reducing exposure to a specific category of price risk. (4) A position taken because it offers the prospect of capital gain. (5) Purposeful ownership of a less than fully diversified portfolio in pursuit of a superior risk-adjusted return.

Time Diversification: The notion that above average returns tend to offset below average returns over long time horizons. It does not necessarily follow, however, that time diversification reduces risk. Paul Samuelson and others have shown that although the likelihood of a loss given investment in a risky asset decreases with time, the potential magnitude of a loss increases with time if risky asset returns are random, suggesting that exposure to risky assets should be invariant to one's horizon. If risky asset returns mean revert, however, investors with a utility function that is more risk averse than a logwealth utility function should be willing to allocate a larger fraction of their wealth to risky assets given a long horizon, than they would given a short horizon.

Value At Risk (VAR): A currency-denominated measurement of the loss a dealer or an end user of financial instruments would experience in the event of, say, a two-standard deviation adverse move in reference prices or rates in the course of a day or other standardized period.

Vulture Fund: A pooled account, created by public or private subscription, that specializes in distressed investments such as high-yield bonds in or near default, fallen angels, or highly leveraged equities.

ENDNOTES

[1] These terms are from G. Gastineau and M. Kritzman, Dictionary of Financial Risk Management, Frank J. Fabozzi Associates, 1996.

BIOGRAPHY

Thomas Schneeweis

Dr. Schneeweis is Professor of Finance at the Isenberg School of Management at the University of Massachusetts in Amherst, Massachusetts and Director of the Center for International Securities and Derivatives Markets (CISDM) at the School of Management. He is co-author of Financial Futures: Fundamentals, Strategies, and Applications (Irwin) and the author of Benefits of Managed Futures and Alternative Investments in the Institutional Portfolio (AIMA).

Tom is on the Board of Directors of the Managed Funds Association, Chairman of the Education Committee of the AIMA, and editor of *The Journal of Alternative Investments* published by Institutional Investor, Inc. He has also published widely in academic and financial practitioner publications such as *The Journal of Finance, JFQA, The Journal of Portfolio Management* and *Financial Analysts Journal.*

Tom is the U.S. Managing Partner of TRS Associates, which was established in 1982 and specializes in multi-advisor fund creation, asset allocation, and risk management services. In addition, he is an outside director for the Managers Funds, a no-load, open-end, management investment company with over ten funds, and for Navesink Investors Limited, an offshore hedge fund.

Joseph F. Pescatore

Joseph Pescatore is a Principal at a large institutional money management firm. His responsibilities include research, product development, and investment education and communications on absolute return strategies. Until recently, Joe was Senior Director of Institutional Marketing at the New York Mercantile Exchange, developing and implementing marketing and education programs on commodities, managed futures and other alternative investments. Before taking that role, he was Director of Global Business Development at the Exchange, leading the development and launch of the world's first 24-hour electronic trading system for natural gas and crude oil futures and options. Prior to joining the NYSE, Joe worked at CSC Consulting.

Joseph graduated from Montclair State University and did post graduate work at Fordham University. He serves on the Board of the Center for International Security and Derivative Markets at the University of Massachusetts and is Chairman of the Managed Funds Association's Exchange Advisory Council.